Street by Street

GLASGOW

CLYDEBANK, COATBRIDGE, EAST KILBRIDE, HAMILTON, PAISLEY

Airdrie, Barrhead, Cambuslang, Cumbernauld, Dumbarton, Erskine, Johnstone, Kirkintilloch, Milngavie, Motherwell, Newton Mearns, Renfrew, Rutherglen, Uddingston, Wishaw

3rd edition October 2007
© Automobile Association Developments Limited 2007

Original edition printed May 2001

 This product includes map data licensed from Ordnance Survey® with the permission of the Controller of Her Majesty's Stationery Office. © Crown copyright 2007. All rights reserved. Licence number 100021153.

The copyright in all PAF is owned by Royal Mail Group plc.

Published by AA Publishing (a trading name of Automobile Association Developments Limited, whose registered office is Fanum House, Basing View, Basingstoke, Hampshire RG21 4EA. Registered number 1878835).

Produced by the Mapping Services Department of The Automobile Association. (A03384)

A CIP Catalogue record for this book is available from the British Library.

Printed by Oriental Press in Dubai

Ref: ML70y

Key to map pages	ii–iii
Key to map symbols	iv–1
Enlarged map pages	2–3
Main map pages	4–181
Index – towns & villages	182
Index – streets	183–214
Index – featured places	214–218
Glasgow Underground	218
Acknowledgements	219

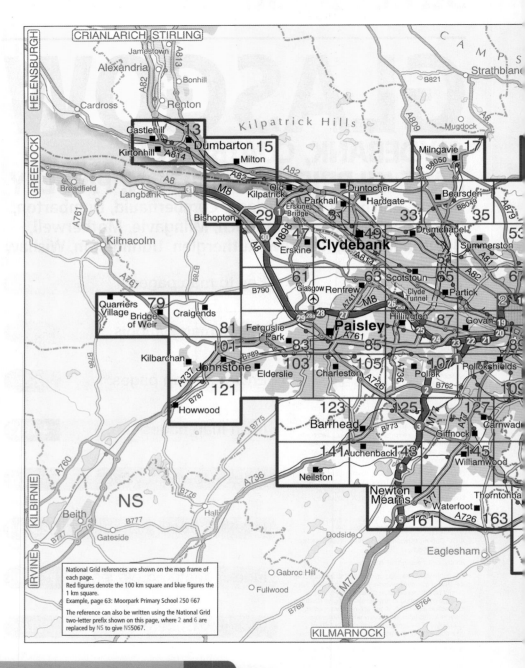

National Grid references are shown on the map frame of each page.
Red figures denote the 100 km square and blue figures the 1 km square.
Example, page 63: Moorpark Primary School 250 667
The reference can also be written using the National Grid two-letter prefix shown on this page, where 2 and 6 are replaced by NS to give NS5067.

Scale of enlarged map pages 1:10,000 6.3 inches to 1 mile

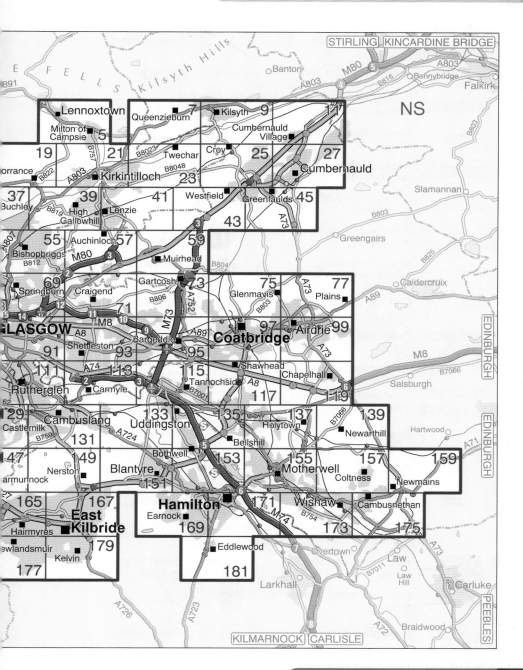

iv

Junction 9	Motorway & junction	LC	Level crossing
Services	Motorway service area	● ● ● ●	Tramway
	Primary road single/dual carriageway	- - - - - - - - -	Ferry route
Services	Primary road service area	....	Airport runway
	A road single/dual carriageway	— ·· — ·· —	County, administrative boundary
	B road single/dual carriageway	ᵛᵛᵛᵛᵛᵛᵛᵛᵛᵛ	Mounds
	Other road single/dual carriageway	**17**	Page continuation 1:15,000
	Minor/private road, access may be restricted	**3**	Page continuation to enlarged scale 1:10,000
← ←	One-way street		River/canal, lake, pier
	Pedestrian area		Aqueduct, lock, weir
- - - - - - -	Track or footpath	465 ▲ Winter Hill	Peak (with height in metres)
	Road under construction		Beach
⁆- - - - -⁅	Road tunnel		Woodland
P	Parking		Park
P+	Park & Ride	† † † † †	Cemetery
	Bus/coach station		Built-up area
	Railway & main railway station		Industrial/business building
	Railway & minor railway station		Leisure building
⊖	Underground station		Retail building
⊖	Light railway & station		Other building
+++++++++	Preserved private railway	**IKEA**	IKEA store

⊓⊓⊓⊓⊓⊓⊓	City wall		♟	Castle
A&E	Hospital with 24-hour A&E department		🏛	Historic house or building
PO	Post Office		Wakehurst Place (NTS)	National Trust property
📖	Public library		Ⓜ	Museum or art gallery
𝒊	Tourist Information Centre		🐎	Roman antiquity
𝒊	Seasonal Tourist Information Centre		⚱	Ancient site, battlefield or monument
🂠🂠	Petrol station, 24 hour Major suppliers only		▦	Industrial interest
✝	Church/chapel		❀	Garden
🚻	Public toilets		◉	Garden Centre Garden Centre Association Member
♿	Toilet with disabled facilities		🌷	Garden Centre Wyevale Garden Centre
PH	Public house AA recommended		🌲	Arboretum
🍴	Restaurant AA inspected		🛒	Farm or animal centre
Madeira Hotel ◼	Hotel AA inspected		🦌	Zoological or wildlife collection
🎭	Theatre or performing arts centre		🦜	Bird collection
📽	Cinema		🐋	Nature reserve
⚑	Golf course		⚔	Aquarium
▲	Camping AA inspected		𝐕	Visitor or heritage centre
⊡	Caravan site AA inspected		ⵣ	Country park
▲⊡	Camping & caravan site AA inspected		◠	Cave
𝕏	Theme park		🌾	Windmill
🏚	Abbey, cathedral or priory		🛢	Distillery, brewery or vineyard

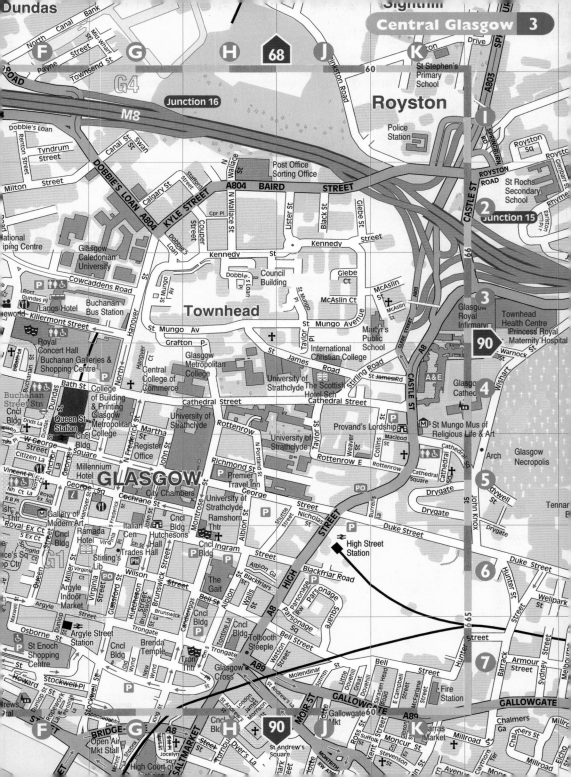

E   F   G   H

65   66

Maiden Castle

Garmore

Spouthead

Shields

I

78

Glorat House

Sheilds Cottage

2

Alloch Dam

3

77

Mount Dam

Lochalsh Crs

Lochiel Drive

A891 CAMPSIE ROAD

Newmill

Valleyfield

Mount Pleasant Crs

Craighead Primary School

Craighead Rd

Derrywood Road

4

Glazert Water

Baldoran Drive

PO

Scott Av

Greta Meek La

Elizabeth Av

Archibald Ter

Marley Way

Laburnum Drive

Chestnut Gdns

Irvine Gdns

James Leeson Ct

Hillside Ter

Cairnview Road

Montgomery Av

Harkness

Birdston Rd

Beechtree Ter

Kirkton Crs

Milton of Campsie

5

Alton

Cannerton Pk

Cannerton Ct

Kincaid Wy

Blair Dr

Glenburn Crs

Kincaid Field

Rundell drive

ANTERMONY R

Linden Lea

Redmoss Road

Maple

Glazert Pl

Newfield Drive

Munro Av

Briar Pk

Cherry Pl

Alder Rd

Limetree Walk

Juniper Drive

Hazel Bank Road

Rowan Av

Willow Dr

Cedar

Poplar Dr

Sycamore Wy

Skinners Hl

65

B757

BIRDSTON

Redmoss Farm

34

66

676

21

E   F   G   H

Glazert Water

E   F   78   G   H   B879

Cedar Rd
Larch Dr
Almond Dr
Cherry La
Wyndford Road

Castlecary **1**

78

Castlecary
House
Hotel
Bridgend Ct
PH

Carnbath Farm Road
Castle view
Castle Court
A80
North Lanarkshire
Falkirk

Napier   Place
Wyndford Rd
Tollpark   Road
CASTLECARY ROAD
Castlecary
Road

2

Napier   Ct
Tollpark Pl
CASTLECARY   ROAD

Cumbernauld
Airport

osh Rd
Napier   Road
Napier
Napier Way
OKI Way

Wardpark

Castlecary
Cottage

3

77

Napier   Road
Napier Pk
Napier
Rd

Dunns Wood Road

Forest Road

CASTLECARY   ROAD

Forest-Road
Whitelees Rd
Whitelees   Road
Whitelees Rd
Castburn
Braesburn
Castburn Rd
Br Rd
Brsbrn Pl

4

Wardpark   Road
Wardpark
Ct
Wardpark
Ct

Council
Building

BrkKenburn Rd
Roseburn Ct
Redburn
Rd
Redburn Rd

Wardpark Pl

Cumbernauld Village

Broom   Road

Whitelees
Primary
School

5

Forest Road

Lilac Hill
Lilac   Av
Lilac
Pl
Ct Ct
Chestnut Av
Lic Ct
Chst Pl

Blackthorn Road
Maple Road
Maple Ct

Ash   Road
Blackthorn Road
Cherry Av
Hornbeam
Hornbeam Rd
Almond   Rd
Almond
Rd
Road

79

E   Cumbernauld
House
F   **27**   G   H

Bruce Road
Pine Pl
Pine
Pine
Pine Gr
Pine

Abronhill
Health
Centre

St Lucys
Primary
School
Elm Dr
Road
Hawthorn Rd
Forest Road

Larch
Larch
Place
Larch Road
Larch Road

PO

Red Burn

Glenhead
Prim School

Abronhill

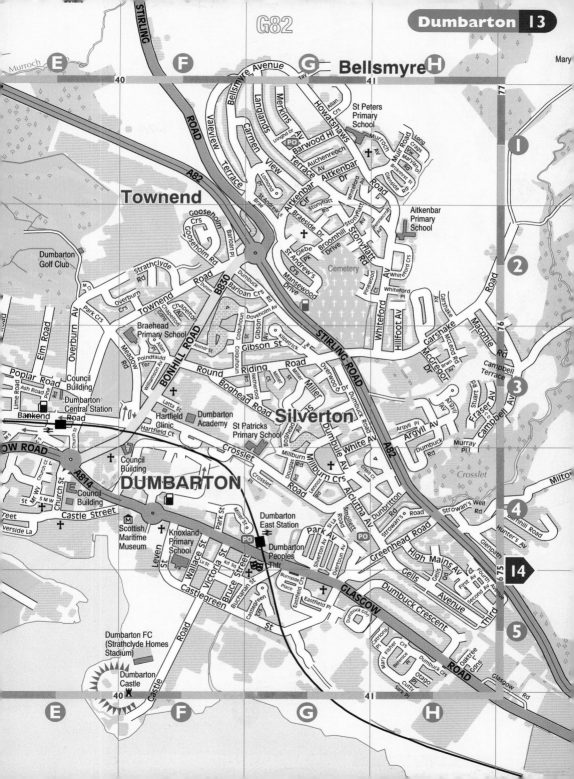

14

A 242 B Overtoun C 43 D

Road
Macphie Rd
96
Garshake
Av
McLeod Rd
McGregor Dr
Campbell
Terrace
Barnhill

1
Stuart
Fraser Av
Campbell Avenue

13
Murroch
Pl

Crosslet

Milton Brae

Strowan

2
Barnhill Road
Hunter's Av
Glenpath

Loch
Bowie

Middleton

Milton Brae

Mains Av
Geils Av
First Av
Fourth Avenue
Second Avenue

Avenue

3
Oaktree
Gdns
Crescent

ROAD
Glasgow Rd

Milton Brae

Milton Court

Milton
Hill

A82
A814

Dumbuck
Colquhoun
Road
Crannog Rd
Lennox
Rd
Hill Vw
Whyte Cr

Milton

4
Travelodge
A82

674

5

Milton Island

West Dunbartonshire
Renfrewshire

A 242 B **28** C 43 D

River Clyde

1 grid square represents 500 metres

E   F   G   H

44   45

76

I

Creigarestie

Greenland
Reservoir

2

Rigangower

75

Greenland

3

Auchentorlie
House

4

Kilpatrick
Braes

674

Bowling

GREAT WESTERN ROAD

A82

5

Manse Road

A814

DUMBARTON ROAD

Scott Av

Clyd Vw Ct

Dmbrtn Rd

Bowling
Station

PO

E   F   G   H

44   29   45

West Dunbarton

Renfr

Roman
Crescent

20

B822

263 **A** 76

I

Kinkell

B

4
64

Redmoss Farm

Redmoss

Glazert Pl

Linden Lea

Cannel

Maple

Munro Rd

Viewpark Drive

Briar Bk

Kinc

Kin

Cherry Pl

D

Alder

Limetree Walk

Juniper Drive

Hazel Bank

Sk

Ro

2 75

Wetshod

Whitehill

Balquharrage

Golf Course

3

SIE RO

Carlston

19

Hayston Golf Club

Springfield

Kirkintilloch Road

Rd

4 674

Golf Course

Kirkintilloch Golf Club

KIRKINTILLOCH

River Kelvin

Hayston

Kelvin Drive

Kelvin Wy

Adamslie Dr

Glasgow Rd

an Dr

Hayston Rd

Claremont Avenue

Norwood Avenue

GLASGOW ROAD A803

Great Drive

Bellevue Road

Bellevue Av

Byars

Road

5

Fraser Gdns

Rob Roy FC

St Marys Primary Sch

Campsie Vw

Woodland Av

Coxdale Av

Melford Av

Beaufort Drive

Roman Road

St
Hi

263
64

A

B

39

C

D

Burnside Av

West Gins Av

Av

I grid square represents 500 metres

River Kelvin

B8023

E   F   7   G   H
    70   71   76

I

Main St

Glen Shirva Road

Barhill Lane

Council Building

Mrryfi

Annieston

Shr L

Wndl Ter

Burnbrae

Park Av

Windy Yetts

Sunnyhill

2

Shirva Farm

Twechar

St Johns Wy

75

Twechar Primary School

Davidson Crs

3

Kelvin View

Johnstone Ter

Differ Av

PO

24

Gartshore Crescent

West Board

4

B8

Hu

Hi

Easterton

B74

Mollins Road

5

9

E   F   42   G   H
    70   71

Mollins

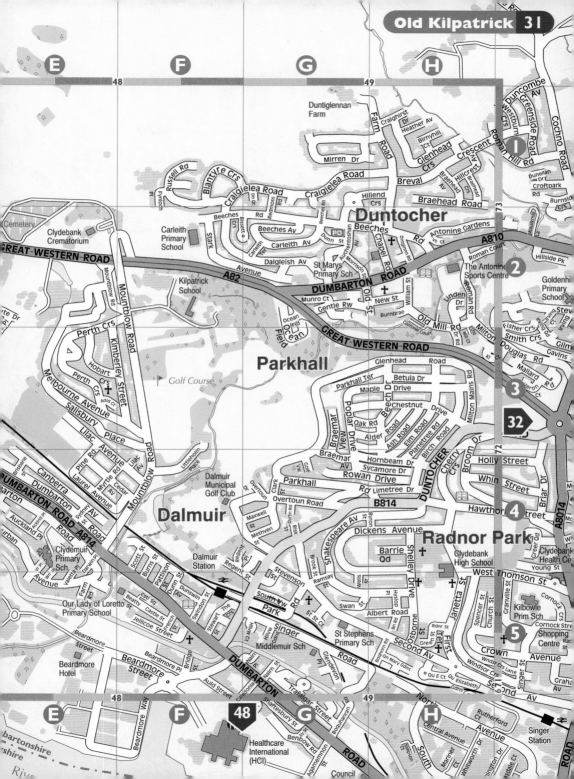

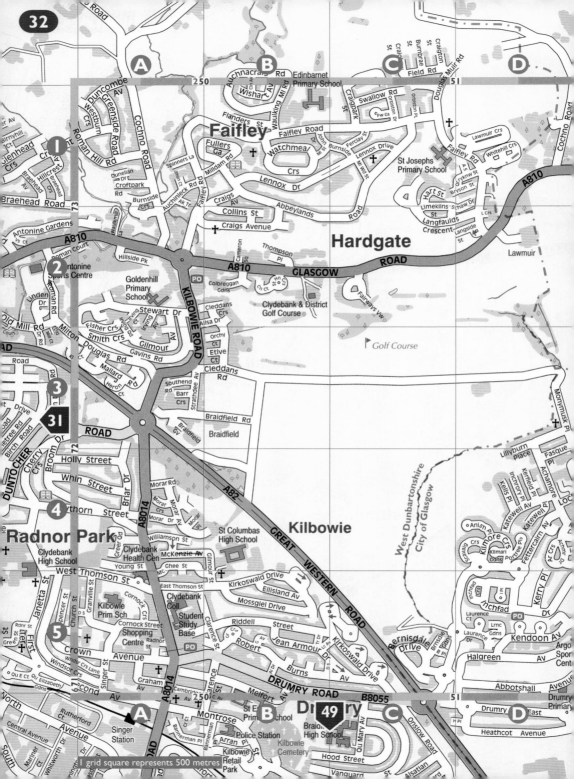

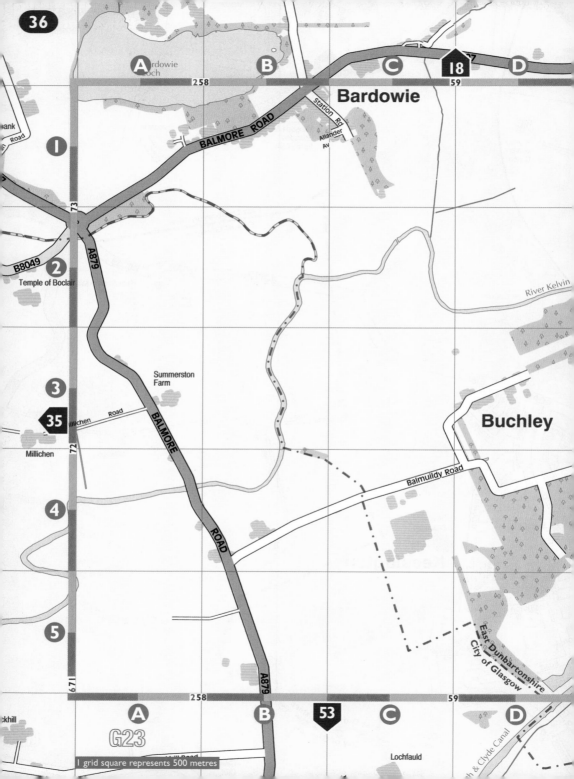

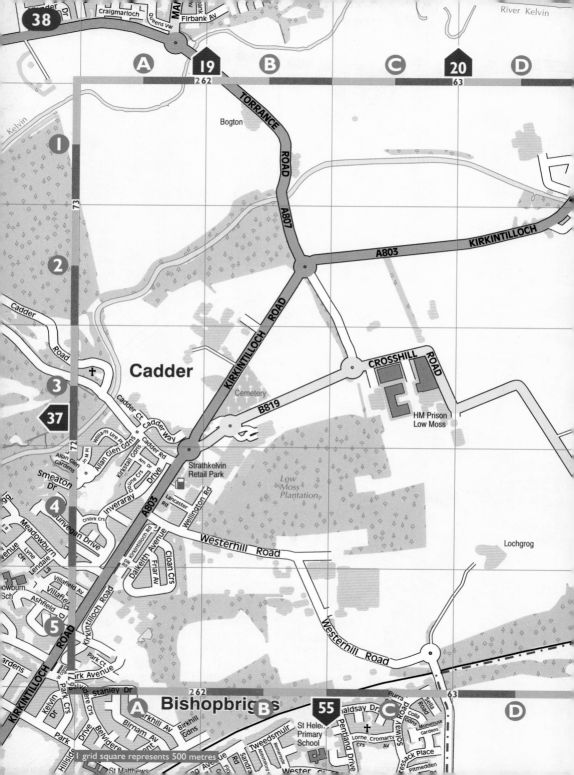

Glenacre Rd
Sandyknowes Rd
Council Building
Lenziemill
Glenacre Road
Kelvin Rd
Kelvin Road
LENZIEMILL

E 7
F 7
G
H
27

B039
JANE
AE
Abbotsford Rd
Abbotsford Pl
Abbe Ct
Telford Pl
Telford Road
B8054
76
77

Greenfaulds Road
Halldon Av
Tannoch Pl
Tannoch Pl
Tannoch Drive
Lenziemill Road
B8039

Greenside

Waterhead

Palacerigg Golf Club

Golf Course

1

2

73

Greenfaulds Station
Greenfaulds
Road

Council Building
Blairlinn Road
Mid Rd
Broomlee Road
Greens Rd
Tower Rd
Limekilns Rd
Belstane Rd
Stirling Road
Blairlinn Vw
BLAIRLINN ROAD

Luggiebank

Luggie Water

Blairlinn

A73

Glenhove

3

72

Coathill

Millcroft Road

Spairdrum Road

Sp Rd
STIRLING ROAD

Muirhead

4

Boglea

Brackenknowe Road

Hulks Road

Windyridge

Staylee

5

671

BLACKBOG RD
B8039

76
77

E
F
STIRLING ROAD
G
H

ellstane
Blackbog Road
Whinrigg

48

Primary School

Beardmore Street

A Beardmore Hotel

Beardmore Street

Beardmore Way

Jellicoe Street

French St

Stewart

Singer

Middlemuir Sch

B

31

Auld Street

Caledon St

BARTON **ROAD**

Shaftesbury St

Trafalgar Street

Benbow Rd

Agamemnon

Glendevon Pl

C

St Stephens Primary Sch

Osborne St

Second Av

North

Central Avenue

South Avenue

D

I

West Dunbartonshire
Renfrewshire

River Clyde

Gladstone St

Healthcare International (HCI)

Council Building

Cable Depot Road

Council Building

CLYDEBANK

Arcadia Bus Centre

DUMBA

West Dunbartonshire
Renfrewshire

Newshot Drive

Meadows D

Meadow Av

Mains River

2

PO

Mains Drive

Mains Wood

Garnieland Road

Carnie Pl

Carnie

Carnie La

Carnie

Carnie Oval

Hwth Crs

Hawthorn Crs

Hawthorn Av

Newshot Island

St Annes Prim Sch

Mai

Parkvale

St Annes Av

Parkvale

St Annes

Carnie Av

Garnie

Hawthorn Crs

Hawthorn Rd

Flures Av

Flures Dr

3

St Annes Wynd

Parkvale Av

Prkvl Gdns

Prkvl Way

Brmlnds Gdns

Garnieland Rd

Broomlands Av

Brmld

Flures Dr

Flures Cres

47

Newshot Drive

Florish Road

Brmlds Ct

WY

M C

Flures Pl Dr

Flures Drive

Park Gv

Winding

Parksail

Dr

Parksail

Bourne Crs

Sandielands Av

Wrightlands Crs

Flures Crs

Torran Drive

Newshot Dr

Nramh

Cem

Park Crs

Bourne

Park Road

Av

Broompark Dr

Northbar House

4 Crs

Luckingsford Road

Luckingsford Av

Lcksgford Dr

Inchinnan

Banchory

Gilbert

Birkhall Av

Inchinnan Primary School

Braemar Road

Balmoral Crs

Old Greenock Rd

Old Greenock Rd

Florish

Old Mains

Freeland Drive

Ladyacres

Ladyacres

WY

Old Greenock Rd

PO

5

GREENOCK ROAD

Town of Inchinnan

GREENOCK ROAD

Portnauld House

A

B

62

C

GREENOCK ROAD

D

PA4

I grid square represents 500 metres

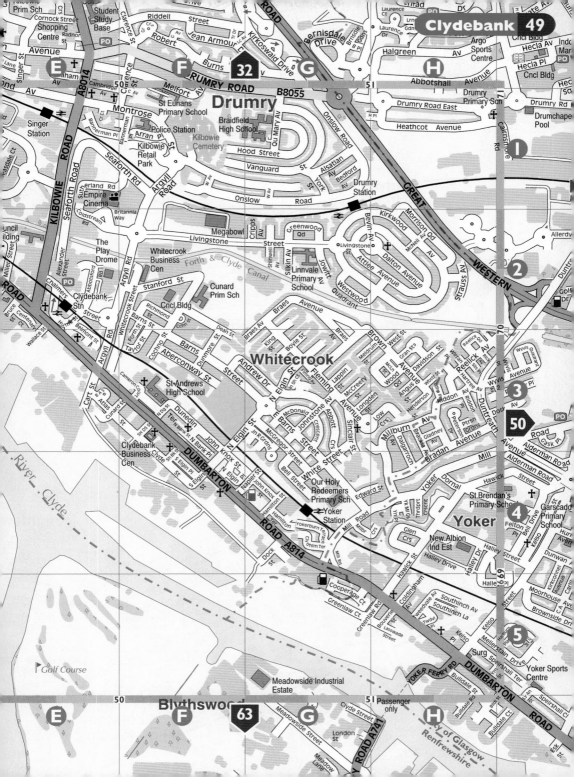

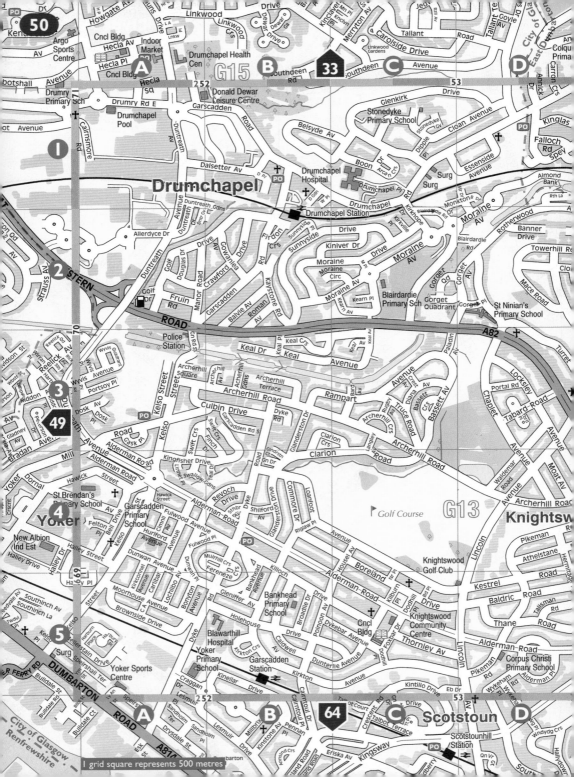

I grid square represents 500 metres

56

B819 Crosshill
CROSS

Loch Farm

A   **B**   **39**   **C**   **D**

264   Gadloch   65

B812

1

Rushyhill   Parkhillhead

Westerhill Road

2

Robroyston Road

70   B812

Lumloch   Langm

AUCHINAIRN ROAD   Road

3   Cardyke Farm

Dunbartonshire
City of G   **55**   Langmuirhead Road

Robroyston

4   North Lanarkshire
          City of Glasgow
Crmw
Ct
Cortmalaw Rd   Auchinleck

Auchinleck   Road

Glenbuck Av   Saughs   Road
Cumnock Road   Saughs   Drive   M80
Auchinleck Av   Saughs Gdns   Saughs Road
5   P Gdn   P Dr   Saughs Av
Aclnnock Con   Drumclog   Bogside
B765   Gdns   Kilkerran
Drive   Saughs Road
Robroyston

A   **B**   **70**   **C**   **D**   **Stepps**
264   Junction 2   65   Whitehill
Bogside Rd   Farm Rd
Dunalastair Drive   Ballalo

1 grid square represents 500 metres   Inglenueuk Av   neuk Crescent   St Fillans Rd   Road

South Crooks

A   2 44   B   **46**   C   45   D

1

68

2

HOUSTON ROAD

Netherfield

3

67

Moss Road

Fulwood

Selvieland

Birkenhead

4

Auchans Road

Knowes

81

5

666

Moss Cottage

M8

A   2 44   B   **82**   C   45   D

Moss Road

60

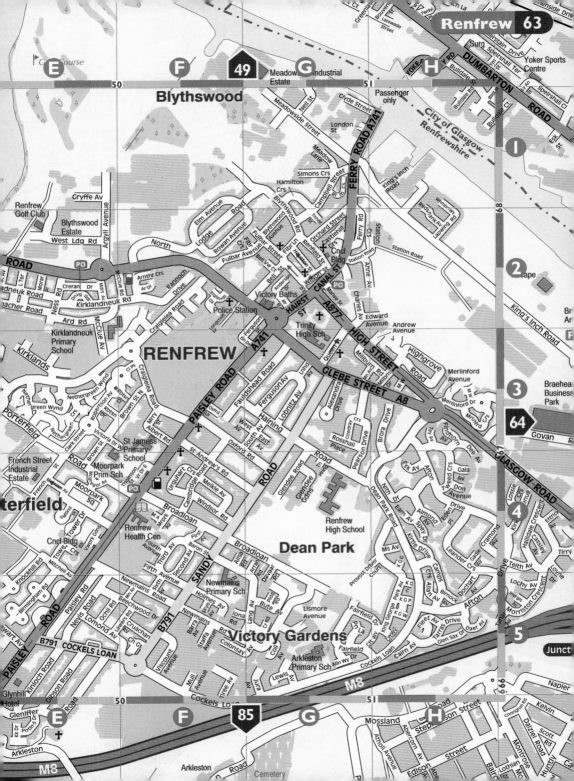

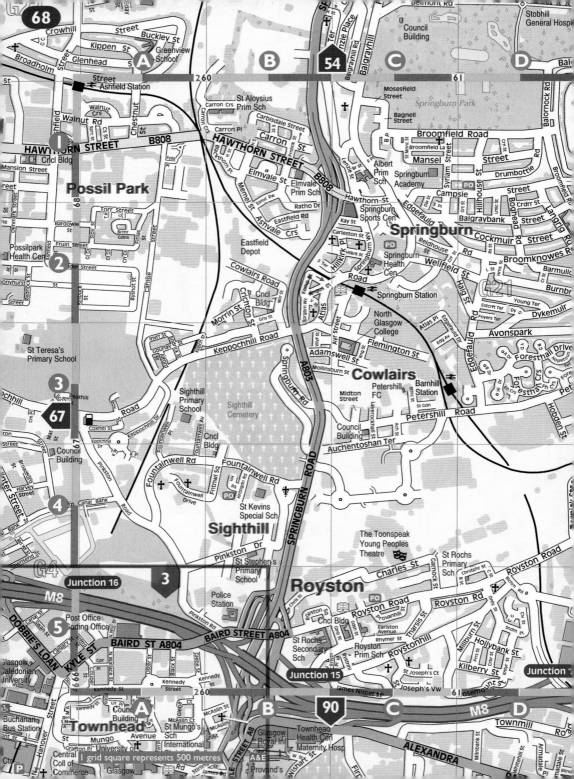

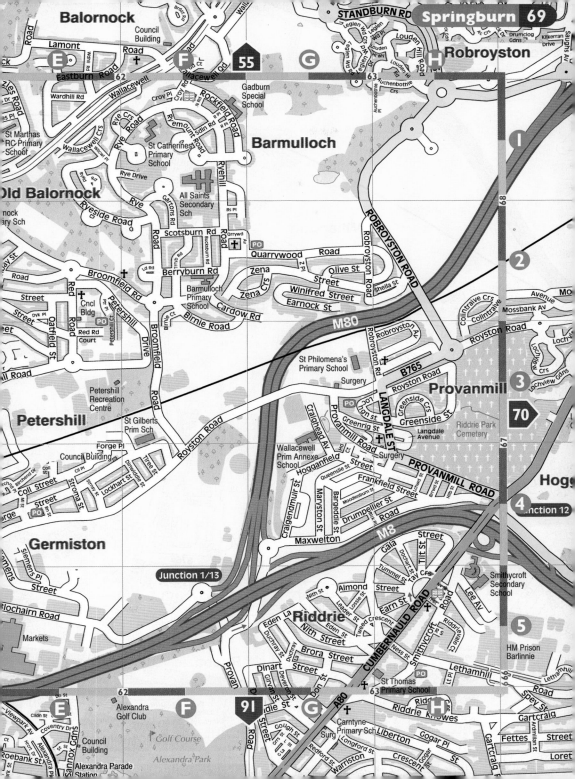

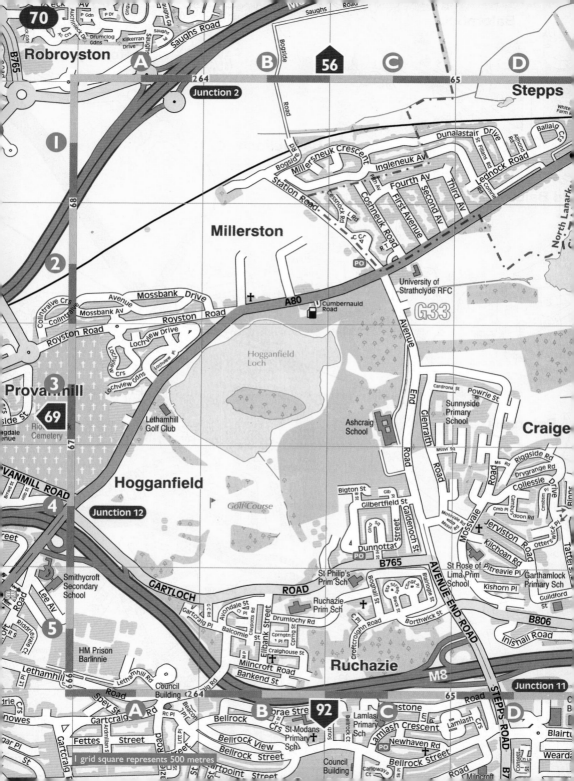

70 Robroyston

A

B **56** **C**

D Stepps

Junction 2

Saughs Road

Bogside Road

Millerston

Millersneuk Crescent

Station Road

Cessnock Rd

Cosnheuk Road

Inglenuek Av

Fourth Av

First Avenue

Second Av

Third Av

Dunalastair Drive

Legnock Road

Ballalo Crs

I

2

Mossbank Drive

Collintrave Crs

Collintrave Avenue

Mossbank Av

Royston Road

A80

Cumbernauld Road

University of Strathclyde RFC

G33

Lochview Drive

Lochview Crs

Lochview Gdns

Lochview Pl

Hogganfield Loch

Avenue End

Cardrona St

Powrie St

Sunnyside Primary School

Craige

3 Provanmill

69 Riddrie Cemetery

Lethamhill Golf Club

Ashcraig School

Glenraith Road

Mssvl Sq

Riggside Rd

Ms Rd

Drygrange Rd

Collessie Drive

Hogganfield

Golf Course

Bigton St

Gilbertfield St

Caldenoch St

Mossvale Rd

Mossvale Road

Cambusdoon Rd

Crnbsm

Jerviston Road

Otters Wick Rd

Tatter

Rinns

4 PROVANMILL ROAD

Junction 12

Dunnottar Street

PO

B765

St Rose of Lima Prim School

Kilchoan Rd

Pitreavie Pl

Kishorn Pl

Garthamlock Primary Sch

Guildford St

Smithycroft Secondary School

Lee Av

GARTLOCH ROAD

Gartcraig Pl

Balcomie

Avondale St

Ellbank Street

Drumlochy Rd

St Philip's Prim Sch

Ruchazie Prim Sch

Boghall St

Croftcroighn Road

Borthwick St

AVENUE END ROAD

B806

Inishall Road

5

HM Prison Barlinnie

Lethamhill Rd

Craighouse St

Milncroft Road

Bankend St

Ruchazie

M8

Junction 11

Lethamhill Road

Council Building

A

Gartcraig Road

Spey St

Bellrock

B Brae Stre **92** **C** stone

D

Bellrock Crs

St Modans Primary Sch

Lamlash Primary Sch

Lamlash Crescent

Lamlash Crs

STEPPS ROAD

Blairtu

Fettes Street

Bellrock View

Bellrock Street

Newhaven Rd

Bellrock Street

Weard

Council Building

Carloway Ct

1 grid square represents 500 metres

E
F
G
H

78
79

I

68

2

Darngavil

Arbuc

Ballochney Road

Road

Ballochney Road

Airdriehill

Meadowhead

Road

Heatheryford
Cdns

Arbuckle

Orch
Dr

Killearn Crs

Cromlix
Grove

Ba

3

Ballochney Road

Spring

Glbank Vw

Cs

Silverdale
Ter

Ashlea
Cdns

Cralglea Ter

Arrondale Rd

Kintyre Crescent

Aberfeloy
Av

Artic
Av

Meadow
View

Ballochnie
Dr

Meadow
View
East
Av

Arkaig
Av

Bellis
Pl

West
Av

Livingston
Drive

Steamlg
St

Moffat View

Ballochnie
View

Road

Annieshill
View

Bruce
Street

Wallace St

Jarvie

PO

Station
Road

Brownie

Av

A89

67

Avenue

Plains

Plains
Primary
School

Victor St

Arden
St

Steamlg St

Main Str

4

A89

St David's
Primary School

Burnhead
Road

B8058

Connor St

Street

A89

Airdrie Road

St Philips
School

Plains
Country Park

5

Easter Mo
Golf Club

699

Clarkston

E

Colliertree
Glebe
Crs

McAllister Avenue

Craighead St

Springwe

Rosebank

Church
Crs

Kg
Crs

F

99

Forrest St

Forrest

Katherine

Tower

G

79

H

Clarkston
Primary

Grahamshill

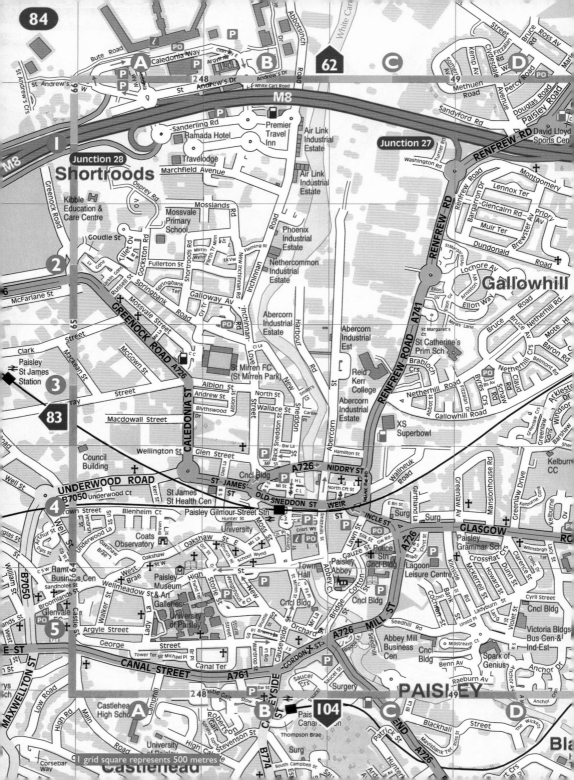

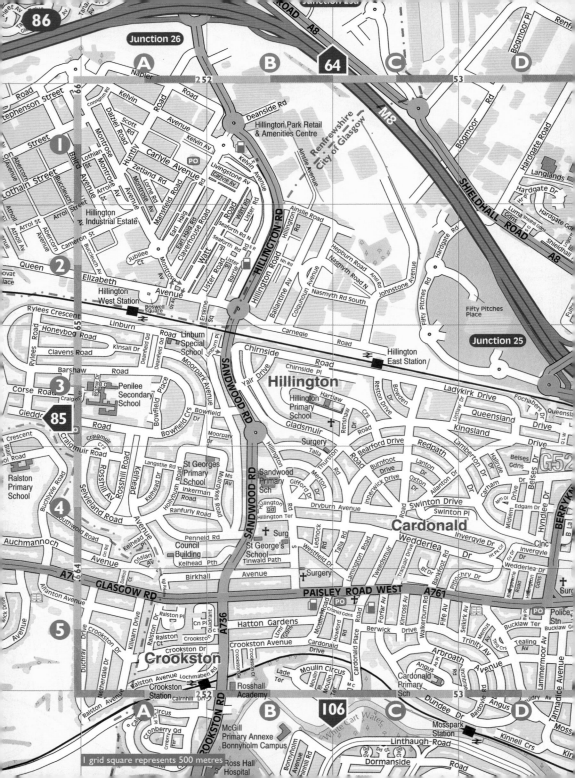

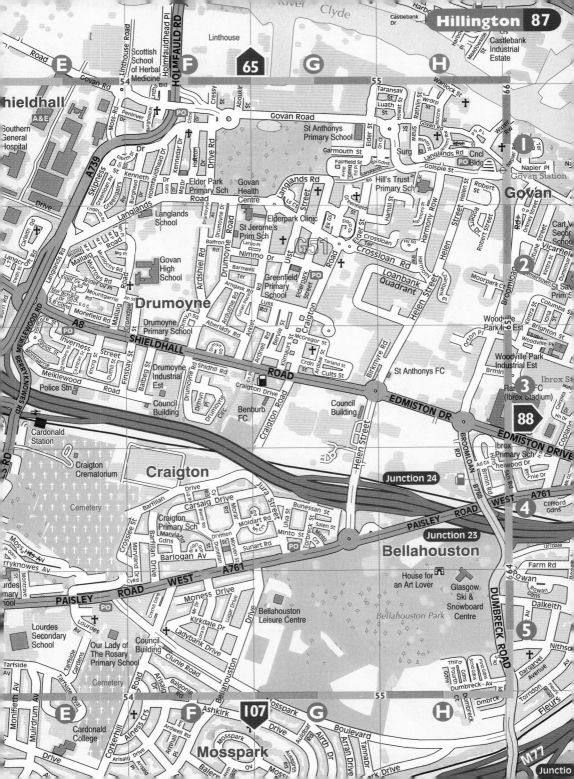

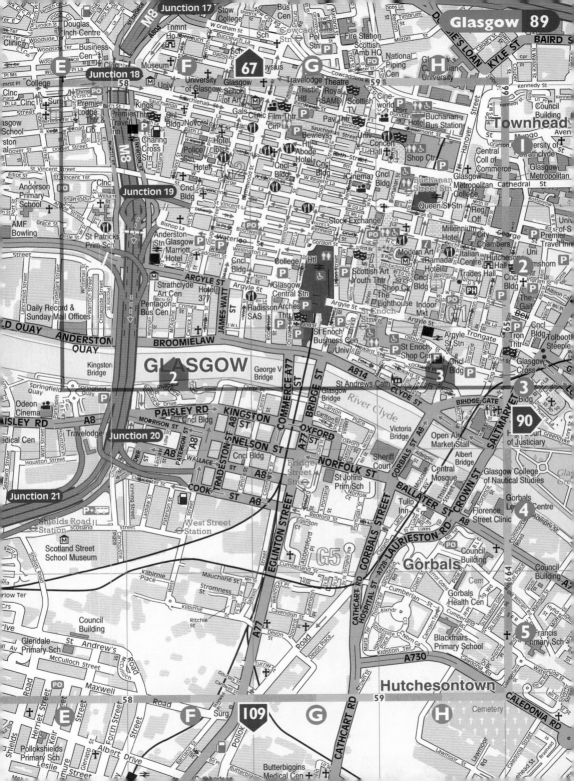

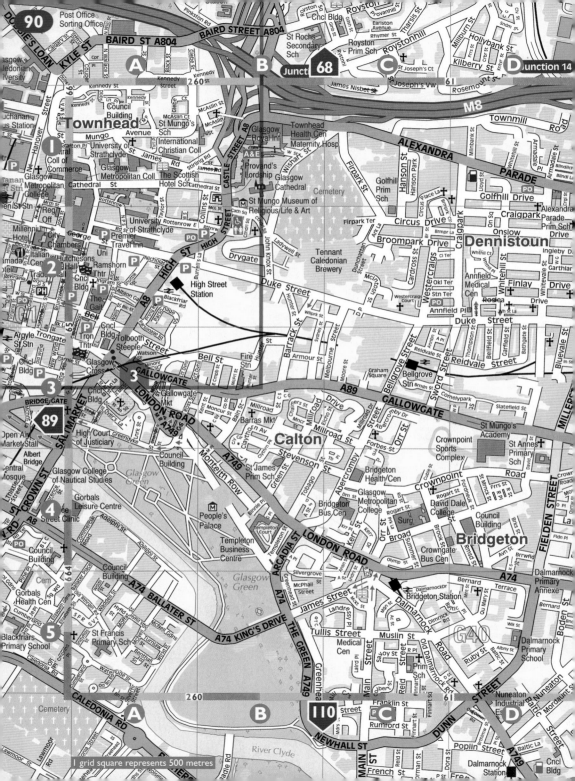

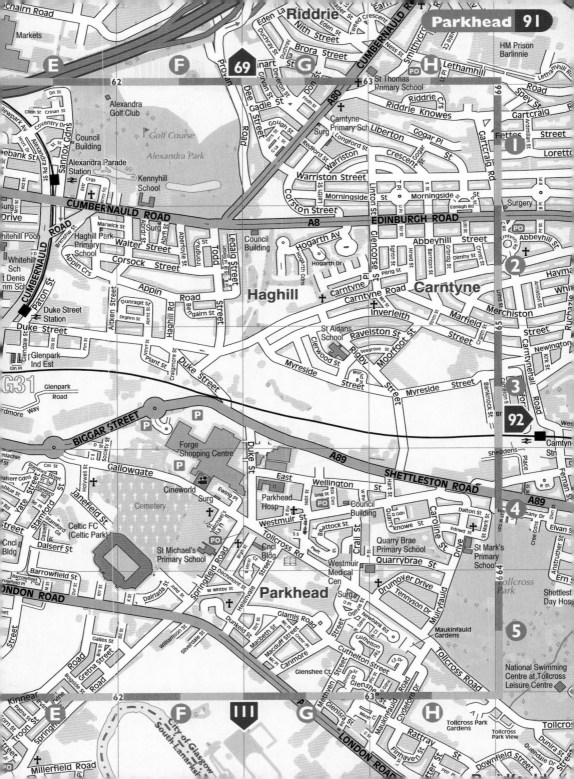

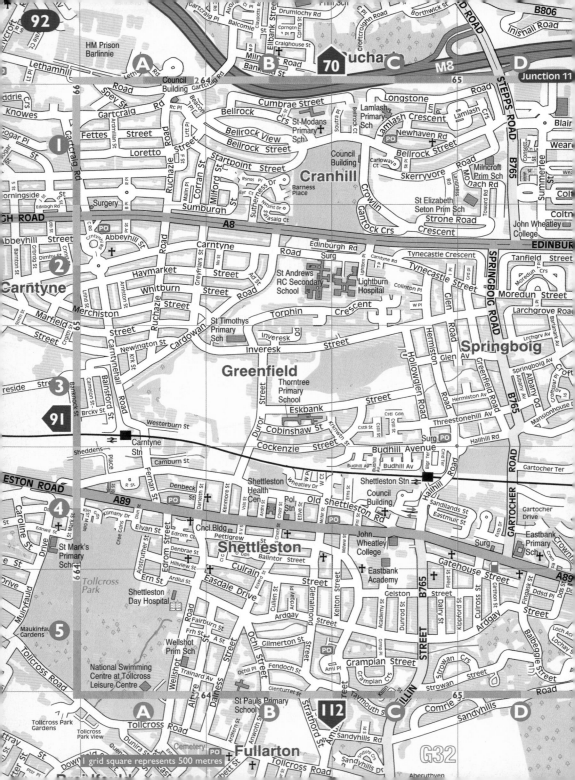

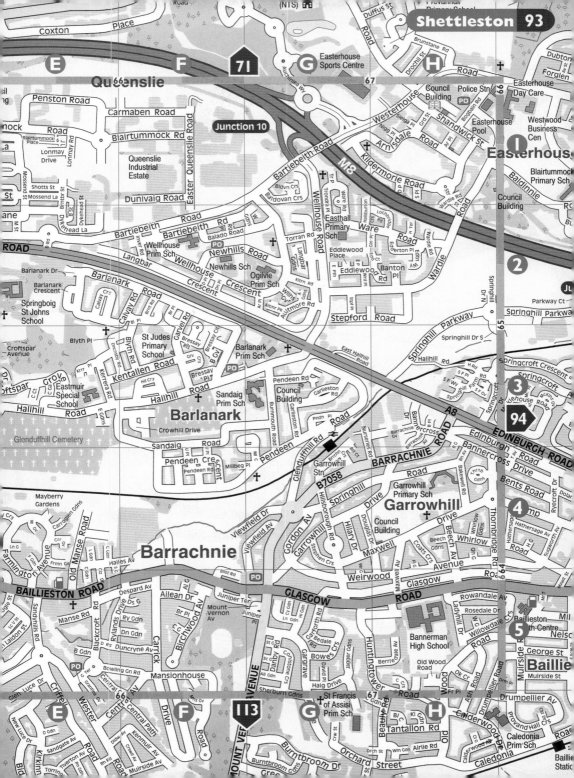

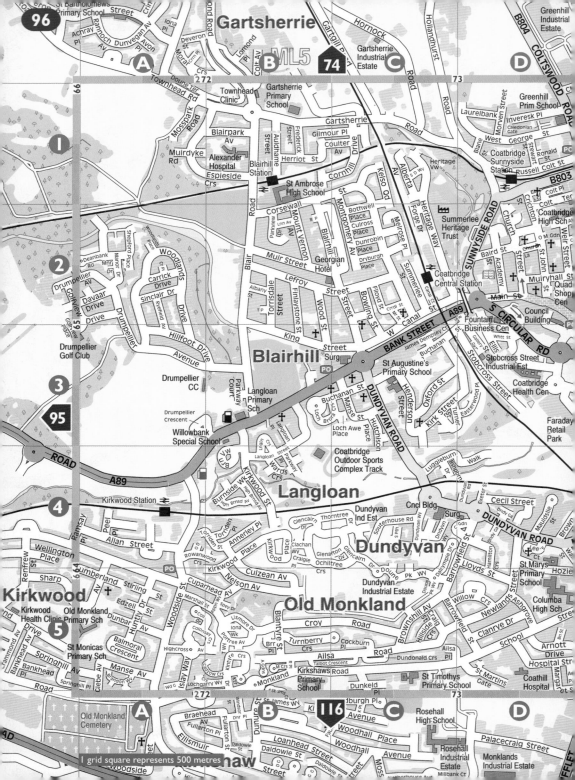

1 grid square represents 500 metres

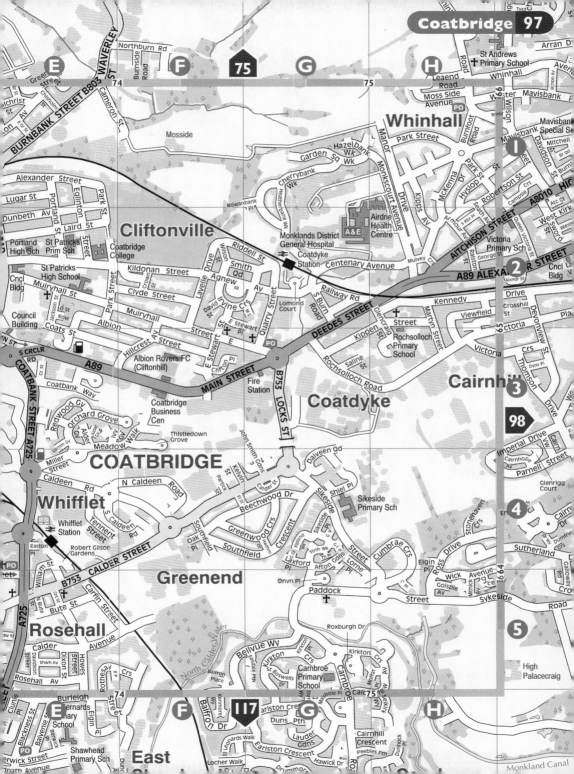

A 240 **B** 761 **C** 41 **D**

80

Chuckie Lane

I

64

BRIDGE

WEIR

OF

Crosslee

Lochermill

The Beech

Stanley Dr

Stanley La

Sandholes Rd

Burnside Avenue

Pannell Farm

Kilbarchan Cemetery

2

Monkland

Kilbarchan Primary School

Park Gdns

Wheatlands Farm

Barnscroft

Locher Road

Glentyan AV

Wheatlands Dr Rd

Park Vw

Meadside Avenue

Road

Taylor AV

West Rd

EAST Rd

Me Pl

Meadside

The Grove

3

Road

Glentyan House

Shuttle St

Taylor AV

Loom Wk

New Street old school

Gateshead Pl

Sq

Kilbarchan

Weavers Ct

Merchants C

Church St

Cedar Ct

Steeple Weaver's Cottage (NTS)

Ewing St

Well Rd

Barn Gn

Fulton Crs

Craigends Dr

Cuninghame Rd

Crescent

Churchill Pl

High Barholm

Low Barholm

Barrhill

4

63

Burntshields

Road

Kibbleston Road

Langside Drive

Station Road

Rock Drive

Station Wnd

Maxky Park

Langside Park

Weirs Pl

Lewis Crs

Lewis Crs

Lewis Td

Quarrybank

Easwald Bank

St Barchan's Rd

Milliken Drive

Milliken Rd

Gladstone Farm

Tandlehill

Burnside Gdns

Dalhousie Rd

Ladysmith Av

PO

KILB

Abbanoy

Rams AV Crs

Olenick Av

Troubridge Crs

Mackenzie Av

Trordg Av

Melfort Gdns

Milliken Pk Rd

5

662

Auchenames

Kibbleston Road

Troubridge Av

Tandlehill Road

Glenart Gy

B787

HU

Huthead Cott

Tandlehill Road

Millikenpark

Milliken Park Station

COCHRANEMILL

A 240 **B** 120 Cartside **C** 41 **D**

Kibbleston

Faulds

Corsford Avenue

Tay Pl

Ness Av

Forth Pl

Ettrick Ter

Teviot

Fordbank Primary

Brookfield

Linwood

JOHNSTONE

Quarrelton

Thornhill

THORN BRAE

Roads and places:

B789 BARROCHAN ROAD

Merchiston Hospital

Merchiston Drive

White House

ROAD

BARROCHAN ROAD

A761

BRIDGE OF WEIR ROAD

A737

Johnstone Hospital

Kintyre Av

Broomward Dr

Ritchie Park

Miller Street

Street

Ritchie

Woodlands Primary Sch

Our Lady of Peace Primary Sch

Linwood High School

East Fulton Primary School

Glimartin Pl

Alford Pl

Stirling

Merchiston Av

Killin

Pentland Av

Clippens

Woodside Rd

Victoria Rd

Black Cart Water

KILBARCHAN ROAD

B787

GRAHAM STREET

MACDOWALL ST

HIGH STREET

Johnstone Swimming Pool

Johnstone Health Cen

Police Stn

Cncl Bldg

Surgery

Surg

St Margarets Primary Sch

Thomson St

Ferguson St

Hagg Pl

Hagg Crs

Hagg Road

Ulundi

Stirling Dr

Ladeside Dr

Shanks Crs

Polson Drive

Floorsburn Crs

Floors St

Buchanan St

Bevan Gv

Jubilee Ter

Cartside

Mc. Laurin Crs

Ryefield

Bute Av

Greenend

Avenue

Dundonald Av

Highcraig Av

Cragview

St David's Primary School

CW Ter

Craigston Rd

North Craigston Rd

Gipson Crs

Quarry Street

Dimity St

Church St

Campbell St

Belth Road

Park Road

Broom

Tower Rd

Hawthorn Rd

Poplar

Heather Place

Sycamore

Willow

Yew Pl

Cedar Av

Maple

Larch Pl

Chestnut Pl

Juniper Place

Holly Pl

Acacia Pl

Aspen Pl

Walnut Crs

Windsor Crs

Castle Av

Balmoral Road

Thornhill Road

Auchenlodment Road

Overton Road

Springfield

Fraser Av

Beith Rd

Elm Lea

Beith Road

McKay Pl

Elm

Birch Crs

Alder Pl

Spruce

Cherry

Hazel Avenue

Pine Crs

Panetree

Rowantree Road

Fir Pl

Thorn Prim Sch

Johnstone Station

THORNHILL

Canal Road

B789

Laighcartside

Gas Street

Brewery St

Mary Street

Ann St

Ellerslie

John Lang St

Armour St

Loudon

Clark St

Rankine St

Collier St

George St

Napier St

PO

Surg

Cncl Bldg

Cncl Bldg

Auchenlodment Primary School

Johnstone High

Junction markers: E · F · 81 · G · H · I · 82 · 2 · 3 · 4 · 102 · 5 · E · F · 121 · G · H

I grid square represents 500 metres

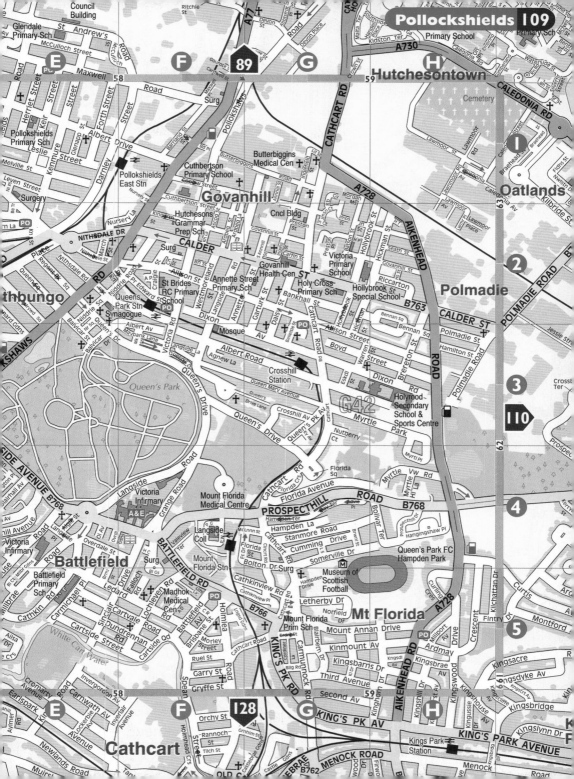

Council Building

Glendale Primary Sch

St Andrew's

Ritchie St

A77

Devon St

Devon Place

Primary School

Primary Sch

McCulloch Street

Maxwell 58

E

F

89

G

H

A730

Hutchesontown

Caledonia Rd

CALEDONIA RD

Herriet Street

Forth Street

Keir St

Albert Drive

Road

Surg

Pollokshaws

Butterbiggins

Cemetery

Lawmoor St

I

Pollokshields Primary Sch

Leslie

Kenmure Street

Glenapp St

Pollokshields East Stn

Cuthbertson Primary School

Butterbiggins Medical Cen

A728

Caledonia Av

Oatlands

Kilbride St

Melville st

Leven street

Nursery

Cuthbertson

Govanhill

Road

Morgan St

Hollybrook St

Hickman

A728

AIKENHEAD

Lawmoor Place

PO

NITHSDALE DR

Hutchesons Grammar Prep Sch

CALDER

Govanhill St

Preston St

Victoria Primary School

seath st

Polmadie

2

thbungo

Queens Park Stn Synagogue

St Brides RC Primary School

Allison Street

Annette Street Primary Sch

Govanhill Health Cen

ST

Holy Cross Primary Sch

Riccarton

Hollybrook Special School

B763

CALDER ST

Polmadie Av

Queen's Drive

DIXON

Annette

Garturk

Daisy

Mosque

Av

Albert Road

Bennan Sq

Allison Street

Hamilton St

Polmadie Road

3

Queen's Park

Agnew La

Crosshill Station

queen Mary Avenue

Boyd

Dixon

Street

Breeton St

110

G42

Myrtle

Holyrood Secondary School & Sports Park

62

Crosst Ter

Queen's Drive

Crosshill Av

Cathcart

Nutberry Ct

Myrtl Pl

Prospect

Langside

Victoria Infirmary

A&E

Grange Road

Mount Florida Medical Centre

Cathcart Rd

Florida Sq

Florida Avenue

PROSPECTHILL

ROAD

Myrtle Rd

Vw Rd

4

SIDE AVENUE B768

Langside Coll

Hampden La

Stanmore Road

Cumming Drive

ROAD

B768

Queen's Park FC Hampden Park

Battlefield

Victoria Infirmary

BATTLEFIELD RD

Mount Florida Stn

Somerville Dr

Museum of Scottish Football

Mt Florida

A728

Curling

5

Battlefield Primary Sch

Madhok Medical Cen

Battlefield

Florida

Bolton Dr Surg

Letherby Dr

Norfield Dr

Mount Annan Drive

PO

Ardmay

Montford

Cartside street

Cartvale Rd

Dundrennan Rd

Brisbane St

Morley Street

Mount Florida Prim Sch

Mount Annan Drive

Kinmount Av

AIKENHEAD RD

Milport Drive

Kingsbrae

Kingswood

Kingsacre

White Cart Water

Invergordon St

Ruel St

Garry St

Gryffe St

KING'S PK RD

Carmunnock Rd

Kingsbarns Dr

Third Avenue

Kingshill

Kingsdyke Av

Cromarty Avenue

Carnwath Av 58

Spean

Second Av 59

KING'S PARK AVENUE

F

128

G

H

Kings Park Station

Cathcart

Orchy St

KING'S PK AV

Rannoch St

Tilch St

MENOCK ROAD

B762

Menock

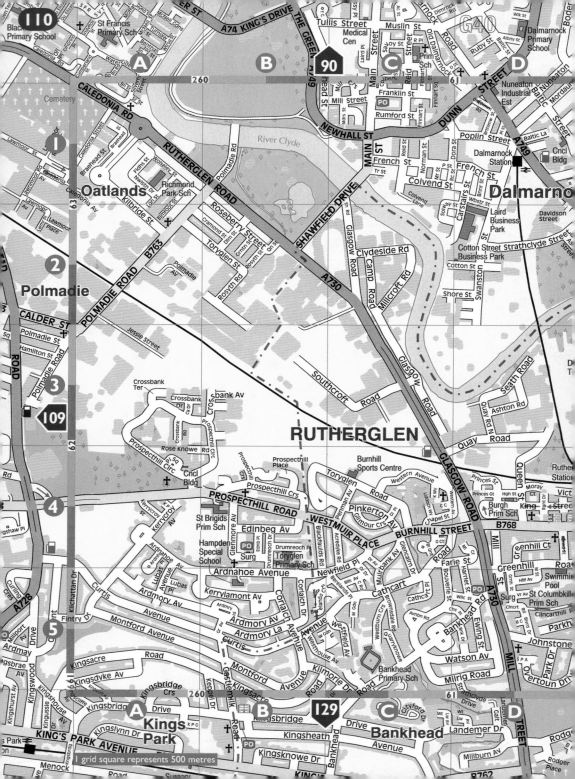

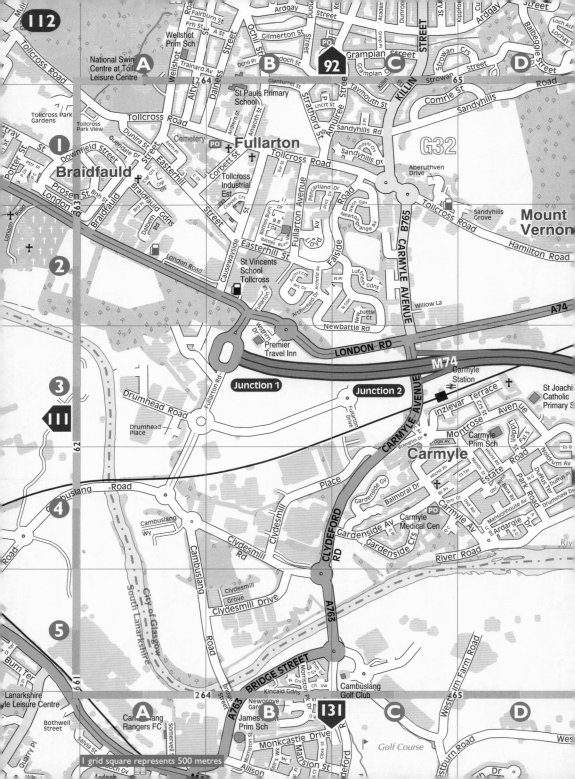

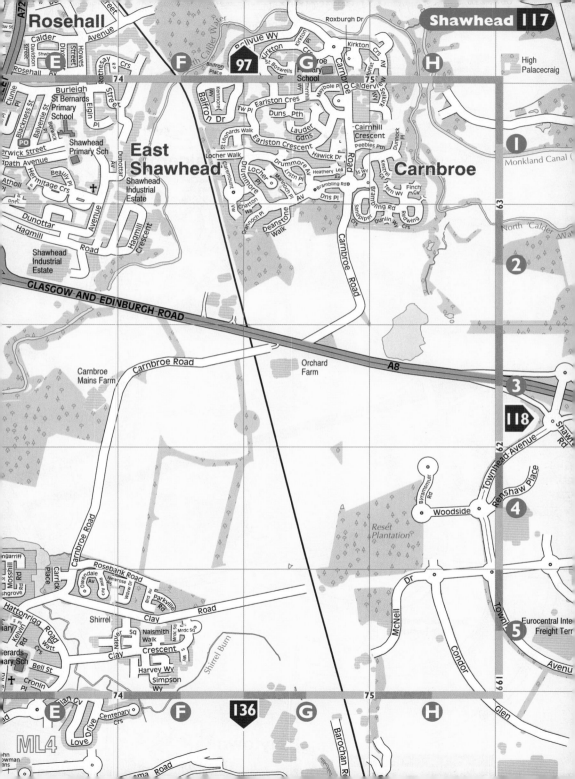

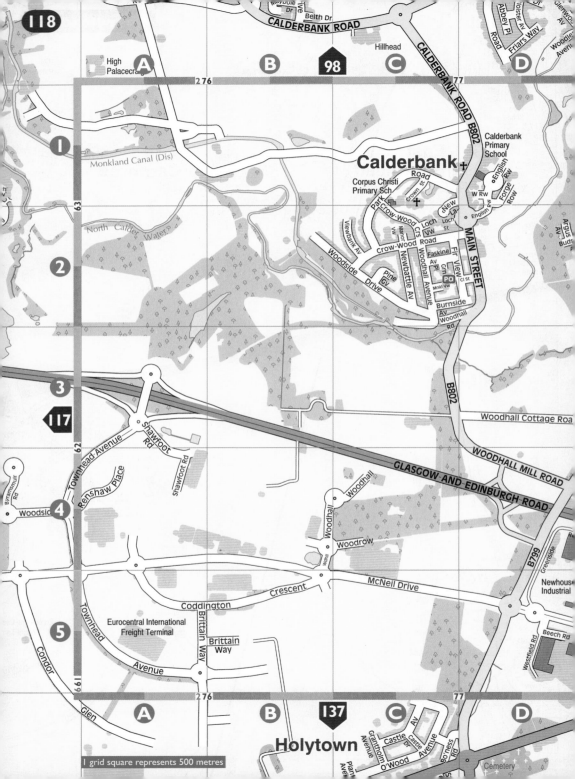

120

Auchenames

Huthead Cott

A 240 **B** **100** **C** Millikenpark **D**

Kibbleston

Tandlehill Road

62 41 Cochranemill

Cartside

Milliken Park Station

Corseford Avenue

Tay Pl
Forb Pl
Ettrick Ter
Teviot

Tweed
Ness Av
Spey Pl
Fordbank Primary School

I

Kibbleston

Faulds

Church
Pa

Avnan Pl

Hallhill

Walpole

St Cuthberts High School

2

Drygate

Kibbleston Road

61

Black Cart Water

A737

Corseford School

Beith

ROAD

St Anthonys Primary School

Swallow Dr

Swan

plover

Linnet Av
Martlet Dr
curlew

Thirdpart Hall

Meikle Corseford

Midton Road

3

Station

Torbracken

Drygait

B787

Midton Road

Howwood Station

Mayfield Crescent
Mayfield Drive

New Avenue
Hallside St
Md Ct

PO

Howwood Primary School

Earlshill Drive

Elliston Rd
Elliston Pl

Sefton Av

George Street

Howwood

Tor Bracken

4

Ulister Crescent
Knm v'w
B787

MAIN STREET

Kild

BOWFIELD RD

Hill Road
Semple View
Hillfoot Drive

Elliston

Bowfield Way

B776

Carsewood Avenue

Skiff Wood

5

B776

North Muirdykes

A 240 **B** PA9 **C** 41 **D**

B776

South

North

1 grid square represents 500 metres

122

Foxbar Rd   Foxbar Rd   Castleview   Castleview Dr

Foxbar Dr   Hollows   Avenue

Hollows crescent

Stanely Grange

Foxbar Crs

A   **B**   **103**   **C**   **D**

Glenburn

Rd Wy

Limecraigs Rd   Limecraigs Crs

Nethercraigs Rd   Wardhouse Rd

Limeview Av

Langcraigs Prim Sch

Bardra

Hollybush Av   Capsegreen Av

47

Craigdhullin Av

Braemount Av

Braehead Rd

Caplaw Rd

Craigmount Av

Langc

246

61

PA2

1   Robertson Park

Gleniffer Braes Country Park

Hillcrest Avenue

Braemount

GLENIFFER ROAD

B775

Sergeantlaw Road

2

60

Paisley Golf Club

Braehead Road

3

Golf Course

Sergeantlaw

4   East Renfrewshire

Renfrewshire

Thornliemuir

Renfrewshire

East Renfrewshire

659

5

Mossneuk Farm

246   Capellie Fm   47

A   **B**   **140**   **C**   **D**

Greenfieldmuir

Killoch Water

1 grid square represents 500 metres

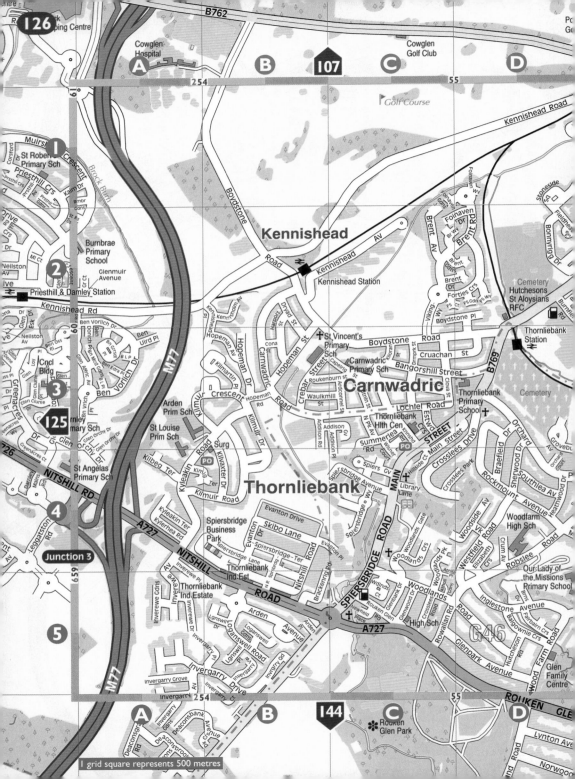

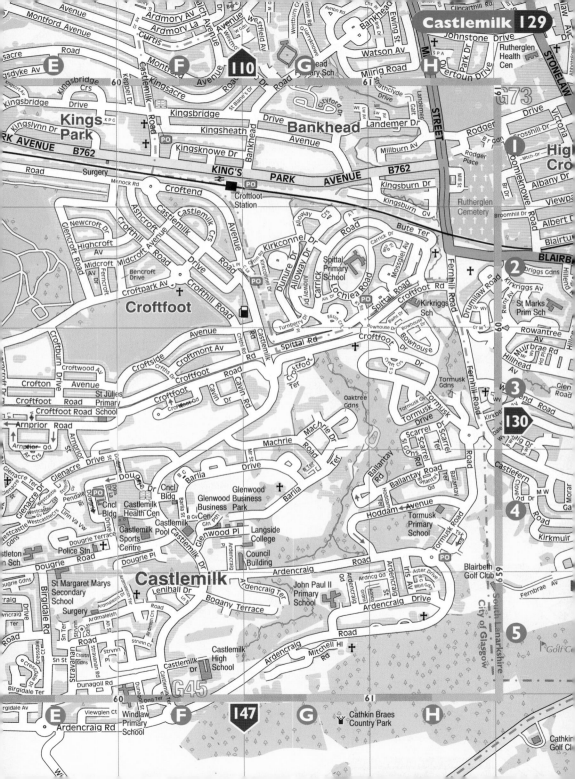

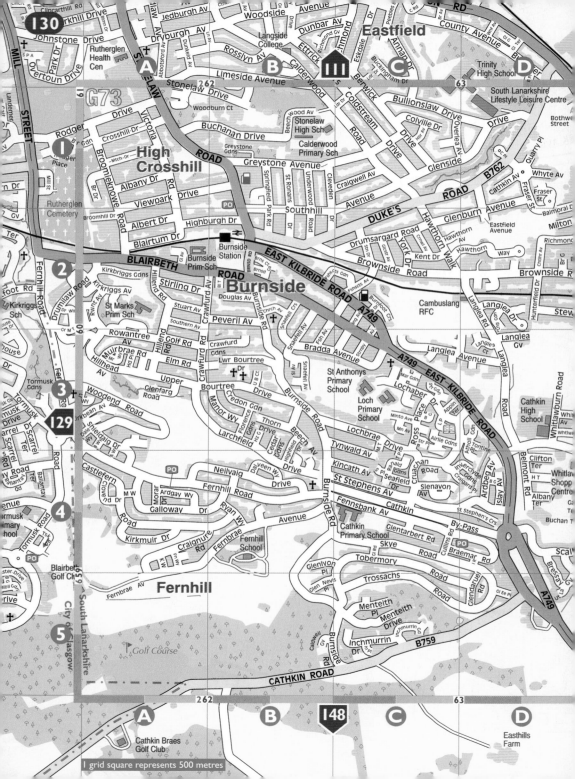

A 266 B ■113 C 67 D

Westburn

Light Burn

Westfarm Wy Westfarm Crs
Newton Gv Grnw Av
Mitchell Av
Lckhr Dr
Westbn Av Lockhart Avenue
Henderson Av Dunlop St
McIver St

I 19 Mill Road Westburn Road
Redpath Drive Findlay Ter
Westburn Rd Arrol Wynd Nth St PO
Dalziel Wynd Nthn St
Dalziel Crs Colville Ct
Northbank Av

Rowan Place
Westburn Cemetery

Old Mill Rd

Newton
St Charles Primary School
Newton Brae
Redlawood Pl
Redlawood Road
Redlawood Rd
Westburn

Westburn Road

Newton Station

Road

Hills Av
Hallside Av Hi Crs
Gate
Acacia Wa
Alder
Azalea Gdns

2 McGregor Court
M Wy MacArthur Wynd Macdougal Dr
Macfarlane Crs Mill Gv Mill Wk
Glencairn Gardens
Cambuslang Recreation Centre
Arn St Annick St
Dunan St
Wiston St
Montgomery St
Medwin St
Graham Av
Gateside Avenue
Mill Road

Ash Wynd As Pl
Ash Wynd
Alder

Hallside
Village Road
Cedar Ct Birch Pl
Cherrytree Dr Cypress Wy
Hallside Rd Bay Willow Ct
C Wy
Hallside Primary Sch
Elm Wy
Beech Crs

3 Hamilton Crs Langcroft Dr
Rosebank Drive
St Cadoc's Primary S
Cairns Primary Sch
Wellside Drive Surg Dn Pk Glen St PO
Dn Pk Dr
131
Overton St
Wiff Clyde Place
Av
Graham Av
Overton Road
Overton School
New Rd
Cncl Bldg
Flemington Industrial Est
Elm Wy
Elder Fir Ct
Hawthorn
Elder Crs
Laburnum Av
Boulevard
Sym Way
Lilac Wynd
Lilac
Spruce Dr
Spruce Wy
Redwood Crs
Redwood Wy

4 Ty Dr Auld Kirk Rd
Greenlees
Gilbertfield Road
Castle Chimmins Av
Lightburn
Helenslea Av
Claude Av
Deans Av
Dechmont
Castle Chimmins Road
Quarry Av
Waterside Gdns
Letterickhills Crs
Hutchinson Pl
Strathclyde Gdns
Carnpole View
Larch
Laurel La
Pine Wd
Oak Wynd
Oak Wynd
Mor Ct
Maple Ct Mulberry Wynd
Magnolia Dr
Magnol Tc

G72

5 Flemington Farm
Spittal Farm

Dalton
HAMILTON ROAD A724

A 266 B ▼150 C 67 D

Mossneuk
Farm

A   246   **B**   122   **C**   47   **D**

Capellie Fm

Greenfieldmuir

I   58

Killoch Water

2

Foreside

Station Brae

3   57

Fereneze Road

G78

Crofthead
Industrial
Estate

Holehouse Brae

Millview
Mdws

Milnthird

Holehouse

Milliview Ter
Marchill Ter
Mdws
Alexander Ter
Orr Ter
Uphill
Ter

Pattiston

4

A736 LOCHLIBO ROAD

The
Grove
Glen Creran
Crs

Glenlivet Rd

Glenorrin
Cr's

Glen Roy

Glen Doll Rd

Gin Finiet
Road

Gin Grn
Glen Mark Rd
Glen Lyon Rd
Glen Muir Rd

Glen Shee Av

Uplawmoor Road

Crumyards

Glen Isla Av

5   6 56

Kilburn

A   Jaapston   246   **B**   **C**   47   **D**

1 grid square represents 500 metres

Craig of
Neilston

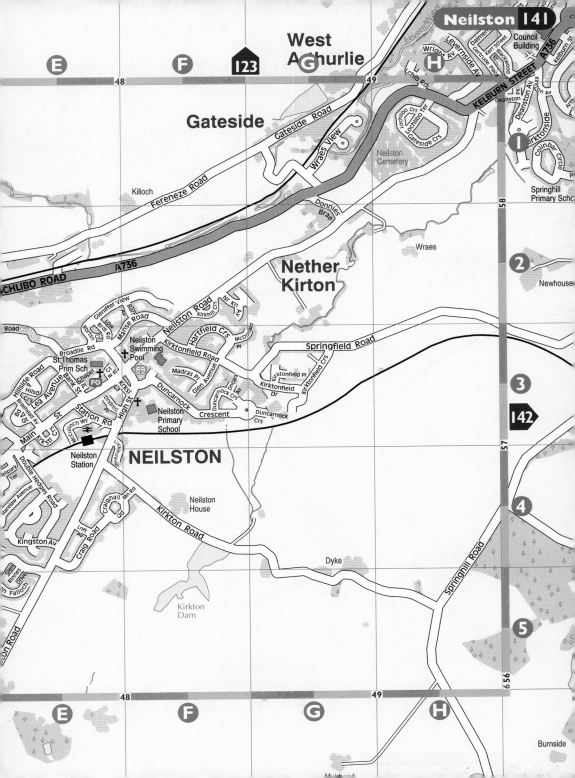

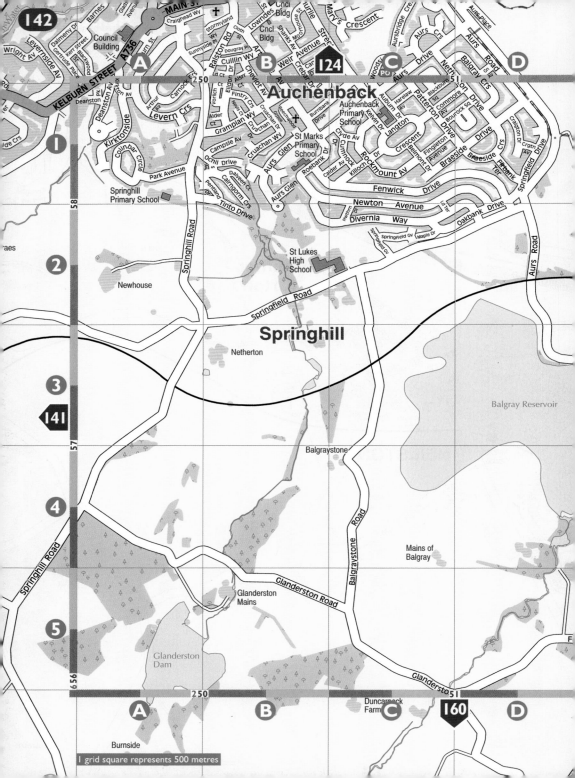

Cresdale Ve
Ardmaleish
Sn St
Cresdale Ct
Strynn
Ardmaleish
Road
Sn Ter
Stravanan
Road
Castlemilk High School
Ardencraig
Road
arkshire
Glasgow
Golf C
Gdns
Cssbn
Castlemilk
Castlemilk
Mitchell Hl Rd
Birgidale Ter
Stravanan Rd
Dr
129
Ardencraig
E
Strynn Pl
Castlemilk Ter
F
G45
G
H
Viewglen Ct
60
Dunagoil St
Dng Ter
Birgidale Av
Ardencraig Rd
Windlaw Primary School
Cathkin Braes Country Park
Cathk Golf C
I
Road
Windlaw
Road
58
Golf Course
P
Gallowhill
2
Hillcrest
Gallowhill Rd
Muir Farm
unnock
CATHKIN ROAD
B759
Stuart
Wm
Cam
3
PO
Manse Rd
Sycamore Way
Cragwell Pk
Kirk Rd
Craigsheen Av
Gleba Av
City of Glasgow
South Lanarkshire
57
148
Bankhead Rd
Waterside Rd
BUSBY ROAD
drive
Macrngs
Parthead Rd
Carmunnock Primary School
Craigsheen Av
Woodland Gardens
Kittochside Road
re La
Picketlaw Dr
Woodside Rd
Woodside Gdns
Parklee Dr
Highfla Farm
aw Farm
Picketlaw Farm
Waterside Gdns
Parklea Farm
4
Waterside Road
Waterbank Road
Kittochside Road
Waterside
Agricultural Museum
M
rnmuir Rd
5
56
Highland Farm
rmunnock
Dykehea Farm
Glen Road
E
F
165
G
H
Stewartfield Wy
Macvicar
Maclaren
McCallum
Cv
Westerfield Road
Macdonald Av
McKay Pl
Mackenzie Gar
Macivor
Crs
Maclem
EAST KILBRIDE ROAD
60
Cemetery
Museum of Scottish Country Life
Glen Rd
Minister's Park
hill Green
Castleglen Road
Macclim Pk
Macdonald Av

E 64 F Turnlaw **131** G 65 H

I

58

2

Golf Cour

B759

Turnlaw

Turnlaw

EAST KILBRIDE ROAD

GLASGOW ROAD

Greenleeshill

Cairnmuir Road

Glasgow Road

Crookedshields

Nerston Residential School

Crookedshields Road

3

150

57

Lettrickhills

4

Nerston Road

Nerston

Kingsgate Retail Park

A749

Chapelside Road

East Kilbride Golf Club

Golf Course

Stoneymeadow Road

HA TON

5

656

Mavor Way

Mavor Avenue

Howard Av

Howard Ct

A749 KINGSWAY

A749

Chapelside Road

Law

Place

64

Howard Av

E 64 F A749 KINGSWAY **167** iew Pl G Othello 65 Bolingbr Calderwood Primary Sch Neville Rd Warwick H Pembroke Road

Long Thorndyke Redgrave Rd Ashcroft Tewkesbury Stratford Salisbury

Bosworth Mowbray Maxwellton Road

Wilson Place

Mavor

Leesburn

Yeow on Pl

Blackbraes Rd Runcinan Pl Geddes Hill Orchard Rae burn Av St

HAMILTON ROAD

Strothers Crs Baillie Baillie Pl Othello McBeth Hamlet Abacy Falstaff Orind Edmund kean

Talbot

A   B   132   C   Flemington Farm   D   Spittal Farm

ROAD   A724

266   67

I

58

2

Dechmont Farm

Crookedshields

3

149

57

Mid Lettrick

Lettrickhills

4

Rotten Calder

Crossbasket   HAMILTON   High

B7012   Hamilton Road

Stoneymeadow Road   A725

5   HAMILTON   ROAD

Gillies Crs

Peploe Drive

Cadell Gdns

Fergusson Pl

Barrie Rd

Thorndyke   Redgrave   Ashcroft   Tewkesbury   Kirkmenan   Wylie

Edmund kean

Long alderwood Primary ch

656   Stratford

Neville Rd

Warwick

Salisbury

Pembroke Road

Mowbray

Maxwellton

Waverley

A   B   167   C   D

266   67

I grid square represents 500 metres

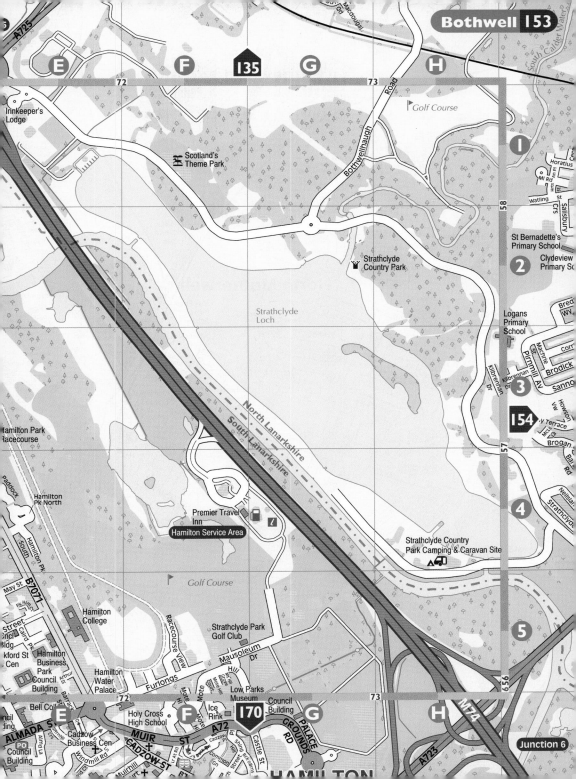

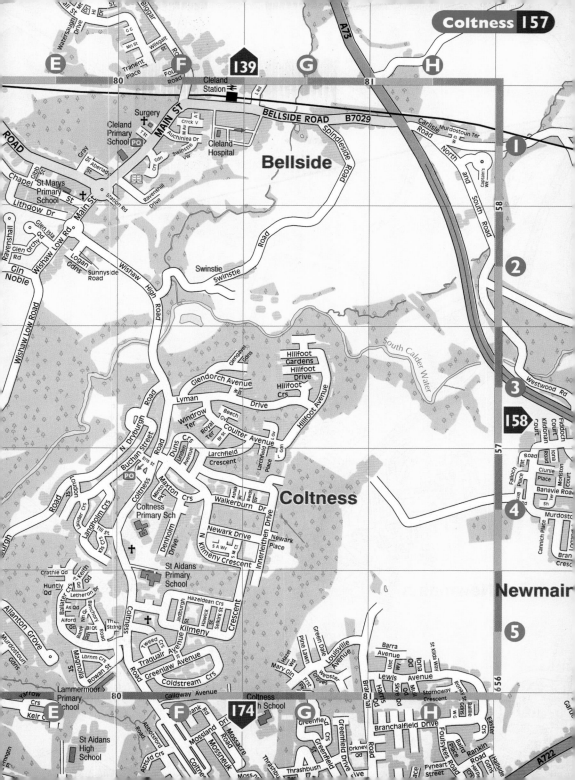

A **B** **C** **D**

282 Shawstonfoot Road 83 Foulburn Road

Hill of
Murdostoun

Carlisle Murdostoun Ter WD
Road Captain's Murdostoun
North Stocks Road

1

58

South

Road **2**

ter Water

Westwood Rd **3**

157

57

Murdostoun
Castle

Underwood
Dr Murray Crs

Devine Ov

Tilt
Fiddoch
Court Iona MCc Rd
Kildonan Road Isla Avenue
Court Moriston Court Robert
Clunie Place Tiree Crescent Barragh Wynd
Falloch Place Banavie Road McMahon DR
SUR Rd Bgn Bell VW McMahon Dr
Cannich Place Murdostoun Coll Street Calder Av
Logandale View Kilmichael Avenue Bonds
AV Duke Prince Drive
Branchaimuir SP Street Place Woodside Crescent
Crescent MB Castle VW Firtree Road
Clark Street King Street Abernethyn Road Firtree
WESTWOOD ROAD Northwood Place Alcath Road
Lawrie Stewart Crescent Drive Muirhouse Avenue Bonkle
street West Eastwood Crindledyke Rd Hawthorn
Place BI PI Crescent Bonkle Road Avenue
St Brigids Park Dr Crindledyke Bonkle Auchter AV Mavisbank
Primary A73 Dougan Dr Gdns Braedale Crs
School Newton Drive Bonkle Road
Claire Manse Rd Medical †
Street Centre

Bonkle

Newmains **4**

5

Crindledyke

A71

St Kilda Way
Iona Stornoway Ronald St Gdns
avenue Crescent Baillie
Rd Easter Kirkgate Bonkle
Drive Rankin Road Gdns Hope St School Rd Road
Foulsykes Road Baird Newmains Brwn Cathb'
Fyneart Road Place Primary Sch St Road
Street Church 282 Little John Gardens PO MAIN STREET MORNINGSIDE ROAD 83

282 **175**

A **B** **C** **D**

MANSE ROAD

I grid square represents 500 metres

656

Bowhousebog
or Liquo

Hartwood Road

Bowhousebog

Old

Mill

Road

Foulburn Road

Castlerigg

Mill Road

Allanbank

PO

A71

Allanton
Primary
School

Redmire Crescent

Darmeid
Place

Hartfield

Allanton

Hartfi

Calder
Rd

Newmark

Coltness

Rd

Allanbank
Street

Hawthorn
Place

Avenue

Springhead
Road

Kingshill
Rd

Houldsworth Cr's

Wilson Road

Allanton Road

Muirhoustoun
Road

Church Road

Cairney
Pl

Brownhill
View

owfield

Mill Road

Cathburn

Daviesdykes

E F G H

84 85

58

57

656

1

2

3

4

5

Fingalton Road

B769

A Glanderston 142 B C 143 D
251 52

56

Netherplace

Duncarnock
Farm

Netherplace Road

Kiloran
Pl
Mey Pl
Kiloran Gv Mey
Ct

I

Cumnock House
Farm

DODSIDE ROAD

Caldcoats

Neth

M77

Burn Brock

2

55

3

Faulds
Farm

Pilmuir

B769

4

54

DODSIDE ROAD

A77

Golf Course

5

East Renfrewshire
Golf Club

A 251 B C 52 D

M77

I grid square represents 500 metres

NEWTON MEARNS

AYR ROAD

A77

A726

Mearns Primary School

The Avenue Shopping Centre

Police Stn
Cncl Bldgs

Hunter Drive

Malletsheugh

Faside House

Maidenhill

Titwood Road

Hazelden Road

Mearns Road

2 Mear

162

Section 5

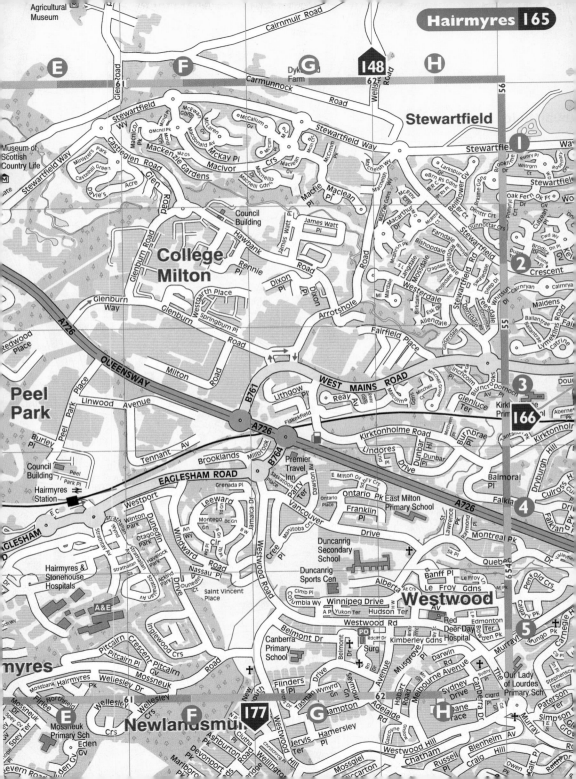

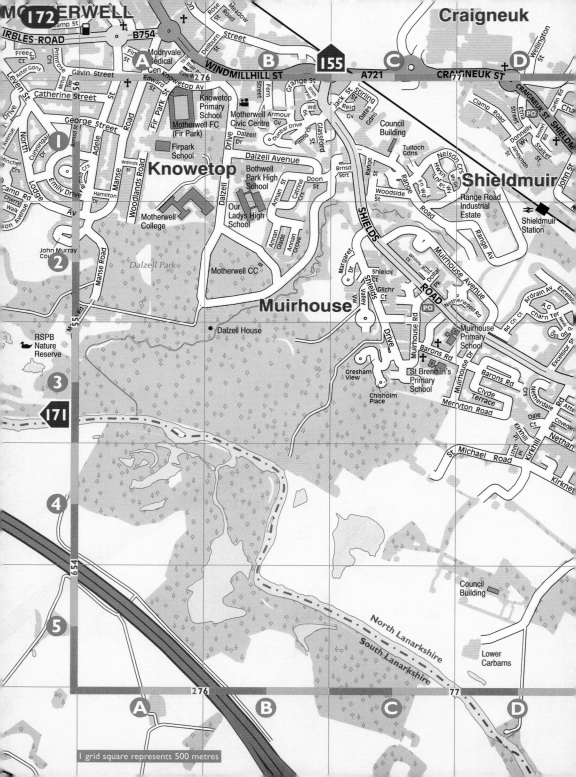

176

A726

176

Hayhill Road

Road

EAGLESHAM ROAD

164

Hai

A 259 **B** **164** **C** 60 **D**

Hayhill

Gill

Hayhill Road

B764

Lawmuir

1

Jackton

Blackadder Pl

Bowmont Pl

Greenhills Road

Tay Pl

Tay GV

Medwin Gdns

Findhorn

Findhorn Ct

Gardenhall

Blaeshill Rd

Avenue

Mossneuk

Wamphray Place

Borthwick

Moffat Ct

Moffat Ct

Allan Ct

Medwin Ct

Douglas Drive

Brodick

Whiteadder Place

Jackton Business Centre

Borthwick Dr

Allan Pl

Milburn Wy

Milburn Gdns

White Cart Water

53

Kirtle Pl

Annan Av

Burnock

Lochar

Dee

2

EAGLESHAM ROAD

Westend

Lendal Pl

Trent

Tyne Place

Swift P

land

Mossneuk

3

Waukers

South Lanarkshire

East Renfrewshire

Lawside

Newhouse

Newland Farm

52

Polnoon Water

Craighall

Jackton Road

Newlands Ro

4

Mains

North Allerton

5

Polnoon

South Allerton

hall Road

Millhall

651

A 259 **B** Nethercraig **C** 60 **D**

Millhouse

Millhall Road

Golf Club

Cadzow Castle

E

170

F

G

H

171

Golf Course

ewood

Avonba Crs
Dungavel Gdns
Avonb
Avonavel Avenue
Tinto Vw
Silverhill

Moore Gdns
Aitken
Austine Dr
Bishop Gdns
Galston Court
Galston Ct
Dunion Court
Fenwick Drive
Fenwick Dr
Means Ct
Means Rd

Chatelherault
Country Park

I

53

Aitken Road

Avon Water

2

3

52

Carscallan

4

Carscallan Road

Elm Court

Beech Av
Chestnut Vw
Larch Rd
Furnace Rd
Battersan Gdns
Rowan Gv

Sunnyside Road

Sunnyside Road

Denholm Gdns
Castle Wynd
Cm Rd

Quarter

Merrick Gardens
Fenavon Road
Limeklinburn Rd
Darngaber Rd
Darngaber Gardens

PO
Quarter
Primary
School

St Torch Gr

5

651

2

73

74

E

F

Knowetop

G

H

Wee Sunnyside Road

Sunnyside Road

Abronhill	27 F2	Carnwadric	126 C3	Foxbar	103 E4
Airdrie	98 B2	Carrickstone	10 B5	Freeland	47 G3
Allanbank	159 G1	Castlecary	11 H1	Fullarton	112 B1
Allanton	159 H2	Castlehead	104 A1	Gallowhill	84 D2
Allanton	171 G4	Castlehill	12 A2	Gallowhill	147 F2
Anniesland	51 E5	Castlemilk	129 F5	Garnkirk	58 A5
Arden	125 G3	Cathcart	128 A1	Garrowhill	93 H4
Auchenback	142 B1	Chapelhall	119 E3	Gartcosh	72 D1
Auchinairn	55 E4	Charleston	104 B2	Garthamlock	71 E4
Auchinloch	57 E1	Chryston	58 B1	Gartlea	98 C3
Auchinraith	152 A3	Clarkston	99 E1	Gartloch	72 B3
Auchinreoch	6 B4	Clarkston	145 G3	Gartness	99 F4
Auchinstarry	8 C4	Cleekhimin	155 G2	Gartsherrie	74 B5
Baillieston	94 A5	Cleland	156 D1	Gateside	141 F1
Balloch	25 F3	Clevans	78 D4	Germiston	69 E4
Balmalloch	7 H1	Cliftonville	97 F2	Giffnock	127 G5
Balmore	18 C5	Clydebank	48 D2	Glasgow	3 G5
Balornock	55 E5	Coatbridge	97 E4	Glenburn	103 H5
Bankhead	129 G1	Coatdyke	97 G3	Glenmavis	75 G2
Bardowie	36 C1	College Milton	165 F2	Gorbals	89 H4
Bargarran	30 A5	Colston	54 B3	Govan	88 A1
Bargeddie	95 F5	Coltness	157 G4	Govanhill	109 F1
Barlanark	93 F3	Condorrat	44 A1	Greenend	97 F5
Barmulloch	69 G1	Corkerhill	107 F2	Greenfaulds	45 E1
Barncluith	170 C4	Cowlairs	68 C5	Greenfield	92 B5
Barrachnie	93 F4	Craigend	47 E2	Greenhead	174 C3
Barrhead	124 B4	Craigend	70 D5	Greenhills	177 H2
Battlefield	109 E4	Craigendoran	81 E3	Haghill	91 G2
Bearsden	34 B3	Craigneuk	98 D3	Hairmyres	164 D5
Bellahouston	87 H4	Craigneuk	155 G5	Hallside	132 B2
Bellshill	135 F3	Craigton	87 F4	Hamilton	170 C1
Bellside	157 G1	Cranhill	92 B1	Hardgate	32 C2
Biggar Road	138 D2	Craigenmuir	71 F2	Hareshaw	139 G2
Birdston	21 E2	Crindledyke	158 C5	Harestanes	22 B5
Birkenshaw	114 D3	Croftfoot	129 F2	Hayston	20 B5
Birniehill	178 D1	Crookfur	144 A4	High Blantyre	150 D4
Bishopbriggs	55 E5	Crookston	86 A5	High Crosshill	130 A1
Bishopton	28 D5	Crosshill	94 C4	High Gallowhill	38 F2
Blackhall	104 D1	Crosslee	80 B2	Highgate	86 B3
Blackwood	24 B5	Crossmill	124 B3	Hogganfield	70 A4
Blairhill	96 B3	Crossmyloof	108 C2	Holehills	76 C4
Blairlinn	45 F5	Croy	24 D1	Holehouse	140 C4
Blairskaith	18 A2	Cumbernauld	26 B4	Holytown	137 F1
Blantyre	151 E3	Cumbernauld Village	11 E5	Houston	80 C1
Blythswood	63 F1	Dalmarnock	110 D1	Howwood	120 B4
Bogside	175 H5	Dalmuir	31 H4	Hurlet	106 A5
Bonkle	158 D4	Dalshannon	43 H5	Hutchesontown	89 H3
Bothwell	152 A1	Dalton	132 D5	Ibrox	88 A3
Bowling	15 H5	Dean Park	63 G4	Inchinnan	46 B4
Braehead	164 C2	Dennistoun	90 D2	Johnstone	101 H4
Braidfauld	111 H1	Dennystown	12 D3	Kelvin	178 D3
Bridgend	58 C1	Dovecothall	124 D3	Kelvindale	51 H5
Bridge of Weir	79 H5	Downhill	66 B3	Kelvinside	67 C1
Bridgeton	90 D4	Drumchapel	50 A1	Kennishead	126 B2
Brookfield	101 E1	Drumgelloch	98 C1	Kessington	35 E4
Broom	144 C5	Drumpellier	95 H2	Kilbarchan	100 C5
Broomhill	65 G3	Drumry	49 F1	Kildrum	32 B4
Broomhouse	113 H2	Dullatur	9 G5	Kildrum	26 D2
Browsburn	98 C4	Dumbarton	13 F4	Kilsyth	8 C1
Brucehill	12 B4	Dumbreck	88 A5	Kings Park	129 E1
Buchley	36 D3	Dundyvan	96 C4	Kirkhill	162 D1
Burnbank	152 C5	Duntocher	31 G2	Kirkintilloch	20 C4
Burnfoot	75 H1	Earnock	169 E4	Kirkshaw	116 A1
Burnside	130 B2	Easterhouse	93 H1	Kirktonhill	12 D5
Busby	146 A5	Eastfield	25 G3	Kirkwood	95 H5
Cadder	38 A3	Eastfield	111 G5	Knightswood	50 D4
Cadzow	180 D1	East Kilbride	166 C5	Knowetop	172 A1
Cairnhill	97 H5	East Mains	166 C5	Kylepark	114 C5
Calderbank	118 C1	East Shawhead	117 F1	Laighstonehall	169 F3
Calderwood	166 C2	Eddlewood	180 D1	Lambhill	53 G4
Calton	90 B3	Elderslie	102 B2	Langloan	96 B4
Cambuslang	131 F3	Erskine	47 F2	Langside	108 D5
Cambusnethan	174 C2	Faifley	32 B1	Lennoxtown	4 C2
Carbrain	26 D4	Fairhill	169 H5	Lenzie	40 A3
Cardonald	86 C4	Fallside	116 A5	Lenziemill	26 B5
Carfin	137 G5	Ferguslie Park	83 G4	Linwood	81 H5
Carmunnock	146 D2	Fernhill	130 A5	Lochwood	72 C5
Carmyle	112 C4	Ferniegair	171 E4	Low Blantyre	151 H1
Carnbroe	117 H1	Flemington	131 H4	Low Waters	170 B4
Carntyne	91 H2	Forgewood	136 B5	Luggiebank	45 G2
Mansewood	127 E1	Radnor Park	31 H4			
Marnock	59 H5	Ranfurly	79 F5			
Maryhill	52 B5	Rashielee	47 F1			
Mearns	162 A2	Rawyards	76 C5			
Meikle Earnock	180 C1	Renfrew	63 F3			
Merrylee	127 G3	Riddrie	69 G5			
Millarston	103 F1	Robroyston	55 H5			
Millersneuk	40 B4	Rogerton	148 C4			
Millerston	70 B2	Rosebank	22 A5			
Millikenpark	100 C5	Rosehall	97 E5			
Milngavie	17 C4	Rossland	46 B1			
Milnwood	136 C3	Royston	3 K1			
Milton	14 C4	Ruchazie	70 C5			
Milton	53 H4	Ruchill	67 F1			
Milton of Campsie	5 H5	Rutherglen	110 B3			
Moffat Mills	99 G2	Saint Leonards	167 F5			
Mollinsburn	43 E4	Scotstoun	64 C1			
Mollinsburn	41 H5	Seafar	26 A4			
Morningside	175 H2	Shawhead	116 C1			
Mossend	136 C2	Shawlands	108 C4			
Mossneuk	176 D2	Sheddens	146 A3			
Mosspark	107 F1	Shettleston	92 B4			
Motherwell	154 D5	Shieldhall	86 D1			
Mountblow	30 D4	Shieldmuir	172 D1			
Mount Vernon	112 D2	Shortroods	83 H1			
Mt Florida	109 G5	Sighthill	68 B4			
Muirend	128 A2	Silverton	13 G3			
Muirhead	58 C4	Silvertonhill	170 A3			
Muirhead	113 H1	Sizginth	22 B4			
Muirhouse	172 B2	Springboig	92 D3			
The Murray	178 B3	Springburn	68 C2			
Neilston	141 F4	Springhill	142 B3			
Nerston	149 F4	Stamperland	146 A2			
Nether Kirton	141 G2	Stepps	70 D1			
Netherlee	127 H4	Stewartfield	165 H1			
Netherplace	160 C1	Stonefield	152 A2			
Netherton	173 F4	Strathbungo	108 D2			
Newarthill	138 C5	Summerston	53 D5			
Newhousemill	167 G5	Swinton	94 B3			
Newlands	127 G1	Tannochside	115 F4			
Newlandsmuir	177 E1	Temple	51 F4			
Newmains	158 A5	Thornliebank	126 B4			
New Stevenston	137 G5	Thornly Park	104 C3			
Newton	132 C1	Thorntonhall	163 H2			
Newton Mearns	161 F1	Thrashbush	76 A5			
Nitshill	125 E2	Torbush	175 G2			
North Motherwell	154 B2	Torrance	19 F4			
Oatlands	110 A1	Townend	13 F1			
Old Balornock	69 E1	Townhead	3 H3			
Oldhall	85 G4	Twechar	23 E2			
Old Kilpatrick	30 A2	Uddingston	133 H2			
Old Monkland	96 B5	Udston	168 D1			
Orbiston	135 G3	Victory Gardens	63 F5			
Oxgang	40 C1	Viewpark	115 H4			
Paisley	104 C1	Wardpark	11 E3			
Parkhall	31 G3	Waterfoot	162 D4			
Parkhead	91 G5	Waterloo	174 C5			
Park Mains	47 H2	Waterside	41 E1			
Parkside	139 F5	Waterside	124 D2			
Partick	65 H4	West Arthurlie	123 G5			
Pather	174 A4	Westburn	132 B1			
Peel Park	165 E5	West Drumoyne	87 F2			
Petersburn	99 F3	Wester Auchinloch	57 E2			
Petershill	69 G3	Westfield	43 G2			
Pilmuir	160 B4	West Mains	166 A4			
Pilmuir	160 B4	West Porton	28 D4			
Plains	77 G4	Westwood	165 H5			
Pollokshaws	108 A4	Whifflet	97 E4			
Pollokshields	108 C1	Whinhall	97 H1			
Polmadie	109 H2	Whitecraigs	144 D4			
Port Dundas	67 H4	Whitecrook	49 G3			
Porterfield	62 D4	Whitehill	152 C3			
Possil Park	67 H1	Whitehills	178 C3			
Priesthill	125 F1	Whiteinch	65 F2			
Provanmill	69 H3	Williamwood	145 E2			
Quarrelton	101 F5	Wishaw	173 H1			
Quarriers Village	78 A1	Yett	137 H4			
Quarter	181 E5	Yoker	49 H4			
Queenslie	93 E1	Yorkhill	88 B1			
Queenzieburn	7 F2					

USING THE STREET INDEX

Street names are listed alphabetically. Each street name is followed by its postal town or area locality, the Postcode District, the page number, and the reference to the square in which the name is found.

Standard index entries are shown as follows:

Abbey Cl *PSLY* PA1 ....**84** B4

Street names and selected addresses not shown on the map due to scale restrictions are shown in the index with an asterisk:

Auchinbee Farm Rd *BALLOCH* G68 *.....**25** F1

GENERAL ABBREVIATIONS

ACC	ACCESS	CLFS	CLIFFS	DR	DRIVE	GDNS	GARDENS	INT	INTERCHANGE
ALY	ALLEY	CMP	CAMP	DRO	DROVE	GLD	GLADE	IS	ISLAND
AP	APPROACH	CNR	CORNER	DRY	DRIVEWAY	GLN	GLEN	JCT	JUNCTION
AR	ARCADE	CO	COUNTY	DWGS	DWELLINGS	GN	GREEN	JTY	JETTY
ASS	ASSOCIATION	COLL	COLLEGE	E	EAST	GND	GROUND	KG	KING
AV	AVENUE	COM	COMMON	EMB	EMBANKMENT	GRA	GRANGE	KNL	KNOLL
BCH	BEACH	COMM	COMMISSION	EMBY	EMBASSY	GRG	GARAGE	L	LAKE
BLDS	BUILDINGS	CON	CONVENT	ESP	ESPLANADE	GT	GREAT	LA	LANE
BND	BEND	COT	COTTAGE	EST	ESTATE	GTWY	GATEWAY	LDG	LODGE
BNK	BANK	COTS	COTTAGES	EX	EXCHANGE	GV	GROVE	LGT	LIGHT
BR	BRIDGE	CP	CAPE	EXPY	EXPRESSWAY	HGR	HIGHER	LK	LOCK
BRK	BROOK	CPS	COPSE	EXT	EXTENSION	HL	HILL	LKS	LAKES
BTM	BOTTOM	CR	CREEK	F/O	FLYOVER	HLS	HILLS	LNDG	LANDING
BUS	BUSINESS	CREM	CREMATORIUM	FC	FOOTBALL CLUB	HO	HOUSE	LTL	LITTLE
BVD	BOULEVARD	CRS	CRESCENT	FK	FORK	HOL	HOLLOW	LWR	LOWER
BY	BYPASS	CSWY	CAUSEWAY	FLD	FIELD	HOSP	HOSPITAL	MAG	MAGISTRATE
CATH	CATHEDRAL	CT	COURT	FLDS	FIELDS	HRB	HARBOUR	MAN	MANSIONS
CEM	CEMETERY	CTRL	CENTRAL	FLS	FALLS	HTH	HEATH	MD	MEAD
CEN	CENTRE	CTS	COURTS	FM	FARM	HTS	HEIGHTS	MDW	MEADOWS
CFT	CROFT	CTYD	COURTYARD	FT	FORT	HVN	HAVEN	MEM	MEMORIAL
CH	CHURCH	CUTT	CUTTINGS	FTS	FLATS	HWY	HIGHWAY	MI	MILL
CHA	CHASE	CV	COVE	FWY	FREEWAY	IMP	IMPERIAL	MKT	MARKET
CHYD	CHURCHYARD	CYN	CANYON	FY	FERRY	IN	INLET	MKTS	MARKETS
CIR	CIRCLE	DEPT	DEPARTMENT	GA	GATE	IND EST	INDUSTRIAL ESTATE	ML	MALL
CIRC	CIRCUS	DL	DALE	GAL	GALLERY	INF	INFIRMARY	MNR	MANOR
CL	CLOSE	DM	DAM	GDN	GARDEN	INFO	INFORMATION	MS	MEWS

MSN......MISSION
MT......MOUNT
MTN......MOUNTAIN
MTS......MOUNTAINS
MUS......MUSEUM
MWY......MOTORWAY
N......NORTH
NE......NORTH EAST
NW......NORTH WEST
O/P......OVERPASS
OFF......OFFICE
ORCH......ORCHARD
OV......OVAL
PAL......PALACE
PAS......PASSAGE
PAV......PAVILION
PDE......PARADE
PH......PUBLIC HOUSE
PK......PARK

PKWY......PARKWAY
PL......PLACE
PLN......PLAIN
PLNS......PLAINS
PLZ......PLAZA
POL......POLICE STATION
PR......PRINCE
PREC......PRECINCT
PREP......PREPARATORY
PRIM......PRIMARY
PROM......PROMENADE
PRS......PRINCESS
PRT......PORT
PT......POINT
PZ......PIAZZA
QD......QUADRANT
QU......QUEEN
QY......QUAY

R......RIVER
RBT......ROUNDABOUT
RD......ROAD
RDG......RIDGE
REP......REPUBLIC
RES......RESERVOIR
RFC......RUGBY FOOTBALL CLUB
RI......RISE
RM......RAMP
RW......ROW
S......SOUTH
SCH......SCHOOL
SE......SOUTH EAST
SER......SERVICE AREA
SH......SHORE
SHOP......SHOPPING
SKWY......SKYWAY
SMT......SUMMIT
SOC......SOCIETY

SP......SPUR
SPR......SPRING
SQ......SQUARE
ST......STREET
STN......STATION
STR......STREAM
STRD......STRAND
SW......SOUTH WEST
TDG......TRADING
TER......TERRACE
THWY......THROUGHWAY
TNL......TUNNEL
TOLL......TOLLWAY
TPK......TURNPIKE
TR......TRACK
TRL......TRAIL
TWR......TOWER
U/P......UNDERPASS
UNI......UNIVERSITY

UPR......UPPER
V......VALE
VA......VALLEY
VIAD......VIADUCT
VIL......VILLA
VIS......VISTA
VLG......VILLAGE
VLS......VILLAS
VW......VIEW
W......WEST
WD......WOOD
WHF......WHARF
WK......WALK
WKS......WALKS
WLS......WELLS
WY......WAY
YD......YARD
YHA......YOUTH HOSTEL

POSTCODE TOWNS AND AREA ABBREVIATIONS

AIRDRIE......Airdrie
BAIL/MDB/MHD......Baillieston/Moodiesburn/Muirhead
BALLOCH......Balloch
BLSH......Bellshill
BLTYR/CAMB......Blantyre/Cambuslang
BNYBR/BNK......Bonnybridge/Banknock
BRHD/NEIL......Barrhead/Neilston
BRWEIR......Bridge of Weir
BSDN......Bearsden
BSHPBGS......Bishopbriggs
BSHPTN......Bishopton
CAR/SHTL/MSPK......Carmyle/Shettleston
CARD/HILL/MSPK......Cardonald/Hillington/Mosspark
CARLUKE......Carluke

CGLE......Central Glasgow east
CGLW......Central Glasgow west
CLYDBK......Clydebank
COWCAD......Cowcaddens
CRG/CRSL/HOU......Craigends/Crosslee/Houston
CRMNK/CLK/EAG......Carmunnock/Clarkston/Eaglesham
CSMK......Castlemilk
CTBR......Coatbridge
CUMB......Cumbernauld
DEN/PKHD......Dennistoun/Parkhead
DMBTN......Dumbarton
DMNK/BRGTN......Dalmarnock/Bridgeton
DRUM......Drumchapel
EKILN......East Kilbride north

EKILS......East Kilbride south
ERSK......Erskine
ESTRH......Easterhouse
GBLS......Gorbals
GIF/THBK......Giffnock/Thornliebank
GOV/IBX......Govan/Ibrox
GVH/MTFL......Govanhill/Mount Florida
HMLTN......Hamilton
HWWD......Howwood
JNSTN......Johnstone
KKNTL......Kirkintilloch
KLBCH......Kilbarchan
KNTSWD......Knightswood
KSYTH......Kilsyth
KVD/HLHD......Kelvindale/Hillhead
KVGV......Kelvingrove
LNPK/KPK......Linn Park/King's Park

LRKH......Larkhall
MLNGV......Milngavie
MRYH/FIRH......Maryhill/Firhill
MTHW......Motherwell
NMRNS......Newton Mearns
OLDK......Old Kilpatrick
PGL......Port Glasgow
PLK/PH/NH......Pollock/Priesthill/Nitshill
PLKSD/SHW......Pollokshields/Shawlands
PLKSW/MSWD......Pollockshaws/Manseswood
PPK/MIL......Possil Park/Milton
PSLY......Paisley
PSLYN/LNWD......Paisley north/Linwood

PSLYS......Paisley south
PTCK......Partick
RNFRW......Renfrew
RUTH......Rutherglen
SCOT......Scotstoun
SHTTS......Shotts
SMSTN......Summerston
SPRGB/BLRNK......Springburn/Balornock
STPS/GTHM/RID......Stepps/Garthamlock/Riddrie
STRHV......Strathaven
UD/BTH/TAN......Uddingston/Bothwell/Tannochside
WISHAW......Wishaw

A

Abbey Cl PSLY PA1......84 B4
Abbeycraig Rd ESTRH G34......94 D1
Abbey Dr SCOT G14......65 F2
Abbeygreen St ESTRH G34......72 D5
Abbeyhill St CAR/SHTL G32......91 H2
Abbeylands Rd CLYDBK G81......32 B2
Abbey Pl AIRDRIE ML6......98 D5
Abbey Rd JNSTN PA5......102 A2
Abbots Ct BALLOCH G68......9 H3
Abbotsford BSHPBGS G64......55 F5
Abbotsford Av HMLTN ML3......152 C4
RUTH G73......111 E5
Abbotsford Brae EKILN G74......166 B2
Abbotsford Ct CUMB G67......45 E1
Abbotsford Crs HMLTN ML3......152 C4
PSLY PA2......102 C5
WISHAW ML2......174 A1
Abbotsford La BLSH ML4......135 G1
GBLS G5......89 G5
Abbotsford Pl CUMB G67......45 E1
BSDN G61......33 H2
CLYDBK G81......49 E2
CUMB G67......45 E1
CUMB G67......26 B5
HMLTN ML3......152 B4
WISHAW ML2......174 B1
Abbotshall Av DRUM G15......32 D5
Abbotsinch Rd PSLYN/LNWD PA3......62 B5
Abbots Ter AIRDRIE ML6......98 D5
Abbot St PLKSD/SHW G41......108 D3
Abbott Crs CLYDBK G81......49 F3
Abercorn Av CARD/HILL/MSPK G52......85 H2
Abercorn Crs HMLTN ML3......170 C3
Abercorn Dr HMLTN ML3......170 C2
Abercorn Pl SMSTN G23......52 D2
Abercorn Rd NMRNS G77......143 H4
Abercorn St CLYDBK G81......32 D1
PSLYN/LNWD PA3......84 C4
Abercrombie Crs BAIL/MDB/MHD G69......95 F4
Abercromby Crs EKILN G74......167 H1
Abercromby Dr DMNK/BRGTN G40......90 C3
Abercromby Pl EKILN G74......167 G1
Abercromby St DMNK/BRGTN G40......90 C4
Aberdalgie Gdns ESTRH G34......94 A1
Aberdalgie Rd ESTRH G34......94 A1
Aberdour Ct BLTYR/CAMB G72......168 B4
Aberdour St DEN/PKHD G31......91 F2
Aberfeldy Av AIRDRIE ML6......77 G3
Aberfeldy St DEN/PKHD G31......91 F1
Aberfoyle St DEN/PKHD G31......91 F2
Aberlady Rd GOV/IBX G51......87 F3
Aberlady St MTHW ML1......157 E1
Aberlour Av BLTYR/CAMB G72......168 C2
Abernethy Dr PSLYN/LNWD PA3......101 H1
Abernethy Rd WISHAW ML2......173 H4
Abernethy Pl NMRNS G77......162 C1
Abernethy St DEN/PKHD G31......91 F2
Aberuthven Dr CAR/SHTL G32......112 C1
Abiegail Pl BLTYR/CAMB G72......151 G1

Aboukir St GOV/IBX G51......87 F1
Aboyne Dr PSLY PA2......104 C3
Acacia Dr BRHD/NEIL G78......123 H2
PSLY PA2......103 G5
Acacia Pl JNSTN PA5......121 H1
Acacia Wy BLTYR/CAMB G72......132 B2
Academy Pk AIRDRIE ML6......98 B2
PLKSD/SHW G41......88 B5
Academy St AIRDRIE ML6......98 B2
CAR/SHTL G32......92 C5
Acer Crs PSLY PA2......103 F5
Acer Gv AIRDRIE ML6......119 F1
Achamore Dr DRUM G15......32 C4
Achamore Gdns DRUM G15......32 C4
Achamore Rd DRUM G15......32 C4
Acherhill Gdns KNTSWD G13......50 B3
Achnasheen Rd AIRDRIE ML6......99 H3
Achray Dr PSLY PA2......103 F3
Achray Pl CTBR ML5......73 H5
MLNGV G62......16 B2
Achray Rd CUMB G67......44 A2
Acorn St DMNK/BRGTN G40......90 C5
Acre Dr MRYH/FIRH G20......52 A2
Acredyke Crs SPRGB/BLRNK G21......55 E4
Acredyke Pl SPRGB/BLRNK G21......55 F5
Acredyke Rd RUTH G73......110 C4
SPRGB/BLRNK G21......55 E4
Acre Rd MRYH/FIRH G20......52 A2
Acre Valley Rd BSHPBGS G64......19 E5
Adam Av AIRDRIE ML6......98 C2
Adams Court La CGLE G1......2 E7
Adamslie Dr KNTSWD G13......49 H3
Adamson St BLSH ML4......136 C2
Adams Pl KSYTH G65......8 B2
Adamswell St SPRGB/BLRNK G21......68 B3
Adamswell Ter BAIL/MDB/MHD G69......59 F1
Addie St MTHW ML1......155 E1
Addiewell Pl CTBR ML5......96 D5
Addiewell St CAR/SHTL G32......92 B2
Addison Gv GIF/THBK G46......126 B3
Addison Rd GIF/THBK G46......126 C3
KVD/HLHD G12......66 C2
Adelaide Ct CLYDBK G81......31 E3
Adelaide Rd EKILS G75......177 G1
Adele St MTHW ML1......172 A1
Adelphi St GBLS G5......89 H4
Admiral St PLKSD/SHW G41......88 D4
Admiralty Gv OLDK G60......30 C3
Admiralty Pl OLDK G60......30 C3
Advie Pl GVH/MTFL G42......109 G4
Affric Dr PSLY PA2......105 E3
Afton Crs BSDN G61......52 A1
Afton Dr RNFRW PA4......63 H4
Afton Gdns BLTYR/CAMB G72......151 E4
CTBR ML5......97 G4
Afton Rd CUMB G67......26 D1
Afton St PLKSD/SHW G41......108 D4
Afton Vw KKNTL G66......21 H4
Agamemnon St CLYDBK G81......48 C2
Agnew Gv BLSH ML4......135 E2
Agnew La GVH/MTFL G42......109 F2
Aikenhead Rd GVH/MTFL G42......109 H2
LNPK/KPK G44......128 D1
Aikman Pl EKILN G74......166 B2
Aikman Rd MTHW ML1......154 A5
Ailean Dr CAR/SHTL G32......93 F5
Ailean Gdns CAR/SHTL G32......93 F5
Aillort Pl EKILN G74......166 B2

Ailort Av LNPK/KPK G44......128 B2
Ailsa Av MTHW ML1......154 A3
Ailsa Ct HMLTN ML3......168 C4
Ailsa Crs MTHW ML1......154 A3
Ailsa Dr CLYDBK G81......32 A2
GIF/THBK G46......145 F2
GVH/MTFL G42......109 E5
KKNTL G66......39 H5
PSLY PA2......104 A5
RUTH G73......129 G2
UD/BTH/TAN G71......134 B3
Ailsa Pl CTBR ML5......96 C5
Ailsa Rd BSHPBGS G64......55 E1
CTBR ML5......96 B5
RNFRW PA4......63 F4
Ainslie Av CARD/HILL/MSPK G52......86 B1
Ainslie Rd CARD/HILL/MSPK G52......86 C2
CUMB G67......27 E2
Airbles Crs MTHW ML1......154 C5
Airbles Dr MTHW ML1......154 C5
Airbles Farm Rd MTHW ML1......171 F1
MTHW ML1......154 B5
Airbles Rd MTHW ML1......154 D5
Airbles St MTHW ML1......154 D5
Airdale Av GIF/THBK G46......127 F5
Airdriehill Rd AIRDRIE ML6......76 D4
Airdrie Rd AIRDRIE ML6......77 G5
CUMB G67......43 F4
KSYTH G65......9 E5
Airgold Dr DRUM G15......33 E4
Airlie Av BSDN G61......34 B1
Airlie Dr BLSH ML4......135 H1
Airlie Gdns RUTH G73......130 C3
Airlie La KVD/HLHD G12......66 A4
Airlie Rd BAIL/MDB/MHD G69......113 H1
Airlie St KVD/HLHD G12......66 A4
Airlour Rd PLKSW/MSWD G43......127 H2
Airth Dr CARD/HILL/MSPK G52......107 G1
Airth La CARD/HILL/MSPK G52......107 G1
Airthrey Av SCOT G14......65 F2
Airthrey La SCOT G14......65 F2
Airth Wy BALLOCH G68......24 C5
Aitchison Ct AIRDRIE ML6......98 A1
Aitchison St AIRDRIE ML6......97 H2
Aitkenbar Cir DMBTN G82......13 C2
Aitkenbar Dr DMBTN G82......13 C1
Aitken Cl WISHAW ML2......158 B3
Aitkenhead Av CTBR ML5......95 C5
Aitkenhead Rd AIRDRIE ML6......119 E2
UD/BTH/TAN G71......115 E4
Aitken Rd HMLTN ML3......181 E2
Aitken St AIRDRIE ML6......76 B5
DEN/PKHD G31......91 E5
Alasdair Ct BRHD/NEIL G78......124 B5
Albany Av CAR/SHTL G32......92 D4
Albany Dr RUTH G73......130 A3
Albany Pl UD/BTH/TAN G71......134 D1
Albany Qd CAR/SHTL G32......92 D4
Albany Rd HMLTN ML3......180 D1
Albany St DMNK/BRGTN G40......90 D5
CTBR ML5......96 B2
Albany Ter BLTYR/CAMB G72......130 D4
Alba Wy HMLTN ML3......180 D1
Alberta Av CTBR ML5......96 C1
EKILS G75......165 H5
Alberta Crs EKILS G75......165 H5
Alberta Pk EKILS G75......165 H5
Albert Av GVH/MTFL G42......109 E3
Albert Crs AIRDRIE ML6......98 C2
Albert Dr BSDN G61......35 E4
PLKSD/SHW G41......88 D5
RUTH G73......130 A2

Albert Pl AIRDRIE ML6......98 C1
Albert Qd MTHW ML1......137 F2
Albert Rd CLYDBK G81......31 G5
GVH/MTFL G42......109 F3
JNSTN PA5......101 F5
KKNTL G66......39 H5
RNFRW PA4......63 F3
Albert St CTBR ML5......96 D2
HMLTN ML3......152 C4
MTHW ML1......155 E3
Albert Ter HMLTN ML3......152 B4
Albion Ga CGLE G1......3 H6
Albion St BAIL/MDB/MHD G69......113 G1
CGLE G1......3 H6
CTBR ML5......96 C2
MTHW ML1......155 E3
PSLYN/LNWD PA3......84 B3
Albion Wy EKILS G75......178 C3
Alcaig Rd CARD/HILL/MSPK G52......107 F2
Alcath Rd WISHAW ML2......158 C4
Alclutha Av DMBTN G82......13 G4
Alder Av HMLTN ML3......170 B4
KKNTL G66......39 G3
Alder Bank UD/BTH/TAN G71......115 H5
Alder Ct BRHD/NEIL G78......142 B1
EKILS G75......177 H5
Alder Crs EKILS G75......177 H5
Alder Gdns MTHW ML1......172 D2
Alder Ga BLTYR/CAMB G72......132 B2
Alder Gv CTBR ML5......97 E3
Alderman Pl KNTSWD G13......50 D5
Alderman Rd KNTSWD G13......50 A4
Alder Pl EKILS G75......177 H5
JNSTN PA5......101 H5
PLKSW/MSWD G43......127 F2
Alder Rd CLYDBK G81......31 G3
CUMB G67......26 B5
DMBTN G82......12 D5
KKNTL G66......6 F5
PLKSW/MSWD G43......127 F2
Alderside Av WISHAW ML2......175 E1
Alderside Gdns UD/BTH/TAN G71......114 D5
Alderstocks EKILS G75......178 B5
Alderston Pl BLSH ML4......135 F3
Aldersyde Pl BLTYR/CAMB G72......151 F1
Aldersyde Ter MTHW ML1......157 F1
Alexander Av UD/BTH/TAN G71......134 D1
Alexander Balfour Gdns HMLTN ML3......170 A4
Alexander Crs GBLS G5......89 H5
Alexander Gdns HMLTN ML3......170 D3
Alexander Gibson Wy MTHW ML1......154 C5
Alexander Pl KKNTL G66......41 H1
Alexander St CLYDBK G81......49 E2
CTBR ML5......97 E1
DMBTN G82......13 G2
WISHAW ML2......173 G2
Alexander Ter BRHD/NEIL G78......140 D4
Alexandra Av STPS/GTHM/RID G33......57 G5
Alexandra Ct DEN/PKHD G31......91 E1
Alexandra Dr PSLY PA2......103 G3
RNFRW PA4......63 G3
Alexandra Gdns KKNTL G66......39 H4
Alexandra Pde DEN/PKHD G31......90 C1
Alexandra Pk KKNTL G66......39 H4
Alexandra Park St DEN/PKHD G31......91 E1
Alexandra Rd KKNTL G66......39 H4
EKILS G75......21 E5

KKNTL G66......20 D5
Alford Pl PSLYN/LNWD PA3......81 F5
Alford Od WISHAW ML2......158 A4
Alford St SPRGB/BLRNK G21......68 A3
Alfred La KVD/HLHD G12......66 D3
Aigle St GVH/MTFL G42......109 E4
Algoma Pl EKILS G75......165 G5
Alice Av BLSH ML4......135 H3
Alice St PSLYS PA2......104 B2
Aline Ct BRHD/NEIL G78......124 A3
Alison Lea EKILN G74......167 F2
Allan Av RNFRW PA4......63 H5
Allanbank St SHOTS ML7......159 G2
Allan Ct EKILS G75......176 D1
Allan Crs DMBTN G82......13 G1
Allandale Av MTHW ML1......138 C2
Allander Av MLNGV G62......36 B1
Allander Dr BSHPBGS G64......19 E5
Allander Gdns BSHPBGS G64......19 F5
Allander Rd MLNGV G62......17 E3
Allander St PPK/MIL G22......67 H2
Allands Av RNFRW PA4......61 H1
Allanfauld Rd CUMB G67......26 B3
Allan Glen Gdns BSHPBGS G64......37 H4
Allan Gv BLSH ML4......136 A1
Allan Pl DMBTN G82......13 E5
DMNK/BRGTN G40......111 E1
EKILS G75......176 D1
Allanshaw Gdns HMLTN ML3......169 G3
Allanshaw Gv HMLTN ML3......169 G3
Allanshaw St HMLTN ML3......169 G3
Allan St CTBR ML5......96 A4
DMNK/BRGTN G40......111 E2
MTHW ML1......155 E3
Allanton Av PSLY PA1......85 H5
Allanton Dr CARD/HILL/MSPK G52......86 C4
Allanton Gv WISHAW ML2......158 B4
Allanton Lea HMLTN ML3......169 H5
Allanton Pl HMLTN ML3......170 B4
Allanton Rd SHOTS ML7......159 F2
Albany Crs MTHW ML1......137 G3
Allendale EKILN G74......165 H2
Allender Rd BSDN G61......51 E1
BSDN G61......34 A5
Allen Wy RNFRW PA4......63 G5
Allerdyce Dr DRUM G15......50 A2
Allershaw Pl WISHAW ML2......173 G5
Allershaw Rd WISHAW ML2......173 G5
Allerton Gdns BAIL/MDB/MHD G69......93 G5
Allison Av ERSK PA8......47 E3
Allison Dr BLTYR/CAMB G72......131 F1
Allison Pl BAIL/MDB/MHD G69......72 D2
GVH/MTFL G42......109 F2
NMRNS G77......161 F2
Allison St GVH/MTFL G42......109 F2
Allnach Pl ESTRH G34......95 E1
Alloway Av PSLYS PA2......105 E4
Alloway Ct KKNTL G66......22 A3
Alloway Crs PSLYS PA2......104 D4
RUTH G73......129 G2
Alloway Dr CLYDBK G81......32 B5
KKNTL G66......22 A3
NMRNS G77......162 B1
PSLYS PA2......105 F4
RUTH G73......129 G2
Alloway Gdns HMLTN ML3......168 C4
KKNTL G66......22 A3
Alloway Gv KKNTL G66......22 A3
Alloway Rd AIRDRIE ML6......99 G1
EKILN G74......167 H2
PLKSW/MSWD G43......127 G1
Alloway Ter KKNTL G66......21 H3
Almada La HMLTN ML3......170 A1
Almada St HMLTN ML3......170 A1
Almond Av RNFRW PA4......63 H4

Almond Bank *BSDN* G61.....50 D1
Almond Crs *PSLYS* PA2.....103 E2
Almond Dr *BSHPTN* PA7.....46 A1
 EKILN G74.....167 E4
 KNNTL G66.....23 F5
Almond Pl *CTBR* ML5.....34 A5
Almond Rd *BSDN* G61.....50 D1
 CUMB G67.....11 H5
 STPS/GTHM/RID G33.....70 D1
Almond St
 STPS/GTHM/RID G33.....69 G5
Almond V *UD/BTH/TAN* G71.....115 F5
Almond Wy *MTHW* ML1.....171 H2
Alness Crs
 CARD/HILL/MSPK G52.....107 E4
Alness St *HMLTN* ML3.....170 A3
Alness Ter *HMLTN* ML3.....170 A3
Alpine Gv *UD/BTH/TAN* G71.....115 E5
Alpine Pth *BLTYR/CAMB* G72.....151 H5
Alpine Wk *BLTYR/CAMB* G72.....151 H5
Alsatian Av *CLYDBK* G81.....49 G1
Alsh Ter *HMLTN* ML3.....169 F4
Alston Av *CTBR* ML5.....97 E1
Altnacreag Gdns
 BAIL/MDB/MHD G69.....42 B5
Alton Rd *PSLY* PA1.....85 F5
Altpatrick Gdns *JNSTN* PA5.....102 A1
Altyre St *CAR/SHTL* G32.....112 A1
Alva Ga
 CARD/HILL/MSPK G52.....107 F3
Alva Ga
 CARD/HILL/MSPK G52.....107 F1
Alva Pl *KNNTL* G66.....40 B4
Alwyn Av *CRG/CRSL/HOU* PA6.....81 E3
Alwyn Ct *EKILN* G74.....166 B2
Alwyn Dr *EKILN* G74.....166 B2
Alyssum Crs *MTHW* ML1.....154 C2
Alyth Crs
 CRMNK/CLK/EAG G76.....146 B2
Alyth Gdns
 CARD/HILL/MSPK G52.....107 F1
 CRMNK/CLK/EAG G76.....146 B2
Amber Ter *BLSH* ML4.....135 H5
Ambleside *EKILS* G75.....177 E2
Ambleside Ri *HMLTN* ML3.....180 C5
Amethyst Av *BLSH* ML4.....135 H5
Amisfield St *MRYH/FIRH* G20.....66 D1
Amochrie Dr *PSLYS* PA2.....103 F4
Amochrie Gln *PSLYS* PA2.....103 F4
Amochrie Rd *PSLYS* PA2.....103 E4
Amochrie Wy *PSLYS* PA2.....103 E3
Amulree Pl *CAR/SHTL* G32.....92 B5
Amulree St *CAR/SHTL* G32.....112 B1
Ancaster Dr *KNTSWD* G13.....51 G5
Ancaster La *KNTSWD* G13.....51 G5
Anchor Av *PSLY* PA1.....84 D5
Anchor Crs *PSLY* PA1.....104 D1
Anchor Dr *PSLY* PA1.....84 D5
Anchor La *CGLE* G1.....2 C5
Anchor Wynd *PSLY* PA1.....104 D1
Ancroft St *MRYH/FIRH* G20.....67 F3
Andersen Ct *EKILS* G75.....178 B3
Anderside *EKILS* G75.....178 B3
Anderson Av *KSYTH* G65.....7
Anderson Ct *BLSH* ML4.....136 A2
Anderson Dr *NMRNS* G77.....161 F1
 RNFRW PA4.....63 H2
Anderson La *AIRDRIE* ML6.....98 B1
Anderson Rd *BSHPTN* PA7.....28 D4
Anderson St *AIRDRIE* ML6.....98 B1
 HMLTN ML3.....152 D5
 MTHW ML1.....154 D5
 PTCK G11.....66 A4
Anderston Quay *KVGV* G3.....89 E3
Andrew Av *KNNTL* G66.....40 A5
 RNFRW PA4.....63 H2
Andrew Dr *CLYDBK* G81.....49 F5
Andrew Paton Wy
 HMLTN ML3.....152 B4
Andrew Sillars Av
 BLTYR/CAMB G72.....131 H2
Andrew St *EKILN* G74.....166 C4
 PSLYN/LNWD PA3.....84 A3
Anford Gdns
 BLTYR/CAMB G72.....151 H3
Anford Pl *BLTYR/CAMB* G72.....151 H3
Angela Wy *UD/BTH/TAN* G71.....134 A1
Angle Ga *SCOT* G14.....65 E2
Angus Av *AIRDRIE* ML6.....98 B4
 BSHPBGS G64.....55 E2
 CARD/HILL/MSPK G52.....106 D1
 EKILN G74.....167 E5
 HMLTN ML3.....170 D2
 MTHW ML1.....154 B2
Angus Ov
 CARD/HILL/MSPK G52.....86 C5
Angus Pl
 CARD/HILL/MSPK G52.....86 C5
 EKILN G74.....167 E5
Angus St *CLYDBK* G81.....49 H5
 SPRGB/BLRNK G21.....68 B2
Anish Pl *DRUM* G15.....32 D4
Anniker Av *EKILS* G75.....178 C2
Annan Av *AIRDRIE* ML6.....119 E3
Annan Crs *AIRDRIE* ML6.....119 E3
Annandale St *GVH/MTFL* G42.....109 G1
Annan Dr *BSDN* G61.....33 H5
 PSLYS PA2.....103 E3
Annan Gld *MTHW* ML1.....172 B2
Annan Pl *MTHW* ML1.....172 B2
Annan St *MTHW* ML1.....120 D1
Annan St *MTHW* ML1.....172 B2
Annbank Pth *DEN/PKHD* G31.....90 C5
Annbank St *DEN/PKHD* G31.....90 C3
Ann Ct *HMLTN* ML3.....152 B5
Anne Av *RNFRW* PA4.....63 G2
Anne Crs *KNNTL* G66.....40 A5
Annerley Pl *CTBR* ML5.....96 B4
Annette St *GVH/MTFL* G42.....109 G2
Annfield Gdns
Annfield Pl *DEN/PKHD* G31.....90 D2
Annick Dr *BSDN* G61.....33 H5
Annick St *BLTYR/CAMB* G72.....132 A2
Anniesdale Av
 STPS/GTHM/RID G33.....57 F5
Annieshill Vw *AIRDRIE* ML6.....77 H4
Anniesland Crs *SCOT* G14.....64 B1

Anniesland Rd *KNTSWD* G13.....51 F5
 SCOT G14.....64 B1
Annieston *KSYTH* G65.....23 F1
Anniversary Av *EKILS* G75.....177 H1
Annsfield Rd *HMLTN* ML3.....180 C1
Ann St *HMLTN* ML3.....152 B5
 JNSTN PA5.....101 H3
Ansdell Av *BLTYR/CAMB* G72.....151 F3
Anson St *DMNK/BRGTN* G40.....90 C5
Anstruther St *CAR/SHTL* G32.....92 A5
Antermony Rd *KNNTL* G66.....21 H5
Anthony St *CGLW* G2.....2
Antigua Wy *EKILS* G75.....165 F4
Anton Crs *KSYTH* G65.....8 C2
Antonine *KNNTL* G66.....22 B3
Antonine Av *MTHW* ML1.....154 B2
Antonine Gdns *CLYDBK* G81.....31 H2
Antonine Rd *BALLOCH* G68.....9 G4
 BSDN G61.....33 G2
Anwoth St *CAR/SHTL* G32.....112 B1
Appin Crs *DEN/PKHD* G31.....91 E2
Appin Rd *DEN/PKHD* G31.....91 E2
Appin Ter *HMLTN* ML3.....168 D1
 RUTH G73.....130 C3
Appin Wy *AIRDRIE* ML6.....75 H2
 CTBR ML5.....96 B5
Appleby St *PPK/MIL* G22.....67 G3
Appleby Gv
 BAIL/MDB/MHD G69.....95 F3
Applecross Gdns
 BAIL/MDB/MHD G69.....42 A5
Applecross Qd *WISHAW* ML2.....157 E5
Applecross Rd *KNNTL* G66.....22 B4
Applecross St *COWCAD* G4.....67 G3
Appledore Crs
 UD/BTH/TAN G71.....134 B4
Apple Wy *EKILS* G75.....178 C2
Apsley St *PTCK* G11.....65 H4
Aqua Av *HMLTN* ML3.....168 D5
Aqua Ct *HMLTN* ML3.....168 D5
Araburn Dr *EKILS* G75.....178 B3
Aranthrue Crs *RNFRW* PA4.....63 F2
Aranthrue Dr *RNFRW* PA4.....63 F2
Aray St *MRYH/FIRH* G20.....52 C5
Arbroath Av
 CARD/HILL/MSPK G52.....86 C5
Arbroath Gv *HMLTN* ML3.....169 G3
Arbuckle Pl *AIRDRIE* ML6.....77 H3
Arcadia Pl *DMNK/BRGTN* G40.....90 B4
Arcadia St *BLSH* ML4.....116 D5
 DMNK/BRGTN G40.....90 B4
Arcan Crs *DRUM* G15.....50 C1
Archerfield Av *CAR/SHTL* G32.....112 B2
Archerfield Crs *CAR/SHTL* G32.....112 B2
Archerfield Dr *CAR/SHTL* G32.....112 B2
Archerfield Gv *CAR/SHTL* G32.....112 B2
Archerhill Av *KNTSWD* G13.....50 B3
Archerhill Crs *KNTSWD* G13.....50 C3
Archerhill Gdns *KNTSWD* G13.....50 C3
Archerhill Rd *KNTSWD* G13.....50 B3
Archerhill Sq *KNTSWD* G13.....50 A3
Archerhill Ter *KNTSWD* G13.....50 B3
Archibald Ter *KNNTL* G66.....5 F4
Archiebald Pl *BLSH* ML4.....136 C3
Arch Wy *KSYTH* G65.....8 B1
Ardargie Dr *CAR/SHTL* G32.....112 D4
Ardargie Gv *CAR/SHTL* G32.....112 D4
Ardargie Pl *CAR/SHTL* G32.....112 D4
Ardbeg Av *AIRDRIE* ML6.....76 B3
 RUTH G73.....130 D3
Ardbeg La *EKILN* G74.....164 B2
 GVH/MTFL G42.....109 F2
Ardbeg Rd *MTHW* ML1.....157 F5
Ardbeg St *GVH/MTFL* G42.....109 F2
Ardconnel St *GIF/THBK* G46.....126 C3
Arden Av *GIF/THBK* G46.....126 B5
Ardenclutch Av *HMLTN* ML3.....169 G1
Arden Ct *HMLTN* ML3.....170 A4
Ardencraig Crs *CSMK* G45.....146 D1
Ardencraig Dr *CSMK* G45.....129 G5
Ardencraig Gdns *CSMK* G45.....129 G5
Ardencraig La *CSMK* G45.....146 D1
Ardencraig Pl *CSMK* G45.....129 G5
Ardencraig Qd *CSMK* G45.....146 D1
Ardencraig Rd *CSMK* G45.....146 D1
Ardencraig St *CSMK* G45.....129 H5
Ardencraig Ter *CSMK* G45.....129 G5
Arden Dr *GIF/THBK* G46.....127 E5
Ardenlea *UD/BTH/TAN* G71.....115 F5
Ardenlea St
 DMNK/BRGTN G40.....111 E1
Arden Pl *GIF/THBK* G46.....126 B5
Arden Rd *HMLTN* ML3.....169 H5
Arden St *AIRDRIE* ML6.....77 H4
Arden Ter *HMLTN* ML3.....169 H5
Ardery St *PTCK* G11.....65 H4
Ardessie Pl *MRYH/FIRH* G20.....66 C1
Ardessie St *SMSTN* G23.....52 C2
Ardfern Rd *AIRDRIE* ML6.....99 H3
Ardfern St *CAR/SHTL* G32.....112 B1
Ardgay Pl *CAR/SHTL* G32.....92 B5
Ardgay St *CAR/SHTL* G32.....92 B5
Ardgay Wy *RUTH* G73.....130 A4
Ardgoil Dr *BALLOCH* G68.....25 E4
Ardgour Dr
 PSLYN/LNWD PA3.....101 H1
Ardgowan Av *PSLYS* PA2.....104 C1
Ardgowan Dr
 UD/BTH/TAN G71.....115 E4
Ardgowan St *PSLYS* PA2.....104 C2
Ardgowan Terrace La *KVGV* G3.....66 C5
Ardgryfe Crs
 CRG/CRSL/HOU PA6.....81 F2
Ardholm St *CAR/SHTL* G32.....92 B4
Ardhu Pl *DRUM* G15.....33 E4
Ardle Rd *PLKSW/MSWD* G43.....127 H2
Ardlui St *CAR/SHTL* G32.....111 H1
Ardmaleish Crs *CSMK* G45.....129 F5
Ardmaleish Dr *CSMK* G45.....129 F5
Ardmaleish Rd *CSMK* G45.....129 F5
Ardmaleish St *CSMK* G45.....129 F5
Ardmaleish Ter *CSMK* G45.....129 F5
Ardmay Crs *LNPK/KPK* G44.....109 H5
Ardmillan St
 STPS/GTHM/RID G33.....92 A1
Ardmore Cresent *AIRDRIE* ML6.....76 B3

Ardmory Av *GVH/MTFL* G42.....110 B5
Ardmory La *LNPK/KPK* G44.....110 B5
Ardmory Pl *GVH/MTFL* G42.....110 B5
Ardnahoe Av *GVH/MTFL* G42.....110 A4
Ardnahoe Pl *GVH/MTFL* G42.....110 A4
Ardneil Rd *GOV/IBX* G51.....87 G3
Ardnish St *GOV/IBX* G51.....87 E2
Ardoch Crs *DMBTN* G82.....12 C5
Ardoch Gv *BLTYR/CAMB* G72.....131 F1
Ardochrig *EKILS* G75.....178 B5
Ardoch Rd *BSDN* G61.....35 E3
Ardoch St *PPK/MIL* G22.....67 H2
Ardo Gdns *GOV/IBX* G51.....88 A4
Ardo Av *MTHW* ML1.....172 D2
Ard Rd *RNFRW* PA4.....63 E2
Ardshiel Rd *GOV/IBX* G51.....87 F2
Ardsloy Pl *SCOT* G14.....64 B2
Ard St *CAR/SHTL* G32.....92 B5
Ardtoe Crs
 STPS/GTHM/RID G33.....71 F1
Ardtoe Pl *STPS/GTHM/RID* G33.....71 F1
Arduthie Rd *GOV/IBX* G51.....87 F2
Ardwell Rd
 CARD/HILL/MSPK G52.....107 F1
Argus Av *AIRDRIE* ML6.....118 D2
Argyle Crs *DMBTN* G82.....12 C3
 HMLTN ML3.....169 H5
Argyle Dr *HMLTN* ML3.....169 F1
Argyle Gdns *KNNTL* G66.....4 B1
Argyle Rd *BSDN* G61.....34 B1
Argyle St *CGLW* G2.....2 A6
 KVGV G3.....88 D2
 PSLY PA1.....84 A5
Argyll Av *DMBTN* G82.....13 H5
 PSLYN/LNWD PA3.....83 E5
 RNFRW PA4.....63 E2
Argyll Gdns *LRKH* ML9.....96 B5
Argyll Pl *BLSH* ML4.....135 G4
 DMBTN G82.....13 H3
 EKILN G74.....167 F2
 KSYTH G65.....8 D1
Argyll Rd *CLYDBK* G81.....49 F2
Arisaig Dr *BSDN* G61.....35 E5
 CARD/HILL/MSPK G52.....107 F1
Arisaig Pl
 CARD/HILL/MSPK G52.....107 F1
Arisdale Crs *NMRNS* G77.....144 B4
Arkaig Av *AIRDRIE* ML6.....77 H4
Arkaig Pl *NMRNS* G77.....162 C1
Arkaig St *WISHAW* ML2.....174 A5
Ark La *DEN/PKHD* G31.....90 C2
Arkleston Crs *PSLYN/LNWD* PA3.....85 E3
Arkleston Dr *PSLY* PA1.....85 E3
Arkleston Rd *PSLY* PA1.....85 E3
Arkle Ter *BLTYR/CAMB* G72.....130 D4
Arklet Rd *GOV/IBX* G51.....87 F3
Arklet Wy *WISHAW* ML2.....157 F5
Arkwrights Wy *PSLY* PA1.....103 G1
Arlington Pl *KVGV* G3.....2 A1
Arlington St *KVGV* G3.....2 A1
Armadale Pl *DEN/PKHD* G31.....90 D1
Armadale St *DEN/PKHD* G31.....90 D1
Armour Av *AIRDRIE* ML6.....97 H2
Armour Ct *BLTYR/CAMB* G72.....151 E4
 KNNTL G66.....22 A4
Armour Dr *KNNTL* G66.....22 A4
Armour Gv *MTHW* ML1.....172 B1
Armour Pl *JNSTN* PA5.....101 H3
 MTHW ML1.....172 B1
Armour St *COWCAD* G4.....90 B3
 JNSTN PA5.....101 H4
Armstrong Crs *UD/BTH/TAN* G71.....115 F4
Armstrong Gv *EKILS* G75.....178 A1
Arnbrae Rd *KSYTH* G65.....7 H1
Arngask Rd *GOV/IBX* G51.....87 F2
Arnhall Pl
 CARD/HILL/MSPK G52.....107 F1
Arnhem St *BLTYR/CAMB* G72.....132 A2
Arnholm Pl
 CARD/HILL/MSPK G52.....107 F1
Arnisdale Pl *ESTRH* G34.....93 H1
Arnisdale Rd *ESTRH* G34.....93 H1
Arnisdale Wy *RUTH* G73.....130 A4
Arnish *ERSK* PA8.....47 H4
Arniston St *CAR/SHTL* G32.....92 A2
Arniston Wy *PSLYN/LNWD* PA3.....84 D2
Arnold Av *BSHPBGS* G64.....54 D2
Arnol Pl *STPS/GTHM/RID* G33.....93 G2
Arnott Dr *CTBR* ML5.....116 B1
Arnott Qd *MTHW* ML1.....154 B1
Arnott Wy *BLTYR/CAMB* G72.....131 F1
Arnprior Crs *CSMK* G45.....129 E5
Arnprior Qd *CSMK* G45.....129 E5
Arnprior Rd *CSMK* G45.....129 E5
Arnprior St *CSMK* G45.....129 E5
Arnside Av *GIF/THBK* G46.....127 E4
Arnton Gv *AIRDRIE* ML6.....119 F4
Arnwood Dr *KVD/HLHD* G12.....65 H1
Arondale Rd *AIRDRIE* ML6.....77 G3
Aron Ter *BLTYR/CAMB* G72.....131 E4
Aros Dr *CARD/HILL/MSPK* G52.....107 F2
Aros La *CARD/HILL/MSPK* G52.....107 F2
Arran *EKILN* G74.....167 H4
Arran Av *DMBTN* G82.....13 E3
 PSLYN/LNWD PA3.....83 E5
Arran Dr *AIRDRIE* ML6.....76 A3
 CARD/HILL/MSPK G52.....107 F1
 CUMB G67.....26 C1
 GIF/THBK G46.....127 E5
 JNSTN PA5.....101 E5
 KNNTL G66.....21 G4
 PSLYS PA2.....104 B5
Arran Gdns *HMLTN* ML3.....180 D1
Arran La *BAIL/MDB/MHD* G69.....95 E5
Arran Pl *CLYDBK* G81.....49 F1
 CTBR ML5.....116
 STPS/GTHM/RID G33.....93 G2
Arran Rd *MTHW* ML1.....154 D1
 RNFRW PA4.....63 G5
Arran Ter *RUTH* G73.....129 G2
Arran Vw *KSYTH* G65.....8 C1
Arran Wy *UD/BTH/TAN* G71.....134 A5
Arrochar Ct *SMSTN* G23.....52 C3
Arrochar Dr *SMSTN* G23.....52 C2
Arrochar St *SMSTN* G23.....52 B2
Arrol Pl *EKILS* G75.....178 D2
Arrol St *CARD/HILL/MSPK* G52.....85 H2

Arrol Wynd *BLTYR/CAMB* G72.....132 A1
Arrotshole Rd *EKILN* G74.....165 G2
Arrowsmith Av *KNTSWD* G13.....51 E3
Arthur Av *AIRDRIE* ML6.....98 A3
Arthurlie Av *BRHD/NEIL* G78.....124 B5
Arthurlie Dr *GIF/THBK* G46.....145 F1
 NMRNS G77.....161 G2
Arthurlie St *BRHD/NEIL* G78.....124 B5
Arthur Rd *PSLYS* PA2.....104 B4
Arthur St
 CRMNK/CLK/EAG G76.....145 H4
 HMLTN ML3.....152 C5
 KVGV G3.....66 C5
 PSLY PA1.....83 H4
Arundel Dr *BSHPBGS* G64.....38 A4
 GVH/MTFL G42.....109 F5
Ascaig Crs
 CARD/HILL/MSPK G52.....107 G1
Ascog Rd *BSDN* G61.....51 G1
Ascog St *GVH/MTFL* G42.....109 F2
Ascot Av *KVD/HLHD* G12.....51 G5
Ash Av *EKILS* G75.....177 H2
Ashbank Crs *AIRDRIE* ML6.....119 F1
Ashburn Gdns *MLNGV* G62.....16 C4
Ashburn Rd *MLNGV* G62.....16 C3
Ashburton La *KVD/HLHD* G12.....52 A5
Ashburton Pk *EKILS* G75.....177 E1
Ashburton Rd *KVD/HLHD* G12.....51 H5
Ashby Crs *KNTSWD* G13.....51 F2
Ash Ct *EKILS* G75.....177 H2
Ashcroft *EKILN* G74.....150 A5
Ashcroft Av *KNNTL* G66.....4 C3
Ashcroft Dr *LNPK/KPK* G44.....129 F1
Ashdale Dr
 CARD/HILL/MSPK G52.....107 F1
Ashdene St *PPK/MIL* G22.....53 G4
Asher Rd *AIRDRIE* ML6.....119 F2
Ashfield *BSHPBGS* G64.....54 C1
Ashfield Rd
 CRMNK/CLK/EAG G76.....145 H4
 MLNGV G62.....17 E4
Ashfield St *PPK/MIL* G22.....67 H2
Ashgill Pl *PPK/MIL* G22.....53 H5
Ashgill Rd *PPK/MIL* G22.....53 G5
Ashgrove *AIRDRIE* ML6.....99 E2
Ash Gv *BSHPBGS* G64.....54 C1
 UD/BTH/TAN G71.....115 G4
Ashgrove Rd *BLSH* ML4.....135 G1
Ashgrove St
 DMNK/BRGTN G40.....110 D2
Ashiestiel Pl *CUMB* G67.....44 C5
Ashiestiel Rd *CUMB* G67.....44 C5
Ashkirk Dr
 CARD/HILL/MSPK G52.....107 F1
Ashkirk Pl *WISHAW* ML2.....157 F4
Ashland Av *HMLTN* ML3.....180 D1
Ashlar Av *BALLOCH* G68.....9 G3
Ashlea Dr *GIF/THBK* G46.....127 G3
Ashlea Gdns *AIRDRIE* ML6.....98 A3
Ashley Dr *UD/BTH/TAN* G71.....134 C1
Ashley La *KVGV* G3.....2 A1
Ashley Pk *UD/BTH/TAN* G71.....135 E1
Ashley Pl *BLTYR/CAMB* G72.....151 F2
Ashley St *KVGV* G3.....2 A1
Ashmore Rd
 PLKSW/MSWD G43.....128 A3
Ash Pl *EKILS* G75.....177 H2
 JNSTN PA5.....101 H4
Ash Rd *BAIL/MDB/MHD* G69.....113 H1
 CLYDBK G81.....31 H1
 CUMB G67.....11 F5
 DMBTN G82.....13 E3
Ashton Gdns
 BAIL/MDB/MHD G69.....
Ashton Grn *EKILN* G74.....166 B4
Ashton La *KVD/HLHD* G12.....66 C4
Ashton Rd *KVD/HLHD* G12.....66 C4
 RUTH G73.....110 D3
Ashton Vw *DMBTN* G82.....12 B3
Ashtree Ct *OLDK* G60.....30 C2
Ashtree Gv *NMRNS* G77.....161 F2
Ashtree Rd *PLKSW/MSWD* G43.....108 B5
Ashvale Crs *SPRGB/BLRNK* G21.....68 B2
Ashwood *WISHAW* ML2.....173 F4
Ashwood Gdns *KNTSWD* G13.....65 G1
Ashworth Ter *HMLTN* ML3.....169 H1
Ash Wynd *BLTYR/CAMB* G72.....132 B3
Aspen Ga *MTHW* ML1.....138 A5
Aspen Dr *SPRGB/BLRNK* G21.....68 C2
Aspen Pl *BLTYR/CAMB* G72.....132 B2
 JNSTN PA5.....101 H5
Aspen Wy *HMLTN* ML3.....170 B3
Asquith Pl *BLSH* ML4.....136 C2
Aster Dr *CSMK* G45.....129 H5
Aster Gdns *MTHW* ML1.....154 D5
 PLK/PH/NH G53.....125 H5
Athelstane Dr *CUMB* G67.....44 C1
Athelstane Rd *KNTSWD* G13.....50 D4
Athena Wy *UD/BTH/TAN* G71.....115 F5
Athole Gdns *KVD/HLHD* G12.....66 B4
Athole La *KVD/HLHD* G12.....66 B4
Atholl Av *BSHPBGS* G64.....19 H4
 CARD/HILL/MSPK G52.....85 H2
Atholl Crs *PSLY* PA1.....85 H4
Atholl Dr *BALLOCH* G68.....24 D5
 GIF/THBK G46.....145 F2
Atholl Gdns *BSDN* G61.....34 B1
 BSHPBGS G64.....37 G5
 GIF/THBK G46.....145 F2
 RUTH G73.....130 D4
Atholl La *BAIL/MDB/MHD* G69.....
Atholl Pl *PSLYN/LNWD* PA3.....81
Atholl St *HMLTN* ML3.....152 B5
Atholl Ter *UD/BTH/TAN* G71.....115 F3
Atlas Pl *SPRGB/BLRNK* G21.....68 B2
Atlas Rd *SPRGB/BLRNK* G21.....68 B2
Atlas St *CLYDBK* G81.....49 E3
Atlin Dr *MTHW* ML1.....138 A5
Attercliffe Av *WISHAW* ML2.....172 D3
Attlee Av *CLYDBK* G81.....49 H2
Attlee Pl *CLYDBK* G81.....49 H2
Attow Rd *PLKSW/MSWD* G43.....127 E2
Auburn Dr *BRHD/NEIL* G78.....142 C1

Auchans Rd
 CRG/CRSL/HOU PA6.....81 G3
Auchenbothie Crs
 STPS/GTHM/RID G33.....69 H1
Auchenbothie Pl
 STPS/GTHM/RID G33.....69 H1
Auchencrow St *ESTRH* G34.....94 C1
Auchencruive *MLNGV* G62.....17 G5
Auchenfoil Rd *KNNTL* G66.....22 B3
Auchendavie Steadings
 KNNTL G66.....22
Auchengeich Gdns
 BAIL/MDB/MHD G69.....59 E1
Auchengeich Rd
 BAIL/MDB/MHD G69.....41 G4
Auchengilloch *EKILS* G75.....178 B3
Auchengreoch Av *JNSTN* PA5.....121 E1
Auchengreoch Rd *JNSTN* PA5.....121 E1
Auchenhowie Rd *MLNGV* G62.....17 G5
Auchenkilns Pk *BALLOCH* G68.....25 F4
Auchenkilns Rd *CUMB* G67.....44 C2
Auchenlodment Rd
 JNSTN PA5.....102 A2
Auchenreoch Av *DMBTN* G82.....13 G1
Auchenstewart Ct
 WISHAW ML2.....174 B2
Auchentorlie Qd *PSLY* PA1.....85 E5
Auchentorlie St *PTCK* G11.....65 G4
Auchentoshan Av *CLYDBK* G81.....31 G2
Auchentoshan Ter
 SPRGB/BLRNK G21.....68 B4
Auchinairn Gdns *BSHPBGS* G64.....55 G3
Auchinairn Rd *BSHPBGS* G64.....54 D3
Auchinbee Farm Rd
 BALLOCH G68.....25 F1
Auchinbee Wy *BALLOCH* G68.....25 F2
Auchincampbell Rd
 HMLTN ML3.....170 A1
Auchinclach Dr *BSDN* G61.....33 H1
Auchingill Pl *ESTRH* G34.....72 C5
Auchingill Rd *ESTRH* G34.....72 C5
Auchingramont Rd
 HMLTN ML3.....170 A1
Auchinlea Dr *MTHW* ML1.....157 F1
Auchinlea Rd *ESTRH* G34.....71 G5
Auchinlea Wy *ESTRH* G34.....71 G5
Auchinleck Av
 STPS/GTHM/RID G33.....55 H5
Auchinleck Crs
 STPS/GTHM/RID G33.....55 H5
Auchinleck Dr
 STPS/GTHM/RID G33.....55 H5
Auchinleck Gdns
 STPS/GTHM/RID G33.....55 H5
Auchinleck Rd *CLYDBK* G81.....32 A1
 STPS/GTHM/RID G33.....56 A4
Auchinleck Ter *CLYDBK* G81.....32 A1
Auchinloch Rd *KNNTL* G66.....40 A1
Auchinloch St
 SPRGB/BLRNK G21.....68 B3
Auchinraith Av *HMLTN* ML3.....152 D5
Auchinraith Rd
 BLTYR/CAMB G72.....151 G4
Auchinraith Ter
 BLTYR/CAMB G72.....151 H4
Auchinvole Crs *KSYTH* G65.....7 H2
Auchmannoch Av *PSLY* PA1.....85 H4
Auchnacraig Rd *CLYDBK* G81.....32 B1
Auchter Av *WISHAW* ML2.....158 D5
Auchterburn Rd *SHOTTS* ML7.....159 G2
Auchter Rd *WISHAW* ML2.....174 D1
Auckland Pk *EKILS* G75.....165 F5
Auckland Pl *CLYDBK* G81.....31 E4
Auckland St *PPK/MIL* G22.....67 G2
Auldbar Rd
 CARD/HILL/MSPK G52.....107 G1
Auldbar Ter *PSLYS* PA2.....104 D2
Auldburn Pl
 PLKSW/MSWD G43.....127 F1
Auldburn Rd
 PLKSW/MSWD G43.....126 D1
Auldearn Rd
 SPRGB/BLRNK G21.....55 F4
Auldgirth Rd
 CARD/HILL/MSPK G52.....107 G1
Auldhouse Av
 PLKSW/MSWD G43.....127 E1
Auldhouse Gdns
 PLKSW/MSWD G43.....127 F1
Auldhouse Rd
 PLKSW/MSWD G43.....127 E1
Auldhouse Ter
 PLKSW/MSWD G43.....127 F1
Auld Kirk Rd
 BLTYR/CAMB G72.....131 H4
Auldmurroch Dr *MLNGV* G62.....16 B3
The Auld Rd *CUMB* G67.....26 C1
Auld's Brae *AIRDRIE* ML6.....98 B1
Auld St *CLYDBK* G81.....31 E4
Aultbea St *PPK/MIL* G22.....53 G5
Aultmore Dr *MTHW* ML1.....137 F5
Aultmore Gdns
 STPS/GTHM/RID G33.....93 G2
Aultmore Pk
 STPS/GTHM/RID G33.....93 G2
Aultmore Rd
 STPS/GTHM/RID G33.....93 G2
Aurs Crs *BRHD/NEIL* G78.....124 C5
Aursbridge Dr
 BRHD/NEIL G78.....124 C5
Aursbridge Crs
 BRHD/NEIL G78.....124 C5
Aurs Dr *BRHD/NEIL* G78.....142 C1
Aurs Gln *BRHD/NEIL* G78.....142 B1
Aurs Pl *BRHD/NEIL* G78.....142 D1
Aurs Rd *BRHD/NEIL* G78.....124 D5
Austen La *KNTSWD* G13.....65 F1
Austen Rd *KNTSWD* G13.....65 F1
Austine Dr *HMLTN* ML3.....181 E1
Avenel Rd *KNTSWD* G13.....51 F2
Avenue End Rd
 STPS/GTHM/RID G33.....70 C4
Avenuehead Rd
 BAIL/MDB/MHD G69.....59 F3
Avenuepark St
 MRYH/FIRH G20.....66 D2
Avenue St *DMNK/BRGTN* G40.....90 D4
 RUTH G73.....111 E3
Aviemore Gdns *BSDN* G61.....34 D3

Aviemore Rd
CARD/HILL/MSPK G52 107 F2
Avoch St ESTRH G34 72 A5
Avon Av BSDN G61 35 E4
Avonbank Crs HMLTN ML3 170 B5
Avonbank Rd RUTH G73 110 C5
Avonbrae Crs HMLTN ML3 170 B5
Avonbridge Dr HMLTN ML3 170 C2
Avondale Av EKILN G74 166 C4
Avondale Dr PSLY PA1 85 E3
Avondale Gdns EKILN G74 166 D5
Avondale Pl EKILN G74 166 D5
Avondale St
STPS/GTHM/RID G33 70 B5
Avon Dr BLSH ML4 136 B3
PSLYN/LNWD PA3 82 A3
Avonhead EKILS G75 178 B3
Avonhead Av CUMB G67 44 B1
Avonhead Gdns CUMB G67 44 B1
Avonhead Pl CUMB G67 44 B1
Avonhead Rd CUMB G67 44 B1
Avon Pl CTBR ML5 74 A5
Avon Rd BSHPBGS G64 54 D3
GIF/THBK G46 127 E5
Avonside Gv HMLTN ML3 170 C2
Avonspark St
SPRGB/BLRNK G21 68 D3
Avon St HMLTN ML3 170 B2
MTHW ML1 154 C5
Aylmer Rd PLKSW/MSWD G43 128 A1
Ayr Dr AIRDRIE ML6 98 B4
Ayr Rd NMRNS G77 160 D3
Ayr St SPRGB/BLRNK G21 68 C3
Ayton Pk North EKILN G74 167 E2
Ayton Pk South EKILN G74 166 D2
Aytoun Dr ERSK PA8 30 A5
Aytoun Rd PLKSD/SHW G41 108 C1
Azalea Gdns
BLTYR/CAMB G72 132 B2

B

Babylon Av BLSH ML4 135 H4
Babylon Dr BLSH ML4 135 H4
Babylon Pl BLSH ML4 135 H5
Babylon Rd BLSH ML4 135 H4
Backbrae St KSYTH G65 8 B2
Back Cswy DEN/PKHD G31 91 G4
Backmuir Crs HMLTN ML3 152 C4
Backmuir Pl HMLTN ML3 152 C4
Backmuir Rd DRUM G15 33 G3
HMLTN ML3 152 C3
Back O' Barns HMLTN ML3 170 B1
Back O' Dykes Rd KKNTL G66 41 E1
Back O' Hl CRG/CRSL/HOU PA6 80 C2
Back O' Hill Rd BSHPBGS G64 18 D3
Back Rd BRWEIR PA11 79 G3
Back Rw HMLTN ML3 170 B1
Back Sneddon St
PSLYN/LNWD PA3 84 B4
Badenheath Pl BALLOCH G68 43 E3
Badenoch Rd KKNTL G66 22 B4
Bagnell St SPRGB/BLRNK G21 68 C1
Bahamas Wy EKILS G75 165 F4
Bailie Dr BSDN G61 34 A1
Baillie Dr EKILN G74 167 E1
UD/BTH/TAN G71 134 B4
Baillie Gdns WISHAW ML2 174 D1
Baillie Pl EKILN G74 167 F1
Baillies La AIRDRIE ML6 98 B1
Bailliesmuir Pl WISHAW ML2 158 B4
Baillieston Rd CAR/SHTL G32 93 F5
UD/BTH/TAN G71 114 A3
Baillie Wynd
UD/BTH/TAN G71 115 F5
Bainsford St CAR/SHTL G32 92 A3
Bain St DMNK/BRGTN G40 90 B3
Baird Av AIRDRIE ML6 76 C4
CARD/HILL/MSPK G52 85 H1
Baird Brae COWCAD G4 67 G3
Baird Crs CUMB G67 44 A1
Baird Dr BSDN G61 34 A3
ERSK PA8 30 A5
Baird Gdns BLTYR/CAMB G72 151 H4
Baird Hl EKILS G75 166 A5
Baird Pl BLSH ML4 116 D5
WISHAW ML2 174 D1
Bairds Crs HMLTN ML3 169 H2
Bairdsland Vw BLSH ML4 136 A2
Baird St COWCAD G4 3 H2
CTBR ML5 96 D2
Baker St PLKSD/SHW G41 108 D3
Bakewell Rd
BAIL/MDB/MHD G69 93 H4
Balaclava St KVGV G3 2 B6
Balado Rd
STPS/GTHM/RID G33 93 F2
Balbeggie St CAR/SHTL G32 92 D5
Balbeg St GOV/IBX G51 87 F3
Balblair Rd
CARD/HILL/MSPK G52 107 G1
Balcarres Av KVD/HLHD G12 66 B1
Balcary Pl AIRDRIE ML6 119 F3
Balcastle Gdns KSYTH G65 7 H1
Balcastle Rd KSYTH G65 7 G1
Balcomie St
STPS/GTHM/RID G33 70 B5
Balcurvie Rd ESTRH G34 71 H4
Baldernock Rd MLNGV G62 17 H3
Baldinnie Rd ESTRH G34 94 A1
Baldoran Dr KKNTL G66 5 F4
Baldorran Crs BALLOCH G68 25 G2
Baldovan Crs
STPS/GTHM/RID G33 93 G1
Baldovie Rd
CARD/HILL/MSPK G52 106 D1
Baldragon Rd ESTRH G34 72 A5
Baldric Rd KNTSWD G13 50 D5
Baldwin Av KNTSWD G13 51 E2
Balerno Dr
CARD/HILL/MSPK G52 107 F1
Balfleurs St MLNGV G62 17 F3
Balfluig St ESTRH G34 71 G5
Balfour St MRYH/FIRH G20 52 C5
Balfour Ter EKILS G75 178 C1
Balfron Crs HMLTN ML3 169 E2
Balfron Dr CTBR ML5 117 F1
Balfron Pl CTBR ML5 97 F5
Balfron Rd GOV/IBX G51 87 F2
PSLY PA1 85 G4
Balgair Dr PSLY PA1 85 E4
Balgair Gdns PPK/MIL G22 67 G2
Balgair St PPK/MIL G22 67 G1
Balgair Ter CAR/SHTL G32 92 C4
Balglass St PPK/MIL G22 67 G2
Balgonie Av PSLYS PA2 103 F3
Balgonie Dr PSLYS PA2 103 H3
Balgonie Rd
CARD/HILL/MSPK G52 107 F1
Balgonie Woods PSLYS PA2 103 H3
Balgownie Crs GIF/THBK G46 126 D5
Balgraybank St
SPRGB/BLRNK G21 68 D2
Balgray Crs BRHD/NEIL G78 124 D5
Balgrayhill Rd
SPRGB/BLRNK G21 54 C5
Balgray Rd NMRNS G77 143 F5
Balgraystone Rd NMRNS G77 142 C5
Balintore St CAR/SHTL G32 92 B4
Baliol La KVGV G3 2 A1
Baliol St KVGV G3 2 A1
Baljaffray Rd BSDN G61 33 F1
Ballagan Pl MLNGV G62 16 B3
Ballaig Av BSDN G61 34 A3
Ballaig Crs
STPS/GTHM/RID G33 70 D1
Ballantay Qd CSMK G45 129 H4
Ballantay Rd CSMK G45 129 H4
Ballantay Ter CSMK G45 129 H4
Ballantine Av
CARD/HILL/MSPK G52 86 B2
Ballantrae EKILN G74 166 A2
Ballantrae Crs NMRNS G77 162 B1
Ballantrae Dr NMRNS G77 162 B1
Ballantrae Rd
BLTYR/CAMB G72 151 H5
Ballater Crs WISHAW ML2 157 E5
Ballater Dr BSDN G61 51 G1
PSLYS PA2 104 C3
RNFRW PA4 48 A4
Ballater Pl GBLS G5 90 A5
Ballater St GBLS G5 89 H4
Ballayne Dr
BAIL/MDB/MHD G69 42 B5
Ballerup Ter EKILS G75 178 B2
Ballindalloch Dr
DEN/PKHD G31 90 D1
Ballindalloch La
DEN/PKHD G31 90 D1
Balloch Gdns
CARD/HILL/MSPK G52 107 G1
Balloch Loop Rd BALLOCH G68 25 E3
Ballochmill Rd RUTH G73 111 G4
Ballochmyle EKILN G74 167 G1
Ballochmyle Crs
PLK/PH/NH G53 106 B4
Ballochmyle Dr
PLK/PH/NH G53 106 B3
Ballochmyle Gdns
PLK/PH/NH G53 106 B4
Ballochmyle Pl
PLK/PH/NH G53 106 B4
Ballochney Rd AIRDRIE ML6 77 E2
Ballochney St AIRDRIE ML6 75 H5
Ballochnie Dr AIRDRIE ML6 77 H3
Ballochnie Vw AIRDRIE ML6 77 G4
Balloch Rd AIRDRIE ML6 99 H3
Balloch Vw CUMB G67 26 B3
Ballogie Rd LNPK/KPK G44 109 G5
Balmalloch Rd KSYTH G65 7 H1
Balmartin Rd SMSTN G23 52 C2
Balmedie ERSK PA8 47 F1
Balmeg Av GIF/THBK G46 145 F2
Balmoral Av AIRDRIE ML6 76 A1
Balmoral Crs CTBR ML5 96 A5
RNFRW PA4 48 B4
Balmoral Dr
BLTYR/CAMB G72 130 D2
BSDN G61 51 H1
BSHPTN PA7 46 B2
CAR/SHTL G32 112 C4
Balmoral Gdns
BLTYR/CAMB G72 133 F5
UD/BTH/TAN G71 115 E3
Balmoral Pl EKILN G74 165 H4
Balmoral Rd JNSTN PA5 102 A4
Balmoral St SCOT G14 64 C3
Balmore Dr HMLTN ML3 180 B1
Balmore Pl PPK/MIL G22 53 G5
Balmore Rd BSHPBGS G64 18 D5
SMSTN G23 53 F4
Balmore Sq PPK/MIL G22 67 G1
Balmuildy Rd BSHPBGS G64 37 G4
SMSTN G23 36 C4
Balornock Rd
SPRGB/BLRNK G21 68 D1
Balruddery Pl BSHPBGS G64 55 G3
Balshagray Av PTCK G11 65 G3
Balshagray Crs PTCK G11 65 F4
Balshagray Dr PTCK G11 65 G3
Balshagray La PTCK G11 65 G3
Balshagray Pl PTCK G11 65 G3
Baltersan Gdns HMLTN ML3 181 F5
Baltic Ct DMNK/BRGTN G40 110 D1
Baltic La DMNK/BRGTN G40 110 D1
Baltic Pl DMNK/BRGTN G40 90 C5
Baltic St DMNK/BRGTN G40 110 D1
Balure Pl DEN/PKHD G31 91 F2
Balure St DEN/PKHD G31 91 F2
Balvaird Crs RUTH G73 110 D5
Balvaird Dr RUTH G73 110 D5
Balvenie Dr MTHW ML1 155 G1
Balvenie St CTBR ML5 117 E1
Balveny St
STPS/GTHM/RID G33 71 E4
Balvicar Dr GVH/MTFL G42 109 E3
Balvicar St GVH/MTFL G42 109 E2
Balvie Av DRUM G15 50 B2
GIF/THBK G46 127 G5
Balvie Crs MLNGV G62 16 D3
Balvie Rd MLNGV G62 16 D3
Banavie La PTCK G11 65 H3
Banavie Rd PTCK G11 66 A3
WISHAW ML2 158 A4
Banchory Av AIRDRIE ML6 76 A1
PLKSW/MSWD G43 127 E2
RNFRW PA4 48 A4
Banchory Crs BSDN G61 51 H1
Banchory Rd WISHAW ML2 157 E5
Baneberry Pth EKILN G74 166 A1
Banff Av AIRDRIE ML6 98 B5
Banff Pl EKILS G75 165 H5
Banff Qd WISHAW ML2 157 E5
Banff St STPS/GTHM/RID G33 70 C4
Bangorshill St GIF/THBK G46 126 C3
Bank Av MLNGV G62 17 E2
Bankbrae Av PLK/PH/NH G53 125 F1
Bankend BRWEIR PA11 79 H4
Bankend Rd BRWEIR PA11 80 A5
DMBTN G82 13 E3
Bankend St
STPS/GTHM/RID G33 70 B5
Bankfield Dr HMLTN ML3 180 D2
Bankfoot Dr
CARD/HILL/MSPK G52 86 C5
Bankfoot Pl NMRNS G77 162 C1
Bankfoot Rd
CARD/HILL/MSPK G52 86 C5
PSLYN/LNWD PA3 83 G4
Bankglen Rd DRUM G15 33 G4
Bankhall St GVH/MTFL G42 109 G2
Bankhead Av AIRDRIE ML6 99 E2
BLSH ML4 136 A4
CTBR ML5 95 H5
KNTSWD G13 50 B5
Bankhead Dr RUTH G73 110 D5
Bankhead Pl AIRDRIE ML6 99 E2
CTBR ML5 95 H5
Bankhead Rd
CRMNK/CLK/EAG G76 147 E3
KKNTL G66 41 E1
RUTH G73 129 G1
Bankholm Pl
CRMNK/CLK/EAG G76 146 A5
Banknock St CAR/SHTL G32 91 H3
Bank Pk EKILS G75 166 A5
Bank Rd CAR/SHTL G32 112 D4
Bankside Av JNSTN PA5 101 G3
Banks Rd KKNTL G66 21 G4
Bank St AIRDRIE ML6 98 B1
BLTYR/CAMB G72 131 F1
BRHD/NEIL G78 141 E3
BRHD/NEIL G78 124 B5
CTBR ML5 96 C3
KVD/HLHD G12 66 D4
PSLY PA1 84 D5
Banktop Pl JNSTN PA5 101 G3
Bank Vw AIRDRIE ML6 119 E2
Bankview Dr KKNTL G66 20 C5
Bannercross Av
BAIL/MDB/MHD G69 93 H4
Bannercross Dr
BAIL/MDB/MHD G69 93 H3
Bannercross Gdns
BAIL/MDB/MHD G69 93 H4
Banner Dr KNTSWD G13 50 D2
Bannerman Dr BLSH ML4 136 C2
Bannerman Pl CLYDBK G81 49 F1
Banner Rd BSDN G61 51 E1
Bannockburn Pl MTHW ML1 137 F5
Bantaskin St MRYH/FIRH G20 52 B4
Banton Pl
STPS/GTHM/RID G33 93 H2
Banton Rd KSYTH G65 9 G1
Banyan Crs UD/BTH/TAN G71 116 A3
Barassie EKILN G74 166 A2
Barassie Ct UD/BTH/TAN G71 134 A5
Barassie Dr BRWEIR PA11 79 F5
Barbados Gn EKILS G75 165 F4
Barbae Pl UD/BTH/TAN G71 134 B4
Barbana Rd EKILN G74 164 D3
Barbegs Crs KSYTH G65 24 D1
Barberry Av PLK/PH/NH G53 125 G5
Barberry Gdns
PLK/PH/NH G53 125 G5
Barberry Pl PLK/PH/NH G53 125 H5
Barbeth Gdns CUMB G67 44 A3
Barbeth Pl CUMB G67 43 H2
Barbeth Rd CUMB G67 43 H2
Barbeth Wy CUMB G67 43 H2
Barbreck Rd PLKSD/SHW G41 109 E2
Barcaldine Av
BAIL/MDB/MHD G69 58 B2
Barcaldine Ter
PLKSD/SHW G41 109 E2
Barcapel Av NMRNS G77 144 B3
Barclay Av JNSTN PA5 102 A2
Barclay Ct OLDK G60 30 C2
Barclay Rd MTHW ML1 154 A4
Barclay St SPRGB/BLRNK G21 68 C1
Barcloy Pl AIRDRIE ML6 119 G3
Barcraigs Dr PSLYS PA2 104 C4
Bard Av KNTSWD G13 50 C3
Bardowie St PPK/MIL G22 67 H2
Bardrain Av JNSTN PA5 102 B2
Bardrain Rd PSLYS PA2 103 H5
Bardrill Dr BSHPBGS G64 54 B2
Bardykes Rd BLTYR/CAMB G72 151 F2
Barfillan Dr
CARD/HILL/MSPK G52 87 F4
Bargany Ct PLK/PH/NH G53 106 B3
Bargany Pl PLK/PH/NH G53 106 B4
Bargany Rd PLK/PH/NH G53 106 B3
Bargaran Rd PLK/PH/NH G53 106 C1
Bargarran Rd ERSK PA8 47 E1
Bargarron Dr
PSLYN/LNWD PA3 84 D2
Bargeddie St
STPS/GTHM/RID G33 69 G4
Barhill La KSYTH G65 23 F1
Bar Hill Pl KSYTH G65 7 H2
Barhill Rd ERSK PA8 47 F1
Barholm Sq
STPS/GTHM/RID G33 71 E5
Barke Rd CUMB G67 26 C2
Barkly Ter EKILS G75 165 H5
Barlae Av
CRMNK/CLK/EAG G76 163 F5
Barlanark Av CAR/SHTL G32 92 D2
Barlanark Crs
STPS/GTHM/RID G33 93 E2
Barlanark Dr
STPS/GTHM/RID G33 93 E2
Barlanark Pl
STPS/GTHM/RID G33 93 F2
Barlanark Rd
STPS/GTHM/RID G33 93 E2
Barlandfauld St KSYTH G65 8 C3
Barlia Dr CSMK G45 129 F4
Barlia Gdns CSMK G45 129 F4
Barlia Gv CSMK G45 129 F4
Barlia St CSMK G45 129 F4
Barlia Ter CSMK G45 129 G4
Barloan Crs DMBTN G82 13 F2
Barloan Pl DMBTN G82 13 F2
Barloch Av MLNGV G62 17 E3
Barloch Rd MLNGV G62 17 F3
Barloch St PPK/MIL G22 67 H2
Barlogan Av
CARD/HILL/MSPK G52 87 F4
Barlogan Qd
CARD/HILL/MSPK G52 87 F4
Barmulloch Rd
SPRGB/BLRNK G21 68 D2
Barnbeth Rd PLK/PH/NH G53 106 C2
Barncluith Av HMLTN ML3 170 D3
Barncluith Rd HMLTN ML3 170 C2
Barnes Rd MRYH/FIRH G20 53 G5
Barness Pl
STPS/GTHM/RID G33 92 B1
Barnes St BRHD/NEIL G78 124 A5
Barnflat St RUTH G73 111 E3
Barn Gn KLBCH PA10 100 B3
Barnhill Dr HMLTN ML3 168 C3
NMRNS G77 161 G3
SPRGB/BLRNK G21 68 D3
Barnhill Rd DMBTN G82 14 A2
Barnkirk Av DRUM G15 33 F5
Barnscroft KLBCH PA10 100 C2
Barnsford Av RNFRW PA4 61 G2
Barnsford Rd RNFRW PA4 61 G3
Barns St CLYDBK G81 49 F3
Barnton St CAR/SHTL G32 91 H2
Barnwell Ter GOV/IBX G51 87 F2
Barochan Crs
PSLYN/LNWD PA3 83 F5
Barochan Rd BLSH ML4 136 C1
CRG/CRSL/HOU PA6 80 D4
PLK/PH/NH G53 106 C1
Baronald Dr KVD/HLHD G12 52 A5
Baronald Ga KVD/HLHD G12 52 A5
Baronald St RUTH G73 111 E3
Baron Ct HMLTN ML3 170 D3
Barone Dr
CRMNK/CLK/EAG G76 145 F2
Baronhall Dr
BLTYR/CAMB G72 151 F2
Baronhill CUMB G67 10 C5
Baron Rd PSLYN/LNWD PA3 84 D3
Baronscourt Dr PSLY PA1 83 E5
Baronscourt Gdns PSLY PA1 83 E5
Baronscourt Rd PSLY PA1 103 E1
Barons Ga UD/BTH/TAN G71 133 H3
Barons Rd MTHW ML1 172 D3
Baron St RNFRW PA4 63 F4
Barony Ct
BAIL/MDB/MHD G69 94 A3
Barony Dr
BAIL/MDB/MHD G69 94 A3
Barony Gdns
BAIL/MDB/MHD G69 94 A4
Barony Pl BALLOCH G68 24 C4
Barony Wynd
BAIL/MDB/MHD G69 94 A4
Barra Av RNFRW PA4 63 F5
WISHAW ML2 157 H5
Barrachnie Av
BAIL/MDB/MHD G69 93 H4
Barrachnie Ct
BAIL/MDB/MHD G69 93 G4
Barrachnie Crs
BAIL/MDB/MHD G69 93 G4
Barrachnie Gv
BAIL/MDB/MHD G69 93 H3
Barrachnie Pl
BAIL/MDB/MHD G69 93 H3
Barrachnie Rd
BAIL/MDB/MHD G69 93 H4
Barrack St COWCAD G4 90 B3
HMLTN ML3 170 A1
Barra Dr AIRDRIE ML6 99 F3
Barra Gdns OLDK G60 30 D3
Barra Pl CTBR ML5 96 B5
Barra Rd OLDK G60 30 D3
Barraston Rd BSHPBGS G64 19 E2
Barra St MRYH/FIRH G20 52 B3
Barr Av BRHD/NEIL G78 141 F2
Barrbridge Rd
BAIL/MDB/MHD G69 95 G5
Barrcraig Rd BRWEIR PA11 79 F4
Barr Crs CLYDBK G81 32 A3
Barr Farm Rd KSYTH G65 8 C3
Barr Gv UD/BTH/TAN G71 115 F4
Barrhead Rd NMRNS G77 143 G5
PLK/PH/NH G53 106 B5
PSLYS PA2 104 C1
Barrhill Ct KKNTL G66 22 A5
Barrhill Crs KLBCH PA10 100 C4
Barrhill Rd KKNTL G66 22 A5
Barriedale Av HMLTN ML3 169 G2
Barriedale Crs
BLTYR/CAMB G72 168 B2
Barrie Qd CLYDBK G81 31 H4
Barrie Rd
CARD/HILL/MSPK G52 86 B2
EKILN G74 150 A5
Barrie St MTHW ML1 154 D4
Barrington Dr COWCAD G4 67 E4
Barrisdale Rd MRYH/FIRH G20 52 C4
WISHAW ML2 158 A4
Barrisdale Wy RUTH G73 130 A3
Barrland Dr GIF/THBK G46 127 F4
Barrland St PLKSD/SHW G41 109 F1
Barrmill Rd
PLKSW/MSWD G43 126 D2
Barrochan Rd
CRG/CRSL/HOU PA6 81 F5
JNSTN PA5 101 F3
Barrowfield Ga
DMNK/BRGTN G40 91 E5
Barrowfield Pl
DMNK/BRGTN G40 91 E5
Barrowfield St CTBR ML5 96 D5
DMNK/BRGTN G40 90 D4
Barrpath KSYTH G65 8 D3
Barr Pl NMRNS G77 143 H5
PSLY PA1 84 A5
Barr St MRYH/FIRH G20 67 F3
MTHW ML1 154 D2
Barr Ter EKILN G74 166 B3
Barrwood Pl
UD/BTH/TAN G71 115 F4
Barrwood St
STPS/GTHM/RID G33 69 H4
Barry Gdns BLTYR/CAMB G72 151 F4
Barscube Ter PSLYS PA2 104 D2
Barshaw Ct
CARD/HILL/MSPK G52 86 A3
Barshaw Dr
CARD/HILL/MSPK G52 86 A3
PSLY PA1 84 D3
Barshaw Pl PSLY PA1 85 G4
Barshaw Rd
CARD/HILL/MSPK G52 85 H3
Barskiven Rd PSLY PA1 83 E5
Barterholm Rd PSLYS PA2 104 C2
Bartholomew St
DMNK/BRGTN G40 110 D1
Bartiebeith Rd
STPS/GTHM/RID G33 93 E2
Bartonhall Rd WISHAW ML2 174 C4
Barty's Rd BLSH ML4 * 136 B2
Barwood Dr ERSK PA8 30 B5
Barwood Hl DMBTN G82 13 G1
Bassett Av KNTSWD G13 50 C3
Bassett Crs KNTSWD G13 50 C3
Bathgate St DEN/PKHD G31 90 D3
Bathgo Av PSLY PA1 85 H5
Bath La CGLW G2 2 B3
Bathlin Crs
BAIL/MDB/MHD G69 42 B5
Bath St CGLW G2 2 B3
Batson St GVH/MTFL G42 109 G2
Battlefield Av GVH/MTFL G42 109 F5
Battlefield Gdns
GVH/MTFL G42 109 F5
Battlefield Rd GVH/MTFL G42 109 F4
Battles Burn Dr
CAR/SHTL G32 112 B2
Battles Burn Ga
CAR/SHTL G32 112 B2
Battles Burn Vw
CAR/SHTL G32 112 B2
Bavelaw St
STPS/GTHM/RID G33 71 E4
Baxter Wynd WISHAW ML2 173 F3
Bayfield Av DRUM G15 33 F5
Bayfield Ter DRUM G15 33 F5
Bay Willow Ct
BLTYR/CAMB G72 132 C3
Beacon Pl
STPS/GTHM/RID G33 92 A1
Beaconsfield Rd
KVD/HLHD G12 66 A1
Beard Crs
BAIL/MDB/MHD G69 73 E1
Beardmore Pl CLYDBK G81 31 F5
Beardmore St CLYDBK G81 31 F5
Beardmore Wy CLYDBK G81 48 B1
DEN/PKHD G31 90 D3
Bearford Dr
CARD/HILL/MSPK G52 86 C4
Bearsden Rd KNTSWD G13 51 G5
Beaton Rd PLKSD/SHW G41 108 D2
Beatrice Dr MTHW ML1 137 E2
Beatrice Gdns
CRG/CRSL/HOU PA6 81 E3
Beatson Wynd
UD/BTH/TAN G71 115 F3
Beattock St DEN/PKHD G31 91 G4
Beattock Wynd HMLTN ML3 169 F2
Beatty St CLYDBK G81 31 F5
Beaufort Av
PLKSW/MSWD G43 127 F1
Beaufort Dr KKNTL G66 20 D5
Beaufort Gdns BSHPBGS G64 54 B2
Beauly Crs AIRDRIE ML6 99 F3
WISHAW ML2 174 A4
Beauly Dr PSLYS PA2 102 D3
Beauly Pl
BAIL/MDB/MHD G69 58 C2
CTBR ML5 117 E1
EKILN G74 166 A3
MRYH/FIRH G20 66 C1
MTHW ML1 137 F3
Beauly Rd
BAIL/MDB/MHD G69 113 H1
Beaumont Ga KVD/HLHD G12 66 B4
Beckfield Crs
STPS/GTHM/RID G33 55 G4
Beckfield Dr
STPS/GTHM/RID G33 55 G4
Beckfield Ga
STPS/GTHM/RID G33 55 G4
Beckfield Gv
STPS/GTHM/RID G33 55 G4
Beckfield Wk
STPS/GTHM/RID G33 55 G4
Beckford St HMLTN ML3 152 D5
Bedale Rd
BAIL/MDB/MHD G69 93 G5
Bedcow Vw KKNTL G66 40 C1
Bedford Av CLYDBK G81 49 G1
Bedford La GBLS G5 89 G4
Bedford St GBLS G5 89 G4
Bedlay Ct
BAIL/MDB/MHD G69 42 B5
Bedlay Vw UD/BTH/TAN G71 115 G3
Beech Av
BAIL/MDB/MHD G69 93 H4
BLTYR/CAMB G72 131 E1
BRWEIR PA11 79 G2
BSDN G61 34 D1
HMLTN ML3 181 F4
JNSTN PA5 102 B2
MTHW ML1 137 G5
NMRNS G77 161 H1
PLKSD/SHW G41 88 A5
PSLYS PA2 104 D3
RUTH G73 130 B3
Beechbank Av AIRDRIE ML6 98 A1
Beech Crs BLTYR/CAMB G72 132 B3
MTHW ML1 137 H1
NMRNS G77 161 H2
Beech Dr CLYDBK G81 31 H3
Beeches Av CLYDBK G81 31 G2
Beeches Rd CLYDBK G81 31 G2

The Beeches
CRG/CRSL/HOU PA6 ......81 E2
JNSTN PA5 ......80 D5
Beech Gdns
BAIL/MDB/MHD D69 ......93 H4
Beech Gv
BAIL/MDB/MHD D69 ......75 F3
EKILS G75 ......177 G2
WISHAW ML2 ......157 F3
Beechgrove Av
UD/BTH/TAN G71 ......115 H5
Beechgrove Qd MTHW ML1 ......137 F2
Beechgrove St
DMNK/BRGTN G40 * 111 E2
Beechlands Av
LNPK/KPK G44 ......127 H5
Beechlands Dr
CRMNK/CLK/EAC G76 ......145 E4
Beechmount Rd KKNTL G66 ......39 H4
Beech Pl BSHPBGS G64 ......55 E3
Beech Rd BSHPBGS G64 ......55 E3
JNSTN PA5 ......101 E5
KKNTL G66 ......39 H2
MTHW ML1 ......118 D5
Beechtree Ter KKNTL G66 ......5 D1
Beechwood WISHAW ML2 ......173 G4
Beechwood Av
CRMNK/CLK/EAC G76 ......145 F4
HMLTN ML3 ......169 G5
RUTH G73 ......130 B1
Beechwood Ct BSDN G61 ......34 C5
CUMB G67 ......26 B3
Beechwood Crs WISHAW ML2 ......174 B3
Beechwood Dr CTBR ML5 ......97 F4
PTCK G11 ......65 G2
RNFRW PA4 ......63 F5
Beechwood Gdns BLSH ML4 ......136 B3
Beechwood Gv
BRHD/NEIL G78 ......142 B1
Beechwood Pl PTCK G11 ......65 G2
Beechwood Rd CUMB G67 ......26 B4
Beechworth Dr MTHW ML1 ......138 A5
Beecroft Pl BLTYR/CAMB G72 ......151 H1
Beith Dr KNTSWD G13 ......50 A4
Beith St AIRDRIE ML6 ......98 B3
JNSTN PA5 ......101 F5
Beith St PTCK G11 ......65 H5
Beith Wy BLTYR/CAMB G72 ......168 C3
Belford Ct MRYH G20 ......161 G3
Belford Gv NMRNS G77 ......161 G3
Belgowan St BLSH ML4 ......116 C5
Belgrave La KVD/HLHD G12 ......66 D3
Belgrave St BLSH ML4 ......135 G1
Belhaven Crs NMRNS G77 ......161 F4
Belhaven Pk
BAIL/MDB/MHD D69 ......58 B4
Belhaven Pl NMRNS G77 ......161 F5
Belhaven Rd HMLTN ML3 ......168 D2
WISHAW ML2 ......173 G3
Belhaven Ter KVD/HLHD G12 ......66 B2
WISHAW ML2 ......173 H2
Belhaven Terrace La
KVD/HLHD G12 ......66 B2
Belhaven Ter West
KVD/HLHD G12 ......66 B2
Belhaven Terrace West La
KVD/HLHD G12 ......66 B2
Bellahouston Dr
CARD/HILL/MSPK G52 ......107 F1
Bellairs Pl BLTYR/CAMB G72 ......151 F1
Bellas Pl AIRDRIE ML6 ......77 H4
Bellcote Rd BALLOCH G68 ......9 H5
Belleisle Av
UD/BTH/TAN G71 ......133 H1
Belleisle Ct BALLOCH G68 ......26 A1
Belleisle Crs BRWEIR PA11 ......79 E4
Belleisle Dr BALLOCH G68 ......26 A1
Belleisle Gdns BALLOCH G68 ......26 A1
Belleisle Gv BALLOCH G68 ......26 A1
Belleisle St GVH/MTFL G42 ......109 G3
Bellevue Av KKNTL G66 ......20 D5
Bellevue Rd KKNTL G66 ......20 D5
Bellfield Crs BRHD/NEIL G78 ......124 A3
Bellfield Dr WISHAW ML2 ......173 H4
Bellfield Rd KKNTL G66 ......20 D5
Bellfield St DEN/PKHD G31 ......90 D3
Bellflower Av
PLK/PH/NH G53 ......125 H4
Bellflower Ct EKILN G74 ......165 H2
Bellflower Gdns
PLK/PH/NH G53 ......125 H4
Bellflower Pl PLK/PH/NH G53 ......125 H4
Bell Gn East EKILS G75 ......166 D5
Bell Gn West EKILS G75 ......166 B5
Bellgrove St DEN/PKHD G31 ......90 C3
Bellrock Ct
STPS/GTHM/RID G33 ......92 C1
Bellrock Crs
STPS/GTHM/RID G33 ......92 B1
Bellrock St
STPS/GTHM/RID G33 ......92 B1
Bellrock Vw
STPS/GTHM/RID G33 ......92 B1
Bells Br KVGV G3 ......88 D1
Belliscroft Av RUTH G73 ......110 C5
Bellslyke Rd AIRDRIE ML6 ......98 A3
Bellshaugh Ct KVD/HLHD G12 ......66 B1
Bellshaugh
Gdns KVD/HLHD G12 ......66 B1
Bellshaugh La KVD/HLHD G12 ......66 B1
Bellshaugh Pl KVD/HLHD G12 ......66 B1
Bellshaugh Rd KVD/HLHD G12 ......66 B1
Bellshill Rd BLSH ML4 ......135 F4
HMLTN ML3 ......152 D2
MTHW ML1 ......136 B3
UD/BTH/TAN G71 ......134 A2
Bellside Rd AIRDRIE ML6 ......119 G2
MTHW ML1 ......157 H1
Bellsmyre Av DMBTN G82 ......13 F1
Bell St AIRDRIE ML6 ......98 A1
BLSH ML4 ......117 E5
CGLE G1 ......3 H6
CLYDBK G81 ......49 G4
RNFRW PA4 ......63 G1
WISHAW ML2 ......173 G2
Belltrees Crs PSLY PA1 ......83 F5
Bell Vw WISHAW ML2 ......158 B4
Bell View Ct RNFRW PA4 ......63 G2

Bellvue Crs BLSH ML4 ......135 G3
Bellvue Wy CTBR ML5 ......97 F3
Bellwood St PLKSD/SHW G41 ......108 D5
Bellziehill Rd BLSH ML4 ......135 F2
Belmont Av UD/BTH/TAN G71 ......114 D5
Belmont Crs KVD/HLHD G12 ......66 D3
Belmont Dr BRHD/NEIL G78 ......142 C1
EKILS G75 ......165 G5
GIF/THBK G46 ......127 E4
RUTH G73 ......111 E5
Belmont La KVD/HLHD G12 ......66 D3
Belmont Rd BLTYR/CAMB G72 ......130 D4
PSLYN/LNWD PA3 ......84 D5
SPRGB/BLRNK G21 ......54 C5
Belmont St CLYDBK G81 ......49 E2
CTBR ML5 ......75 H5
KSYTH G65 ......8 A1
KVD/HLHD G12 ......66 D3
MRYH/FIRH G20 ......67 E3
Belses Dr
CARD/HILL/MSPK G52 ......86 D4
Belses Gdns
CARD/HILL/MSPK G52 ......86 D4
Belstane Pl UD/BTH/TAN G71 ......134 B4
Belstane Rd CUMB G67 ......45 E3
Belsyde Av DRUM G15 ......50 B1
Beltane St KVGV G3 2
WISHAW ML2 ......173 H3
Beltonfoot Wy WISHAW ML2 ......173 G3
Beltrees Av PLK/PH/NH G53 ......106 B3
Beltrees Crs PLK/PH/NH G53 ......106 B3
Beltrees Rd PLK/PH/NH G53 ......106 B3
Belvidere Crs BLSH ML4 ......136 A3
BSHPBGS G64 ......54 D1
Belvidere Rd BLSH ML4 ......135 H5
Belvoir Pl BLTYR/CAMB G72 ......151 G2
Bemersyde BSHPBGS G64 ......55 F1
Bemersyde Av
PLKSW/MSWD G43 ......127 E2
Bemersyde Rd PSLYS PA2 ......102 D4
Ben Alder Dr PSLYS PA2 ......105 G3
Benalder St PTCK G11 ......66 E5
Benbecula EKILN G74 ......167 H4
Benbow Rd CLYDBK G81 ......48 C1
Bencloich Crs KKNTL G66 ......4 C1
Bencloich Rd KKNTL G66 ......4 C2
Bencroft Dr LNPK/KPK G44 ......129 F2
Ben Donich Pl
PLK/PH/NH G53 ......126 A2
Ben Edra Pl PLK/PH/NH G53 ......126 A3
Benford Av MTHW ML1 ......138 A5
Benford Knowe MTHW ML1 ......138 A3
Bengairn St DEN/PKHD G31 ......91 F2
Bengal Pl PLKSW/MSWD G43 ......108 B5
Bengal St PLKSW/MSWD G43 ......108 B5
Ben Garrisdale Pl
PLK/PH/NH G53 ......126 A3
Benhar Pl
STPS/GTHM/RID G33 ......92 A2
Benholm St CAR/SHTL G32 ......112 A1
Ben Hope Av PLK/PH/NH G53 ......126 A3
Ben Laga Pl PLK/PH/NH G53 ......126 A3
Ben Lawers Dr BALLOCH G68 ......25 E3
PSLYS PA2 ......105 G2
Ben Ledi Av PSLYS PA2 ......105 G2
Ben Ledi Crs BALLOCH G68 ......25 F3
Ben Loyal Av PSLYS PA2 ......105 G2
Ben Lui Dr PSLYS PA2 ......105 G3
Ben Lui Pl BALLOCH G68 ......25 F3
PLK/PH/NH G53 ......126 A3
Ben Macdui Gdns
PSLYS PA2 ......105 G2
Ben More Dr BALLOCH G68 ......25 F3
PSLYS PA2 ......105 G2
Bennan Pl EKILS G75 ......177 H4
Bennan Sq GVH/MTFL G42 ......109 H3
Ben An PSLY PA1 ......
Ben Nevis Rd PSLYS PA2 ......105 G2
Ben Nevis Wy BALLOCH G68 ......25 E3
Benny Lynch Ct GBLS G5 ......89 H4
Ben Oss Pl PLK/PH/NH G53 ......125 H3
Benson St CTBR ML5 ......96 D5
Benston Pl JNSTN PA5 ......101 F5
Benston Rd JNSTN PA5 ......101 F5
Bent Crs UD/BTH/TAN G71 ......134 C1
Benthall St GBLS G5 ......90 A5
Bentinck St KVGV G3 ......66 D5
Bent Rd AIRDRIE ML6 ......119 E1
HMLTN ML3 ......169 H2
Bents Rd BAIL/MDB/MHD D69 ......94 A4
Ben Uird Pl PLK/PH/NH G53 ......126 A3
Ben Vane Av PSLYS PA2 ......105 F3
Ben Venue Rd BALLOCH G68 ......25 E3
Benview Rd
CRMNK/CLK/EAC G76 ......145 H3
Benview St MRYH/FIRH G20 ......67 E3
Benview Ter PSLYS PA2 ......105 E3
Ben Vorlich Dr
PLK/PH/NH G53 ......126 A3
Ben Vorlich Pl
PLK/PH/NH G53 ......126 A3
Benvue Rd KKNTL G66 ......4 C5
Ben Wyvis Dr PSLYS PA2 ......105 F3
Berelands Crs GVH/MTFL G42 ......110 B5
Berelands Pl RUTH G73 ......110 D5
Berenice Pl DMBTN G82 ......13 H5
Beresford Av SCOT G14 ......65 F2
Berkeley St KVGV G3 ......88 D1
Berkeley Terrace La KVGV G3 ......89 E1
Berl Av CRG/CRSL/HOU PA6 ......80 D1
Bernadette Crs MTHW ML1 ......138 A4
Bernadette St MTHW ML1 ......138 A4
Bernard St DMNK/BRGTN G40 ......90 D5
Bernard Ter
DMNK/BRGTN G40 ......90 D5
Berneray St PPK/MIL G22 ......53 H4
Bernisdale Dr DRUM G15 ......32 C5
Bernisdale Gdns DRUM G15 ......32 C5
Bernisdale Pl DRUM G15 ......32 C5
Berridale Av LNPK/KPK G44 ......128 B2
Berriedale EKILS G75 ......164 D5
Berriedale Av
BAIL/MDB/MHD D69 ......93 H5
Berriedale Crs
BLTYR/CAMB G72 ......168 B2
Berriedale Qd WISHAW ML2 ......157 E5
Berriedale Ter
BLTYR/CAMB G72 ......168 B2

Berryburn Rd
SPRGB/BLRNK G21 ......69 F2
Berryhill Crs WISHAW ML2 ......173 F5
Berryhill Dr GIF/THBK G46 ......127 E5
Berryhill Rd CUMB G67 ......26 A4
GIF/THBK G46 ......145 E1
Berryknowe Av
BAIL/MDB/MHD D69 ......58 B4
Berryknowe La
CARD/HILL/MSPK G52 ......86 D4
Berryknowes Av
CARD/HILL/MSPK G52 ......86 D4
Berryknowes Rd
GOV/IBX G51 ......87 E3
Bertram St HMLTN ML3 ......152 B5
PLKSD/SHW G41 ......108 D3
Bervie St GOV/IBX G51 ......87 H3
Berwick Crs AIRDRIE ML6 ......98 A4
PSLYN/LNWD PA3 ......81 H4
Berwick Dr
CARD/HILL/MSPK G52 ......86 C5
RUTH G73 ......111 G5
Berwick Pl CTBR ML5 ......117 E1
EKILN G74 ......167 F2
Berwick St CTBR ML5 ......117 E1
HMLTN ML3 ......152 C5
Bessemer Dr EKILS G75 ......178 D5
Bethal La EKILS G75 ......177 F4
Betula Dr CLYDBK G81 ......31 H3
Bevan Gv JNSTN PA5 ......101 F4
Beveridge Ter BLSH ML4 ......136 C3
Beverley Rd
PLKSW/MSWD G43 ......127 G1
Bevin Av CLYDBK G81 ......49 G1
Bideford Crs CAR/SHTL G32 ......113 E1
The Bield WISHAW ML2 ......174 B3
Biggar Rd AIRDRIE ML6 ......119 G4
MTHW ML1 ......138 D2
Biggar St DEN/PKHD G31 ......91 E3
Bigton St STPS/GTHM/RID G33 ......70 C4
Billings Rd MTHW ML1 ......154 A5
Bilsland Ct MRYH/FIRH G20 ......67 G1
Bilsland Dr MRYH/FIRH G20 ......67 F1
Binend Rd PLK/PH/NH G53 ......106 D4
Binniehill Rd BALLOCH G68 ......25 H3
Binnie Pl DMNK/BRGTN G40 ......90 A4
Binns Rd STPS/GTHM/RID G33 ......70 D4
Birch Av
CRMNK/CLK/EAC G76 ......146 A4
Birch Brae HMLTN ML3 ......170 A4
Birch Cl BLTYR/CAMB G72 ......131 H1
Birch Crs
CRMNK/CLK/EAC G76 ......146 A4
JNSTN PA5 ......101 H5
Birch Dr BLTYR/CAMB G72 ......131 H1
KKNTL G66 ......40 D1
Birchend Dr
SPRGB/BLRNK G21 ......69 E4
Birchend Pl
SPRGB/BLRNK G21 ......68 D4
Birchfield Dr SCOT G14 ......64 C2
Birchfield Rd HMLTN ML3 ......169 F2
Birchgrove
CRG/CRSL/HOU PA6 ......81 G2
Birch Gv UD/BTH/TAN G71 ......115 G5
Birch Knowe BSHPBGS G64 ......55 E3
Birchlea Dr GIF/THBK G46 ......127 G3
Birchmount Ct AIRDRIE ML6 ......99 E1
Birch Pl BLTYR/CAMB G72 ......151 G2
BLTYR/CAMB G72 ......132 C3
Birch Qd AIRDRIE ML6 ......99 E2
Birch Rd CLYDBK G81 ......31 H4
CUMB G67 ......27 G2
DMBTN G82 ......13 E3
Birch St GBLS G5 ......110 A1
MTHW ML1 ......137 G2
Birch Vw BSDN G61 ......34 D3
Birchview Dr
CRMNK/CLK/EAC G76 ......146 A5
Birchwood Av CAR/SHTL G32 ......93 F3
Birchwood Dr PSLYS PA2 ......103 G3
Birchwood Gv
BAIL/MDB/MHD D69 ......95 F3
Birchwood Pl CAR/SHTL G32 ......93 F3
Birdsfield Dr
BLTYR/CAMB G72 ......151 G2
Birdsfield St HMLTN ML3 ......152 A4
Birdston Rd KKNTL G66 ......21 E1
SPRGB/BLRNK G21 ......55 F5
Birgidale Av CSMK G45 ......147 E1
Birgidale Rd CSMK G45 ......129 E5
Birgidale Ter CSMK G45 ......129 E5
Birkdale EKILN G74 ......165 H2
Birkdale Ct UD/BTH/TAN G71 ......134 A5
Birkdale Crs BALLOCH G68 ......10 C4
Birkdale Wd BALLOCH G68 ......10 C4
Birkenburn Rd CUMB G67 ......11 H4
Birken Rd KKNTL G66 ......40 B1
Birkenshaw St DEN/PKHD G31 ......91 E2
Birkhall Av
CARD/HILL/MSPK G52 ......86 A5
RNFRW PA4 ......48 A4
Birkhall Dr BSDN G61 ......51 G1
Birkhill Av BSHPBGS G64 ......55 E1
Birkhill Gdns BSHPBGS G64 ......55 E1
Birkmyre Rd GOV/IBX G51 ......87 G3
Birkshaw Brae WISHAW ML2 ......173 H5
Birkshaw Pl WISHAW ML2 ......173 H5
Birkwood Pl NMRNS G77 ......161 G5
Birkwood St
DMNK/BRGTN G40 ......111 E3
Birmingham Rd RNFRW PA4 ......63 G5
Birnam Av BSHPBGS G64 ......55 E1
Birnam Crs BSDN G61 ......35 E3
Birnam Pl HMLTN ML3 ......168 D2
NMRNS G77 ......162 C1
Birness Dr
PLKSW/MSWD G43 ......108 C5
Birnie Ct SPRGB/BLRNK G21 ......69 F2
Birnie Rd SPRGB/BLRNK G21 ......69 F2
Birnock Av RNFRW PA4 ......63 H5
Birrell St CLYDBK G81 ......31 H1
Birrell Rd MLNGV G62 ......16 C2
Birrens Rd MTHW ML1 ......154 B2
Birsay Rd PPK/MIL G22 ......53 G4
Bishop Gdns BSHPBGS G64 ......54 B1

Bishop La CGLW G2 ......2 B5
Bishopmill Pl
SPRGB/BLRNK G21 ......69 F2
Bishops Ga EKILN G74 ......164 B2
Bishopsgate Dr
SPRGB/BLRNK G21 ......54 B4
Bishops Pk EKILN G74 ......164 A2
Bissett St CLYDBK G81 ......31 F2
Blackadder Pl EKILS G75 ......176 C1
Blackbog Rd AIRDRIE ML6 ......45 E5
Blackbraes Dr EKILN G74 ......167 E1
Blackburn Crs DMBTN G82 ......12 C5
KKNTL G66 ......40 D1
Blackburn Sq
BRHD/NEIL G78 ......142 C1
Blackburn St GOV/IBX G51 ......88 D3
Blackbyres Ct
BRHD/NEIL G78 ......124 C3
Blackbyres Rd
BRHD/NEIL G78 ......124 C3
Blackcraig Av DRUM G15 ......33 F5
Blackcroft Gdns
CAR/SHTL G32 ......93 E5
Blackcroft Rd CAR/SHTL G32 ......93 E5
Blackdyke Rd KKNTL G66 ......21 G5
Blackfarm Rd NMRNS G77 ......162 A1
Blackfaulds Rd RUTH G73 ......110 B5
Blackford Rd PSLYS PA2 ......104 D1
Blackfriar Rd CGLE G1 ......3 J6
Blackfriars St CGLE G1 ......3 H5
Blackhall La PSLY PA1 ......104 C1
Blackhall St PSLY PA1 ......104 C1
Blackhill Pl
STPS/GTHM/RID G33 ......69 G4
Blackhill Rd SMSTN G23 ......53 E1
Blackhouse Av NMRNS G77 ......162 A1
Blackhouse Gdns
NMRNS G77 ......162 A1
Blackhouse Rd NMRNS G77 ......162 A1
Blackie St KVGV G3 ......88 C1
Blacklands Pl KKNTL G66 ......40 C4
Blacklands Rd EKILN G74 ......166 A4
Blacklaw Dr EKILN G74 ......167 F4
Blacklaw La PSLYN/LNWD PA3 ......84 B4
Blackmoor Pl MTHW ML1 ......137 F4
Blackmoss Dr BLSH ML4 ......135 G3
Blackness St CTBR ML5 ......117 E1
Blackey Burn Dr
PLK/PH/NH G53 ......106 A2
Blackstone Av
PLK/PH/NH G53 ......106 D4
Blackstone Crs
PLK/PH/NH G53 ......106 D3
Blackstone Rd
PSLYN/LNWD PA3 ......83 F1
Blackstoun Av
PSLYN/LNWD PA3 ......83 G4
Blackstoun Ov
PSLYN/LNWD PA3 ......83 G4
Blackstoun Rd
PSLYN/LNWD PA3 ......83 G4
Black St AIRDRIE ML6 ......76 C5
COWCAD G4 ......3 J2
Blackthorn Av KKNTL G66 ......39 F3
Blackthorn Gv KKNTL G66 ......39 F3
Blackthorn Rd CUMB G67 ......27 G2
UD/BTH/TAN G71 ......115 H4
Blackthorn St PPK/MIL G22 ......68 B1
Blackwood Av NMRNS G77 ......161 G5
Blackwood Gdns MTHW ML1 ......154 B3
Blackwood Rd BALLOCH G68 ......24 C4
MLNGV G62 ......16 D2
Blackwood St BRHD/NEIL G78 ......142 A1
MRYH/FIRH G20 ......67 E2
Blackwood Ter JNSTN PA5 ......121 E1
Bladda La PSLY PA1 ......84 C5
Blades Ct BAIL/MDB/MHD D69 ......59 F5
Bladnoch Dr DRUM G15 ......50 D1
Blaeberry Pl BALLOCH G68 ......25 E3
Blaeloch Av CSMK G45 ......146 D1
Blaeloch Dr CSMK G45 ......146 C1
Blaeloch Ter CSMK G45 ......146 C1
Blaeshill Rd EKILS G75 ......164 D5
Blairatholl Av PTCK G11 ......65 H3
Blairatholl Crs NMRNS G77 ......162 C1
Blairatholl Gdns HMLTN ML3 ......169 F1
PTCK G11 ......65 H3
Blair Atholl Ga NMRNS G77 ......162 C1
Blair Atholl Wynd
MTHW ML1 ......137 G5
Blairbeth Dr LNPK/KPK G44 ......109 G5
Blairbeth Rd RUTH G73 ......130 A2
Blairbeth Ter RUTH G73 ......130 B2
Blairbuie Dr MRYH/FIRH G20 ......52 A1
Blair Crs BAIL/MDB/MHD D69 ......113 H1
Blairdardie Rd DRUM G15 ......50 D2
Blairdenan Av
BAIL/MDB/MHD D69 ......42 A5
Blairdenon Dr BALLOCH G68 ......25 G2
Blair Dr KKNTL G66 ......5 E1
Blair Gdns BSHPBGS G64 ......19 F4
NMRNS G77 ......143 G5
Blairgowrie Rd
CARD/HILL/MSPK G52 ......86 D5
Blairhall Av PLKSD/SHW G41 ......109 E4
Blairhill Av KKNTL G66 ......40 D5
Blairhill Pl CTBR ML5 ......96 B2
Blairhill St CTBR ML5 ......96 B2
Blairholm Dr BLSH ML4 ......136 A4
Blairlinn Rd CUMB G67 ......45 F2
Blairlinn Vw CUMB G67 ......45 F2
Blairlogie St
STPS/GTHM/RID G33 ......70 C5
Blairmore Av PSLY PA1 ......85 F4
Blairpark Av CTBR ML5 ......96 B1
Blair Pth MTHW ML1 ......155 E5
Blair Rd CTBR ML5 ......96 B2
PSLY PA1 ......85 H5
Blairston Av
UD/BTH/TAN G71 ......152 C1
Blairston Gdns
UD/BTH/TAN G71 ......152 C1
Blairtum Dr RUTH G73 ......130 A2
Blairtummock Pl
STPS/GTHM/RID G33 ......93 E1
Blairtummock Rd
STPS/GTHM/RID G33 ......92 D1
Blake Rd CUMB G67 ......26 D2
Blane Dr MLNGV G62 ......17 F2
Blanefield Gdns KNTSWD G13 ......51 G2
Blane St CTBR ML5 ......96 D1
Blaneview
STPS/GTHM/RID G33 ......71 E2
Blantyre Crs CLYDBK G81 ......31 F1
Blantyre Dr BSHPTN PA7 ......28 D4
Blantyre Farm Rd
BLTYR/CAMB G72 ......133 G5
UD/BTH/TAN G71 ......114 C4
Blantyre Gdns BALLOCH G68 ......24 C4
Blantyre Mill Rd
UD/BTH/TAN G71 ......134 B5
Blantyre Rd
UD/BTH/TAN G71 ......134 B5
Blantyre St CTBR ML5 ......96 B5
KVGV G3 ......66 C5
Blaven Ct BAIL/MDB/MHD D69 ......85 G5
Blawarthill St SCOT G14 ......64 A1
Bleachfield MLNGV G62 ......16 D2
Bleasdale Ct CLYDBK G81 ......49 E1
Blenheim Av EKILS G75 ......177 H1
STPS/GTHM/RID G33 ......57 E5
Blenheim Ct KSYTH G65 ......8 B1
PSLY PA1 ......84 A4
STPS/GTHM/RID G33 ......57 E5
Blochairn Rd
SPRGB/BLRNK G21 ......68 D3
Bluebell Gdns CSMK G45 ......129 H5
MTHW ML1 ......136 B5
Bluebell Wy AIRDRIE ML6 ......76 A4
KKNTL G66 ......4 D3
Bluebell Wynd WISHAW ML2 ......173 G5
Bluevale St DEN/PKHD G31 ......90 D3
Blythe Pl STPS/GTHM/RID G33 ......93 F2
Blyth Pl STPS/GTHM/RID G33 ......93 E3
Blyth Rd STPS/GTHM/RID G33 ......93 F3
Blythswood Av RNFRW PA4 ......63 G2
Blythswood Dr
PSLYN/LNWD PA3 ......84 A3
Blythswood Rd RNFRW PA4 ......63 G1
Blythswood Sq CGLW G2 ......2 C4
Blythswood St CGLW G2 ......2 D5
The Boardwalk EKILS G75 ......178 D2
Bobbins Ga PSLY PA1 ......103 G3
Boclair Av BSDN G61 ......34 C4
Boclair Crs BSDN G61 ......34 D4
BSHPBGS G64 ......54 C1
Boclair Rd BSDN G61 ......34 D4
BSHPBGS G64 ......54 C1
Boclair St KNTSWD G13 ......51 F3
Bodden Sq MTHW ML1 ......119 F5
Boden Qd MTHW ML1 ......154 A3
Boden St DMNK/BRGTN G40 ......90 D5
Bodmin Gdns
BAIL/MDB/MHD D69 ......42 A5
Bogany Ter CSMK G45 ......129 A5
Bogbain Rd ESTRH G34 ......93 H1
Boggknowe
UD/BTH/TAN G71 ......114 C4
Boghall St
STPS/GTHM/RID G33 ......70 C5
Boghead Av DMBTN G82 ......13 G3
Boghead Rd DMBTN G82 ......13 F3
KKNTL G66 ......39 F3
SPRGB/BLRNK G21 ......68 D1
Bogleshole Rd
BLTYR/CAMB G72 ......111 H5
Bogmoor Pl GOV/IBX G51 ......64 D5
Bogmoor Rd GOV/IBX G51 ......86 D1
Bogside Rd KSYTH G65 ......8 B3
STPS/GTHM/RID G33 ......70 B1
Bogside St DMNK/BRGTN G40 ......91 E5
Bogstonhill Rd
CRG/CRSL/HOU PA6 ......80 C1
Bogs Vw BLSH ML4 ......135 G4
Bogton Av LNPK/KPK G44 ......128 A3
Bogton Avenue La
LNPK/KPK G44 ......128 A3
Boydston Rd PLKSD/SHW G41 ......109 F1
Bolingbroke EKILN G74 ......167 F1
Bolivar Ter GVH/MTFL G42 ......109 H4
Bolton Dr GVH/MTFL G42 ......109 F4
Bon Accord Rd
CRMNK/CLK/EAC G76 ......146 A4
Bon Accord Sq CLYDBK G81 ......49 E3
Bonar Crs BRWEIR PA11 ......79 H4
Bonar La BRWEIR PA11 ......79 H4
Bonawe St MRYH/FIRH G20 ......67 E2
Bonds Dr WISHAW ML2 ......158 A3
Bo'Ness Rd AIRDRIE ML6 ......119 E3
MTHW ML1 ......118 A4
Boness St DMNK/BRGTN G40 ......91 E5
Bonhill Rd DMBTN G82 ......13 F3
Bonhill St PPK/MIL G22 ......67 G3
Bonkle Gdns WISHAW ML2 ......158 C5
Bonkle Rd WISHAW ML2 ......158 C5
Bonnar St DMNK/BRGTN G40 ......110 D1
Bonnaughton Rd BSDN G61 ......33 G2
Bonnyholm Av
PLK/PH/NH G53 ......106 B1
Bonnyrigg Dr
PLKSW/MSWD G43 ......126 D2
Bontine Av DMBTN G82 ......12 C3
Bonyton Av KNTSWD G13 ......50 A5
Boon Dr DRUM G15 ......50 C1
Boquhanran Rd CLYDBK G81 ......48 C1
Borden La KNTSWD G13 ......65 H1
Borden Rd KNTSWD G13 ......65 H1
Border Wy KKNTL G66 ......21 G5
Boreland Dr HMLTN ML3 ......168 D3
KNTSWD G13 ......50 C5
Boreland Pl KNTSWD G13 ......50 C5
Bore Rd AIRDRIE ML6 ......98 C1
Borgie Crs BLTYR/CAMB G72 ......131 F2
Borland Rd BSDN G61 ......34 D5
Borron St COWCAD G4 ......67 H5
Borrowdale EKILS G75 ......177 E3
Borthwick Dr EKILS G75 ......176 C1
Borthwick Pl
BAIL/MDB/MHD D69 ......73 E2

Borthwick St
STPS/GTHM/RID G33 70 C5
Bosfield Cnr EKILN G74 166 C2
Bosfield Pl EKILN G74 166 C2
Bosfield Rd EKILN G74 166 B2
Boswell Ct GVH/MTFL G42 109 E5
Boswell Dr BLTYR/CAMB G72 151 G3
Boswell Pk EKILN G74 167 F1
Boswell Sq
CARD/HILL/MSPK G52 86 A2
Bosworth Rd EKILN G74 167 F1
Botanic Crs MRYH/FIRH G20 66 C2
Bothlin Dr
STPS/GTHM/RID G33 57 E5
Bothlyn Av KKNTL G66 40 B1
Bothlyn Crs
BAIL/MDB/MHD G69 58 D4
Bothlyn Rd
BAIL/MDB/MHD G69 58 C3
Bothwellhaugh Qd
BLSH ML4 135 G4
Bothwellhaugh Rd
MTHW ML1 153 G1
Bothwell La CGLW G2 2 C5
KVD/HLHD G12 66 D4
Bothwell Pl BLSH ML4 135 E1
Bothwellpark Rd
UD/BTH/TAN G71 134 C5
Bothwell Pl CTBR ML5 96 C2
PSLYS PA2 102 D4
Bothwell Rd HMLTN ML3 152 D3
UD/BTH/TAN G71 134 A3
Bothwell St
BLTYR/CAMB G72 130 D1
CGLW G2 2 C5
HMLTN ML3 152 D5
Bourhill Ct WISHAW ML2 173 E3
Bourne Ct RNFRW PA4 48 A4
Bourne Crs RNFRW PA4 48 A4
Bourne St HMLTN ML3 170 C2
Bourock Sq BRHD/NEIL G78 142 C1
Bourtree Rd HMLTN ML3 168 D4
Bouverie St RUTH G73 110 C4
SCOT G14 49 H5
Bowden Dr
CARD/HILL/MSPK G52 86 C3
Bowden Gv WISHAW ML2 157 G4
Bowden Pk EKILS G75 165 H5
Bower St KVD/HLHD G12 66 D3
Bowerwalls St
BRHD/NEIL G78 124 D3
Bowes Crs
BAIL/MDB/MHD G69 93 G5
Bowfield Crs
CARD/HILL/MSPK G52 86 A3
Bowfield Dr
CARD/HILL/MSPK G52 86 A3
Bowfield Pl
CARD/HILL/MSPK G52 86 A3
Bowfield Rd HWWD PA9 120 A4
Bowfield Wy HWWD PA9 120 A4
Bowhill Rd AIRDRIE ML6 119 F3
Bowhousebrae Rd
AIRDRIE ML6 99 F4
Bowhouse Dr CSMK G45 129 H3
Bowhouse Rd AIRDRIE ML6 99 G5
Bowie St DMBTN G82 12 D4
Bowling Green La SCOT G14 65 E3
Bowling Green Rd
BAIL/MDB/MHD G69 58 C3
CAR/SHTL G32 93 E5
LNPK/KPK G44 128 B2
SCOT G14 65 E3
Bowling Green St BLSH ML4 136 A2
Bowling Green Vw
BLTYR/CAMB G72 132 C3
Bowling St CTBR ML5 96 C2
Bowman St GVH/MTFL G42 109 F2
Bowmont Pl EKILS G75 176 D1
Bowmont Ter KVD/HLHD G12 66 B3
Bowmore Crs EKILN G74 164 B2
Bowmore Gdns RUTH G73 130 D4
UD/BTH/TAN G71 114 D4
Bowmore Rd
CARD/HILL/MSPK G52 87 F4
Bowmount Gdns
KVD/HLHD G12 66 B3
Bowyer Vennel BLSH ML4 135 G1
Boyd Dr MTHW ML1 154 A3
Boydstone Pl GIF/THBK G46 126 D2
Boydstone Rd
PLKSW/MSWD G43 126 B1
Boyd St GVH/MTFL G42 109 G3
Boylestone Rd
BRHD/NEIL G78 123 H3
Boyle St CLYDBK G81 49 G3
Boyndie St ESTRH G34 94 A1
Brabloch Crs
PSLYN/LNWD PA3 84 C3
Bracadale Dr
BAIL/MDB/MHD G69 94 C5
Bracadale Gdns
BAIL/MDB/MHD G69 94 C5
Bracadale Gv
BAIL/MDB/MHD G69 94 B5
Bracadale Rd
BAIL/MDB/MHD G69 94 B5
Brackenbrae Av BSHPBGS G64 54 B1
Brackenbrae Rd
BSHPBGS G64 54 C2
Brackendene
CRG/CRSL/HOU PA6 81 E2
Brackenhill Dr HMLTN ML3 180 B1
Brackenhurst St DMBTN G82 13 H1
Brackenrig Crs
CRMNK/CLK/EAG G76 163 F5
Brackenrig Rd GIF/THBK G46 126 B5
Bracken St MTHW ML1 137 F4
PPK/MIL G22 53 G5
Bracken Ter UD/BTH/TAN G71 134 B4
Brackla Av CLYDBK G81 49 H3
Braco Av AIRDRIE ML6 119 E3
Bradan Av KNTSWD G13 49 H4
Bradda Av RUTH G73 130 B3
Bradfield Av KVD/HLHD G12 66 B1
Bradley Ct
STPS/GTHM/RID G33 71 G1
Bradshaw Crs HMLTN ML3 168 D2
Brady Crs
BAIL/MDB/MHD G69 42 B5
Braedale Av AIRDRIE ML6 98 C2
MTHW ML1 154 A4
Braedale Crs WISHAW ML2 158 C5
Braeface Rd CUMB G67 26 A3
Braefield Dr GIF/THBK G46 126 D4
Braefoot Av MLNGV G62 17 E5
Braefoot Crs PSLYS PA2 104 C4
Braehead BLTYR/CAMB G72 151 G4
Braehead Av BRHD/NEIL G78 141 E3
CLYDBK G81 31 H1
CTBR ML5 116 A1
MLNGV G62 16 D4
Braehead Crs CLYDBK G81 31 H1
Braehead Dr BLSH ML4 135 G3
Braehead Pl BLSH ML4 135 G3
Braehead Qd BRHD/NEIL G78 141 E3
MTHW ML1 138 A3
Braehead Rd CLYDBK G81 31 H1
CUMB G67 26 D2
EKILN G74 164 B2
PSLYS PA2 122 D2
Braehead St GBLS G5 110 A1
KKNTL G66 21 E4
Braemar Av CLYDBK G81 31 G4
Braemar Ct LNPK/KPK G44 127 H3
Braemar Crs BSDN G61 51 G1
PSLYS PA2 104 C3
Braemar Dr JNSTN PA5 102 A3
Braemar Rd RNFRW PA4 48 A4
RUTH G73 130 C4
Braemar St GVH/MTFL G42 109 E5
HMLTN ML3 152 C4
Braemar Vw CLYDBK G81 31 G4
Braemore Gdns PPK/MIL G22 68 A2
Braemount Av PSLYS PA2 122 D1
Braes Av CLYDBK G81 49 G3
Braesburn Ct CUMB G67 11 H4
Braesburn Pl CUMB G67 11 H4
Braesburn Rd CUMB G67 11 H4
Braeside Av
BAIL/MDB/MHD G69 59 E1
MLNGV G62 17 E5
RUTH G73 111 F5
Braeside Crs
BAIL/MDB/MHD G69 95 E4
BRHD/NEIL G78 142 D1
Braeside Dr BRHD/NEIL G78 142 C1
DMBTN G82 13 G2
Braeside Gdns HMLTN ML3 170 B5
Braeside Pl BLTYR/CAMB G72 131 G3
Braeside Rd MTHW ML1 138 A3
Braeside St MRYH/FIRH G20 67 E3
Braes O' Yetts KKNTL G66 22 A5
Braeval Wy
STPS/GTHM/RID G33 71 F1
Braeview Av PSLYS PA2 103 G5
Braeview Dr PSLYS PA2 103 G5
Braeview Gdns PSLYS PA2 103 G5
Braeview Pl EKILN G74 166 D1
Braeview Rd PSLYS PA2 103 G5
Braid Av MTHW ML1 156 B1
Braidbar Farm Rd
GIF/THBK G46 127 G4
Braidbar Rd GIF/THBK G46 127 F4
Braidcraft Rd
PLK/PH/NH G53 106 D3
Braidcraft Ter
PLK/PH/NH G53 107 E3
Braidfauld Gdns
CAR/SHTL G32 112 A1
Braidfauld Pl CAR/SHTL G32 112 A2
Braidfauld St CAR/SHTL G32 112 A2
Braidfield Gv CLYDBK G81 32 A3
Braidfield Rd CLYDBK G81 32 B3
Braidholm Crs GIF/THBK G46 127 F3
Braidholm Rd GIF/THBK G46 127 G3
Braidhurst St MTHW ML1 154 D2
Braidley Crs EKILS G75 178 B3
Braidpark Dr GIF/THBK G46 127 G4
Braids Cir PSLYS PA2 104 B3
Braids Dr PLK/PH/NH G53 106 B3
Braid Sq COWCAD G4 67 F4
Braid's Rd PSLYS PA2 104 B3
Braid St COWCAD G4 67 F4
Braidwood Pl
PSLYN/LNWD PA3 81 G5
Braidwood St WISHAW ML2 157 F3
Bramah Av EKILS G75 178 C1
Bramble Ct KKNTL G66 4 A2
Brambling Ct WISHAW ML2 173 H4
Brambling Rd CTBR ML5 117 H1
Bramley Dr BLSH ML4 116 D4
Bramley Pl AIRDRIE ML6 99 F3
KKNTL G66 40 B4
Brampton EKILS G75 177 E2
Branchalfield Dr
WISHAW ML2 174 D1
Branchalmuir Crs
WISHAW ML2 158 A4
Branchal Rd WISHAW ML2 157 G5
Branchock Av
BLTYR/CAMB G72 132 A3
Brancumhall Rd EKILN G74 167 G2
Brandon Dr BSDN G61 34 B1
Brandon Gdns
BLTYR/CAMB G72 130 D2
Brandon Ga BLSH ML4 136 A2
Brandon Pl BLSH ML4 135 F4
Brandon St DEN/PKHD G31 90 C3
HMLTN ML3 170 B2
MTHW ML1 154 D4
Brandon Wy CTBR ML5 96 A5
Brand Pl GOV/IBX G51 88 B3
Brand St GOV/IBX G51 88 C3
Brankholm Brae HMLTN ML3 168 C1
Branklyn Cl KNTSWD G13 51 E5
Branklyn Ct KNTSWD G13 51 E5
Branklyn Crs KNTSWD G13 51 E5
Branklyn Gv KNTSWD G13 51 E5
Branklyn Pl KNTSWD G13 51 E5
Brannock Av MTHW ML1 138 A3
Brannock Pl MTHW ML1 138 A3
Brannock Rd MTHW ML1 138 A4
Brassey St MRYH/FIRH G20 52 D5
Breadalbane Crs MTHW ML1 154 C1
Breadalbane Gdns RUTH G73 130 C3
Breadalbane St KVGV G3 89 E1
Breadie Dr MLNGV G62 16 D5
Breamish Pl EKILS G75 177 E2
Bream Pl CRG/CRSL/HOU PA6 81 E3
Brechin Rd BSHPBGS G64 55 F2
Brechin St KVGV G3 88 D1
Breck Av PSLYS PA2 102 C5
Brediland Rd
PSLYN/LNWD PA3 81 H5
PSLYS PA2 102 D5
Bredin Wy MTHW ML1 154 A2
Bredisholm Crs
UD/BTH/TAN G71 115 H3
Bredisholm Dr
BAIL/MDB/MHD G69 94 B5
Bredisholm Rd
BAIL/MDB/MHD G69 94 C5
Bredisholm Ter
BAIL/MDB/MHD G69 94 B5
Brendon Av EKILS G75 177 F4
Brenfield Av LNPK/KPK G44 128 A3
Brenfield Dr LNPK/KPK G44 128 A3
Brenfield Rd LNPK/KPK G44 128 A3
Brent Av GIF/THBK G46 126 C2
Brent Ct EKILN G74 166 B2
Brent Crs CRG/CRSL/HOU PA6 80 D3
Brent Dr GIF/THBK G46 126 C2
Brent Gdns GIF/THBK G46 126 C2
Brent Rd EKILN G74 166 B2
GIF/THBK G46 126 D2
Brent Wy GIF/THBK G46 126 C2
Brentwood Av
PLK/PH/NH G53 125 F3
Brentwood Dr
PLK/PH/NH G53 125 F3
Brentwood Sq
PLK/PH/NH G53 125 G3
Brereton St GVH/MTFL G42 109 H3
Bressay EKILN G74 166 B2
Bressay Cl
STPS/GTHM/RID G33 93 F3
Bressay Gv BLTYR/CAMB G72 130 D4
STPS/GTHM/RID G33 93 F3
Bressay Pl
STPS/GTHM/RID G33 93 F3
Bressay Rd
STPS/GTHM/RID G33 93 F3
Breval Crs CLYDBK G81 31 H1
Brewery St JNSTN PA5 101 G3
Brewster Av PSLYN/LNWD PA3 84 D2
Briar Bank KKNTL G66 5 F5
Briarcroft Dr
STPS/GTHM/RID G33 55 G5
Briarcroft Pl
STPS/GTHM/RID G33 55 H5
Briarcroft Rd
STPS/GTHM/RID G33 55 H4
Briar Dr CLYDBK G81 32 A4
Briar Gdns
PLKSW/MSWD G43 127 G2
Briar Gv PLKSW/MSWD G43 127 G2
Briarlea Dr GIF/THBK G46 127 F3
Briar Neuk BSHPBGS G64 55 E3
Briar Rd KKNTL G66 21 H5
PLKSW/MSWD G43 127 G2
Briar Wk KKNTL G66 22 A5
Briarwell La MLNGV G62 17 F4
Briarwell Rd MLNGV G62 17 F4
Briarwood Ct CAR/SHTL G32 113 F2
Briarwood Rd WISHAW ML2 173 F1
Brick La PSLYN/LNWD PA3 84 C4
Bridgeburn Dr
BAIL/MDB/MHD G69 58 D1
Bridgeford Av BLSH ML4 117 F5
Bridgegait MLNGV G62 17 G5
Bridge-Gate CGLE G1 89 H3
Bridgend Ct BALLOCH G68 11 H1
Bridgend Crs
BAIL/MDB/MHD G69 58 D1
Bridgend Pl
BAIL/MDB/MHD G69 58 D1
Bridge of Weir Rd
CRG/CRSL/HOU PA6 80 C2
JNSTN PA5 100 D1
PSLYN/LNWD PA3 82 A4
Bridge St BLTYR/CAMB G72 131 F1
CLYDBK G81 31 F5
DMBTN G82 12 D4
GBLS G5 89 G3
HMLTN ML3 169 H3
PSLY PA1 84 C5
PSLYN/LNWD PA3 82 B4
WISHAW ML2 173 F2
Bridgeton Cross
DMNK/BRGTN G40 90 C4
Bridgeway Ct KKNTL G66 40 C1
Bridgeway Rd KKNTL G66 40 C1
Bridgeway Ter KKNTL G66 40 C1
Bridie Ter EKILN G74 167 F1
Brierie Av CRG/CRSL/HOU PA6 80 C2
Brierie Gdns
CRG/CRSL/HOU PA6 80 C3
Brierie Hill Ct
CRG/CRSL/HOU PA6 80 C3
Brierie-Hill Gv
CRG/CRSL/HOU PA6 80 C3
Brierie-Hill Rd
CRG/CRSL/HOU PA6 80 B3
Brierie La CRG/CRSL/HOU PA6 80 B3
Brigbrae Av BLSH ML4 136 B4
Brigham Pl SMSTN G23 52 D3
Brighton Pl GOV/IBX G51 88 A3
Brighton St GOV/IBX G51 88 A3
Brightside Av
UD/BTH/TAN G71 134 A2
Brig O'Lea Ter BRHD/NEIL G78 140 D4
Brigside Gdns HMLTN ML3 170 D3
Brisbane Ct GIF/THBK G46 127 G4
Brisbane Rd BSHPTN PA7 29 E5
Brisbane St CLYDBK G81 31 E4
GVH/MTFL G42 109 F5
Brisbane Ter EKILS G75 177 H1
Britannia Wy CLYDBK G81 49 E2
Brittain Wy MTHW ML1 118 A5
Broad Cairn Ct MTHW ML1 172 D3
Broadford St COWCAD G4 67 H4
Broadholm St PPK/MIL G22 53 H5
Broadleys Av BSHPBGS G64 54 C1
Broadlie Ct BRHD/NEIL G78 141 E3
Broadlie Dr KNTSWD G13 50 B5
Broadlie Rd BRHD/NEIL G78 140 D3
Broadloan RNFRW PA4 63 F4
Broadmoss Av NMRNS G77 162 D1
Broad Sq BLTYR/CAMB G72 151 F2
Broad St DMNK/BRGTN G40 90 C4
The Broad Wy WISHAW ML2 173 F1
Broadwood Dr
LNPK/KPK G44 128 C1
Brockburn Crs
PLK/PH/NH G53 106 C4
Brockburn Rd
PLK/PH/NH G53 106 C3
Brockburn Ter
PLK/PH/NH G53 106 D4
Brocklinn Pk EKILS G75 176 D1
Brock Ov PLK/PH/NH G53 125 H1
Brock Pl PLK/PH/NH G53 106 D5
Brock Rd PLK/PH/NH G53 125 G1
Brock Ter PLK/PH/NH G53 125 H1
Brockville St CAR/SHTL G32 92 A3
Brodick Av MTHW ML1 154 A3
Brodick Dr EKILN G74 166 A2
Brodick Pl NMRNS G77 160 D2
Brodick St SPRGB/BLRNK G21 68 D5
Brodie Gdns
BAIL/MDB/MHD G69 94 B3
Brodie Gv
BAIL/MDB/MHD G69 94 B3
Brodie Park Av PSLYS PA2 104 B2
Brodie Park Crs PSLYS PA2 104 A2
Brodie Park Gdns PSLYS PA2 104 B2
Brodie Pl EKILN G74 166 A2
Brodie Rd SPRGB/BLRNK G21 55 F4
Brogan Crs MTHW ML1 154 A3
Bron Wy CUMB G67 26 C4
Brookfield Av
STPS/GTHM/RID G33 55 G4
Brookfield Cnr
STPS/GTHM/RID G33 55 G4
Brookfield Dr
STPS/GTHM/RID G33 55 G4
Brookfield Gdns
STPS/GTHM/RID G33 55 G4
Brookfield Ga
STPS/GTHM/RID G33 55 G4
Brookfield Pl
STPS/GTHM/RID G33 55 H4
Brookfield Rd
STPS/GTHM/RID G33 55 G4
Brooklands EKILN G74 165 F4
Brooklands Av
UD/BTH/TAN G71 114 D5
Brooklea Dr GIF/THBK G46 127 F2
Brooklime Dr EKILN G74 165 H1
Brooklime Gdns EKILN G74 165 H2
Brookside St
DMNK/BRGTN G40 90 D4
Brook St CLYDBK G81 31 G4
DMNK/BRGTN G40 90 C4
Broom Av ERSK PA8 47 G4
Broomburn Dr NMRNS G77 162 A1
Broom Crs BRHD/NEIL G78 123 H2
EKILS G75 178 A3
Broomcroft Rd NMRNS G77 144 D4
Broom Dr CLYDBK G81 31 H4
Broomfield
CRG/CRSL/HOU PA6 81 E2
Broomfield Av
BLTYR/CAMB G72 111 G5
NMRNS G77 162 A2
Broomfield La
SPRGB/BLRNK G21 68 C1
Broomfield Pl
SPRGB/BLRNK G21 68 C1
Broomfield Rd GIF/THBK G46 144 D4
SPRGB/BLRNK G21 68 C1
Broomfield St AIRDRIE ML6 98 C2
Broomfield Ter
UD/BTH/TAN G71 115 E3
Broomfield Wk KKNTL G66 21 F5
Broom Gdns KKNTL G66 39 G2
Broomhill Av CAR/SHTL G32 112 C4
NMRNS G77 162 B1
PTCK G11 65 G4
Broomhill Crs BLSH ML4 135 G4
ERSK PA8 47 G4
Broomhill Dr DMBTN G82 13 G2
PTCK G11 65 G3
RUTH G73 130 A2
Broomhill Farm Ms KKNTL G66 21 G4
Broomhill Gdns NMRNS G77 162 A1
PTCK G11 65 G3
Broomhill La PTCK G11 65 G3
Broomhill Pl PTCK G11 65 G4
Broomhill Ter PTCK G11 65 G4
Broomieknowe Dr RUTH G73 130 A1
Broomieknowe Gdns
RUTH G73 129 H1
Broomieknowe Rd
RUTH G73 130 A1
Broomielaw CGLW G2 2 B7
Broomknoll St AIRDRIE ML6 98 B2
Broomknowe BALLOCH G68 25 H2
Broomknowes Av KKNTL G66 40 B4
Broomknowes Rd
SPRGB/BLRNK G21 68 D2
Broomlands Av ERSK PA8 48 A3
Broomlands Crs ERSK PA8 48 A3
Broomlands Gdns ERSK PA8 48 A3
Broomlands Rd CUMB G67 26 C5
Broomlands St PSLY PA1 83 H5
Broomlands Wy ERSK PA8 48 B3
Broomlea Crs RNFRW PA4 47 H4
Broomlee Rd CUMB G67 45 E2
Broomley Dr GIF/THBK G46 145 F1
Broomley La GIF/THBK G46 145 F1
Broomloan Pl GOV/IBX G51 87 H3
Broomloan Rd GOV/IBX G51 87 H4
Broompark Av
BLTYR/CAMB G72 151 F4
Broompark Circ
DEN/PKHD G31 90 C1
Broompark Crs AIRDRIE ML6 76 B4
Broompark Dr DEN/PKHD G31 90 C2
NMRNS G77 144 C4
RNFRW PA4 48 A4
Broompark La
DEN/PKHD G31 90 C2
Broompark Rd
BLTYR/CAMB G72 151 F3
WISHAW ML2 173 E1
Broompark St DEN/PKHD G31 90 C2
Broom Pl BRWEIR PA11 79 H3
CTBR ML5 116 C1
MTHW ML1 137 H3
PLKSW/MSWD G43 127 G2
Broom Rd CUMB G67 11 F5
NMRNS G77 144 D4
PLKSW/MSWD G43 127 G2
Broom Rd East NMRNS G77 162 C2
Broomside Crs MTHW ML1 172 A1
Broomside St MTHW ML1 171 H1
Broomstone Av NMRNS G77 162 A2
Broom Ter JNSTN PA5 101 G5
Broomton Rd
SPRGB/BLRNK G21 55 F4
Broomvale Dr NMRNS G77 144 C5
Broomward Dr JNSTN PA5 102 A1
Brora Crs HMLTN ML3 169 E5
Brora Dr BSDN G61 35 E4
GIF/THBK G46 127 G5
RNFRW PA4 63 H3
Brora Gdns BSHPBGS G64 55 E2
Brora Rd BSHPBGS G64 55 E2
Brora St STPS/GTHM/RID G33 69 G5
Broughton EKILS G75 178 B4
Broughton Dr SMSTN G23 52 D3
Broughton Gdns SMSTN G23 52 D2
Broughton Pl CTBR ML5 117 E1
HMLTN ML3 169 F2
Broughton Rd SMSTN G23 52 D3
Brouster Hl EKILN G74 166 B4
Brouster Pl EKILN G74 166 B4
Brown Av CLYDBK G81 49 G3
DMBTN G82 13 H3
Brown Ct
STPS/GTHM/RID G33 71 F1
Brownhill Rd
PLKSW/MSWD G43 127 E3
Brownhill Vw WISHAW ML2 159 E4
Brownieside Pl AIRDRIE ML6 77 H3
Brownlie St GVH/MTFL G42 109 G4
Brown Pl BLTYR/CAMB G72 131 F1
Brown Rd CUMB G67 26 B3
Brownsburn Rd AIRDRIE ML6 98 C5
Brownsdale Rd RUTH G73 110 C5
Brownsfield Crs RNFRW PA4 61 G1
Brownsfield Rd RNFRW PA4 61 G1
Brownshill Av CTBR ML5 96 C5
Brownside Av
BLTYR/CAMB G72 130 D2
BRHD/NEIL G78 123 H2
Brownside Crs
BRHD/NEIL G78 123 H2
Brownside Dr
BRHD/NEIL G78 123 H2
KNTSWD G13 50 A5
Brownside Gv
BRHD/NEIL G78 123 H2
Brownside Rd RUTH G73 130 C2
Brownsland Ct
BAIL/MDB/MHD G69 59 F5
Brown's La PSLY PA1 84 B5
Brown St CGLW G2 2 C6
CTBR ML5 96 D4
MTHW ML1 155 E2
PSLY PA1 83 H4
RNFRW PA4 63 E4
WISHAW ML2 175 F1
Brown St North RNFRW PA4 63 F3
Browside Av PSLYS PA2 103 H5
Bruce Av BLTYR/CAMB G72 131 F4
JNSTN PA5 121 F1
MTHW ML1 154 C3
PSLYN/LNWD PA3 84 D2
Brucefield Pl ESTRH G34 94 C1
Brucehill Rd DMBTN G82 12 B3
Bruce Pl EKILS G75 178 C1
Bruce Rd BSHPTN PA7 28 D5
MTHW ML1 137 G5
PLKSD/SHW G41 88 D5
PSLYN/LNWD PA3 84 D3
RNFRW PA4 62 D5
Bruce St AIRDRIE ML6 77 H4
BLSH ML4 136 A2
CLYDBK G81 49 E2
CTBR ML5 97 E1
DMBTN G82 13 F5
Bruce Ter BLTYR/CAMB G72 151 H1
EKILS G75 178 C1
Brunel Wy EKILS G75 166 C5
Brunstane Rd ESTRH G34 71 H5
Brunswick La CGLE G1 3 G7
Brunswick St CGLE G1 3 G7
Brunton St LNPK/KPK G44 128 B2
Brunton Ter LNPK/KPK G44 128 A3
Bruntsfield Av
PLK/PH/NH G53 125 G4
Bruntsfield Gdns
PLK/PH/NH G53 125 G4
Bryan St HMLTN ML3 152 C5
Bryce Pl EKILS G75 177 H2
Brydson Pl PSLYN/LNWD PA3 82 A3
Bryon Ct UD/BTH/TAN G71 134 C5
Bryson Ct HMLTN ML3 180 D1
Bryson St CLYDBK G81 32 C1
Buccleuch Av
CARD/HILL/MSPK G52 85 H1
CRMNK/CLK/EAG G76 145 G3
Buccleuch Dr BSDN G61 34 B1
Buccleuch La KVGV G3 2 C2
Buccleuch St KVGV G3 2 B2
Buchanan Av BSHPTN PA7 29 E4
Buchanan Ct
STPS/GTHM/RID G33 57 G5
Buchanan Crs BSHPBGS G64 55 F3
HMLTN ML3 169 G3
Buchanan Dr BSDN G61 34 D4
BSHPBGS G64 55 F3
KKNTL G66 40 A4
NMRNS G77 144 B3
RUTH G73 130 A1
Buchanan Ga
STPS/GTHM/RID G33 57 G5
Buchanan Gv
BAIL/MDB/MHD G69 94 A4
Buchanan Pl BSHPBGS G64 19 F4
Buchanan St AIRDRIE ML6 98 B1
BAIL/MDB/MHD G69 94 A5
CGLE G1 2 E6
CTBR ML5 96 C3
DMBTN G82 13 F5
JNSTN PA5 101 F4
MLNGV G62 17 F3

Buchanan Wy JNSTN PA5..........101 F4
Buchandyke Rd EKILN G74.......167 E1
Buchan Gn EKILN G74............167 E2
Buchan Rd AIRDRIE ML6.........137 C5
Buchan St HMLTN ML3............169 H5
  WISHAW ML2......................157 F4
Buchan Ter BLTYR/CAMB G72...130 D4
Buchlyvie Gdns BSHPBGS G64....54 C3
Buchlyvie Rd PSLY PA1...........85 H4
Buchlyvie St ESTRH G34..........94 A2
Buckingham Ct HMLTN ML3 ....168 D1
Buckingham Dr
  CAR/SHTL G32.................112 C4
  RUTH G73.......................111 G5
Buckingham St
  KVD/HLHD G12.................66 C3
Buckingham Ter
  KVD/HLHD G12.................66 C3
Bucklaw Pl
  CARD/HILL/MSPK G52........86 D5
Bucklaw Pl
  CARD/HILL/MSPK G52........86 D5
Bucklaw Ter
  CARD/HILL/MSPK G52........86 D5
Buckley St PPK/MIL G22........54 A1
Buckshorn Rd
  SPRGB/BLRNK G21............69 F2
Buckthorne Pl
  PLK/PH/NH G53...............125 G5
Buddon St DMNK/BRGTN G40....91 F5
Budhill Av CAR/SHTL G32.......92 C4
Budshaw Av AIRDRIE ML6.......118 D2
Bulldale Ct SCOT G14............63 H1
Bulldale Rd SCOT G14...........63 H1
Bulldale St SCOT G14............63 H1
Buller Cl BLTYR/CAMB G72.....133 C5
Buller Crs BLTYR/CAMB G72....133 F5
Bullionslaw Dr RUTH G75.......130 C1
Bulloch Rd GIF/THBK G46.......127 G5
Bull Rd CRMNK/CLK/EAG G76..146 A4
Bullwood Av PLK/PH/NH G53...106 A3
Bullwood Ct PLK/PH/NH G53...106 A3
Bullwood Dr PLK/PH/NH G53...106 A3
Bullwood Gdns
  PLK/PH/NH G53...............106 A3
Bullwood Pl PLK/PH/NH G53...106 A3
Bunbury Ter EKILS G75.........165 H5
Bunessan St
  CARD/HILL/MSPK G52........87 G4
Bunhouse Rd KVGV G3..........88 D2
Burghead Dr GOV/IBX G51......87 F1
Burghead Pl GOV/IBX G51......87 F1
Burgher St DEN/PKHD G31.....91 F4
Burgh Hall La PTCK G11........66 A4
Burgh Hall St PTCK G11........66 A4
Burgh La KVD/HLHD G12........66 C3
Burleigh Rd
  UD/BTH/TAN G71..............134 C4
Burleigh St CTBR ML5...........117 E1
  GOV/IBX G51....................87 H1
Burley Pl EKILN G74.............165 E3
Burlington Av KVD/HLHD G12 ..52 A4
Burmola St PPK/MIL G22........67 G2
Burnacre Gdns
  UD/BTH/TAN G71..............114 D5
Burnawn Gdns
  STPS/GTHM/RID G33..........55 G4
Burnawn Gv
  STPS/GTHM/RID G33..........55 G4
Burnawn Pl
  STPS/GTHM/RID G33..........55 G4
Burnbank Centre
  HMLTN ML3.....................152 B5
Burnbank Dr BRHD/NEIL G78..142 B1
Burnbank Gdns
  MRYH/FIRH G20................67 F4
Burnbank La MRYH/FIRH G20...67 F4
Burnbank Rd HMLTN ML3.......169 G1
Burnbank St AIRDRIE ML6.......98 A1
  CTBR ML5........................97 E1
Burnbank Ter COWCAD G4......67 E4
  KSYTH G65........................8 C1
Burnblea Gdns HMLTN ML3....170 B3
Burnblea St HMLTN ML3.......170 A3
  KSYTH G65........................23 F1
Burnbrae Av
  BAIL/MDB/MHD G69...........59 F1
  BSDN G61........................34 D1
Burnbrae Dr JNSTN PA5........102 C1
  PSLYN/LNWD PA3..............82 C5
  RUTH G73.......................130 C2
Burnbrae Gdns
  PLK/PH/NH G53...............125 H2
Burnbrae Pl EKILN G74.........165 H4
Burnbrae Rd
  BAIL/MDB/MHD G69...........41 E5
  BLTYR/CAMB G72..............151 E2
  KKNTL G66.......................57 C1
  PSLYN/LNWD PA3..............82 A5
Burnbrae St
  SPRGB/BLRNK G21.............68 D2
Burncleuch Av
  BLTYR/CAMB G72..............131 F3
Burncrooks Av BSDN G61.......34 A1
  EKILN G74......................165 H5
Burndyke Ct GOV/IBX G51.....88 B2
Burndyke Sq GOV/IBX G51.....88 B2
Burnet Rose Ct EKILN G74.....165 H4
Burnet Rose Gdns EKILN G74...165 H4
Burnet Rose Pl EKILN G74.....165 H1
Burnett Ct
  BAIL/MDB/MHD G69............58 B3
Burnett Rd
  STPS/GTHM/RID G33..........93 F2
Burnfield Dr
  PLKSW/MSWD G43............93 H5
Burnfield Gdns
  GIF/THBK G46...................127 E3
Burnfield Rd GIF/THBK G46....126 D2
Burnfoot Crs PSLYS PA2........103 H5
  RUTH G73.......................130 C2
Burnfoot Dr
  CARD/HILL/MSPK G52........86 C4
Burnfoot Rd AIRDRIE ML6.......97 H1

Burngreen KSYTH G65.............8 B2
Burnhall Pl WISHAW ML2......174 C4
Burnhall Rd WISHAW ML2.....174 B3
Burnhall St WISHAW ML2.....174 B3
Burnham Rd SCOT G14..........64 B2
Burnhaven ERSK PA8............47 F1
Burnhead Rd AIRDRIE ML6......77 H5
  BALLOCH G68....................25 H3
  PLKSW/MSWD G43............127 H2
Burnhead St
  UD/BTH/TAN G71..............115 G5
Burnhill Dr RUTH G73...........110 C4
Burnhill St RUTH G73...........110 C4
Burnhouse Av BALLOCH G68....25 F3
Burnhouse Brae NMRNS G77..162 B2
Burnhouse Crs HMLTN ML3....169 G4
Burnhouse Rd HMLTN ML3.....169 G4
Burnhouse St MRYH/FIRH G20..52 C5
Burniebrae AIRDRIE ML6........97 H1
Burniebrae Rd AIRDRIE ML6...119 F1
Burnlea Crs
  CRC/CRSL/HOU PA6...........80 B1
Burnlip Rd BSDN G61............74 D2
Burnmouth Pl BSDN G61........34 D3
Burnmouth Rd
  STPS/GTHM/RID G33...........93 G3
Burnock Pl EKILS G75...........176 D1
Burnpark Av
  UD/BTH/TAN G71..............114 C5
Burns Pl BSHPTN PA7...........111 H5
Burns Av BSHPTN PA7...........29 E3
Bürns Crs AIRDRIE ML6...........98 C3
Burns Dr JNSTN PA5.............121 F1
  KKNTL G66.......................22 A4
Burns Gdns BLTYR/CAMB G72..151 E1
Burns Gv GIF/THBK G46.........126 D5
Burnside BSDN G61...............33 H1
Burnside Av AIRDRIE ML6......118 C2
  BLSH ML4.........................135 A4
  BRHD/NEIL G78.................124 A3
  JNSTN PA5......................100 D1
  KKNTL G66........................39 G1
Burnside Ct BSDN G61...........33 H1
  RUTH G73........................130 B2
Burnside Crs
  BLTYR/CAMB G72..............152 A4
  CLYDBK G81......................32 A2
Burnside Gdns
  CRMNK/CLK/EAG G76........145 G3
  KLBCH PA10.....................100 C4
Burnside Ga RUTH G73..........130 B2
Burnside La HMLTN ML3.......170 B3
Burnside Pl DMBTN G82.........13 G3
Burnside Rd GIF/THBK G46....145 E4
  GIF/THBK G46...................145 E4
  JNSTN PA5.......................102 B3
  MTHW ML1......................138 A3
  RUTH G73........................130 B2
Burnside St MTHW ML1........172 C1
Burnside Vw CTBR ML5..........96 B4
  EKILS G75.......................177 F4
Burnside Wk CTBR ML5..........96 B4
Burns La AIRDRIE ML6...........119 E1
Burns Pk EKILN G74.............166 D3
  CUMB G67.......................26 C2
  KKNTL G66.......................39 G1
Burns St CLYDBK G81.............31 F5
  COWCAD G4......................67 G4
  HMLTN ML3.....................170 A3
Burntbroom Dr
  BAIL/MDB/MHD G69...........113 G1
Burntbroom Gdns
  BAIL/MDB/MHD G69...........113 G1
Burntbroom St
  STPS/GTHM/RID G33...........93 E2
Burn Ter BLTYR/CAMB G72....111 H5
Burn Vw CUMB G67..............27 E2
Burnwood Dr AIRDRIE ML6......99 H3
Burra Gdns BSHPBGS G64.......55 G1
Burrell Ct PLKSD/SHW G41....108 B2
Burrell's La COWCAD G4...........3 K5
Burrelton Rd
  PLKSW/MSWD G43............128 A2
Burte Ct BLSH ML4...............116 D4
Busby Rd BLSH ML4..............135 C4
  CRMNK/CLK/EAG G76........147 F1
  CRMNK/CLK/EAG G76........145 H3
Bush Crs WISHAW ML2..........174 B3
Bushes Av PSLYS PA2...........104 A3
Busheyhill St
  BLTYR/CAMB G72..............131 F2
Bute EKILN G74...................167 E4
Bute Av MTHW ML1.............154 B3
Bute Crs BSDN G61...............65 G5
  OLDK G60.........................50 D3
  PSLYS PA2.......................104 A5
Bute Dr JNSTN PA5..............101 E5
  OLDK G60.........................30 D3
Bute Gdns KVD/HLHD G12......66 C4
  LNPK/KPK G44.................128 A4
  OLDK G60.........................30 D2
Bute La KVD/HLHD G12..........66 C4
Bute Pl OLDK G60..................31 E5
Bute Rd KKNTL G66...............62 A5
  PSLYN/LNWD PA3..............82 A5
Bute St CTBR ML5................97 E5
  HMLTN ML3.....................152 C4
Bute Ter UD/BTH/TAN G71.....129 H2
  UD/BTH/TAN G71..............115 G5
Butterbiggins Rd
  GVH/MTFL G42..................109 G1
Butterburnpark St
  HMLTN ML3.....................170 A4
Butterfield Pl GVH/MTFL G42 ..109 F1
Buttermere EKILS G75...........177 E5
Byars Rd KKNTL G66..............20 D5
Byramsmuir Rd MTHW ML1...117 H4
Byrebush Rd
  PLK/PH/NH G53................106 D3
Byres Av PSLYN/LNWD PA3.....84 D1
Byres Crs PSLYN/LNWD PA3....84 D1
Byresknowe La MTHW ML1....155 H3
Byres Rd JNSTN PA5.............102 C2
  KVD/HLHD G12..................66 C4
  MTHW ML1.......................138 B3

Byrestone Av NMRNS G77......162 D1
Byron St CLYDBK G81.............31 G4
  PTCK G11.........................65 G4
Byshot St PPK/MIL G22.........68 A2

C

Cable Depot Rd CLYDBK G81....48 D1
Cadder Av BAIL/MDB/MHD G69..73 E1
Cadder Ct BSHPBGS G64.........38 A5
Cadder Pl MRYH/FIRH G20......52 D4
Cadder Rd BSHPBGS G64........37 H2
  MRYH/FIRH G20.................52 D4
Cadder Wy BSHPBGS G64.......38 A5
Cadder's Sheuch KSYTH G65.....9 F2
Cadoc St BLTYR/CAMB G72....131 G2
Cadogan St CCLW G2...............2 C5
Cadzow Av GIF/THBK G46......145 E2
  HMLTN ML3.....................152 C5
Cadzow Crs CTBR ML5...........96 A5
Cadzow Dr BLTYR/CAMB G72..131 F2
Cadzow La HMLTN ML3.........170 B1
Cadzow Pk HMLTN ML3.........170 B1
Cadzow Rd HMLTN ML3........181 F5
Cadzow St CGLW G2................2 C5
  HMLTN ML3.....................170 B1
  MTHW ML1......................154 C4
Caird Dr PTCK G11................66 A4
Caird Gdns HMLTN ML3........152 D5
Caird Pk HMLTN ML3............153 E5
Caird St HMLTN ML3.............152 D5
Cairn Av RNFRW PA4..............63 H5
Cairnban St GOV/IBX G51.......87 E3
Cairnbrook Rd ESTRH G34.......94 B1
Cairn Ct EKILN G74...............166 B1
Cairndow Av LNPK/KPK G44...128 A3
Cairndow Avenue La
  LNPK/KPK G44.................128 A3
Cairndow Ct LNPK/KPK G44...128 A3
Cairn Dr PSLYN/LNWD PA3.....82 A3
Cairnhill Crs CTBR ML5..........117 E4
Cairney Pl WISHAW ML2.......159 E4
Cairngorm Crs HMLTN ML3....180 B1
Cairngorm Crs
  BRHD/NEIL G78.................142 B1
  BSDN G61........................33 G2
  PSLYS PA2......................104 A3
  WISHAW ML2...................173 G2
Cairngorm Gdns BALLOCH G68..25 F4
Cairngorm Rd PLK/PH/NH G53..125 G2
Cairngorm Rd
  PLKSW/MSWD G43............127 F2
Cairnhill Av
  CARD/HILL/MSPK G52........106 A1
Cairnhill Circ
  CARD/HILL/MSPK G52........106 A1
Cairnhill Dr
  CARD/HILL/MSPK G52........106 A1
Cairnhill Pl
  CARD/HILL/MSPK G52........106 A1
Cairnhill Rd AIRDRIE ML6.......98 A4
Cairnhill Vw BSDN G61..........51 F1
Cairnhope Av AIRDRIE ML6.....98 A4
Cairnlea Dr GOV/IBX G51.......88 A3
Cairnlea Gdns BLSH ML4........136 A4
Cairnlea Rd MLNGV G62.........16 C2
Cairnmuir Rd
  CRMNK/CLK/EAG G76........148 A5
Cairnoch HI BSHPBGS G64.......25 C5
Cairn Pl EKILN G74...............166 B1
Cairnryan EKILN G74............166 A2
Cairnryan Crs
  BLTYR/CAMB G72..............168 C2
Cairns Av BLTYR/CAMB G72...131 G2
Cairns Dr MLNGV G62.............17 E3
Cairnsmore Dr BSDN G61.......33 G1
Cairnsmore Rd DRUM G15......49 H1
Cairns Rd BLTYR/CAMB G72...131 G3
  BSHPTN PA7......................28 D4
Cairn St SPRGB/BLRNK G21....54 C5
Cairnswell Av
  BLTYR/CAMB G72..............131 H3
Cairnswell Pl
  BLTYR/CAMB G72..............131 H3
Cairntoul Ct BALLOCH G68......25 F4
Cairntoul Dr SCOT G14...........50 B5
Cairntoul Pl SCOT G14............50 B5
Cairn Vw AIRDRIE ML6............98 A3
  KKNTL G66........................40 D1
Cairnview Rd KKNTL G66..........5 F1
Cairnwood Dr AIRDRIE ML6.....98 A4
Caithness Rd EKILN G74........167 G2
Caithness St
  BLTYR/CAMB G72..............151 F4
  MRYH/FIRH G20.................67 E2
Cala Sona Ct WISHAW ML2....173 F5
Calcots Pl ESTRH G34.............72 B5
Caldarvan St PPK/MIL G22......67 F3
Caldeen Rd CTBR ML5............97 E4
Calder Av BRHD/NEIL G78.....142 C1
  CTBR ML5.........................97 E5
Caldebank Rd AIRDRIE ML6.....98 C5
Calderbank Ter MTHW ML1....155 E3
Calderbraes Av
  UD/BTH/TAN G71..............114 D4
Caldercuilt Rd
  MRYH/FIRH G20.................52 B3
Calder Dr BLSH ML4..............135 H3
  BLTYR/CAMB G72..............131 F2
Calder Ga BSHPBGS G64........37 G4
Calderglen Av
  BLTYR/CAMB G72..............133 F4
Calderglen Rd EKILN G74......167 H4
Caldergrove MTHW ML1........154 D3
Calderpark Av AIRDRIE ML6.....99 E2
Calderpark Ct
  UD/BTH/TAN G71..............114 A2
Calderpark Crs
  UD/BTH/TAN G71..............114 A2
Calderpark Pl
  UD/BTH/TAN G71..............114 A2

MLNGV G62........................16 D4
Calderpark Rd
  UD/BTH/TAN G71..............114 A2
Calderpark Ter
  UD/BTH/TAN G71..............114 A2
Calder Pl BAIL/MDB/MHD G69..94 A5
Calder St BLSH ML4..............136 B3
  BLTYR/CAMB G72..............133 F2
  GVH/MTFL G42..................109 G2
  SHOTTS ML7.....................159 G2
Calderside Gv EKILN G74......167 H5
Calderside Rd EKILN G74......167 G5
Calder St AIRDRIE ML6..........118 D2
  BLTYR/CAMB G72..............151 G2
  CTBR ML5.........................97 E5
  GVH/MTFL G42..................109 F2
Caldervale St AIRDRIE ML6......99 F5
Calder Vw HMLTN ML3..........155 E5
Calderview Av CTBR ML5.......117 G1
Calderwood Av
  BAIL/MDB/MHD G69...........113 H1
  BLTYR/CAMB G72..............151 G4
Calderwood Dr
  BAIL/MDB/MHD G69...........113 H1
Calderwood Gdns
  BAIL/MDB/MHD G69...........113 H1
  EKILN G74.......................167 H2
Calderwood Rd EKILN G74.....167 E3
  PLKSW/MSWD G43............127 G1
Caldwell Av KNTSWD G13......50 B5
  PSLYN/LNWD PA3..............101 G1
Caldwell Gv BLSH ML4..........116 D4
  RUTH G73........................130 D5
Caldwell Qd MTHW ML1.......154 B5
Caledonia Av GBLS G5..........109 H1
  RUTH G73........................111 E4
Caledonia Ct
  PSLYN/LNWD PA3..............84 A3
Caledonia Dr
  BAIL/MDB/MHD G69...........114 A1
  MTHW ML1......................138 B3
Caledonian Av BLSH ML4......135 G3
Caledonian Crs EKILN G74.....166 D4
Caledonian Crs
  KVD/HLHD G12..................66 D4
Caledonian Ga BSHPBGS G64..96 D1
Caledonian Rd WISHAW ML2..173 H3
Caledonia Rd
  BAIL/MDB/MHD G69...........113 H1
  GBLS G5..........................109 H1
Caledonia St CLYDBK G81.......48 C3
  GBLS G5..........................110 A1
  PSLYN/LNWD PA3..............84 A4
Caledonia Ter DMBTN G82......12 B4
Caledonia Wy
  PSLYN/LNWD PA3..............84 A5
Caledonia Wy East
  PSLYN/LNWD PA3..............62 A5
Caledonia Wy West
  PSLYN/LNWD PA3..............62 A5
Caledon La KVD/HLHD G12.....66 B4
Caledon St KVD/HLHD G12.....66 B4
Calfhill Rd PLK/PH/NH G53....106 C1
Calfmuir Rd KKNTL G66...........40 D2
Calgary Pk EKILS G75...........166 A5
Calgary St COWCAD G4............3 G2
Calico Wy KKNTL G66..............4 A1
Callaghan Wynd
  BLTYR/CAMB G72..............151 E2
Callander Ct BALLOCH G68......26 B1
Callander Rd AIRDRIE ML6.....119 E3
  BALLOCH G68.....................26 B1
Callander St MRYH/FIRH G20..67 F3
Callieburn Ct BSHPBGS G64....54 D3
Callieburn Rd BSHPBGS G64...54 D3
Callon St AIRDRIE ML6............98 B2
Cally Av DRUM G15...............33 F5
Calside PSLYS PA2...............104 B3
Calside Av PSLYS PA2...........104 A2
Calton Entry
  DMNK/BRGTN G40..............90 B3
Calvay Crs
  STPS/GTHM/RID G33..........93 E2
Calvay Rd
  STPS/GTHM/RID G33..........93 F2
Cambourne Rd
  BAIL/MDB/MHD G69...........42 A5
Cambridge Av CLYDBK G81.....49 F1
Cambridge Rd RNFRW PA4.....63 F4
Cambridge St KVGV G3............2 D3
Camburn St CAR/SHTL G32.....92 A4
Cambusdoon Rd
  STPS/GTHM/RID G33..........70 D4
Cambuskenneth Gdns
  CAR/SHTL G32....................93 E4
Cambuslang Rd
  CAR/SHTL G32...................111 F3
Cambuslang Wy
  CAR/SHTL G32...................112 A4
Cambusnethan St
  WISHAW ML2...................174 D1
Cambus Pl
  STPS/GTHM/RID G33..........70 D4
Camden Ter GBLS G5............89 H5
Camellia Dr WISHAW ML2.....175 H4
Cameron Crs
  BLTYR/CAMB G72..............151 G3
Cameron Dr BSHPTN PA7.......29 E5
  CRMNK/CLK/EAG G76........147 F3
  HMLTN ML3.....................169 H3
Cameron Dr BSDN G61...........34 C5
  NMRNS G77....................144 B4
Cameron Pl BLSH ML4..........117 H1
Cameron Sq CLYDBK G81.......32 B2
Cameron St
  CARD/HILL/MSPK G52........85 H2
  CTBR ML5........................116 C1
  MTHW ML1......................154 C4
Cameron Wy
  BLTYR/CAMB G72..............151 G2
Camlachie St DEN/PKHD G31..91 E4
  DMNK/BRGTN G40..............90 D4
Campbell Av BSHPTN PA7......29 E4
  DMBTN G82.......................13 H3

Campbell Crs NMRNS G77.....144 B4
  UD/BTH/TAN G71..............131 H3
Campbell Dr BRHD/NEIL G78.124 B5
  BSDN G61........................34 A3
  DMBTN G82.......................13 H3
Campbell La HMLTN ML3.......170 B2
Campbell Pl BSHPBGS G64....19 F4
  JNSTN PA5.......................101 G4
  MRYH/FIRH G20.................52 D4
  RNFRW PA4.......................63 G2
  WISHAW ML2...................174 B2
Campbell Ter DMBTN G82.....13 H3
Camphill Gdns BSHPTN PA7...46 B1
Campion Rd MTHW ML1........154 D2
Camp Rd BAIL/MDB/MHD G69..94 A4
  MTHW ML1......................171 H1
  RUTH G73.......................110 C2
Campsie Av RNFRW PA4.........63 H4
Campsie Crs AIRDRIE ML6.....142 B1
Campsie Crs AIRDRIE ML6.....34 A1
Campsie Dr BSDN G61............34 A1
  MLNGV G62.......................17 F5
  PSLYN/LNWD PA3..............82 B5
  PSLYS PA2......................104 A4
  RNFRW PA4.......................84 D1
Campsie Gdns
  CRMNK/CLK/EAG G76........145 F2
Campsie Pl
  BAIL/MDB/MHD G69............19 H3
Campsie Rd BSHPBGS G64.....19 H3
  EKILS G75.......................177 F5
  KKNTL G66.........................5 E4
  WISHAW ML2...................173 F1
Campsie St SPRGB/BLRNK G21..68 C1
Campsie Vw
  BAIL/MDB/MHD G69............95 E4
  BAIL/MDB/MHD G69............95 H3
  BLTYR/CAMB G72..............132 B4
  CUMB G67........................26 D3
  HMLTN ML3.....................168 D5
  KKNTL G66........................20 C5
  STPS/GTHM/RID G33..........71 E2
  UD/BTH/TAN G71..............115 F4
Campston Pl
  STPS/GTHM/RID G33..........70 D5
Camp St MTHW ML1.............154 D3
Camsbusmore Pl
  STPS/GTHM/RID G33..........70 D4
Camstradden Dr East
  BSDN G61........................33 H4
Camstradden Dr West
  BSDN G61........................33 H4
Camus Pl DRUM G15.............33 E4
Canal Av JNSTN PA5.............101 H4
Canal Ct CTBR ML5................96 C2
Canal La KKNTL G66..............21 F4
Canal Rd JNSTN PA5............101 H4
Canal St CLYDBK G81............49 F2
  JNSTN PA5.......................101 H3
  KKNTL G66........................21 F4
  RNFRW PA4.......................63 G2
Canal Ter PSLY PA1...............84 B5
Canberra Av CLYDBK G81.......31 E4
Canberra Dr EKILS G75.........165 H5
Cander Rigg BSHPBGS G64....37 H4
Canderigg CGLE G1................3 H7
Candren Rd PSLYN/LNWD PA3..82 C3
Canmore Pl DEN/PKHD G31....91 G5
Canmore St DEN/PKHD G31....91 G5
Cannich Dr PSLYS PA2..........105 E3
Cannich Pl WISHAW ML2......158 A4
Canniesburn Qd BSDN G61....51 F1
Canniesburn Rd BSDN G61....50 D1
Canonbie Av EKILN G74........166 C1
Canonbie St ESTRH G34.........72 C5
Canterbury EKILS G75...........177 H1
Cantieslaw Dr EKILN G74......166 D2
Canting Wy GOV/IBX G51.......88 B2
Canyon Rd WISHAW ML2......173 E5
Cap Cot EKILN G74...............168 B2
Capel Av NMRNS G77...........144 C4
Capel Gv EKILN G74.............167 E2
Capelrig Dr EKILN G74..........167 E2
  NMRNS G77....................144 B2
Capelrig La NMRNS G77.......144 A4
Capelrig Rd NMRNS G77.......161 G1
Capelrig St GIF/THBK G46.....126 C3
Caplaw Pl WISHAW ML2.......173 G2
Caplethill Rd PSLYS PA2........123 G1
Caprington St
  STPS/GTHM/RID G33..........70 B5
Captain's Wk MTHW ML1.....157 H1
Cara Dr GOV/IBX G51............87 E1
Carbarns WISHAW ML2.........173 E4
Carbarns East WISHAW ML2..173 E4
Carbarns Rd WISHAW ML2....173 E4
Carbarns West WISHAW ML2..173 E4
Carberry Rd PLKSD/SHW G41..108 C2
Carbeth Rd MLNGV G62.........16 D4
Carbisdale St PPK/MIL G22....68 B1
Carbost St SMSTN G23..........52 C1
Carbrook St PSLY PA1............83 H5
  SPRGB/BLRNK G21.............68 C4
Cardarrach St
  SPRGB/BLRNK G21.............68 D2
Cardean Rd BLSH ML4..........116 D5
Cardell Av PSLYS PA2...........103 F1
Cardell Crs AIRDRIE ML6.......119 E2
Cardell Dr PSLYS PA2...........103 F1
Cardell Rd PSLYS PA2...........103 F1
Cardonald Dr
  CARD/HILL/MSPK G52........86 B5

Cardonald Gdns
CARD/HILL/MSPK G52 86 B5
Cardonald Place Rd
CARD/HILL/MSPK G52 86 C5
Cardowan Dr *BALLOCH* G68 24 C4
STPS/GTHM/RID G33 71 E1
Cardowan Pk
UD/BTH/TAN G71 115 G3
Cardowan Rd *CAR/SHTL* G32 92 A3
STPS/GTHM/RID G33 57 F5
Cardow Rd *SPRGB/BLRNK* G21 69 F2
Cardrona St
STPS/GTHM/RID G33 70 C3
Cardross Pl *BALLOCH* G68 25 F3
Cardross Rd *DMBTN* G82 12 B3
Cardross St *DEN/PKHD* G31 90 C2
Cardwell St *GBLS* G5 89 F5
Cardyke St *SPRGB/BLRNK* G21 68 D2
Careston Pl *BSHPBGS* G64 55 G2
Carey Gdns *MTHW* ML1 157 F1
Carfin Mill Rd *MTHW* ML1 155 H2
Carfin Rd *MTHW* ML1 138 A5
WISHAW ML2 172 D1
Carfin St *CTBR* ML5 97 E5
GVH/MTFL G42 109 G2
MTHW ML1 137 G4
Carfrae St *KVGV* G3 88 B1
Cargill Sq *BSHPBGS* G64 55 F3
Carham Dr
CARD/HILL/MSPK G52 86 D4
Carillon Rd *GOV/IBX* G51 88 B4
Carisbrooke Crs *BSHPBGS* G64 38 A4
Carlaverock Rd
PLKSW/MSWD G43 127 G1
Carleith Av *CLYDBK* G81 31 G2
Carleith Qd *GOV/IBX* G51 87 E2
Carleith Ter *CLYDBK* G81 31 G2
Carleston St
SPRGB/BLRNK G21 68 C2
Carleton Ct *GIF/THBK* G46 127 F3
Carleton Dr *GIF/THBK* G46 127 F3
Carleton Ga *GIF/THBK* G46 127 F3
Carlibar Av *KNTSWD* G13 50 A5
Carlibar Dr *BRHD/NEIL* G78 124 B4
Carlibar Gdns
BRHD/NEIL G78 124 B4
Carlibar Rd *BRHD/NEIL* G78 124 B4
Carlile Pl *PSLYN/LNWD* PA3 84 B3
Carlins Pl *KKNTL* G66 4 B2
Carlisle Rd *AIRDRIE* ML6 98 D4
HMLTN ML3 170 D3
MTHW ML1 157 H1
Carlisle St *PPK/MIL* G22 68 A2
Carloway Ct
STPS/GTHM/RID G33 92 C1
Carlowrie Av
BLTYR/CAMB G72 133 F5
Carlton Ct *GBLS* G5 89 G3
Carlton Pl *GBLS* G5 89 G3
Carlyle Av
CARD/HILL/MSPK G52 86 B1
Carlyle Dr *EKILN* G74 166 D3
Carmaben Rd
STPS/GTHM/RID G33 93 E1
Carment Dr *PLKSD/SHW* G41 108 C4
Carmen Vw *DMBTN* G82 13 F1
Carmichael Pl *GVH/MTFL* G42 109 E5
Carmichael St *GOV/IBX* G51 88 A3
Carmunnock By-Pass
CRMNK/CLK/EAG G76 146 D4
Carmunnock Rd
CRMNK/CLK/EAG G76 146 C4
CSMK G45 146 D1
EKILN G74 165 H3
LNPK/KPK G44 128 D2
Carmyle Av *CAR/SHTL* G32 112 C4
Carmyle Gdns *CTBR* ML5 116 B1
Carna Dr *LNPK/KPK* G44 128 D2
Carnarvon St *KVGV* G3 2 A1
Carnbroe Rd *BLSH* ML4 117 E4
Carneddans Rd *MLNGV* G62 16 A1
Carnegie Hl *EKILS* G75 166 A5
Carnegie Pl *EKILS* G75 166 A5
Carnegie Rd
CARD/HILL/MSPK G52 86 B3
Carnoch St *SMSTN* G23 52 C2
Carnock Crs *BRHD/NEIL* G78 142 A1
Carnock Rd *PLK/PH/NH* G53 106 D4
Carnoustie Ct
UD/BTH/TAN G71 134 A5
Carnoustie Crs *BSHPBGS* G64 55 F2
EKILS G75 177 F2
Carnoustie Pl *BLSH* ML4 116 D5
GBLS G5 89 E4
Carnoustie St *GBLS* G5 89 E4
Carnoustie Wy *BALLOCH* G68 10 B4
Carntynehall Rd
CAR/SHTL G32 92 A3
Carntyne Pl *CAR/SHTL* G32 91 G2
Carntyne Rd *CAR/SHTL* G32 91 G2
Carnwadric Rd *GIF/THBK* G46 126 B3
Carnwath Av
PLKSW/MSWD G43 128 A1
Caroline St *DEN/PKHD* G31 91 H4
Carolside Av
CRMNK/CLK/EAG G76 145 H3
Carolside Dr *DRUM* G15 33 G5
Carousel Crs *WISHAW* ML2 174 B2
Carradale Crs *BALLOCH* G68 24 D5
Carradale St *CTBR* ML5 96 C2
Carrbridge Dr *MRYH/FIRH* G20 52 C5
Carresbrook Av *KKNTL* G66 40 D2
Carriagehill Av *PSLYS* PA2 104 B2
Carriagehill Dr *PSLYS* PA2 104 B3
Carrickarden Rd *BSDN* G61 34 C5
Carrick Ct *KKNTL* G66 22 A3
Carrick Crs *GIF/THBK* G46 145 F1
Carrick Dr *CAR/SHTL* G32 93 F5
CTBR ML5 96 A2
RUTH G73 129 H2
Carrick Gdns *BLSH* ML4 116 D4
BLTYR/CAMB G72 151 G4
HMLTN ML3 168 D3
Carrick Gv *CAR/SHTL* G32 93 F5
Carrick Pl *BLSH* ML4 117 E4
CTBR ML5 96 A2
CTBR ML5 74 B1
Carrick Rd *BSHPBGS* G64 55 F2
BSHPTN PA7 46 B1
CUMB G67 26 C1
EKILN G74 166 C2
RUTH G73 129 G2
Carrickstone Rd *BALLOCH* G68 26 A1
Carrickstone Vw
BALLOCH G68 10 B5
Carrick St *CGLW* G2 2 C7
Carrick Ter *DMBTN* G82 12 A3
Carrick V *MTHW* ML1 157 F1
Carrickvale Ct *BALLOCH* G68 10 A5
Carrington St *COWCAD* G4 67 E4
Carroglen Gdns *CAR/SHTL* G32 93 E4
Carroglen Gv *CAR/SHTL* G32 93 E4
Carroll Crs *MTHW* ML1 137 H5
Carron Ct *HMLTN* ML3 169 G4
Carron Crs *BSDN* G61 33 H5
BSHPBGS G64 55 E2
KKNTL G66 40 B4
PPK/MIL G22 68 B1
Carron Dr *BSHPTN* PA7 46 B1
Carron Pl *CTBR* ML5 74 A5
EKILS G75 178 C3
PPK/MIL G22 68 B1
Carron St *PPK/MIL* G22 68 B1
WISHAW ML2 174 A4
Carrour Gdns *BSHPBGS* G64 54 C1
Carr Qd *BLSH* ML4 136 C2
Carruth Rd *BRWEIR* PA11 79 F3
Carsaig Dr
CARD/HILL/MSPK G52 87 F4
Carscallan Rd *HMLTN* ML3 180 D2
Carsegreen Av *PSLYS* PA2 122 C1
Carseview Dr *BSDN* G61 34 D2
Carsewood Av *HWWD* PA9 120 A4
Carstairs St
DMNK/BRGTN G40 110 D2
Carswell Gdns
PLKSD/SHW G41 108 D2
Carswell Rd *NMRNS* G77 143 F5
Cartbank Gv *LNPK/KPK* G44 128 B3
Cartcraigs Rd
PLKSW/MSWD G43 127 E1
Cartha Crs *PSLYS* PA2 104 D1
Cartha St *PLKSD/SHW* G41 108 C5
Cartsbridge Rd
CRMNK/CLK/EAG G76 145 H4
Cartside Av *JNSTN* PA5 101 E5
RNFRW PA4 61 G2
Cartside Dr
CRMNK/CLK/EAG G76 146 B4
Cartside Pl
CRMNK/CLK/EAG G76 146 A5
Cartside Qd *GVH/MTFL* G42 109 F5
Cartside Rd
CRMNK/CLK/EAG G76 146 A5
Cartside St *GVH/MTFL* G42 109 E5
Cart St *CLYDBK* G81 49 E3
Cartvale La *PSLYN/LNWD* PA3 84 B3
Cartvale Rd *GVH/MTFL* G42 109 E5
Cartview Ct
CRMNK/CLK/EAG G76 146 A4
Caskie Dr *BLTYR/CAMB* G72 151 H1
Cassels Gv *MTHW* ML1 154 B1
Cassels St *MTHW* ML1 154 D2
Cassidy Dr *JNSTN* PA5 101 G3
Cassiltoun Gdns *CSMK* G45 129 E5
Cassley Av *RNFRW* PA4 64 A4
Castburn Rd *CUMB* G67 11 H4
Castle Av *JNSTN* PA5 102 A3
MTHW ML1 137 G1
UD/BTH/TAN G71 133 H4
Castlebank Ct *KNTSWD* G13 51 F5
Castlebank Crs *PTCK* G11 65 H5
Castlebank Dr *PTCK* G11 65 H5
Castlebank Gdns *KNTSWD* G13 51 F5
Castlebank Pl *PTCK* G11 65 G5
Castlebank St *PTCK* G11 65 G5
Castlebank Vls *KNTSWD* G13 51 F5
Castlebay Dr *PPK/MIL* G22 53 H2
Castlebay Pl *PPK/MIL* G22 53 H3
Castlebay St *PPK/MIL* G22 53 H3
Castlebrae *DMBTN* G82 12 B2
Castlebrae Gdns
LNPK/KPK G44 128 C1
Castlecary Rd *BALLOCH* G68 11 E4
Castle Chimmins Av
BLTYR/CAMB G72 132 A3
Castle Chimmins Rd
BLTYR/CAMB G72 132 A4
Castle Ct *BALLOCH* G68 11 H2
KKNTL G66 21 F5
Castle Crs *BSHPTN* PA7 46 A1
Castlecroft Gdns
UD/BTH/TAN G71 134 A2
Castle Dr *MTHW* ML1 137 G1
Castlefern Rd *RUTH* G73 129 H4
Castlefield Gdns *EKILS* G75 177 G3
Castle Gait *PSLY* PA1 104 B1
Castle Gdns
BAIL/MDB/MHD G69 59 E2
PSLYS PA2 103 F1
Castle Ga *NMRNS* G77 162 B2
UD/BTH/TAN G71 133 H2
Castleglen Rd *EKILN* G74 165 E1
Castlegreen Crs *DMBTN* G82 13 G5
Castlegreen St *DMBTN* G82 13 F5
Castlehill Crs *AIRDRIE* ML6 119 G3
HMLTN ML3 171 G4
RNFRW PA4 63 G2
Castlehill Dr *NMRNS* G77 162 A1
Castlehill Gdns *HMLTN* ML3 170 C3
Castlehill Gn *EKILN* G74 165 E1
Castlehill Qd *DMBTN* G82 12 B2
Castlehill Rd *BSDN* G61 33 G2
DMBTN G82 12 B2
WISHAW ML2 173 G5
Castlelaw Gdns *CAR/SHTL* G32 92 C3
Castlelaw St *CAR/SHTL* G32 92 C3
Castle Mains Rd *MLNGV* G62 16 C4
Castlemilk Crs *LNPK/KPK* G44 129 F2
Castlemilk Dr *CSMK* G45 129 F5
Castlemilk Rd *LNPK/KPK* G44 129 G3
LNPK/KPK G44 110 B5
Castlemilk Ter *CSMK* G45 129 F5
Castlemount Av *NMRNS* G77 162 A2
Castle Qd *AIRDRIE* ML6 99 E2
Castle Rd *AIRDRIE* ML6 99 E2
BRWEIR PA11 79 G2
JNSTN PA5 102 B1
NMRNS G77 161 F1
Castle Sq *CLYDBK* G81 31 F5
Castle St *AIRDRIE* ML6 118 D2
BAIL/MDB/MHD G69 113 G1
CLYDBK G81 31 F5
COWCAD G4 3 K4
DMBTN G82 13 E4
HMLTN ML3 170 C1
PSLY PA1 83 H5
PTCK G11 66 B5
RUTH G73 111 E4
Castleton Av *NMRNS* G77 162 B2
SPRGB/BLRNK G21 54 B4
Castleton Crs *NMRNS* G77 162 A2
Castleton Dr *NMRNS* G77 162 A2
Castleton Gv *NMRNS* G77 162 A2
Castleview *BALLOCH* G68 11 G2
Castle Vw *WISHAW* ML2 158 B4
Castleview Av *PSLYS* PA2 103 F5
Castleview Dr *PSLYS* PA2 103 F5
Castle Wy *CUMB* G67 27 E2
Castle Wynd *HMLTN* ML3 181 E5
UD/BTH/TAN G71 134 C5
Cathay St *PPK/MIL* G22 53 H3
Cathburn Rd *WISHAW* ML2 175 H1
Cathcart Crs *PSLYS* PA2 104 D1
Cathcart Pl *RUTH* G73 110 C5
Cathcart Rd *GBLS* G5 89 G5
GVH/MTFL G42 109 F5
RUTH G73 110 C5
Cathedral Sq *COWCAD* G4 3 K5
Cathedral St *CGLE* G1 3 G4
Catherine St *MTHW* ML1 171 H1
Catherine Wy *MTHW* ML1 137 E4
Cathkin Av *BLTYR/CAMB* G72 130 D1
RUTH G73 111 F5
Cathkin By-Pass *RUTH* G73 130 C4
Cathkin Crs *BALLOCH* G68 10 A5
Cathkin Dr
CRMNK/CLK/EAG G76 145 F2
Cathkin Pl *BLTYR/CAMB* G72 130 D1
Cathkin Rd
CRMNK/CLK/EAG G76 147 F2
GVH/MTFL G42 109 E5
UD/BTH/TAN G71 114 D3
Cathkinview Pl
GVH/MTFL G42 109 F5
Cathkinview Rd
GVH/MTFL G42 109 F5
Catrine *EKILN* G74 166 A3
Catrine Ct *PLK/PH/NH* G53 106 B4
Catrine Crs *MTHW* ML1 172 B1
Catrine Gdns
PLK/PH/NH G53 106 B4
Catrine Pl *PLK/PH/NH* G53 106 B4
Catrine Rd *PLK/PH/NH* G53 106 B4
Catriona Pl *DMBTN* G82 13 H5
Cauldstream Pl *MLNGV* G62 16 C4
Causewayside
Crs *CAR/SHTL* G32 112 B2
Causewayside St
CAR/SHTL G32 112 B2
Causeyside St *PSLY* PA1 104 B1
Cavendish Dr *NMRNS* G77 144 C4
Cavendish Pl *GBLS* G5 89 G5
Cavendish St *GBLS* G5 89 G5
Cavin Dr *CSMK* G45 129 F3
Cavin Rd *CSMK* G45 129 F3
Cawder Ct *BALLOCH* G68 9 H5
Cawder Pl *BALLOCH* G68 10 A5
Cawder Rd *BALLOCH* G68 10 A5
Cawder Vw *BALLOCH* G68 10 A5
Cawder Wy *BALLOCH* G68 10 A5
Cawdor Crs *AIRDRIE* ML6 119 F1
BSHPTN PA7 46 A1
Cawdor Wy *EKILN* G74 166 A2
Cayton Gdns
BAIL/MDB/MHD G69 93 G5
Cecil St *CRMNK/CLK/EAG* G76 145 H3
CTBR ML5 96 D4
KVD/HLHD G12 66 C3
Cedar Av *CLYDBK* G81 31 E4
JNSTN PA5 121 G1
UD/BTH/TAN G71 115 G4
Cedar Ct *BLTYR/CAMB* G72 132 B3
EKILS G75 177 H3
KLBCH PA10 100 B3
MRYH/FIRH G20 67 G4
Cedar Crs *HMLTN* ML3 170 B4
Cedar Dr *EKILS* G75 177 H3
KKNTL G66 39 H3
KKNTL G66 5 G5
UD/BTH/TAN G71 116 A4
Cedar Gdns *MTHW* ML1 137 H3
RUTH G73 130 B4
Cedar Gv *BAIL/MDB/MHD* G69 95 F3
Cedar La *MTHW* ML1 137 G2
Cedar Pl *BLTYR/CAMB* G72 151 F2
EKILS G75 177 H3
Cedar Rd *BSHPBGS* G64 55 E3
CUMB G67 27 F2
Cedar St *MRYH/FIRH* G20 67 F4
Cedar Wk *MTHW* ML1 138 A5
Cedarwood *WISHAW* ML2 173 E4
Cedarwood Av *NMRNS* G77 162 A1
NMRNS G77 144 C5
Cedarwood Rd *NMRNS* G77 162 A1
Cedric Pl *KNTSWD* G13 51 E4
Cedric Rd *KNTSWD* G13 51 E4
Celtic St *MRYH/FIRH* G20 52 B4
Cemetery Rd
BLTYR/CAMB G72 151 F4
CARD/HILL/MSPK G52 87 E5
Centenary Av *AIRDRIE* ML6 97 G2
Centenary Ct *BRHD/NEIL* G78 124 A5
CLYDBK G81 49 E2
Centenary Crs *BLSH* ML4 136 A1
Centenary Gdns *CTBR* ML5 96 C4
HMLTN ML3 170 B3
Centenary Qd *MTHW* ML1 137 F2
Central Av *BLTYR/CAMB* G72 151 H5
BLTYR/CAMB G72 131 E1
CAR/SHTL G32 113 E1
CLYDBK G81 48 D1
MTHW ML1 137 E2
PTCK G11 65 G4
UD/BTH/TAN G71 134 D1
Central Gv *CAR/SHTL* G32 93 E5
Central Pth *CAR/SHTL* G32 113 F1
Central Rd *PSLY* PA1 84 B4
Central Wy *CUMB* G67 26 A5
PSLY PA1 84 B4
Centre St *AIRDRIE* ML6 118 D2
CTBR ML5 59 H5
GBLS G5 89 G3
Centre Wy *BRHD/NEIL* G78 124 A4
Centrewest *EKILN* G74 166 B4
Centurion Pl *MTHW* ML1 154 A1
Ceres Gdns *BSHPBGS* G64 55 G2
Ceres Pl *MTHW* ML1 154 C2
Cessnock Rd
STPS/GTHM/RID G33 70 B1
Cessnock St *GOV/IBX* G51 88 B4
Chalmers Crs *EKILS* G75 178 C1
Chalmers Dr *EKILS* G75 178 C1
Chalmers Ga
DMNK/BRGTN G40 90 B3
Chalmers St *CLYDBK* G81 49 E2
DMNK/BRGTN G40 90 B3
Chamberlain La *KNTSWD* G13 65 F1
Chamberlain Rd *KNTSWD* G13 65 F1
Chancellor St *PTCK* G11 66 A4
Chantinghall Rd *HMLTN* ML3 169 G2
Chantinghall Ter *HMLTN* ML3 169 G2
Chapel Ct *RUTH* G73 110 C4
Chapel Crs *HMLTN* ML3 180 D2
Chapelcross Av *AIRDRIE* ML6 76 B5
Chapelhill Rd *PSLYS* PA2 104 D2
Chapelknowe Rd *MTHW* ML1 156 A1
Chapel Pl *BRHD/NEIL* G78 141 E3
Chapel Rd *CLYDBK* G81 31 H2
WISHAW ML2 175 G4
Chapelside Av *AIRDRIE* ML6 98 B1
Chapelside Rd *EKILN* G74 149 G5
Chapel St *AIRDRIE* ML6 98 B1
KKNTL G66 4 B2
MRYH/FIRH G20 66 D1
MTHW ML1 157 E1
RUTH G73 110 C4
Chapelton Av *BSDN* G61 34 C4
DMBTN G82 13 F2
Chapelton Gdns *BSDN* G61 34 C4
DMBTN G82 13 F2
Chapelton Rd *CUMB* G67 44 C2
Chapelton St *PPK/MIL* G22 53 H5
Chaplet Av *KNTSWD* G13 50 D3
Chapman Av *CTBR* ML5 59 H5
Chapman St *GVH/MTFL* G42 109 F2
Chappell St *BRHD/NEIL* G78 124 A4
Charing Cross La *KVGV* G3 2 A3
Charles Av *RNFRW* PA4 63 G2
Charles Crs *KKNTL* G66 40 A5
Charleson Rw *KSYTH* G65 24 D2
Charles Qd *MTHW* ML1 137 F2
Charles St *KSYTH* G65 8 B1
SPRGB/BLRNK G21 68 C5
WISHAW ML2 172 D1
Charlotte Av *BSHPBGS* G64 19 F5
Charlotte Pl *PSLYS* PA2 104 B2
Charlotte St *CGLE* G1 90 A3
DMBTN G82 12 C3
Charn Ter *MTHW* ML1 172 D2
Charnwood Av *JNSTN* PA5 121 E1
Chassels St *CTBR* ML5 96 D1
Chateau Gv *HMLTN* ML3 170 D3
Chatelherault Av
BLTYR/CAMB G72 130 D2
Chatelherault Crs
HMLTN ML3 170 B5
Chatham *EKILS* G75 177 H1
Chatton St *SMSTN* G23 52 C2
Chatton Wk *CTBR* ML5 117 G2
Cheapside St *KVGV* G3 2 A6
Chelmsford Dr *KVD/HLHD* G12 66 A1
Cherry Av *CUMB* G67 11 G5
Cherry Bank *KKNTL* G66 39 G3
Cherrybank Rd
PLKSW/MSWD G43 128 A2
Cherrybank Wk *AIRDRIE* ML6 97 G1
Cherry Crs *CLYDBK* G81 31 H4
Cherry Gv
BAIL/MDB/MHD G69 95 G3
Cherry Pl *BSHPBGS* G64 55 E3
JNSTN PA5 101 H5
KKNTL G66 5 F5
MTHW ML1 137 G3
UD/BTH/TAN G71 116 A4
Cherryridge Dr
BAIL/MDB/MHD G69 95 G3
Cherrytree Dr
BLTYR/CAMB G72 132 B3
Cherrytree Wynd *EKILS* G75 178 C1
Cherry Wk *MTHW* ML1 171 H2
Cherrywood Rd *JNSTN* PA5 102 B2
Chesterfield Av
KVD/HLHD G12 65 H1
Chesters Crs *MTHW* ML1 154 B2
Chesters Pl *RUTH* G73 110 C5
Chesters Rd *BSDN* G61 33 H4
Chester St *CAR/SHTL* G32 92 B4
Chestnut Av *BSHPTN* PA7 28 C3
CUMB G67 11 G5
Chestnut Ct *CUMB* G67 11 G5
KKNTL G66 5 F5
Chestnut Crs *EKILS* G75 177 H2
HMLTN ML3 170 B3
UD/BTH/TAN G71 115 H5
Chestnut Dr *CLYDBK* G81 31 H3
KKNTL G66 39 G2
Chestnut Gv
BAIL/MDB/MHD G69 59 H5
BLTYR/CAMB G72 151 F2
MTHW ML1 171 G1
Chestnut La *MLNGV* G62 16 C4
Chestnut Pl *CUMB* G67 11 G5
JNSTN PA5 121 H1
Chestnut St *PPK/MIL* G22 68 A1
Chestnut Wk *KKNTL* G66 4 B3
Chestnut Wy
BLTYR/CAMB G72 132 B3
HMLTN ML3 181 F4
Cheviot Av *BRHD/NEIL* G78 124 B5
Cheviot Crs *EKILS* G75 177 F4
WISHAW ML2 173 G2
Cheviot Dr *NMRNS* G77 161 F2
Cheviot Rd *HMLTN* ML3 170 C3
PLKSW/MSWD G43 127 F2
PSLYS PA2 104 A4
Cheviot St *BLTYR/CAMB* G72 151 F3
Chirmorie Crs
PLK/PH/NH G53 106 B3
Chirmorie Pl *PLK/PH/NH* G53 106 B3
Chirnside Pl
CARD/HILL/MSPK G52 86 B3
Chirnside Rd
CARD/HILL/MSPK G52 86 B3
Chisholm Av *BSHPTN* PA7 29 F5
Chisholm Dr *NMRNS* G77 144 B4
Chisholm Pl *MTHW* ML1 172 C3
Chisholm St *CTBR* ML5 97 E1
Chisolm St *CGLE* G1 3 H7
Chrighton Gn
UD/BTH/TAN G71 115 F4
Chriss Av *HMLTN* ML3 180 D1
Christchurch Pl *EKILS* G75 177 G1
Christian St
PLKSW/MSWD G43 108 B5
Christie La *PSLYN/LNWD* PA3 84 B4
Christie St *BLSH* ML4 136 C3
PSLY PA1 84 C4
Christopher St
SPRGB/BLRNK G21 68 D5
Chryston Rd
BAIL/MDB/MHD G69 58 C3
KKNTL G66 41 F2
Chuckie La *JNSTN* PA5 100 D1
Church Av *RUTH* G73 130 B2
STPS/GTHM/RID G33 57 E5
WISHAW ML2 175 E1
Church Ct *DMBTN* G82 13 E4
HMLTN ML3 170 B1
Church Crs *AIRDRIE* ML6 77 F5
Church Hl *PSLY* PA1 84 B4
Churchill Av *EKILN* G74 166 C4
JNSTN PA5 120 D1
Churchill Crs
UD/BTH/TAN G71 134 C4
Churchill Dr *BSHPTN* PA7 29 E5
PTCK G11 65 H3
Churchill Pl *KLBCH* PA10 100 B4
Church La *CTBR* ML5 96 D2
Church Manse La
BRWEIR PA11 79 G3
Church Pl *OLDK* G60 30 B2
Church Rd
BAIL/MDB/MHD G69 58 B4
BRWEIR PA11 79 H4
CRMNK/CLK/EAG G76 146 A4
GIF/THBK G46 127 F5
WISHAW ML2 159 E4
Church St
BAIL/MDB/MHD G69 94 B5
BLTYR/CAMB G72 151 H3
CLYDBK G81 31 H5
CTBR ML5 96 D2
DMBTN G82 13 E4
HMLTN ML3 170 B1
JNSTN PA5 101 G3
KLBCH PA10 100 B3
KSYTH G65 8 B2
MTHW ML1 138 C3
PTCK G11 66 B5
UD/BTH/TAN G71 133 H2
Church Vw *BLTYR/CAMB* G72 112 B5
CTBR ML5 96 D2
Church View Gdns *BLSH* ML4 135 H2
Circus Dr *DEN/PKHD* G31 90 C2
Circus Place La
DEN/PKHD G31 90 C2
Citadel Pl *MTHW* ML1 154 B2
Citizen La *CGLE* G1 3 F5
Citrus Crs *UD/BTH/TAN* G71 115 H4
Cityford Dr *RUTH* G73 129 G1
Civic St *COWCAD* G4 2 D1
Civic Wy *KKNTL* G66 39 H1
Clachan Dr *GOV/IBX* G51 87 F1
The Clachan *WISHAW* ML2 174 A2
Clachan Wy *CTBR* ML5 96 B4
Claddens Pl *KKNTL* G66 40 C4
PPK/MIL G22 53 G5
Claddens Qd *PPK/MIL* G22 53 H5
Claddens St *PPK/MIL* G22 53 G5
Cladence Gv *EKILS* G75 178 C3
Claire St *WISHAW* ML2 158 A5
Clairinsh Gdns *RNFRW* PA4 63 F5
Clairmont Gdns *KVGV* G3 67 E5
Clair Rd *BSHPBGS* G64 55 G2
Clamp Rd *WISHAW* ML2 172 D1
Clamps Gv *EKILN* G74 166 D5
Clamps Ter *EKILN* G74 166 D5
Clamps Wd *EKILN* G74 166 D5
Clanrye Dr *CTBR* ML5 96 D5
Clapperhow Rd *MTHW* ML1 155 F1
Claremont Av *KKNTL* G66 20 D5
Claremont Dr *MLNGV* G62 17 E3
Claremont Gdns *MLNGV* G62 17 E4
Claremont Pas *KVGV* G3 67 E5
Claremont Pl *KVGV* G3 67 E5
Claremont St *KVGV* G3 88 D1
Claremont Ter *KVGV* G3 67 E5
Claremont Terrace La
KVGV G3 66 D5
Claremount Av
GIF/THBK G46 127 F5
Claremount Vw *CTBR* ML5 117 F2
Clarence Dr *PSLY* PA1 84 D4
PTCK G11 65 H3
Clarence Gdns *PTCK* G11 65 H3
Clarence La *KVD/HLHD* G12 66 A3
Clarence St *CLYDBK* G81 49 F1
PSLY PA1 84 D4
Clarendon Pl *MRYH/FIRH* G20 67 F4
Clarendon Rd *WISHAW* ML2 173 F4
Clarendon St *MRYH/FIRH* G20 67 F4
Clare St *SPRGB/BLRNK* G21 68 D5
Clarinda Ct *KKNTL* G66 22 A3
Clarinda Pl *MTHW* ML1 137 H4
Clarion Crs *KNTSWD* G13 50 B3
Clarion Rd *KNTSWD* G13 50 B4
Clarkin Av *EKILS* G75 177 F4
Clark Pl *NMRNS* G77 161 E1
Clarkston Av *LNPK/KPK* G44 128 A3
Clarkston Dr *AIRDRIE* ML6 99 E2
Clarkston Rd
CRMNK/CLK/EAG G76 145 H2
LNPK/KPK G44 128 B2
Clark St *AIRDRIE* ML6 98 C2
CLYDBK G81 31 G4
JNSTN PA5 101 G3
PSLYN/LNWD PA3 83 H3
RNFRW PA4 63 E3
WISHAW ML2 158 A4

Clark Wy BLSH ML4......116 C5
Clarkwell Rd HMLTN ML3......168 D2
Clarkwell Ter HMLTN ML3......169 E2
Clathic Av BSDN G61......34 C5
Claude Av BLTYR/CAMB G72......132 B4
Clay Ct PSLYN/LNWD PA3......84 D3
Clavens Rd
  CARD/HILL/MSPK C52......85 H3
Claverhouse Pl PSLYS PA2......104 D1
Claverhouse Rd
  CARD/HILL/MSPK C52......86 A2
Clavering St East PSLY PA1......83 H4
Clavering St West PSLY PA1......83 H5
Clay Crs BLSH ML4......117 E5
Clayhouse Rd
  STPS/GTHM/RID G33......71 F2
Claymore Dr
  CRG/CRSL/HOU PA6......81 E3
Claypotts Pl
  STPS/GTHM/RID G33......70 B5
Claypotts Rd
  STPS/GTHM/RID G33......70 B5
Clay Rd BLSH ML4......117 F5
Clayslaps Rd KVGV G3......66 C5
Claythorn Av
  DMNK/BRGTN G40......90 B4
Claythorn Circ
  DMNK/BRGTN G40......90 B3
Claythorn Pk
  DMNK/BRGTN G40......90 B4
Claythorn St
  DMNK/BRGTN G40......90 B3
Clayton Ter DEN/PKHD G31......90 D2
Clearfield Av HMLTN ML3......169 G1
Cleddans Crs CLYDBK G81......32 B2
Cleddans Rd CLYDBK G81......32 B1
  KKNTL G66......21 G4
Cleddans Vw AIRDRIE ML6......75 H2
Cleddens Ct BSHPBGS G64......54 D2
Cleeves Qd PLK/PH/NH G53......125 F2
Cleeves Rd PLK/PH/NH G53......125 F2
Cleghorn St PPK/MIL G22......67 G3
Cleish Av BSDN G61......16 A5
Cleland La GBLS G5......89 H4
Cleland Rd EKILN G74......166 D2
Cleland Rd MTHW ML1......138 C5
  WISHAW ML2......173 H2
Cleland St GBLS G5......89 H4
Clelland Av BSHPBGS G64......54 D3
Clerwood St CAR/SHTL G32......91 G5
Cleuch Gdns
  CRMNK/CLK/EAG G76......145 G2
Clevans Rd BRWEIR PA11......79 E4
Cleveden Crs KVD/HLHD G12......66 A1
Cleveden Crescent La
  KVD/HLHD G12......66 B1
Cleveden Dr KVD/HLHD G12......66 A1
  RUTH G73......130 B1
Cleveden Drive La
  KVD/HLHD G12......66 B2
Cleveden Gdns
  KVD/HLHD G12......66 B1
Cleveden La KVD/HLHD G12......52 A5
Cleveden Rd KVD/HLHD G12......66 B2
  KVD/HLHD G12......52 A5
Cleveland La KVGV G5......2 A3
Cleveland St KVGV G3......2 A5
Clifford Gdns GOV/IBX G51......88 A4
Clifford La GOV/IBX G51......88 C4
Clifford St GOV/IBX G51......88 B4
Cliff Rd KVGV G3......67 F5
Clifton Pl CTBR ML5......97 H3
  KVGV G5......88 D1
Clifton Rd GIF/THBK G46......127 E4
Clifton St KVGV G3......66 C5
Clincarthill Rd RUTH G73......110 D5
Clincart Rd GVH/MTFL G42......109 G4
Clippens Rd
  CRG/CRSL/HOU PA6......81 F3
  PSLYN/LNWD PA3......101 H1
Cloan Av DRUM G15......50 C1
Cloan Crs BSHPBGS G64......38 A4
Clober Farm La MLNGV G62......16 D1
Cloberfield MLNGV G62......16 D1
Cloberfield Gdns MLNGV G62......16 D2
Cloberhill Rd KNTSWD G13......50 D2
Clober Rd MLNGV G62......16 D2
Clochbar Av MLNGV G62......16 D1
Clochbar Gdns MLNGV G62......16 D2
Clochoderick Av KLBCH PA10......100 C4
Cloch St STPS/GTHM/RID G33......92 B1
Clockerhill Pl MTHW ML1......138 D1
Cloister Av AIRDRIE ML6......98 D5
Closeburn St PPK/MIL G22......67 H2
Cloth St BRHD/NEIL G78......124 B5
Clouden Rd CUMB G67......26 D5
Cloudhowe Ter
  BLTYR/CAMB G72......151 F2
Clouston Ct MRYH/FIRH G20......66 D2
Clouston La MRYH/FIRH G20......66 C2
Clova Pl UD/BTH/TAN G71......134 A1
Clova St GIF/THBK G46......126 C3
Cloverbank Gdns
  SPRGB/BLRNK G21......68 D5
Cloverbank St
  SPRGB/BLRNK G21......68 D5
Clovergate BSHPBGS G64......54 B2
Cloverhill Pl
  BAIL/MDB/MHD G69......58 B3
Cloverhill Ter EKILN G74......166 B4
Cloverhill Vw EKILN G74......166 A4
Clunie Pl CTBR ML5......117 E1
Clunie Av MTHW ML1......158 A4
Clunie Pl
  CARD/HILL/MSPK C52......87 F5
  CLYDBK G81......51 H1
Cluny Av BSDN G61......51 H1
Cluny Dr BSDN G61......32 B1
  NMRNS G77......143 G5
  PSLYN/LNWD PA3......84 D3
Cluny Gdns SCOT G14......65 F2
Clutha Pl EKILS G75......177 F1
Clutha St GOV/IBX G51......88 C3
Clyde Av BRHD/NEIL G78......142 C1
  BSHPBGS G64......19 F5
  HMLTN ML3......171 G4
  UD/BTH/TAN G71......152 A1

Clydebrae Dr
  UD/BTH/TAN G71......152 C2
Clydebrae St GOV/IBX G51......88 A1
Clyde Dr BLSH ML4......136 B3
Clydeford Dr CAR/SHTL G32......111 H1
  UD/BTH/TAN G71......114 C5
Clydeford Rd
  BLTYR/CAMB G72......131 G1
  CAR/SHTL G32......112 C4
Clydeholm Rd SCOT G14......65 E4
Clydeholm Ter CLYDBK G81......49 G4
Clydeneuk Dr
  UD/BTH/TAN G71......114 C5
Clyde Pl BLTYR/CAMB G72......132 C5
  GBLS G5......2 C7
  JNSTN PA5......120 D1
  MTHW ML1......137 F3
Clyde Rd PSLYN/LNWD PA3......85 E2
Clydesdale Av HMLTN ML3......180 D2
  PSLYN/LNWD PA3......62 D5
  WISHAW ML2......173 G4
Clydesdale Pl HMLTN ML3......180 D2
Clydesdale St BLSH ML4......137 E3
  HMLTN ML3......169 H1
Clydeshore Rd DMBTN G82......12 C5
Clydeside Rd RUTH G73......110 C2
Clydesmill Dr CAR/SHTL G32......112 B5
Clydesmill Gv CAR/SHTL G32......112 B5
Clydesmill Pl CAR/SHTL G32......112 B4
Clydesmill Rd CAR/SHTL G32......112 B4
Clyde St CGLE G1......2 E5
  CLYDBK G81......49 F4
  CTBR ML5......97 F2
  RNFRW PA4......63 G1
Clyde Ter MTHW ML1......172 D3
  UD/BTH/TAN G71......171 E5
Clydevale UD/BTH/TAN G71......152 C1
Clyde Valley Av MTHW ML1......171 H1
Clyde Vw HMLTN ML3......169 G4
  PSLYS PA2......105 E2
Clydeview UD/BTH/TAN G71......152 C1
Clyde View Ct GOV/IBX G51......15 F5
Clydeview Ter CAR/SHTL G32......112 D4
Clynder St GOV/IBX G51......88 A3
Clyth Dr GIF/THBK G46......127 G5
Coach Pl KSYTH G65......8 C5
Coach Rd KSYTH G65......8 C3
Coalburn Rd
  UD/BTH/TAN G71......134 C2
Coalhall Av MTHW ML1......155 F1
Coalhill St DEN/PKHD G31......91 E4
Coatbank St CTBR ML5......97 E3
Coatbank Wy CTBR ML5......97 E3
Coatbridge Rd AIRDRIE ML6......75 H1
  BAIL/MDB/MHD G69......94 B4
Coathill St CTBR ML5......74 C1
Coathill St CTBR ML5......96 D5
Coats Crs BAIL/MDB/MHD G69......93 H4
Coats Dr PSLYS PA2......103 C1
Coatshill Av
  BLTYR/CAMB G72......151 F1
Coats St CTBR ML5......97 E2
Cobbett Rd MTHW ML1......154 A5
Cobbleton Rd MTHW ML1......137 E5
Cobington Pl
  STPS/GTHM/RID G33......70 D5
Cobinshaw St CAR/SHTL G32......92 B4
Coburg St GBLS G5......89 G4
Cochno Rd CLYDBK G81......32 D1
Cochno St CLYDBK G81......49 F1
Cochranemill Rd JNSTN PA5......100 D5
Cochrane St
  PSLYN/LNWD PA3......82 A3
Cochrane St BLSH ML4......135 H2
  BRHD/NEIL G78......124 A5
  CGLE G1......3 G5
Cochran St PSLY PA1......84 C5
Cockburn Pl CTBR ML5......96 C5
Cockels Loan RNFRW PA4......85 F1
Cockenzie St CAR/SHTL G32......92 B4
Cockhill Wy BLSH ML4......135 E1
Cockmuir St
  SPRGB/BLRNK G21......68 D2
Coddington Crs BLSH ML4......118 A5
Cogan Pl BRHD/NEIL G78......124 A5
Cogan Rd PLKSW/MSWD G43......127 F1
Cogan St BRHD/NEIL G78......124 A5
  PLKSW/MSWD G43......108 B5
Colbert St DMNK/BRGTN G40......110 C1
Colbreggan Ct CLYDBK G81......32 B2
Colbreggan Gdns CLYDBK G81......32 B2
Colchester Dr KVD/HLHD G12......51 H5
Coldingham Av SCOT G14......49 H5
Coldstream Crs WISHAW ML2......157 F5
Coldstream Dr PSLYS PA2......103 F3
  RUTH G73......130 C1
Coldstream Pl
  SPRGB/BLRNK G21......67 H3
Coldstream Rd CLYDBK G81......49 E2
Coldstream St
  BLTYR/CAMB G72......151 G3
Colebrooke La KVD/HLHD G12......66 D3
Colebrooke Pl
  KVD/HLHD G12......66 D3
Colebrooke St
  BLTYR/CAMB G72......131 F1
  KVD/HLHD G12......66 D3
Colebrooke Ter
  KVD/HLHD G12......66 D3
Coleridge EKILS G75......177 F1
Coleridge Av
  UD/BTH/TAN G71......134 C5
Colfin St ESTRH G34......72 B5
Colgrain Av MRYH/FIRH G20......53 G5
Colgrain St MRYH/FIRH G20......67 F1
Colgrave Crs CAR/SHTL G32......112 A1
Colinbar Cir BRHD/NEIL G78......142 A1
Colinslee Av PSLYS PA2......104 C3
Colinslee Crs PSLYS PA2......104 C3
Colinslee Dr PSLYS PA2......104 C3
Colinslie Rd PLK/PH/NH G53......106 D4
Colinton Gdns
  BAIL/MDB/MHD G69......58 B2
Colintraive Av
  STPS/GTHM/RID G33......69 G4
Colintraive Crs
  STPS/GTHM/RID G33......69 H3
Coll EKILN G74......179 F1

Collace Av BRWEIR PA11......79 G4
Colla Gdns BSHPBGS G64......55 G4
Coll Av RNFRW PA4......63 G5
Coll Dr CTBR ML5......96 A5
College Ga BSDN G61......33 H1
College St DMBTN G82......13 E3
Collessie Dr
  STPS/GTHM/RID G33......70 D4
Collier St JNSTN PA5......99 E1
Collina St MRYH/FIRH G20......52 B5
Collins St CLYDBK G81......32 B2
  COWCAD G4......3 K5
Coll Pl AIRDRIE ML6......98 D4
  SPRGB/BLRNK G21......69 E4
Collree Gdns ESTRH G34......94 B2
Coll St SPRGB/BLRNK G21......69 E4
  WISHAW ML2......158 A2
Collylinn Rd BSDN G61......34 B4
Colmonell Av KNTSWD G13......50 A4
Colonsay Av RNFRW PA4......63 G5
Colonsay Crs CTBR ML5......96 A5
Colonsay Dr NMRNS G77......143 G5
Colonsay Rd
  CARD/HILL/MSPK C52......87 F4
  PSLYS PA2......104 A3
Colquhoun DMBTN G82......13 F5
Colquhoun Av
  CARD/HILL/MSPK C52......86 B2
Colquhoun Dr BSDN G61......34 A3
Colquhoun Rd DMBTN G82......13 G4
Colquhoun St DMBTN G82......13 G3
Colson Pl BLSH ML4......136 B4
Colston Av BSHPBGS G64......54 C4
Colston Dr BSHPBGS G64......54 C4
Colston Gdns BSHPBGS G64......54 B4
Colston Gv BSHPBGS G64......54 C4
Colston Pth BSHPBGS G64......54 B4
Colston Rd AIRDRIE ML6......98 D2
  BSHPBGS G64......54 C4
Colston Rd AIRDRIE ML6......98 D2
  BSHPBGS G64......54 C4
Colston Ter AIRDRIE ML6......98 D2
Coltmuir Crs BSHPBGS G64......54 B4
Coltmuir Dr BSHPBGS G64......54 B4
Coltmuir Gdns BSHPBGS G64......54 B4
Coltmuir St PPK/MIL G22......53 H5
Coltness La STPS/GTHM/RID G33......92 D2
Coltness St WISHAW ML2......174 B1
Coltness St
  STPS/GTHM/RID G33......92 D1
Coltpark Av BSHPBGS G64......54 B3
Coltpark La BSHPBGS G64......54 B3
Colt Pl CTBR ML5......96 D2
Coltsfoot Dr PLK/PH/NH G53......125 G4
Coltswood Rd CTBR ML5......74 D5
Colt Ter CTBR ML5......96 D2
Columba Ct
  UD/BTH/TAN G71......115 H5
Columba Crs MTHW ML1......154 C1
  MTHW ML1......136 C5
Columba St GOV/IBX G51......88 A3
Colvend Dr RUTH G73......130 A3
Colvend La
  DMNK/BRGTN G40......110 C1
Colvend St
  DMNK/BRGTN G40......110 C1
Colville Cl BLTYR/CAMB G72......132 A2
Colville Ct MTHW ML1......155 H1
Colville Dr RUTH G73......130 C1
Colvilles Pl EKILS G75......179 E2
Colvilles Rd EKILS G75......178 D3
Colwood Gdns
  PLK/PH/NH G53......125 F5
Colwood Pl PLK/PH/NH G53......125 F4
Colwood Sq PLK/PH/NH G53......125 F5
Colwyn Ct AIRDRIE ML6......76 B5
Colzium Vw KSYTH G65......8 C2
Combe Qd BLSH ML4......135 H4
Comedie Rd
  STPS/GTHM/RID G33......71 F2
Comely Bank HMLTN ML3......169 E2
Comelybank La DMBTN G82......12 C3
Comelybank Rd DMBTN G82......12 C3
Comelypark St
  DEN/PKHD G31......90 C3
Commerce St GBLS G5......89 G4
Commercial Rd
  BRI'D/NEIL G78......124 B4
  GBLS G5......90 A4
Common Gn HMLTN ML3......170 B1
Commonhead Av
  AIRDRIE ML6......76 A5
Commonhead La AIRDRIE ML6......76 A5
Commonhead Rd ESTRH G34......94 D1
Commonhead St AIRDRIE ML6......76 A5
Commonside St AIRDRIE ML6......76 A5
Commore Av BRHD/NEIL G78......142 C1
Commore Dr KNTSWD G13......50 A4
Community Av BLSH ML4......135 H5
Community Pl BLSH ML4......136 A4
Community Rd BLSH ML4......135 H4
Comrie Crs HMLTN ML3......168 C4
Comrie Rd
  STPS/GTHM/RID G33......70 D1
Comrie St CAR/SHTL G32......112 C1
Cona St GIF/THBK G46......126 B3
Condor Gln MTHW ML1......117 H5
Condorrat Ring Rd CUMB G67......43 H2
Condorrat Rd CUMB G67......44 A4
Congress Rd KVGV G3......88 D2
Congress Wy KVGV G3......88 D2
Conifer Pl KKNTL G66......39 G2
Conisborough Cl ESTRH G34......71 H5
Conisborough Rd ESTRH G34......71 G4
Coniston EKILS G75......177 E5
Coniston Crs HMLTN ML3......180 C5
Coniston Dr BLSH ML4......136 A4
Conistone Crs
  BAIL/MDB/MHD G69......93 G5

Connal St DMNK/BRGTN G40......111 E1
Connell Crs MLNGV G62......17 G4
Conniston St CAR/SHTL G32......91 H2
Connor Rd BRHD/NEIL G78......124 A4
Connor St AIRDRIE ML6......77 F5
Conon Av BSDN G61......34 A5
Conservation Pl
  WISHAW ML2......174 A4
Consett La
  STPS/GTHM/RID G33......92 D1
Consett St
  STPS/GTHM/RID G33......92 D1
Constance St MTHW ML1......154 B1
Constantine Rd MTHW ML1......154 B1
Constarry Rd KSYTH G65......24 D1
Consul Wy MTHW ML1......154 B1
Contin Pl MRYH/FIRH G20......66 C1
Cook St GBLS G5......89 F4
Coolgardie Gn EKILS G75......177 H1
Coolgardie Pl EKILS G75......177 H1
Cooperage Ct SCOT G14......64 A1
Co-operative Ter JNSTN PA5......101 H3
Copenhagen Av EKILS G75......178 D2
Copland Pl GOV/IBX G51......88 A3
Copland Qd GOV/IBX G51......88 A3
Copland Rd GOV/IBX G51......88 A4
Coplaw St GVH/MTFL G42......109 F5
Copperfield La
  UD/BTH/TAN G71......115 F5
Copperwood Crs HMLTN ML3......152 C5
Copperwood Wynd
  HMLTN ML3......152 C5
Coralmount Gdns KKNTL G66......40 B1
Corbett Ct CAR/SHTL G32......112 A1
Corbett St CAR/SHTL G32......112 A1
Corbie Pl MLNGV G62......16 C3
Cordiner La LNPK/KPK G44......109 G5
Cordiner St LNPK/KPK G44......109 G5
Corkerhill Gdns
  CARD/HILL/MSPK C52......87 F5
Corkerhill Pl
  CARD/HILL/MSPK C52......107 E2
Corkerhill Rd
  PLK/PH/NH G53......107 E2
Corlaich Av GVH/MTFL G42......110 B5
Corlaich Dr GVH/MTFL G42......110 B5
Corless Ct UD/BTH/TAN G71......134 B2
Cormack Av BSHPBGS G64......19 G4
Cormorant Av
  CRG/CRSL/HOU PA6......81 E4
Cornaig Rd PLK/PH/NH G53......106 C4
Cornalee Gdns
  PLK/PH/NH G53......106 B4
Cornalee Pl PLK/PH/NH G53......106 B4
Cornalee Rd PLK/PH/NH G53......106 C4
Cornelian Ter BLSH ML4......135 H3
Cornelia St MTHW ML1......154 A1
Cornhill Dr CTBR ML5......96 A5
Cornhill St SPRGB/BLRNK G21......68 D1
Cornmill Ct CLYDBK G81......31 H2
Cornock Crs CLYDBK G81......32 A5
Cornock St CLYDBK G81......32 A5
Corn St COWCAD G4......67 G4
Cornwall Av RUTH G73......130 C2
Cornwall St EKILN G74......166 A4
  PLKSD/SHW G41......88 C4
Cornwall St South
  PLKSD/SHW G41......88 C4
Coronation Ct MTHW ML1......137 E3
Coronation Pl
  BAIL/MDB/MHD G69......58 D4
Coronation St MTHW ML1......137 E3
Coronation St WISHAW ML2......174 C2
Coronation Wy BSDN G61......51 H1
Corpach Pl ESTRH G34......72 C5
Corra Linn HMLTN ML3......169 F2
Corran Av NMRNS G77......143 H4
Corran St
  STPS/GTHM/RID G33......92 A1
Correen Gdns BSDN G61......33 G1
Corrie Brae KSYTH G65......8 A1
Corrie Dr MTHW ML1......154 A3
  PSLY PA1......85 H5
Corrie Gdns EKILS G75......177 G4
Corrie Gv LNPK/KPK G44......128 A3
Corrie Pl KKNTL G66......40 B4
Corrie Rd KSYTH G65......8 C2
Corrie Vw BALLOCH G68......24 D5
Corrour Rd NMRNS G77......143 H4
  PLKSW/MSWD G43......108 C5
Corsebar Av PSLYS PA2......103 H2
Corsebar Crs PSLYS PA2......103 H3
Corsebar Dr PSLYS PA2......103 H2
Corsebar La PSLYS PA2......103 G3
Corsebar Rd PSLYS PA2......103 G3
Corsebar Wy PSLYS PA2......103 H1
Corse Dr BRHD/NEIL G78......123 H4
Corseford Av JNSTN PA5......120 D1
Corsehill Pl ESTRH G34......94 B1
Corsehill St ESTRH G34......94 B1
Corselet Rd BRHD/NEIL G78......143 F1
  PLK/PH/NH G53......125 F5
Corse Rd
  CARD/HILL/MSPK C52......85 H3
Corsewall Av CAR/SHTL G32......113 F1
Corsewall St CTBR ML5......96 B2
Corsford Dr PLK/PH/NH G53......125 H1
Corsock Av HMLTN ML3......168 D3
Corsock St DEN/PKHD G31......91 E1
Corston St STPS/GTHM/RID G33......91 G1
Cortachy Pl BSHPBGS G64......55 G2
Cortmalaw Cl
  STPS/GTHM/RID G33......55 H4
Coruisk Dr
  CRMNK/CLK/EAG G76......145 G2
Corunna St KVGV G3......88 C2
Coshneuk Rd
  STPS/GTHM/RID G33......70 C1
Cotton Av PSLYN/LNWD PA3......82 D4
Cotton St DMNK/BRGTN G40......110 C2
  PSLY PA1......84 B5
Cotton V MTHW ML1......156 B2
Coulin Gdns PPK/MIL G22......67 H3
Coulter Av CTBR ML5......96 C1
  WISHAW ML2......157 F3

Countess Ga
  UD/BTH/TAN G71......133 H4
County Av BLTYR/CAMB G72......111 G5
County Dr PSLY PA1......84 B4
County Sq PSLY PA1......84 B4
Couper Pl COWCAD G4......3 H2
Couper St COWCAD G4......3 H2
Coursington Crs MTHW ML1......155 E3
Coursington Gdns
  MTHW ML1......155 E3
Coursington Pl MTHW ML1......155 E3
Coursington Rd MTHW ML1......154 D3
Courthill BSDN G61......34 A2
Courthill Av LNPK/KPK G44......128 C2
Courthill Crs KSYTH G65......8 C2
Coustonholm Rd
  PLKSW/MSWD G43......108 C5
Couther Qd AIRDRIE ML6......76 A4
Covanburn Av HMLTN ML3......170 C4
Covenant Pl WISHAW ML2......172 D3
Coventry Dr DEN/PKHD G31......91 E1
Cowal Crs KKNTL G66......21 G5
Cowal Dr PSLYN/LNWD PA3......101 H1
Cowal Rd MRYH/FIRH G20......52 B4
Cowal St MRYH/FIRH G20......52 B4
Cowan Crs BRHD/NEIL G78......124 C5
Cowan La KVD/HLHD G12......66 D4
Cowan Rd BALLOCH G68......25 G3
Cowan St KVD/HLHD G12......66 D4
Cowan Wilson Av
  BLTYR/CAMB G72......151 G2
Cowan Wynd
  UD/BTH/TAN G71......115 F4
Cowcaddens Rd COWCAD G4......3 F3
  COWCAD G4......2 D2
Cowcaddens St CCLW G2......2 D2
Cowdenhill Circ KNTSWD G13......51 E3
Cowdenhill Pl KNTSWD G13......51 E3
Cowdenhill Rd KNTSWD G13......50 D3
Cowdray Crs RNFRW PA4......63 G3
Cowgate KKNTL G66......21 E5
Cowglen Rd PLK/PH/NH G53......106 D5
Cowlairs Rd SPRGB/BLRNK G21......68 B2
Coxdale Av KKNTL G66......20 D5
Coxhill St SPRGB/BLRNK G21......68 A3
Coxton Pl
  STPS/GTHM/RID G33......71 E5
Coylton Crs HMLTN ML3......168 C4
Coylton Rd
  PLKSW/MSWD G43......128 A2
Crabb Qd MTHW ML1......154 B1
Cragdale EKILN G74......165 H2
Craggan Dr SCOT G14......50 A5
Crags Av PSLYS PA2......104 C2
Crags Crs PSLYS PA2......104 C2
Crags Rd PSLYS PA2......104 C2
Cragwell Pk
  CRMNK/CLK/EAG G76......147 F3
Craigallian Av
  BLTYR/CAMB G72......132 A4
  MLNGV G62......17 E2
Craigancur La
  PLKSW/MSWD G43......127 F3
Craigard Pl RUTH G73......130 C4
Craigash Qd MLNGV G62......16 C3
Craigash Rd MLNGV G62......16 C3
Craigbank Dr
  PLK/PH/NH G53......125 F1
Craigbank St
  STPS/GTHM/RID G33......70 C2
Craigbarnet Crs
  STPS/GTHM/RID G33......70 C2
Craigbarnet Rd MLNGV G62......16 B3
Craigbet Av BRWEIR PA11......78 B1
Craigbet Crs BRWEIR PA11......78 B1
Craigbet Pl BRWEIR PA11......78 B1
Craigbo Av SMSTN G23......52 C2
Craigbog Av JNSTN PA5......121 E1
Craigbo Rd SMSTN G23......52 C2
Craigbo St SMSTN G23......52 C2
Craigburn Av
  CRG/CRSL/HOU PA6......81 F4
Craigburn Crs
  CRG/CRSL/HOU PA6......81 F4
Craigburn Pl
  CRG/CRSL/HOU PA6......81 F4
Craigburn St HMLTN ML3......170 A5
Craigdhu Av AIRDRIE ML6......99 F2
  MLNGV G62......16 D4
Craigdhu Rd BSDN G61......16 D5
  MLNGV G62......16 D4
Craigdonald Pl JNSTN PA5......101 H3
Craigellan Rd
  PLKSW/MSWD G43......127 G1
Craigelvan Av CUMB G67......43 G1
Craigelvan Ct CUMB G67......43 G2
Craigelvan Dr CUMB G67......43 G2
Craigelvan Gdns CUMB G67......43 G2
Craigelvan Gv CUMB G67......43 G2
Craigelvan Pl CUMB G67......43 G2
Craigelvan Vw CUMB G67......43 G2
Craigenbay Crs KKNTL G66......40 A3
Craigenbay Rd KKNTL G66......40 A4
Craigenbay St
  SPRGB/BLRNK G21......69 E2
Craigend Crs MLNGV G62......16 D3
Craigend Dr CTBR ML5......95 G5
Craigend Dr West
  MLNGV G62......16 C3
Craigendmuir Rd
  STPS/GTHM/RID G33......71 F2
Craigendmuir St
  STPS/GTHM/RID G33......69 G4
Craigendon Ov PSLYS PA2......122 D1
Craigendon Rd PSLYS PA2......122 D1
Craigend Pl KNTSWD G13......51 F5
Craigend Rd CUMB G67......43 G3
Craigends Ct KLBCH PA10......100 C3
Craigends Dr KLBCH PA10......100 C3
Craigends Rd
  CRG/CRSL/HOU PA6......81 E4
Craigend St KNTSWD G13......51 F5
Craigend Vw CUMB G67......43 G3
Craigenfeoch Av JNSTN PA5......101 E5
Craigens Rd AIRDRIE ML6......99 H4
Craigfaulds Av PSLYS PA2......103 G2
Craigfell Ct HMLTN ML3......168 D3
Craigflower Gdns
  PLK/PH/NH G53......125 F5
Craigflower Rd
  PLK/PH/NH G53......125 F5

Craig Gdns NMRNS G77 ....161 F1
Craighalbert Rd BALLOCH G68....25 G2
Craighalbert Wy BALLOCH G68....25 C1
Craighall Gd BRHD/NEIL G78.....141 H4
Craighall Rd COWCAD G4............67 G4
Craighead Av
  STPS/GTHM/RID G33................69 C3
Craighead Rd MLNGV G62...........16 B3
Craighead St AIRDRIE ML6............5 C4
Craighead St AIRDRIE ML6..........99 F1
Craighead Wy
  BRHD/NEIL G78.....................124 A5
Craig Hl EKILS G75...................177 H1
Craighill Dr
  CRMNK/CLK/EAG G76.............145 G4
Craighill Gv
  CRMNK/CLK/EAG G76.............145 G4
Craighirst Dr CLYDBK G81..........31 H1
Craighirst Rd MLNGV G62..........16 B5
Craighlaw Av
  CRMNK/CLK/EAG G76.............163 E3
Craighlaw Dr
  CRMNK/CLK/EAG G76.............163 E3
Craigholme
  CRG/CRSL/HOU PA6................81 E1
Craighouse St
  STPS/GTHM/RID G33................70 B3
Craighton Gdns KKNTL G66..........4 D2
Craighurst Rd MLNGV G62..........16 B3
Craigieburn Dr PSLYS PA2.........103 H4
Craigieburn Gdns
  MRYH/FIRH G20.......................52 A3
Craigieburn Rd CUMB G67..........26 B4
Craigie Dr NMRNS G77..............161 G2
Craigiehall Av ERSK PA8.............47 F4
Craigiehall Crs ERSK PA8............47 F4
Craigiehall Pl GOV/IBX G51........88 C5
Craigiehall St GOV/IBX G51.......88 C5
Craigiehall Wy ERSK PA8............47 G4
Craigielea Crs MLNGV G62.........16 C3
Craigielea Dr
  PSLYN/LNWD PA3....................83 G3
Craigielea Pk RNFRW PA4..........63 F3
Craigielea Rd CLYDBK G81..........31 C1
  RNFRW PA4.............................63 F3
Craigielea St DEN/PKHD G31......91 E1
Craigie Pk KKNTL G66................40 B5
Craigie Pl CTBR ML5..................96 B4
Craigie St GVH/MTFL G42.........109 F2
Craigievar St NMRNS G77..........143 G5
Craigievar St
  STPS/GTHM/RID G33................71 F4
Craiglea Pl AIRDRIE ML6.............98 D1
Craiglea Ter AIRDRIE ML6...........98 D1
Craiglee EKILS G75...................178 B4
Craiglee St CAR/SHTL G32.........91 H5
Craiglinn BALLOCH G68.............25 E3
Craiglinn Park Rd
  BALLOCH G68.........................25 E4
Craiglockhart Dr
  STPS/GTHM/RID G33................71 G4
Craiglockhart Pl
  STPS/GTHM/RID G33................71 G4
Craiglockhart St
  STPS/GTHM/RID G33................71 G5
Craigmaddie Gdns
  BSHPBGS G64.........................19 E5
Craigmaddie Terrace La
  KVGV G3..................................66 D5
Craigmarloch Av
  BSHPBGS G64.........................19 F5
Craigmillar Av WISHAW ML2.......17 F3
Craigmillar Pl
  BAIL/MDB/MHD G69................72 D1
Craigmillar Rd
  GVH/MTFL G42......................109 F5
Craigmochan Av AIRDRIE ML6....76 A4
Craigmont Dr MRYH/FIRH G20....52 D5
Craigmont St MRYH/FIRH G20....52 D5
Craigmore Rd BSDN G61............33 G1
Craigmore St DEN/PKHD G31.....91 F3
Craigmount Av PSLYS PA2........122 D1
Craigmuir Crs
  CARD/HILL/MSPK G52.............86 A5
Craigmuir Pl
  BLTYR/CAMB G72...................151 E4
Craigmuir Pl
  CARD/HILL/MSPK G52.............85 H5
Craigmuir Rd
  BLTYR/CAMB G72...................151 E4
  CARD/HILL/MSPK G52.............85 H5
Craigneil St
  STPS/GTHM/RID G33................71 F4
Craigneith Ct EKILN G74...........167 H1
Craignethan Rd
  GIF/THBK G46.........................144 D3
Craigneuk Av AIRDRIE ML6........98 D3
Craigneuk St MTHW ML1...........155 H1
Craigneuk St MTHW ML1...........155 C5
  WISHAW ML2..........................171 D1
Craignure Crs AIRDRIE ML6........99 F2
Craignure Rd RUTH G73............130 A4
Craigpark DEN/PKHD G31..........90 D2
Craigpark Dr DEN/PKHD G31.....90 D2
Craigpark Pl AIRDRIE ML6..........99 C3
Craigpark St CLYDBK G81..........32 C1
Craig St AIRDRIE ML6.................98 A2
  BLTYR/CAMB G72...................151 H3
  CTBR ML5.................................96 C5
Craigston Rd JNSTN PA5...........101 G2
Craigton Crs NMRNS G77..........143 G5
Craigton Dr BRHD/NEIL G78......142 A1
  MLNGV G62............................16 D2
  NMRNS G77............................143 H5

Craigton Gdns MLNGV G62.........16 D2
Craigton Pl BLTYR/CAMB G72....151 G1
Craigton Pl GOV/IBX G51............87 F3
  GOV/IBX G51...........................87 C3
Craigton Rd GOV/IBX G51...........87 G3
  MLNGV G62............................16 D3
Craigvale Crs AIRDRIE ML6.........99 F2
Craigvicar Gdns
  CAR/SHTL G32..........................93 E4
Craigview Av JNSTN PA5...........101 E5
Craigview Rd KKNTL ML1...........154 D2
Craigview Ter JNSTN PA5...........101 E5
Craigwell Av RUTH G73..............130 C1
Crail Cl BLTYR/CAMB G72...........168 C2
Crail St DEN/PKHD G31................91 F3
Crammond Av CTBR ML5............117 H5
Cramond Av RNFRW PA4.............63 H4
Cramond St GBLS G5..................110 A2
Cramond Ter CAR/SHTL G32........92 C4
Cranborne Rd KVD/HLHD G12.....65 H1
Cranbrooke Dr
  MRYH/FIRH G20.......................52 C4
Crannog Rd DMBTN G82..............14 B4
Cranston St KVGV G3....................2 A5
Cranworth La KVD/HLHD G12......66 C3
Cranworth St KVD/HLHD G12......66 C3
Crarae Av BSDN G61...................51 F1
Crarea Pl NMRNS G77................143 F5
Crathes Ct LNPK/KPK G44..........127 H5
Crathie Dr AIRDRIE ML6..............76 A2
  PTCK G11..................................65 H4
Crathie Pl NMRNS G77...............162 C1
Crathie Qd WISHAW ML2...........157 H5
Crawford Av KKNTL G66..............40 B5
Crawford Crs
  BLTYR/CAMB G72...................151 G2
  UD/BTH/TAN G71....................114 C5
Crawford Dr DRUM G15..............50 B2
  EKILN G74..............................167 E3
Crawford Hl EKILN G74..............167 E3
Crawford Rd
  CRG/CRSL/HOU PA6................81 E2
  MLNGV G62............................16 D1
Crawford St HMLTN ML3............152 B5
  MTHW ML1.............................154 C4
Crawfurd Av RUTH G73..............130 A2
Crawfurd Dr
  PSLYN/LNWD PA3....................83 C3
Crawfurd Gdns RUTH G73..........130 B3
Crawfurd Rd RUTH G73..............130 A3
Crawriggs Av KKNTL G66............40 A2
Craw Rd PSLYS PA2..................103 H1
Creamery Rd WISHAW ML2........173 H4
Crebar Dr BRHD/NEIL G78..........124 B5
Crebar St GIF/THBK G46.............126 B3
Credon Dr AIRDRIE ML6..............98 B4
Credon St CAR/SHTL G32...........130 B3
Cree Av BSDN G61.......................55 G2
Cree Gdns CAR/SHTL G32...........92 A4
Cree Pl EKILS G75......................165 G4
Creighton Gv EKILN G74............166 B4
Creran Ct HMLTN ML3................169 F4
Creran Dr RNFRW PA4................63 E3
Crescent Rd KNTSWD G13...........64 C1
The Crescent CLYDBK G81..........31 F5
  CRMNK/CLK/EAG G76.............146 B5
Cressdale Ct CSMK G45.............129 E5
Cressdale Dr CSMK G45.............129 E5
Cresswell Gv NMRNS G77..........161 G2
Cresswell La KVD/HLHD G12......66 C3
Cresswell Pl NMRNS G77...........161 G3
Cresswell St KVD/HLHD G12......66 C3
Cressy St GOV/IBX G51................87 E1
Crest Av KNTSWD G13................50 C5
Crestlea Av PSLYS PA2..............104 B4
Crichton St CTBR ML5..................96 D1
  SPRGB/BLRNK G21.................68 B2
Crieff Av AIRDRIE ML6................118 D3
Criffell Gdns CAR/SHTL G32.......113 E1
Criffell Rd CAR/SHTL G32............93 E4
Crighton Wynd BLSH ML4..........134 D2
Crimea St CGLW G2.......................7 H1
Crimond Pl KSYTH G65.................7 H1
Crinan Crs CTBR ML5...................74 A5
Crinan Gdns BSHPBGS G64.........55 F2
Crinan Pl BLSH ML4...................136 A3
Crinan St DEN/PKHD G31............91 F1
Crindledyke Crs WISHAW ML2...158 B5
Cripps Av CLYDBK G81................49 G2
Croftbank Av
  UD/BTH/TAN G71....................152 C1
Croftbank Crs
  UD/BTH/TAN G71....................152 C1
Croftbank Ga
  UD/BTH/TAN G71....................152 C1
Croftbank St
  SPRGB/BLRNK G21...................68 C2
Croftburn Dr LNPK/KPK G44......128 C4
Croftcot Av BLSH ML4................135 G4
Croftcroighan Rd
  STPS/GTHM/RID G33................70 D3
Croftend Av LNPK/KPK G44.......129 F1
Croftend La LNPK/KPK G44........129 F2
Croftfoot Crs CSMK G45.............129 H3
Croftfoot Dr CSMK G45..............129 G4
Croftfoot Pl
  BAIL/MDB/MHD G69................59 F5
Croftfoot Qd CSMK G45.............129 F5
Croftfoot Rd CSMK G45..............129 E3
Croftfoot St CSMK G45...............129 G3
Croftfoot Ter CSMK G45..............129 G3
Crofthead Crs BLSH ML4............135 G4
Crofthead Dr KKNTL G66...............4 A1
Crofthead St
  UD/BTH/TAN G71....................134 A2
Crofthill Av UD/BTH/TAN G71.....134 A1
Crofthill Rd LNPK/KPK G44........129 F1
Crofthouse Dr
  LNPK/KPK G44........................129 F5
Croftmont Av LNPK/KPK G44.....129 F4
Croftmoraig Av
  BAIL/MDB/MHD G69................42 B4
Crofton Av LNPK/KPK G44.........129 E4
Croftpark Av LNPK/KPK G44......129 F2
Croftpark Crs
  BLTYR/CAMB G72...................151 H4
Croftpark Rd CLYDBK G81..........32 A1

Croftpark St BLSH ML4...............135 H1
Croft Rd BLTYR/CAMB G72.........131 G2
  EKILS G75..............................178 B1
Croftside Av LNPK/KPK G44.......129 F5
Croftspar Av CAR/SHTL G32........93 E3
Croftspar Ct CAR/SHTL G32........93 E5
Croftspar Dr CAR/SHTL G32........93 D5
Croftspar Ga CAR/SHTL G32.......93 E3
Croftspar Gv CAR/SHTL G32.......93 D5
Croftspar Pl CAR/SHTL G32........92 D3
Croftwood BSHPBGS G64.............55 E3
Croft Wy RNFRW PA4..................63 H5
Croftwood Av LNPK/KPK G44....129 E3
Croftwood Rd HMLTN ML3.........170 A4
Croft Wynd
  UD/BTH/TAN G71....................134 B1
Crogal Crs AIRDRIE ML6.............119 E2
Cromalt Av EKILS G75................177 C4
Cromalt Crs BSDN G61................16 A5
Cromarty Av BSHPBGS G64.........55 C1
Cromarty Crs BSDN G61..............34 C1
Cromarty Gdns
  CRMNK/CLK/EAG G76.............146 B1
Cromarty Pl
  BAIL/MDB/MHD G69................58 C2
  EKILN G74..............................167 F2
Cromarty Rd AIRDRIE ML6...........98 A5
Crombie Gdns
  BAIL/MDB/MHD G69................113 G1
Cromdale St GOV/IBX G51...........87 F3
Cromdale Wy MTHW ML1...........137 F5
Cromer Gdns MRYH/FIRH G20.....67 F1
Crompton Av LNPK/KPK G44......128 C2
Cromptons Gv PSLY PA1.............103 C1
Cromwell La COWCAD G4............67 F4
Cromwell St MRYH/FIRH G20......67 F4
Cronan Dr HMLTN ML3...............168 D1
Cronberry Qd
  CARD/HILL/MSPK G52.............106 A1
Cronberry Ter
  CARD/HILL/MSPK G52.............106 A1
Cronin Pl BLSH ML4...................116 B4
Cronulla Pl KSYTH G65..................8 C2
Crookedshields Rd
  EKILN G74..............................149 G3
Crookfur Rd NMRNS G77...........143 H4
Crookston Av
  CARD/HILL/MSPK G52.............86 B5
Crookston Ct
  CARD/HILL/MSPK G52.............86 B5
Crookston Dr
  CARD/HILL/MSPK G52.............86 B5
Crookston Gv
  CARD/HILL/MSPK G52.............86 B5
Crookston Pl
  CARD/HILL/MSPK G52.............86 A5
Crookston Qd
  CARD/HILL/MSPK G52.............86 A5
Crookston Rd
  CARD/HILL/MSPK G52.............86 A5
Crookston Ter
  CARD/HILL/MSPK G52.............86 B5
Crosbie Dr PSLYS PA2................102 D5
Crosbie La MRYH/FIRH G20.........52 B3
Crosbie St MRYH/FIRH G20.........52 B3
Crosbie Wd PSLYS PA2..............103 G3
Cross Arthurlie St
  BRHD/NEIL G78......................124 A4
Crossbank Av CVH/MTFL G42....110 B3
Crossbank Dr GVH/MTFL G42....110 A3
Crossbank Rd
  GVH/MTFL G42.......................110 A3
Crossbank Ter
  GVH/MTFL G42.......................110 A3
Crossburn Av MLNGV G62...........16 D4
Crossdykes KKNTL G66...............40 D1
Crossflat Crs PSLY PA1................84 D4
Crossford Dr SMSTN G23.............52 D2
Cross Gates BLSH ML4...............135 H5
Crosshill Av GVH/MTFL G42.......109 G5
  KKNTL G66..............................40 A2
Crosshill Dr MTHW ML1.............137 H4
  RUTH G73..............................130 A1
Crosshill Rd BSHPBGS G64..........38 C5
  KKNTL G66..............................39 E4
  KKNTL G66..............................66 B4
  MTHW ML1.............................155 E4
Crosshouse Rd EKILS G75..........177 E5
Crosslea Gdns
  CRG/CRSL/HOU PA6................80 C3
Crosslee Crs
  CRG/CRSL/HOU PA6................80 D2
Crosslee Pk
  CRG/CRSL/HOU PA6................80 D3
Crosslees Dr BRWEIR PA11..........80 B5
Crosslees Pk GIF/THBK G46........126 C4
Crosslees Rd GIF/THBK G46........126 C5
Crosslee St
  CARD/HILL/MSPK G52.............87 E4
Crosslet Ct DMBTN G82..............13 C4
Crosslet Pl DMBTN G82..............13 C4
Crosslet Rd DMBTN G82..............13 H4
Crossloan Rd GOV/IBX G51.........87 G2
Crossloan Ter GOV/IBX G51.........87 C2
Crossmill Av BRHD/NEIL G78.....124 C3
Crossmyloof Gdns
  PLKSD/SHW G41......................108 C3
Crosspoint Dr SMSTN G23...........52 D2
Cross Rd PSLYS PA2..................103 G2
Cross Stone Pl MTHW ML1.........154 D4
Cross St CAR/SHTL G32...............112 D3
Crossveggate MLNGV G62..........17 F4
Crossview Av
  BAIL/MDB/MHD G69................94 C4
Crossview Pl
  BAIL/MDB/MHD G69................94 C4
Crossways
  CRG/CRSL/HOU PA6................81 E1
Crovie Rd PLK/PH/NH G53..........106 B5
Crow Av MTHW ML1...................137 G2
Crowflats Rd
  UD/BTH/TAN G71....................133 H1
Crowflat Vw
  UD/BTH/TAN G71....................115 H3
Crowhill Crs AIRDRIE ML6............76 A4

Crowhill Dr
  STPS/GTHM/RID G33................93 F3
Crowhill Rd BSHPBGS G64..........54 C2
Crowhill St PPK/MIL G22..............53 H5
Crow La KNTSWD G13.................65 G3
Crowlin Crs
  STPS/GTHM/RID G33................92 C1
Crown Av CLYDBK G81................31 H5
Crown Circ KVD/HLHD G12.........66 B5
Crown Gdns KVD/HLHD G12........66 B5
Crownhall Pl CAR/SHTL G32........92 D4
Crownhall Rd CAR/SHTL G32......92 D4
Crownhill Ct AIRDRIE ML6............76 A4
Crownpoint Rd
  DEN/PKHD G31........................90 C4
Crown Rd North
  KVD/HLHD G12.......................66 A3
Crown Rd South
  KVD/HLHD G12.......................66 A3
Crown St AIRDRIE ML6...............118 C1
  BAIL/MDB/MHD G69................113 G1
  CTBR ML5.................................97 F2
  GBLS G5...................................89 H5
Crown Ter KVD/HLHD G12...........66 A3
Crow Rd KKNTL G66......................4 A1
Crowwood Dr AIRDRIE ML6.........99 E2
Crow-Wood Rd AIRDRIE ML6......13 H5
Crow Wood Rd
  BAIL/MDB/MHD G69................58 A4
Croy Av NMRNS G77..................144 D5
Croy Pl SPRGB/BLRNK G21.........69 F1
Croy Rd CTBR ML5.....................116 A2
Cruachan Av PSLYS PA2............104 B4
  RNFRW PA4.............................63 F5
Cruachan Dr BRHD/NEIL G78.....142 B1
  NMRNS G77............................161 G1
Cruachan Rd BSDN G61..............33 G1
  RUTH G73..............................130 C4
Cruachan St GIF/THBK G46........126 D3
Cruachan Wy
  BRHD/NEIL G78......................142 B1
Cruden St GOV/IBX G51...............87 F3
Crum Av GIF/THBK G46...............126 D4
Crusader Av KNTSWD G13...........51 E2
Cubie St DMNK/BRGTN G40.........90 C4
Cuckoo Wy MTHW ML1..............137 G2
Cuilhill Rd
  BAIL/MDB/MHD G69................95 F3
Cuillin Pl AIRDRIE ML6................119 G3
The Cuillins
  BAIL/MDB/MHD G69................114 B4
Cuillin Wy BRHD/NEIL G78.........124 B5
Cuilmuir Ter KSYTH G65..............24 D1
Cuilmuir Vw KSYTH G65..............24 D1
Cuilbin Dr KNTSWD G13..............50 A5
Cullen La EKILS G75...................178 A1
Cullen Pl UD/BTH/TAN G71.........115 F4
Cullen Rd EKILS G75...................178 A1
  MTHW ML1.............................154 B5
Cullen St CAR/SHTL G32.............92 B5
Cullins Rd RUTH G73..................130 C4
Cullion Wy MTHW ML1...............138 C2
Culloch Rd BSDN G61..................16 A5
Culloden Av BLSH ML4...............136 C5
Culloden St DEN/PKHD G31.........91 E1
Culrain Gdns CAR/SHTL G32.......92 B4
Culrain St CAR/SHTL G32............92 B4
Culross Hl EKILN G74.................166 A4
Culross Pl CTBR ML5....................96 C2
  EKILN G74..............................166 A4
Culross St CAR/SHTL G32...........92 D5
Culross Wy
  BAIL/MDB/MHD G69................42 B5
Cult Rd KKNTL G66.......................40 B5
Cults St GOV/IBX G51.................87 F3
Culvain Av BSDN G61..................33 H1
Culzean AIRDRIE ML6..................96 A1
Culzean Av CTBR ML5..................96 B5
Culzean Crs
  BAIL/MDB/MHD G69................93 H5
  NMRNS G77............................144 D5
Culzean Dr CAR/SHTL G32..........93 E4
  MTHW ML1.............................137 F4
Culzean Pl EKILN G74.................166 A2
Cumberland Pl CTBR ML5............95 H5
  GBLS G5...................................89 H5
Cumberland St GBLS G5..............89 H5
Cumbernauld Rd
  BAIL/MDB/MHD G69................59 F1
  CUMB G67................................43 E4
  DEN/PKHD G31........................91 F2
  STPS/GTHM/RID G33................70 B2
  STPS/GTHM/RID G33................92 B1
Cumbrae Ct CLYDBK G81............49 E5
Cumbrae Crs CTBR ML5...............97 H4
Cumbrae Crs North
  DMBTN G82............................12 B2
Cumbrae Crs South
  DMBTN G82............................12 A2
Cumbrae Dr MTHW ML1.............154 B3
Cumbrae Pl CTBR ML5.................97 H5
Cumbrae Rd PSLYS PA2.............104 B5
  RNFRW PA4.............................63 G5
Cumbrae St
  STPS/GTHM/RID G33................92 B1
Cumlodden Dr
  MRYH/FIRH G20.......................52 B4
Cumming Dr GVH/MTFL G42.....109 G4
Cumnock Dr AIRDRIE ML6...........98 D5
  BRHD/NEIL G78......................142 C1
Cumnock Rd
  STPS/GTHM/RID G33................55 H5
Cumroch Rd KKNTL G66................4 A1
Cunard St CLYDBK G81...............49 F3
Cunninghame Rd KLBCH PA10...100 C3
Cunningair Dr MTHW ML1...........171 H1
Cunningham Dr GIF/THBK G46...127 F4
Cunninghame Dr EKILN G74.......166 B4
Cunningham Gdns
  CRG/CRSL/HOU PA6................81 E2

Cunningham Rd
  CARD/HILL/MSPK G52.............86 A1
Cunningham St MTHW ML1........154 C4
Cuparhead Av CTBR ML5.............96 A5
Curfew Rd KNTSWD G13.............51 E3
Curle St SCOT G14.......................65 G3
Curlew Pl JNSTN PA5.................120 D2
Curling Crs GVH/MTFL G42........109 H5
Curlinghaugh Crs
  WISHAW ML2..........................174 B2
Curlingmire EKILS G75...............178 B3
Curran Av WISHAW ML2.............173 F4
Currie Ct JNSTN PA5...................53 E5
Currie St MRYH/FIRH G20............53 D5
Curtis Av LNPK/KPK G44............128 D1
Curzon St MRYH/FIRH G20.........52 D5
Cuthbertson St
  PLKSD/SHW G41......................109 F1
Cuthbert St
  UD/BTH/TAN G71....................115 C5
Cuthelton Dr DEN/PKHD G31.....115 C5
Cuthelton St DEN/PKHD G31.......91 C5
Cuthelton Ter DEN/PKHD G31......91 H5
The Cut UD/BTH/TAN G71..........134 A2
Cutty Sark Pl DMBTN G82...........13 H5
Cypress Av BLTYR/CAMB G72....151 F2
  UD/BTH/TAN G71....................115 F4
Cypress Ct EKILS G75................177 H3
  HMLTN ML3............................170 B3
  KKNTL G66..............................39 G2
Cypress Crs EKILS G75..............177 H3
Cypress Gv
  BAIL/MDB/MHD G69................95 F3
  BRWEIR PA11...........................78 C1
Cypress Pl EKILS G75.................177 H3
Cypress St PPK/MIL G22..............54 A4
Cypress Wy BLTYR/CAMB G72...132 C3
Cyprus Av JNSTN PA5................102 A2
Cyril St PSLY PA1.........................84 D5

D

Daer Av RNFRW PA4....................63 H5
Daer Wy HMLTN ML3.................169 F3
Daffodil Wy MTHW ML1.............154 C4
Dairsie Gdns BSHPBGS G64.........55 G3
Dairsie St LNPK/KPK G44...........128 A3
Daisy St GVH/MTFL G42.............109 H5
Dakala Ct WISHAW ML2.............173 H3
Dalbeattie Braes
  AIRDRIE ML6...........................119 F3
Dalbeth Rd CAR/SHTL G32.........112 A2
Dalcharn Pl ESTRH G34...............93 H1
Dalcraig Crs
  BLTYR/CAMB G72...................151 F1
Dalcross St PTCK G11..................66 B4
Dalcruin Gdns
  BAIL/MDB/MHD G69................42 B4
Daldowie Rd
  UD/BTH/TAN G71....................113 H2
Daldowie St CTBR ML5...............116 B3
Dale Av EKILS G75......................177 H3
Dale Ct WISHAW ML2.................172 D3
Daleview Av KVD/HLHD G12........52 A5
Daleview Dr
  CRMNK/CLK/EAG G76.............145 G4
Daleview Gv
  CRMNK/CLK/EAG G76.............145 G4
Dale Wy RUTH G73.....................129 H3
Dalgarroch Av CLYDBK G81.........49 H5
Dalgleish Av CLYDBK G81............31 G2
Dalgraig Crs
  BLTYR/CAMB G72...................133 F5
Dalhousie Gdns BSHPBGS G64.....54 C1
Dalhousie La KVGV G3...................2 C2
Dalhousie Rd KLBCH PA10.........100 C3
Dalhousie St COWCAD G4.............2 D2
Dailea Dr ESTRH G34..................72 C5
Dailea Pl ESTRH G34..................72 C5
Dalintober St GBLS G5..................89 F4
Dalkeith Av BSHPBGS G64...........55 A4
  PLKSD/SHW G41....................108 A4
Dalkeith Rd BSHPBGS G64..........38 A4
Dalmacoulter Rd AIRDRIE ML6....76 C3
Dalmahoy Crs BRWEIR PA11.......79 E5
Dalmahoy St CAR/SHTL G32........92 H2
Dalmally St MRYH/FIRH G20.......67 E3
Dalmarnock Ct
  DMNK/BRGTN G40..................111 E1
Dalmarnock Dr
  DMNK/BRGTN G40....................90 C5
Dalmarnock Rd
  DMNK/BRGTN G40..................111 E2
  DMNK/BRGTN G40..................90 C5
Dalmary Dr PSLY PA1...................85 E3
Dalmellington Ct EKILN G74.......166 A5
  PLK/PH/NH G53......................106 B4
Dalmellington Dr EKILN G74.......166 A5
  PLK/PH/NH G53......................106 B4
Dalmellington Rd
  PLK/PH/NH G53......................127 B4
Dalmeny Av GIF/THBK G46.........127 F4
Dalmeny Dr BRHD/NEIL G78......141 A3
Dalmeny Rd HMLTN ML3.............170 A3
Dalmeny St GBLS G5..................110 B2
Dalmore Crs MTHW ML1...............17 F1
Dalmore Dr AIRDRIE ML6.............98 B5
Dalnair Pl MLNGV G62.................16 B5
Dalnair St KVGV G3.....................66 B5
Dainess St CAR/SHTL G32..........112 C1
Dalnottar Av OLDK G60................30 C2
Dalnottar Dr OLDK G60................30 C3
Dalnottar Gdns OLDK G60............30 C3
Dalnottar Hill Rd OLDK G60.........30 C2
Dalnottar Ter OLDK G60...............30 C2
Dalreoch Av
  BAIL/MDB/MHD G69................94 B4
Dalreoch Ct DMBTN G82..............12 C3
Dalriada Crs MTHW ML1.............154 C1
Dalriada St DMNK/BRGTN G40....91 F5
Dalry Gdns HMLTN ML3..............168 C3

Dalrymple Dr CTBR ML5 ......96 C5
　EKILN G74 ......166 B3
　NMRNS G77 ......162 B1
Dalry Pl AIRDRIE ML6 ......119 F4
Dalry Rd UD/BTH/TAN G71 ......115 G5
Dalry St CAR/SHTL G32 ......92 C5
Dalserf Crs GIF/THBK G46 ......145 E1
Dalserf Gdns DEN/PKHD G31 ......91 G4
Dalserf Pl DEN/PKHD G31 ......91 G4
Dalsetter Av DRUM G15 ......50 A1
Dalsetter Pl DRUM G15 ......50 B1
Dalshannon Pl CUMB G67 ......43 H1
Dalshannon Rd CUMB G67 ......44 A1
Dalshannon Vw CUMB G67 ......43 H1
Dalsholm Pl MRYH/FIRH G20 ......52 A3
Dalsholm Rd MRYH/FIRH G20 ......52 B3
Dalskeith Av
　PSLYN/LNWD PA3 ......83 F4
Dalskeith Crs
　PSLYN/LNWD PA3 ......83 F4
Dalskeith Rd
　PSLYN/LNWD PA3 ......83 F5
Dalswinton Pth ESTRH G34 ......94 B1
Dalswinton St ESTRH G34 ......94 B1
Dalton Av CLYDBK G81 ......49 H2
Dalton Hl HMLTN ML3 ......168 D3
Dalton St DEN/PKHD G31 ......91 H4
Dalveen Ct BRHD/NEIL G78 ......142 B1
Dalveen Dr UD/BTH/TAN G71 ......114 D4
Dalveen Qd CTBR ML5 ......97 G4
Dalveen St CAR/SHTL G32 ......92 A4
Dalveen Wy RUTH G73 ......130 B4
Dalwhinnie Av
　BLTYR/CAMB G72 ......133 F5
Daly Gdns BLTYR/CAMB G72 ......151 G1
Dalziel Av MTHW ML1 ......137 F2
Dalziel Dr MTHW ML1 ......172 B2
Dalziel Crs BLTYR/CAMB G72 ......132 A1
Dalziel Dr PLKSD/SHW G41 ......108 B1
Dalziel Gv BLTYR/CAMB G72 ......132 A1
Dalziel Pl BLTYR/CAMB G72 ......132 A1
Dalziel Rd
　CARD/HILL/MSPK G52 ......86 A1
Dalziel St HMLTN ML3 ......152 C5
　HMLTN ML3 ......154 D3
Dalziel Wy BLTYR/CAMB G72 ......132 A1
Damshot Crs
　PLK/PH/NH G53 ......107 E4
Damshot Rd PLK/PH/NH G53 ......107 E5
Danby Rd
　BAIL/MDB/MHD G69 ......93 G5
Danes Av SCOT G14 ......64 D2
Danes Crs SCOT G14 ......64 C1
Danes Dr SCOT G14 ......64 D2
Danes La North SCOT G14 ......64 D2
Danes La South SCOT G14 ......64 D2
Daniel McLaughlin Pl
　KNTL G66 ......21 G4
Dargarvel Av PLKSD/SHW G41 ......88 C5
Dargavel Av BSHPTN PA7 ......46 A1
　BSHPTN PA7 ......29 E5
Dargavel Rd ERSK PA8 ......46 C2
Darkwood Crs
　PSLYN/LNWD PA3 ......83 G3
Darkwood Dr
　PSLYN/LNWD PA3 ......83 G3
Darleith St CAR/SHTL G32 ......92 A4
Darley Pl HMLTN ML3 ......169 F3
Darley Rd BALLOCH G68 ......10 A5
Darluith Rd PSLYN/LNWD PA3 ......81 F5
Darnaway Av
　STPS/GTHM/RID G33 ......71 E4
Darnaway Dr
　STPS/GTHM/RID G33 ......71 E4
Darnaway St
　STPS/GTHM/RID G33 ......71 E4
Darngaber Gdns HMLTN ML3 ......181 E5
Darngaber Rd HMLTN ML3 ......181 E5
Darnick St SPRGB/BLRNK G21 ......68 D4
Darnley Crs BSHPBGS G64 ......37 G5
Darnley Gdns
　PLKSD/SHW G41 ......108 D2
Darnley Mains Rd
　PLK/PH/NH G53 ......125 H4
Darnley Pl PLKSD/SHW G41 ......108 D2
Darnley Rd BRHD/NEIL G78 ......124 D4
　PLKSD/SHW G41 ......108 D2
Darnley St BLTYR/CAMB G72 ......158 B4
Darragh on WISHAW ML2 ......158 B4
Darroch Dr ERSK PA8 ......30 A5
Darroch Wy CUMB G67 ......26 C2
Dartford St PPK/MIL G22 ......67 G3
Darvel Crs PSLY PA1 ......85 H5
Darvel Dr NMRNS G77 ......144 D5
Darwin Pl CLYDBK G81 ......31 E5
Darwin Rd EKILS G75 ......165 H5
Davaar EKILN G74 ......167 F4
Davaar Dr CTBR ML5 ......116 A1
　MTHW ML1 ......136 B5
　PSLY PA2 ......104 B4
Davaar Pl NMRNS G77 ......143 H4
Davaar Rd RNFRW PA4 ......63 G5
Davaar St DMNK/BRGTN G40 ......91 E5
Daventry Dr KVD/HLHD G12 ......65 H1
David Gray Dr KNTL G66 ......22 A4
David Pl BAIL/MDB/MHD G69 ......93 G5
Davidson Crs KSYTH G65 ......23 F2
Davidson Gdns CAR/SHTL G32 ......92 D3
Davidson Qd CLYDBK G81 ......31 G1
Davidson St AIRDRIE ML6 ......98 A1
　CLYDBK G81 ......49 H3
　CTBR ML5 ......97 E5
　DMNK/BRGTN G40 ......110 D2
Davidson Pl KKNTL G66 ......40 C4
David St CTBR ML5 ......97 F2
　DMNK/BRGTN G40 ......90 D4
Davieland Rd GIF/THBK G46 ......144 D1
Davie's Acre EKILN G74 ......165 E1
Davies Qd MTHW ML1 ......136 C5
Davington Dr HMLTN ML3 ......168 C3
Daviot St GOV/IBX G51 ......87 E3
Dawson Av EKILS G75 ......165 G4
Dawson Pl COWCAD G4 ......67 G3
Dawson Rd COWCAD G4 ......67 G3
Deaconsbank Av
　GIF/THBK G46 ......144 A1
Deaconsbank Crs
　GIF/THBK G46 ......144 B1

Deaconsbrook Rd
　GIF/THBK G46 ......144 A1
Deaconsgrange Rd
　GIF/THBK G46 ......144 A1
Deacons Rd KSYTH G65 ......8 B2
Deacons Vw GIF/THBK G46 ......144 A1
Dealston Rd BRHD/NEIL G78 ......124 A3
Deanbank Rd CTBR ML5 ......96 A2
Deanbrae St
　UD/BTH/TAN G71 ......134 B2
Dean Crs BAIL/MDB/MHD G69 ......58 C2
　HMLTN ML3 ......169 H4
Deanfield Qd
　CARD/HILL/MSPK G52 ......86 A3
Dean Park Av
　UD/BTH/TAN G71 ......134 B5
Dean Park Dr
　BLTYR/CAMB G72 ......132 A3
Dean Park Rd RNFRW PA4 ......63 G4
Deans Av BLTYR/CAMB G72 ......132 A4
Deanside Rd
　CARD/HILL/MSPK G52 ......86 B1
Deanston Av BRHD/NEIL G78 ......142 A1
Deanston Dr
　PLKSD/SHW G41 ......108 D4
Deanstone Pl CTBR ML5 ......117 G1
Deanstone Wk CTBR ML5 ......117 G1
Deanston Dr CTBR ML5 ......116 B1
Deanston Pk BRHD/NEIL G78 ......141 H1
Dean St BLSH ML4 ......136 A2
　CLYDBK G81 ......49 F2
Deanwood Av LNPK/KPK G44 ......128 A4
Deanwood Rd
　LNPK/KPK G44 ......128 A4
Dechmont Av
　BLTYR/CAMB G72 ......132 A4
　MTHW ML1 ......154 B3
Dechmont Gdns
　BLTYR/CAMB G72 ......151 F1
Dechmont Pl
　BLTYR/CAMB G72 ......132 A4
Dechmont Rd
　UD/BTH/TAN G71 ......114 D3
　HMLTN ML3 ......169 H5
Dechmont Vw BLSH ML4 ......135 G4
　UD/BTH/TAN G71 ......115 F5
Dee Av PSLY PA2 ......103 E2
　RNFRW PA4 ......63 H3
Dee Crs PSLY PA2 ......103 E2
Deedes St AIRDRIE ML6 ......97 G3
Dee Dr PSLY PA2 ......103 E3
Deep Dl EKILN G74 ......165 H2
Deepdene Rd
　BAIL/MDB/MHD G69 ......59 E2
　BSDN G61 ......51 E1
Dee Pl EKILS G75 ......176 D1
　JNSTN PA5 ......120 D1
Deerdykes Ct North
　BALLOCH G68 ......43 F2
Deerdykes Ct South
　BALLOCH G68 ......43 F3
Deerdykes Pl BALLOCH G68 ......43 F2
Deerdykes Rd BALLOCH G68 ......43 E3
Deerdykes Vw BALLOCH G68 ......43 E3
Deer Park Ct HMLTN ML3 ......180 D1
Deer Park Pl HMLTN ML3 ......181 E1
Dee St STPS/GTHM/RID G33 ......91 G1
Dee Ter HMLTN ML3 ......169 G5
Delhi Av CLYDBK G81 ......30 D4
Delhmont St MTHW ML1 ......155 F5
The Dell BLSH ML4 ......136 C4
Delny Pl STPS/GTHM/RID G33 ......93 F2
Delvin Rd LNPK/KPK G44 ......128 B2
Dempsey Rd BLSH ML4 ......135 G4
Denbak Av HMLTN ML3 ......169 F3
Denbeath Ct HMLTN ML3 ......171 F5
Denbeck St CAR/SHTL G32 ......92 A4
Denbrae St CAR/SHTL G32 ......92 A4
Denewood Av PSLY PA2 ......104 A4
Denham St PPK/MIL G22 ......67 H3
Denholm Crs EKILS G75 ......166 B5
　WISHAW ML2 ......157 F2
Denholm Dr GIF/THBK G46 ......145 F2
　WISHAW ML2 ......157 F2
Denholm Gdns HMLTN ML3 ......181 E5
Denholm Gn EKILS G75 ......166 B5
Denholm Ter HMLTN ML3 ......168 D2
Denmark St PPK/MIL G22 ......67 H2
Denmilne Rd
　BAIL/MDB/MHD G69 ......94 C2
Denmilne St ESTRH G34 ......94 B1
Dennistoun Forge
　DMBTN G82 ......12 D3
Dentdale EKILN G74 ......165 H2
Deramore Av GIF/THBK G46 ......144 D3
Derby St KVGV G3 ......88 D1
Derby Terrace La KVGV G3 ......66 C5
Derby Wynd MTHW ML1 ......155 G1
Derrywood Rd KKNTL G66 ......5 G4
Derwent Dr CTBR ML5 ......73 H4
Derwent St PPK/MIL G22 ......67 G2
Derwentwater EKILS G75 ......177 E2
Despard Av CAR/SHTL G32 ......93 E5
Despard Gdns CAR/SHTL G32 ......93 F5
Deveron Av GIF/THBK G46 ......127 G1
Deveron Rd BSDN G61 ......50 D1
　EKILN G74 ......167 G4
　MTHW ML1 ......137 G2
Deveron St CTBR ML5 ......74 A5
　CTBR ML5 ......73 H5
　STPS/GTHM/RID G33 ......69 G5
Devine Gv WISHAW ML2 ......158 B3
Devlin Ct BLTYR/CAMB G72 ......151 H3
Devlin Gv BLTYR/CAMB G72 ......151 H3
Devol Crs PLK/PH/NH G53 ......106 C4
Devondale Av
　BLTYR/CAMB G72 ......151 F1
Devon Gdns BSHPBGS G64 ......37 G5
Devonhill Av HMLTN ML3 ......180 D1
Devon Pl PLKSD/SHW G41 ......89 G5
Devonport Pk EKILS G75 ......177 F1
Devonshire Gardens La
　KVD/HLHD G12 ......66 A2
Devonshire Ter
　KVD/HLHD G12 ......66 A2

Devonshire Terrace La
　KVD/HLHD G12 ......66 A2
Devon St GBLS G5 ......89 G5
Devonview Pl AIRDRIE ML6 ......98 A3
Devonview St AIRDRIE ML6 ......98 A2
Devon Wk BALLOCH G68 ......24 C5
Devon Wy MTHW ML1 ......154 A4
Dewar Cl UD/BTH/TAN G71 ......115 F3
Dewar Dr DRUM G15 ......33 F5
Dewar Ga DRUM G15 ......33 F5
Dewar Rd
　STPS/GTHM/RID G33 ......71 H2
　STPS/GTHM/RID G33 ......57 H5
Diamond St BLSH ML4 ......135 H4
Diana Av KNTSWD G13 ......50 C3
Diana Qd MTHW ML1 ......137 F2
Dickens Av CLYDBK G81 ......31 G1
Dicks Pk EKILS G75 ......166 A5
Dick St MRYH/FIRH G20 ......67 E3
Differ Av KSYTH G65 ......24 C5
Dilwara Av SCOT G14 ......65 F4
Dimity St JNSTN PA5 ......101 G4
Dimsdale Crs WISHAW ML2 ......174 B4
Dimsdale Rd WISHAW ML2 ......174 B4
Dinard Dr GIF/THBK G46 ......127 F3
Dinart St STPS/GTHM/RID G33 ......69 G5
Dinduff St ESTRH G34 ......72 B5
Dinmont Av PSLY PA2 ......103 E3
Dinmont Crs MTHW ML1 ......155 F5
Dinmont Rd PLKSD/SHW G41 ......108 C3
Dinwiddie St
　SPRGB/BLRNK G21 ......69 F4
Dinyra Pl CTBR ML5 ......59 H5
Dippie Pl DRUM G15 ......50 A1
Dirleton Dr PLKSD/SHW G41 ......108 D4
　PSLYS PA2 ......103 F3
Dirleton Ga BSDN G61 ......51 E1
　BSDN G61 ......34 A5
Divernia Wy BRHD/NEIL G78 ......142 C2
Dixon Av DMBTN G82 ......12 D4
　GVH/MTFL G42 ......109 F2
Dixon Dr DMBTN G82 ......12 C5
Dixon Pl EKILN G74 ......165 G2
Dixon Rd GVH/MTFL G42 ......109 H3
Dixon St CCLE G1 ......2 E7
　GBLS G5 ......89 H3
　HMLTN ML3 ......170 A2
　PSLY PA1 ......84 D5
Dickens Gv MTHW ML1 ......138 A5
Dobbie's Loan COWCAD G4 ......3 G2
Dobbie's Loan Pl COWCAD G4 ......3 H5
Dochart Av RNFRW PA4 ......63 H5
Dochart Dr CTBR ML5 ......73 H4
Dochart St
　STPS/GTHM/RID G33 ......69 H4
Dock St CLYDBK G81 ......49 G4
Dodhill Pl KNTSWD G13 ......50 C5
Dodside Gdns CAR/SHTL G32 ......92 D5
Dodside St CAR/SHTL G32 ......92 D5
Dolan St BAIL/MDB/MHD G69 ......94 A4
Dollar Pk MTHW ML1 ......172 C2
Dollar Ter MRYH/FIRH G20 ......52 B3
Dolphin Rd PLKSD/SHW G41 ......108 C2
Dominica Gn EKILS G75 ......165 F4
Donaldfield Rd BRWEIR PA11 ......79 G2
Donaldson Av KKNTL G66 ......39 H1
Donaldson Dr RNFRW PA4 ......63 F3
Donaldson Gn
　UD/BTH/TAN G71 ......115 G4
Donaldson St HMLTN ML3 ......152 B5
　KKNTL G66 ......39 H1
Donaldswood Pk PSLYS PA2 ......103 H4
Donaldswood Rd PSLYS PA2 ......103 H5
Donald Ter HMLTN ML3 ......169 H4
Donald Wy UD/BTH/TAN G71 ......115 F5
Don Av RNFRW PA4 ......63 H4
Don Ct HMLTN ML3 ......169 F5
Don Dr PSLYS PA2 ......103 E3
Donhoe Ct BSHPBGS G64 ......54 D2
Donnelly Wy WISHAW ML2 ......157 E1
Donnies Brae BRHD/NEIL G78 ......141 G2
Don Pl JNSTN PA5 ......120 D1
Don St STPS/GTHM/RID G33 ......91 G1
Doon Crs BSDN G61 ......34 A5
Doonfoot Gdns EKILN G74 ......166 A3
Doonfoot Rd
　PLKSW/MSWD G43 ......127 F1
Doon Pl KKNTL G66 ......21 H3
Doon Rd KKNTL G66 ......21 H4
Doon Side CUMB G67 ......26 D3
Doon St CLYDBK G81 ......32 B5
　MTHW ML1 ......172 B1
Doon Wy KKNTL G66 ......22 A3
Dorain Rd MTHW ML1 ......138 A4
Dorchester Av KVD/HLHD G12 ......51 H5
Dorchester Ct KVD/HLHD G12 ......51 H5
Dorchester Pl KVD/HLHD G12 ......65 H5
Dorian Dr
　CRMNK/CLK/EAG G76 ......145 E2
Dorlin Rd
　STPS/GTHM/RID G33 ......71 F1
Dormanside Ct
　PLK/PH/NH G53 ......106 C1
Dormanside Ga
　PLK/PH/NH G53 ......106 C1
Dormanside Gv
　PLK/PH/NH G53 ......106 C1
Dormanside Pl
　PLK/PH/NH G53 ......106 D2
Dormanside Rd
　PLK/PH/NH G53 ......106 C1
Dornal Av KNTSWD G13 ......49 H4
Dornford Av CAR/SHTL G32 ......113 E2
Dornford Rd CAR/SHTL G32 ......113 E2
Dornie Dr CAR/SHTL G32 ......112 C4
Dornoch Av GIF/THBK G46 ......145 F1
Dornoch Ct BLSH ML4 ......135 H2
Dornoch Pl
　BAIL/MDB/MHD G69 ......58 C2
　EKILN G74 ......165 H3
Dornoch Rd BSDN G61 ......51 E1
　MTHW ML1 ......137 G2
Dornoch St DMNK/BRGTN G40 ......90 D4
Dornoch Wy AIRDRIE ML6 ......98 A4
　BALLOCH G68 ......10 C5
　BLTYR/CAMB G72 ......168 C1

Dorset Rd KVGV G3 ......89 E1
Dosk Av KNTSWD G13 ......50 A3
　KNTSWD G13 ......49 H3
Dosk Pl KNTSWD G13 ......50 A3
Double Hedges Rd
　BRHD/NEIL G78 ......141 E4
Dougalston Av MLNGV G62 ......17 F4
Dougalston Crs MLNGV G62 ......17 F4
Dougalston Gdns North
　MLNGV G62 ......17 F4
Dougalston Gdns South
　MLNGV G62 ......17 F4
Dougan Dr WISHAW ML2 ......158 C5
Douglas Av CAR/SHTL G32 ......112 C3
　GIF/THBK G46 ......145 F1
　JNSTN PA5 ......102 A2
　KKNTL G66 ......40 A2
　RUTH G73 ......130 B2
Douglas Crs AIRDRIE ML6 ......98 B3
　ERSK PA8 ......48 C1
　HMLTN ML3 ......180 D5
　UD/BTH/TAN G71 ......115 G4
Douglasdale EKILN G74 ......166 A3
Douglas Dr
　BAIL/MDB/MHD G69 ......93 G4
　BLSH ML4 ......136 C3
　BLTYR/CAMB G72 ......131 E5
　DRUM G15 ......50 A2
　EKILS G75 ......176 D1
　NMRNS G77 ......144 B4
　UD/BTH/TAN G71 ......152 B1
Douglas Drive La CSMK G45 ......129 E4
Douglas Gdns BSDN G61 ......34 B3
　GIF/THBK G46 ......145 F1
　UD/BTH/TAN G71 ......134 A2
Douglas Ga BLTYR/CAMB G72 ......131 F2
Douglas La CGLW G2 ......2 C4
Douglas Muir Dr MLNGV G62 ......16 A3
Douglas Muir Gdns
　MLNGV G62 ......16 A2
Douglas Muir Pl MLNGV G62 ......16 A2
Douglas Muir Rd CLYDBK G81 ......32 C1
　MLNGV G62 ......16 B3
Douglas Park Crs BSDN G61 ......34 D2
Douglas Park La HMLTN ML3 ......169 H1
Douglas Pl BSDN G61 ......34 C2
　HMLTN ML3 ......180 D2
　KKNTL G66 ......40 A3
Douglas Rd DMBTN G82 ......13 G2
　PSLYN/LNWD PA3 ......84 B1
Douglas St AIRDRIE ML6 ......98 B5
　BLTYR/CAMB G72 ......151 F4
　CGLW G2 ......2 C4
　HMLTN ML3 ......169 H1
　MLNGV G62 ......17 E4
　MTHW ML1 ......154 C3
　PSLY PA1 ......83 H5
　UD/BTH/TAN G71 ......115 G5
Dougray Pl BRHD/NEIL G78 ......124 B5
Dougrie Dr CSMK G45 ......129 E4
Dougrie Pl CSMK G45 ......129 F4
Dougrie Rd CSMK G45 ......128 D5
Dougrie St CSMK G45 ......129 F4
Dougrie Ter CSMK G45 ......129 E4
Doune Crs AIRDRIE ML6 ......119 E3
　BSHPBGS G64 ......38 A4
　NMRNS G77 ......144 A5
Doune Gdns MRYH/FIRH G20 ......66 D3
Doune Gardens La
　MRYH/FIRH G20 ......66 D3
Doune Park Wy CTBR ML5 ......96 C5
Doune Qd MRYH/FIRH G20 ......66 D3
Doune Ter CTBR ML5 ......74 A5
Dovecot PLKSW/MSWD G43 ......108 B4
Dovecote Vw KKNTL G66 ......40 C1
Dovecotwood KSYTH G65 ......8 B1
Doveholm DMBTN G82 ......13 F2
Doveholm Av DMBTN G82 ......13 G2
Dove Pl EKILS G75 ......177 E2
　KVGV G3 ......74 A4
Dove St PLK/PH/NH G53 ......125 F2
Dove Wynd BLSH ML4 ......116 C5
Dowan Rd CUMB G67 ......25 H4
Dowanhill St PTCK G11 ......66 B4
Dowan Rd MLNGV G62 ......35 H1
Dowanside La KVD/HLHD G12 ......66 B3
Dowanside Rd KVD/HLHD G12 ......66 B3
Downcraig Dr CSMK G45 ......128 C5
Downcraig Gv CSMK G45 ......128 D5
Downcraig Rd CSMK G45 ......128 C5
Downcraig Ter CSMK G45 ......129 E5
Downfield Dr HMLTN ML3 ......180 B1
Downfield Gdns
　UD/BTH/TAN G71 ......134 A5
Downfield St CAR/SHTL G32 ......111 H1
Downhill St KVD/HLHD G12 ......66 A3
Downiebrae Rd RUTH G73 ......111 E2
Downie Cl UD/BTH/TAN G71 ......115 G4
Downie St HMLTN ML3 ......180 D1
Downs St SPRGB/BLRNK G21 ......68 B2
Dowrie Crs PLK/PH/NH G53 ......106 C3
Draffen St MTHW ML1 ......155 E3
Drakemire Av CSMK G45 ......128 D3
Drakemire Dr CSMK G45 ......128 C5
Drake St DMNK/BRGTN G40 ......90 B5
Dreghorn St DEN/PKHD G31 ......91 F2
Drimnin Rd
　STPS/GTHM/RID G33 ......71 G1
Drive Rd GOV/IBX G51 ......87 F1
Drochil St ESTRH G34 ......71 H5
Drove Hl BALLOCH G68 ......25 E2
Drumabethie Rd AIRDRIE ML6 ......98 C1
Drumbeg Dr PLK/PH/NH G53 ......125 F1
Drumbeg Pth
　BLTYR/CAMB G72 ......168 B2
Drumbeg Ter MLNGV G62 ......16 B5
Drumbottie Rd
　SPRGB/BLRNK G21 ......68 D1
Drumby Crs
　CRMNK/CLK/EAG G76 ......145 G1
Drumcarn Dr MLNGV G62 ......16 D4
Drumcavel Rd
　BAIL/MDB/MHD G69 ......58 C1
Drumchapel Gdns DRUM G15 ......50 B1
Drumchapel Pl DRUM G15 ......50 C1

Drumchapel Rd DRUM G15 ......50 C1
Drumclair Pl AIRDRIE ML6 ......99 E2
Drumclog Av MLNGV G62 ......17 E1
Drumclog Gdns
　STPS/GTHM/RID G33 ......56 A5
Drumcross Rd BSHPTN PA7 ......29 G5
　PLK/PH/NH G53 ......106 D3
Drumduff EKILS G75 ......178 A5
Drumfearn Rd
　MRYH/FIRH G20 ......66 G1
Drumgelloch St AIRDRIE ML6 ......99 G1
Drumglass Vw KSYTH G65 ......24 D1
Drumhead Pl CAR/SHTL G32 ......112 A3
Drumhead Rd CAR/SHTL G32 ......112 A3
Drumhill KKNTL G66 ......22 B3
Drumilaw Rd RUTH G73 ......129 H2
Drumilaw Wy RUTH G73 ......129 H2
Drumlaken Av SMSTN G23 ......52 B2
Drumlaken Ct SMSTN G23 ......52 B2
Drumlaken St SMSTN G23 ......52 B2
Drumlanrig Av ESTRH G34 ......94 C1
Drumlanrig Crs
　BAIL/MDB/MHD G69 ......72 D2
Drumlanrig Pl ESTRH G34 ......94 C1
Drumlin Dr MLNGV G62 ......16 D5
Drumloch Gdns EKILS G75 ......178 B3
Drumlochy Rd
　STPS/GTHM/RID G33 ......70 B5
Drum Mains Pk BALLOCH G68 ......24 B5
Drummond Av RUTH G73 ......110 C4
Drummond Dr PSLY PA1 ......85 G5
　WISHAW ML2 ......174 A3
Drummond Hl EKILN G74 ......167 E2
Drummond Pl EKILN G74 ......167 E2
Drummore Av CTBR ML5 ......117 G1
Drummore Rd DRUM G15 ......33 H4
Drumnessie Ct BALLOCH G68 ......43 G1
Drumnessie Rd BALLOCH G68 ......43 G1
Drumnessie Vw BALLOCH G68 ......24 D5
Drumover Av AIRDRIE ML6 ......119 G3
Drumover Dr DEN/PKHD G31 ......91 H5
Drumoyne Av GOV/IBX G51 ......87 F2
Drumoyne Circ GOV/IBX G51 ......87 F2
Drumoyne Dr GOV/IBX G51 ......87 F1
Drumoyne Pl GOV/IBX G51 ......87 F2
Drumoyne Qd GOV/IBX G51 ......87 F2
Drumoyne Rd GOV/IBX G51 ......87 F2
Drumoyne Sq GOV/IBX G51 ......87 F1
Drumpark St CTBR ML5 ......95 G5
　GIF/THBK G46 ......126 C3
Drumpellier Av
　BAIL/MDB/MHD G69 ......114 A1
　CTBR ML5 ......96 B1
　CUMB G67 ......44 B1
Drumpellier Ct CUMB G67 ......44 B1
Drumpellier Crs CTBR ML5 ......96 A3
Drumpellier Gdns CUMB G67 ......44 B1
Drumpellier Gv CUMB G67 ......44 B1
Drumpellier Pl
　BAIL/MDB/MHD G69 ......94 A5
　CUMB G67 ......44 B1
Drumpellier Rd
　BAIL/MDB/MHD G69 ......113 H1
Drumpellier St
　STPS/GTHM/RID G33 ......69 G2
Drumreoch Dr
　GVH/MTFL G42 ......110 B5
Drumreoch Pl
　GVH/MTFL G42 ......110 B5
Drumry Rd CLYDBK G81 ......32 B5
Drumry Rd East DRUM G15 ......49 H1
Drumsack Av
　BAIL/MDB/MHD G69 ......58 B3
Drumsargard Rd RUTH G73 ......130 C2
Drumshangie Pl AIRDRIE ML6 ......76 B4
Drumshaw Dr CAR/SHTL G32 ......112 D4
Drumtrocher St KSYTH G65 ......8 B2
Drury St CGLE G1 ......2 E5
Dryad St GIF/THBK G46 ......126 B2
Dryburgh Av PSLYS PA2 ......103 F3
　RUTH G73 ......111 E5
Dryburgh Gdns
　MRYH/FIRH G20 ......67 E3
Dryburgh Hl EKILN G74 ......166 A4
Dryburgh La EKILN G74 ......166 A4
Dryburgh Pl CTBR ML5 ......96 C2
Dryburgh Rd BSDN G61 ......33 H2
　WISHAW ML2 ......173 H1
Dryburgh St HMLTN ML3 ......152 C4
Dryburgh Wk
　BAIL/MDB/MHD G69 ......42 B5
Dryburn Av
　CARD/HILL/MSPK G52 ......86 B4
Dryden St HMLTN ML3 ......152 C4
Drygait HWD PA9 ......120 B3
Drygate COWCAD G4 ......3 K5
Drygrange Rd
　STPS/GTHM/RID G33 ......70 D4
Drymen Pl KKNTL G66 ......40 A5
Drymen Rd BSDN G61 ......34 C5
Drymen St
　CARD/HILL/MSPK G52 ......87 E4
Drynoch Pl PPK/MIL G22 ......53 G4
Drysdale St SCOT G14 ......64 A1
Duart Dr EKILN G74 ......166 A2
　JNSTN PA5 ......102 A3
　NMRNS G77 ......144 D5
Duart St MRYH/FIRH G20 ......52 B3
Duart Wy
　BAIL/MDB/MHD G69 ......72 D2
Dubs Rd BRHD/NEIL G78 ......124 D4
Dubton St ESTRH G34 ......72 A5
Duchall Pl SCOT G14 ......64 C2
Duchess Ct HMLTN ML3 ......170 D3
Duchess Palace RUTH G73 ......111 F4
Duchess Rd RUTH G73 ......111 F3
Duchray Dr PSLY PA1 ......86 A5
Duchray La
　STPS/GTHM/RID G33 ......69 G5
Duchray St
　STPS/GTHM/RID G33 ......69 G5
Dudhope St
　STPS/GTHM/RID G33 ......71 E4

Dudley Dr CTBR ML5 ......73 H4
 KVD/HLHD G12 ......65 H3
Dudley La KVD/HLHD G12......65 H3
Duffus Dr CAR/SHTL G32 ......112 D4
Duffus St ESTRH G34 ......71 G5
Duffus Ter CAR/SHTL G32 ......112 D4
Duich Gdns SMSTN G23 ......52 D2
Duisdale Rd CAR/SHTL G32 ......112 D4
Dukes Ga UD/BTH/TAN G71 ......133 H5
Dukes Pl HMLTN ML3 ......180 D2
Dukes Rd
 BAIL/MDB/MHD G69 ......95 E4
 RUTH G73 ......130 C2
Duke St COWCAD G3 ......3 K6
 DEN/PKHD G31 ......91 G5
 HMLTN ML3 ......170 B2
 MTHW ML1 ......170 D2
 PSLYS PA2 ......104 B2
 WISHAW ML2 ......158 A4
Dulnain St BLTYR/CAMB G72 ......132 A2
Duisie Rd SPRGB/BLRNK G21 ......55 F5
Dumbarton Rd CLYDBK G81
 OLDK G60 ......30 B1
 OLDK G60 ......15 C5
 SCOT G14 ......64 B2
 SCOT G14 ......49 H5
Dumbreck Av
 PLKSD/SHW G41 ......107 H1
Dumbreck Ct
 PLKSD/SHW G41 ......107 H1
Dumbreck Pl KKNTL G66 ......40 B4
Dumbreck Rd
 PLKSD/SHW G41 ......108 A2
Dumbreck Sq PLKSD/SHW G41...87 F1
Dumbrock Rd MLNGV G62 ......16 B4
Dumbuck Gdns DMBTN G82 ......13 G5
Dumbuck Rd DMBTN G82 ......13 H5
Dumbuie Av DMBTN G82 ......13 G5
Dumfries Crs AIRDRIE ML6 ......98 A4
Dumgoyne Av MLNGV G62 ......16 B4
Dumgoyne Dr BSDN G61 ......34 A1
Dumgoyne Gdns MLNGV G62 ...16 D4
Dumgoyne Pl
 CRMNK/CLK/EAG G76 ......145 F5
Dunagoil Rd CSMK G45 ......129 E5
Dunagoil St CSMK G45 ......129 F5
Dunagoil Ter CSMK G45 ......147 F1
Dunalastair Dr
 STPS/GTHM/RID G33 ......70 C1
Dunan Pl STPS/GTHM/RID G33...93 F2
Dunard Rd RUTH G73 ......111 E5
Dunard St MRYH/FIRH G20 ......67 E3
Dunaskin St PTCK G11 ......66 B5
Dunavon Pl CTBR ML5 ......97 G5
Dunbar Av CTBR ML5 ......96 A5
 JNSTN PA5 ......101 F5
 RUTH G73 ......111 F5
Dunbar Dr MTHW ML1 ......172 B1
Dunbar Hl EKILN G74 ......165 H4
Dunbar La MTHW ML1 ......172 B1
Dunbar Pl EKILN G74 ......165 H4
Dunbar Rd PSLYS PA2 ......103 F3
Dunbar St HMLTN ML3 ......152 C5
Dunbeath Av
 BLTYR/CAMB G72 ......168 B2
Dunbeith Pl MRYH/FIRH G20 ...66 D2
Dunbeth Av CTBR ML5 ......97 E2
Dunbeth Rd CTBR ML5 ......97 E1
Dunblane Dr EKILN G74 ......166 C5
Dunblane Pl EKILN G74 ......166 C5
Dunblane St COWCAD G4 ......2 E2
Dunbritton Rd BALLOCH G68 ...25 G5
Duncan Av SCOT G14 ......64 D3
Duncan Ct MTHW ML1 ......154 C1
Duncan La SCOT G14 ......64 D3
Duncan La North SCOT G14 ...64 D3
Duncan La South SCOT G14 ...64 D3
Duncan McIntosh Rd
 BALLOCH G68 ......10 D3
Duncann ERSK PA8 ......47 H4
Duncansby Dr
 BLTYR/CAMB G72 ......168 B2
Duncansby Rd
 STPS/GTHM/RID G33 ......93 F3
Duncan St CLYDBK G81 ......31 H5
Duncarnock Av
 BRHD/NEIL G78 ......141 F3
Duncarnock Crs
 BRHD/NEIL G78 ......141 F3
Dunchattan Pl DEN/PKHD G31...90 C2
Dunchattan St
 DEN/PKHD G31 ......90 C2
Dunchurch Rd PSLY PA1 ......85 G4
Dunclutha Dr
 UD/BTH/TAN G71 ......152 B1
Dunclutha St
 DMNK/BRGTN G40 ......111 E2
Duncolm Pl MLNGV G62 ......16 B3
Duncombe St MRYH/FIRH G20...52 A2
Duncombe Vw CLYDBK G81 ...32 A1
Duncraig Crs JNSTN PA5 ......120 D1
Duncrub Dr BSHPBGS G64 ......54 B2
Duncruin St MRYH/FIRH G20 ...52 A2
Duncruin Ter MRYH/FIRH G20...52 C4
Duncryne Av CAR/SHTL G32 ...93 E5
Duncryne Gdns CAR/SHTL G32...93 F5
Duncryne Pl BSHPBGS G64 ...54 B3
Duncryne Rd CAR/SHTL G32 ...93 F5
Dundaff Hl BALLOCH G68 ......25 G5
Dundas Av BSHPBGS G64
Dundas Ct EKILN G74 ......166 B3
Dundashill COWCAD G4 ......67 G4
Dundas La CGLE G1 ......3 F4
Dundas St CGLE G1 ......3 F5
Dundee Dr
 CARD/HILL/MSPK G52 ......106 C1
Dundonald Av JNSTN PA5 ......101 E5
Dundonald Ct CTBR ML5 ......96 D5
 NMRNS G77 ......162 B1
Dundonald Dr HMLTN ML3 ......180 D1
Dundonald Pl
 BRHD/NEIL G78 ......141 E3
Dundonald Rd KVD/HLHD G12...66 B2
 PSLYN/LNWD PA3 ......84 D2
Dundonald St
 BLTYR/CAMB G72 ......151 F2

Dundrennan Dr AIRDRIE ML6 ...119 F2
Dundrennan Rd
 GVH/MTFL G42 ......109 E5
Dundyvan Ga CTBR ML5 ......96 D4
Dundyvan La WISHAW ML2 ...173 H5
Dundyvan Rd CTBR ML5 ......96 D4
Dundyvan Wy CTBR ML5 ......173 H5
Dunearn Pl PSLYS PA2 ......104 D1
Dunearn St COWCAD G4 ......67 G4
Dunedin Ct EKILS 165 F5
Dunedin Dr EKILS G75 ......165 H4
Dunedin Ter CLYDBK G81 ......49 F5
Dunellan Av
 BAIL/MDB/MHD G69 ......59 F1
Dunellan Ct
 BAIL/MDB/MHD G69 ......59 F1
Dunellan Crs
 BAIL/MDB/MHD G69 ......59 F1
Dunellan Dr CLYDBK G81 ......32 A1
Dunellan Gdns
 BAIL/MDB/MHD G69 ......59 F1
Dunellan Gv
 BAIL/MDB/MHD G69 ......59 F1
Dunellan Pl
 BAIL/MDB/MHD G69 ......59 F1
Dunellan Rd MLNGV G62 ......16 A3
Dunellan St
 CARD/HILL/MSPK G52 ......87 F4
Dungavel Gdns HMLTN ML3...170 B5
Dungeonhill Rd ESTRH G34 ...94 C1
Dunglass Av SCOT G14 ......64 D2
Dunglass La SCOT G14 ......64 D2
Dunglass La North SCOT G14...64 D2
Dunglass La South SCOT G14...64 D2
Dunglass Pl MLNGV G62 ......16 C2
 NMRNS G77 ......143 F5
Dunglass Sq EKILN G74 ......166 B2
Dungoil Av BALLOCH G68 ......25 F2
Dungoil Rd KKNTL G66 ......40 B4
Dungoyne St MRYH/FIRH G20...52 B3
Dunira St CAR/SHTL G32 ......112 A1
Dunivaig Rd
 STPS/GTHM/RID G33 ......93 F1
Dunkeld Av RUTH G73 ......111 E5
Dunkeld Dr BSDN G61 ......35 E2
Dunkeld Pl CTBR ML5 ......96 C5
 HMLTN ML3 ......168 D2
 NMRNS G77 ......162 C1
Dunkeld St DEN/PKHD G31 ...91 F5
Dunkenny Rd DRUM G15 ......33 E4
Dunlin EKILN G74 ......166 B2
 KVD/HLHD G12 ......51 H5
Dunlin Ct BLSH ML4 ......116 B4
Dunlin Crs CRG/CRSL/HOU PA6...80 D2
Dunlin Wy CTBR ML5 ......117 H2
Dunlop Crs UD/BTH/TAN G71...152 C1
Dunlop Gv UD/BTH/TAN G71...115 H4
Dunlop Pl MLNGV G62 ......16 D2
Dunlop St BLTYR/CAMB G72 ...132 B1
 CGLE G1 ......89 H3
 CGLW G2 ......3 F7
 PSLYN/LNWD PA3 ......82 B5
Dunmore Dr MLNGV G62 ......17 G5
Dunmore St CLYDBK G81 ......49 F3
Dunnachie Dr CTBR ML5 ......95 G5
Dunnet Av AIRDRIE ML6 ......76 A1
Dunnet Gv BLTYR/CAMB G72...168 C1
Dunnet Dr
 CRG/CRSL/HOU PA6 ......80 C2
Dunnichen Gdns
 BSHPBGS G64 ......55 G2
Dunnikier Wk BALLOCH G68...24 C4
Dunning St DEN/PKHD G31 ...91 G5
Dunnock Pl CTBR ML5 ......117 H1
Dunnottar Crs EKILN G74 ......165 H2
Dunnottar St EKILN G74 ......165 H2
 STPS/GTHM/RID G33 ......70 C4
Dunn St DEN/PKHD G31 ......91 F5
 DMNK/BRGTN G40 ......110 C1
 PSLY PA1 ......84 D4
Dunns Wood Rd CUMB G67 ...11 G3
Dunolie Pl
 BAIL/MDB/MHD G69 ......72 D1
Dunolly Dr NMRNS G77 ......161 G5
Dunolly St SPRGB/BLRNK G21...68 D5
Dunottar Av CTBR ML5 ......117 E2
Dunottar Pl CTBR ML5 ......117 E1
Dunphail Dr ESTRH G34 ......94 C1
Dunphail Rd ESTRH G34 ......94 C1
Dunragit St DEN/PKHD G31 ...91 F2
Dunrobin Av JNSTN PA5 ......102 B3
Dunrobin Ct EKILN G74 ......166 A2
Dunrobin Crs EKILN G74 ......166 A2
Dunrobin Dr EKILN G74 ......166 A2
Dunrobin Pl CTBR ML5 ......96 C2
Dunrobin Rd AIRDRIE ML6 ......99 E3
Dunrobin St DEN/PKHD G31 ...91 E4
Dunrod Hl EKILN G74 ......166 C2
Dunrod St CAR/SHTL G32 ......92 C5
Dunscore Brae HMLTN ML3 ...168 D3
Duns Crs WISHAW ML2 ......157 F4
Dunside Dr PLK/PH/NH G53 ...125 F1
Dunskaith Pl ESTRH G34 ......94 C1
Dunskaith St ESTRH G34 ......94 C1
Dunsmore Rd BSHPTN PA7 ...28 D4
Dunsmuir St GOV/IBX G51 ...88 A2
Duns Pth CTBR ML5 ......117 G1
Dunswin Av CLYDBK G81 ......31 F5
Dunsyre Pl SMSTN G23 ......52 D2
Dunsyre St
 STPS/GTHM/RID G33 ......91 H1
Duntarvie Av ESTRH G34 ......94 B1
Duntarvie Cl ESTRH G34 ......94 B1
Duntarvie Crs ESTRH G34 ......94 B1
Duntarvie Dr ESTRH G34 ......94 A1
Duntarvie Gdns ESTRH G34 ...94 B1
Duntarvie Gv ESTRH G34 ......94 B1
Duntarvie Pl ESTRH G34 ......94 A1
Duntarvie Qd ESTRH G34 ......94 B1
Duntarvie Rd ESTRH G34 ......94 A1
Dunterlie Av KNTSWD G13 ...50 B5
Dunterlie Ct BRHD/NEIL G78...124 B4
Duntiblae KKNTL G66 ......40 D1
Duntiblae Rd KKNTL G66 ......40 D1

Duntiglennan Rd CLYDBK G81...31 H2
Duntocher Rd BSDN G61 ......33 G2
 CLYDBK G81 ......31 H4
Duntreath Av DRUM G15 ......50 A2
 KNTSWD G13 ......49 H3
Duntreath Dr DRUM G15 ......50 A2
Duntreath Gdns DRUM G15 ...50 A2
Duntreath Gv DRUM G15 ......50 A2
Duntreath Ter KSYTH G65 ......8 B2
Duntroon St DEN/PKHD G31 ...91 E1
Dunure Dr HMLTN ML3 ......168 C5
 NMRNS G77 ......162 B1
 RUTH G73 ......129 G2
Dunure Pl CTBR ML5 ......116 B1
 NMRNS G77 ......162 B1
Dunure St CTBR ML5 ......116 B1
 MRYH/FIRH G20 ......52 C4
Dunvegan AIRDRIE ML6 ......75 H2
Dunvegan Av CTBR ML5 ......74 A5
 JNSTN PA5 ......102 A3
Dunvegan Dr BSHPBGS G64...37 H4
 NMRNS G77 ......161 G5
Dunvegan Pl EKILN G74 ......166 A2
 UD/BTH/TAN G71 ......114 C4
Dunvegan Qd RNFRW PA4 ...63 G2
Dunwan Av KNTSWD G13 ......50 A5
Dunwan Pl KNTSWD G13 ......50 A5
Dunwan Av CLYDBK G81 ......31 E4
Durham St PLKSD/SHW G41 ...88 C4
Durisdeer Dr HMLTN ML3 ......168 D4
Durness Av BSDN G61 ......35 E3
Durris Gdns CAR/SHTL G32 ...113 E1
Durrockstock Crs PSLYS PA2...103 E5
Durrockstock Rd PSLYS PA2...103 E5
Durward EKILN G74 ......167 H1
Durward Av PLKSD/SHW G41...108 C3
Durward Ct PLKSD/SHW G41...108 C3
Durward Crs PSLYS PA2 ......103 E2
Duthie Park Gdns
 KNTSWD G13 ......51 E5
Duthil St GOV/IBX G51 ......87 E3
Dyce Av AIRDRIE ML6 ......97 H5
Dyce La PTCK G11 ......65 H4
Dyer's La CGLE G1 ......90 A3
Dyfrig St BLTYR/CAMB G72 ...151 F2
Dykebar Av KNTSWD G13 ......50 B5
Dykebar Crs PSLYS PA2 ......105 E2
Dykehead Av AIRDRIE ML6 ...76 A4
Dykehead La
 STPS/GTHM/RID G33 ......93 E2
Dykehead Rd AIRDRIE ML6 ...76 A4
 BAIL/MDB/MHD G69 ......95 F4
 BALLOCH G68 ......25 H2
 KSYTH G65 ......7 E1
Dykehead St
 STPS/GTHM/RID G33 ......93 E2
Dykemuir Pl
 SPRGB/BLRNK G21 ......69 E2
Dykemuir Qd
 SPRGB/BLRNK G21 ......68 D2
Dykemuir St
 SPRGB/BLRNK G21 ......68 D2
Dyke Rd KNTSWD G13 ......50 B4
Dyke St BAIL/MDB/MHD G69...94 B4
 CTBR ML5 ......95 G5
Dysart Ct BALLOCH G68 ......24 C4
Dysart Dr BLTYR/CAMB G72 ...168 B2
Dysart Wy AIRDRIE ML6 ......99 H3

E

Eagle Crs BSDN G61 ......33 G2
Eaglesham Ct EKILS G75 ......165 E4
 GOV/IBX G51 ......88 D3
Eaglesham Pl GOV/IBX G51 ...88 D3
Eaglesham Rd
 CRMNK/CLK/EAG G76 ......176 A2
 EKILS G75 ......164 D4
 NMRNS G77 ......161 G2
Eagle St COWCAD G4 ......67 H4
Earlbank Av SCOT G14 ......64 D2
Earlbank La North SCOT G14...64 D2
Earlbank La South SCOT G14...64 D2
Earl Haig Rd
 CARD/HILL/MSPK G52 ......86 A2
Earl La SCOT G14 ......64 D3
Earl Pl BRWEIR PA11 ......79 G4
 SCOT G14 ......64 D2
Earlsburn Rd KKNTL G66 ......40 B4
Earlscourt
 BAIL/MDB/MHD G69 ......59 E2
Earlsgate CRG/CRSL/HOU PA6...80 C2
Earl's Ga UD/BTH/TAN G71 ...133 H4
Earl's Hl BALLOCH G68 ......25 F3
Earlspark Av
 PLKSW/MSWD G43 ......128 A1
Earlston Av
 SPRGB/BLRNK G21 ......68 C5
Earlston Crs CTBR ML5 ......117 F1
Earlston Pl SPRGB/BLRNK G21...68 C5
Earlston St WISHAW ML2 ......157 F4
Earl St SCOT G14 ......64 C2
Earlybraes Gdns
 STPS/GTHM/RID G33 ......93 E3
Earn Av BLSH ML4 ......116 A3
 BSDN G61 ......35 E4
 RNFRW PA4 ......63 H4
Earnbrae Gdns
Earnock Av MTHW ML1 ......154 A3
Earnock Gdns HMLTN ML3...169 E4
Earnock Rd HMLTN ML3 ......168 D3
Earnock St HMLTN ML3 ......169 F1
 STPS/GTHM/RID G33 ......69 G4
Earnside St CAR/SHTL G32 ...92 C4
Earn St STPS/GTHM/RID G33...69 H4
Easdale EKILN G74 ......179 E1
Easdale Dr CAR/SHTL G32 ......92 A5
Easdale Pl CTBR ML5 ......117 G1
Easdale Ri HMLTN ML3 ......169 G4
Easdale Rd NMRNS G77 ......143 G5
East Academy St
 WISHAW ML2 ......174 A3

East Av AIRDRIE ML6 ......77 H3
 BLTYR/CAMB G72 ......151 H5
 MTHW ML1 ......137 G5
 RNFRW PA4 ......63 G3
 UD/BTH/TAN G71 ......116 B4
Eastbank Dr CAR/SHTL G32 ...92 D4
East Barns St CLYDBK G81 ...49 G3
East Bath La CGLW G2 ......3 F4
East Buchanan St PSLY PA1...84 C4
Eastburn Crs
 SPRGB/BLRNK G21 ......55 E5
Eastburn Rd
 SPRGB/BLRNK G21 ......69 E1
East Burnside St KSYTH G65 ...8 B2
East Campbell St CGLE G1 ...3 K7
Eastcote Av SCOT G14 ......65 F2
Eastcroft RUTH G73 ......111 E4
Eastcroft Ter
 SPRGB/BLRNK G21 ......68 D2
East Dean St BLSH ML4 ......136 A2
Eastend Av MTHW ML1 ......155 G5
Easterbrae MTHW ML1 ......171 G1
Easter Craigs DEN/PKHD G31...91 E1
Easter Crs WISHAW ML2 ......174 D1
Easter Garngaber Rd
 KKNTL G66 ......40 B3
Easterhill Pl CAR/SHTL G32...112 A1
Easterhill St CAR/SHTL G32 ...112 A1
Easterhouse Pl
 BAIL/MDB/MHD G69 ......94 B1
Eastermains KKNTL G66 ......22 A5
Easter Ms UD/BTH/TAN G71...133 F2
Easter Queenslie Rd
 STPS/GTHM/RID G33 ......93 F1
Easter Rd
 CRMNK/CLK/EAG G76 ......146 B5
Easterton Av
Easter Wood Crs
 UD/BTH/TAN G71 ......115 E4
Easterwood Pl CTBR ML5 ......96 D3
Eastfield Av
 BLTYR/CAMB G72 ......130 D3
Eastfield Crs DMBTN G82 ......13 G5
Eastfield Pl DMBTN G82 ......13 G5
Eastfield Rd BALLOCH G68 ...25 G2
 SPRGB/BLRNK G21 ......68 B2
Eastfield Ter BLSH ML4 ......136 C3
Eastgate BAIL/MDB/MHD G69...73 F1
East Ga WISHAW ML2 ......158 A1
East George St CTBR ML5 ...97 E1
East Glebe Ter HMLTN ML3...170 A3
East Greenlees Av
 BLTYR/CAMB G72 ......131 H4
East Greenlees Crs
 BLTYR/CAMB G72 ......131 G4
East Greenlees Dr
 BLTYR/CAMB G72 ......131 G4
East Greenlees Gv
 BLTYR/CAMB G72 ......131 E5
East Greenlees Rd
 BLTYR/CAMB G72 ......131 G4
East Hallhill Rd
 STPS/GTHM/RID G33 93
East Hamilton St
 WISHAW ML2 ......174 A3
East High St AIRDRIE ML6 ......98 A3
 KKNTL G66 ......21 E4
East Kilbride Rd
 BLTYR/CAMB G72 ......131 E5
 CRMNK/CLK/EAG G76 ......147 E1
 RUTH G73 ......130 C3
East La PSLY PA1 ......85 E4
Eastlea Pl AIRDRIE ML6 ......98 C3
East Mains Rd EKILN G74 ...166 B3
East Milton Gv EKILS G75 ...165 G4
Eastmuir St CAR/SHTL G32 ...92 C4
 WISHAW ML2 ......174 D2
Easton Pl CTBR ML5 ......97 E4
East Rd KLBCH PA10 ......100 B3
East Scott Ter HMLTN ML3 ...170 A4
Eastside KKNTL G66 ......21 F4
East Springfield Ter
 BSHPBGS 55 E3
East Stewart Pl CTBR ML5 ...97 F3
East Stewart St CTBR ML5 ...97 F3
East Thomson St CLYDBK G81...32 A5
East Thornlie St
 WISHAW ML2 ......174 A3
East Wellbrae Crs
 HMLTN ML3 ......169 G4
East Wellington St
 DEN/PKHD G31 ......91 G4
Eastwood Av GIF/THBK G46 ...127 F5
 PLKSD/SHW G41 ......108 C4
Eastwood Crs GIF/THBK G46...126 D3
Eastwood Dr WISHAW ML2 ...158 B5
Eastwoodmains Rd
 GIF/THBK G46 ......145 F1
Eastwood Rd
 BAIL/MDB/MHD G69 ......59 F1
Eastwood Vw
 BLTYR/CAMB G72 ......132 D1
Easwald Bank KLBCH PA10...100 C4
Ebroch Dr KSYTH G65 ......8 C2
Ebroch Pk KSYTH G65 ......8 C2
Eccles St PPK/MIL G22 ......54 A5
Eckford St CAR/SHTL G32 ...92 B5
Eday St PPK/MIL G22 ......54 A3
Edderton Pl ESTRH G34 ......93 H2
Edderton Wy ESTRH G34 ......93 H2
Eddlewood Ct
 STPS/GTHM/RID G33 ......93 E3
Eddlewood Pth
 STPS/GTHM/RID G33 ......93 E3
Eddlewood Pl
 STPS/GTHM/RID G33 ......93 E3
Eddlewood Rd
 STPS/GTHM/RID G33 ......93 E3
Eden Dr EKILS G75 ......177 E2
Eden Gdns EKILS G75 ......177 E1
Eden Gv EKILS G75 ......177 E1
Edenhall Ct NMRNS G77 ......161 G3
Edenhall Gv NMRNS G77 ......161 G3

Eden La STPS/GTHM/RID G33...69 G5
Eden Pk UD/BTH/TAN G71 ...134 A5
Eden Pl RNFRW PA4 ......63 H4
Edenside BALLOCH G68 ......10 D3
Eden St STPS/GTHM/RID G33...69 G5
Edenwood Dr DEN/PKHD G31...91 H4
Edgam Dr
 CARD/HILL/MSPK G52 ......86 D4
Edgefauld Av
 SPRGB/BLRNK G21 ......68 C2
Edgefauld Dr
 SPRGB/BLRNK G21 ......68 C2
Edgefauld Pl
 SPRGB/BLRNK G21 ......68 C1
Edgefauld Rd
 SPRGB/BLRNK G21 ......68 C2
Edgehill La PTCK G11 ......65 H2
Edgehill Rd BSDN G61 ......34 B2
 PTCK G11 ......65 G2
Edgemont St
 PLKSD/SHW G41 ......108 D4
Edinbeg Av
 CAR/SHTL G32 ......110 B4
Edinbeg Pl CVH/MTFL G42 ...110 B4
Edington Gdns
 BAIL/MDB/MHD G69 ......42 A5
Edington St COWCAD G4 ......67 C4
Edison St
 CARD/HILL/MSPK G52 ......85 H1
Edmiston Dr GOV/IBX G51 ...87 H3
 PSLYN/LNWD PA3 ......81 G5
Edmonstone Dr KSYTH G65 ...8 B3
Edmonton Ter EKILS G75 ......165 H5
Edmund Kean EKILN G74 ...149 H5
Edrom Ct CAR/SHTL G32 ......92 A4
Edrom St CAR/SHTL G32 ......92 A5
Edward Av RNFRW PA4 ......63 G2
Edward St
 STPS/GTHM/RID G33 ......71 E1
Edward St
 BAIL/MDB/MHD G69 ......95 E4
 CLYDBK G81 ......49 H4
 HMLTN ML3 ......170 A3
 KSYTH G65 ......8 B1
 MTHW ML1 ......172 A1
Edwin St GOV/IBX G51 ......88 C4
Edzell Ct SCOT G14 ......65 E4
Edzell Dr JNSTN PA5 ......102 C2
 NMRNS G77 ......161 H1
Edzell Gdns BSHPBGS G64 ...54 A3
 WISHAW ML2 ......173 H5
Edzell Pl SCOT G14 ......65 E3
Edzell St CTBR ML5 ......96 A5
 SCOT G14 ......65 E4
Egidia Av GIF/THBK G46 ......127 E5
Egilsay Pl PPK/MIL G22 ......53 H5
Egilsay St PPK/MIL G22 ......53 H5
Egilsay Ter PPK/MIL G22 ......53 H5
Eglinton Ct CBLS G5 ......89 G4
Eglinton Dr GIF/THBK G46 ...127 F5
Eglinton St CTBR ML5 ......97 E2
 GBLS G5 ......89 G5
Egmont Pk EKILS G75 ......177 F1
Eider EKILN G74 ......179 E1
Eider Av EKILS G75 ......177 F1
Eider Gv EKILS G75 ......177 F1
Eider Pl EKILS G75 ......177 F1
Eighth St UD/BTH/TAN G71 ...114 D3
Eildon Crs AIRDRIE ML6 ......119 G3
Eildon Dr BRHD/NEIL G78 ...142 B1
Eildon Rd KKNTL G66 ......21 H5
Eileen Gdns BSHPBGS G64 ...54 D1
Elcho St DMNK/BRGTN G40 ...90 C3
Elderbank BSDN G61 ......34 B5
Elder Crs BLTYR/CAMB G72 ...132 B3
Elder Gv UD/BTH/TAN G71 ...115 G5
Elder Grove Av GOV/IBX G51...87 E2
Elder Grove Ct GOV/IBX G51...87 E2
Elder Grove Pl GOV/IBX G51...87 E2
Elderpark Gdns GOV/IBX G51...87 G2
Elderpark Gv GOV/IBX G51 ...87 G2
Elderpark St GOV/IBX G51 ...87 G2
Elderslie St KVGV G3 ......89 E1
Elder St GOV/IBX G51 ......87 G2
Elders Wy WISHAW ML2 ......158 A3
Elder Wy MTHW ML1 ......138 A5
Eldin Pl JNSTN PA5 ......79 H5
 JNSTN PA5
Eldon Gdns BSHPBGS G64 ...54 B2
Eldon St KVGV G3 ......66 D4
Elgin Av EKILN G74 ......166 C2
Elgin Gdns
 CRMNK/CLK/EAG G76 ......146 A2
Elgin Pl AIRDRIE ML6 ......98 A3
 CTBR ML5 ......117 E1
 KSYTH G65 ......8 B1
Elgin Rd BSDN G61 ......34 D5
Elgin St DEN/PKHD G31 ......90 D2
Elgin Ter HMLTN ML3 ......168 D1
Elgin Wy BLSH ML4 ......135 H1
Elibank St
 STPS/GTHM/RID G33 ......70 B5
Elie St BLTYR/CAMB G72 ......168 C2
 KVD/HLHD G12 ......66 B4
Eliot Ter HMLTN ML3 ......170 A3
Eliot St KVGV G3 ......88 D1
Eliot Ct MTHW ML1 ......154 C1
Elizabeth Av KKNTL G66 ......5 F4
Elizabeth Crs GIF/THBK G46...126 D4
Elizabeth Qd MTHW ML1 ......137 E2
Elizabeth St GOV/IBX G51 ...88 B3
Elizabeth Wynd HMLTN ML3...180 C1
Ella Gdns BLSH ML4 ......136 B3
Ellangowan Ct MLNGV G62 ...17 E3
Ellangowan Rd MLNGV G62 ...17 E3
 PLKSD/SHW G41 ......108 A4
Ellergreen Rd BSDN G61 ......34 B4
Ellerslie St JNSTN PA5 ......101 H3
Ellesmere St PPK/MIL G22 ...67 F2
Elliot Av GIF/THBK G46 ......127 F5
 PSLYS PA2 ......102 C5
Elliot Crs EKILN G74 ......167 E3
Elliot Dr GIF/THBK G46 ......127 F5

Elliot St *KVGV* G3 ... 88 D2
Elisiland *EKILN* G74 ... 167 G2
KKNTL C66 ... 22 B3
Elisiland Av *CLYDBK* G81 ... 32 B5
Elisiland Crs *RUTH* G73 ... 129 G2
Elisiland Dr *BLTYR/CAMB* G72 151 E4
KKNTL G66 ... 22 A3
Elisiland Rd
CRMNK/CLK/EAG G76 ... 145 H5
CUMB G67 ... 26 D3
PLKSW/MSWD G43 ... 127 G1
Elisiland Farm Rd
BAIL/MDB/MHD G69 ... 94 C5
Ellismuir Pl
BAIL/MDB/MHD G69 ... 94 B5
Ellismuir Rd
BAIL/MDB/MHD G69 ... 94 B5
Ellismuir St *CTBR* ML5 ... 116 A1
Ellismuir Wy
UD/BTH/TAN G71 ... 115 F3
Ellis St *CTBR* ML5 ... 96 D3
Elliston Av *PLK/PH/NH* G53 ... 125 H2
Elliston Crs *PLK/PH/NH* G53 ... 125 H2
Elliston Dr *PLK/PH/NH* G53 ... 125 H2
Elliston Pl *HWWD* PA9 ... 120 A4
Elliston Rd *HWWD* PA9 ... 120 A4
Ellis Wy *MTHW* ML1 ... 155 H5
Ellon Dr *PSLYN/LNWD* PA3 ... 101 H1
Ellon Gv *PSLYN/LNWD* PA3 ... 84 C2
Elrig *EKILS* G75 ... 178 A3
Elm Av *KKNTL* G66 ... 39 H2
RNFRW PA4 ... 63 F2
Elm Bank *BSHPBGS* G64 ... 55 E2
KKNTL G66 ... 21 F5
Elmbank Av
UD/BTH/TAN G71 ... 115 G5
Elmbank Crs *CGLW* G2 ... 2 B3
HMLTN ML3 ... 169 F1
Elmbank St *BLSH* ML4 ... 135 H2
CGLW G2 ... 2 B4
Elm Ct *HMLTN* ML3 ... 181 F4
Elm Crs *UD/BTH/TAN* G71 ... 116 A5
Elm Dr *AIRDRIE* ML6 ... 119 F1
BLTYR/CAMB G72 ... 131 H1
JNSTN PA5 ... 121 H1
Elmfoot St *GBLS* G5 ... 110 A2
Elm Gdns *BSDN* G61 ... 34 B2
Elmhurst *MTHW* ML1 ... 171 G1
Elmira Rd
BAIL/MDB/MHD G69 ... 58 B4
Elm La East *SCOT* G14 ... 65 E3
Elm La West *SCOT* G14 ... 65 E3
Elm Lea *JNSTN* PA5 ... 102 A2
Elmore Av *LNPK/KPK* G44 ... 128 C3
Elm Pl *EKILS* G75 ... 177 H2
Elm Qd *AIRDRIE* ML6 ... 99 E3
Elm Rd *BRWEIR* PA11 ... 79 H1
CLYDBK G81 ... 31 H3
DMBTN G82 ... 13 F3
MTHW ML1 ... 137 F5
PSLYS PA2 ... 104 D3
RUTH G73 ... 130 A3
Elmslie Ct
BAIL/MDB/MHD G69 ... 94 B5
Elm St *BLTYR/CAMB* G72 ... 151 E4
CRMNK/CLK/EAG G76 ... 146 A4
CTBR ML5 ... 97 F4
KKNTL G66 ... 40 A2
MTHW ML1 ... 154 C3
SCOT G14 ... 65 E3
Elmvale Rw
SPRGB/BLRNK G21 ... 68 C3
Elmvale st *SPRGB/BLRNK* G21 68 B3
Elm View Ct *BLSH* ML4 ... 136 C3
Elm Wk *BSDN* G61 ... 34 B2
Elm Wy *BLTYR/CAMB* G72 ... 132 B3
Elmwood *WISHAW* ML2 ... 173 H4
Elmwood Av *NMRNS* G77 ... 144
PTCK G11 ... 65 G2
Elmwood Ct
UD/BTH/TAN G71 ... 134 B5
Elmwood La *PTCK* G11 ... 65 G2
Elphinstone Pl *EKILS* G75 ... 178 C2
Elphinstone Pl *GOV/IBX* G51 ... 88 B2
Elphinstone Rd
GIF/THBK G46 ... 144 D3
Elphin St *SMSTN* G23 ... 52 C2
Elrig Rd *LNPK/KPK* G44 ... 128 A3
Elspeth Gdns *BSHPBGS* G64 ... 55 F1
Eltham St *PPK/MIL* G22 ... 67 G3
Elvan Pl *EKILS* G75 ... 177 F1
Elvan St *CAR/SHTL* G32 ... 92 A4
MTHW ML1 ... 154 C4
Embo Dr *KNTSWD* G13 ... 50 C5
Emerald Ter *BLSH* ML4 ... 135 H3
Emerson Rd *BSHPBGS* G64 ... 54 D2
Emerson Rd West
BSHPBGS G64 ... 54 D2
Emily Dr *MTHW* ML1 ... 171 H1
Emma Jay Rd *BLSH* ML4 ... 136 B4
Empire Wy *MTHW* ML1 ... 154 B1
Endfield Av *KVD/HLHD* G12 ... 52 A5
Endrick Bank *BSHPBGS* G64 ... 37 H4
Endrick Dr *BSDN* G61 ... 34 C4
PSLY PA1 ... 85 H4
Endrick St *SPRGB/BLRNK* G21 ... 68 A3
English Rw *AIRDRIE* ML6 ... 118 D2
English St *WISHAW* ML2 ... 173 E2
Ennerdale *EKILS* G75 ... 177 E2
Ennisfree Rd
BLTYR/CAMB G72 ... 151 G2
Ensay St *PPK/MIL* G22 ... 54 A4
Enterkin st *CAR/SHTL* G32 ... 92 A5
Eriboll Pl *PPK/MIL* G22 ... 53 G4
Eriboll St *PPK/MIL* G22 ... 53 G4
Ericht Rd *PLKSW/MSWD* G43 ... 127 F2
Eriska Av *SCOT* G14 ... 64 B1
Eriskay Av *HMLTN* ML3 ... 169 E3
NMRNS G77 ... 143 G5
Eriskay Crs *NMRNS* G77 ... 143 G5
Eriskay Dr *OLDK* G60 ... 30 D3
Ermelo Gdns *EKILS* G75 ... 177 G4
Erradale Pl *PPK/MIL* G22 ... 53 F4
Erradale St *PPK/MIL* G22 ... 53 F4
Errogie St *ESTRH* G34 ... 94 A1
Errol Gdns *GBLS* G5 ... 89 H5
Erskine Av *PLKSD/SHW* G41 ... 88 A5

Erskine Br *OLDK* G60 ... 30 B3
Erskine Crs *AIRDRIE* ML6 ... 98 A4
Erskinefauld Rd
PSLYN/LNWD PA3 ... 82 A3
Erskine Ferry Rd *OLDK* G60 ... 30 B3
Erskine Rd *GIF/THBK* G46 ... 145 E4
Erskine Sq
CARD/HILL/MSPK G52 ... 86 A2
Ervie St *ESTRH* G34 ... 94 B2
Esdaile Ct *MTHW* ML1 ... 137 H4
Esk Av *RNFRW* PA4 ... 63 H4
Eskbank St *CAR/SHTL* G32 ... 92 B3
Esk Di *EKILN* G74 ... 165 H2
Eskdale Dr *RUTH* G73 ... 111 G5
Eskdale Rd *BSDN* G61 ... 51 E1
Eskdale St *GVH/MTFL* G42 ... 109 G3
Esk Dr *PSLYS* PA2 ... 102 D3
Esk St *SCOT* G14 ... 64 A1
Esmond St *KVGV* G3 ... 66 B5
Espedair St *PSLYS* PA2 ... 104 B1
Espieside Crs *CTBR* ML5 ... 96 B1
Essenside Av *DRUM* G15 ... 50 D1
Essex Dr *SCOT* G14 ... 65 F2
Essex La *SCOT* G14 ... 65 F3
Esslemont Av *SCOT* G14 ... 64 C2
Estate Qd *CAR/SHTL* G32 ... 112 D4
Estate Rd *CAR/SHTL* G32 ... 112 D4
Etive Av *BSDN* G61 ... 35 E4
HMLTN ML3 ... 169 F4
Etive Ct *CLYDBK* G81 ... 32 B3
CUMB G67 ... 44 A2
Etive Crs *BSHPBGS* G64 ... 55 E2
CUMB G67 ... 44 A2
WISHAW ML2 ... 174 A5
Etive Dr *AIRDRIE* ML6 ... 98 B1
BSHPTN PA7 ... 46 B1
CUMB G67 ... 44 A2
GIF/THBK G46 ... 145 G1
Etive St *CAR/SHTL* G32 ... 92 B4
WISHAW ML2 ... 174 A4
Etna St *WISHAW* ML2 ... 172 D1
Eton La *KVD/HLHD* G12 ... 66 D4
Ettrick Av *BLSH* ML4 ... 116 D5
RNFRW PA4 ... 63 H4
Ettrick Crs *RUTH* G73 ... 111 F5
BSHPTN PA7 ... 46 B1
Ettrick Hi *EKILN* G74 ... 166 D2
Ettrick Pl *PLKSW/MSWD* G43 ... 108 C5
Ettrick St *WISHAW* ML2 ... 156 D5
Ettrick Ter *JNSTN* PA5 ... 120 D1
Evan Crs *GIF/THBK* G46 ... 127 G5
Evan Dr *GIF/THBK* G46 ... 145 G1
Evanton Dr *GIF/THBK* G46 ... 126 A4
Evanton Pl *GIF/THBK* G46 ... 126 A4
Everard Ct *SPRGB/BLRNK* G21 ... 54 B4
Everard Dr *SPRGB/BLRNK* G21 ... 54 B5
Everard Pl *SPRGB/BLRNK* G21 ... 54 B4
Everard Qd *SPRGB/BLRNK* G21 ... 54 B4
Eversley St *CAR/SHTL* G32 ... 112 B1
Everton Rd *PLK/PH/NH* G53 ... 106 D2
Ewart Crs *HMLTN* ML3 ... 169 F2
Ewart La *HMLTN* ML3 ... 169 G4
Ewing Pl *DEN/PKHD* G31 ... 91 F4
Ewing St *KLBCH* PA10 ... 100 B3
RUTH G73 ... 110 D5
Ewing Wk *MLNGV* G62 ... 17 G4
Excelsior St *MTHW* ML1 ... 173 E2
MTHW ML1 ... 172 D3
Exchange Pl *CGLE* G1 ... 3 F5
Exeter Dr *PTCK* G11 ... 65 H4
Exeter La *PTCK* G11 ... 65 H4
Exeter St *CTBR* ML5 ... 96 D4
Eynort St *PPK/MIL* G22 ... 53 F4
Eyrepoint Ct
STPS/GTHM/RID G33 ... 92 B1

F

Factory Rd *MTHW* ML1 ... 154 D5
Fagan Ct *BLTYR/CAMB* G72 ... 151 H1
Faifley Rd *CLYDBK* G81 ... 32 B1
Fairbairn Crs *GIF/THBK* G46 ... 126 D5
Fairburn St *CAR/SHTL* G32 ... 92 A5
Fairfax Av *LNPK/KPK* G44 ... 128 D2
Fairfield Ct
CRMNK/CLK/EAG G76 ... 145 H5
Fairfield Dr
CRMNK/CLK/EAG G76 ... 145 H5
RNFRW PA4 ... 63 G5
Fairfield Gdns *GOV/IBX* G51 ... 87 G1
Fairfield Pl *EKILN* G74 ... 165 G5
GOV/IBX G51 ... 87 G1
HMLTN ML3 ... 169 H5
UD/BTH/TAN G71 ... 134 C5
Fairfield St *GOV/IBX* G51 ... 87 G1
Fairford Dr *CUMB* G67 ... 44 C2
Fairhaven Av *AIRDRIE* ML6 ... 99 F3
Fairhaven Rd *SMSTN* G23 ... 52 D3
Fairhill Av *HMLTN* ML3 ... 169 H4
Fairhill Crs *HMLTN* ML3 ... 169 H4
Fairhill Pl *HMLTN* ML3 ... 180 B1
Fairholm Av *HMLTN* ML3 ... 171 H4
Fairholm St *CAR/SHTL* G32 ... 112 A1
Fairley St *GOV/IBX* G51 ... 88 A3
Fairlie *EKILN* G74 ... 166 A3
Fairlie Park Dr *PTCK* G11 ... 65 H4
Fair Oaks
CRMNK/CLK/EAG G76 ... 147 F2
Fairway *BSDN* G61 ... 33 E3
Fairway Av *PSLYS* PA2 ... 104 A5
The Fairways *JNSTN* PA5 ... 121 E2
UD/BTH/TAN G71 ... 134 D4
Fairways Vw *CLYDBK* G81 ... 32 C1
Fairweather Pl *NMRNS* G77 ... 161 G2
Fairyknowe Ct
UD/BTH/TAN G71 ... 134 C5
Fairyknowe Gdns
UD/BTH/TAN G71 ... 134 C5
Faith Av *BRWEIR* PA11 ... 78 C1
Falconbridge Rd *EKILN* G74 ... 167 F1
Falcon Crs *PSLYN/LNWD* PA3 ... 83 G4
Falconer Ter *HMLTN* ML3 ... 169 H4
Falcon Rd *JNSTN* PA5 ... 121 E3

Falcon Ter *MRYH/FIRH* G20 ... 52 B3
Falcon Terrace La
MRYH/FIRH G20 ... 52 B3
Falfield St *GBLS* G5 ... 89 F5
Falkland Av *NMRNS* G77 ... 144 D4
Falkland Crs *BSHPBGS* G64 ... 55 G3
Falkland Dr *EKILN* G74 ... 165 H4
Falkland La *KVD/HLHD* G12 ... 66 A4
Falkland Pk *EKILN* G74 ... 166 A4
Falkland Pl *CTBR* ML5 ... 117 E1
EKILN G74 ... 166 A4
Falkland St *KVD/HLHD* G12 ... 66 A4
Falloch Pl *WISHAW* ML2 ... 158 A4
Falloch Rd *BSDN* G61 ... 50 D1
GVH/MTFL G42 ... 109 F5
MLNGV G62 ... 16 C2
Fallside Av *UD/BTH/TAN* G71 ... 134 D1
Fallside Rd *UD/BTH/TAN* G71 ... 134 B5
Falside Av *PSLYS* PA2 ... 104 B3
Falside Rd *CAR/SHTL* G32 ... 112 B2
PSLYS PA2 ... 104 A3
Falstaff *EKILN* G74 ... 149 H5
Faraday Av *WISHAW* ML2 ... 174 B2
Fara St *SMSTN* G23 ... 53 E3
Farie St *RUTH* G73 ... 110 C4
Farm Ct *UD/BTH/TAN* G71 ... 134 C3
Farm Crs *MTHW* ML1 ... 138 C3
Farme Castle Ct *RUTH* G73 ... 111 F3
Farmeloan Rd *RUTH* G73 ... 111 E3
Farmgate Sq *BLSH* ML4 ... 135 G3
Farmington Av *CAR/SHTL* G32 ... 93 E4
Farmington Gdns
CAR/SHTL G32 ... 93 E4
Farmington Gv *CAR/SHTL* G32 ... 93 E4
Farm La *BLSH* ML4 ... 135 G4
Farm Pk *KKNTL* G66 ... 40 A4
Farm Rd *BLTYR/CAMB* G72 ... 151 G4
CLYDBK G81 ... 31 E4
HMLTN ML3 ... 169 E1
PLKSD/SHW G41 ... 88 A4
Farm St *MTHW* ML1 ... 154 C3
Farm Ter *HMLTN* ML3 ... 169 E1
Farndale *EKILN* G74 ... 165 H2
Farne Dr *LNPK/KPK* G44 ... 128 C3
Farnell St *COWCAD* G4 ... 67 G4
Farrier Ct *JNSTN* PA5 ... 101 G3
Faskally Av *BSHPBGS* G64 ... 37 F5
Faskin Crs *PLK/PH/NH* G53 ... 106 A5
Faskine Av *AIRDRIE* ML6 ... 118 C2
Faskin Pl *PLK/PH/NH* G53 ... 106 A5
Faskin Rd *PLK/PH/NH* G53 ... 106 A5
Fasque Pl *DRUM* G15 ... 32 D4
Fauldhouse St *GBLS* G5 ... 110 A1
Faulds *BAIL/MDB/MHD* G69 ... 94 B4
Faulds Gdns
BAIL/MDB/MHD G69 ... 94 B4
Fauldshead Rd *RNFRW* PA4 ... 63 F3
Fauldspark Crs
BAIL/MDB/MHD G69 ... 94 B3
Fauldswood Crs *PSLYS* PA2 ... 103 G3
Fauldswood Dr *PSLYS* PA2 ... 103 G3
Faulkner Gv *MTHW* ML1 ... 156 C2
Fearnach Pl *MRYH/FIRH* G20 ... 52 A4
Fearnmore Rd
MRYH/FIRH G20 ... 52 C4
Fells View AV *KKNTL* G66 ... 21 H4
Felton Pl *KNTSWD* G13 ... 50 A5
Fendoch St *CAR/SHTL* G32 ... 92 B5
Fenella St *CAR/SHTL* G32 ... 92 C4
Fennsbank Av *RUTH* G73 ... 130 C4
Fenwick Dr *BRHD/NEIL* G78 ... 142 C1
HMLTN ML3 ... 181 E1
Fenwick Pl *GIF/THBK* G46 ... 126 C5
Fenwick Rd *GIF/THBK* G46 ... 127 E4
Ferclay St *CLYDBK* G81 ... 32 C1
Fereneze Av *BRHD/NEIL* G78 ... 124 A4
CRMNK/CLK/EAG G76 ... 145 H2
RNFRW PA4 ... 84 D1
Fereneze Crs *HMLTN* ML3 ... 169 E2
Fereneze Dr *PSLYS* PA2 ... 103 H5
Fereneze Gv *BRHD/NEIL* G78 ... 124 A4
Fereneze Rd *BRHD/NEIL* G78 ... 140 A3
Fergus Av *PSLYN/LNWD* PA3 ... 83 H4
Fergus Ct *MRYH/FIRH* G20 ... 66 D2
Fergus Dr *MRYH/FIRH* G20 ... 66 D2
PSLYN/LNWD PA3 ... 83 H4
Ferguslie *PSLY* PA1 ... 83 G5
Ferguslie Park Av
PSLYN/LNWD PA3 ... 83 F5
Ferguslie Park Crs
PSLYN/LNWD PA3 ... 83 G5
Ferguslie Wk *PSLY* PA1 ... 83 G5
Fergus La *MLNGV* G62 ... 17 G4
RNFRW PA4 ... 63 G5
Ferguson Dr *MTHW* ML1 ... 171 H2
Ferguson St *AIRDRIE* ML6 ... 76 B4
JNSTN PA5 ... 101 G3
RNFRW PA4 ... 63 F2
Ferguston Rd *BSDN* G61 ... 34 C4
Fernan St *CAR/SHTL* G32 ... 92 A4
Fern Av *BSHPBGS* G64 ... 55 E3
ERSK PA8 ... 47 G4
KKNTL G66 ... 39 H2
First Av *BSDN* G61 ... 34 D3
DMBTN G82 ... 13 H5
KKNTL G66 ... 40 A3
LNPK/KPK G44 ... 128 A1
RNFRW PA4 ... 63 F4
STPS/GTHM/RID G33 ... 70 C1
UD/BTH/TAN G71 ... 115 E4
Fernbank Av
BLTYR/CAMB G72 ... 131 H3
Fernbank St *PPK/MIL* G22 ... 68 B1
Fernbrae Av *RUTH* G73 ... 130 A4
Fernbrae Wy *RUTH* G73 ... 130 A4
Ferncroft Dr *LNPK/KPK* G44 ... 129 E2
Ferndale Ct *SMSTN* G23 ... 52 C3
Ferndale Dr *SMSTN* G23 ... 52 C3
Ferndale Gdns *SMSTN* G23 ... 52 C3
Ferndale Pl *SMSTN* G23 ... 52 C3
Fern Dr *BRHD/NEIL* G78 ... 124 A3
Ferness Ov *SPRGB/BLRNK* G21 ... 55 H1
Ferness Pl *SPRGB/BLRNK* G21 ... 55 H1
Ferness Rd *SPRGB/BLRNK* G21 ... 55 H1
Fern Gv *BAIL/MDB/MHD* G69 ... 59 F5
Ferngrove Av *KVD/HLHD* G12 ... 52 A5
Fernhill Gra
UD/BTH/TAN G71 ... 152 B1
Fernhill Rd *CSMK* G45 ... 129 H3
Fernie Gdns *MRYH/FIRH* G20 ... 52 D4

Fernington Pl *WISHAW* ML2 ... 174 A1
Fernington Pl *WISHAW* ML2 ... 174 H1
Fern La *KKNTL* G66 ... 21 G1
KVD/HLHD G12 ... 65 G4
Fernlea *BSDN* G61 ... 34 B5
Fernleigh Rd
PLKSW/MSWD G43 ... 127 G2
Fernslea Av
BLTYR/CAMB G72 ... 151 E4
Fern St *MTHW* ML1 ... 172 B1
Ferryden St *SCOT* G14 ... 65 F4
Ferry Rd *BSHPTN* PA7 ... 28 D4
KVGV G3 ... 66 B5
RNFRW PA4 ... 63 G2
UD/BTH/TAN G71 ... 133 H1
Fersit St *PLKSW/MSWD* G43 ... 127 F1
Fetlar Dr *LNPK/KPK* G44 ... 128 D2
Fettar Rd *BRWEIR* PA11 ... 79 G3
Fettercairn Av *DRUM* G15 ... 32 D4
Fettes St *STPS/GTHM/RID* G33 ... 92 A1
Fiddoch Ct *WISHAW* ML2 ... 158 A3
Fidra St *STPS/GTHM/RID* G33 ... 92 A1
Fielden Pl *DMNK/BRGTN* G40 ... 90 D4
Fielden St *DMNK/BRGTN* G40 ... 90 D4
Field Gv
CRMNK/CLK/EAG G76 ... 146 A5
Fieldhead Dr
PLKSW/MSWD G43 ... 126 D2
Fieldhead Sq
PLKSW/MSWD G43 ... 126 D2
Field Rd *CRMNK/CLK/EAG* G76 146 A5
Field St *HMLTN* ML3 ... 170 A4
Fife Av *AIRDRIE* ML6 ... 98 A4
CARD/HILL/MSPK G52 ... 86 C5
Fife Crs *UD/BTH/TAN* G71 ... 152 B1
Fife Dr *MTHW* ML1 ... 137 H3
Fife Wy *BSHPBGS* G64 ... 55 G3
Fifth Av *AIRDRIE* ML6 ... 98 D3
KVD/HLHD G12 ... 65 G1
RNFRW PA4 ... 63 F4
STPS/GTHM/RID G33 ... 70 C1
Fifth Rd *BLTYR/CAMB* G72 ... 151 H5
Fifty Pitches Pl *GOV/IBX* G51 ... 86 A3
Fifty Pitches Rd *GOV/IBX* G51 ... 86 C2
Finart Dr *PSLYS* PA2 ... 105 E3
Finch Dr *KNTSWD* G13 ... 50 A3
Finch Gv *CTBR* ML5 ... 117 H1
Finch Pl *JNSTN* PA5 ... 121 E2
Finch Wy *BLSH* ML4 ... 116 B5
Findhorn Av *PSLYS* PA2 ... 103 E3
RNFRW PA4 ... 63 H3
Findhorn Ct *EKILS* G75 ... 164 C5
Findhorn Pl *EKILS* G75 ... 164 C5
Findhorn St
STPS/GTHM/RID G33 ... 91 G1
Findlay St *KSYTH* G65 ... 8 B2
MTHW ML1 ... 155 E5
Findlay Ter *BLTYR/CAMB* G72 ... 132 A1
Findochty
STPS/GTHM/RID G33 ... 71 F5
Fingal La *MRYH/FIRH* G20 ... 52 B4
Fingal St *MRYH/FIRH* G20 ... 52 C4
Fingalton Rd *NMRNS* G77 ... 142 D5
Fingask St *CAR/SHTL* G32 ... 92 D5
Finglas Av *PSLYS* PA2 ... 105 E3
Finglen Pl *PLK/PH/NH* G53 ... 125 G5
Fingleton Av *BRHD/NEIL* G78 ... 142 C1
Finhaven St *CAR/SHTL* G32 ... 111 H1
Finlarig St *ESTRH* G34 ... 94 B2
Finlas Pl *PPK/MIL* G22 ... 68 A1
Finlas St *PPK/MIL* G22 ... 68 A1
Finlay Dr *DEN/PKHD* G31 ... 90 D2
PSLYN/LNWD PA3 ... 101 G1
Finlay Ri *MLNGV* G62 ... 17 G5
Finlayson Dr *AIRDRIE* ML6 ... 99 F2
Finlayson St *CTBR* ML5 ... 96 B5
Finnart Sq
DMNK/BRGTN G40 ... 110 C1
Finnart St *DMNK/BRGTN* G40 ... 110 C1
Finnieston Sq *KVGV* G3 ... 88 D1
Finnie Wynd *MTHW* ML1 ... 172 C1
Finnieston St *KVGV* G3 ... 2 A7
Finsbay St *GOV/IBX* G51 ... 87 E3
Fintaig La *WISHAW* ML2 ... 174 D2
Fintrie Ter *HMLTN* ML3 ... 168 D1
Fintry Av *PSLYS* PA2 ... 104 B4
Fintry Crs *BRHD/NEIL* G78 ... 142 B1
BSHPBGS G64 ... 55 G2
Fintry Dr *LNPK/KPK* G44 ... 109 H5
Fintry Gdns *BSDN* G61 ... 16 C5
Fintry Pl *EKILS* G75 ... 177 F4
Firbank Av *BSHPBGS* G64 ... 19 F1
Firbank Qd *AIRDRIE* ML6 ... 119 F1
Firbank Ter *BRHD/NEIL* G78 ... 142 D2
Fir Ct *BLTYR/CAMB* G72 ... 132 B3
Firdon Crs *DRUM* G15 ... 50 B2
Fir Dr *EKILS* G75 ... 177 F5
Fir Gv *UD/BTH/TAN* G71 ... 115 H5
Firhill Av *AIRDRIE* ML6 ... 98 A3
Firhill Rd *MRYH/FIRH* G20 ... 67 F2
Firhill St *MRYH/FIRH* G20 ... 67 F2
Fir La *EKILS* G75 ... 177 E1
Firpark Rd *BSHPBGS* G64 ... 55 E3
Firpark St *DEN/PKHD* G31 ... 90 C2
Fir Park St *MTHW* ML1 ... 172 A1
Firpark Ter *DEN/PKHD* G31 ... 90 C2
Fir Pl *BAIL/MDB/MHD* G69 ... 113 H1
BLTYR/CAMB G72 ... 132 B1
JNSTN PA5 ... 101 H5
First Gdns *PLKSD/SHW* G41 ... 87 H5
First Rd *BLTYR/CAMB* G72 ... 151 H5
First St *UD/BTH/TAN* G71 ... 115 E4
Firtree Pl *WISHAW* ML2 ... 158 C4
Firtree Rd *WISHAW* ML2 ... 158 C4
Fir Vw *AIRDRIE* ML6 ... 118 C4
Firwood Crs *NMRNS* G77 ... 161 H1
Firwood Dr *LNPK/KPK* G44 ... 128 D2
Firwood Rd *NMRNS* G77 ... 144 B5
Fischer Gdns *PSLY* PA1 ... 83 E5

Fisher Av *KSYTH* G65 ... 8 B2
PSLY PA1 ... 83 E5
Fisher Crs *CLYDBK* G81 ... 32 A3
Fisher Dr *PSLY* PA1 ... 83 E5
Fishers Rd *RNFRW* PA4 ... 43 F5
Fishescoates Av *RUTH* G73 ... 130 C2
Fishescoates Gdns *RUTH* G73 ... 130 B2
Fitzalan Dr *PSLYN/LNWD* PA3 ... 84 D3
Fitzalan Rd *RNFRW* PA4 ... 62 D5
Fitzroy La *KVGV* G3 ... 88 D1
Flakefield *EKILN* G74 ... 165 G3
Flanders St *CLYDBK* G81 ... 32 B1
Flaxfield Gv *MTHW* ML1 ... 136 C5
Flaxmill Av *WISHAW* ML2 ... 173 E1
Flax Rd *UD/BTH/TAN* G71 ... 134 B2
Fleet Av *RNFRW* PA4 ... 63 H5
Fleet St *CAR/SHTL* G32 ... 92 C5
Fleming Av
BAIL/MDB/MHD G69 ... 58 B4
CLYDBK G81 ... 49 G3
Fleming Ct *HMLTN* ML3 ... 168 D1
MTHW ML1 ... 172 B1
Fleming Pl *EKILS* G75 ... 166 A5
Fleming Rd *BLSH* ML4 ... 136 A1
BSHPTN PA7 ... 29 E5
CRC/CRSL/HOU PA6 ... 80 D1
CUMB G67 ... 26 B3
Fleming St *DEN/PKHD* G31 ... 91 E4
PSLYN/LNWD PA3 ... 84 B2
Flemington Pl
SPRGB/BLRNK G21 ... 68 C3
Flemington Wy
BAIL/MDB/MHD G69 ... 58 B3
Fleming Wy *HMLTN* ML3 ... 168 C1
Flenders Av
CRMNK/CLK/EAG G76 ... 145 F4
Flenders Rd
CRMNK/CLK/EAG G76 ... 145 F4
Fleurs Av *PLKSD/SHW* G41 ... 108 A1
Fleurs Rd *PLKSD/SHW* G41 ... 88 A5
Flinders Pl *EKILS* G75 ... 177 G1
Flloyd St *CTBR* ML5 ... 96 C2
Floorsburn Crs *JNSTN* PA5 ... 101 F4
Floors St
CRMNK/CLK/EAG G76 ... 162 D4
Floors St *JNSTN* PA5 ... 101 G4
Flora Gdns *BSHPBGS* G64 ... 55 F1
Florence Dr *GIF/THBK* G46 ... 127 F5
Florence Gdns *RUTH* G73 ... 130 B3
Florence St *GBLS* G5 ... 89 H4
Florida Av *GVH/MTFL* G42 ... 109 G4
Florida Crs *GVH/MTFL* G42 ... 109 G4
Florida Dr *GVH/MTFL* G42 ... 109 F4
Florida Gdns
BAIL/MDB/MHD G69 ... 93 H4
Florida Sq *GVH/MTFL* G42 ... 109 G4
Florida St *GVH/MTFL* G42 ... 109 G4
Florish Rd *ERSK* PA8 ... 48 A3
Flour Mill Wynd
BAIL/MDB/MHD G69 ... 42 B5
Flowerdale Pl
PLK/PH/NH G53 ... 125 G4
Flowerhill St *AIRDRIE* ML6 ... 98 C1
Flures Av *ERSK* PA8 ... 48 B3
Flures Crs *ERSK* PA8 ... 48 B3
Flures Dr *ERSK* PA8 ... 48 B3
Flures Pl *ERSK* PA8 ... 48 B3
Fochabers Dr
CARD/HILL/MSPK G52 ... 86 D3
Foinaven Dr *GIF/THBK* G46 ... 126 D2
Foinaven Gdns
GIF/THBK G46 ... 126 D1
Foinaven Wy *GIF/THBK* G46 ... 126 D1
Foinavon Rd *BLSH* ML3 ... 181 E5
Foots Rd
CRMNK/CLK/EAG G76 ... 162 D4
Forbes Dr
DMNK/BRGTN G40 ... 90 C3
MTHW ML1 ... 136 A5
Forbes Pl *PSLY* PA1 ... 84 B5
Forbes St *DMNK/BRGTN* G40 ... 90 C3
Fordneuk St
DMNK/BRGTN G40 ... 90 D4
Fordoun St *ESTRH* G34 ... 94 C1
Ford Rd *KVD/HLHD* G12 ... 66 C2
NMRNS G77 ... 161 G2
Fordyce St *PTCK* G11 ... 66 A4
Foremount Terrace La
KVD/HLHD G12 ... 66 B3
Fore Rw *HMLTN* ML3 ... 170 B1
Forest Av *BLSH* ML4 ... 136 A4
HMLTN ML3 ... 180 D2
Forest Dr *UD/BTH/TAN* G71 ... 134 B4
Forest Gdns *KKNTL* G66 ... 39 F4
Foresthall Crs
SPRGB/BLRNK G21 ... 68 C3
Foresthall Dr
SPRGB/BLRNK G21 ... 68 C3
Forest La *HMLTN* ML3 ... 180 D2
Forest Pk *WISHAW* ML2 ... 157 G5
Forest Pl *KKNTL* G66 ... 39 F4
PSLYS PA2 ... 104 B2
Fore St *SCOT* G14 ... 64 D2
Forest Rd *CUMB* G67 ... 11 F4
CUMB G67 ... 27 F1
Forfar Av
CARD/HILL/MSPK G52 ... 86 C5
Forfar Crs *BSHPBGS* G64 ... 55 F3
Forgan Gdns *BSHPBGS* G64 ... 55 H3
Forge Dr *CTBR* ML5 ... 96 C2
Forge Pl *SPRGB/BLRNK* G21 ... 69 E4
Forge Rd *AIRDRIE* ML6 ... 118 C4
Forge Row *AIRDRIE* ML6 ... 118 C4
Forge St *SPRGB/BLRNK* G21 ... 69 E4
Forgewood Pth *AIRDRIE* ML6 ... 99 H5
Forgewood Rd *MTHW* ML1 ... 136 B5
Forglen St *ESTRH* G34 ... 72 A5
Formby Dr *SMSTN* G23 ... 52 C3
Forres Av *GIF/THBK* G46 ... 127 G4
Forres Crs *BLSH* ML4 ... 135 H1
Forres Ga *GIF/THBK* G46 ... 127 G5
Forres Gv *EKILN* G74 ... 166 C4
Forres St *HMLTN* ML3 ... 157 E5
SMSTN G23 ... 52 D2
Forrester Ct *BSHPBGS* G64 ... 54 D3
Forrestfield Crs *NMRNS* G77 ... 144 D5
Forrestfield Gdns
NMRNS G77 ... 144 B5
Forrestfield St
SPRGB/BLRNK G21 ... 68 D3

Forrest Ga HMLTN ML3 169 G4
UD/BTH/TAN G71 115 G3
Forrest St AIRDRIE ML6 99 F1
BLTYR/CAMB G72 152 A3
DMNK/BRGTN G40 90 D4
Forsa Ct EKILS G75 177 H4
Forsyth St AIRDRIE ML6 98 C1
Forteviot Av
BAIL/MDB/MHD G69 94 B4
Forteviot Pl
BAIL/MDB/MHD G69 94 B4
Forth Av PSLYS PA2 102 D3
Forth Ct EKILS G75 176 D1
Forth Crs EKILS G75 176 D1
Forth Gv EKILS G75 176 D1
Forth Pl JNSTN PA5 120 D1
Forth Rd BLTYR/CAMB G72 151 H5
BSDN G61 51 E1
BSHPBGS G64 19 F5
Forth St CLYDBK G81 49 F3
PLKSD/SHW G41 109 E1
Forth Ter HMLTN ML3 169 G5
Forties Ct GIF/THBK G46 126 C2
Forties Crs GIF/THBK G46 126 C2
Forties Gdns GIF/THBK G46 126 D2
Forties Rd
CRG/CRSL/HOU PA6 80 D3
Forties Wy GIF/THBK G46 126 D2
Fortieth Av EKILS G75 178 C3
Fortingall Av KVD/HLHD G12 52 B5
Fortingall Pl KVD/HLHD G12 52 B5
Fortingall Rd
BLTYR/CAMB G72 152 A5
Fortrose Ct BLTYR/CAMB G72 168 B2
Fortrose St PTCK G11 66 A4
Fort St MTHW ML1 154 B2
Forum Pl MTHW ML1 154 B1
Fossil Gv KKNTL G66 22 A4
Foswell Dr DRUM G15 33 E3
Foswell Pl DRUM G15 32 D3
Fotheringay La
PLKSD/SHW G41 108 C2
Fotheringay Rd
PLKSD/SHW G41 108 C2
Foulis La KNTSWD G13 51 G5
Foulis St KNTSWD G13 51 G5
Foulsykes Rd WISHAW ML2 174 D1
Foundry La BRHD/NEIL G78 124 B5
Foundry Rd MTHW ML1 139 F5
Fountain Av RNFRW PA4 61 G2
Fountain Crs RNFRW PA4 61 G1
Fountain Dr RNFRW PA4 61 H2
Fountainwell Av
SPRGB/BLRNK G21 68 A4
Fountainwell Dr
SPRGB/BLRNK G21 68 A4
Fountainwell Pl
SPRGB/BLRNK G21 68 A4
Fountainwell Rd COWCAD G4 68 A4
Fountainwell Sq
SPRGB/BLRNK G21 68 B4
Fourth Av DMBTN G82 13 H5
KKNTL G66 57 E2
RNFRW PA4 63 F4
STPS/GTHM/RID G33 70 C1
Fourth Gdns PLKSD/SHW G41 87 H5
Fourth St UD/BTH/TAN G71 115 E3
Four Windings
CRG/CRSL/HOU PA6 80 C1
Fowler Pl EKILS G75 178 D2
Fowlis Dr NMRNS G77 143 H4
Foxbar Crs PSLYS PA2 102 D5
Foxbar Dr KNTSWD G13 50 C5
PSLYS PA2 102 D5
Foxbar Rd PSLYS PA2 102 B5
Foxes Gv KKNTL G66 40 B3
Foxglove Pl PLK/PH/NH G53 125 G4
Fox Gv MTHW ML1 154 A3
Foxhills Pl SMSTN G23 52 D2
Foxknowe Gdns CLYDBK G81 32 C1
Foxley St CAR/SHTL G32 112 D3
Fox St CGLE G1 2 E7
Foyers Ter SPRGB/BLRNK G21 68 D2
Foy Gdn BLSH ML4 116 D4
Francis St GBLS G5 89 F5
Frankfield Rd
STPS/GTHM/RID G33 71 F1
Frankfield St
STPS/GTHM/RID G33 69 G4
Frankfort St PLKSD/SHW G41 108 D3
Franklin Pl EKILS G75 165 G4
Franklin St
DMNK/BRGTN G40 110 C1
Fraser Av BSHPTN PA7 28 D4
DMBTN G82 13 H3
JNSTN PA5 101 H4
NMRNS G77 144 B4
RUTH G73 111 F5
Fraser Crs HMLTN ML3 169 G3
Fraser Gdns KKNTL G66 20 D5
Fraser St BLTYR/CAMB G72 130 D1
MTHW ML1 139 E5
Frazer St DMNK/BRGTN G40 91 E4
Frederick St CTBR ML5 96 B1
Freeland Ct PLK/PH/NH G53 125 H1
Freeland Crs PLK/PH/NH G53 125 G1
Freeland Dr BRWEIR PA11 79 G2
PLK/PH/NH G53 125 G1
RNFRW PA4 47 H5
Freeland Pl KKNTL G66 21 F5
Freeland Rd ERSK PA8 47 G4
Freelands Crs OLDK G60 30 C3
Freelands Rd OLDK G60 30 D4
Freeneuk La
BLTYR/CAMB G72 131 G1
Freeneuk Wynd
BLTYR/CAMB G72 131 G1
Freesia Ct MTHW ML1 154 D5
French St CLYDBK G81 31 F5
DMNK/BRGTN G40 110 D1
RNFRW PA4 63 E4
WISHAW ML2 174 A2
Freuchie St
BAIL/MDB/MHD G69 94 A2
Frew St AIRDRIE ML6 98 B1
Friar Av BSHPBGS G64 38 A4
Friarscourt Av KNTSWD G13 51 E3
Friarscourt Rd
BAIL/MDB/MHD G69 58 A2
Friars Cft KKNTL G66 21 G5
Friarshall Ga PSLYS PA2 104 A2
Friars Pl KNTSWD G13 51 E3
Friars Wy AIRDRIE ML6 98 D5
Friarton Rd
PLKSW/MSWD G43 128 A2
Frood St MTHW ML1 154 B1
Fruin Av NMRNS G77 144 B5
Fruin Dr WISHAW ML2 174 D2
Fruin Ri HMLTN ML3 168 D3
Fruin Rd DRUM G15 50 A2
Fruin St PPK/MIL G22 67 H2
Fulbar Av RNFRW PA4 63 F2
Fulbar Ct RNFRW PA4 63 F2
Fulbar Crs PSLYS PA2 103 E2
Fulbar Gdns PSLYS PA2 103 E2
Fulbar La RNFRW PA4 63 G2
Fulbar Rd GOV/IBX G51 86 D2
PSLYS PA2 103 E2
Fulbar St RNFRW PA4 63 G2
Fullarton Av CAR/SHTL G32 112 B2
Fullarton Dr CAR/SHTL G32 112 C3
Fullarton La CAR/SHTL G32 112 B2
Fullarton Pl CTBR ML5 116 A1
Fullarton Rd BALLOCH G68 10 A5
CAR/SHTL G32 112 B3
Fullarton St CTBR ML5 116 B1
Fullers Ga CLYDBK G81 32 B1
Fullerton St
PSLYN/LNWD PA3 84 A2
Fullerton Ter
PSLYN/LNWD PA3 84 B2
Fulmar Pk EKILN G74 166 A2
Fulmar Pl JNSTN PA5 120 D3
Fulton Crs KLBCH PA10 100 B3
Fulton Dr CRG/CRSL/HOU PA6 81 F3
Fulton Gdns
CRG/CRSL/HOU PA6 81 F3
Fulton Rd MLNGV G62 17 F4
Fulton St KNTSWD G13 51 F4
Fulwood Av KNTSWD G13 50 A4
PSLYN/LNWD PA3 82 A3
Fulwood Pl KNTSWD G13 50 A4
The Furlongs HMLTN ML3 170 A1
Furnace Rd HMLTN ML3 181 F5
Fyneart St WISHAW ML2 174 D1
Fyne Av BLSH ML4 116 B5
Fyne Ct HMLTN ML3 169 F4
Fynloch Pl CLYDBK G81 31 F1
Fyvie Av PLKSW/MSWD G43 126 D2
Fyvie Crs AIRDRIE ML6 99 F2

G

Gadie Av RNFRW PA4 63 H4
Gadie St STPS/GTHM/RID G33 91 G1
Gadloch Av KKNTL G66 57 E1
Gadloch St PPK/MIL G22 53 H5
Gadloch Vw KKNTL G66 57 E1
Gadsburn Ct
SPRGB/BLRNK G21 55 F5
Gadshill St SPRGB/BLRNK G21 68 C5
Gailes Pk UD/BTH/TAN G71 134 A5
Gailes Rd BALLOCH G68 10 B5
Gailes St DMNK/BRGTN G40 91 E5
Gainburn Ct CUMB G67 43 G2
Gainburn Crs CUMB G67 43 G3
Gainburn Gdns CUMB G67 43 G3
Gainburn Pl CUMB G67 43 G2
Gainburn Vw CUMB G67 43 H2
Gainside Rd CTBR ML5 59 H5
Gairbraid Av MRYH/FIRH G20 52 B5
Gairbraid Ct MRYH/FIRH G20 52 B5
Gairbraid Pl MRYH/FIRH G20 52 C5
Gairbraid Ter
BAIL/MDB/MHD G69 95 F4
Gair Crs WISHAW ML2 174 A4
Gala Av RNFRW PA4 63 H4
Gala Crs WISHAW ML2 173 H1
Gala St STPS/GTHM/RID G33 69 H4
Galbraith Dr GOV/IBX G51 87 E1
MLNGV G62 16 D5
Galdenoch St
STPS/GTHM/RID G33 70 C4
Gallacher Av PSLYS PA2 103 F3
Gallacher Ct MTHW ML1 172 C2
Gallan Av SMSTN G23 52 D2
Gallery Gv CTBR ML5 96 D3
Galloway Av HMLTN ML3 180 C1
PSLYN/LNWD PA3 84 A2
WISHAW ML2 174 B1
Galloway Dr RUTH G73 130 A4
Galloway Rd AIRDRIE ML6 98 A5
EKILN G74 167 F2
Galloway St
SPRGB/BLRNK G21 54 C5
Galloway Ter
PSLYN/LNWD PA3 84 A2
Gallowflat St RUTH G73 111 E4
Gallowgate CGLE G1 3 J7
DEN/PKHD G31 91 E4
DMNK/BRGTN G40 90 C3
Gallowhill Av KKNTL G66 39 H2
Gallowhill Rd
CRMNK/CLK/EAG G76 147 F2
KKNTL G66 39 H2
PSLYN/LNWD PA3 84 C3
Galston Av NMRNS G77 144 D5
Galston Ct HMLTN ML3 181 E1
Galston St PLK/PH/NH G53 125 E1
Galt Pl EKILS G75 178 A1
Gamrie Dr PLK/PH/NH G53 106 B5
Gamrie Gdns PLK/PH/NH G53 106 B5
Gamrie Rd PLK/PH/NH G53 106 B4
Gannochy Dr BSHPBGS G64 55 F2
Gantock Crs
STPS/GTHM/RID G33 92 C2
Gara Rd AIRDRIE ML6 99 E4
Gardenhall EKILS G75 164 C5
Gardenhall Ct EKILS G75 164 D5
Gardenside Av CAR/SHTL G32 112 C4
UD/BTH/TAN G71 133 H1
Gardenside Crs CAR/SHTL G32 112 C4
Gardenside Gv CAR/SHTL G32 112 C4
Gardenside Pl CAR/SHTL G32 112 C4
Gardenside Rd HMLTN ML3 170 A3
Gardenside St
UD/BTH/TAN G71 133 H1
Garden Square Wk
AIRDRIE ML6 97 G1
Gardner Gv UD/BTH/TAN G71 115 F4
Gardner St PTCK G11 66 A4
Gardyne St ESTRH G34 71 H5
Gareloch Av AIRDRIE ML6 76 A4
PSLYS PA2 103 F2
Garfield Av BLSH ML4 136 B3
Garfield Dr BLSH ML4 136 B3
Garfield Pl
STPS/GTHM/RID G33 57 F5
Garfield St DEN/PKHD G31 90 D3
Garforth Rd
BAIL/MDB/MHD G69 93 G5
Gargrave Av
BAIL/MDB/MHD G69 93 G5
Garion Dr KNTSWD G13 64 C1
Garlieston Rd
STPS/GTHM/RID G33 93 G3
Garmouth Ct GOV/IBX G51 87 H1
Garmouth Gdns GOV/IBX G51 87 G1
Garmouth St GOV/IBX G51 87 G1
Garnethill St KVGV G3 2 C2
Garnet St KVGV G3 2 B2
Garngaber Av KKNTL G66 40 A3
Garngaber Ct KKNTL G66 40 B3
Garnhall Farm Rd
BALLOCH G68 11 G2
Garnie Av ERSK PA8 48 A3
Garnieland Rd ERSK PA8 48 A3
Garnie La ERSK PA8 48 A3
Garnie Ov ERSK PA8 48 A2
Garnie Pl ERSK PA8 48 A2
Garnkirk La
STPS/GTHM/RID G33 71 F1
Garnock Pk EKILN G74 167 E4
Garnock St SPRGB/BLRNK G21 68 C4
Garnqueen Crs CTBR ML5 73 H1
Garrell Av KSYTH G65 8 B1
Garrell Pl KSYTH G65 8 A2
Garrell Rd KSYTH G65 8 A2
Garrell Wy CUMB G67 26 A3
KSYTH G65 8 A2
Garret Pl BALLOCH G68 9 H5
Garrick Av NMRNS G77 161 G3
Garrioch Crs MRYH/FIRH G20 66 C1
Garrioch Dr MRYH/FIRH G20 66 C1
Garrioch Ga MRYH/FIRH G20 66 C1
Garriochmill Rd
MRYH/FIRH G20 66 C2
Garrioch Qd MRYH/FIRH G20 66 C1
Garrioch Rd MRYH/FIRH G20 66 C2
Garrowhill Dr
BAIL/MDB/MHD G69 93 G4
Garry Av BSDN G61 51 H1
Garry Dr PSLYS PA2 103 F2
Garry St LNPK/KPK G44 109 F5
Garscadden Rd DRUM G15 50 A1
Garscadden Rd South
DRUM G15 50 A3
Garscube Rd COWCAD G4 2 D2
MRYH/FIRH G20 67 F3
Garshake Av DMBTN G82 13 H2
Garshake Rd DMBTN G82 13 H3
Gartartan Rd PSLY PA1 86 A4
Gartcarron Hl BALLOCH G68 25 G2
Gartcloss Rd CTBR ML5 73 H4
Gartconnell Dr BSDN G61 34 B2
Gartconnell Gdns BSDN G61 34 B2
Gartconnell Rd BSDN G61 34 B2
Gartconner Av KKNTL G66 22 B5
Gartcosh Rd
BAIL/MDB/MHD G69 95 F1
Gartcosh Wk BLSH ML4 135 G2
Gartcraig Pl
STPS/GTHM/RID G33 70 A5
Gartcraig Rd
STPS/GTHM/RID G33 91 H1
Gartferry Av
BAIL/MDB/MHD G69 58 D1
Gartferry Rd
BAIL/MDB/MHD G69 58 C1
Gartferry St
SPRGB/BLRNK G21 68 D2
Gartfield St AIRDRIE ML6 98 C3
Gartgill Rd CTBR ML5 74 B4
Garthamlock Rd ESTRH G34 71 F5
Garthland Dr DEN/PKHD G31 90 D2
Garthland La PSLY PA1 84 C4
Garth St CGLE G1 3 G6
Gartlea Av AIRDRIE ML6 98 C2
Gartleahill AIRDRIE ML6 98 C2
Gartlea Rd AIRDRIE ML6 98 B2
Gartliston Rd CTBR ML5 74 C3
Gartliston Ter
BAIL/MDB/MHD G69 95 F4
Gartloch Rd
BAIL/MDB/MHD G69 72 D3
ESTRH G34 71 G4
STPS/GTHM/RID G33 70 A5
Gartly St LNPK/KPK G44 128 A3
Gartmore Gdns
UD/BTH/TAN G71 114 D4
Gartmore Rd PSLY PA1 85 F5
Gartmore Ter
BLTYR/CAMB G72 130 D4
Gartness Dr AIRDRIE ML6 99 F4
Gartness Rd AIRDRIE ML6 119 H1
Gartocher Dr CAR/SHTL G32 92 D4
Gartocher Rd CAR/SHTL G32 92 D4
Gartocher Ter CAR/SHTL G32 92 D4
Gartons Rd SPRGB/BLRNK G21 69 F1
Gartsherrie Rd CTBR ML5 96 B1
Gartshore Crs KSYTH G65 23 F3
Gartshore Gdns BALLOCH G68 24 C4
Gartshore Rd BALLOCH G68 42 C2
Garturk St CTBR ML5 97 E5
GVH/MTFL G42 109 G2
Garvald St DMNK/BRGTN G40 111 E1
Garve Av LNPK/KPK G44 128 B3
Garvel Crs
STPS/GTHM/RID G33 93 F3
Garvel Pl MLNGV G62 16 B3
Garvel Rd MLNGV G62 16 B3
STPS/GTHM/RID G33 93 F3
Garvin Lea BLSH ML4 116 D4
Garvock Dr
PLKSW/MSWD G43 127 E2
Garwhitter Dr MLNGV G62 17 F3
Gascoyne EKILS G75 177 H1
Gask Pl KNTSWD G13 50 A3
Gas St JNSTN PA5 101 H3
Gatehouse St CAR/SHTL G32 92 C4
Gateshead Pl KLBCH PA10 100 B3
Gateside Av
BLTYR/CAMB G72 132 A2
KSYTH G65 7 H2
Gateside Crs AIRDRIE ML6 98 B1
BRHD/NEIL G78 141 H1
Gateside Pk KSYTH G65 7 H2
Gateside Rd BRHD/NEIL G78 141 G1
WISHAW ML2 173 F1
Gateside St DEN/PKHD G31 91 E3
HMLTN ML3 170 B2
The Gateway EKILN G74 166 D1
Gauldry Av
CARD/HILL/MSPK G52 106 D1
Gauze St PSLY PA1 84 C4
Gavell Rd KSYTH G65 7 G3
Gavinburn Gdns OLDK G60 30 A1
Gavinburn Pl OLDK G60 30 B1
Gavin's Mill Rd MLNGV G62 17 E4
Gavins Rd CLYDBK G81 32 A3
Gavin St MTHW ML1 154 D5
Gavinton St LNPK/KPK G44 128 A2
Gayne Dr CTBR ML5 59 H5
Gean Ct CUMB G67 27 H1
Geary St SMSTN G23 52 C2
Geddes Hl EKILN G74 167 E1
Geddes Rd SPRGB/BLRNK G21 55 F4
Geelong Gdns KKNTL G66 4 B1
Geils Av DMBTN G82 13 H5
Geils Qd DMBTN G82 13 H5
Gelston St CAR/SHTL G32 92 C5
Gemmel Pl NMRNS G77 161 E1
Gentle Rw CLYDBK G81 31 G2
George Av CLYDBK G81 32 B5
George Crs CLYDBK G81 32 B5
George Gray St RUTH G73 111 F4
George La PSLY PA1 84 B5
George Mann Ter RUTH G73 129 H3
George Pl PSLY PA1 84 B5
George Reith Av
KVD/HLHD G12 65 G1
George Sq CGLE G1 3 F5
George St AIRDRIE ML6 119 E1
AIRDRIE ML6 97 H2
BAIL/MDB/MHD G69 94 A5
BRHD/NEIL G78 124 A4
CGLE G1 3 H5
HMLTN ML3 152 B5
HWWD PA9 120 A4
JNSTN PA5 101 G3
MTHW ML1 171 H1
PSLY PA1 83 H5
George V Br CGLE G1 2 D7
Gerard Pl BLSH ML4 117 E5
Germiston Ct EKILS G75 177 F4
Germiston Crs EKILS G75 177 F4
Gertrude Pl BRHD/NEIL G78 123 H5
Ghillies La MTHW ML1 154 B1
Gibbon Crs EKILN G74 167 F2
Gibb St AIRDRIE ML6 119 E1
MTHW ML1 157 E1
Gibson Av DMBTN G82 13 G3
Gibson Crs JNSTN PA5 101 F4
Gibson Qd MTHW ML1 154 B1
Gibson Rd RNFRW PA4 85 E1
Gibson St DMBTN G82 13 F3
DMNK/BRGTN G40 90 B3
KVD/HLHD G12 66 D4
Giffnock Park Av
GIF/THBK G46 127 F3
Gifford Dr
CARD/HILL/MSPK G52 86 B4
Gifford Pl CTBR ML5 116 B1
Gifford Wynd PSLYS PA2 103 E2
Gigha Qd WISHAW ML2 173 F4
Gilbertfield Pl
STPS/GTHM/RID G33 70 C4
Gilbertfield Rd
BLTYR/CAMB G72 132 A4
Gilbertfield St
STPS/GTHM/RID G33 70 C4
Gilbert St KVGV G3 88 B1
Gilchrist St CTBR ML5 97 E1
Gilchrist Wy WISHAW ML2 174 B4
Gilderdale EKILN G74 165 H3
Gilhill St MRYH/FIRH G20 52 C4
Gillies Crs EKILN G74 150 A5
Gillies La BAIL/MDB/MHD G69 94 B5
Gilmartin Rd
PSLYN/LNWD PA3 81 G5
Gilmerton St CAR/SHTL G32 92 B5
Gilmour Av CLYDBK G81 32 A3
EKILN G74 164 A3
Gilmour Crs RUTH G73 110 C4
Gilmour Dr HMLTN ML3 169 E3
Gilmour Pl BLSH ML4 135 F2
CTBR ML5 96 B1
Gilmour St CLYDBK G81 32 B4
PSLY PA1 84 B4
Gilmourton Crs NMRNS G77 161 G2
Gimmerscroft Crs
AIRDRIE ML6 99 G3
Girdons Wy UD/BTH/TAN G71 133 H1
Girthon St CAR/SHTL G32 92 D5
Girvan Crs AIRDRIE ML6 119 E3
Girvan St STPS/GTHM/RID G33 69 G5
Gladney Av KNTSWD G13 49 H3
Gladsmuir Rd
CARD/HILL/MSPK G52 86 B3
Gladstone Av BRHD/NEIL G78 124 A5
JNSTN PA5 121 E2
Gladstone Ct HMLTN ML3 152 B5
Gladstone St BLSH ML4 136 A2
CLYDBK G81 48 B1
COWCAD G4 67 F4
Glaive Rd KNTSWD G13 51 E2
Glamis Av JNSTN PA5 102 A3
NMRNS G77 144 C5
Glamis Ct MTHW ML1 137 H4
Glamis Crs BLTYR/CAMB G72 168 C2
Glamis Dr EKILN G74 166 C2
Glamis Rd DEN/PKHD G31 91 G5
Glanderston Av
BRHD/NEIL G78 124 D5
NMRNS G77 143 G4
Glanderston Ct KNTSWD G13 50 B4
Glanderston Dr KNTSWD G13 50 B4
Glanderston Ga NMRNS G77 143 H4
Glanderston Rd NMRNS G77 142 C5
Glasgow Br GBLS G5 2 E7
KKNTL G66 39 E1
Glasgow & Edinburgh Rd
BAIL/MDB/MHD G69 115 G1
CTBR ML5 117 E2
MTHW ML1 118 C4
Glasgow Harbour Ter
PTCK G11 65 H5
Glasgow Rd
BAIL/MDB/MHD G69 95 G3
BAIL/MDB/MHD G69 93 H5
BLTYR/CAMB G72 151 G2
BRHD/NEIL G78 124 C3
CLYDBK G81 32 B2
CRMNK/CLK/EAG G76 163 E3
CUMB G67 44 B1
DMBTN G82 12 D4
EKILN G74 149 F3
KKNTL G66 20 C5
KSYTH G65 7 F3
MLNGV G62 17 F5
PLK/PH/NH G53 124 D2
PSLY PA1 84 D4
RNFRW PA4 63 H4
RUTH G73 110 C4
UD/BTH/TAN G71 114 D5
WISHAW ML2 173 E1
Glasgow St KVD/HLHD G12 66 D3
Glassel Rd ESTRH G34 72 C5
Glasserton Pl
PLKSW/MSWD G43 128 A2
Glasserton Rd
PLKSW/MSWD G43 128 A2
Glassford St CGLE G1 3 G6
MTHW ML1 172 B1
Glaudhall Av
BAIL/MDB/MHD G69 58 D4
Glazert Meadow KKNTL G66 4 C3
Glazert Pl KKNTL G66 5 F5
Glebe Av
CRMNK/CLK/EAG G76 147 E3
CTBR ML5 116 A1
UD/BTH/TAN G71 134 C5
Glebe Ct COWCAD G4 3 J3
Glebe Crs AIRDRIE ML6 99 E1
HMLTN ML3 169 H3
Glebe Gdns
CRG/CRSL/HOU PA6 80 C1
Glebe Hollow
UD/BTH/TAN G71 134 C5
Glebe La NMRNS G77 161 G1
Glebe Pk DMBTN G82 13 G2
Glebe Pl BLTYR/CAMB G72 131 G2
RUTH G73 110 C4
Glebe Rd NMRNS G77 161 G1
Glebe St BLSH ML4 135 G2
COWCAD G4 3 J2
EKILN G74 166 C4
HMLTN ML3 170 A3
RNFRW PA4 63 G3
The Glebe UD/BTH/TAN G71 134 B5
Glebe Wynd
UD/BTH/TAN G71 134 C5
Gleddoch Rd
CARD/HILL/MSPK G52 85 H3
Gleddoch Vw DMBTN G82 12 C5
Gledstane Rd BSHPTN PA7 46 A1
Glenacre Crs
UD/BTH/TAN G71 114 D4
Glenacre Dr AIRDRIE ML6 99 E3
CSMK G45 129 E4
Glenacre Rd CUMB G67 26 B5
Glenacre St CSMK G45 129 E4
Glenacre Ter CSMK G45 129 E4
Glen Affric EKILN G74 167 E4
Glen Affric Av
PLK/PH/NH G53 125 H3
Glen Affric Dr AIRDRIE ML6 119 E3
Glen Affric Wy AIRDRIE ML6 119 E3
Glenafton Gv CTBR ML5 96 C4
Glenafton Vw HMLTN ML3 169 G5
Glen Alby Pl PLK/PH/NH G53 125 H3
Glenallan Ter MTHW ML1 136 C5
Glen Almond EKILN G74 167 F3
Glenalmond St CAR/SHTL G32 92 B5
Glenalva Ct KSYTH G65 8 B1
Glenapp Av PSLYS PA2 105 F3
Glenapp Rd PSLYS PA2 105 E3
Glenapp St PLKSD/SHW G41 109 E1
Glenarklet Dr PSLYS PA2 104 D3
Glen Arroch EKILN G74 167 E4
Glenartney
CRG/CRSL/HOU PA6 80 B1
Glenartney Rd
BAIL/MDB/MHD G69 58 B2
Glenashdale Wy PSLYS PA2 104 D3
Glen Av BAIL/MDB/MHD G69 59 E1
BRHD/NEIL G78 141 F3
CAR/SHTL G32 92 C3
Glenavon Ct HMLTN ML3 169 G5
Glen Avon Dr AIRDRIE ML6 119 E3
Glenavon Rd
MRYH/FIRH G20 52 C4
Glenbank Av KKNTL G66 40 A4
Glenbank Dr GIF/THBK G46 126 C5
Glenbank Rd KKNTL G66 40 A4
Glenbarr St
SPRGB/BLRNK G21 68 C5
Glen Bervie EKILN G74 167 E3
Glenbervie Pl NMRNS G77 143 F5
SMSTN G23 52 C2
Glenboig Rd
BAIL/MDB/MHD G69 59 G4
Glen Brae BRWEIR PA11 79 G3
Glenbrittle Dr PSLYS PA2 104 D3
Glenbrittle Wy PSLYS PA2 104 D3
Glenbuck Av
STPS/GTHM/RID G33 56 A5
Glenbuck Dr
STPS/GTHM/RID G33 56 A5
Glenburn Av
BAIL/MDB/MHD G69 94 B4
BAIL/MDB/MHD G69 59 E2
BLTYR/CAMB G72 130 C2
MTHW ML1 137 H3
Glenburn Crs KKNTL G66 5 G5
PSLYS PA2 104 A5
UD/BTH/TAN G71 115 G4

Glenburn Gdns
  BAIL/MDB/MHD G69 ....59 H5
  BSHPBGS G64 ....54 C1
Glenburnie Pl ESTRH G34 ....93 H2
Glenburn La MRYH/FIRH G20 ....52 D4
Glenburn Rd BSDN G61 ....34 A3
  EKILN G74 ....
  GIF/THBK G46 ....145 E1
  HMLTN ML3 ....169 G2
  PSLYS PA2 ....103 G4
Glenburn St MRYH/FIRH G20 ....52 D4
Glenburn Ter MTHW ML1 ....155 G1
Glenburn Wy EKILN G74 ....165 E2
Glencairn Av WISHAW ML2 .....173 G5
Glencairn Ct RUTH G73 ....110 C4
Glencairn Dr
  BAIL/MDB/MHD G69 ....58 D1
  CTBR ML5 ....96 C4
  PLKSD/SHW G41 ....108 D2
  RUTH G73 ....110 C4
Glencairn Gdns
  BLTYR/CAMB G72 ....132 A2
  PLKSD/SHW G41 ....108 D2
Glencairn La PLKSD/SHW G41 ...108 D2
Glencairn Rd CUMB G67 ....27 E3
  DMBTN G82 ....12 B4
  PSLYN/LNWD PA3 ....84 D2
Glencairn St MTHW ML1 ....154 D5
Glencalder Crs BLSH ML4 .....136 B4
Glen Cally EKILN G74 ....167 E4
Glencally Av PSLYS PA2 ......105 E3
Glen Cannich EKILN G74 ......167 E4
Glen Carron EKILN G74 ....167 E4
Glencart Gv KLBCH PA10 ......100 D5
Glencleland Rd WISHAW ML2 ..173 E1
Glenclora Dr PSLYS PA2 ......104 D3
Glen Clova EKILN G74 ....167 E3
Glen Clova Dr BALLOCH G68 ....25 F3
Glencloy St MRYH/FIRH G20 ....52 A3
Glen Clunie EKILN G74 ....167 G3
Glen Clunie Dr
  PLK/PH/NH G53 ....125 H3
Glen Clunie Pl
  PLK/PH/NH G53 ....125 H3
Glencoats Crs
  PSLYN/LNWD PA3 ....83 G4
Glencoats Dr
  PSLYN/LNWD PA3 ....83 F5
Glencoe Dr MTHW ML1 ....137 F2
Glencoe Pl HMLTN ML3 ....169 G5
  KNTSWD G13 ....51 E5
Glencoe Rd RUTH G73 ....130 C4
Glencoe St KNTSWD G13 ....51 E5
Glen Cona Dr
  PLK/PH/NH G53 ....125 H2
Glencorse Rd PSLYS PA2 .....103 H2
Glencorse St CAR/SHTL G32 ....91 H2
Glencraig St AIRDRIE ML6 .....97 H3
Glen Creran Crs
  BRHD/NEIL G78 ....140 C4
Glen Crs KNTSWD G13 ....49 H4
Glencroft Av
  UD/BTH/TAN G71 ....114 D4
Glencroft Rd LNPK/KPK G44 ...129 E2
Glencryan Rd CUMB G67 ....26 D4
Glendale Av AIRDRIE ML6 ......99 E3
Glendale Crs BSHPBGS G64 .....55 F3
Glendale Dr BSHPBGS G64 ......55 F4
Glendale Gv CTBR ML5 ....116 B1
Glendale Pl BSHPBGS G64 ......55 F4
  DEN/PKHD G31 ....91 E3
Glendale St DEN/PKHD G31 .....91 E3
Glendaruel Av BSDN G61 ....35 G4
Glendaruel Rd RUTH G73 .....131 E5
Glendarvel Gdns PPK/MIL G22 ..68 A2
Glendee Gdns RNFRW PA4 ....63 G4
Glendee Rd RNFRW PA4 ....63 G4
Glen Dene Wy
  PLK/PH/NH G53 ....125 H3
Glendentan Rd BRWEIR PA11 ....79 F5
Glen Derry EKILN G74 ....167 G2
Glen Dessary EKILN G74 ......167 H3
Glendeveron Wy MTHW ML1 ....137 G5
Glen Devon EKILN G74 ....167 G4
Glendevon Pl CLYDBK G81 ......31 G5
  HMLTN ML3 ....169 G5
Glendevon Sq
  STPS/GTHM/RID G33 ....70 C4
Glen Dewar Pl
  PLK/PH/NH G53 ....125 H3
Glendinning Rd KNTSWD G13 ....51 F2
Glen Dochart Dr BALLOCH G68 ..25 F3
Glendoick Pl NMRNS G77 .....143 F5
Glen Doll EKILN G74 ....167 F4
Glen Doll Rd BRHD/NEIL G78 ..140 D4
Glendorch Av WISHAW ML2 ....158 A4
Glendore St SCOT G14 ....65 F4
Glen Douglas Dr BALLOCH G68 ..25 G1
Glendoune Rd
  CRMNK/CLK/EAG G76 ....145 H5
Glen Dr MTHW ML1 ....137 G2
Glenduffhill Rd
  BAIL/MDB/MHD G69 ....93 G4
Glen Dye EKILN G74 ....167 E3
Glen Eagles Av EKILN G74 ...167 H4
Gleneagles Av BALLOCH G68 ...10 C5
Gleneagles Dr BSHPBGS G64 ...37 H5
Gleneagles Gdns BSHPBGS G64 .37 H5
Gleneagles La North
  SCOT G14 ....64 D2
Gleneagles La South
  SCOT G14 ....64 D3
Gleneagles Pk
  UD/BTH/TAN G71 ....134 A1
Glenelg Crs KKNTL G66 ....22 A4
Glenelg Qd ESTRH G34 ....72 C5
Glenelm Pl BLSH ML4 ....135 H1
Glen Esk EKILN G74 ....167 F5
Glenesk Crs PLK/PH/NH G53 ..125 H3
Glen Esk Dr PLK/PH/NH G53 ..125 H3
Glenesk Pl PLK/PH/NH G53 ...125 H3
Glen Etive Pl RUTH G73 .....130 D5
Glen Falloch Crs
  BRHD/NEIL G78 ....140 C4
Glen Falloch Wy BALLOCH G68 ..9 G5
Glen Farg EKILN G74 ....167 F4
Glenfarg Crs BSDN G61 ....35 E4

Glenfarg Rd RUTH G73 ....130 A3
Glenfarg St MRYH/FIRH G20 ...67 F4
Glenfarm Rd MTHW ML1 ......138 B3
Glen Farrar EKILN G74 ......167 F4
Glen Feshie EKILN G74 ......167 E5
Glenfield Av PSLYS PA2 .....123 F1
Glenfield Crs PSLYS PA2 ....123 F1
Glenfield Gdns PSLYS PA2 ...123 E1
Glenfield Gv PSLYS PA2 .....123 E1
Glenfield Rd EKILS G75 .....178 D2
  PSLYS PA2 ....103 H5
Glen Finlet Rd
  BRHD/NEIL G78 ....140 C5
Glenfinnan Dr BSDN G61 ......35 F5
Glenfinnan Pl MRYH/FIRH G20 .52 C5
Glenfinnan Rd MRYH/FIRH G20 .52 C5
Glenfinnan Rd
  MRYH/FIRH G20 ....66 C1
Glenfruin Crs PSLYS PA2 ....105 E3
Glenfruin Dr AIRDRIE ML6 ...119 E3
Glenfruin Rd
  BLTYR/CAMB G72 ....151 F1
Glen Fyne Rd BALLOCH G68 ....25 G1
Glen Gairn EKILN G74 ....167 F4
Glen Gairn Crs
  BRHD/NEIL G78 ....140 D4
Glen Garrel Pl KSYTH G65 .....7 H1
Glengarriff Rd BLSH ML4 ....117 E4
Glen Garry EKILN G74 ....167 E5
Glengarry Dr
  CARD/HILL/MSPK G52 ....86 D4
Glengavel Crs
  STPS/GTHM/RID G33 ....56 A5
Glengavel Gdns WISHAW ML2 ..157 G3
Glen Gavin Wy PSLYS PA2 ....104 B5
Glengowan Rd BRWEIR PA11 ....79 F5
Glen Gv EKILS G75 ....178 A1
Glengyre Pl ESTRH G34 ....94 C1
Glengyre St ESTRH G34 ....94 B1
Glenhead Crs CLYDBK G81 .....31 H1
  PPK/MIL G22 ....53 H5
Glenhead Dr MTHW ML1 ......171 H1
Glenhead Rd CLYDBK G81 ......31 H5
  KKNTL G66 ....40 C1
Glenhead St PPK/MIL G22 .....53 H5
Glenheath Dr CTBR ML5 ....73 H1
Glenholme Av PSLYS PA2 .....103 G3
Glenhove Rd CUMB G67 ....26 C5
Gleniffer Av KNTSWD G13 .....50 B5
Gleniffer Crs JNSTN PA5 ....102 B5
Gleniffer Rd BRHD/NEIL G78 .123 H2
Gleniffer Rd RNFRW PA4 ......85 E1
Gleniffer Vw BRHD/NEIL G78 .141 E2
Glen Isla EKILN G74 ....167 H3
Glen Isla Av BRHD/NEIL G78 .140 D5
Glenisla Av
  BAIL/MDB/MHD G69 ....42 B5
Glen Isla Qd MTHW ML1 .....157 E2
Glenisla St DEN/PKHD G31 ...111 G1
Glenkirk Dr DRUM G15 ....50 C1
Glen Kyle Dr PLK/PH/NH G53 .125 H5
Glen La PSLYN/LNWD PA3 ......84 B4
Glen Lednock Dr BALLOCH G68 .25 G1
Glen Lee EKILN G74 ....167 H3
Glenlee St HMLTN ML3 ....152 A5
Glen Lethnot EKILN G74 .....167 H3
Glen Livet Pl PLK/PH/NH G53 125 H5
Glenlivet Rd BRHD/NEIL G78 .140 D4
Glen Lochay Gdns
  BALLOCH G68 ....25 F1
Glenlora Dr PLK/PH/NH G53 ..125 F1
Glenlora Ter PLK/PH/NH G53 .106 C5
Glen Loy Pl PLK/PH/NH G53 ..125 H3
Glen Luce Dr CAR/SHTL G32 ..113 E1
Glenluce Gdns
  BAIL/MDB/MHD G69 ....42 B5
Glenluce Ter EKILN G74 .....165 H5
Glenluggie Rd KKNTL G66 .....40 D1
Glenlui Av RUTH G73 ....130 A2
Glen Luss Gdns BALLOCH G68 ..25 F3
Glen Luss Pl CTBR ML5 ....97 C4
  PLK/PH/NH G53 ....125 H5
Glen Lyon EKILN G74 ....167 H4
Glen Lyon Ct BALLOCH G68 ....25 F1
Glenlyon Ct HMLTN ML3 ......169 H5
Glenlyon Pl RUTH G73 ....130 B5
Glen Lyon Rd BRHD/NEIL G78 .140 D4
Glen Mallie EKILN G74 ......167 H4
Glenmalloch Pl JNSTN PA5 ..102 B1
Glenmanor Av
  BAIL/MDB/MHD G69 ....41 H5
Glen Mark EKILN G74 ....167 H3
Glenmarklet Crs PSLYS PA2 .104 D5
Glen Mark Rd
  BRHD/NEIL G78 ....140 D4
Glenmavis Rd AIRDRIE ML6 ....75 H3
Glenmavis St COWCAD G4 ....2 E2
Glen More EKILN G74 ....166 D4
Glenmore Av BLSH ML4 ......136 A1
  GVH/MTFL G42 ....110 B4
Glenmore Rd MTHW ML1 ......137 H5
Glen Moriston EKILN G74 ....167 H4
Glen Moriston Rd
  BALLOCH G68 ....25 F1
  PLK/PH/NH G53 ....125 H5
Glenmoss Av ERSK PA8 ....47 E2
Glen Moy EKILN G74 ....167 H4
Glenmuir Dr PLK/PH/NH G53 ..125 H2
Glen Muir Rd BRHD/NEIL G78 .140 D5
Glen Nevis EKILN G74 ....167 H5
Glen Nevis Pl RUTH G73 .....130 B5
Glen Noble MTHW ML1 ....139 E5
Glenochil Rd AIRDRIE ML6 ..119 E3
Glen Ogilvie EKILN G74 .....167 H3
Glen Ogle St CAR/SHTL G32 ...92 D5
Glenorchard Rd BSHPBGS G64 .18 B2
Glen Orchy Ct BALLOCH G68 ....9 F5
Glen Orchy Dr BALLOCH G68 ...25 F5
  PLK/PH/NH G53 ....125 H5
Glen Orchy Pl AIRDRIE ML6 .119 E3
  BALLOCH G68 ....9 F5
Glen Orchy Rd MTHW ML1 ....157 F2
Glen Ord Rd MTHW ML1 ......137 G5
Glenorrin Wy BRHD/NEIL G78 .140 D4

Glenpark AIRDRIE ML6 ....99 F3
Glenpark Av GIF/THBK G46 ...126 C5
Glenpark Gdns
  BLTYR/CAMB G72 ....111 H5
Glenpark Rd DEN/PKHD G31 ....91 E5
Glenpark St WISHAW ML2 ....173 H1
Glenpark Ter
  BLTYR/CAMB G72 ....111 H5
Glenpath DMBTN G82 ....13 H4
Glenpatrick Rd JNSTN PA5 ..102 B3
Glenpatrick Rd
  CRMNK/CLK/EAG G76 ....145 H5
Glen Prosen EKILN G74 ......167 F5
Glen Quoich EKILN G74 ......167 G2
Glenraith Rd
  STPS/GTHM/RID G33 ....70 C3
Glen Rannoch Dr AIRDRIE ML6 119 E3
Glenrigg Ct AIRDRIE ML6 .....98 A4
Glen Rinnes Dr
  BRHD/NEIL G78 ....141 E5
Glen Rd AIRDRIE ML6 ....99 F3
  BSHTN PA7 ....28 D4
  CAR/SHTL G32 ....92 C2
  EKILN G74 ....165 H1
  MTHW ML1 ....119 E5
  OLDK G60 ....30 C2
  WISHAW ML2 ....173 H1
Glen Rosa Gdns BALLOCH G68 ..25 F1
Glen Roy Dr BRHD/NEIL G78 ..140 D4
Glen Sannox Dr BALLOCH G68 ..25 G1
Glen Sannox Gv BALLOCH G68 ..25 G1
Glen Sannox Loan
  BALLOCH G68 ....25 F1
Glen Sannox Vw BALLOCH G68 ..25 F1
Glen Sannox Wy BALLOCH G68 ..25 F1
Glen Sannox Wynd
  BALLOCH G68 ....25 F1
Glen Sax Dr RNFRW PA4 ....63 H5
Glen Shee EKILN G74 ....167 F3
Glen Shee Av BRHD/NEIL G78 .140 D5
Glenshee Gdns
  DEN/PKHD G31 ....111 H1
Glenshee St DEN/PKHD G31 ...91 G5
Glenshee Ter HMLTN ML3 ....169 G5
Glenshiel Av PSLYS PA2 .....104 D3
Glenshira Av PSLYS PA2 ....104 D3
Glen Shirva Rd KSYTH G65 ....23 F1
Glenside Av PLK/PH/NH G53 .106 C2
Glenside Dr RUTH G73 ....130 C1
Glenside Rd DMBTN G82 ....13 H1
Glenspean Pl CTBR ML5 ....97 G4
Glenspean St
  PLKSW/MSWD G43 ....127 G1
Glen St BLTYR/CAMB G72 ....132 A5
  BRHD/NEIL G78 ....124 B4
  MTHW ML1 ....138 A3
  PSLYN/LNWD PA3 ....84 A4
Glentanar Dr
  BAIL/MDB/MHD G69 ....59 F1
Glentanar Pl PPK/MIL G22 ....53 G4
Glentanar Rd PPK/MIL G22 ....53 G4
Glen Tanner EKILN G74 ......167 G3
Glen Tarbert Dr
  BRHD/NEIL G78 ....140 D4
Glentarbert Rd RUTH G73 ...130 C4
Glen Tennet EKILN G74 ......167 F5
Glentore Qd AIRDRIE ML6 .....76 B4
Glentrool Gdns
  BAIL/MDB/MHD G69 ....42 B5
  PPK/MIL G22 ....68 A2
Glen Turret EKILN G74 ......167 G3
Glentyan Av KLBCH PA10 .....100 B2
Glentyan Dr PLK/PH/NH G53 .125 H1
Glentyan Ter PLK/PH/NH G53 106 B5
Glen Urquhart EKILN G74 ....167 H4
Glen Vw CUMB G67 ....27 E2
  HMLTN ML3 ....180 D2
Glenview AIRDRIE ML6 ....99 E3
Glenview Crs
  BAIL/MDB/MHD G69 ....42 A5
Glenview Pl
  BLTYR/CAMB G72 ....151 G1
Glenville Av GIF/THBK G46 ..126 C5
Glenville Ga
  CRMNK/CLK/EAG G76 ....146 B5
Glenville Ter
  CRMNK/CLK/EAG G76 ....146 B5
Glenward Av KKNTL G66 ....4 C3
Glenwell St AIRDRIE ML6 .....99 H3
Glenwood Av AIRDRIE ML6 ....98 D5
Glenwood Ct KKNTL G66 ....39 F5
Glenwood Dr GIF/THBK G46 ..126 C5
Glenwood Gdns KKNTL G66 .....39 F5
Glenwood Pth CSMK G45 .....129 F4
Glenwood Pl CSMK G45 ......129 F4
  KKNTL G66 ....39 F5
Glenwood Rd KKNTL G66 ......39 F5
Glorat Av KKNTL G66 ....4 C1
Gloucester Av
  CRMNK/CLK/EAG G76 ....145 G3
  RUTH G73 ....130 C2
Gloucester St GBLS G5 ....89 F4
Gockston Rd
  PSLYN/LNWD PA3 ....84 A2
Gogar Pl STPS/GTHM/RID G33 .91 H1
Gogar St STPS/GTHM/RID G33 .91 H1
Goil Av BLSH ML4 ....135 E1
Goldberry Av SCOT G14 ....64 C1
Goldcrest Ct WISHAW ML2 ...173 G4
Goldenacre Pl AIRDRIE ML6 .119 H2
Goldeneive Vw
  CRG/CRSL/HOU PA6 ....80 B3
Goldie Rd UD/BTH/TAN G71 ..134 B3
Golf Course Rd BRWEIR PA11 .79 E3
  BSHPBGS G64 ....18 B5
Golf Dr DRUM G15 ....50 A2
  PSLY PA1 ....85 H5
Golfhill Dr DEN/PKHD G31 ....90 D1
Golfhill Qd AIRDRIE ML6 .....76 B4
Golfhill Rd WISHAW ML2 ....157 F1
Golf Pl BLSH ML4 ....136 A4
Golf Rd BSHPTN PA7 ....28 D5
  CRMNK/CLK/EAG G76 ....145 G2
  RUTH G73 ....130 A3

Golf Vw CLYDBK G81 ....31 G4
Golfview BSDN G61 ....33 G3
Golfview Dr CTBR ML5 ....95 H2
Golfview Pl CTBR ML5 ....95 H2
Golspie Av AIRDRIE ML6 .....97 H1
Golspie St GOV/IBX G51 .....87 H1
Golspie Wy BLTYR/CAMB G72 .168 D2
Goosedubbs CGLE G1 ....3 H6
Gooseholm Crs DMBTN G82 ....13 F2
Gooseholm Rd DMBTN G82 .....13 F1
Gopher Av UD/BTH/TAN G71 ..115 G4
Gorbals St GBLS G5 ....89 H4
Gordon Av
  BAIL/MDB/MHD G69 ....93 G4
  BSHPTN PA7 ....28 D4
  CARD/HILL/MSPK G52 ....86 D2
  LNPK/KPK G44 ....127 H5
Gordon Dr EKILN G74 ....167 E2
  LNPK/KPK G44 ....127 H5
Gordon La CGLE G1 ....2 E5
Gordon Pl BLSH ML4 ....135 G4
Gordon Rd HMLTN ML3 ....169 H4
  LNPK/KPK G44 ....127 H5
Gordon St CGLE G1 ....2 E5
  PSLY PA1 ....84 B5
Gordon Ter BLTYR/CAMB G72 .151 F1
  HMLTN ML3 ....169 E2
Gorebridge St CAR/SHTL G32 .91 H2
Gorget Av KNTSWD G13 ....50 D2
Gorget Pl KNTSWD G13 ....50 D2
Gorget Qd KNTSWD G13 ....50 C2
Gorse Crs BRWEIR PA11 ....79 F4
Gorsehall St MTHW ML1 .....139 E5
Gorse Pl UD/BTH/TAN G71 ...115 G4
Gorsewood BSHPBGS G64 ....54 B2
Gorstan Pl MRYH/FIRH G20 ...66 C1
Gorstan St SMSTN G23 ....52 C3
Gosford La SCOT G14 ....64 B2
Goudie St PSLYN/LNWD PA3 ...84 A2
Gough St STPS/GTHM/RID G33 .91 G1
Gourlay BSHPBGS G64 ....21 G5
Gourlay St SPRGB/BLRNK G21 .68 B2
Gourock St GBLS G5 ....89 F4
Govanhill St GVH/MTFL G42 .109 H2
Govan Rd GOV/IBX G51 ....65 H5
Gowanbank Gdns JNSTN PA5 ..101 F4
Gowanlea Av DRUM G15 ....50 B2
Gowanlea Dr GIF/THBK G46 ..127 G3
Gowanlea Ter
  UD/BTH/TAN G71 ....115 G5
Gower St PLKSD/SHW G41 ......88 B4
Gower Ter PLKSD/SHW G41 ....88 B4
Gowkhall Av MTHW ML1 ......138 C4
Goyle Av DRUM G15 ....51 E1
Grace Av BAIL/MDB/MHD G69 ..95 E4
Grace St KVGV G3 ....88 D3
Grace Wynd HMLTN ML3 ......170 B2
Graeme Ct MTHW ML1 ....137 E2
Graffham Av GIF/THBK G46 ..127 G4
Grafton Pl COWCAD G4 ....3 G4
Graham Av BLTYR/CAMB G72 ..132 C5
  CLYDBK G81 ....32 A5
  EKILN G74 ....166 B3
  HMLTN ML3 ....181 H1
Graham Rd DMBTN G82 ....12 C5
Grahamsdyke Rd KKNTL G66 ...21 G4
Grahamshill Av AIRDRIE ML6 .99 E1
Grahamshill St AIRDRIE ML6 .99 E1
Graham Sq DEN/PKHD G31 ......6 J5
Grahamston Ct PSLYS PA2 ...105 F4
Grahamston Crs PSLYS PA2 ..105 F4
Grahamston Pk
  BRHD/NEIL G78 ....124 B2
Grahamston Pl PSLYS PA2 ...105 E4
Grahamston Rd PSLYS PA2 ...124 B1
Graham St AIRDRIE ML6 ....98 B2
  BRHD/NEIL G78 ....124 A3
  HMLTN ML3 ....170 B2
  JNSTN PA5 ....101 F4
  MTHW ML1 ....137 F2
  WISHAW ML2 ....174 C2
Graham Ter BSHPBGS G64 .....55 E4
Graignestock Pl
  DMNK/BRGTN G40 ....90 B4
Graignestock St
  DMNK/BRGTN G40 ....90 B4
Graigside Pl BALLOCH G68 ....43 G1
Grainger Rd BSHPBGS G64 ....55 G2
Grampian Av PSLYS PA2 .....104 A5
Grampian Ct BSDN G61 ....16 A5
Grampian Crs AIRDRIE ML6 ..119 E3
  CAR/SHTL G32 ....92 C5
Grampian Pl CAR/SHTL G32 ...92 C5
Grampian Rd WISHAW ML2 ...173 G5
Grampian St CAR/SHTL G32 ...92 C5
Grampian Wy BALLOCH G68 ....25 H1
  BRHD/NEIL G78 ....141 G4
  BSDN G61 ....16 A5
Granby La KVD/HLHD G12 ......66 C4
Grandtully Dr KVD/HLHD G12 .52 B5
Grange Av MLNGV G62 ....17 F3
  WISHAW ML2 ....173 H4
Grange Gdns
  UD/BTH/TAN G71 ....152 B1
Grangeneuk Gdns
  BALLOCH G68 ....25 G4
Grange Rd BSDN G61 ....34 B1
  GVH/MTFL G42 ....109 G4
Grange St MTHW ML1 ....172 B1
Grannoch Pl CTBR ML5 ......117 F1
Grant Ct HMLTN ML3 ....180 C2
Grantholm Av MTHW ML1 .....139 H2
Grantlea Gv CAR/SHTL G32 ...93 E5
Grantlea Ter CAR/SHTL G32 ..93 E5
Grantley Gdns
  PLKSD/SHW G41 ....108 C4
Grantley St PLKSD/SHW G41 .108 C4
Grantoffen Pth EKILS G75 ..178 A3
Grant Pl WISHAW ML2 ....157 F5
Grantown Av AIRDRIE ML6 ....99 F3
Grantown Gdns AIRDRIE ML6 ..76 A2
Grants Av PSLYS PA2 ....104 A3
Grants Crs PSLYS PA2 ......104 A4
Grants Pl PSLYS PA2 ....104 A4
  PSLYS PA2 ....103 H4
Grants Wy PSLYS PA2 ....104 A3
Granville St CLYDBK G81 .....32 A5
  KVGV G3 ....2 A3

Grasmere EKILS G75 ....177 E3
Grasmere Ct HMLTN ML3 .....180 D2
Grathellen Ct MTHW ML1 ....155 F2
Gray Dr BSDN G61 ....34 C5
Grayshill Rd BALLOCH G68 ...44 A2
Gray's Rd UD/BTH/TAN G71 ..134 C2
Grayston Mnr
  BAIL/MDB/MHD G69 ....58 D2
Gray St KKNTL G66 ....41 E1
  KVGV G3 ....2 A1
  MTHW ML1 ....157 E1
Great Dovehill CGLE G1 ....3 J7
Great George La
  KVD/HLHD G12 ....66 C4
Great George St
  KVD/HLHD G12 ....66 D4
Great Hamilton St PSLYS PA2 104 B3
Great Kelvin La
  KVD/HLHD G12 ....66 D4
Great Western Rd
  CLYDBK G81 ....32 B4
  KNTSWD G13 ....50 D3
  OLDK G60 ....31 E2
  OLDK G60 ....15 E5
Great Western Ter
  KVD/HLHD G12 ....66 B2
Great Western Terrace La
  KVD/HLHD G12 ....66 B2
Greenacres MTHW ML1 ....154 B5
Greenacres Ct
  PLK/PH/NH G53 ....125 H3
Greenacres Dr
  PLK/PH/NH G53 ....125 H3
Greenacres Wy
  PLK/PH/NH G53 ....125 H3
Greenan Av LNPK/KPK G44 ...110 B5
Greenbank Av GIF/THBK G46 .145 E5
Greenbank Dr PSLYS PA2 ....104 A5
Greenbank Rd WISHAW ML2 ..174 D2
  BALLOCH G68 ....25 G3
Green Dl WISHAW ML2 ....157 G5
Greenbank St RUTH G73 .....90 A3
Greendyke St CGLE G1 ....90 A3
Greenend Av JNSTN PA5 .....121 E1
Greenend Pl CAR/SHTL G32 ...92 D2
Greenend Vw BLSH ML4 ......135 G3
Greenfarm Rd NMRNS G77 ...143 G5
Green Farm Rd
  PSLYN/LNWD PA3 ....82 A3
Greenfaulds Crs CUMB G67 ...26 C5
Greenfaulds Rd CUMB G67 ....44 C1
Greenfield Dr WISHAW ML2 ..174 C1
Greenfield Qd MTHW ML1 ...138 C3
Greenfield Rd CAR/SHTL G32 .92 D3
  CRMNK/CLK/EAG G76 ....146 B5
  WISHAW ML2 ....152 B5
Greenfield St GOV/IBX G51 ..87 G2
  WISHAW ML2 ....174 C1
Greengairs Av GOV/IBX G51 .87 F1
Greenhall Pl
  BLTYR/CAMB G72 ....151 F4
Greenhead Rd BSDN G61 .....34 C4
  DMBTN G82 ....13 H4
  RNFRW PA4 ....47 H4
  WISHAW ML2 ....174 C2
Greenhead St
  DMNK/BRGTN G40 ....90 B5
Greenhill BSHPBGS G64 ......55 E4
Greenhill Av
  BAIL/MDB/MHD G69 ....58 D4
  GIF/THBK G46 ....145 F1
Greenhill Ct RUTH G73 .....110 A3
Greenhill Crs JNSTN PA5 ...102 A2
  PSLYN/LNWD PA3 ....82 B3
Greenhill Dr PSLYN/LNWD PA3 82 B4
Greenhill Rd MTHW ML1 .....139 H2
  PSLYN/LNWD PA3 ....82 B3
  RUTH G73 ....110 A3
Greenhills Crs EKILS G75 ..177 F5
Greenhills Rd EKILS G75 ...176 D1
  EKILS G75 ....177 G5
Greenhill St RUTH G73 .....110 D5
Greenholm Av
  CRMNK/CLK/EAG G76 ....145 H3
  UD/BTH/TAN G71 ....114 D5
Greenholme St
  LNPK/KPK G44 ....127 G1
Greenknowe Rd
  PLKSW/MSWD G43 ....127 E1
Greenlaw Av PSLY PA1 ....84 D4
  WISHAW ML2 ....157 F5
Greenlaw Crs PSLY PA1 .....84 D3
Greenlaw Dr PSLY PA1 ......84 D4
Greenlaw Gdns PSLY PA1 ....84 D3
Greenlaw Rd NMRNS G77 ....161 G5
  SCOT G14 ....49 G5
Greenlea Rd
  BAIL/MDB/MHD G69 ....58 A3
Greenlea St KNTSWD G13 .....51 F5
Greenlees Gdns
  BLTYR/CAMB G72 ....131 E4
Greenlees Pk
  BLTYR/CAMB G72 ....131 F4
Greenlees Rd
  BLTYR/CAMB G72 ....131 E3
Greenloan Av GOV/IBX G51 ..87 F1
Greenmoss Pl BLSH ML4 .....136 A2
Greenmount PPK/MIL G22 ....53 F4
Greenock Av LNPK/KPK G44 ..128 C2
Greenock Rd BSHPTN PA7 ....29 E3
  PSLYN/LNWD PA3 ....84 A3
  RNFRW PA4 ....47 G5
Green Pl AIRDRIE ML6 ......118 C2
  UD/BTH/TAN G71 ....134 A1
Greenrig UD/BTH/TAN G71 ...134 A1
Green Rd PSLYS PA2 ....103 F1
  RUTH G73 ....110 A3
Greenrigg Rd CUMB G67 .....26 D4
Greenrig St
  UD/BTH/TAN G71 ....134 A1
Greenshields Rd
  BAIL/MDB/MHD G69 ....93 H4
Greenside
  CRMNK/CLK/EAG G76 ....147 F2
Greenside Crs
  STPS/GTHM/RID G33 ....69 H3

Greenside Rd CLYDBK G81 32 A1
MTHW ML1 118 D5
WISHAW ML2 174 B3
Greenside St CTBR ML5 97 E1
MTHW ML1 138 C3
STPS/GTHM/RID G33 69 H3
Greens Rd CUMB G67 45 E2
Green St CLYDBK G81 31 H5
DMNK/BRGTN G40 90 B4
UD/BTH/TAN G71 134 C5
The Green DMNK/BRGTN G40 90 B5
Greentree Dr
BAIL/MDB/MHD G69 113 G1
Greenview St
PLKSW/MSWD G43 108 B4
Greenways Av PSLYS PA2 103 F2
Greenways Ct PSLYS PA2 103 F2
Greenwood Av
BLTYR/CAMB G72 132 A1
Greenwood Crs CTBR ML5 97 F4
Greenwood Dr BSDN G61 34 D4
JNSTN PA5 121 F1
Greenwood Qd CLYDBK G81 49 G2
Greenwood Rd
CRMNK/CLK/EAG G76 145 G3
Greer Qd CLYDBK G81 32 A4
Grenada Pl EKILS G75 165 F4
Grenadier Gdns MTHW ML1 171 G2
Grenadier Pk
BLTYR/CAMB G72 131 F3
Grenville Dr
BLTYR/CAMB G72 131 E3
Gresham Vw MTHW ML1 172 C3
Greta Meek La KKNTL G66 5 G4
Gretna St DMNK/BRGTN G40 91 E5
Greyfriars Rd
UD/BTH/TAN G71 114 B4
Greyfriars St CAR/SHTL G32 92 A2
Greystone Av RUTH G73 130 B1
Greystone Gdns RUTH G73 130 B1
Greywood St KNTSWD G13 51 F4
Grierson La
STPS/GTHM/RID G33 91 G1
Grierson St
STPS/GTHM/RID G33 91 G1
Grieve Cft UD/BTH/TAN G71 152 B1
Grieve Rd CUMB G67 26 C2
Griffen Av PSLY PA1 82 D4
Griffin Pl BLSH ML4 116 D4
Griqua Ter UD/BTH/TAN G71 134 C5
Grogarry Rd DRUM G15 33 F4
Grosvenor Crescent La
KVD/HLHD G12 66 C3
Grosvenor La KVD/HLHD G12 66 C3
Grosvenor Ter KVD/HLHD G12 66 C3
Groveburn Av GIF/THBK G46 126 D3
Grove Pk KKNTL G66 40 A4
Grovepark Ct MRYH/FIRH G20 67 F4
Grove Park Gdns
MRYH/FIRH G20 67 F4
Grovepark Pl MRYH/FIRH G20 67 F3
Grovepark St MRYH/FIRH G20 67 F4
The Groves BSHPBGS G64 55 F3
The Grove BRHD/NEIL G78 140 D4
BRWEIR PA11 79 H5
BSHPTN PA7 28 D5
GIF/THBK G46 145 E2
KLBCH PA10 100 B3
Grove Wd UD/BTH/TAN G71 116 A3
Grudie St ESTRH G34 93 H1
Gryfebank Av
CRG/CRSL/HOU PA6 81 F2
Gryfebank Cl
CRG/CRSL/HOU PA6 81 F2
Gryfebank Crs
CRG/CRSL/HOU PA6 81 F2
Gryfebank Wy
CRG/CRSL/HOU PA6 81 F2
Gryfe Rd BRWEIR PA11 79 G4
Gryfewood Crs
CRG/CRSL/HOU PA6 81 F2
Gryfewood Wy
CRG/CRSL/HOU PA6 81 F2
Gryffe Av BRWEIR PA11 79 G2
RNFRW PA4 63 E1
Gryffe Crs PSLYS PA2 103 E3
Gryffe Gv BRWEIR PA11 79 G3
Gryffe St LNPK/KPK G44 128 B1
Guildford St
STPS/GTHM/RID G33 70 D5
Gullane Crs BALLOCH G68 10 B4
Gullane Dr CTBR ML5 116 B2
Gullane St PTCK G11 66 A5
Gullion Pk EKILN G74 166 D1
Gunn Ms WISHAW ML2 173 G3
Gunn Qd BLSH ML4 135 F4
Guthrie Dr UD/BTH/TAN G71 115 F3
Guthrie Pl BSHPBGS G64 19 G5
EKILN G74 166 G3
Guthrie St HMLTN ML3 170 A1
MRYH/FIRH G20 52 C5
Gyle Pl WISHAW ML2 174 D2

H

Haberlea Av PLK/PH/NH G53 125 H4
Haberlea Gdns
PLK/PH/NH G53 125 H5
Haddington Wy CTBR ML5 116 B1
Haddow Gv UD/BTH/TAN G71 115 F4
Haddow St HMLTN ML3 170 B2
Hadrian Ter MTHW ML1 154 B2
Hagart Rd CRG/CRSL/HOU PA6 80 C1
Hagen Dr MTHW ML1 156 B2
Hagg Crs JNSTN PA5 101 F3
Hagg Pl JNSTN PA5 101 F3
Hagg Rd JNSTN PA5 101 F4
Haggs La PLKSD/SHW G41 108 B2
Haggs Rd PLKSD/SHW G41 108 B3
Haggswood Av
PLKSD/SHW G41 108 B2
Haghill Rd DEN/PKHD G31 91 F3
Hagmill Crs CTBR ML5 117 F2
Hagmill Rd CTBR ML5 117 E2
Haig Dr BAIL/MDB/MHD G69 93 G5
Haig St SPRGB/BLRNK G21 68 C2
Hailes Av CAR/SHTL G32 93 E4
Haining Rd RNFRW PA4 63 G3
The Haining RNFRW PA4 63 G4
Hairmyres Dr EKILS G75 164 D5
Hairmyres La EKILS G75 164 D4
Hairmyres Pk EKILS G75 165 E5
Hairmyres St GVH/MTFL G42 109 H2
Hairst St RNFRW PA4 63 G2
Halbeath Av DRUM G15 33 E5
Halbert St PLKSD/SHW G41 108 D3
Haldane La SCOT G14 65 E3
Haldane Pl EKILS G75 178 C1
Haldane St SCOT G14 65 E3
Halfmerk North EKILN G74 166 D3
Halfmerk South EKILN G74 166 D3
Halgreen Av DRUM G15 32 D5
Halidon Av CUMB G67 45 E1
Halkirk Ga BLTYR/CAMB G72 168 B1
Hallbrae St
STPS/GTHM/RID G33 69 H4
Hallcraig St AIRDRIE ML6 98 B1
Halley Dr KNTSWD G13 49 H5
Halley Pl KNTSWD G13 49 H5
Halley St KNTSWD G13 49 H4
Hallforest St
STPS/GTHM/RID G33 70 C4
Hallhill Crs
STPS/GTHM/RID G33 93 F3
Hallhill Rd CAR/SHTL G32 93 E3
CAR/SHTL G32 92 D3
JNSTN PA5 120 D2
Halliburton Crs ESTRH G34 93 H2
Halliburton Ter ESTRH G34 93 H2
Hallidale Crs RNFRW PA4 64 A4
Hallinan Gdns WISHAW ML2 173 G4
Hall Pl STPS/GTHM/RID G33 71 G1
Hallrule Dr
CARD/HILL/MSPK G52 86 D4
Hallside Av BLTYR/CAMB G72 132 B2
Hallside Bvd
BLTYR/CAMB G72 132 C4
Hallside Crs
BLTYR/CAMB G72 132 B2
Hallside Dr BLTYR/CAMB G72 132 B2
Hallside Gdns WISHAW ML2 174 D1
Hallside Pl GBLS G5 89 H5
Hallside Rd BLTYR/CAMB G72 132 C3
Hallside St HWWD PA9 120 A4
Hall St CLYDBK G81 49 E2
HMLTN ML3 170 A4
MTHW ML1 137 F3
Hallydown Dr KNTSWD G13 64 D1
Halpin Cl BLSH ML4 135 E2
Halton Gdns
BAIL/MDB/MHD G69 93 G5
Haltons Pth
UD/BTH/TAN G71 134 B1
Hamersley Pl EKILS G75 177 G1
Hamilcomb Rd BLSH ML4 135 H4
Hamill Dr KSYTH G65 8 D2
Hamilton Av PLKSD/SHW G41 108 A1
Hamilton Crs
BLTYR/CAMB G72 131 H3
BSDN G61 34 B1
BSHPTN PA7 28 C5
CTBR ML5 96 D5
RNFRW PA4 63 G1
Hamilton Dr AIRDRIE ML6 76 C5
ERSK PA8 30 A5
GIF/THBK G46 127 G5
KVD/HLHD G12 66 D3
MTHW ML1 172 A1
UD/BTH/TAN G71 152 C1
Hamilton Drive La
KVD/HLHD G12 66 D3
Hamiltonhill Crs PPK/MIL G22 67 G2
Hamiltonhill Rd PPK/MIL G22 67 G3
Hamilton Park Av
KVD/HLHD G12 66 D3
Hamilton Pk North
HMLTN ML3 153 E4
Hamilton Pk South
HMLTN ML3 153 E4
Hamilton Pl EKILS G75 178 B1
HMLTN ML3 180 D2
MTHW ML1 137 H3
Hamilton Rd
BAIL/MDB/MHD G69 113 G2
BLSH ML4 135 H2
BLTYR/CAMB G72 150 D5
CAR/SHTL G32 112 D2
EKILN G74 167 E1
MTHW ML1 154 C4
RUTH G73 111 E5
UD/BTH/TAN G71 152 C1
UD/BTH/TAN G71 114 A3
Hamilton St CLYDBK G81 49 G4
GVH/MTFL G42 109 H3
PSLYN/LNWD PA3 84 C4
Hamilton Ter CLYDBK G81 49 G4
Hamilton Vw
UD/BTH/TAN G71 115 F5
Hamlet EKILN G74 149 H5
Hampden Dr LNPK/KPK G44 109 G5
Hampden La GVH/MTFL G42 109 G4
Hampden Ter GVH/MTFL G42 109 G4
Handel Pl GBLS G5 89 H5
Hangingshaw Pl
GVH/MTFL G42 109 H4
Hanover Cl GVH/MTFL G42 109 F4
Hanover Ct CGLE G1 3 G4
Hanover St CGLE G1 3 F5
Hanson Pk DEN/PKHD G31 90 C1
Hanson St DEN/PKHD G31 90 C1
Hapland Av PLK/PH/NH G53 106 D2
Hapland Rd PLK/PH/NH G53 106 D2
Harbour La PSLYN/LNWD PA3 84 B4
Harbour Pl PTCK G11 65 H5
Harbour Rd PSLYN/LNWD PA3 84 B2
Harburn Pl SCOT G14 50 A5
SMSTN G23 52 D2
Harbury Pl SCOT G14 50 A5
Harcourt Dr DEN/PKHD G31 91 E1
Hardgate Dr GOV/IBX G51 86 D1
Hardgate Gdns GOV/IBX G51 86 D2
Hardgate Pl GOV/IBX G51 86 D2
Hardgate Rd GOV/IBX G51 86 D1
Hardie Av RUTH G73 111 F4
Hardie St BLTYR/CAMB G72 151 G3
HMLTN ML3 169 H3
MTHW ML1 154 D2
Hardmuir Gdns KKNTL G66 21 G4
Hardridge Av
CARD/HILL/MSPK G52 107 F2
Hardridge Pl
CARD/HILL/MSPK G52 107 F2
Hardridge Rd
CARD/HILL/MSPK G52 107 E2
Harefield Dr SCOT G14 64 C1
Harelaw Av BRHD/NEIL G78 141 E4
LNPK/KPK G44 127 H3
Harelaw Crs PSLYS PA2 103 H5
Hareshaw Rd MTHW ML1 139 G2
Harestanes Gdns KKNTL G66 22 A4
Harestone Crs WISHAW ML2 174 B3
Harestone Rd WISHAW ML2 174 B3
Harhill St GOV/IBX G51 87 H2
Harkins Av BLTYR/CAMB G72 151 F3
Harkness Av KKNTL G66 5 F5
Harland St SCOT G14 64 D3
Harley St GOV/IBX G51 88 B4
Harmetray St PPK/MIL G22 54 A5
Harmony Pl GOV/IBX G51 87 H2
Harmony Rw GOV/IBX G51 87 H2
Harmony Sq GOV/IBX G51 87 H2
Harmsworth St PTCK G11 65 F4
Harper Crs WISHAW ML2 174 D1
Harport St GIF/THBK G46 126 B3
Harriet Pl PLKSW/MSWD G43 127 E1
Harriet St RUTH G73 110 D4
Harrington Rd EKILN G74 166 B4
Harris Cl NMRNS G77 143 G4
Harris Crs OLDK G60 30 C3
Harris Dr OLDK G60 30 C3
Harris Gdns OLDK G60 30 D3
Harrison Dr GOV/IBX G51 88 A3
Harris Qd WISHAW ML2 174 D1
Harris Rd OLDK G60 30 C3
SMSTN G23 52 C2
Harrow Ct DRUM G15 33 E5
Harrow Pl DRUM G15 33 E5
Hartfield Ct DMBTN G82 13 F3
Hartfield Crs BRHD/NEIL G78 141 F3
Hartfield Ter PSLYS PA2 104 C2
Hartlaw Crs
CARD/HILL/MSPK G52 86 B3
Hartree Av KNTSWD G13 49 H3
Hartstone Rd
PLK/PH/NH G53 106 C5
Hart St CLYDBK G81 32 C1
DEN/PKHD G31 91 H4
PSLYN/LNWD PA3 82 A4
Hartwood Gdns NMRNS G77 161 G3
Hartwood Rd SHOTTS ML7 159 G1
Harvest Dr MTHW ML1 171 H1
Harvey St COWCAD G4 67 H4
Harvey Wy BLSH ML4 117 F5
Harvie Av NMRNS G77 144 A4
Harvie St GOV/IBX G51 88 C3
Harwood Gdns
BAIL/MDB/MHD G69 42 B5
Harwood St CAR/SHTL G32 91 H2
Hastie St KVGV G3 66 C5
Hastings EKILS G75 177 F1
Hatfield Dr KVD/HLHD G12 65 G1
Hathaway Dr GIF/THBK G46 127 E5
Hathaway La MRYH/FIRH G20 66 D1
Hathaway St
MRYH/FIRH G20 66 D1
Hathersage Av
BAIL/MDB/MHD G69 94 A4
Hathersage Dr
BAIL/MDB/MHD G69 94 A4
Hathersage Gdns
BAIL/MDB/MHD G69 94 A4
Hatton Gdns
CARD/HILL/MSPK G52 86 B5
Hatton Pl MTHW ML1 137 H5
Hattonrigg Rd BLSH ML4 117 E5
Hatton Ter MTHW ML1 137 H5
Haughburn Pl
PLK/PH/NH G53 106 C5
Haughburn Rd
PLK/PH/NH G53 106 C5
Haughburn Ter
PLK/PH/NH G53 106 D5
Haugh Pl HMLTN ML3 170 B4
Haugh Rd KSYTH G65 8 A2
KVGV G3 88 C1
Haughton Av KSYTH G65 8 C2
Haughview Rd MTHW ML1 154 A4
Havelock La PTCK G11 66 B4
Havelock Pk EKILS G75 165 F4
Havelock St PTCK G11 66 B4
Haven Pk EKILS G75 177 E2
Havoc Rd DMBTN G82 12 A4
Hawbank Rd EKILN G74 165 F2
Hawick Av PSLYS PA2 103 G3
Hawick Dr CTBR ML5 117 G1
Hawick St KNTSWD G13 50 A4
KNTSWD G13 49 H5
WISHAW ML2 157 F5
Hawkhead Av PSLYS PA2 * 105 E3
Hawkhead Rd PSLY PA1 85 E5
PSLYS PA2 105 F2
Hawkwood EKILS G75 178 A4
Hawkwood Rd AIRDRIE ML6 76 A2
Hawthorn Av
BLTYR/CAMB G72 130 C2
BSDN G61 34 D1
BSHPBGS G64 55 E3
DMBTN G82 12 A3
ERSK PA8 48 B3
JNSTN PA5 101 H5
KKNTL G66 39 H3
WISHAW ML2 158 D4
Hawthorn Crs ERSK PA8 48 B3
Hawthornden Gdns
SMSTN G23 52 D1
Hawthorn Dr AIRDRIE ML6 99 E3
BRHD/NEIL G78 142 C2
CTBR ML5 97 G4
MTHW ML1 137 G4
WISHAW ML2 174 B3
Hawthorn Gdns BLSH ML4 136 B3
BLTYR/CAMB G72 132 B3
CRMNK/CLK/EAG G76 145 H4
Hawthorn Hl HMLTN ML3 170 B4
Hawthornhill Rd DMBTN G82 12 A2
Hawthorn Pl SHOTTS ML7 159 G2
Hawthorn Qd PPK/MIL G22 67 H1
Hawthorn Rd
CRMNK/CLK/EAG G76 145 H4
CUMB G67 27 H1
ERSK PA8 48 B3
Hawthorn St BSHPBGS G64 19 G4
CLYDBK G81 31 H4
PPK/MIL G22 67 H1
Hawthorn Ter EKILS G75 177 G2
UD/BTH/TAN G71 115 G5
Hawthorn Wk
BLTYR/CAMB G72 130 C2
Hawthorn Wy
BLTYR/CAMB G72 130 D2
ERSK PA8 48 B3
Hay Av BSHPTN PA7 29 F5
Hayburn Crs PTCK G11 65 H3
Hayburn Ga PTCK G11 66 A4
Hayburn La KVD/HLHD G12 65 H3
Hayburn St PTCK G11 65 A5
Hayfield St GBLS G5 90 A5
Hayhill Rd EKILN G74 176 A1
Hayle Gdns
BAIL/MDB/MHD G69 42 A5
Haymarket St CAR/SHTL G32 92 A2
Haystack Pl KKNTL G66 40 A4
Hayston Crs PPK/MIL G22 67 G1
Hayston Rd BALLOCH G68 26 B1
KKNTL G66 20 C5
Hayston St PPK/MIL G22 67 G1
Haywood St PPK/MIL G22 53 G5
Hazel Av BSDN G61 34 D1
JNSTN PA5 101 H5
KKNTL G66 40 A2
LNPK/KPK G44 128 A3
Hazel Bank KKNTL G66 20 D1
Hazelbank Wk AIRDRIE ML6 97 G1
Hazeldean Crs WISHAW ML2 157 F5
Hazel Dene BSHPBGS G64 55 E2
Hazelden Pk LNPK/KPK G44 127 H3
Hazelden Rd NMRNS G77 161 F5
Hazelfield Gv AIRDRIE ML6 119 F3
Hazel Gdns MTHW ML1 171 H2
Hazel Gv KKNTL G66 40 A2
Hazelhead EKILN G74 167 E3
Hazellea Dr GIF/THBK G46 127 G3
Hazel Pk HMLTN ML3 170 B3
Hazel Rd CUMB G67 27 F2
Hazel Ter UD/BTH/TAN G71 115 G5
Hazelton MTHW ML1 154 C5
Hazel Wd WISHAW ML2 157 G5
Hazelwood Av NMRNS G77 161 H1
PSLYS PA2 102 D5
Hazelwood Dr
BLTYR/CAMB G72 151 F2
Hazelwood Gdns RUTH G73 130 B3
Hazelwood Gv
BAIL/MDB/MHD G69 95 F3
Hazelwood La BRWEIR PA11 79 G4
Hazelwood Rd BRWEIR PA11 79 G5
PLKSD/SHW G41 88 B5
Hazlitt Gdns MRYH/FIRH G20 53 F5
Hazlitt Pl MRYH/FIRH G20 53 F5
Hazlitt St MRYH/FIRH G20 53 G5
Headhouse Ct EKILS G75 166 A5
Heath Av BSHPBGS G64 55 E3
KKNTL G66 39 H4
Heathcliffe Av
BLTYR/CAMB G72 151 F1
Heathcot Av DRUM G15 49 H1
Heathcot Pl DRUM G15 49 G1
Heather Av BRHD/NEIL G78 123 H2
BSDN G61 16 B5
CLYDBK G81 31 H1
MTHW ML1 137 F2
Heatherbank Av
BAIL/MDB/MHD G69 72 B3
Heatherbank Dr
BAIL/MDB/MHD G69 72 A3
Heatherbank Gv
BAIL/MDB/MHD G69 72 B3
Heatherbank Wk AIRDRIE ML6 97 G1
Heatherbrae BSHPBGS G64 54 B2
Heather Dr KKNTL G66 39 F4
Heather Gdns KKNTL G66 39 F4
UD/BTH/TAN G71 115 H5
Heather Pl JNSTN PA5 101 H5
Heather Vw KKNTL G66 4 C1
Heatheryford Gdns
AIRDRIE ML6 77 H3
Heathery Knowe EKILS G75 178 B1
Heatheryknowe Rd
BAIL/MDB/MHD G69 94 D1
Heathery Lea Av CTBR ML5 117 G1
Heathery Rd WISHAW ML2 173 G2
Heathfield Av
BAIL/MDB/MHD G69 59 F1
Heathfield Dr MLNGV G62 17 F2
Heathfield St
STPS/GTHM/RID G33 92 D1
Heathside Rd GIF/THBK G46 127 G4
Heathwood Dr GIF/THBK G46 126 D4
Hecla Av DRUM G15 33 E5
Hecla Pl DRUM G15 33 E5
Hecla Sq DRUM G15 50 A1
Hector Rd PLKSD/SHW G41 108 C4
Helensburgh Dr KNTSWD G13 51 E5
Helenslea BLTYR/CAMB G72 132 A3
Helenslea Pl BLSH ML4 135 G3
Helenslee Ct DMBTN G82 12 C4
Helenslee Crs DMBTN G82 12 C4
Helenslee Rd DMBTN G82 12 C4
Helen St GOV/IBX G51 87 G4
Helenvale Ct DEN/PKHD G31 91 G4
Helenvale St DEN/PKHD G31 91 F4
Helmsdale Av
BLTYR/CAMB G72 133 F4
Helmsdale Cl
BLTYR/CAMB G72 168 C1
Helmsdale Dr PSLYS PA2 103 E2
Hemlock St KNTSWD G13 51 G4
Henderland Dr BSDN G61 51 F1
Henderland Rd BSDN G61 51 G2
Henderson Av
BLTYR/CAMB G72 132 A1
Henderson St MTHW ML1 154 C3
Henderson St AIRDRIE ML6 98 C1
CLYDBK G81 49 H3
CTBR ML5 96 C3
MRYH/FIRH G20 67 E3
PSLY PA1 84 A4
Henrietta St SCOT G14 64 D3
Henry Qd MTHW ML1 138 D2
Henry St BRHD/NEIL G78 124 A4
Hepburn Hl HMLTN ML3 169 G5
Hepburn Rd
CARD/HILL/MSPK G52 86 B2
Herald Av KNTSWD G13 51 E2
Herald Gv MTHW ML1 171 G1
Herbertson Gv
BLTYR/CAMB G72 151 E1
Herbertson St
BLTYR/CAMB G72 151 H3
Herbert St MRYH/FIRH G20 67 E3
Heriot Av PSLYS PA2 103 E4
Heriot Crs BSHPBGS G64 37 H5
Heriot Rd KKNTL G66 39 H5
Heritage Ct NMRNS G77 144 B5
Heritage Vw CTBR ML5 96 C1
Heritage Wy CTBR ML5 96 C1
Herma St SMSTN G23 52 D3
Hermes Wy BLSH ML4 137 E2
Hermiston Av CAR/SHTL G32 92 C3
Hermiston Rd CAR/SHTL G32 92 C3
Hermitage Av KNTSWD G13 50 D4
Hermitage Crs CTBR ML5 117 E1
Herndon Ct NMRNS G77 144 D4
Heron Ct CLYDBK G81 32 A3
Heron Pl JNSTN PA5 121 E2
Herries Rd PLKSD/SHW G41 108 B3
Herriet St PLKSD/SHW G41 109 E1
Herriot St CTBR ML5 96 B1
Herschell St KNTSWD G13 51 G5
Hertford Av KVD/HLHD G12 52 A5
Hewett Crs
CRG/CRSL/HOU PA6 80 D2
Hexham Gdns
PLKSD/SHW G41 108 C3
Heys St BRHD/NEIL G78 124 B5
Hickman St GVH/MTFL G42 109 H2
Hickman Ter GVH/MTFL G42 109 H2
Hickory Crs UD/BTH/TAN G71 115 H3
Hickory St PPK/MIL G22 68 B1
High Barholm KLBCH PA10 100 C3
High Barrwood Rd KSYTH G65 8 D2
High Beeches
CRMNK/CLK/EAG G76 147 F2
High Blantyre Rd
HMLTN ML3 152 B5
Highburgh Dr RUTH G73 130 A2
Highburgh Rd KVD/HLHD G12 66 B4
High Burnside Av CTBR ML5 96 B4
High Calside PSLYS PA2 104 A1
High Common Rd EKILN G74 167 F5
Highcraig Av JNSTN PA5 101 E5
High Craigends KSYTH G65 8 C2
Highcroft Av LNPK/KPK G44 129 E2
Highcross Av CTBR ML5 96 A5
Higherness Wy CTBR ML5 116 B1
Highfield Av PSLYS PA2 103 H5
Highfield Ct KKNTL G66 21 H5
Highfield Crs MTHW ML1 155 F2
PSLYS PA2 104 A5
Highfield Dr
CRMNK/CLK/EAG G76 145 G3
KVD/HLHD G12 52 A5
RUTH G73 130 B4
Highfield Pl EKILN G74 166 D2
KVD/HLHD G12 52 A5
Highfield Rd KKNTL G66 21 G4
High Flender Rd
CRMNK/CLK/EAG G76 145 G5
High Graighall Rd COWCAD G4 67 G4
Highgrove Rd RNFRW PA4 63 H3
High Kirk Vw JNSTN PA5 101 G4
Highland Av
BLTYR/CAMB G72 151 F2
Highland La GOV/IBX G51 88 B1
Highland Pk KSYTH G65 8 B1
High Mains Av DMBTN G82 13 H4
High Parksail ERSK PA8 47 H3
High Parks Crs HMLTN ML3 180 D2
High Patrick St HMLTN ML3 170 B3
High Rd MTHW ML1 154 C3
PSLYS PA2 103 H1
Highstonehall Rd
HMLTN ML3 168 D5
High St AIRDRIE ML6 98 A1
BRHD/NEIL G78 141 E3
CGLE G1 3 J6
DMBTN G82 12 D4
JNSTN PA5 101 G5
MTHW ML1 138 B3
PSLY PA1 84 A5
RNFRW PA4 63 G3
RUTH G73 110 D4
High Whitehills Rd EKILS G75 178 B3
Hilary Dr BAIL/MDB/MHD G69 93 G4
Hillary Av RUTH G73 130 C1
Hill Av NMRNS G77 161 F1
Hillbare St GOV/IBX G51 87 E3
Hill Crs CRMNK/CLK/EAG G76 146 A4
Hillcrest BAIL/MDB/MHD G69 58 C3
CRMNK/CLK/EAG G76 147 E2
Hillcrest Av CAR/SHTL G32 112 C4
CLYDBK G81 31 H1
CTBR ML5 97 F3
CUMB G67 26 A5
LNPK/KPK G44 127 H3
PSLYS PA2 122 C1
WISHAW ML2 173 F2
Hillcrest Dr NMRNS G77 144 D5
Hillcrest Rd BSDN G61 34 C4
CAR/SHTL G32 112 D4
KSYTH G65 7 E2
UD/BTH/TAN G71 115 F5
Hillcrest St MLNGV G62 17 F3
Hillcrest Ter
UD/BTH/TAN G71 134 C4
Hillcroft Ter BSHPBGS G64 54 C3
Hillend Crs CLYDBK G81 31 H1
CRMNK/CLK/EAG G76 145 F4
Hillend Rd
CRMNK/CLK/EAG G76 145 G4
PPK/MIL G22 53 F4
RUTH G73 130 A3
Hillfoot CRG/CRSL/HOU PA6 81 E3
Hillfoot Av DMBTN G82 13 H3
RUTH G73 110 D5
WISHAW ML2 157 G3
Hillfoot Crs WISHAW ML2 157 G3

Hillfoot *BSDN* G61......**34** D3
  CTBR ML5......**96** A3
  HWWD PA9......**120** A4
  WISHAW ML2......**157** G5
Hillfoot Gdns
  UD/BTH/TAN G71......**114** D4
  WISHAW ML2......**157** G5
Hillfoot Rd *AIRDRIE* ML6......**98** C5
Hillfoot St *DEN/PKHD* G31......**90** D2
Hillhead Av
  BAIL/MDB/MHD G69......**59** E1
  MTHW ML1......**137** F5
  RUTH G73......**138** D3
Hillhead Crs *HMLTN* ML3......**168** D2
  MTHW ML1......**137** F5
Hillhead Dr *AIRDRIE* ML6......**98** B3
  MTHW ML1......**155** F1
Hillhead Pl *RUTH* G73......**130** A3
Hillhead Rd *KNTSL* G66......**21** F4
  SPRGB/BLRNK G21......**55** G4
Hillhead St *KVD/HLHD* G12......**66** C4
  MLNGV G62......**17** E3
Hillhead Ter *HMLTN* ML3......**168** D2
Hillhouse Crs *HMLTN* ML3......**169** E2
Hillhouse Rd
  BLTYR/CAMB G72......**168** C1
  HMLTN ML3......**169** E2
Hillhouse St
  SPRGB/BLRNK G21......**68** D5
Hillhouse Ter *HMLTN* ML3 *......**169** E2
Hillington Gdns
  CARD/HILL/MSPK G52......**86** D5
Hillington Park Circ
  CARD/HILL/MSPK G52......**86** D4
Hillington Qd
  CARD/HILL/MSPK G52......**86** B4
Hillington Rd
  CARD/HILL/MSPK G52......**86** B2
Hillington Rd South
  CARD/HILL/MSPK G52......**86** B4
Hillington Ter
  CARD/HILL/MSPK G52......**86** B4
Hillkirk Pl *SPRGB/BLRNK* G21......**68** C2
Hillkirk St *SPRGB/BLRNK* G21......**68** C2
Hillneuk Av *BSDN* G61......**34** C3
Hillneuk Dr *BSDN* G61......**34** D3
Hillpark Av *PSLYS* PA2......**104** A3
Hillpark Dr
  PLKSW/MSWD G43......**127** F1
Hill Pl *BLSH* ML4......**135** G4
  MTHW ML1......**137** H5
Hillrigg Av *AIRDRIE* ML6......**98** D1
Hill Rd *CUMB* G67......**26** A3
  HWWD PA9......**120** A4
Hillsborough La
  KVD/HLHD G12......**66** D3
Hillsborough Rd
  BAIL/MDB/MHD G69......**93** G4
Hillside *CRG/CRSL/HOU* PA6......**81** E3
  KSYTH G65......**8** D5
Hillside Av *BSDN* G61......**34** C3
  CRMNK/CLK/EAG G76......**145** G5
Hillside Ct *CAR/SHTL* G32......**126** C4
Hillside Crs *BRHD/NEIL* G78......**141** E3
  CTBR ML5......**96** C5
  HMLTN ML3......**169** H5
  MTHW ML1......**138** A4
Hillside Dr *BRHD/NEIL* G78......**123** H4
  BSDN G61......**34** D3
  BSHPBGS G64......**54** A1
Hillside Gardens La *PTCK* G11......**66** A3
Hillside Gv *BRHD/NEIL* G78......**123** H5
Hillside La *HMLTN* ML3......**169** H5
Hillside Pk *CLYDBK* G81......**32** A2
Hillside Qd
  PLKSW/MSWD G43......**127** E2
Hillside Rd *BRHD/NEIL* G78......**123** G5
  PLKSW/MSWD G43......**127** E2
  PSLYS PA2......**104** D2
Hillside Ter *HMLTN* ML3......**169** H5
  KKNTL G66......**5** F5
Hill St *AIRDRIE* ML6......**119** E2
  DMBTN G82......**12** C4
  HMLTN ML3......**169** E2
  KVGV G3......**2** C4
  WISHAW ML2......**173** H3
Hillswick Crs *PPK/MIL* G22......**53** G3
Hill Ter *MTHW* ML1......**137** H5
Hilltop Av *BLSH* ML4......**116** D5
Hilltop Rd
  BAIL/MDB/MHD G69......**59** E1
Hill Vw *DMBTN* G82......**14** C4
  EKILS G75......**166** B5
Hillview Av *KKNTL* G66......**4** C1
  KSYTH G65......**8** D3
Hillview Ct *CLYDBK* G81......**31** G5
Hillview Crs *BLSH* ML4......**116** D4
  UD/BTH/TAN G71......**114** D4
Hillview Dr *BLTYR/CAMB* G72......**151** G1
  CRMNK/CLK/EAG G76......**145** G5
Hillview Gdns *CLYDBK* G81......**31** G5
Hillview Pl
  CRMNK/CLK/EAG G76......**145** H3
  NMRNS G77......**161** G1
Hillview Rd *BRWEIR* PA11......**79** H4
  JNSTN PA5......**102** B2
Hillview St *CAR/SHTL* G32......**92** A4
Hiltonbank St *HMLTN* ML3......**169** H2
Hilton Gdns *KNTSWD* G13......**51** H5
Hilton Pk *BSHPBGS* G64......**37** G5
Hilton Rd *BSHPBGS* G64......**37** G5
  MLNGV G62......**16** C3
Hilton Ter *BLTYR/CAMB* G72......**130** D4
  BSHPBGS G64......**37** G5
  KNTSWD G13......**51** H5
Hilton Vw *BLSH* ML4......**116** D4
Hinshaw St *MRYH/FIRH* G20......**67** F3
Hinshelwood Dr *GOV/IBX* G51......**87** H4
Hinshelwood Pl *GOV/IBX* G51......**88** A4
Hobart Crs *CLYDBK* G81......**31** E3
Hobart Qd *WISHAW* ML2......**174** D3
Hobart Rd *EKILS* G75......**177** H1
Hobart St *PPK/MIL* G22......**67** G2
Hobden St *SPRGB/BLRNK* G21......**68** D3
Hoddam Av *CSMK* G45......**129** G4
Hoddam Ter *CSMK* G45......**129** H4
Hogan Wy *MTHW* ML1......**156** B2
Hogarth Av *CAR/SHTL* G32......**91** G2
Hogarth Ct *CAR/SHTL* G32......**91** G2

Hogarth Gdns *CAR/SHTL* G32......**91** G2
Hogganfield Ct
  STPS/GTHM/RID G33......**69** G4
Hogganfield St
  STPS/GTHM/RID G33......**69** G4
Hogg Av *JNSTN* PA5......**101** F5
Hogg Rd *AIRDRIE* ML6......**99** E5
Hogg St *AIRDRIE* ML6......**98** B2
Holeburn La
  PLKSW/MSWD G43......**127** F1
Holeburn Rd
  PLKSW/MSWD G43......**127** F1
Holehills Dr *AIRDRIE* ML6......**76** C4
Holehills Pl *AIRDRIE* ML6......**76** C4
Holehouse Brae
  BRHD/NEIL G78......**140** D3
Holehouse Dr *KNTSWD* G13......**50** B5
Holehouse Ter
  BRHD/NEIL G78......**140** D3
Hollandbush Gv *HMLTN* ML3......**169** H5
Hollandhurst Rd *CTBR* ML5......**74** C5
Holland St *CCLW* G2......**2** B4
Hollinwell Rd *SMSTN* G23......**52** B3
Hollowglen Rd *CAR/SHTL* G32......**92** C3
Hollows Av *PSLYS* PA2......**103** E5
Hollows Crs *PSLYS* PA2......**103** E5
Hollybank Pl
  BLTYR/CAMB G72......**131** G3
Hollybank St
  SPRGB/BLRNK G21......**68** D5
Hollybrook Pl *GVH/MTFL* G42......**109** G2
Hollybrook St *GVH/MTFL* G42......**109** G3
Hollybush Av *PSLYS* PA2......**122** C1
Hollybush Rd
  CARD/HILL/MSPK G52......**86** A4
Holly Dr *DMBTN* G82......**13** H2
  SPRGB/BLRNK G21......**68** D3
Holly Gv *BLSH* ML4......**137** E2
Hollyhill Gv
  BAIL/MDB/MHD G69......**95** F3
Hollymount *BSDN* G61......**51** G1
Holly Pl *JNSTN* PA5......**121** H1
Holly St *AIRDRIE* ML6......**98** D2
Hollytree Gdns *KKNTL* G66......**4** A2
Holm Av *PSLYS* PA2......**104** C2
Holmbank Av
  PLKSD/SHW G41......**108** C5
Holmbrae Av
  UD/BTH/TAN G71......**115** E5
Holmbrae Rd
  UD/BTH/TAN G71......**115** E5
Holmbyre Rd *CSMK* G45......**146** C1
Holmbyre Ter *CSMK* G45......**128** D5
Holme Av *UD/BTH/TAN* G71......**114** D5
Holmes Av *RNFRW* PA4......**63** F5
Holmes Qd *BLSH* ML4......**136** A4
Holmfauldhead Dr
  GOV/IBX G51......**87** F1
Holmfauldhead Pl
  GOV/IBX G51......**65** F3
Holmfauld Rd *GOV/IBX* G51......**87** F1
Holm Gdns *BLSH* ML4......**136** B3
Holmhead Crs *LNPK/KPK* G44......**128** B1
Holmhead Pl *LNPK/KPK* G44......**128** B1
Holmhill Av *BLTYR/CAMB* G72......**131** F3
Holmhills Dr
  BLTYR/CAMB G72......**131** E4
Holmhills Gdns
  BLTYR/CAMB G72......**131** E4
Holmhills Gv
  BLTYR/CAMB G72......**131** E4
Holmhills Pl
  BLTYR/CAMB G72......**131** E4
Holmhills Rd
  BLTYR/CAMB G72......**131** E4
Holmhills Ter
  BLTYR/CAMB G72......**131** E3
Holm La *EKILN* G74......**166** A4
Holmlea Rd *GVH/MTFL* G42......**109** F5
Holmpark *BSHPTN* PA7......**28** D5
Holm Pl *PSLYN/LNWD* PA3......**82** A4
Holms Crs *ERSK* PA8......**47** E1
Holms Pl *BAIL/MDB/MHD* G69......**58** D4
Holm St *CGLE* G2......**2** D6
  MTHW ML1......**137** F4
Holmswood Av
  BLTYR/CAMB G72......**151** G2
Holmwood Av
  UD/BTH/TAN G71......**115** E5
Holmwood Gdns
  UD/BTH/TAN G71......**134** A1
Holyknowe Crs *KKNTL* G66......**4** C1
Holyknowe Rd *KKNTL* G66......**4** C2
Holyrood Crs *MRYH/FIRH* G20......**67** E4
Holyrood Qd *MRYH/FIRH* G20......**67** E4
Holyrood St *HMLTN* ML3......**152** B5
Holytown Rd *BLSH* ML4......**136** D2
Holywell St *DEN/PKHD* G31......**91** E4
Homer Pl *BLSH* ML4......**136** D2
Homeston Av
  UD/BTH/TAN G71......**134** B4
Honeybog Rd
  CARD/HILL/MSPK G52......**85** H3
Honeywell Av
  STPS/GTHM/RID G33......**71** H2
Honeywell Crs
  STPS/GTHM/RID G33......**71** H3
Honeywell Dr
  STPS/GTHM/RID G33......**71** H2
Honeywell Rd
  STPS/GTHM/RID G33......**71** H2
Hood St *CLYDBK* G81......**49** F1
Hooper Pl *BLSH* ML4......**136** A1
Hope Av *BRWEIR* PA11......**78** B1
Hopefield Av *KVD/HLHD* G12......**66** B1
Hopehill Gdns
  MRYH/FIRH G20......**67** F3
Hopehill Rd *MRYH/FIRH* G20......**67** F3
Hopeman *ERSK* PA8......**30** B5
Hopeman Av *GIF/THBK* G46......**126** B3
Hopeman Dr *GIF/THBK* G46......**126** B3
Hopeman Rd *GIF/THBK* G46......**126** B3
Hopeman St *GIF/THBK* G46......**126** B3
Hopepark Dr *BALLOCH* G68......**24** C3
Hope St *BLSH* ML4......**136** B2
  CGLW G2......**2** C5
  HMLTN ML3......**170** B2

  MTHW ML1......**154** D3
  WISHAW ML2......**175** F1
Hopetoun Pl *SMSTN* G23......**52** D1
Hopetoun Ter
  SPRGB/BLRNK G21......**68** D3
Horatius St *MTHW* ML1......**154** A1
Hornal Rd *UD/BTH/TAN* G71......**134** B3
Hornbeam Dr *CLYDBK* G81......**31** G4
Hornbeam Rd *CUMB* G67......**11** G5
  UD/BTH/TAN G71......**115** G4
Horne St *PPK/MIL* G22......**68** B1
Hornock Rd *CTBR* ML5......**74** C5
Hornshill Dr *MTHW* ML1......**139** E5
Hornshill Farm Rd
  STPS/GTHM/RID G33......**57** F5
Hornshill St
  SPRGB/BLRNK G21......**68** D2
Horsborgh Av *KSYTH* G65......**8** B1
Horse Shoe Rd *BSDN* G61......**34** B4
Horsewood Rd *BRWEIR* PA11......**79** F4
Horslethill Rd *KVD/HLHD* G12......**66** B3
Horslet St *CTBR* ML5......**95** H5
Hospital Rd *WISHAW* ML2......**174** B4
Hospital St *CTBR* ML5......**96** D5
  GBLS G5......**89** G5
Hotspur St *MRYH/FIRH* G20......**66** D1
Houldsworth Crs
  SHOTTS ML7......**159** H2
Houldsworth La *KVGV* G3......**88** D3
Householmill Crs
  PLK/PH/NH G53......**125** H1
Householmuir Pl
  PLK/PH/NH G53......**106** C5
Householmuir Rd
  PLK/PH/NH G53......**125** F2
Householwood Crs
  PLK/PH/NH G53......**106** C5
Householwood Rd
  PLK/PH/NH G53......**106** C5
Housel Av *KNTSWD* G13......**50** C5
Houstonfield Qd
  CRG/CRSL/HOU PA6......**80** D1
Houston Pl *GBLS* G5......**89** E3
  JNSTN PA5......**102** B2
Houston Rd *BRWEIR* PA11......**79** H2
  CRG/CRSL/HOU PA6......**80** D1
  RNFRW PA4......**61** F2
Houston St *HMLTN* ML3......**170** A4
  PLKSD/SHW G41......**89** E4
  RNFRW PA4......**63** G2
  WISHAW ML2......**174** C3
Houston Ter *EKILN* G74......**166** A3
Houstoun Sq *JNSTN* PA5......**101** G3
Howard Av *EKILN* G74......**149** F5
Howard Ct *EKILN* G74......**149** F5
Howard St *CGLE* G2......**2** E7
  PSLY PA1......**84** D4
Howatshaws Rd *DMBTN* G82......**13** G1
Howat St *GOV/IBX* G51......**87** H1
Howden Av *MTHW* ML1......**119** E4
Howden Dr
  PSLYN/LNWD PA3......**101** H1
Howden Pl *MTHW* ML1......**137** F2
Howe Gdns *UD/BTH/TAN* G71......**115** F5
Howe Rd *KSYTH* G65......**8** B3
Howes St *CTBR* ML5......**97** E5
Howford Rd
  CARD/HILL/MSPK G52......**86** C5
Howgate Av *DRUM* G15......**33** E5
Howgate Rd *HMLTN* ML3......**169** H5
Howieshill Av
  BLTYR/CAMB G72......**131** G2
Howieshill Rd
  BLTYR/CAMB G72......**131** G3
Howletnest Rd *AIRDRIE* ML6......**98** D3
Howlet Pl *HMLTN* ML3......**170** B4
Howson Lea *MTHW* ML1......**172** C1
Howson Vw *MTHW* ML1......**154** A3
Howth Dr *KNTSWD* G13......**51** G3
Howth Ter *KNTSWD* G13......**51** G3
Hoylake Pk *UD/BTH/TAN* G71......**134** A5
Hoylake Pl *SMSTN* G23......**52** D2
Hozier Crs *UD/BTH/TAN* G71......**115** E4
Hozier St *CTBR* ML5......**96** D5
Hudson Ter *EKILS* G75......**165** G5
Hudson Wy *EKILS* G75......**165** H5
Hughenden Dr *KVD/HLHD* G12......**66** A2
Hughenden Gdns
  KVD/HLHD G12......**65** H2
Hughenden La *KVD/HLHD* G12......**66** A2
Hughenden Rd
  KVD/HLHD G12......**66** A2
Hugh Murray Gv
  BLTYR/CAMB G72......**131** H2
Hugo St *MRYH/FIRH* G20......**67** E1
Huks Rd *AIRDRIE* ML6......**45** G5
Humbie Ct *NMRNS* G77......**161** H5
Humbie Gv *NMRNS* G77......**161** H5
Humbie Lawns *NMRNS* G77......**161** H5
Humbie Rd
  CRMNK/CLK/EAG G76......**162** C5
  NMRNS G77......**161** H5
Hume Dr *UD/BTH/TAN* G71......**134** B4
Hume Pl *EKILS* G75......**166** A5
Hume Rd *CUMB* G67......**26** C3
Hume St *CLYDBK* G81......**49** E2
Hunter Dr *NMRNS* G77......**161** E2
Hunterfield Dr
  BLTYR/CAMB G72......**130** D2
Hunterhill Av *PSLYS* PA2......**104** C1
Hunterhill Rd *PSLYS* PA2......**104** C1
Hunter Pl *KLBCH* PA10......**100** B4
  MLNGV G62......**16** C4
Hunter Rd *HMLTN* ML3......**152** C4
  MLNGV G62......**16** C4
  RUTH G73......**111** F3
Hunter's Av *DMBTN* G82......**13** H4
Hunters Crs *EKILN* G74......**149** H1
Huntersfield Rd *JNSTN* PA5......**100** D5
Hunters Gv *EKILN* G74......**150** A1
Hunters Hill Ct
  SPRGB/BLRNK G21......**54** C5
Huntershill Rd *BSHPBGS* G64......**54** C3
Huntershill St
  SPRGB/BLRNK G21......**54** B5
Huntershill Wy *BSHPBGS* G64......**54** B5
Hunters Pl *EKILN* G74......**167** F2
Hunter St *AIRDRIE* ML6......**76** A1
  BLSH ML4......**135** H2

  COWCAD G4......**3** K7
  EKILN G74......**166** C5
  PSLY PA1......**84** B4
Hunt Hl *BALLOCH* G68......**24** A4
Hunthill La *UD/BTH/TAN* G71......**151** E4
Hunthill Pl
  CRMNK/CLK/EAG G76......**146** B5
Hunthill Rd *BLTYR/CAMB* G72......**151** E4
Huntingdon Rd
  SPRGB/BLRNK G21......**68** B5
Huntingdon Sq
  SPRGB/BLRNK G21......**68** B5
Hunting Lodge Gdns
  HMLTN ML3......**170** D3
Huntingtower Rd
  BAIL/MDB/MHD G69......**93** G5
Huntley Gdns *KVD/HLHD* G12......**66** B3
Huntly Av *BLSH* ML4......**135** H1
  GIF/THBK G46......**127** G4
Huntly Ct *BSHPBGS* G64......**54** D3
Huntly Dr *BLTYR/CAMB* G72......**151** E4
  BSDN G61......**34** B1
  CTBR ML5......**96** A5
Huntly Gdns
  BLTYR/CAMB G72......**168** C2
  KVD/HLHD G12......**66** B3
Huntly Qd *WISHAW* ML2......**157** E5
Huntly Rd
  CARD/HILL/MSPK G52......**86** A1
  KVD/HLHD G12......**66** B3
Huntly Ter *PSLYS* PA2......**104** D3
Hurlawcrook Rd *EKILS* G75......**178** D5
Hurlet Rd *PSLYS* PA2......**106** C5
Hurlford Av *KNTSWD* G13......**50** B5
Hurly Hawkin *BSHPBGS* G64......**55** G3
Hutcheson Rd *GIF/THBK* G46......**126** D5
Hutcheson St *CGLE* G2......**3** G7
Hutchinson Pl
  BLTYR/CAMB G72......**132** B4
Hutchison Dr *BSDN* G61......**51** H1
Hutchison Pl *CTBR* ML5......**8** B1
Hutchison St *HMLTN* ML3......**170** A5
Hutton *KVD/HLHD* G12......**51** H5
Hutton Av *CRG/CRSL/HOU* PA6......**80** D1
Hutton Dr *EKILN* G74......**166** C1
  GOV/IBX G51......**87** F1
Huxley Pl *MRYH/FIRH* G20......**53** E5
Huxley St *MRYH/FIRH* G20......**53** E5
Hydepark St *KVGV* G3......**89** E4
Hyndal Av *PLK/PH/NH* G53......**106** D3
Hyndland Av *PTCK* G11......**66** A4
Hyndland Rd *KVD/HLHD* G12......**66** A3
Hyndland St *PTCK* G11......**66** B4
Hyndlee Dr
  CARD/HILL/MSPK G52......**86** D4
Hyndshaw Rd *WISHAW* ML2......**175** H5
Hyslop Pl *CLYDBK* G81......**31** H5
Hyslop St *AIRDRIE* ML6......**97** H1

I

Iain Dr *BSDN* G61......**33** H2
Iain Rd *BSDN* G61......**33** H2
Ian Smith Ct *CLYDBK* G81......**49** G2
Ibroxholm Ov *GOV/IBX* G51......**88** A4
Ibroxholm Pl *GOV/IBX* G51......**88** A4
Ibrox St *GOV/IBX* G51......**88** B3
Ibrox Ter *GOV/IBX* G51......**88** A3
Ida Qd *BLSH* ML4......**135** G2
Iddesleigh Av *MLNGV* G62......**17** E3
Ilay Av *BSDN* G61......**51** H1
Ilay Ct *BSDN* G61......**51** H1
Ilay Rd *BSDN* G61......**51** H1
Imlach Pl *MTHW* ML1......**154** C5
Imperial Dr *AIRDRIE* ML6......**98** A4
Imperial Wy
  UD/BTH/TAN G71......**134** B5
Inchbrae Dr
  CARD/HILL/MSPK G52......**86** D5
Inchcolm Gdns
  BAIL/MDB/MHD G69......**42** A5
Inchcolm Pl *EKILN* G74......**165** H3
Inchfad Dr *DRUM* G15......**32** D5
Inchfad Pl *DRUM* G15......**32** D5
Inchfad Rd *DRUM* G15......**32** D5
Inch Garvie *EKILN* G74......**167** G4
Inchgower Rd
  STPS/GTHM/RID G33......**57** F5
Inchholm La *PTCK* G11......**65** H3
Inchinnan Dr *RNFRW* PA4......**61** H2
Inchinnan Rd *BLSH* ML4......**116** C5
  PSLYN/LNWD PA3......**84** B2
Inch Keith *EKILN* G74......**167** G4
Inchkeith Pl *CAR/SHTL* G32......**92** D2
Inchlaggan Pl *DRUM* G15......**32** D4
Inchlee St *SCOT* G14......**65** F4
Inch Marnock *EKILN* G74......**167** F5
Inch Murrin *EKILN* G74......**167** G4
Inchmurrin Av *KKNTL* G66......**22** B5
Inchmurrin Gdns *RUTH* G73......**130** C5
Inchmurrin Pl *RUTH* G73......**130** C5
Inchnock Av
  BAIL/MDB/MHD G69......**59** F5
Inchoch Gv
  STPS/GTHM/RID G33......**71** H4
Inchoch St
  STPS/GTHM/RID G33......**71** H4
Inchrory Pl *DRUM* G15......**32** D4
Inchwood Ct *BALLOCH* G68......**43** H1
Inchwood Pl *BALLOCH* G68......**43** H1
Inchwood Rd *BALLOCH* G68......**43** G1
Incle St *PSLY* PA1......**84** C4
India Dr *RNFRW* PA4......**61** H1
India St *CCLE* G2......**2** B5
Industry St *KKNTL* G66......**40** A1
Inga St *MRYH/FIRH* G20......**53** D4
Ingerbreck Av *RUTH* G73......**130** C2
Ingleby Dr *DEN/PKHD* G31......**90** D2
Inglefield Ct *AIRDRIE* ML6......**98** A3
Inglefield St *GVH/MTFL* G42......**109** G2
Ingleneuk Av
  STPS/GTHM/RID G33......**57** G1
Inglestone Av *GIF/THBK* G46......**126** D5
Inglewood Crs *EKILS* G75......**165** F5
  PSLYS PA2......**102** D2

Inglis Pl *EKILS* G75......**178** B1
Inglis St *DEN/PKHD* G31......**90** D3
  WISHAW ML2......**173** E4
Ingliston Dr *BSHPTN* PA7......**28** C5
Ingram St *CGLE* G1......**3** H6
Inishail Rd
  STPS/GTHM/RID G33......**70** D3
Inkerman Rd
  CARD/HILL/MSPK G52......**86** A4
Innellan Gdns *MRYH/FIRH* G20......**52** A4
Innellan Pl *MRYH/FIRH* G20......**52** A4
Innerleithen Dr *WISHAW* ML2......**157** G4
Innermanse Qd *MTHW* ML1......**138** C2
Innerwick Dr
  CARD/HILL/MSPK G52......**86** C4
Innes Ct *EKILN* G74......**166** B1
International Av
  BLTYR/CAMB G72......**168** C1
Inveraray Dr *BSHPBGS* G64......**38** A4
Inveraray Gdns *MRYH/FIRH* G20......**137** H5
Inverarish *ERSK* PA8......**47** H4
Inverary Dr
  BAIL/MDB/MHD G69......**72** D2
Invercanny Dr *DRUM* G15......**33** E4
Invercanny Pl *DRUM* G15......**33** F4
Invercargill *EKILS* G75......**177** F1
Inverclyde Ct *EKILS* G75......**177** G4
Inverclyde Gdns *RUTH* G73......**130** D4
Inveresk Pl *CTBR* ML5......**96** D1
Inveresk Qd *CAR/SHTL* G32......**92** B3
Inveresk St *CAR/SHTL* G32......**92** B3
Inverewe Av *GIF/THBK* G46......**126** A5
Inverewe Dr *GIF/THBK* G46......**126** A5
Inverewe Gdns
  GIF/THBK G46......**126** A4
Inverewe Pl *GIF/THBK* G46......**126** A4
Inverewe Wy *NMRNS* G77......**143** F5
Invergarry Av *GIF/THBK* G46......**144** A1
Invergarry Ct *GIF/THBK* G46......**126** A5
Invergarry Dr *GIF/THBK* G46......**126** A5
Invergarry Gdns
  GIF/THBK G46......**144** A1
Invergarry Gv *GIF/THBK* G46......**126** A5
Invergarry Pl *GIF/THBK* G46......**126** A5
Invergarry Quad
  GIF/THBK G46......**126** A5
Invergarry Vw *GIF/THBK* G46......**126** B5
Inverglas Av *RNFRW* PA4......**64** A5
Invergordon Av
  PLKSW/MSWD G43......**109** E5
Invergordon Pl *AIRDRIE* ML6......**98** D3
Invergyle Dr
  CARD/HILL/MSPK G52......**86** C4
Inverkar Dr *PSLYS* PA2......**103** F2
Inverlair Av *LNPK/KPK* G44......**128** B1
Inverleith St *CAR/SHTL* G32......**91** G4
Inverlochy St
  STPS/GTHM/RID G33......**71** E2
Inverness St *GOV/IBX* G51......**87** E3
Inveroran Dr *BSDN* G61......**35** E3
Inver Rd *STPS/GTHM/RID* G33......**93** F1
Invershin Dr *MRYH/FIRH* G20......**66** C1
Inverurie St *SPRGB/BLRNK* G21......**68** B3
Invervale Av *AIRDRIE* ML6......**99** G3
Inzievar Ter *CAR/SHTL* G32......**112** C3
Iona Av *EKILN* G74......**166** D1
Iona Crs *OLDK* G60......**30** D3
Iona Dr *PSLYS* PA2......**104** A5
Iona Gdns *OLDK* G60......**30** D3
Iona Pl *CTBR* ML5......**74** A5
Iona Qd *WISHAW* ML2......**157** H5
Iona Rdg *HMLTN* ML3......**168** D4
Iona Rd *RNFRW* PA4......**63** E5
  RUTH G73......**130** D4
  WISHAW ML2......**158** A4
Iona St *GOV/IBX* G51......**88** A2
  MTHW ML1......**154** C1
Iona Wk *CTBR* ML5......**96** B5
Iona Wy *KKNTL* G66......**22** A5
Iris Av *CSMK* G45......**129** H4
Irongray St *DEN/PKHD* G31......**91** F2
Irvine Ct *DMNK/BRGTN* G40......**111** F2
Irvine Crs *CTBR* ML5......**97** F1
Irvine Dr *PSLYN/LNWD* PA3......**81** G4
Irvine Gdns *KKNTL* G66......**5** F5
Irvine Pl *KSYTH* G65......**8** B1
Irvine St *DMNK/BRGTN* G40......**111** E2
  DMNK/BRGTN G40......**111** H3
Irvine Ter *HMLTN* ML3......**170** A5
Irving Av *CLYDBK* G81......**32** A3
Irving Ct *CLYDBK* G81......**32** A3
Irving Qd *CLYDBK* G81......**32** A2
Isabella Gdns *HMLTN* ML3......**171** E4
Iser La *PLKSD/SHW* G41......**108** D4
Isla Av *WISHAW* ML2......**158** A4
Island Rd *CUMB* G67......**25** H5
Islay Av *RUTH* G73......**130** D4
Islay Crs *HMLTN* ML3......**169** E3
  OLDK G60......**30** D3
  PSLYS PA2......**104** A5
Islay Dr *NMRNS* G77......**143** G5
  OLDK G60......**30** D3
Islay Gdns *WISHAW* ML2......**173** F4
Islay Rd *KKNTL* G66......**22** A5
Islay Wy *CTBR* ML5......**96** A5
Ivanhoe *EKILN* G74......**167** G1
Ivanhoe Crs *WISHAW* ML2......**174** B2
Ivanhoe Dr *KKNTL* G66......**21** H5
Ivanhoe Rd *CUMB* G67......**26** B5
  KNTSWD G13......**51** E3
  PSLYS PA2......**102** D3
Ivybank Av *BLTYR/CAMB* G72......**131** H3
Ivy Pl *BLTYR/CAMB* G72......**151** F3
  MTHW ML1......**137** F4
Ivy Rd *UD/BTH/TAN* G71......**115** H4
Ivy Ter *MTHW* ML1......**137** F2
Ivy Wy *AIRDRIE* ML6......**119** F1

J

Jackson Dr
  STPS/GTHM/RID G33......**71** H1
Jackson Pl *BSDN* G61......**34** B5

Jackson St CTBR ML5 ...97 E2
Jack's Rd UD/BTH/TAN G71 ...134 A1
Jack St HMLTN ML3 ...170 A5
  MTHW ML1 ...172 C1
Jackton Rd EKILS G75 ...176 C3
Jacobite Pl BLSH ML4 ...136 C3
Jagger Gdns
  BAIL/MDB/MHD G69 ...93 G5
Jamaica St EKILS G65 ...165 G4
Jamaica St CGLE G1 ...2 E7
James Dempsey Ct CTBR ML5 ...96 C5
James Dempsey Gdns
  CTBR ML5 * ...96 C5
James Dunlop Gdns
  BSHPBGS G64 ...55 E4
James Gray St
  PLKSD/SHW G41 ...108 D4
James Hamilton Dr
  BLSH ML4 ...136 B1
James Healy Dr HMLTN ML3 ...180 C1
James Leeson Ct KKNTL G66 ...5 F4
James Morrison St CGLE G1 ...90 A3
James Nisbet St
  SPRGB/BLRNK G21 ...90 C1
James St BLSH ML4 ...116 B5
  DMNK/BRGTN G40 ...90 B5
  MTHW ML1 ...154 C3
James Vw MTHW ML1 ...137 F4
James Watt Av EKILS G75 ...166 D5
James Watt Pl EKILN G74 ...165 G2
James Watt Rd MLNGV G62 ...16 D2
James Watt St CCLW G2 ...2 C7
Jamieson Ct CLYDBK G81 ...32 A1
  GVH/MTFL G42 ...109 G2
Jamieson Dr EKILN G74 ...166 D3
Jamieson St GVH/MTFL G42 ...109 G2
Janebank Av
  BLTYR/CAMB G72 ...131 H3
Janefield Av JNSTN PA5 ...101 F4
Janefield Pl
  BLTYR/CAMB G72 ...151 F4
  KKNTL G66 ...4 B1
Jane Pl GBLS G5 ...89 H5
Jane Rae Gdns CLYDBK G81 ...49 G3
Jane's Brae CUMB G67 ...26 B5
Janesmith St WISHAW ML2 ...172 D1
Janetta St CLYDBK G81 ...31 H5
Jardine St MRYH/FIRH G20 ...67 E3
Jardine Ter
  BAIL/MDB/MHD G69 ...73 E1
Jarvie Av KSYTH G65 ...8 B3
Jarvie Wy PLSYS PA2 ...102 D4
Jasmine Pl CUMB G67 ...44 A1
Java St MTHW ML1 ...154 B1
Jean Armour Dr CLYDBK G81 ...32 A5
Jeanette Av HMLTN ML3 ...180 C1
Jedburgh Av DRUM G15 ...33 G5
Jedburgh Dr DRUM G15 ...33 H5
Jeffrey Pl KSYTH G65 ...8 A1
Jellicoe St CLYDBK G81 ...31 F5
Jennys Well Ct PSLYS PA2 ...105 G2
Jenys Well Rd PSLYS PA2 ...105 G2
Jervis Ter EKILS G75 ...177 G1
Jerviston Ct MTHW ML1 ...155 F1
Jerviston Rd MTHW ML1 ...155 F1
  STPS/GTHM/RID G33 ...70 D4
Jerviston St MTHW ML1 ...155 F1
Jerviswood MTHW ML1 ...155 F1
Jessie St GVH/MTFL G42 ...110 A3
Joanna Ter BLTYR/CAMB G72 ...151 G2
John Bowman Gdns
  BLSH ML4 ...136 A1
John Brannan Wy
  UD/BTH/TAN G71 ...135 E1
John Brown Pl
  BAIL/MDB/MHD G69 ...58 B3
John Burnside Dr CLYDBK G81 ...32 B1
John Hendry Rd
  UD/BTH/TAN G71 ...134 B3
John Knox St CLYDBK G81 ...49 G4
  COWCAD G4 ...3 K5
John Lang St JNSTN PA5 ...101 H3
John Murray Ct MTHW ML1 ...171 H4
Johnsburn Dr
  PLK/PH/NH G53 ...125 G1
Johnsburn Rd
  PLK/PH/NH G53 ...125 G1
Johnshaven St
  PLKSW/MSWD G43 ...108 B5
John Smith Ct AIRDRIE ML6 ...98 A1
John Smith Gdns CTBR ML5 ...97 F3
John Smith Ga
  BRHD/NEIL G78 ...124 B3
Johnstone Av
  CARD/HILL/MSPK G52 ...86 C2
  CLYDBK G81 ...49 G3
Johnstone Dr RUTH G73 ...110 D5
Johnstone Rd HMLTN ML3 ...170 B3
Johnstone St BLSH ML4 ...136 B3
Johnstone Ter KKNTL G66 ...23 F3
Johnston Rd
  BAIL/MDB/MHD G69 ...59 F3
Johnston St AIRDRIE ML6 ...98 C1
  PSLY PA1 ...84 B5
John St BLSH ML4 ...136 B3
  BLTYR/CAMB G72 ...151 H1
  BRHD/NEIL G78 ...124 A4
  CGLE G1 ...3 G6
  HMLTN ML3 ...170 B2
  KKNTL G66 ...21 F4
  MTHW ML1 ...172 D1
John Wilson Dr KSYTH G65 ...7 H1
Jones Wynd MTHW ML1 ...156 A5
Joppa St STPS/GTHM/RID G33 ...91 H1
Jordanhill Crs KNTSWD G13 ...65 E1

Jordanhill Dr KNTSWD G13 ...65 E1
Jordanhill La KNTSWD G13 ...65 F1
Jordan St SCOT G14 ...65 E4
Jordanvale Av SCOT G14 ...65 E4
Jowitt Av CLYDBK G81 ...49 G2
Jubilee Ct
  CARD/HILL/MSPK G52 ...86 A2
Jubilee Gdns BSDN G61 ...34 B4
Jubilee Ter JNSTN PA5 ...101 E3
Julian Av KVD/HLHD G12 ...66 B2
Julian La KVD/HLHD G12 ...66 B2
Juniper Av BRWEIR PA11 ...78 C2
  EKILS G75 ...178 A2
Juniper Ct KKNTL G66 ...39 G5
Juniper Dr KKNTL G66 ...20 D1
Juniper Gv HMLTN ML3 ...170 C5
Juniper Pl
  BAIL/MDB/MHD G69 ...93 G5
  JNSTN PA5 ...101 E3
  UD/BTH/TAN G71 ...116 A4
Juniper Rd UD/BTH/TAN G71 ...116 A4
Juniper Ter CAR/SHTL G32 ...93 F5
Juno St MTHW ML1 ...154 C1
Jupiter St MTHW ML1 ...154 C1
Jura EKILN G74 ...179 E1
Jura Av RNFRW PA4 ...63 G5
Jura Ct BLTYR/CAMB G72 ...133 F4
Jura Dr BLTYR/CAMB G72 ...133 F4
  NMRNS G77 ...143 G4
  OLDK G60 ...30 D3
Jura Gdns HMLTN ML3 ...169 F3
Jura Qd WISHAW ML2 ...173 F4
Jura Rd OLDK G60 ...30 D3
  PSLYS PA2 ...104 A5
Jura St CARD/HILL/MSPK G52 ...87 G4
Jura Wynd CTBR ML5 ...59 H5

K

Kaim Dr PLK/PH/NH G53 ...125 H1
Katewell Av DRUM G15 ...32 D4
Katewell Pl DRUM G15 ...32 D4
Katherine St AIRDRIE ML6 ...99 F1
Katrine Av BLSH ML4 ...135 C1
  BSHPBGS G64 ...55 E2
Katrine Crs AIRDRIE ML6 ...76 A5
Katrine Dr NMRNS G77 ...162 C1
  PSLYS PA2 ...103 F3
Katrine Pl BLTYR/CAMB G72 ...131 F1
  CTBR ML5 ...74 A5
Kay Gdns MTHW ML1 ...154 A3
Kaystone Rd DRUM G15 ...50 B2
Kay St SPRGB/BLRNK G21 ...68 C2
Keal Av DRUM G15 ...50 B3
Keal Crs DRUM G15 ...50 B3
Keal Dr DRUM G15 ...50 B3
Keal Pl DRUM G15 ...50 B3
Kearn Av DRUM G15 ...50 C2
Kearn Pl DRUM G15 ...50 C2
Keats Pk UD/BTH/TAN G71 ...134 B5
Keil Crs DMBTN G82 ...12 C4
Keir Gv WISHAW ML2 ...174 A1
Keir Dr BSHPBGS G64 ...54 C1
Keir Hardie Av MTHW ML1 ...137 D2
Keir Hardie Dr BLSH ML4 ...135 G3
  KSYTH G65 ...8 B3
Keir St PLKSD/SHW G41 ...109 E1
Keir's Wk BLTYR/CAMB G72 ...131 F1
Keith Av GIF/THBK G46 ...127 G4
Keith Ct PTCK G11 ...66 B4
Keith Qd WISHAW ML2 ...157 F5
Keith St HMLTN ML3 ...170 C1
  PTCK G11 ...66 B4
Kelbourne Crs BLSH ML4 ...135 G2
Kelbourne St MRYH/FIRH G20 ...66 D2
Kelburne Dr PSLY PA1 ...85 E4
Kelburne Gdns
  BAIL/MDB/MHD G69 ...113 H1
  PSLY PA1 ...84 D4
Kelburne Gv PSLY PA1 ...84 D4
Kelburn St BRHD/NEIL G78 ...141 H1
Kelhead Av
  CARD/HILL/MSPK G52 ...86 A4
Kelhead Dr
  CARD/HILL/MSPK G52 ...86 A4
Kelhead Pth
  CARD/HILL/MSPK G52 ...86 A4
Kelhead Pl
  CARD/HILL/MSPK G52 ...86 A4
Kellie Gv EKILN G74 ...166 A2
Kelso Av BRWEIR PA11 ...79 F4
  PSLYS PA2 ...103 F3
Kelso Crs WISHAW ML2 ...157 E4
Kelso Dr EKILN G74 ...166 D2
Kelso Gdns
  BAIL/MDB/MHD G69 ...42 A5
Kelso Pl SCOT G14 ...49 H5
Kelso Qd CTBR ML5 ...96 C1
Kelso St KNTSWD G13 ...50 A4
  SCOT G14 ...49 H5
Kelton St CAR/SHTL G32 ...92 C5
Kelvin Av
  CARD/HILL/MSPK G52 ...86 B1
Kelvin Ct EKILS G75 ...178 D2
Kelvin Crs BSDN G61 ...51 G1
Kelvindale Gdns
  MRYH/FIRH G20 ...52 B5
Kelvindale Pl MRYH/FIRH G20 ...52 C5
Kelvindale Rd KVD/HLHD G12 ...66 B1
Kelvin Dr AIRDRIE ML6 ...76 C5
  BAIL/MDB/MHD G69 ...58 D2
  BRHD/NEIL G78 ...142 C1
  BSHPBGS G64 ...54 D1
  EKILS G75 ...178 C2
  KKNTL G66 ...20 C5
  MRYH/FIRH G20 ...66 C2
Kelvin Gdns HMLTN ML3 ...168 D1
  KSYTH G65 ...8 B3
Kelvingrove St KVGV G3 ...88 C1
Kelvinhaugh Ga KVGV G3 ...88 C1
Kelvinhaugh Pl KVGV G3 ...88 C1
Kelvinhaugh St KVGV G3 ...88 C1
Kelvin Pk South EKILS G75 ...178 D4
Kelvin Pl EKILS G75 ...178 D1

Kelvin Rd BLSH ML4 ...117 E5
  CUMB G67 ...26 C5
  EKILS G75 ...178 D1
  MLNGV G62 ...16 D3
  UD/BTH/TAN G71 ...116 C5
Kelvin Rd North CUMB G67 ...26 C5
Kelvinside Av MRYH/FIRH G20 ...66 D2
Kelvinside Dr MRYH/FIRH G20 ...67 E2
Kelvinside Gdns
  MRYH/FIRH G20 ...66 D2
Kelvinside Gdns East
  MRYH/FIRH G20 ...67 E3
Kelvinside Gardens La
  MRYH/FIRH G20 ...66 D2
Kelvinside Ter South
  KVD/HLHD G12 ...66 D3
Kelvinside Ter West
  MRYH/FIRH G20 ...66 D3
Kelvin St CTBR ML5 ...97 F4
Kelvinvale KKNTL G66 ...21 F4
Kelvin Vw BSHPBGS G64 ...19 G5
  KSYTH G65 ...23 F1
Kelvin Wy KKNTL G66 ...20 C5
  KSYTH G65 ...8 A1
  KVGV G3 ...66 C5
Kemp Av PSLYN/LNWD PA3 ...62 D5
Kempsthorn Cresent
  PLK/PH/NH G53 ...106 C3
Kempsthorn Pl
  PLK/PH/NH G53 ...106 C3
Kempsthorn Rd
  PLK/PH/NH G53 ...106 C3
Kemp St HMLTN ML3 ...170 A2
  SPRGB/BLRNK G21 ...68 B2
Kenbank Crs BRWEIR PA11 ...79 G3
Kenbank Rd BRWEIR PA11 ...79 G3
Kendal Av GIF/THBK G46 ...127 G4
  KVD/HLHD G12 ...51 H5
Kendal Dr KVD/HLHD G12 ...51 H5
Kendon Av DRUM G15 ...32 D5
Kenilburn Av AIRDRIE ML6 ...76 C4
Kenilburn Crs AIRDRIE ML6 ...76 C4
Kenilworth EKILN G74 ...167 G1
Kenilworth Av
  PLKSD/SHW G41 ...108 C4
  PSLYS PA2 ...103 E4
  WISHAW ML2 ...174 A3
Kenilworth Ct CUMB G67 ...26 A5
Kenilworth Crs BLSH ML4 ...135 C1
  BSDN G61 ...33 H2
  HMLTN ML3 ...169 E5
Kenilworth Dr AIRDRIE ML6 ...98 D1
Kenilworth Rd KKNTL G66 ...21 G5
Kenmar Gdns
  UD/BTH/TAN G71 ...114 D4
Kenmar Ter HMLTN ML3 ...152 C5
Kenmore Gdns BSDN G61 ...35 E3
Kenmore Rd CUMB G67 ...26 C3
Kenmore St CAR/SHTL G32 ...92 B4
Kenmore Wy CTBR ML5 ...117 F1
Kenmuiraid Pl BLSH ML4 ...135 G4
Kenmuir Av CAR/SHTL G32 ...113 F1
Kenmuirhill Rd
  CAR/SHTL G32 ...113 E3
Kenmuir Rd CAR/SHTL G32 ...113 E4
Kenmuir St CTBR ML5 ...95 G5
Kenmure Av BSHPBGS G64 ...54 C2
Kenmure Crs BSHPBGS G64 ...54 C2
Kenmure Dr BSHPBGS G64 ...54 C2
Kenmure Gdns BSHPBGS G64 ...54 C2
Kenmure La BSHPBGS G64 ...54 C2
Kenmure Rd GIF/THBK G46 ...145 G4
Kenmure St PLKSD/SHW G41 ...109 E1
Kenmure Wy RUTH G73 ...130 A4
Kennedar Dr GOV/IBX G51 ...87 F1
Kennedy Dr AIRDRIE ML6 ...97 H2
Kennedy St COWCAD G4 ...3 J2
  WISHAW ML2 ...174 B2
Kennelburn Rd AIRDRIE ML6 ...119 E3
Kenneth Rd MTHW ML1 ...154 B5
Kennihill AIRDRIE ML6 ...76 B5
Kennihill Qd AIRDRIE ML6 ...76 B5
Kennishead Av GIF/THBK G46 ...126 B2
Kennishead Pl GIF/THBK G46 ...126 B2
Kennisholm Av
  GIF/THBK G46 ...126 B2
Kennyhill Sq DEN/PKHD G31 ...91 E1
Kensington Dr GIF/THBK G46 ...145 G1
Kensington Ga KVD/HLHD G12 ...66 B2
Kensington Gate La
  KVD/HLHD G12 ...66 B2
Kensington Rd KVD/HLHD G12 ...66 B2
Kentallen Rd
  STPS/GTHM/RID G33 ...93 E3
Kent Dr RUTH G73 ...130 C2
Kentigern Ter BSHPBGS G64 ...54 D3
Kentmere Cl EKILS G75 ...177 F2
Kentmere Dr EKILS G75 ...177 F2
Kentmere Pl EKILS G75 ...177 F2
Kent Pl EKILS G75 ...177 E2
Kent Rd KVGV G3 ...88 D1
Kent St DMNK/BRGTN G40 ...90 A5
Keppel Dr LNPK/KPK G44 ...110 B5
Keppochhill Dr
  SPRGB/BLRNK G21 ...68 A4
Keppochhill Pl
  SPRGB/BLRNK G21 ...68 A4
Keppochhill Rd PPK/MIL G22 ...67 H3
  SPRGB/BLRNK G21 ...68 A4
Keppochhill Wy
  SPRGB/BLRNK G21 ...68 A4
Keppoch St
  SPRGB/BLRNK G21 ...68 A3
Kerfield Pl DRUM G15 ...32 D4
Kerr Av HMLTN ML3 ...169 F4
Kerr Dr DMNK/BRGTN G40 ...90 C4
  MTHW ML1 ...154 A3
Kerrera Pl
  STPS/GTHM/RID G33 ...93 E3
Kerrera Rd
  STPS/GTHM/RID G33 ...93 E3
Kerr Gdns UD/BTH/TAN G71 ...115 F4
Ker Rd MLNGV G62 ...16 C2

Kerr Pl DMNK/BRGTN G40 ...90 C4
Kerr St BLTYR/CAMB G72 ...151 H2
  BRHD/NEIL G78 ...123 H5
  DMNK/BRGTN G40 ...90 C4
  KKNTL G66 ...4 C2
  PSLYN/LNWD PA3 ...84 A4
Kerrycroy Av GVH/MTFL G42 ...110 A4
Kerrycroy Pl GVH/MTFL G42 ...110 A4
Kerrycroy St GVH/MTFL G42 ...110 A4
Kerrydale St
  DMNK/BRGTN G40 ...91 E5
Kerrylamont Av
  GVH/MTFL G42 ...110 B5
Kerry Pl DRUM G15 ...32 D5
Kersland Dr MLNGV G62 ...17 E3
Kersland La MLNGV G62 ...17 E3
  MLNGV G62 ...17 E3
Kersland St KVD/HLHD G12 ...66 D3
Kessington Dr BSDN G61 ...35 E4
Kessington Rd BSDN G61 ...35 E5
Kessington Sq BSDN G61 ...35 F5
Kessock Dr PPK/MIL G22 ...67 G3
Kessock Pl PPK/MIL G22 ...67 G3
Kestrel Ct CLYDBK G81 ...31 H1
  CTBR ML5 ...117 H1
Kestrel Pl JNSTN PA5 ...121 E2
Kestrel Rd KNTSWD G13 ...50 D5
Kethers La MTHW ML1 ...154 B4
Keswick Dr HMLTN ML3 ...180 C2
Keswick Rd EKILS G75 ...177 E3
Kethers St MTHW ML1 ...154 A4
Kew Gdns UD/BTH/TAN G71 ...115 G5
Kew La KVD/HLHD G12 ...66 C3
Kew Ter KVD/HLHD G12 ...66 C3
Keystone Av MLNGV G62 ...17 E5
Keystone Qd MLNGV G62 ...16 D5
Keystone Rd MLNGV G62 ...17 E5
Kibbleston Rd KLBCH PA10 ...120 A2
Kidston Ter GBLS G5 ...89 H5
Kierhill Rd BALLOCH G68 ...25 F3
Kilallan Av BRWEIR PA11 ...79 F2
Kilbarchan Rd BRWEIR PA11 ...80 A5
  JNSTN PA5 ...101 E5
  KLBCH PA10 ...100 D4
Kilbeg Ter GIF/THBK G46 ...126 B4
Kilberry St SPRGB/BLRNK G21 ...68 D5
Kilbirnie Pl GBLS G5 ...89 F5
Kilbirnie St GBLS G5 ...89 F5
Kilbowie Pl AIRDRIE ML6 ...98 D1
Kilbowie Rd CLYDBK G81 ...49 E2
  CUMB G67 ...26 C4
Kilbreck Gdns BSDN G61 ...16 A5
Kilbrennan Dr MTHW ML1 ...153 H3
Kilbrennan Rd
  PSLYN/LNWD PA3 ...82 A3
Kilbride St GBLS G5 ...110 A1
Kilbride Vw UD/BTH/TAN G71 ...115 F5
Kilburn Gv BLTYR/CAMB G72 ...151 G1
Kilburn Pl KNTSWD G13 ...50 C5
Kilchattan Dr LNPK/KPK G44 ...109 H5
Kilchoan Rd
  STPS/GTHM/RID G33 ...70 D4
Kildale Av RUTH G73 ...110 D5
Kildale Wy RUTH G73 ...110 D5
Kildary Av LNPK/KPK G44 ...128 B2
Kildary Rd LNPK/KPK G44 ...128 B2
Kildermorie Rd ESTRH G34 ...93 H1
Kildonan Ct WISHAW ML2 ...158 A3
Kildonan Dr PTCK G11 ...66 A4
Kildonan Pl MTHW ML1 ...154 B3
Kildonan St CTBR ML5 ...97 F2
Kildrostan St
  PLKSD/SHW G41 ...109 E2
Kildrum Rd CUMB G67 ...27 E1
Kildrum Rd CUMB G67 ...27 E1
Kilearn Rd PSLYN/LNWD PA3 ...85 E2
Kilearn Wy PSLYN/LNWD PA3 ...85 E2
Kilfinan St PPK/MIL G22 ...53 G5
Kilgarth St CTBR ML5 ...116 A1
Kilgraston Rd BRWEIR PA11 ...79 F4
Kilkerran Ct NMRNS G77 ...161 E1
Kilkerran Dr
  STPS/GTHM/RID G33 ...56 A5
Kilkerran Pk NMRNS G77 ...161 E1
Kilkerran Wy NMRNS G77 ...161 E1
Killearn Crs AIRDRIE ML6 ...119 H3
Killearn Dr PSLY PA1 ...85 H5
Killearn St PPK/MIL G22 ...67 G2
Killermont Av
  UD/BTH/TAN G71 ...133 H5
Killermont Rd BSDN G61 ...34 D4
Killermont St CGLW G2 ...3 F5
Killermont Vw
  MRYH/FIRH G20 ...51 H1
Killiegrew Rd
  PLKSD/SHW G41 ...108 C2
Killin Dr PSLYN/LNWD PA3 ...101 C1
Killin St CAR/SHTL G32 ...112 C1
Killoch Av PSLYN/LNWD PA3 ...83 F4
Killoch Dr BRHD/NEIL G78 ...142 C1
  KNTSWD G13 ...50 B4
Killoch La PSLYN/LNWD PA3 ...83 F4
Killoch Rd PSLYN/LNWD PA3 ...83 F4
Killoch Wy PSLYN/LNWD PA3 ...83 F4
Kilmacolm Rd BRWEIR PA11 ...79 E1
Kilmailing Rd LNPK/KPK G44 ...128 C2
Kilmair Pl MRYH/FIRH G20 ...66 C1
Kilmaluag Ter GIF/THBK G46 ...126 A4
Kilmany Dr CAR/SHTL G32 ...92 A4
Kilmany Gdns CAR/SHTL G32 ...92 A4
Kilmardinny Av BSDN G61 ...34 D2
Kilmardinny Crs BSDN G61 ...34 D2
Kilmardinny Ga BSDN G61 ...34 D2
Kilmardinny Gv BSDN G61 ...34 D2
Kilmari Gdns DRUM G15 ...32 D4
Kilmarnock Rd
  PLKSW/MSWD G43 ...127 G1
Kilmartin Pl GIF/THBK G46 ...126 B3
  UD/BTH/TAN G71 ...115 F3
Kilmaurs Dr GIF/THBK G46 ...127 H4
Kilmaurs St GOV/IBX G51 ...87 G3
Kilmeny Crs WISHAW ML2 ...157 H5
Kilmichael Av WISHAW ML2 ...158 A4
Kilmore Crs DRUM G15 ...32 D4

Kilmorie Dr RUTH G73 ...110 B5
Kilmory Av UD/BTH/TAN G71 ...115 F5
Kilmory Ct EKILS G75 ...177 H4
Kilmory Dr NMRNS G77 ...144 B4
Kilmory Gdns GIF/THBK G46 ...145 G4
Kilmory Rd CARLUKE ML8 ...126 B3
Kilmuir Crs GIF/THBK G46 ...126 B3
Kilmuir Dr GIF/THBK G46 ...126 B3
  UD/BTH/TAN G71 ...115 F3
Kilmun St MRYH/FIRH G20 ...52 C4
Kilnburn Rd MTHW ML1 ...154 B3
Kilncroft La PSLYS PA2 ...104 B3
Kilnside Rd PSLY PA1 ...84 C4
Kilnwell Qd MTHW ML1 ...154 C3
Kiloran Gv NMRNS G77 ...160 D1
Kiloran Pl NMRNS G77 ...160 D1
Kiloran St GIF/THBK G46 ...126 C3
Kilpatrick Av PSLYS PA2 ...103 G2
Kilpatrick Crs PSLYS PA2 ...104 A3
Kilpatrick Dr BSDN G61 ...16 A5
  EKILS G75 ...177 G5
  ERSK PA8 ...47 F1
  RNFRW PA4 ...85 E1
  STPS/GTHM/RID G33 ...71 E1
Kilpatrick Gdns
  CRMNK/CLK/EAG G76 ...145 G3
Kilpatrick Vw DMBTN G82 ...13 G3
Kilpatrick Wy
  UD/BTH/TAN G71 ...115 F5
Kilsyth Gdns EKILS G75 ...177 F5
Kilsyth Rd KKNTL G66 ...7 F3
Kiltarie Crs AIRDRIE ML6 ...99 G3
Kiltearn Rd
  STPS/GTHM/RID G33 ...93 G2
Kilvaxter Dr GIF/THBK G46 ...126 B3
Kilwinning Crs AIRDRIE ML6 ...77 F5
  HMLTN ML3 ...168 D4
Kimberley Gdns EKILS G75 ...165 H5
Kimberley St CLYDBK G81 ...31 E3
  WISHAW ML2 ...172 D2
Kinalty Rd LNPK/KPK G44 ...128 B2
Kinarvie Crs PLK/PH/NH G53 ...106 A3
Kinarvie Gdns PLK/PH/NH G53 ...106 A3
Kinarvie Pl PLK/PH/NH G53 ...106 A3
Kinarvie Rd PLK/PH/NH G53 ...106 A3
Kinarvie Ter PLK/PH/NH G53 ...106 A3
Kinbuck St PPK/MIL G22 ...68 A2
Kincaid Fld KKNTL G66 ...21 H5
Kincaid Gdns
  BLTYR/CAMB G72 ...131 F1
Kincaid Wy KKNTL G66 ...21 H5
Kincardine Dr BSHPBGS G64 ...55 F3
Kincardine Pl BSHPBGS G64 ...55 F3
  EKILN G74 ...167 F2
Kincardine Sq
  STPS/GTHM/RID G33 ...71 E5
Kincath Av RUTH G73 ...130 D4
Kinclaven Av DRUM G15 ...33 G5
Kinclaven Pl DRUM G15 ...33 G5
Kincraig St GOV/IBX G51 ...87 E3
Kinellan Rd BSDN G61 ...51 G2
Kinellar Dr SCOT G14 ...50 C5
Kinfauns Dr DRUM G15 ...33 E5
  NMRNS G77 ...144 C5
Kingarth La GVH/MTFL G42 ...109 F2
Kingarth St HMLTN ML3 ...170 A5
  GVH/MTFL G42 ...109 F2
King Edward La KNTSWD G13 ...65 G1
King Edward Rd KNTSWD G13 ...65 G1
Kingfisher Dr KNTSWD G13 ...50 A4
King George Ct RNFRW PA4 ...63 H5
King George Gdns RNFRW PA4 ...63 H5
King George Park Av
  RNFRW PA4 ...63 H5
King George Wy RNFRW PA4 ...63 H5
Kinghorn Dr LNPK/KPK G44 ...128 D1
Kinglas Rd BSDN G61 ...50 D1
King Pl BAIL/MDB/MHD G69 ...59 H2
Kingsacre Rd LNPK/KPK G44 ...109 H5
Kingsbarns Dr LNPK/KPK G44 ...109 G5
Kingsborough Gdns
  KVD/HLHD G12 ...66 A2
Kingsborough Ga
  KVD/HLHD G12 ...66 A3
Kingsborough La
  KVD/HLHD G12 ...66 A3
Kingsborough La East
  KVD/HLHD G12 ...66 A3
Kingsbrae Av LNPK/KPK G44 ...109 H5
Kingsbridge Crs
  LNPK/KPK G44 ...129 E1
Kingsbridge Dr
  LNPK/KPK G44 ...128 D1
Kingsburgh Dr PSLY PA1 ...85 E4
Kingsburn Dr RUTH G73 ...129 H1
Kingsburn Gv RUTH G73 ...129 H1
Kingscliffe Av LNPK/KPK G44 ...128 D1
Kingscourt Av LNPK/KPK G44 ...129 E1
Kings Crs BLTYR/CAMB G72 ...132 B1
Kings Crs JNSTN PA5 ...102 B1
King's Dr BALLOCH G68 ...90 B5
  DMNK/BRGTN G40 ...90 B5
  MTHW ML1 ...137 G4
  NMRNS G77 ...162 A2
Kingsdyke Av LNPK/KPK G44 ...110 A5
Kingsford Av LNPK/KPK G44 ...127 H3
Kingsford Ct NMRNS G77 ...143 H4
King's Gdns NMRNS G77 ...162 B2
Kingsheath Av RUTH G73 ...129 F1
Kingshill Av BALLOCH G68 ...24 C3
Kingshill Dr LNPK/KPK G44 ...128 D1
Kingshill Rd SHOTTS ML7 ...159 H4
Kinghouse Av
  LNPK/KPK G44 ...128 D1
Kingshurst Av LNPK/KPK G44 ...109 H5
Kings inch Dr GOV/IBX G51 ...64 C5
Kings Inch Pl RNFRW PA4 ...64 B3
Kings Inch Rd RNFRW PA4 ...64 A2
Kingsknowe Dr RUTH G73 ...129 F1
Kingsland Dr
  CARD/HILL/MSPK G52 ...86 C3
Kingslea Rd
  CRC/CRSL/HOU PA6 ...80 C1
Kingsley Av GVH/MTFL G42 ...109 G3
Kingsley Ct UD/BTH/TAN G71 ...115 F5
Kingslynn Dr LNPK/KPK G44 ...128 D1
Kingsmuir Dr BALLOCH G68 ...24 C3
Kings Pk BSHPBGS G64 ...19 G4

King's Park Av
LNPK/KPK G44 ......129 E1
LNPK/KPK G44 ......128 D1
King's Park Rd
GVH/MTFL G42......109 G5
King's Pl PPK/MIL G22......53 G5
Kingston Av AIRDRIE ML6......98 D2
BRHD/NEIL G78......141 E4
UD/BTH/TAN G71......115 F4
Kingston Br GBLS G5......2 B7
Kingston Flats KSYTH G65......8 B7
Kingston Gv BSHPTN PA7......29 E5
Kingston Rd BRHD/NEIL G78......140 D5
BSHPTN PA7......29 E5
KSYTH G65......8 B1
Kingston St GBLS G5......89 F3
King St CLYDBK G81......49 F1
CTBR ML5......96 B3
HMLTN ML3......169 E1
KSYTH G65......8 B2
PSLY PA1......83 H4
RUTH G73......110 D4
WISHAW ML2......174 A3
King Street La RUTH G73......110 D4
King's Vw BALLOCH G68......10 B4
King's Wy DMBTN G82......12 C2
Kingsway EKILN G74......166 D3
KKNTL G66......22 B5
KSYTH G65......8 B1
SCOT G14......64 C1
Kingsway ct SCOT G14......64 C1
Kingswood Dr
LNPK/KPK G44......129 E1
Kingswood Rd BSHPTN PA7......28 C4
Kingussie Dr LNPK/KPK G44......128 C2
Kiniver Dr ERSK PA8......50 C2
Kinkell Gdns KKNTL G66......22 B3
Kinloch Av BLTYR/CAMB G72......131 G3
PSLYN/LNWD PA3......101 H1
Kinloch Dr MTHW ML1......136 C5
Kinloch Rd NMRNS G77......143 H4
RNFRW PA4......63 E5
Kinloch St DMNK/BRGTN G40......91 E5
Kinloss Pl EKILN G74......166 D3
Kinmount Av LNPK/KPK G44......109 G5
Kinnaird Av NMRNS G77......144 D5
Kinnaird Crs BSDN G61......35 E3
Kinnaird Dr PSLYN/LNWD PA3......82 A2
Kinnaird Pl BSHPBGS G64......55 E3
Kinnear Rd
DMNK/BRGTN G40......111 E1
Kinneil Av HMLTN ML3......169 E3
Kinnell Av
CARD/HILL/MSPK G52......106 D1
Kinnell Crs
CARD/HILL/MSPK G52......106 D1
Kinnell Pl
CARD/HILL/MSPK G52......107 E1
Kinning St GBLS G5......89 E4
Kinnoul La KVD/HLHD G12......66 B3
Kinnoull Pl BLTYR/CAMB G72......151 G3
Kinpurnie Rd PSLY PA1......85 G4
Kinross Av
CARD/HILL/MSPK G52......86 C5
Kinross Dr EKILN G74......167 G2
Kinsail Dr
CARD/HILL/MSPK G52......86 A3
Kinsbridge Park Ga
LNPK/KPK G44......129 E1
Kinstone Av SCOT G14......64 B1
Kintessack Pl BSHPBGS G64......55 G1
Kintillo Dr KNTSWD G13......50 C5
Kintore Pk HMLTN ML3......180 B1
Kintore Rd
PLKSW/MSWD G43......128 A1
Kintra St GOV/IBX G51......88 A3
Kintyre Av PSLYN/LNWD PA3......101 H2
Kintyre Crs AIRDRIE ML6......77 G5
CTBR ML5......96 B5
NMRNS G77......143 H5
Kintyre Dr CTBR ML5......96 B5
Kintyre Gdns KKNTL G66......22 B3
Kintyre Rd BLTYR/CAMB G72......151 F2
Kintyre St SPRGB/BLRNK G21......68 B5
Kipland Wk CTBR ML5......97 G4
Kippen Dr
CRMNK/CLK/EAG G76......146 C5
Kippen St AIRDRIE ML6......97 G3
PPK/MIL G22......54 A5
Kippford Pl AIRDRIE ML6......119 G3
Kipps Av AIRDRIE ML6......97 H1
Kirkaig Av RNFRW PA4......64 A4
Kirkandrews Pl AIRDRIE ML6......119 H3
Kirkbean Av RUTH G73......129 H3
Kirkbriggs Gdns RUTH G73......130 A2
Kirkburn Av
BLTYR/CAMB G72......131 F3
Kirkcaldy Rd
PLKSD/SHW G41......108 C2
Kirkconnel Av BALLOCH G68......24 C4
KNTSWD G13......50 C5
Kirkconnel Dr RUTH G73......129 F2
Kirk Crs OLDK G60......30 B1
Kirkcudbright Pl EKILN G74......167 G1
Kirkdale Dr
CARD/HILL/MSPK G52......87 F5
Kirkdene Av NMRNS G77......145 E5
Kirkdene Bank NMRNS G77......145 E5
Kirkdene Crs NMRNS G77......145 E5
Kirkdene Gv NMRNS G77......162 C1
Kirkdene Pl NMRNS G77......145 E5
Kirkfield Bank Wy
HMLTN ML3......169 F2
Kirkfield Rd
UD/BTH/TAN G71......134 B4
Kirkgate WISHAW ML2......175 E1
Kirkhall Rd MTHW ML1......138 A3
Kirkhill Av BLTYR/CAMB G72......131 F4
Kirkhill Crs BRHD/NEIL G78......141 F2
Kirkhill Dr MRYH/FIRH G20......66 C1
Kirkhill Gdns
BLTYR/CAMB G72......131 F4
Kirkhill Gv BLTYR/CAMB G72......131 F4
Kirkhill Pl MRYH/FIRH G20......66 C1
WISHAW ML2......172 D3

Kirkhill Rd
BAIL/MDB/MHD G69......73 E1
NMRNS G77......145 E5
UD/BTH/TAN G71......114 D4
WISHAW ML2......172 D3
Kirkhill St WISHAW ML2......173 H4
Kirkhope Dr DRUM G15......50 C2
Kirkinner Rd CAR/SHTL G32......113 E1
Kirkintilloch Rd BSHPBGS G64......54 C5
BSHPBGS G64......38 A5
KKNTL G66......40 A1
KKNTL G66......20 C3
Kirkland Gv JNSTN PA5......101 G5
Kirklandneuk Rd RNFRW PA4......62 D2
Kirklands RNFRW PA4......63 E3
Kirklands Crs KSYTH G65......8 B1
UD/BTH/TAN G71......134 B4
Kirklands Dr NMRNS G77......161 G5
Kirklands Pl NMRNS G77......161 G5
Kirklands Rd NMRNS G77......161 G5
Kirkland St MRYH/FIRH G20......67 E3
MTHW ML1......154 C5
Kirk La BSDN G61......34 C3
PLKSW/MSWD G43......108 B5
Kirklea Gdns
PSLYN/LNWD PA3......83 F4
Kirklee Circ KVD/HLHD G12......66 B2
Kirklee Gdns KVD/HLHD G12......66 B2
Kirklee Gardens La
KVD/HLHD G12......66 C2
Kirklee Pl KVD/HLHD G12......66 C2
Kirklee Qd KVD/HLHD G12......66 C2
Kirklee Quadrant La
KVD/HLHD G12......66 C2
Kirklee Rd BLSH ML4......136 C5
KVD/HLHD G12......66 B2
MTHW ML1......154 D1
Kirklee Ter KVD/HLHD G12......66 B2
Kirklee Terrace La
KVD/HLHD G12......66 C2
Kirklee Terrace Rd
KVD/HLHD G12......66 C2
Kirkliston St CAR/SHTL G32......92 A3
Kirkmaiden Wy
BLTYR/CAMB G72......168 C2
Kirkmichael Av PTCK G11......65 H5
Kirkmichael Gdns PTCK G11......65 H5
Kirkmuir Dr RUTH G73......130 A4
Kirkness St AIRDRIE ML6......98 B1
Kirknethan WISHAW ML2......172 D4
Kirknewton St CAR/SHTL G32......92 B3
Kirkoswald EKILN G74......167 E4
Kirkoswald Dr CLYDBK G81......32 C5
Kirkoswald Rd MTHW ML1......138 B3
PLKSW/MSWD G43......127 G1
Kirkpatrick St
DMNK/BRGTN G40......90 D4
Kirk Pl BSDN G61......34 B3
CUMB G67......43 H1
Kirkriggs Av RUTH G73......130 A2
Kirk Rd BSDN G61......34 B3
CRMNK/CLK/EAG G76......147 E3
MTHW ML1......119 E5
WISHAW ML2......174 C2
Kirkshaw Ct JNSTN PA5......101 G5
Kirkshaws Av CTBR ML5......116 B1
Kirkshaws Pl CTBR ML5......116 C1
Kirkshaws Rd CTBR ML5......116 B1
Kirkstall Gdns BSHPBGS G64......38 A5
Kirkstone Ct EKILS G75......177 E2
Kirk St CTBR ML5......96 C3
MLNGV G62......16 C3
MTHW ML1......154 D5
Kirkstyle Crs AIRDRIE ML6......76 A4
BRHD/NEIL G78......141 E5
Kirkstyle Pl AIRDRIE ML6......75 H4
Kirksyde Av KKNTL G66......40 A1
Kirkton ERSK PA8......47 G3
Kirkton Av BLTYR/CAMB G72......151 F5
BRHD/NEIL G78......124 A5
KNTSWD G13......50 B5
Kirkton Crs CTBR ML5......97 G5
KKNTL G66......5 G5
KNTSWD G13......50 B5
Kirktonfield Crs
BRHD/NEIL G78......141 E3
Kirktonfield Dr
BRHD/NEIL G78......141 E3
Kirktonfield Pl
BRHD/NEIL G78......141 E3
Kirktonfield Rd
BRHD/NEIL G78......141 F3
Kirkton Ga EKILN G74......166 B3
Kirktonholme Crs EKILN G74......166 A3
Kirktonholme Rd EKILN G74......165 G3
Kirkton Pl EKILN G74......166 B3
Kirkton Rd BLTYR/CAMB G72......151 F5
EKILN G74......166 D3
UD/BTH/TAN G71......115 H5
Kirkton Rd BLTYR/CAMB G72......131 G2
BRHD/NEIL G78......124 A5
DMBTN G82......12 C5
Kirktonside BRHD/NEIL G78......142 A1
Kirkvale Ct NMRNS G77......145 E5
Kirkvale Crs NMRNS G77......145 E5
Kirkvale Dr NMRNS G77......145 E5
Kirkview CUMB G67......43 H2
Kirkview Crs NMRNS G77......161 H2
Kirkview Gdns
UD/BTH/TAN G71......114 D4
Kirkville Pl DRUM G15......50 C2
Kirkwall CUMB G67......10 D5
Kirkwall Av BLTYR/CAMB G72......133 F5
Kirkwell Rd LNPK/KPK G44......128 C2
Kirkwood Av CLYDBK G81......49 H2
STPS/GTHM/RID G33......71 G1
Kirkwood Pl CTBR ML5......96 B5
Kirkwood Rd
UD/BTH/TAN G71......115 G4
Kirkwood St CTBR ML5......96 B4
GOV/IBX G51......88 B4
RUTH G73......110 D4
Kirn St MRYH/FIRH G20......52 A5
Kirriemuir EKILN G74......150 A5
Kirriemuir Av
CARD/HILL/MSPK G52......106 D1
Kirriemuir Gdns BSHPBGS G64......55 F1

Kirriemuir Pl
CARD/HILL/MSPK G52......86 D5
Kirriemuir Rd BSHPBGS G64......55 F1
Kirtle Dr RNFRW PA4......63 H4
Kirtle Pl EKILS G75......176 D1
Kishorn Pl
STPS/GTHM/RID G33......70 D5
Kitchener St WISHAW ML2......173 H2
Kittoch Pl EKILN G74......166 C5
Kittochside Rd
CRMNK/CLK/EAG G76......147 F5
Kittoch St EKILN G74......166 B5
Klondike Ct MTHW ML1......137 G4
Knapdale St PPK/MIL G22......53 F4
Knightsbridge St
KNTSWD G13......51 E5
Knightscliffe Av KNTSWD G13......51 E4
Knights Ga UD/BTH/TAN G71......133 H2
Knightswood Ct KNTSWD G13......51 E5
Knightswood Rd KNTSWD G13......51 E4
Knightswood Ter
BLTYR/CAMB G72......151 H1
Knivysbridge Pl BLSH ML4......135 G4
Knockburnie Rd
UD/BTH/TAN G71......134 B4
Knockhall St
STPS/GTHM/RID G33......71 E4
Knockhill Dr LNPK/KPK G44......109 G5
Knockhill Rd RNFRW PA4......63 E5
Knockmilly Pl
BAIL/MDB/MHD G69......42 B5
Knockside Av PLYS PA2......104 A5
Knollpark Dr
CRMNK/CLK/EAG G76......145 G3
Knowe Crs MTHW ML1......138 A3
Knowehead Dr
UD/BTH/TAN G71......133 H1
Knowehead Gdns
PLKSD/SHW G41......109 E1
UD/BTH/TAN G71......133 H1
Knowehead Rd WISHAW ML2......174 B3
Knowehead Ter
PLKSD/SHW G41......108 D1
Knowenoble St MTHW ML1......139 E5
Knowe Rd
BAIL/MDB/MHD G69......58 B4
PSLYN/LNWD PA3......85 E2
Knowes Av NMRNS G77......144 B5
Knowes Rd NMRNS G77......144 B5
Knowes St MLNGV G62......16 C5
Knowetap St MRYH/FIRH G20......52 D4
Knowetop Av MTHW ML1......155 E5
Knowetop Crs DMBTN G82......12 B2
Knox Av BRWEIR PA11......79 G3
Knoxland Sq DMBTN G82......13 E4
Knox Pl NMRNS G77......161 E1
Knox St AIRDRIE ML6......98 C1
PSLY PA1......83 G5
Kronborg Wy EKILS G75......178 A3
Kyleakin Dr
BLTYR/CAMB G72......133 E5
Kyleakin Rd GIF/THBK G46......126 A4
Kyleakin Ter GIF/THBK G46......126 A4
Kyle Dr GIF/THBK G46......127 H4
Kyle Gv MTHW ML1......137 F4
Kylemore Crs MTHW ML1......154 C1
Kylepark Av
UD/BTH/TAN G71......133 G1
Kylepark Crs
UD/BTH/TAN G71......114 C5
Kylepark Dr
UD/BTH/TAN G71......114 C5
Kyle Qd WISHAW ML2......173 H4
Kylerhea Rd GIF/THBK G46......126 A4
Kyle Rd CUMB G67......26 D3
Kyle Sq RUTH G73......129 H3
Kyle St COWCAD G4......3 G2
MTHW ML1......154 A3
Kyle Ter DMBTN G82......12 A3

L

La Belle Allee KVCV G3......66 D5
La Belle Pl KVCV G3......66 D5
Laberge Gdns MTHW ML1......137 G3
Laburnum Av
BLTYR/CAMB G72......132 B4
EKILS G75......177 H2
Laburnum Ct EKILS G75......177 H2
Laburnum Crs WISHAW ML2......157 E5
Laburnum Dr KKNTL G66......5 F5
Laburnum Gdns KKNTL G66......39 G5
Laburnum Gv CTBR ML5......97 E4
Laburnum Lea HMLTN ML3......170 B4
Laburnum Pl JNSTN PA5......121 H1
Laburnum Rd BAIL/MDB/MHD G69......58 D1
PLKSD/SHW G41......88 C5
UD/BTH/TAN G71......115 H5
Lachlan Crs ERSK PA8......46 D2
Lacy St PSLY PA1......84 D4
Ladder Ct EKILS G75......177 G4
Ladeside Ci NMRNS G77......143 H4
Ladeside Dr JNSTN PA5......101 E4
KSYTH G65......8 C1
Lade Ter CARD/HILL/MSPK G52......86 B5
Ladhope Pl KNTSWD G13......49 H4
Ladyacres RNFRW PA4......48 A5
Ladyacres Wy RNFRW PA4......48 A5
Lady Ann Crs AIRDRIE ML6......98 D3
Ladybank BALLOCH G68......10 A4
Ladybank Ct EKILN G74......166 B3
Ladybank Dr
CARD/HILL/MSPK G52......87 F5
Ladybank Gdns EKILN G74......166 B3
Ladyburn St PSLY PA1......84 D5
Ladyhill Dr
BAIL/MDB/MHD G69......93 H5
Lady Isle Crs
UD/BTH/TAN G71......133 H1
Lady Jane Ga
UD/BTH/TAN G71......133 H3
Ladykirk Crs PLYS PA2......104 C1
Ladykirk Dr
CARD/HILL/MSPK G52......86 C3
Ladykirk Wy EKILN G74......166 C1
Lady La PSLY PA1......84 A5

Ladyloan Av DRUM G15......33 E4
Ladyloan Ct DRUM G15......32 D4
Ladyloan Gdns DRUM G15......33 E4
Ladyloan Pl DRUM G15......33 E4
Ladymuir Crs
CARD/HILL/MSPK G52......106 D2
Ladymuir Dr ERSK PA8......47 E2
Ladysmith Av KLBCH PA10......100 C4
Ladysmith Dr EKILS G75......177 F4
Ladysmith St WISHAW ML2......172 D2
Lady Watson Gdns
HMLTN ML3......169 F3
Ladywell Rd MTHW ML1......154 A4
Ladywell St COWCAD G4......90 D2
Lady Wilson St AIRDRIE ML6......98 D2
Ladywood MLNGV G62......17 F3
Laggan Qd AIRDRIE ML6......75 H5
Laggan Rd AIRDRIE ML6......98 A5
BSHPBGS G64......55 E2
NMRNS G77......144 A3
PLKSW/MSWD G43......127 H2
Laggan Ter RNFRW PA4......63 E2
Laidlaw Av MTHW ML1......137 E4
Laidlaw Gdns
UD/BTH/TAN G71......115 E3
Laidlaw St GBLS G5......89 E4
Laidon Rd AIRDRIE ML6......99 E4
Laighcartside St JNSTN PA5......101 H3
Laighlands Rd
UD/BTH/TAN G71......134 C5
Laighmuir St
UD/BTH/TAN G71......134 A2
Laighpark Av BSHPTN PA7......29 E5
Laighpark Vw
PSLYN/LNWD PA3......84 B2
Laigh Rd NMRNS G77......145 E5
Laightonhall Rd
HMLTN ML3......169 G3
Laightoun Ct CUMB G67......43 H2
Laightoun Dr CUMB G67......43 H2
Laightoun Gdns CUMB G67......43 H2
Lainshaw Dr CSMK G45......128 C3
Laird Gv UD/BTH/TAN G71......115 F4
Laird Pl DMNK/BRGTN G40......90 C5
Lairds Ga UD/BTH/TAN G71......133 G2
Laird's Hill Ct KSYTH G65......7 G2
Laird's Hill Pl KSYTH G65......7 G2
Laird St CTBR ML5......97 E2
Lairg Dr BLTYR/CAMB G72......133 G5
Lairhills Rd EKILS G75......178 C1
Lairhill Rd EKILS G75......178 B1
Lamberton Dr
CARD/HILL/MSPK G52......86 D4
Lambhill Qd PLKSD/SHW G41......88 C4
Lambhill St PLKSD/SHW G41......88 C4
Lambie Crs NMRNS G77......143 H5
Lamb St HMLTN ML3......170 B2
PPK/MIL G22......53 G4
Lamerton Rd CUMB G67......27 E3
Lamington Rd
CARD/HILL/MSPK G52......86 C5
Lamlash Crs
STPS/GTHM/RID G33......92 C1
Lamlash Pl EKILS G75......177 G4
STPS/GTHM/RID G33......92 C1
MTHW ML1......154 B3
Lammermoor EKILN G74......167 H1
Lammermoor Av
CARD/HILL/MSPK G52......106 C1
Lammermoor Ct PSLYS PA2......104 A4
Lammermoor Dr CUMB G67......44 D1
Lammermoor Rd KKNTL G66......40 C1
Lammermoor Ter
WISHAW ML2......174 A2
Lammermuir Ct PSLYS PA2......104 A4
Lammermuir Dr PSLYS PA2......104 A4
Lammermuir Gdns BSDN G61......33 H1
Lammermuir Wy
AIRDRIE ML6......119 G3
Lamont Av BSHPTN PA7......29 F5
Lamont Rd SPRGB/BLRNK G21......55 E5
Lanark Av AIRDRIE ML6......119 F4
Lanark St CGLE G1......90 A3
Lancaster Crs AIRDRIE ML6......119 F4
Lancaster Crs KVD/HLHD G12......66 C2
Lancaster Crescent La
KVD/HLHD G12......66 B2
Lancaster Rd BSHPBGS G64......38 A4
Lancefield Quay KVCV G3......88 D2
Lancefield St KVCV G3......89 E2
Landemer Dr RUTH G73......129 G3
Landemer Gait RUTH G73......129 H1
Landressy Pl
DMNK/BRGTN G40......90 C5
Landressy St
DMNK/BRGTN G40......90 C5
Landsdowne Gdns
HMLTN ML3......170 C2
The Lane BALLOCH G68......9 H4
Lanfine Rd PSLY PA1......85 F5
Langa St MRYH/FIRH G20......52 D4
Lang Av BSHPTN PA7......29 F5
RNFRW PA4......63 F4
Langbar Crs
STPS/GTHM/RID G33......93 F2
Langbar Gdns
STPS/GTHM/RID G33......93 F2
Langbyres Rd MTHW ML1......157 G1
Langcraigs Dr PSLYS PA2......103 H4
Langcraigs Ct PSLYS PA2......103 H5
Langcraigs Ter PSLYS PA2......122 D1
Langcroft Dr
BLTYR/CAMB G72......131 H5
Langcroft Pl GOV/IBX G51......87 F3
Langcroft Rd GOV/IBX G51......87 F3
Langcroft Ter GOV/IBX G51......87 F3
Langdale EKILN G74......165 G2
Langdale Av
STPS/GTHM/RID G33......69 H3
Langdales Av BALLOCH G68......25 H5
Langdale St
STPS/GTHM/RID G33......69 H3
Langhaulds Crs CLYDBK G81......32 D2
Langford Dr PLK/PH/NH G53......125 F4
Langford Pl PLK/PH/NH G53......125 F4
Langhaul Av PLK/PH/NH G53......106 A3
Langhaul Pl PLK/PH/NH G53......106 A3
Langhaul Rd PLK/PH/NH G53......106 A3
Langhill Dr BALLOCH G68......25 H2

Langholm EKILS G75......177 E2
Langholm Crs WISHAW ML2......157 E4
Langholm Dr
PSLYN/LNWD PA3......84 B4
Langlands Av EKILS G75......178 C4
GOV/IBX G51......87 E2
Langlands Ct EKILS G75......178 D4
GOV/IBX G51......87 G1
Langlands Dr EKILS G75......178 D4
GOV/IBX G51......86 D1
Langlands Pl EKILS G75......178 C4
Langlands Rd GOV/IBX G51......87 E2
Langlands Sq EKILS G75......178 C4
Langlea Ter DMBTN G82......13 G1
Langlea Av BLTYR/CAMB G72......130 C3
Langlea Ct BLTYR/CAMB G72......130 D3
Langlea Dr BLTYR/CAMB G72......130 D2
Langlea Gdns
BLTYR/CAMB G72......130 D2
Langlea Gv BLTYR/CAMB G72......130 C3
Langlea Rd BLTYR/CAMB G72......130 C3
Langlees Av NMRNS G77......162 C1
Langley Av KNTSWD G13......50 C3
Langloan Crs CTBR ML5......96 B3
Langloan Pl CTBR ML5......96 B3
Langloan St CTBR ML5......96 B3
Langmuir Av KKNTL G66......21 G5
Langmuirhead Rd
STPS/GTHM/RID G33......56 B3
Langmuir Rd
BAIL/MDB/MHD G69......95 F4
KKNTL G66......21 H4
Langmuir Wy
BAIL/MDB/MHD G69......95 G4
Langness Rd
STPS/GTHM/RID G33......92 B1
Langorth Av HMLTN ML3......169 E3
Lang Pl JNSTN PA5......101 F3
Langrig Rd NMRNS G77......161 F2
PPK/MIL G22......54 A2
Langshot St GOV/IBX G51......88 C4
Langside Av PLKSD/SHW G41......108 D3
UD/BTH/TAN G71......134 C2
Langside Dr KLBCH PA10......100 B4
PLKSW/MSWD G43......127 H3
Langside Gdns
GVH/MTFL G42......109 E5
Langside La GVH/MTFL G42......109 F3
Langside Pl PLKSD/SHW G41......108 D4
Langside Rd GVH/MTFL G42......109 F4
UD/BTH/TAN G71......134 C5
Langside St CLYDBK G81......32 C2
Langstile Rd
CARD/HILL/MSPK G52......86 A4
Lang St PSLY PA1......85 E5
Langton Crs BRHD/NEIL G78......142 C1
PLK/PH/NH G53......106 D3
Langton Gdns
BAIL/MDB/MHD G69......93 G5
Langton Pl NMRNS G77......143 H5
Langton Rd PLK/PH/NH G53......106 D3
Langtree Av GIF/THBK G46......144 D1
Lanrig Pl BAIL/MDB/MHD G69......58 B3
Lanrig Rd BAIL/MDB/MHD G69......58 B3
Lansbury Gdns
PSLYN/LNWD PA3......84 A2
Lansdowne Crs
MRYH/FIRH G20......67 E4
Lansdowne Crescent La
MRYH/FIRH G20......67 E4
Lansdowne Dr BALLOCH G68......9 H4
Lantana Gv MTHW ML1......154 C2
Lanton Dr
CARD/HILL/MSPK G52......86 C4
Lanton Pth AIRDRIE ML6......119 F3
Lanton Rd
PLKSW/MSWD G43......127 H2
Lappin St CLYDBK G81......49 G5
Lapwing Rd RNFRW PA4......63 H2
Larbert St COWCAD G4......2 E2
Larch Av BSHPBGS G64......55 E3
KKNTL G66......39 H3
Larch Ct BLTYR/CAMB G72......132 B4
Larch Ct BLTYR/CAMB G72......151 F2
CUMB G67......27 G1
EKILS G75......178 B2
Larch Crs KKNTL G66......39 H3
Larch Dr EKILS G75......177 G3
The Larches
BAIL/MDB/MHD G69......42 B4
Larchfield Av NMRNS G77......161 H1
SCOT G14......64 C2
Larchfield Crs WISHAW ML2......157 F4
Larchfield Dr RUTH G73......130 B3
Larchfield Gdns WISHAW ML2......157 G4
Larchfield Gv WISHAW ML2......157 G3
Larchfield Pl SCOT G14......64 C2
WISHAW ML2......157 G4
Larchfield Rd
BAIL/MDB/MHD G69......59 E1
BSDN G61......51 G2
Larch Gv CUMB G67......27 G1
HMLTN ML3......170 B3
KKNTL G66......39 H3
Larchgrove Av CAR/SHTL G32......93 E4
Larchgrove Pl CAR/SHTL G32......92 D3
Larchgrove Rd CAR/SHTL G32......92 D4
Larch Pl BLTYR/CAMB G72......132 B4
CUMB G67......27 H1
EKILS G75......177 H1
JNSTN PA5......102 A2
UD/BTH/TAN G71......116 A4
Larch Rd CUMB G67......27 G1
PLKSD/SHW G41......88 A5
Larch Wy HMLTN ML3......181 F4
Larchwood Ter
BRHD/NEIL G78......142 C1
Largie Rd PLKSW/MSWD G43......128 A2
Largo La BLTYR/CAMB G72......168 C2
Largo Pl GOV/IBX G51......87 E2
Larkfield Ct
BLTYR/CAMB G72......151 F4
Larkfield Dr KKNTL G66......40 B3

Larkfield Rd GVH/MTFL G42 ....109 G1
Larkin Gdns PSLYN/LNWD PA3....84 A2
Larkin Wy BLSH ML4 ....116 C5
Larkspur Dr EKILN G74 ....165 H1
Lark Wy BLSH ML4 ....116 C5
Lasswade St SCOT G14 ....49 H5
Latherton Dr MRYH/FIRH G20.....66 A1
Latimer Gdns
  CARD/HILL/MSPK G52 ....86 B5
Latta St DMBTN G82 ....13 F3
Lauchope Rd MTHW ML1 ....119 E5
Lauchope St AIRDRIE ML6 ....119 F2
Lauder Crs WISHAW ML2 ....157 E4
Lauderdale Dr NMRNS G77 ....161 G2
Lauderdale Gdns
  KVD/HLHD G12.............................66 A2
Lauderdale La KVD/HLHD G12......66 A3
Lauder Dr PSLYN/LNWD PA3.........82 A4
  RUTH G73 ....130 C1
Lauder Gdns
  BLTYR/CAMB G72 ....133 F5
  CTBR ML5...................................117 G1
Lauder Gn EKILN G74 ....167 E1
Lauder Gr MTHW ML1..................138 A4
Laundry La
  STPS/GTHM/RID G33....................70 D1
Lauranne Pl BLSH ML4.................135 F2
Laurel Av CLYDBK G81 ....31 E4
  KKNTL G66 ....40 A2
Laurelbank CTBR ML5....................95 D1
Laurel Bank HMLTN ML3..............169 H5
Laurel Park Gdns
  KNTSWD G13 ....64 D1
Laurel Pl EKILS G75 ....178 A3
  PTCK G11...................................65 H4
The Laurels MTHW ML1................137 G5
  NMRNS G77 ....144 A5
Laurel St PTCK G11 ....65 H4
Laurel Wy BRHD/NEIL G78...........124 A4
  BRWEIR PA11 ....79 H3
Laurel Wynd
  BLTYR/CAMB G72 ....132 C4
Laurence Ct DRUM G15 ....32 D5
Laurence Dr BSDN G61 ....34 A2
  DRUM G15 ....32 D5
Laurence Gdns DRUM G15 ....32 D5
Lauren Vw AIRDRIE ML6.................98 A2
Lauren Wy PSLYS PA2 ....103 E3
Laurieston Crs AIRDRIE ML6........119 H3
Lauriestone Pl CTBR ML5..............117 C1
Laurieston Rd GBLS G5 ....89 H4
Lauriston Gv NMRNS G77.............143 G5
Lavelle Dr CTBR ML5......................97 F2
Lavender Ct
  UD/BTH/TAN G71.......................115 H5
Lavender Dr EKILS G75 ....178 A3
Laverock Av HMLTN ML3 ....170 D3
Laverockhall St
  SPRGB/BLRNK G21 ....68 C3
Laverock Rd AIRDRIE ML6..............76 C4
Laverock Ter
  BAIL/MDB/MHD G69 ....59 G2
Law Dr MTHW ML1 ....137 H5
Lawers Dr BSDN G61......................33 H2
Lawers Rd
  PLKSW/MSWD G43 ....127 G2
  RNFRW PA4 ....63 E5
Lawfield Av NMRNS G77 ....145 E5
Lawhill Av LNPK/KPK G44 ....129 E3
Lawhope Mill Rd
  AIRDRIE ML6 ....119 H1
Lawmarnock Crs
  BRWEIR PA11 ....79 F4
Lawmarnock Rd
  BRWEIR PA11 ....79 F5
Lawmoor Av GBLS G5 ....109 H2
Lawmoor Pl GBLS G5....................109 H3
Lawmoor Rd GBLS G5...................109 H1
Lawmoor St GBLS G5....................109 H1
Lawmuir Crs CLYDBK G81 ....32 D1
Lawmuir Pl BLSH ML4...................135 H4
Lawmuir Rd BLSH ML4..................135 H4
Lawnmoor Rd GBLS G5.................109 H1
Lawn Pk MLNGV G62 ....17 G4
Lawn St PSLY PA1 ....84 C4
Law Pl W EKILN G74 ....
Lawrence Av GIF/THBK G46..........145 G1
Lawrence St PTCK G11 ....66 B4
Lawrie Pl MTHW ML1 ....156 B1
Lawrie St PTCK G11 ....66 A4
  WISHAW ML2 ....158 A5
Lawson Av MTHW ML1..................171 H3
Law St DMNK/BRGTN G40..............90 D4
Laxford Av LNPK/KPK G44............128 B3
Laxford Rd ERSK PA8 ....46 D2
Laxton Dr KKNTL G66 ....40 B4
Lea Av BRHD/NEIL G78.................141 E3
Leabank Av PSLYS PA2 ....104 B4
Leadburn Rd
  SPRGB/BLRNK G21 ....69 F2
Leadburn St
  STPS/GTHM/RID G33....................91 H2
Leader St
  STPS/GTHM/RID G33....................69 G5
Leaend Rd AIRDRIE ML6.................75 H5
Leander Crs BLSH ML4..................136 D2
  RNFRW PA4 ....63 H4
Learmont Pl MLNGV G62 ....16 D1
Leathem Pl WISHAW ML2 ....172 D4
Leathen Pl ERSK PA8 ....46 D2
Leckethill Av BALLOCH G68 ....43 G1
Leckethill Ct BALLOCH G68 ....43 G1
Leckethill Pl BALLOCH G68 ....43 G1
Leckethill Vw BALLOCH G68 ....43 G1
Leckie Dr HMLTN ML3...................169 H2
Leckie St PLKSD/SHW G41 ....108 A4
Ledaig Pl DEN/PKHD G31 ....91 F2

Ledaig St DEN/PKHD G31 ....91 F2
Ledard Rd GVH/MTFL G42............109 E5
Ledcameroch Crs BSDN G61...........34 A4
Ledcameroch Pk BSDN G61............34 A4
Ledcameroch Rd BSDN G61............34 A4
Ledgate KKNTL G66 ....21 F4
Ledgowan Pl MRYH/FIRH G20.......52 C5
Ledi Dr BSDN G61...........................33 G1
Ledi Rd PLKSW/MSWD G43...........127 F2
Ledmore Dr DRUM G15 ....33 G1
Lednock Rd
  CARD/HILL/MSPK G52 ....86 B4
  STPS/GTHM/RID G33....................70 D1
Ledvinka Crs HMLTN ML3.............152 B6
Lee Av STPS/GTHM/RID G33..........69 H5
Leebank Dr LNPK/KPK G44...........146 A1
Leeburn Av
  CRG/CRSL/HOU PA6.....................80 D2
Leeburn Gdns
  CRG/CRSL/HOU PA6.....................80 D2
Leechlee Rd HMLTN ML3 ....170 B2
Lee Crs BSHPBGS G64 ....54 C3
Leefield Dr LNPK/KPK G44............128 A3
Leehill Rd SPRGB/BLRNK G21........54 B4
Lee Pl BLSH ML4 ....136 C5
Leesburn Pl EKILN G74..................166 C1
Lee's Ct CTBR ML5...........................96 D4
Leesland UD/BTH/TAN G71............115 F4
Leeward Cr EKILS G75....................165 F4
Leewood Dr LNPK/KPK G44...........128 B5
Le Froy Gdns EKILS G75................165 H5
Le Froy La EKILS G75....................165 H5
Lefroy St CTBR ML5.........................96 B2
Legbrannock Av MTHW ML1..........138 A1
Legbrannock Crs MTHW ML1.........138 A3
Legbrannock Rd MTHW ML1..........138 A3
Leggate Wy BLSH ML4...................116 B1
Leggatston Rd
  PLK/PH/NH G53........................125 H4
Leglen Wood Crs
  SPRGB/BLRNK G21 ....55 G5
Leglen Wood Dr
  SPRGB/BLRNK G21 ....55 G5
Leglen Wood Pl
  SPRGB/BLRNK G21 ....55 G5
Leglen Wood Rd
  SPRGB/BLRNK G21 ....55 G5
Leicester Av KVD/HLHD G12...........66 A1
Leighton St MRYH/FIRH G20..........52 D5
  WISHAW ML2 ....174 A5
Leithland Rd JNSTN PA5................102 C4
Leithland Av PLK/PH/NH G53.......106 C3
Leithland Rd PLK/PH/NH G53.......106 C3
Leith St STPS/GTHM/RID G33.........91 G1
Leman Dr CRG/CRSL/HOU PA6.......81 E3
Leman Gv CRG/CRSL/HOU PA6.......81 E3
Lembert Dr
  CRMNK/CLK/EAG G76.................145 G2
Lendale La BSHPBGS G64 ....52 B5
Lendalfoot Gdns HMLTN ML3 ......168 C4
Lendal Pl EKILS G75 ....176 D2
Lendel Pl GOV/IBX G51 ....88 C4
Lenihall Dr CSMK G45 ....129 F5
Lenihall Ter CSMK G45..................129 F5
Lennox Av BSHPTN PA7 ....29 E5
  CTBR ML5...................................96 B2
  MLNGV G62 ....17 E4
  SCOT G14 ....64 D3
Lennox Ct KSYTH G65.......................8 B2
Lennox Crs BSHPBGS G64...............54 C3
Lennox Dr BSDN G61......................34 C1
  CLYDBK G81 ....32 C1
  NMRNS G77 ....161 H5
Lennox Gdns SCOT G14 ....64 D4
Lennox La East SCOT G14...............65 E3
Lennox La West SCOT G14..............64 D3
Lennox Rd CUMB G67.....................26 B3
  DMBTN G82 ....13 G4
  KKNTL G66 ....20 D1
Lennox St DMBTN G82 ....13 F4
  MRYH/FIRH G20..........................52 B4
  WISHAW ML2 ....174 D1
Lennox Ter PSLYN/LNWD PA3.........84 D1
Lentran St ESTRH G34.....................94 C2
Leny St MRYH/FIRH G20.................67 E2
Lenziemill Rd CUMB G67................44 D2
Lenzie Pl SPRGB/BLRNK G21..........54 C5
Lenzie Rd KKNTL G66......................57 E4
  STPS/GTHM/RID G33....................57 E4
Lenzie St SPRGB/BLRNK G21..........68 C1
Lenzie Ter SPRGB/BLRNK G21........54 B5
Leonard Gv MTHW ML1.................156 B1
Lesley Od BLSH ML4 ....135 G5
Leslie Av BSHPTN PA7 ....29 E5
  NMRNS G77 ....144 B3
Leslie Rd PLKSD/SHW G41............108 D2
Leslie St MTHW ML1 ....155 G5
  PLKSD/SHW G41........................109 E1
Lesmuir Dr SCOT G14......................64 B1
Lesmuir Pl SCOT G14 ....64 B1
Letham Ct
  PLKSW/MSWD G43 ....127 H2
Letham Dr BSHPBGS G64................55 F3
  PLKSW/MSWD G43 ....127 H2
Letham Gra BALLOCH G68 ....26 B1
Lethamhill Pl
  STPS/GTHM/RID G33....................69 H5
Lethamhill Rd
  STPS/GTHM/RID G33....................69 H5
Letham Ov BSHPBGS G64...............55 G3
Lethbridge Pl EKILS G75...............165 H5
Letherby Dr LNPK/KPK G44...........109 G5
Letheron Dr WISHAW ML2.............157 E5
Lethington Av
  PLKSD/SHW G41........................108 D4
Lethington Pl
  PLKSD/SHW G41........................108 D4
Lethington Rd
  GIF/THBK G46...........................144 D3
Letterfearn Rd SMSTN G23.............52 D2
Letterickhills Crs
  BLTYR/CAMB G72 ....132 B4
Leven Av BSHPBGS G64 ....55 E2
Leven Ct BRHD/NEIL G78...............124 A2
Leven Dr BSDN G61 ....34 B2
  HMLTN ML3 ....169 G5
Levenford Ter DMBTN G82 ....12 D4
Leven Pl ERSK PA8 ....46 D2
Leven Qd AIRDRIE ML6....................76 A4
Leven Rd CTBR ML5.........................73 H5

Leven St DMBTN G82 ....13 F4
  MTHW ML1 ....154 D5
  PLKSD/SHW G41........................109 E1
Leven Ter MTHW ML1....................137 H5
Leven Wy EKILS G75 ....177 E2
Leven Bridge Ct
  PLK/PH/NH G53........................106 A3
Levern Bridge Gv
  PLK/PH/NH G53........................125 E1
  PLK/PH/NH G53........................106 B5
Levern Bridge Pl
  PLK/PH/NH G53........................125 E1
Levern Bridge Rd
  PLK/PH/NH G53........................125 E1
Levern Bridge Wy
  PLK/PH/NH G53........................125 E1
Levern Crs BRHD/NEIL G78...........142 A1
Leverndale Ct
  PLK/PH/NH G53........................106 A3
Leverndale Rd
  PLK/PH/NH G53........................106 A3
Levern Gdns BRHD/NEIL G78........124 A4
Levern Grove Ct
  PLK/PH/NH G53........................125 E1
Levernside Av
  BRHD/NEIL G78.........................123 H5
  PLK/PH/NH G53........................106 D4
Levernside Crs
  PLK/PH/NH G53........................106 C3
Levernside Rd
  PLK/PH/NH G53........................106 C3
Lewis Av RNFRW PA4 ....63 G5
Lewis Ct KLBCH PA10....................100 D4
  OLDK G60....................................30 D3
Lewis Dr OLDK G60 ....30 D3
Lewis Gdns BSDN G61 ....33 G2
  OLDK G60....................................30 D3
Lewis Gv OLDK G60 ....30 D3
Lewis Pl AIRDRIE ML6.....................99 E4
  NMRNS G77 ....143 G4
  OLDK G60....................................30 D3
Lewiston Dr SMSTN G23.................52 C2
Lewiston Pl SMSTN G23.................52 C2
Lewiston Rd SMSTN G23.................52 C2
Lexwell Av JNSTN PA5...................102 C1
Leyden Gdns MRYH/FIRH G20........66 D1
Leyden St MRYH/FIRH G20.............66 D1
Leyland Av HMLTN ML3.................169 F5
Leys Pk HMLTN ML3.......................169 F1
The Leys BSHPBGS G64 ....54 D2
Libberton Wy HMLTN ML3.............169 F1
Liberton St
  STPS/GTHM/RID G33....................91 H1
Liberty Av
  BAIL/MDB/MHD G69 ....95 E4
Liberty Rd BLSH ML4.....................135 H4
Libo Av PLK/PH/NH G53................107 E3
Libo Pl ERSK PA8.............................46 D1
Library Gdns
  BLTYR/CAMB G72 ....131 E1
Library La GIF/THBK G46...............126 C4
Library Rd WISHAW ML2 ....174 A2
Lickprivick Rd EKILS G75..............177 G1
Liddell St GOV/IBX G51 ....88 A5
Liddells Ct BSHPBGS G64 ....54 D2
Liddell St CAR/SHTL G32...............112 D5
Liddel Rd CUMB G67 ....26 A4
Liddesdale Pl PLSYS PA2 ....103 G1
Liddesdale Pl HWL HIL............125 H1
Liddesdale Rd PPK/MIL G22...........54 B4
Liddesdale Sq PPK/MIL G22...........54 B4
Liddesdale Ter PPK/MIL G22..........54 B4
Liddoch Wy RUTH G73 ....110 C4
Liff Gdns BSHPBGS G64 ....55 G3
Liff Pl ESTRH G34...........................72 B5
Lightburn Pl CAR/SHTL G32...........92 C2
Lightburn Rd
  BLTYR/CAMB G72 ....132 A3
  CUMB G67....................................11 G5
Lilac Ct CUMB G67 ....11 H5
Lilac Crs UD/BTH/TAN G71............115 H4
Lilac Gdns BSHPBGS G64...............55 E3
Lilac Gv WISHAW ML2 ....173 G4
  CUMB G67....................................11 H5
Lilac Hl CUMB G67..........................11 H5
  HMLTN ML3 ....170 C5
Lilac Pl CUMB G67...........................11 H5
Lila Wynd
  BLTYR/CAMB G72 ....132 C3
Lilybank Pl DRUM G15....................32 D4
Lilybank Av AIRDRIE ML6................98 C3
  BAIL/MDB/MHD G69 ....58 B4
  BLTYR/CAMB G72 ....131 G3
Lilybank Gdns
  KVD/HLHD G12.............................66 C4
Lilybank Gardens La
  KVD/HLHD G12.............................66 C4
Lilybank St HMLTN ML3 ....169 H1
Lilybank Ter KVD/HLHD G12...........66 C4
Lilybank Terrace La
  KVD/HLHD G12.............................66 C4
Lily St DMNK/BRGTN G40..............110 D1
Limecraigs Av PSLYS PA2 ....103 H5
Limecraigs Rd PSLYS PA2.............103 H5
Limes Av AIRDRIE ML6....................98 D2
  CUMB G67....................................27 G2
Lime Gv BLTYR/CAMB G72............151 F1
  KKNTL G66 ....40 A3
  MTHW ML1 ....137 G3
Limegrove St BLSH ML4.................116 D5
Limekilns Rd CUMB G67 ....45 E2
Limekilns St CLYDBK G81 ....32 C2
Lime La SCOT G14 ....65 E3
Lime Rd DMBTN G82 ....13 E3
Limeside Av RUTH G73...................111 F5
Limeside Gdns RUTH G73..............111 F5
Lime St SCOT G14 ....65 E3
Limetree Av
  UD/BTH/TAN G71.......................115 G4
Limetree Crs HMLTN ML3.............152 B6
Limetree Crs NMRNS G77.............161 G1
Limetree Dr CLYDBK G81 ....31 H4
Limetree Od
  UD/BTH/TAN G71.......................115 H4
Limetree Wk KKNTL G66................20 D1
Limeview Av PSLYS PA2 ....103 G5
Limeview Crs PSLYS PA2 ....103 G5
Limeview Rd PSLYS PA2................103 G5
Limeview Wy PSLYS PA2...............103 G5

Limewood Pl
  BAIL/MDB/MHD G69 ....95 F3
Linacre Dr CAR/SHTL G32...............93 E2
Linacre Gdns CAR/SHTL G32..........93 E2
Linburn Pl
  CARD/HILL/MSPK G52 ....86 D3
  ERSK PA8 ....46 D2
Lincoln Av KNTSWD G13.................50 D4
  UD/BTH/TAN G71.......................115 F3
Lincoln Ct CTBR ML5.......................96 D1
Lincuan Av GIF/THBK G46.............145 G2
Lindams UD/BTH/TAN G71............134 A2
Linden Av WISHAW ML2................157 F4
Linden Dr CLYDBK G81....................31 H2
Linden Lea HMLTN ML3.................169 G1
  KKNTL G66 ....5 F5
Linden St KNTSWD G13...................51 G4
Lindores Av RUTH G73...................111 E5
Lindores Dr EKILN G74..................165 G4
Lindores St GVH/MTFL G42...........109 G4
Lindrick Dr SMSTN G23..................52 C5
Lindsaybeg Ct
  BAIL/MDB/MHD G69 ....58 B3
Lindsaybeg Rd
  BAIL/MDB/MHD G69 ....58 B3
  KKNTL G66 ....40 B5
Lindsay Dr KVD/HLHD G12.............52 A4
Lindsayfield Av EKILS G75............177 H4
Lindsayfield Rd EKILS G75............177 G4
Lindsay Gv EKILN G74...................166 D4
Lindsay Pl EKILN G74....................166 D4
  KVD/HLHD G12.............................52 A5
Lindsay Rd EKILN G74...................166 C4
Lindsay Ter KKNTL G66.....................4 C2
Lindum Crs MTHW ML1.................154 B2
Lindum St MTHW ML1...................154 A2
Linfern Rd KVD/HLHD G12.............66 A3
Linghope Pl WISHAW ML2.............175 G5
Lingley Av AIRDRIE ML6..................98 B5
Linhead Dr PLK/PH/NH G53..........125 H1
Linhope Pl EKILS G75....................176 D1
Links Rd CAR/SHTL G32................113 E1
The Links BALLOCH G68 ....44 D5
Linksview Rd MTHW ML1..............155 G1
Linkwood Av DRUM G15..................33 E5
Linkwood Crs DRUM G15................33 E5
Linkwood Dr DRUM G15..................33 E5
Linkwood Gdns DRUM G15.............33 E5
Linkwood Pl DRUM G15...................33 E5
Linlithgow Gdns
  CAR/SHTL G32............................93 E4
Linlithgow Pl
  BAIL/MDB/MHD G69 ....72 D1
Linn Crs PSLYS PA2 ....103 G5
Linn Dr LNPK/KPK G44 ....128 A4
Linnet Av JNSTN PA5.....................120 D2
Linnet Pl KNTSWD G13...................50 A5
Linnet Rd BLSH ML4......................136 A3
Linnet Wy BLSH ML4 ....116 C4
Linn Gdns BALLOCH G68 ....25 E5
Linn Ga BALLOCH G68 ....25 E5
Linn Gln KKNTL G66 ....4 D2
Linnhead Dr PLK/PH/NH G53........125 G2
Linnhead Pl SCOT G14....................64 C2
Linnhe Av BSHPBGS G64 ....55 E2
  HMLTN ML3 ....169 F4
  LNPK/KPK G44..........................128 B3
Linnhe Crs WISHAW ML2..............173 G4
Linnhe Dr BRHD/NEIL G78............124 A2
Linnhe Pl BLTYR/CAMB G72..........133 F5
  ERSK PA8 ....46 D2
Linnpark Av LNPK/KPK G44..........128 A5
Linn Park Gdns JNSTN PA5...........101 H4
Linnvale Wy BALLOCH G68 ....43 E4
Linn Valley Vw CSMK G45.............129 E4
Linnwell Crs PSLYS PA2................104 A5
Linside Av PSLY PA1 ....84 D5
Linthaugh Rd
  PLK/PH/NH G53........................106 C1
Linthaugh Ter
  PLK/PH/NH G53........................107 E3
Linthouse Buildings
  GOV/IBX G51 ....87 F1
Linthouse Rd GOV/IBX G51............65 E5
Lintie Rd MTHW ML1.....................137 H5
Lintlaw BLTYR/CAMB G72.............151 E5
Lintlaw Dr
  CARD/HILL/MSPK G52 ....86 C3
Lintmill Ter BRHD/NEIL G78..........140 D4
Lint Mill Wy BALLOCH G68.............25 E3
Linton St STPS/GTHM/RID G33.......91 H1
Lintwhite Crs BRWEIR PA11...........79 H4
Linwood Av
  CRMNK/CLK/EAG G76.................146 A4
  EKILN G74 ....165 E3
Linwood Crs PSLY PA1 ....84 C4
Linwood Rd PSLY PA1......................82 D5
Linwood Ter HMLTN ML3...............169 G1
Lion Bank KKNTL G66 ....21 F4
Lismore EKILN G74 ....167 F5
Lismore Av MTHW ML1 ....171 H4
  RNFRW PA4 ....63 G5
Lismore Dr CTBR ML5......................96 B5
  PSLYN/LNWD PA3......................101 G1
  PSLYS PA2 ....104 A3
Lismore Gdns KLBCH PA10............100 D5
Lismore Hl HMLTN ML3..................168 C4
Lismore Pl AIRDRIE ML6..................99 E2
  BAIL/MDB/MHD G69 ....42 B5
  NMRNS G77 ....143 G5
Lismore Rd KVD/HLHD G12............66 A2
Lister Gdns
  CRMNK/CLK/EAG G76.................146 B5
Lister Pl CARD/HILL/MSPK G52......86 B2
Lister Rd
  CARD/HILL/MSPK G52 ....86 B2
Lister St COWCAD G4 ....67 H2
Lister St BLTYR/CAMB G72 ....151 F5
Lithgow Crs PSLYS PA2..................104 D2
Lithgow Pl HMLTN ML3 ....157 E1
Lithgow Pl EKILN G74....................165 G5
Little Dovehill CGLE G1 ....3 J7
Littlehill St SPRGB/BLRNK G21.......68 D2
Littleholm Pl CLYDBK G81...............31 G3
Little John Gdns WISHAW ML2......175 E1
Littlemill Av BALLOCH G68 ....24 C4

Littlemill Crs PLK/PH/NH G53........106 C4
Littlemill Dr PLK/PH/NH G53.........106 B4
Littlemill Gdns
  PLK/PH/NH G53........................106 B4
Littlemill La OLDK G60....................15 F5
Littlemill Wy MTHW ML1...............155 G1
Littleston Gdns ERSK PA8 ....47 E2
Little St KVGV G3.............................89 E2
Littleton St SMSTN G23..................52 C2
Littleton Dr AIRDRIE ML6................77 H4
Livingstone Av
  CARD/HILL/MSPK G52 ....86 B1
Livingstone Bvd
  BLTYR/CAMB G72 ....151 F5
Livingstone Crs
  BLTYR/CAMB G72 ....151 G1
  EKILS G75..................................178 A5
Livingstone Dr EKILS G75.............166 A5
Livingstone La
  BLTYR/CAMB G72 ....131 F5
Livingstone Pl AIRDRIE ML6............98 C3
Livingston Dr CLYDBK G81..............49 G2
  HMLTN ML3 ....169 F5
Lloyd Av CAR/SHTL G32.................112 B2
Lloyd Dr MTHW ML1......................155 F1
Lloyds St CTBR ML5.........................96 D4
Lloyd St DEN/PKHD G31 ....90 D1
  RUTH G73 ....111 E3
Loanbank Pl GOV/IBX G51..............87 H2
Loanbank Qd GOV/IBX G51.............87 H2
Loancroft Av
  BAIL/MDB/MHD G69 ....94 B1
Loancroft Gdns
  UD/BTH/TAN G71.......................133 H2
Loancroft Ga
  UD/BTH/TAN G71.......................133 H2
Loancroft Pl
  BAIL/MDB/MHD G69 ....94 A1
Loanfoot Av BRHD/NEIL G78.........141 E4
  KNTSWD G13 ....50 B4
Loanfoot Rd
  BLTYR/CAMB G72 ....151 G5
Loanhead Av MTHW ML1...............138 A4
  PSLYN/LNWD PA3......................81 H5
  RNFRW PA4 ....63 G3
Loanhead Crs MTHW ML1.............138 A4
Loanhead Rd MTHW ML1...............137 H4
  PSLYN/LNWD PA3......................81 H5
Loanhead St CAR/SHTL G32...........92 A2
  CTBR ML5...................................116 B1
Loaninghead Dr DMBTN G82...........13 G1
The Loaning GIF/THBK G46............144 D3
  KKNTL G66 ....39 H1
  MTHW ML1 ....154 B3
The Loan MLNGV G62 ....16 A1
Lobnitz Av RNFRW PA4....................63 G3
Lochaber Dr RUTH G73..................130 C3
Lochaber Pl EKILN G74..................166 C2
Lochaber Rd BSDN G61...................52 A1
Loch Achray St CAR/SHTL G32........92 D5
Lochaline Av PSLYS PA2 ....103 F2
Lochaline Dr LNPK/KPK G44..........128 B3
Lochalsh Crs KKNTL G66 ....4 C3
Lochalsh Dr PSLYS PA2..................103 E2
Lochalsh Pl BLTYR/CAMB G72.......133 E5
Lochar Crs PLK/PH/NH G53...........107 E2
Lochard Dr PSLYS PA2...................103 F3
Lochay St EKILS G75......................176 D1
Loch Assynt EKILN G74..................166 D5
Loch Awe EKILN G74......................166 D5
Loch Awe Pl CTBR ML5....................96 C3
Lochay St CAR/SHTL G32................92 D5
Lochbrae Dr RUTH G73..................130 C3
Lochbridge Rd ESTRH G34..............93 H2
Lochbroom Dr NMRNS G77............144 C4
  PSLYS PA2 ....103 F2
Loch Brora Crs CTBR ML5................96 B3
Lochbuie La AIRDRIE ML6................75 H2
Lochburn Crs MRYH/FIRH G20........52 D4
Lochburn Pass
  MRYH/FIRH G20..........................52 D4
Lochburn Rd MRYH/FIRH G20.........52 C4
Lochdochart Rd ESTRH G34.............94 C1
Lochearn Crs AIRDRIE ML6..............98 A4
  PSLYS PA2 ....103 F2
Lochend Av
  BAIL/MDB/MHD G69 ....58 D5
Lochend Crs BSDN G61...................34 A4
Lochend Dr BSDN G61.....................34 A4
Lochend Rd
  BAIL/MDB/MHD G69 ....73 E1
  BAIL/MDB/MHD G69 ....59 E4
  BSDN G61....................................34 B5
  ESTRH G34 ....72 A5
Lochend St MTHW ML1..................155 E4
Locher Av CRG/CRSL/HOU PA6........81 F2
Locherburn Av
  CRMNK/CLK/EAG G76.................146 A4
  EKILN G74 ....165 E3
Locherburn Pl
  CRG/CRSL/HOU PA6.....................81 F3
Locher Crs
  CRG/CRSL/HOU PA6.....................81 F3
Locher Gait
  CRG/CRSL/HOU PA6.....................81 F3
Locher Gdns
  CRG/CRSL/HOU PA6.....................81 F3
Locher Rd BRWEIR PA11................100 A1
Locher Wk CTBR ML5.......................97 G4
Locher Wy
  CRG/CRSL/HOU PA6.....................81 F3
Lochfauld Rd SMSTN G23...............53 G1
Lochfield Crs PSLYS PA2................104 C3
Lochfield Dr PSLYS PA2.................104 D3
Lochfield Gdns ESTRH G34.............72 B5
Lochgarry Wy CTBR ML5.................96 A5
Lochgilp St MRYH/FIRH G20...........52 B4
Loch Goil EKILN G74 ....166 D4
Lochgoin Av DRUM G15...................32 D4
Lochgreen Pl CTBR ML5 ....73 H5
  HMLTN ML3 ....180 B1
Lochgreen St
  STPS/GTHM/RID G33....................69 G3
Lochhead Av
  PSLYN/LNWD PA3......................82 A4
Lochiel La RUTH G73......................130 C3
Lochiel Rd GIF/THBK G46...............126 C5
Lochinch Pl NMRNS G77................143 F5
Lochinvar Rd CUMB G67..................44 C1

Lochinver Crs
  BLTYR/CAMB G72 ....**168** B2
  PSLYS PA2 ....**103** F2
Lochinver Dr *LNPK/KPK* G44 ...**128** B2
Lochinver Gv
  STPS/GTHM/RID G33 ....**131** G2
Loch Laidon St *CAR/SHTL* G32 ...**93** B5
Loch Laxford *EKILN* G74 ....**167** G1
Lochlea *EKILN* G74 ....**167** G1
Loch Lea *KNTTL* G66 ....**57** F2
Lochlea Av *CLYDBK* G81 ....**32** B5
Lochlea Rd
  CRMNK/CLK/EAG G76 ....**145** H5
  CUMB G67 ....**26** D2
  PLKSW/MSWD G43 ....**127** G1
  RUTH G73 ....**129** G2
Lochlea Wy *MTHW* ML1 ....**138** B3
Lochleven La *GVH/MTFL* G42 ....**109** F5
Lochleven Rd *GVH/MTFL* G42 ....**109** F5
Lochlibo Av *KNTSWD* G13 ....**50** A5
Lochlibo Crs *BRHD/NEIL* G78 ...**141** H1
Lochlibo Rd *BRHD/NEIL* G78 ...**140** B4
Lochlibo Ter *BRHD/NEIL* G78 ...**141** H1
Loch Long *EKILN* G74 ....**166** D5
Loch Loyal *EKILN* G74 ....**167** G1
Lochmaben Rd
  BAIL/MDB/MHD G69 ....**73** G2
  CARD/HILL/MSPK G52 ......**86** A5
Lochmaddy Av
  LNPK/KPK G44 ....**128** B3
Loch Maree *EKILN* G74 ....**167** G5
Loch Meadie *EKILN* G74 ....**167** E5
Lochnagar Dr *BSDN* G61 ....**33** C1
Loch Naver *EKILN* G74 ....**167** G1
Lochore Av *PSLYN/LNWD* PA3 ...**84** D2
Loch Pk *WISHAW* ML2 ....**174** D3
Loch Pl *BRWEIR* PA11 ....**79** G3
Lochranza *EKILN* G74 ....**177** H4
Lochranza La *EKILS* G75 ......**177** H4
Loch Rd *AIRDRIE* ML6 ....**119** G2
  BRWEIR PA11 ....**79** G3
  KNTTL G66 ....**40** B1
  MLNGV G62 ....**17** F2
  STPS/GTHM/RID G33 ....**71** E1
Loch Shin *EKILN* G74 ....**167** G5
Lochside *BAIL/MDB/MHD* G69 ....**59** E5
  BSDN G61 ....**34** C5
Lochside Crs *AIRDRIE* ML6 .....**76** B5
Lochside St *PLKSD/SHW* G41 ...**108** D3
Loch St *AIRDRIE* ML6 ....**118** C2
Loch Striven *EKILN* G74 ......**166** D4
Loch Torridon *EKILN* G74 .....**167** G5
Loch Vw *AIRDRIE* ML6 ....**118** C2
Lochview Dr
  STPS/GTHM/RID G33 ....**70** A3
Lochview Gdns
  STPS/GTHM/RID G33 ....**70** A3
Lochview Pl
  STPS/GTHM/RID G33 ....**70** A3
Lochview Qd *BLSH* ML4 ....**135** G4
Lochview Rd *BSDN* G61 ....**34** B5
  CTBR ML5 ....**73** H5
Loch Voil St *CAR/SHTL* G32 ....**93** E5
Lochwood Loan
  BAIL/MDB/MHD G69 ....**42** B5
Lochwood St
  STPS/GTHM/RID G33 ....**69** H4
Lochy Av *RNFRW* PA4 ....**64** A5
Lochy Pl *ERSK* PA8 ....**47** F2
Lochy St *WISHAW* ML2 ....**173** H4
Locke Gv *MTHW* ML1 ....**156** C1
Lockerbie Av
  STPS/GTHM/RID G33 ....**70** D2
Locket Yett Vw *BLSH* ML4 .....**135** G2
Lockhart Av *BLTYR/CAMB* G72 ...**132** A1
Lockhart Ct *NMRNS* G77 ......**161** G3
Lockhart Pl
  UD/BTH/TAN G71 * **114** A2
  WISHAW ML2 ....**174** D1
Lockhart St *HMLTN* ML3 ......**170** C2
  SPRGB/BLRNK G21 ....**69** E4
Lockhart Ter *EKILN* G74 ......**167** E5
Locksley Av *CUMB* G67 ....**44** D2
  KNTSWD G13 ....**50** D3
Locksley Crs *CUMB* G67 ....**44** D2
Locksley Pl *CUMB* G67 ....**44** D2
Locksley Rd *CUMB* G67 ....**44** D2
  PSLYS PA2 ....**103** E5
Locks St *CTBR* ML5 ....**97** G3
Logan Av *NMRNS* G77 ....**143** H4
Logandale Av *WISHAW* ML2 ....**158** A4
Logan Dr *BALLOCH* G68 ....**25** H2
  PSLYN/LNWD PA3 ....**83** H4
Logan Gdns *MTHW* ML1 ....**157** E2
Loganlea Dr *MTHW* ML1 ....**155** F1
Logans Rd *MTHW* ML1 ....**154** A2
Logan St *BLTYR/CAMB* G72 .....**151** H5
  GBLS G5 ....**110** A2
Loganswell Dr *GIF/THBK* G46 ...**126** B5
Loganswell Gdns
  GIF/THBK G46 ....**126** B5
Loganswell Pl *GIF/THBK* G46 ...**126** B5
Loganswell Rd
  GIF/THBK G46 ....**126** B5
Logie Pk *EKILN* G74 ....**166** D2
Logie Sq *EKILN* G74 ....**166** D2
Lomax St
  STPS/GTHM/RID G33 ....**91** G1
Lomond *EKILS* G75 ....**178** B3
Lomond Av *RNFRW* PA4 ....**63** G5
Lomond Crs *BRHD/NEIL* G78 ....**124** B5
  CUMB G67 ....**44** B1
  CUMB G67 ....**44** B1
Lomond Crs *BRWEIR* PA11 .....**79** F3
  CUMB G67 ....**44** B1
  PSLYS PA2 ....**104** A4
Lomond Dr *AIRDRIE* ML6 ....**119** H5
  BRHD/NEIL G78 ....**124** A3
  BSHPBGS G64 ....**37** G5
  CUMB G67 ....**44** B1
  DMBTN G82 ....**13** C1
  NMRNS G77 ....**144** A3
  UD/BTH/TAN G71 ....**134** C4
  WISHAW ML2 ....**173** H4

Lomond Gdns *JNSTN* PA5 ....**102** B2
Lomond Gv *CUMB* G67 ....**44** B1
Lomond Pl *CTBR* ML5 ....**74** B5
  CUMB G67 ....**44** A1
  ERSK PA8 ....**47** F2
  STPS/GTHM/RID G33 ....**71** E2
Lomond Rd *BSDN* G61 ....**51** F1
  BSHPBGS G64 ....**54** B5
  CTBR ML5 ....**74** A4
  KNTTL G66 ....**40** A3
  UD/BTH/TAN G71 ....**115** E5
London Dr *CAR/SHTL* G32 ......**113** F2
London La *CGLE* G1 ....**3** H7
London Rd *CGLE* G1 ....**90** A5
  DMNK/BRGTN G40 ....**90** B4
London St *RNFRW* PA4 ....**63** G1
Lonend *PSLY* PA1 ....**104** C1
Longay Pl *PPK/MIL* G22 ....**53** H5
Longay St *PPK/MIL* G22 ....**53** H5
Long Crags Vw *DMBTN* G82 ....**13** H1
Longcroft Dr *RNFRW* PA4 ......**63** F3
Longden St *CLYDBK* G81 ....**49** G3
Long Dr *EKILS* G75 ....**178** D1
Longford St
  STPS/GTHM/RID G33 ....**91** G1
Longlee *BAIL/MDB/MHD* G69 ....**94** A5
Longmeadow *JNSTN* PA5 ....**100** B8
Longmorn Pl *MTHW* ML1 ....**155** C1
Long Rw *BAIL/MDB/MHD* G69 ...**94** B3
  KKNTL G66 ....**41** E1
Longstone Rd
  STPS/GTHM/RID G33 ....**92** C1
Longwill Ter *CUMB* G67 ....**26** D1
Lonmay Dr
  STPS/GTHM/RID G33 ....**93** E1
Lonmay Rd
  STPS/GTHM/RID G33 ....**93** E1
Lonsdale Av *GIF/THBK* G46 ....**127** F4
Loom Wk *KLBCH* PA10 ....**100** B3
Lora Dr *CARD/HILL/MSPK* G52 ...**87** F5
Loretto Pl
  STPS/GTHM/RID G33 ....**92** A1
Loretto St
  STPS/GTHM/RID G33 ....**92** A1
Lorimer Crs *EKILS* G75 ....**178** A1
Lorn Av *BAIL/MDB/MHD* G69 ....**58** C3
Lorne Dr *MTHW* ML1 ....**136** C5
  PSLYN/LNWD PA3 ....**101** H1
Lorne Pl *CTBR* ML5 ....**97** G5
Lorne Rd
  CARD/HILL/MSPK G52 ......**86** A1
Lorne St *GOV/IBX* G51 ....**88** C3
  HMLTN ML3 ....**169** H1
Lorne Ter *BLTYR/CAMB* G72 ....**131** E4
Lorn Pl *KKNTL* G66 ....**22** C4
Lorraine Gdns *KVD/HLHD* G12 ...**66** B2
Lorraine Gardens La
  KVD/HLHD G12 ....**66** B2
Lorraine Rd *KVD/HLHD* G12 ....**66** B2
Loskin Dr *PPK/MIL* G22 ....**53** G4
Lossie Crs *RNFRW* PA4 ....**64** A4
Lossie St
  STPS/GTHM/RID G33 ....**69** G5
Lothian Crs *PSLYS* PA2 ....**104** A3
Lothian Dr
  CRMNK/CLK/EAG G76 ....**145** G2
Lothian Gdns
  MRYH/FIRH G20 ....**66** D3
Lothian St
  CARD/HILL/MSPK G52 ......**86** A1
Lothian Wy *EKILN* G74 ....**167** F2
Louden Hill Pl
  STPS/GTHM/RID G33 * **55** H5
Louden Hill Rd
  STPS/GTHM/RID G33 ....**55** H5
Louden Hill Wy
  SPRGB/BLRNK G21 ....**55** H5
Loudon Gdns *JNSTN* PA5 ......**101** H3
Loudonhill Av *HMLTN* ML3 .....**170** C5
Loudon Rd
  STPS/GTHM/RID G33 ....**70** C2
Loudon St *WISHAW* ML2 ....**157** H4
Louise Gdns *BLSH* ML4 ....**157** E2
Louisville Av *WISHAW* ML2 ....**157** H5
Lounsdale Av *PSLYS* PA2 .....**103** G1
Lounsdale Crs *PSLYS* PA2 .....**103** G1
Lounsdale Dr *PSLYS* PA2 .....**103** G1
Lounsdale Pl *SCOT* G14 ......**64** C2
Lounsdale Rd *PSLYS* PA2 .....**103** G2
Lourdes Av
  CARD/HILL/MSPK G52 ......**87** G5
Lovat Av *BSDN* G61 ....**34** B1
Lovat Dr *KKNTL* G66 ....**20** C5
Lovat Pl *CARD/HILL/MSPK* G52 ..**85** H2
  RUTH G73 ....**130** C3
Love Av *BRWEIR* PA11 ....**78** B1
Love Dr *BLSH* ML4 ....**136** A1
Love St *PSLYN/LNWD* PA3 .....**84** B3
Low Barholm *KLBCH* PA10 ....**100** C3
Low Broadlie Rd
  BRHD/NEIL G78 ....**141** E2
Low Craigends *KSYTH* G65 ....**8** C2
Low Crs *CLYDBK* G81 ....**49** H3
Lower Auchingramont Rd
  HMLTN ML3 ....**170** B1
Lower Bourtree Dr
  RUTH G73 ....**130** B3
Lower Millgate
  UD/BTH/TAN G71 ....**134** A1
Lower Mill Rd
  CRMNK/CLK/EAG G76 ......**146** A4
Lowndes St
  BRHD/NEIL G78 ....**124** B5
Low Parksail *ERSK* PA8 ......**47** H5
Low Patrick St *HMLTN* ML3 ...**170** C2
Low Rd *PSLYS* PA2 ....**103** H1
Lowther Av *BSDN* G61 ....**33** H1
Lowther Ter *KVD/HLHD* G12 ...**66** B2
Low Waters Rd *HMLTN* ML3 ...**170** A5
Loyal Av *ERSK* PA8 ....**47** F2

Loyal Pl *ERSK* PA8 ....**47** E2
Loyne Dr *RNFRW* PA4 ....**64** A5
Luath St *GOV/IBX* G51 ....**87** H1
Lubas Av *GVH/MTFL* G42 ......**110** A5
Lubas Pl *GVH/MTFL* G42 ......**110** A5
Lubnaig Dr *ERSK* PA8 ....**46** D2
Lubnaig Gdns *BSDN* G61 ......**33** H1
Lubnaig Pl *AIRDRIE* ML6 ......**75** H4
Lubnaig Rd
  PLKSW/MSWD G43 ....**127** H2
Luckiesfauld *BRHD/NEIL* G78 ...**141** E3
Luckingsford Av *RNFRW* PA4 ...**48** A4
Luckingsford Dr *RNFRW* PA4 ...**47** H4
Luckingsford Rd *RNFRW* PA4 ...**47** H4
Lucy Brae *UD/BTH/TAN* G71 ...**114** D4
Luffness Gdns
  CAR/SHTL G32 ....**112** C2
Lugar Dr
  CARD/HILL/MSPK G52 ......**87** F5
Lugar Pl *LNPK/KPK* G44 ......**129** F2
Lugar St *CTBR* ML5 ....**97** E1
Luggiebank Pl
  BAIL/MDB/MHD G69 ....**95** F5
Luggiebank Rd *KKNTL* G66 ....**21** F5
Luggieburn Wk *CTBR* ML5 ....**96** D4
Luggie Vw *CUMB* G67 ....**43** H1
Luing Rd
  CARD/HILL/MSPK G52 ......**87** F4
Luma Gdns *GOV/IBX* G51 ......**86** D2
Lumloch St
  SPRGB/BLRNK G21 ....**68** D2
Lumsden La *KVGV* G3 ....**66** C5
Lumsden St *KVGV* G3 ....**88** C1
Lunan Dr *BSHPBGS* G64 ....**55** F3
Lunan Pl *GOV/IBX* G51 ....**87** F2
Luncarty Pl *CAR/SHTL* G32 ...**112** B1
Luncarty St *CAR/SHTL* G32 ...**112** A1
Lunderston Dr
  PLK/PH/NH G53 ....**106** B5
Lundie Gdns *BSHPBGS* G64 ....**55** G3
Lundie St *CAR/SHTL* G32 .....**111** H1
Luss Brae *HMLTN* ML3 ....**168** D5
Lusset Gln *OLDK* G60 ....**30** C2
Lusset Rd *OLDK* G60 ....**30** C2
Luss Rd *GOV/IBX* G51 ....**87** G2
Lybster Wy *BLTYR/CAMB* G72 ...**168** B2
Lye Brae *CUMB* G67 ....**26** C3
Lyell Gv *EKILN* G74 ....**166** B2
Lyell Pl *EKILN* G74 ....**166** B2
Lyle Crs *BSHPTN* PA7 ....**28** A3
Lyle Pl *PSLYS* PA2 ....**104** D2
Lyle Rd *AIRDRIE* ML6 ....**99** G2
Lylesland Ct *PSLYS* PA2 .....**104** B3
Lyle Sq *MLNGV* G62 ....**16** C3
Lyman Dr *WISHAW* ML2 ......**157** F5
Lymekilns Rd *EKILN* G74 .....**166** A3
Lyndale Pl *MRYH/FIRH* G20 ...**52** C3
Lyndale Rd *MRYH/FIRH* G20 ...**52** C3
Lyndhurst Gdns
  MRYH/FIRH G20 ....**67** E5
Lyndhurst Gardens La
  MRYH/FIRH G20 ....**67** E5
Lynebank Av *NMRNS* G77 .....**161** G5
Lynebank Pl *NMRNS* G77 .....**161** G5
Lyne Cft *BSHPBGS* G64 ....**37** H4
Lynedoch Crs *KVGV* G3 ....**67** E5
Lynedoch Crescent La
  KVGV G3 ....**67** E5
Lynedoch Pl *KVGV* G3 ....**67** E5
Lynedoch St *KVGV* G3 ....**67** E5
Lyne St *WISHAW* ML2 ....**156** D5
Lynnburn Av *BLSH* ML4 ......**135** H2
Lynn Dr *MLNGV* G62 ....**17** G3
Lynne Dr *SMSTN* G23 ....**52** D2
Lynnhurst *UD/BTH/TAN* G71 ...**115** E5
Lynwood Rd *WISHAW* ML2 ....**174** A4
Lynton Av *GIF/THBK* G46 .....**144** D1
Lyoncross Av
  BRHD/NEIL G78 ....**124** C5
Lyoncross Crs
  BRHD/NEIL G78 ....**124** C4
Lyoncross Rd
  PLK/PH/NH G53 ....**106** C2
Lyon Rd *ERSK* PA8 ....**46** D2
  PSLYN/LNWD PA3 ....**82** A5
  PSLYS PA2 ....**103** E3
Lyons Qd *WISHAW* ML2 ......**173** E3
Lysa Vale Pl *BLSH* ML4 ......**135** G2
Lytham Dr *SMSTN* G23 ....**52** D2
Lytham Mdw
  UD/BTH/TAN G71 ....**133** H5
Lyttelton *EKILS* G75 ....**177** G3

M

Mabel St *MTHW* ML1 ....**154** D5
Macadam Gdns *BLSH* ML4 ....**135** H4
Macadam Pl *EKILS* G75 ......**166** B5
Macallan Ms *MTHW* ML1 .....**137** G5
Macarthur Av *AIRDRIE* ML6 ...**98** A3
Macarthur Ct *EKILN* G74 .....**165** H1
Macarthur Crs *EKILN* G74 ....**165** H1
Macarthur Dr *EKILN* G74 .....**165** H1
Macarthur Gdns *EKILN* G74 ...**165** H1
Macarthur Wynd
  BLTYR/CAMB G72 ....**131** H2
Macbeth *EKILN* G74 ....**149** G5
Macbeth Pl *DEN/PKHD* G31 ...**91** G5
Macbeth St *DEN/PKHD* G31 ...**91** G5
Mac Callum Dr
  BLTYR/CAMB G72 ....**131** H4
Maccrimmon Pk *EKILN* G74 ...**165** G1
Macdonald Av *EKILN* G74 ....**165** H1
Macdonald Av *MTHW* ML1 ...**155** G5
Macdonald Gv *BLSH* ML4 .....**135** H4
Macdonald St *MTHW* ML1 ...**155** G5
  RUTH G73 ....**110** D4
Macdougal Dr
  BLTYR/CAMB G72 ....**131** H2
Macdougall St
  PLKSW/MSWD G43 ....**108** B5
Macdougal Qd *BLSH* ML4 .....**135** G4
Macdowall St *JNSTN* PA5 ....**101** G3
  PSLYN/LNWD PA3 ....**84** A3
Macduff Pl *DEN/PKHD* G31 ...**91** G5

Macduff St *DEN/PKHD* G31 ....**91** G5
Macedonian Gv *MTHW* ML1 ...**137** H3
Mace Rd *KNTSWD* G13 ....**50** D2
Macfarlane Crs
  BLTYR/CAMB G72 ....**132** A2
Macfarlane Rd *BSDN* G61 .....**34** C5
Macfie Pl *EKILN* G74 ....**165** G1
Macgregor Ct
  BLTYR/CAMB G72 ....**131** H2
Machrie Dr *CSMK* G45 ....**129** G3
  NMRNS G77 ....**144** B4
Machrie Gn *EKILS* G75 ......**177** G4
Machrie Rd *CSMK* G45 ....**129** G3
Machrie St *CSMK* G45 ....**129** G3
  MTHW ML1 ....**154** A3
Macinnes Dr *MTHW* ML1 .....**137** G5
Macintosh Pl *EKILS* G75 ....**177** H1
Macintyre St *KVGV* G3 ....**2** A5
Macivor Crs *EKILN* G74 ......**165** F1
Mackean St *PSLYN/LNWD* PA3 ..**83** H5
Mackeith St
  DMNK/BRGTN G40 ....**90** C5
Mackenzie Dr *KLBCH* PA10 ...**100** C5
Mackenzie Gdns *EKILN* G74 ...**165** F1
Mackenzie Ter *BLSH* ML4 ....**135** H1
Mackie's Mill Rd *JNSTN* PA5 ..**102** C5
Mackinley Pl *NMRNS* G77 ....**161** G5
Mackintosh Ct
  DEN/PKHD G31 ....**90** C1
Mack St *AIRDRIE* ML6 ....**98** B1
Maclay Pk *KLBCH* PA10 ......**100** B4
Maclean Ct *EKILN* G74 ......**165** G1
Maclean Gv *EKILN* G74 ......**165** G1
Maclean Pl *EKILN* G74 ......**165** G1
Maclean Sq *GOV/IBX* G51 ....**88** C3
Maclean St *CLYDBK* G81 .....**49** G3
  GOV/IBX G51 ....**88** C3
Maclehose Rd *CUMB* G67 .....**27** E2
Maclellan Rd *BRHD/NEIL* G78 ..**141** F4
Maclellan St *PLKSD/SHW* G41 ..**88** C4
Maclean Ct *EKILN* G74 ......**167** E3
Macleod St *COWCAD* G4 ....**3** K5
Macleod Wy
  BLTYR/CAMB G72 ....**131** H2
Macmillan Gdns
  UD/BTH/TAN G71 ....**115** F4
Macneill Dr *EKILN* G74 ......**165** F1
Macneill Gdns *EKILN* G74 ....**165** F1
Macneish Wy *EKILN* G74 .....**165** F1
Macnicol Ct *EKILN* G74 ......**165** F1
Macnicol Pk *EKILN* G74 ......**165** F1
Macnicol Pl *EKILN* G74 ......**165** F1
Macpherson Pk *EKILN* G74 ...**165** H2
Macphie Rd *DMBTN* G82 .....**13** H2
Macrae Gdns *EKILN* G74 .....**166** D1
Macrimmon Pl *EKILS* G75 ....**166** B5
Mactaggart Rd *CUMB* G67 ....**26** A5
Madison Av *LNPK/KPK* G44 ...**128** C2
Madras St *BRHD/NEIL* G78 ...**141** F3
Madras St *DMNK/BRGTN* G40 ..**110** A1
Mafeking St *GOV/IBX* G51 ....**88** A3
  WISHAW ML2 ....**158** A5
Mafeking Ter *BRHD/NEIL* G78 ..**140** D4
Magna St *MTHW* ML1 ....**154** A2
Magnolia Dr
  BLTYR/CAMB G72 ....**132** C4
Magnolia Pl
  UD/BTH/TAN G71 ....**115** H4
Magnolia St *WISHAW* ML2 ...**157** E5
Magnolia Ter
  BLTYR/CAMB G72 ....**132** C4
Magnus Crs *LNPK/KPK* G44 ...**128** C3
Magnus Rd
  CRG/CRSL/HOU PA6 ....**80** D3
Mahon Ct
  BAIL/MDB/MHD G69 ....**59** E5
Maidens *EKILN* G74 ....**166** A2
Maidens Av *NMRNS* G77 .....**144** D5
Maidland Rd *PLK/PH/NH* G53 ..**106** D5
Mailerbeg Gdns
  BAIL/MDB/MHD G69 ....**42** A5
Mailing Av *BSHPBGS* G64 ....**55** E1
Mainhill Av
  BAIL/MDB/MHD G69 ....**94** B4
Mainhill Dr
  BAIL/MDB/MHD G69 ....**94** B4
Mainhill Pl
  BAIL/MDB/MHD G69 ....**94** B4
Mainhill Rd
  BAIL/MDB/MHD G69 ....**95** E4
Main Rd *CUMB* G67 ....**43** F4
  JNSTN PA5 ....**102** B1
  PSLYS PA2 ....**104** A1
Mains Av *GIF/THBK* G46 .....**145** E1
Mainscroft *ERSK* PA8 ....**47** H2
Mains Dr *ERSK* PA8 ....**47** H2
Mainshill Av *ERSK* PA8 ......**47** G2
Mainshill Gdns *ERSK* PA8 ....**47** G2
Mains Pl *BLSH* ML4 ....**135** H4
Mains River *ERSK* PA8 ....**47** H2
Mains Rd *EKILN* G74 ....**148** D5
  KSYTH G65 ....**7** F3
Main St *AIRDRIE* ML6 ....**119** F2
  AIRDRIE ML6 ....**94** A5
  BAIL/MDB/MHD G69 ....**58** C2
  BLSH ML4 ....**135** H4
  BLTYR/CAMB G72 ....**151** F4
  BRHD/NEIL G78 ....**141** E3
  BRWEIR PA11 ....**79** G3
  BSDN G61 ....**34** D1
  BSHPBGS G64 ....**37** G1
  CTBR ML5 ....**95** E5
  CTBR ML5 ....**74** A1
  CUMB G67 ....**10** D5
  DMNK/BRGTN G40 ....**110** C1
  EKILN G74 ....**166** C1
  GIF/THBK G46 ....**126** C4
  HWWD PA9 ....**120** A4
  KKNTL G66 ....**40** A1
  KSYTH G65 ....**23** H1
  MLNGV G62 ....**16** C5
  MTHW ML1 ....**171** H5
  MTHW ML1 ....**137** H3
  UD/BTH/TAN G71 ....**133** D1
  WISHAW ML2 ....**175** H2
  WISHAW ML2 ....**173** H2
Mains Wd *ERSK* PA8 ....**48** A2

Mair St *GOV/IBX* G51 ....**88** D3
Maitland Dr *BSHPBGS* G64 ....**19** F4
Maitland Pl *RNFRW* PA4 ......**63** F4
Maitland St *COWCAD* G4 ......**2** E1
Malborough La North
  PTCK G11 ....**65** G3
Malborough La
  South *PTCK* G11 ....**65** G3
Malcolm Gdns *EKILN* G74 ....**165** H1
Malcolm St *MTHW* ML1 ......**154** B4
Malin Pl *STPS/GTHM/RID* G33 ..**92** A1
Mallaig Pl *GOV/IBX* G51 .....**87** E2
Mallaig Rd *GOV/IBX* G51 .....**87** E2
Mallard Crs *EKILS* G75 ....**177** F3
Mallard Pl *EKILS* G75 ....**177** F3
Mallard Rd *CLYDBK* G81 .....**32** A2
Mallard Ter *EKILS* G75 ......**177** F3
Malleable Gdns *MTHW* ML1 ...**136** B5
Malleny Gv *NMRNS* G77 ......**161** G2
Malletsheugh Rd *NMRNS* G77 .**161** E2
Malloch Crs *JNSTN* PA5 .....**102** A2
Malloch Pl *EKILN* G74 ......**167** E5
Malloch St *MRYH/FIRH* G20 ..**66** D1
Mallot's Vw *NMRNS* G77 .....**161** E2
Malov Ct *EKILS* G75 ....**178** B3
Malta Ter *GBLS* G5 ....**89** G5
Maltbarns St *MRYH/FIRH* G20 ..**67** F3
Mambeg Dr *GOV/IBX* G51 .....**87** F1
Mamore Pl
  PLKSW/MSWD G43 ....**127** F1
Mamore St
  PLKSW/MSWD G43 ....**127** F1
Manchester Dr *KVD/HLHD* G12 .**51** H5
Manderston Meadow
  NMRNS G77 ....**161** E1
Manitoba Crs *EKILS* G75 ....**165** G4
Mannering *EKILN* G74 ....**165** H4
Mannering Ct
  PLKSD/SHW G41 ....**108** B4
Mannering Rd
  PLKSD/SHW G41 ....**102** D4
Mannoch Pl *DMBTN* ML5 .....**117** G1
Mannofield *BSDN* G61 ....**34** A4
Manor Dr *AIRDRIE* ML6 ....**96** C2
  CTBR ML5 ....**96** C2
Manor Ga *NMRNS* G77 ....**162** A2
Manor Park Av *PSLYS* PA2 ...**103** G3
Manor Rd
  BAIL/MDB/MHD G69 ....**73** E1
  DRUM G15 ....**50** A3
  PSLYS PA2 ....**103** E3
  SCOT G14 ....**65** F1
Manor Vw *AIRDRIE* ML6 .....**118** C2
Manor Wy *RUTH* G73 ....**130** B3
Manresa Pl *COWCAD* G4 .....**67** G4
Manse Av *BSDN* G61 ....**34** C4
  CTBR ML5 ....**96** B5
  UD/BTH/TAN G71 ....**134** C4
Manse Brae *LNPK/KPK* G44 ...**128** C1
Manse Ct *BRHD/NEIL* G78 ....**124** C4
  KSYTH G65 ....**8** B3
Manse Crs *CRG/CRSL/HOU* PA6 ..**80** C1
Mansefield Av
  BLTYR/CAMB G72 ....**131** F3
Mansefield Crs *CLYDBK* G60 ...**30** B2
Manse La *EKILN* G74 ....**166** C2
Mansel St *SPRGB/BLRNK* G21 ..**54** B5
Manse Pl *AIRDRIE* ML6 ......**98** B2
Manse Rd
  BAIL/MDB/MHD G69 ....**94** D3
  BRHD/NEIL G78 ....**141** E3
  BSDN G61 ....**34** C3
  CAR/SHTL G32 ....**93** E5
  CRMNK/CLK/EAG G76 ....**147** E5
  KSYTH G65 ....**8** B3
  MTHW ML1 ....**171** H5
  OLDK G60 ....**15** G5
  WISHAW ML2 ....**173** H3
Manse Road Gdns *BSDN* G61 ...**34** C3
Manse St *CTBR* ML5 ....**96** B5
  RNFRW PA4 ....**63** G2
Manse Vw *MTHW* ML1 ....**138** C3
Mansewood Dr *DMBTN* G82 ....**13** H1
Mansewood Rd
  GIF/THBK G46 ....**127** E3
Mansfield Crs
  CRMNK/CLK/EAG G76 ....**145** G4
Mansfield Rd *BLSH* ML4 ......**135** G5
  BAIL/MDB/MHD G69 ....**58** A4
  CRMNK/CLK/EAG G76 ....**145** H4
  HMLTN ML3 ....**180** D1
Mansfield St *PTCK* G11 ......**66** B4
Mansion Ct *BLTYR/CAMB* G72 ..**131** F1
Mansionhouse Av
  CAR/SHTL G32 ....**112** D4
Mansionhouse Dr
  CAR/SHTL G32 ....**92** A3
Mansionhouse Gdns
  PLKSD/SHW G41 ....**108** D5
Mansionhouse Gv
  CAR/SHTL G32 ....**113** F1
Mansionhouse Rd
  CAR/SHTL G32 ....**113** F1
  PLKSD/SHW G41 ....**84** D4
  PSLY PA1 ....**84** D4
Mansion St *BLTYR/CAMB* G72 ..**151** F1
  PPK/MIL G22 ....**67** H1
Manson Pl *EKILS* G75 ....**178** D3
Maple Av *DMBTN* G82 ....**12** D3
  KKNTL G66 ....**5** F5
  NMRNS G77 ....**161** G1
Maple Bank *HMLTN* ML3 .....**170** C3
Maple Ct *CUMB* G67 ....**44** A1
Maple Crs *BLTYR/CAMB* G72 ...**132** C4
Maple Dr *BRHD/NEIL* G78 ....**142** C2
  CLYDBK G81 ....**31** G3
  JNSTN PA5 ....**121** G1
  KKNTL G66 ....**5** F5
Maple Gv *BAIL/MDB/MHD* G69 ..**95** F3
  UD/BTH/TAN G71 ....**116** A4
Maple Qd *AIRDRIE* ML6 ......**99** E3
Maple Rd *CUMB* G67 ....**44** A1
  MTHW ML1 ....**137** G2
  PLKSD/SHW G41 ....**88** B5
Maple Ter *EKILS* G75 ....**177** G2
Maplewood *WISHAW* ML2 .....**173** G4
Mar Av *BSHPTN* PA7 ....**29** E5

Marchbank Gdns *PSLY* PA1 .....85 G5
Marchfield Av
  PSLYN/LNWD PA3 ....84 A1
Marchglen Pl *GOV/IBX* G51 ....87 E2
Marchmont Gdns
  ....54 C1
Marchmont Ter
  KVD/HLHD G12 ....66 B5
March St *PLKSD/SHW* G41 ...109 E2
Mardale *EKILN* G74 ....165 H4
Mardale Wy *MTHW* ML1 65
Mar Dr *BSDN* G61 ....34 C1
Maree Dr
  CARD/HILL/MSPK G52 ....87 F5
  CUMB G67 ....44 A1
Maree Gdns *BSHPBGS* G64 ....55 E2
Maree Rd *PSLYS* PA2 ....103 F2
Marfield St *CAR/SHTL* G32 ....91 H2
Mar Gdns *RUTH* G73 ....130 C3
Mariner Ct *CLYDBK* G81 ....48 C1
Marion St *BLSH* ML4 ....136 C2
Mariscat Rd *PLKSD/SHW* G41 ...108 D2
Marius Crs *WISHAW* ML2 ....154 B2
Marjory Rd *PSLYN/LNWD* PA3 ...84 C2
Markdow Av *PLK/PH/NH* G53 ...106 B3
Market Cl *KSYTH* G65 8
Markethill Rd *EKILN* G74 ....166 B2
Markhill Rd *KKNTL* G66 65
  UD/BTH/TAN G71 ....115 H5
Market St *AIRDRIE* ML6 ....98 B2
  KSYTH G65 8
  UD/BTH/TAN G71 115
Marlach Pl *PLK/PH/NH* G53 ...106 B4
Marlborough Av *PTCK* G11 ....65 G3
Marlborough Pk *EKILS* G75 ...177 F1
Marldon La *PTCK* G11 ....65 G3
Marley Wy *MTHW* ML1 ....S E4
Marlfield Gdns *BLSH* ML4 ....116 D5
Marlow Ter *PLKSD/SHW* G41 ...88 D5
Marlow Ter *PLKSD/SHW* G41 ...88 D5
Marmion Crs *MTHW* ML1 ....136 C5
Marmion Dr *KKNTL* G66 ....21 H5
Marmion Pl *CUMB* G67 ....44 D1
Marmion Rd *CUMB* G67 ....44 D1
  PSLYS PA2 ....102 D4
Marne St *DEN/PKHD* G31 ....91 E2
Marnock Ter *PSLYS* PA2 ....104 D2
Marquis Av *HMLTN* ML3 ....152 C5
Marrswood Gn *HMLTN* ML3 ...169 G1
Marrwood Av *KKNTL* G66 ....41 G2
Marshall La *WISHAW* ML2 ....173 H2
Marshall's La *PSLY* PA1 ....84 B5
Marshall St *CTBR* ML5 ....96 A5
  WISHAW ML2 ....173 G3
Martha St *CGLE* G1 ....3 G4
Martin Ct *HMLTN* ML3 ....169 H2
Martin Crs
  BAIL/MDB/MHD G69 ....94 B4
Martin Pl *MTHW* ML1 ....137 H4
Martinside *EKILS* G75 ....178 B3
Martin St *CTBR* ML5 ....97 G2
  DMNK/BRGTN G40 ....110 C1
Martlet Dr *JNSTN* PA5 ....120 D2
Martyn St *CCLE* G1 4
Martyn St *AIRDRIE* ML6 ....97 H5
Martyrs Pl *BSHPBGS* G64 ....54 D1
Marwick St *DEN/PKHD* G31 ....91 E2
Mary Dr *BLSH* ML4 ....135 F4
Mary Fisher Crs *DMBTN* G82 ...1
Mary Gln *WISHAW* ML2 ....157 G5
Maryhill Rd *BSDN* G61 ....51 H1
  COWCAD G4 ....2 B1
  MRYH/FIRH G20 ....67 E3
Maryknowe Rd *MTHW* ML1 ...155 H1
Maryland Dr
  CARD/HILL/MSPK G52 ....87 F4
Maryland Gdns
  CARD/HILL/MSPK G52 ....87 F4
Maryland Rd *DMBTN* G82 ....13 H4
Mary Rae Rd *BLSH* ML4 ....135 F5
Maryston St
  STPS/GTHM/RID G33 ....69 G4
Mary St *HMLTN* ML3 ....170 A3
  JNSTN PA5 ....101 H5
  PSLYS PA2 ....104 B2
Maryville Av *GIF/THBK* G46 ...127 F5
Maryville Gdns *GIF/THBK* G46 ..127 F5
Maryville Vw
  UD/BTH/TAN G71 ....114 C3
Marywell Pth *BALLOCH* G68 ...24 D5
Marywood Sq
  PLKSD/SHW G41 ....109 E2
Mary Young Pl
  CRMNK/CLK/EAG G76 ...146 A4
Masonfield Av *BALLOCH* G68 ...25 H5
Mason La *MTHW* ML1 ....154 D4
Masterton St *COWCAD* G4 ....67 H3
Masterton Wy
  UD/BTH/TAN G71 ....115 G3
Matherton Av *NMRNS* G77 ...145 E5
Mathieson Crs
  STPS/GTHM/RID G33 ....71 G1
Mathieson Rd *RUTH* G73 ....111 F3
Matilda Rd *PLKSD/SHW* G41 ...88 D5
Mauchline *EKILN* G74 ....164 D1
Mauchline Av *KKNTL* G66 ....22 A3
Mauchline Ct *HMLTN* ML3 ....168 C3
Mauchline St *GBLS* G5 ....89 F5
Maukinfauld Ct
  CAR/SHTL G32 ....111 G1
Maukinfauld Gdns
  DEN/PKHD G31 ....91 H5
Maukinfauld Rd
  CAR/SHTL G32 ....111 H1

Mauldslie St *BLSH* ML4 ....135 H3
  CTBR ML5 ....96 D4
  DMNK/BRGTN G40 ....91 E5
Maule Dr *PTCK* G11 ....65 H4
Mausoleum Dr *HMLTN* ML3 ...153 G5
Mavis Bank *BSHPBGS* G64 ....54 C5
Mavisbank Gdns *BLSH* ML4 ...135 H1
  GOV/IBX G51 ....88 D3
Mavisbank Rd *GOV/IBX* G51 ...88 D3
Mavisbank St *AIRDRIE* ML6 ...98 A1
  WISHAW ML2 ....158 D4
Mavisbank Ter *JNSTN* PA5 ...101 G4
  PSLY PA1 ....104 C1
Mavor Av *BRHD/NEIL* G78 ...123 H4
Maxton Av *BRHD/NEIL* G78 ...123 H4
Maxton Crs *WISHAW* ML2 ....157 F4
Maxton Gv *BRHD/NEIL* G78 ...123 H5
Maxton Ter *BLTYR/CAMB* G72 ...131 E4
Maxwell Av
  BAIL/MDB/MHD G69 ....93 H5
  BSDN G61 ....51 F1
  PLKSD/SHW G41 ....88 D5
Maxwell Crs
  BLTYR/CAMB G72 ....151 G4
Maxwell Dr
  BAIL/MDB/MHD G69 ....93 G4
  EKILN G74 ....166 C3
  ERSK PA8 ....30 A5
  PLKSD/SHW G41 ....88 B5
Maxwell Gdns *PLKSD/SHW* G41 ..88 C5
Maxwell Gv *PLKSD/SHW* G41 ...88 C5
Maxwell La *PLKSD/SHW* G41 ...88 D5
Maxwell Pl *BRWEIR* PA11 ....79 C5
  PLKSD/SHW G41 ....109 F1
  UD/BTH/TAN G71 ....134 B1
Maxwell Rd *BSHPTN* PA7 ....29 G5
  PLKSD/SHW G41 ....89 E5
Maxwell St
  BAIL/MDB/MHD G69 ....94 A5
  CGLE G1 ....3 F7
  PLKSD/SHW G41 ....88 D4
  PSLYN/LNWD PA3 ....84 B4
Maxwellton Av *EKILN* G74 ....166 D3
Maxwellton Rd *EKILN* G74 ....167 E2
  EKILN G74 ....167 F1
  PSLYN/LNWD PA3 ....83 H4
Maxwellton St *PSLYS* PA2 ...103 H1
Maxwelton Rd
  STPS/GTHM/RID G33 ....69 G4
Maybank La *GVH/MTFL* G42 ...109 F3
Maybank St *GVH/MTFL* G42 ...109 F3
Mayberry Crs *CAR/SHTL* G32 ...93 B4
Mayberry Gdns *CAR/SHTL* G32 ...93 B4
Mayberry Gv *CAR/SHTL* G32 ...93 B4
Mayberry Pl
  BLTYR/CAMB G72 ....151 G2
Maybole Crs *NMRNS* G77 ...162 B1
Maybole Dr *AIRDRIE* ML6 ....98 B5
Maybole Gdns *HMLTN* ML3 ...168 C3
Maybole Gv *NMRNS* G77 ....162 B1
Maybole Pl *CTBR* ML5 ....117 G1
Maybole St *PLK/PH/NH* G53 ...125 E1
Mayfield Av
  CRMNK/CLK/EAG G76 ...145 H3
Mayfield Crs *HWWD* PA9 ...120 A3
Mayfield Dr *HWWD* PA9 ...120 A3
Mayfield Pl *HWWD* PA9 ...120 A3
Mayfield Rd *HMLTN* ML3 ...116 D1
  HMLTN ML3 ....169 E1
Mayfield St *MRYH/FIRH* G20 ...67 E1
May Gdns *WISHAW* ML2 ....173 H2
May Rd *PSLYS* PA2 ....104 B5
May St *HMLTN* ML3 ....153 E5
May Ter *GIF/THBK* G46 ....127 F4
  GVH/MTFL G42 ....109 G4
Gay Wynd *HMLTN* ML3 ....152 D5
McAllister Av *AIRDRIE* ML6 ...99 E1
McAlpine St *CCLW* G2 ....2 B7
  WISHAW ML2 ....174 A3
McArdle Av *MTHW* ML1 ....154 A3
McArthur Pk *KKNTL* G66 ....39 H1
McArthur St
  PLKSW/MSWD G43 ....108 B5
McAslin Ct *COWCAD* G4 ....3 J3
McAslin St *COWCAD* G4 ....3 K3
McBride Pth
  STPS/GTHM/RID G33 ....71 F1
McCallum Av *RUTH* G73 ....111 E5
McCallum Ct *EKILN* G74 ....165 G4
McCallum Gdns *BLSH* ML4 ...135 G5
McCallum Gv *EKILN* G74 ....165 F1
McCallum Pl *EKILN* G74 ....165 G1
McCarrison Rd *WISHAW* ML2 ...158 B4
McCash Pl *KKNTL* G66 ....39 H1
McCloy Gdns *PLK/PH/NH* G53 ...125 G2
McClue Av *RNFRW* PA4 ....63 E2
McClue Rd *RNFRW* PA4 ....63 E2
McCormack Gdns *MTHW* ML1 ...138 B5
McCracken Av *RNFRW* PA4 ....63 E4
McCracken Dr
  UD/BTH/TAN G71 ....115 H4
McCreery St *CLYDBK* G81 ....49 G5
McCrorie Pl *KLBCH* PA10 ....100 B2
McCulloch Av
  BRHD/NEIL G78 ....141 E5
McCulloch St *PLKSD/SHW* G41 ...89 E5
McCulloch Wy
  BRHD/NEIL G78 ....141 E5
McDonald Av *JNSTN* PA5 ....101 F5
McDonald Crs *CLYDBK* G81 ...49 G5
McDonald Pl *BRHD/NEIL* G78 ...141 F5
  MTHW ML1 ....137 F2
McEwan Gdns *EKILN* G74 ....165 F1
McFarlane St *COWCAD* G4 ....3 K7
  PSLYN/LNWD PA3 ....83 H2
McGhee St *CLYDBK* G81 ....32 A5
McGoldrick Pl
  STPS/GTHM/RID G33 ....71 G1
McGowan Pl *HMLTN* ML3 ....152 B5
McGregor Av *AIRDRIE* ML6 ....99 E1
  RNFRW PA4 ....63 E4
McGregor Dr *DMBTN* G82 ....13 H1
McGregor Rd *CUMB* G67 ....26 A4
McGregor St *CLYDBK* G81 ....49 H2
  GOV/IBX G51 ....87 G2
  WISHAW ML2 ....173 H2
McGrigor Rd *MLNGV* G62 ....16 D2
McGurk Wy *BLSH* ML4 ....135 E1
McInnes Ct *WISHAW* ML2 ....174 A3

McIntosh Qd *BLSH* ML4 ....135 G5
McIntosh St *DEN/PKHD* G31 ...90 C2
McIntosh Wy *MTHW* ML1 ....171 F1
McIntyre Pl *PSLYS* PA2 ....104 A2
McIntyre Ter
  BLTYR/CAMB G72 ....131 F1
McIver St *BLTYR/CAMB* G72 ...132 A1
McKay Crs *JNSTN* PA5 ....101 H4
McKay Pl *EKILN* G74 ....165 F1
  NMRNS G77 ....161 F1
McKechnie St *GOV/IBX* G51 ...87 H1
McKenna Dr *AIRDRIE* ML6 ...119 E4
McKenzie Av *CLYDBK* G81 ....32 A4
McKenzie St *PSLYN/LNWD* PA3 ..83 H4
McKeown Gdns *BLSH* ML4 ...136 C5
McKerrell St *PSLY* PA1 ....84 D5
McLaren Av *RNFRW* PA4 ....63 F5
McLaren Ct *GIF/THBK* G46 ...145 E1
McLaren Crs *MRYH/FIRH* G20 ...52 D4
McLaren Dr *BLSH* ML4 ....136 C3
McLaren Gdns
  MRYH/FIRH G20 ....52 D4
McLaren Gv *EKILN* G74 ....165 F1
McLaurin Crs *JNSTN* PA5 ...101 E5
McLean Dr *BLSH* ML4 ....135 G5
McLean Pl *PSLYN/LNWD* PA3 ...84 A2
McLees La *MTHW* ML1 ....154 A3
McLennan St *GVH/MTFL* G42 ...109 G4
McLeod Rd *DMBTN* G82 ....13 H3
McMahon Dr *WISHAW* ML2 ...158 B4
McMahon Gv *BLSH* ML4 ....136 A1
McMillan Rd *WISHAW* ML2 ...173 G3
McNair St *CAR/SHTL* G32 ....92 B4
McNeil Av *CLYDBK* G81 ....49 H2
McNeil Dr *MTHW* ML1 ....137 H1
McNeil Gdns *GBLS* G5 ....90 A5
McNeil St *GBLS* G5 ....90 A5
McPhail Av *MTHW* ML1 ....138 C2
McPhail St *DMNK/BRGTN* G40 ...90 B5
McPherson Crs *AIRDRIE* ML6 ...119 F4
McPherson Dr
  UD/BTH/TAN G71 ....134 C4
McPherson St *BLSH* ML4 ....136 C2
McShannon Gv *BLSH* ML4 ....135 H4
McSparran Rd *KSYTH* G65 ....24 D1
McCulloch Wy
  STPS/GTHM/RID G33 ....71 F1
Meadow Av
  BLTYR/CAMB G72 ....151 G4
  ERSK PA8 ....30 B5
Meadowbank Pl *NMRNS* G77 ...144 A5
Meadowbank St *DMBTN* G82 ...13 E3
Meadowburn *BSHPBGS* G64 ...37 H4
Meadowburn Av *KKNTL* G66 ...40 B3
  NMRNS G77 ....144 A5
Meadowburn Rd
  WISHAW ML2 ....174 B2
Meadow Ct *EKILS* G75 ....177 H4
Meadow Ct *DMBTN* G82 ....13 E2
Meadowfield Pl *WISHAW* ML2 ..158 D4
Meadowhead Av
  BAIL/MDB/MHD G69 ....59 E4
Meadowhead Av *AIRDRIE* ML6 ...77 G3
  WISHAW ML2 ....173 H1
Meadowhill *NMRNS* G77 ....144 A4
Meadow La *RNFRW* PA4 ....63 G1
Meadowpark St
  DEN/PKHD G31 ....91 E2
Meadow Rd *NMRNS* G77 ....143 H4
Meadow Rd *DMBTN* G82 ....13 E2
  MTHW ML1 ....155 F5
  PTCK G11 ....65 H5
Meadows Dr *ERSK* PA8 ....47 H2
Meadowside *HMLTN* ML3 ....180 D2
Meadowside Av *JNSTN* PA5 ...102 C2
Meadowside Gdns
  AIRDRIE ML6 ....99 E2
Meadowside Pl *AIRDRIE* ML6 ...99 E2
Meadowside Rd *KSYTH* G65 ....7 E2
Meadowside St *GOV/IBX* G51 ...65 H5
  RNFRW PA4 ....63 G1
The Meadows
  CRG/CRSL/HOU PA6 ....81 F2
Meadow Vw *AIRDRIE* ML6 ....97 E5
Meadow Wy *WISHAW* ML2 ....27 E2
  CUMB G67 ....27 E2
Meadow Wk *CTBR* ML5 ....97 E4
Meadow Wy *NMRNS* G77 ....144 A5
Meadowwell St *CAR/SHTL* G32 ...92 D4
Meadside Av *KLBCH* PA10 ....100 B2
Meadside Rd *KLBCH* PA10 ....100 B2
Mealkirk St *CLYDBK* G81 ....32 B1
Mealybrae Rd *BSHPBGS* G64 ...18 B2
Mearns Ct *HMLTN* ML3 ....181 E1
Mearnscroft Gdns
  NMRNS G77 ....162 A2
Mearnscroft Rd *NMRNS* G77 ...162 A3
Mearnskirk Rd *NMRNS* G77 ...161 G4
Mearns Rd *MTHW* ML1 ....154 B2
  NMRNS G77 ....144 D5
Medlar Ct *BLTYR/CAMB* G72 ...132 C4
Medlar Rd *CUMB* G67 ....27 F3
Medrox Gdns *CUMB* G67 ....45 G1
Medwin Ct *EKILS* G75 ....176 D1
Medwin Gdns *EKILS* G75 ....176 D1
Medwin St *BLTYR/CAMB* G72 ...132 A2
Medwyn St *SCOT* G14 ....65 H4
Meek Pl *BLTYR/CAMB* G72 ....151 G4
Meetinghouse La *PSLY* PA1 ....84 B4
Megan St *DMNK/BRGTN* G40 ...90 C5
Meikle Av *RNFRW* PA4 ....63 G4
Meikle Bin Brae *KKNTL* G66 ....4 C3
Meikle Crs *HMLTN* ML3 ....180 A1
Meikle Earnock Rd
  HMLTN ML3 ....180 A1
Meiklehill Ct *KKNTL* G66 ....21 H4
Meiklehill Rd *KKNTL* G66 ....21 H4
Meiklerig Crs
  PLK/PH/NH G53 ....106 D2
Meikleriggs Dr *PSLYS* PA2 ...103 F3
Meikle Rd *PLK/PH/NH* G53 ...106 D3
Meiklewood Rd *GOV/IBX* G51 ...87 E3
Melbourne Av *CLYDBK* G81 ...31 E3
  EKILS G75 ....177 H1
Melbourne Ct *GIF/THBK* G46 ...127 G4
Melbourne Gn *EKILS* G75 ....165 H5
Melbourne St
  DMNK/BRGTN G40 ....90 C3

Meldon Pl *GOV/IBX* G51 ....87 E2
Meldrum Gdns
  PLKSD/SHW G41 ....108 C2
Meldrum Mains *AIRDRIE* ML6 ...75 H2
Meldrum St *CLYDBK* G81 ....49 H2
Melford Av *GIF/THBK* G46 ...127 G5
  KKNTL G66 ....20 D5
Melford Rd *BLSH* ML4 ....135 F1
Melford Av *CLYDBK* G81 ....32 B5
  PLKSD/SHW G41 ....109 E2
Melfort Gdns *KLBCH* PA10 ....100 D3
  PLKSD/SHW G41 ....168 D2
Mellerstain Dr *SCOT* G14 ....49 H5
Melness Pl *GOV/IBX* G51 ....87 E2
Melrose Av *AIRDRIE* ML6 ....119 E2
  BAIL/MDB/MHD G69 ....95 E4
  MTHW ML1 ....137 G2
  PSLYN/LNWD PA3 ....83 H3
  PSLYS PA2 ....103 F4
  RUTH G73 ....111 E5
Melrose Crs *WISHAW* ML2 ....156 D5
Melrose Gdns
  MRYH/FIRH G20 ....67 E3
Melrose Pl *BLTYR/CAMB* G72 ...151 E5
  CTBR ML5 ....96 C2
Melrose Rd *CUMB* G67 ....44 C1
Melrose St *COWCAD* G4 ....2 B1
  HMLTN ML3 ....152 C5
Melrose Ter *EKILN* G74 ....166 C4
  HMLTN ML3 ....152 C4
Melvaig Pl *MRYH/FIRH* G20 ...66 C1
Melvick Pl *GOV/IBX* G51 ....87 E2
Melville Crs *MTHW* ML1 ....154 D4
Melville Gdns *BSHPBGS* G64 ...54 C1
Melville St *PLKSD/SHW* G41 ...109 E1
Memel St *PPK/MIL* G22 ....68 A5
Memorial Wy *MTHW* ML1 ....137 H1
Memus Av
  CARD/HILL/MSPK G52 ....86 D5
Mendip La *EKILS* G75 ....177 H4
Mennock Ct *HMLTN* ML3 ....168 D3
Mennock St *MTHW* ML1 ....139 F5
Mennock Rd *LNPK/KPK* G44 ...128 D1
Menteith Av *BSHPBGS* G64 ...55 E2
Menteith Dr *RUTH* G73 ....130 C5
Menteith Gdns *BSDN* G61 ....16 A5
Menteith Pl *RUTH* G73 ....130 C5
Menteith Rd *MTHW* ML1 ....154 C1
Menzies Dr *SPRGB/BLRNK* G21 ...68 D1
Menzies Pl *SPRGB/BLRNK* G21 ...68 D1
Menzies Rd
  SPRGB/BLRNK G21 ....68 D1
Merchant La *CGLE* G1 ....3 G6
Merchants Cl *KLBCH* PA10 ...100 B3
Merchiston Av
  PSLYN/LNWD PA3 ....81 H4
Merchiston St *JNSTN* PA5 ...101 E1
Merchiston St *CAR/SHTL* G32 ...91 H2
Mere Ct *BALLOCH* G68 ....9 H4
Merkins Av *DMBTN* G82 ....13 H2
Merkland Ct *KKNTL* G66 ....22 A4
Merkland Pl *PTCK* G11 ....66 A4
Merkland Rd *KKNTL* G66 ....22 A4
Merkland St *PTCK* G11 ....66 A4
Merkland Wy *EKILS* G75 ....177 H3
Merksworth Wy
  COV/IBX G51 ....65 G5
  HMLTN ML3 ....115 G5
Merlewood Av
  UD/BTH/TAN G71 ....134 C3
Merlin Av *BLSH* ML4 ....116 D4
Merlinford Av *RNFRW* PA4 ...63 H3
Merlinford Crs *RNFRW* PA4 ...63 H3
Merlinford Dr *RNFRW* PA4 ...63 H3
Merlinford Wy *RNFRW* PA4 ...63 H3
Merlin Wy *PSLYN/LNWD* PA3 ...85 E2
Merrick Av *BSDN* G61 ....34 A1
Merrick Gdns
  GOV/IBX G51 ....88 B4
  HMLTN ML3 ....169 G5
Merrick Ter *UD/BTH/TAN* G71 ...115 G5
Merrick Wy *RUTH* G73 ....130 A4
Merryburn Av *GIF/THBK* G46 ...127 G3
Merry St *BLTYR/CAMB* G72 ...151 H4
Merrycrest Av *GIF/THBK* G46 ...127 G3
Merrycroft Av *GIF/THBK* G46 ...127 G3
Merryflats *KSYTH* G65 ....23 F1
Merryland Pl *GOV/IBX* G51 ...88 B2
Merryland St *GOV/IBX* G51 ...88 B2
Merrylee Crs *GIF/THBK* G46 ...127 G2
Merrylee Pk *GIF/THBK* G46 ...127 F2
Merrylee Park Av
  ....127 G3
Merrylee Rd
  BLTYR/CAMB G72 ....151 E5
Merrystone St *CTBR* ML5 ....96 B2
Merry St *MTHW* ML1 ....154 D3
Merryton Av *DRUM* G15 ....33 G4
  GIF/THBK G46 ....127 G3
Merryton Ct *HMLTN* ML3 ....180 D1
Merryton Gdns *DRUM* G15 ....33 G4
Merryton Rd *MTHW* ML1 ....172 A5
Merryton St *GIF/THBK* G46 ...127 F2
Merryvale Av *GIF/THBK* G46 ...127 G2
Merryvale Pl *GIF/THBK* G46 ...127 G2
Meryon Gdns *CAR/SHTL* G32 ...113 E1
Meryon Rd *CAR/SHTL* G32 ...113 E1
Methil St *SCOT* G14 ....65 E4
Methil Wy *BLTYR/CAMB* G72 ...151 G2
Methlan Park Gdns
  DMBTN G82 ....12 C5
Methlick Av *AIRDRIE* ML6 ....97 H5
Methuen Rd *PSLYN/LNWD* PA3 ..84 D1
Methven Av *BSDN* G61 ....35 E3
Methven Pl *EKILN* G74 ....165 H4
Methven Rd *GIF/THBK* G46 ...144 D4
Methven St *CLYDBK* G81 ....31 H2
  DEN/PKHD G31 ....111 G1
Metropole La *CGLE* G1 ....89 H3
Mews La *PSLYN/LNWD* PA3 ...84 C2
Mey Ct *NMRNS* G77 ....160 D1
Mey Pl *NMRNS* G77 ....160 D1
Michael McParland Dr
  BSHPBGS G64 ....19 F5
Michael Ter *AIRDRIE* ML6 ....119 E5
Micklehouse Ov
  BAIL/MDB/MHD G69 ....94 A3
Micklehouse Pl
  BAIL/MDB/MHD G69 ....94 A3

Micklehouse Rd
  BAIL/MDB/MHD G69 ....94 A3
Micklehouse Wynd
  BAIL/MDB/MHD G69 ....94 A3
Mid Av *BLSH* ML4 ....136 D2
Mid Barrwood Rd *KSYTH* G65 ...8 E2
Mid Barwood Rd *KSYTH* G65 ....9 E2
Mid Carbarns *WISHAW* ML2 ...173 E4
Midcroft Av *LNPK/KPK* G44 ...129 F2
Middlefield *EKILS* G75 ....178 B3
Middlemuir Rd *KKNTL* G66 ....40 A2
Middlerigg Rd *BALLOCH* G68 ...24 D3
Middlesex Gdns
  PLKSD/SHW G41 ....88 D4
Middlesex St *PLKSD/SHW* G41 ..88 D4
Middle Ward St *CLYDBK* G81 ...32 C1
Midfaulds Av *RNFRW* PA4 ....64 A4
Midland St *CGLE* G1 ....2 E7
Midlem Dr
  CARD/HILL/MSPK G52 ....86 D4
Midlem Ov
  CARD/HILL/MSPK G52 ....86 D4
Midlock St *GOV/IBX* G51 ....88 B4
Midlothian Dr
  PLKSD/SHW G41 ....108 C3
Mid Pk *EKILS* G75 ....166 B5
Mid Rd *CUMB* G67 ....68 B3
Milford *EKILN* G74 ....166 B3
Milford St
  STPS/GTHM/RID G33 ....92 B1
Millands Av *BLTYR/CAMB* G72 ...151 F1
Millarbank St
  SPRGB/BLRNK G21 ....68 B2
Millard Av *MTHW* ML1 ....137 G5
Millar Gv *HMLTN* ML3 ....169 G2
Millarston Av *PSLY* PA1 ....103 E1
Millarston Dr *PSLY* PA1 ....103 E1
Millars Pl *KKNTL* G66 ....40 A4
Millarston Av *PSLY* PA1 ....103 E1
Millarston Dr *PSLY* PA1 ....84 C4
Millbank Av *BLSH* ML4 ....136 A4
Millbank Ct *CTBR* ML5 ....116 C1
Millbank Rd *WISHAW* ML2 ....173 G3
Millbeg Crs
  STPS/GTHM/RID G33 ....93 G4
Millbeg Pl
  STPS/GTHM/RID G33 ....93 F4
Mill Brae *BRWEIR* PA11 ....79 F4
Millbrae Av
  BAIL/MDB/MHD G69 ....58 C3
Millbrae Crs *CLYDBK* G81 ....49 H3
  GVH/MTFL G42 ....109 E4
Millbrae Gdns *GVH/MTFL* G42 ...109 E5
Millbrae Rd *GVH/MTFL* G42 ...108 D5
Millbrix Av *SCOT* G14 ....64 C1
Millbrook *EKILN* G74 ....165 F4
Millburn Av *CLYDBK* G81 ....49 H3
  RNFRW PA4 ....63 G3
  RUTH G73 ....129 H1
Millburn Ct *EKILS* G75 ....176 D2
Millburn Crs *DMBTN* G82 ....13 G4
Millburn Dr *RNFRW* PA4 ....63 G3
Millburn Gdns *EKILS* G75 ....176 D1
Millburn Rd *DMBTN* G82 ....13 G3
  RNFRW PA4 ....63 H3
Millburn St *SPRGB/BLRNK* G21 ...68 C5
  MTHW ML1 ....155 F5
  SPRGB/BLRNK G21 ....68 D5
Millburn Wy *EKILS* G75 ....176 D1
  RNFRW PA4 ....63 H3
Mill Ct *HMLTN* ML3 ....169 H3
  RUTH G73 ....111 E5
Mill Crs *BSHPBGS* G64 ....19 G4
  DMNK/BRGTN G40 ....110 C1
Millcroft Rd *AIRDRIE* ML6 ....45 F4
  CUMB G67 ....44 C4
  RUTH G73 ....110 C2
Milldam Rd *CLYDBK* G81 ....32 B1
Millennium Ct *ESTRH* G34 ....94 B1
Millennium Gdns *ESTRH* G34 ...94 B2
Miller Cl *BSHPBGS* G64 ....54 C3
Miller Ct *DMBTN* G82 ....13 G3
Miller Dr *BSHPBGS* G64 ....55 G2
Millerfield Pl
  DMNK/BRGTN G40 ....111 E1
Miller Field Pl *HMLTN* ML3 ...170 C1
Millerfield Rd
  DMNK/BRGTN G40 ....111 E1
Miller Gdns *BSHPBGS* G64 ....55 G2
Millersneuk Av *KKNTL* G66 ....40 A4
Millersneuk Crs
  STPS/GTHM/RID G33 ....70 B1
Millersneuk Dr *KKNTL* G66 ....40 A4
Millersneuk Rd *KKNTL* G66 ....40 A4
Miller's Pl *AIRDRIE* ML6 ....98 D2
Millers Pl *DEN/PKHD* G31 ....90 D3
Miller St *BAIL/MDB/MHD* G69 ...94 A3
  CGLW G2 ....3 F6
  CLYDBK G81 ....49 E2
  CTBR ML5 ....116 C1
  DMBTN G82 ....13 E2
  HMLTN ML3 ....170 C2
  JNSTN PA5 ....102 A1
  WISHAW ML2 ....173 H2
Miller Wk *BSHPBGS* G64 ....55 G2
Millfield Av *ERSK* PA8 ....47 F2
  MTHW ML1 ....155 E2
Millfield Crs *ERSK* PA8 ....47 F2
Millfield Dr *ERSK* PA8 ....47 G2
Millfield Gdns *ERSK* PA8 ....47 F2
Millfield Hill *ERSK* PA8 ....47 F2
Millfield La *ERSK* PA8 ....47 F2
Millfield Mdw *ERSK* PA8 ....47 F2
Millfield Pl *ERSK* PA8 ....47 F2
Millfield Vw *ERSK* PA8 ....47 E2
Millfield Wk *ERSK* PA8 ....47 G2
Millfield Wynd *ERSK* PA8 ....47 F2
Millford Dr *PSLYN/LNWD* PA3 ...82 A4

Millgate Av UD/BTH/TAN G71 115 E4
Millgate Ct UD/BTH/TAN G71 115 E5
Millgate Rd HMLTN ML3 169 H4
Mill Gv BLTYR/CAMB G72 132 A2
HMLTN ML3 169 H3
Millheugh Pl
BLTYR/CAMB G72 151 F4
Millholm Rd LNPK/KPK G44 128 C3
Millhouse Crs MRYH/FIRH G20 52 A4
Millhouse Dr MRYH/FIRH G20 52 B4
Millichen Rd SMSTN G23 35 H3
Milliken Dr KLBCH PA10 100 D4
Milliken Park Rd KLBCH PA10 100 D5
Milliken Rd KLBCH PA10 100 D4
Mill Loan AIRDRIE ML6 98 B1
Mill of Gryffe La BRWEIR PA11 79 G3
Mill of Gryffe Rd
BRWEIR PA11 79 G3
Mill Pl PSLYN/LNWD PA3 81 H5
UD/BTH/TAN G71 134 A1
Millport Av LNPK/KPK G44 109 H5
Mill Rig EKILS G75 178 A3
Mill Ri KKNTL G66 40 A4
Mill Rd AIRDRIE ML6 76 B5
BLTYR/CAMB G72 131 H1
CLYDBK G81 49 G4
HMLTN ML3 169 H4
KSYTH G65 7 E3
MTHW ML1 155 E2
SHOTTS ML7 159 G2
UD/BTH/TAN G71 152 B1
WISHAW ML2 175 H2
Millroad Dr DMNK/BRGTN G40 90 C3
Millroad St DMNK/BRGTN G40 90 B3
Millstream Ct PSLY PA1 84 C5
Mill St DMNK/BRGTN G40 110 C1
PSLY PA1 84 C5
Millview BRHD/NEIL G78 124 C4
Millview Mdw
BRHD/NEIL G78 140 D3
Millview Pl PLK/PH/NH G53 125 G3
Millview Ter BRHD/NEIL G78 140 D3
Mill Wk BLTYR/CAMB G72 132 A2
Mill Wy KKNTL G66 40 D1
Millwood St PLKSD/SHW G41 108 D4
Milnbank St DEN/PKHD G31 90 D1
Milncroft Pl
STPS/GTHM/RID G33 70 B5
Milncroft Rd
STPS/GTHM/RID G33 70 B5
Milner La KNTSWD G13 65 F1
Milner Rd KNTSWD G13 65 F1
Milne Wy UD/BTH/TAN G71 134 B1
Milngavie Rd BSDN G61 34 C5
Milnpark Gdns
PLKSD/SHW G41 88 C4
Milnpark St PLKSD/SHW G41 88 D4
Milnwood Dr MTHW ML1 136 B5
Milovaig Av SMSTN G23 52 C1
Milovaig St SMSTN G23 52 C2
Milrig Rd RUTH G73 110 C5
Milroy Gdns BLSH ML4 116 D4
Milton Av BLTYR/CAMB G72 130 D2
Milton Brae DMBTN G82 14 A2
Milton Ct DMBTN G82 14 C3
Milton Douglas Rd
CLYDBK G81 31 H2
Milton Dr BSHPBGS G64 54 B4
Milton Gdns
UD/BTH/TAN G71 114 D4
Milton Hl DMBTN G82 14 C4
Milton Mains Rd CLYDBK G81 31 H3
Milton Rd EKILN G74 165 F3
KKNTL G66 4 C3
Milton St AIRDRIE ML6 98 B1
COWCAD G4 3 F2
HMLTN ML3 152 B5
MTHW ML1 154 D2
Milton Ter HMLTN ML3 152 B5
Milverton Av BSDN G61 33 H2
Milverton Rd GIF/THBK G46 144 D1
Mimosa Rd BRWEIR PA11 79 G3
Minard Rd PLKSD/SHW G41 108 D3
Minard Wy UD/BTH/TAN G71 115 F5
Mincher Crs MTHW ML1 171 H1
Minch Wy AIRDRIE ML6 99 E4
Minella Gdns BLSH ML4 116 D4
Minerva St KVGV G3 88 D1
Minerva Wy KVGV G3 88 C1
Mingarry La MRYH/FIRH G20 66 D2
Mingarry St MRYH/FIRH G20 66 D2
Mingulay Crs PPK/MIL G22 54 A3
Mingulay Pl PPK/MIL G22 54 B3
Mingulay St PPK/MIL G22 54 B3
Ministers Pk EKILN G74 165 E1
Minmoir Rd PLK/PH/NH G53 106 A5
Minstrel Rd KNTSWD G13 51 E2
Minto Av RUTH G73 130 C3
Minto Crs
CARD/HILL/MSPK G52 87 G4
Minto Pk WISHAW ML2 157 F4
Minto St
CARD/HILL/MSPK G52 87 G4
Mireton St PPK/MIL G22 67 G1
Mirin Dr PSLYN/LNWD PA3 84 B2
Mirren Dr CLYDBK G81 31 G1
Mirrin Wynd PSLYN/LNWD PA3 84 A2
Mirrlees Dr KVD/HLHD G12 66 B2
Mirrlees La KVD/HLHD G12 66 B2
Mission Pl MTHW ML1 154 D2
Mitchell Av BLTYR/CAMB G72 132 B1
RNFRW PA4 63 E4
Mitchell Ct EKILN G74 165 H3
Mitchell Dr MLNGV G62 17 G4
RUTH G73 130 A1
Mitchell Gv EKILN G74 165 H3
Mitchell Hill Rd CSMK G45 129 G5
Mitchell La CGLE G1 2 E6
Mitchell Rd CUMB G67 26 C3
Mitchell St AIRDRIE ML6 98 A1
CGLE G1 2 E6
CTBR ML5 95 G4
Mitchison Rd CUMB G67 26 C2
Mitre Ct PTCK G11 65 G3
Mitre La SCOT G14 65 E2
Mitre La West SCOT G14 65 E2
Mitre Rd PTCK G11 65 G2
Moat Av KNTSWD G13 50 D4
Mochrum Rd
PLKSW/MSWD G43 127 H1
Moffat Ct EKILS G75 176 D1
Moffathill AIRDRIE ML6 99 F5
Moffat Pl BLTYR/CAMB G72 151 G1
CTBR ML5 97 G5
EKILS G75 176 D1
Moffat Rd AIRDRIE ML6 99 G2
Moffat St GBLS G5 90 A5
Moffat Vw AIRDRIE ML6 77 H4
Mogarth Av PSLYS PA2 103 E4
Moidart Av RNFRW PA4 63 E2
Moidart Ct BRHD/NEIL G78 124 A3
Moidart Crs
CARD/HILL/MSPK G52 87 F4
Moidart Gdns KKNTL G66 22 B4
NMRNS G77 144 B4
Moidart Pl
CARD/HILL/MSPK G52 87 F4
Moidart Rd
CARD/HILL/MSPK G52 87 F4
Moir St CGLE G1 90 A3
Molendinar St CGLE G1 3 J7
Molendinar Ter
BRHD/NEIL G78 140 D4
Mollinsburn Rd CUMB G67 43 F5
Mollinsburn St
SPRGB/BLRNK G21 68 B3
Mollins Ct BALLOCH G68 43 E3
Mollins Rd BALLOCH G68 42 D3
Monach Rd
STPS/GTHM/RID G33 92 D1
Monar Dr PPK/MIL G22 67 G3
Monar St PPK/MIL G22 67 G3
Monart Pl MRYH/FIRH G20 67 E2
Moncrieff Av KKNTL G66 40 A3
Moncrieffe Rd AIRDRIE ML6 99 E5
Moncrieff Gdns KKNTL G66 40 A3
Moncrieff St
PSLYN/LNWD PA3 84 B4
Moncur St DMNK/BRGTN G40 90 B3
Moness Dr
CARD/HILL/MSPK G52 87 F5
Money Gv MTHW ML1 172 C1
Monieburgh Crs KSYTH G65 8 C1
Monieburgh Rd KSYTH G65 8 C1
Monifieth Av
CARD/HILL/MSPK G52 107 E1
Monikie Gdns BSHPBGS G64 55 G2
Monkcastle Dr
BLTYR/CAMB G72 131 F1
Monkland Av KKNTL G66 40 A2
Monkland St AIRDRIE ML6 98 C2
Monkland Vw AIRDRIE ML6 118 C2
UD/BTH/TAN G71 115 F3
Monkland View Crs
BAIL/MDB/MHD G69 95 F4
Monksbridge Av KNTSWD G13 50 D2
Monkscourt Av AIRDRIE ML6 97 H1
Monkscroft Av PTCK G11 65 H3
Monkscroft Ct PTCK G11 65 H4
Monks Rd AIRDRIE ML6 98 D5
Monkton Brae
BAIL/MDB/MHD G69 58 B2
Monkton Cresent CTBR ML5 96 B5
Monkton Dr DRUM G15 50 C2
Monkton Gdns NMRNS G77 162 B1
Monmouth Av KVD/HLHD G12 65 H1
Monreith Av BSDN G61 51 F1
Monreith Rd
PLKSW/MSWD G43 127 H1
Monreith Rd East
LNPK/KPK G44 128 B2
Monroe Dr UD/BTH/TAN G71 115 E3
Monroe Pl UD/BTH/TAN G71 115 E3
Montague La KVD/HLHD G12 66 A2
Montague St COWCAD G4 67 E4
Montalto Av MTHW ML1 155 F1
Montclair Pl PSLYN/LNWD PA3 81 H5
Montego Gn EKILS G75 165 F4
Monteith Dr
CRMNK/CLK/EAG G76 146 B2
Monteith Gdns
CRMNK/CLK/EAG G76 146 A2
Monteith Pl
DMNK/BRGTN G40 90 B4
Monteith Rw CGLE G1 90 A3
Montford Av LNPK/KPK G44 110 B5
Montgarrie St GOV/IBX G51 87 E3
Montgomery Av CTBR ML5 96 C1
PSLYN/LNWD PA3 85 E1
Montgomery Crs
WISHAW ML2 173 F4
Montgomery Dr
GIF/THBK G46 145 F1
KLBCH PA10 100 B2
Montgomery Pl EKILN G74 166 C3
Montgomery Rd
PSLYN/LNWD PA3 84 D1
Montgomery St
BLTYR/CAMB G72 132 A2
DMNK/BRGTN G40 90 D5
EKILN G74 166 C3
Montgomery Ter KKNTL G66 5 F5
Montport Ga BRHD/NEIL G78 124 D4
Montraive St RUTH G73 111 F3
Montrave St
CARD/HILL/MSPK G52 87 E5
Montreal Pk EKILS G75 165 H4
Montrose Av CAR/SHTL G32 112 C3
CARD/HILL/MSPK G52 86 A2
Montrose Crs HMLTN ML3 170 A1
Montrose Dr BSDN G61 34 B1
Montrose Gdns
BLTYR/CAMB G72 133 F5
KSYTH G65 8 A1
MLNGV G62 17 E2
Montrose Pl PSLYN/LNWD PA3 81 H5
Montrose Rd PSLYS PA2 103 E4
Montrose St CGLE G1 3 H6
CLYDBK G81 49 E1
MTHW ML1 154 C1
Montrose Ter BRWEIR PA11 79 G4
BSHPBGS G64 55 F4
Monymusk Gdns
BSHPBGS G64 55 G1
Monymusk Pl DRUM G15 32 D3
Moodiesburn St
STPS/GTHM/RID G33 69 G4
Moorburn Av GIF/THBK G46 127 E4
Moorburn Pl
PSLYN/LNWD PA3 81 G5
Moorcroft Dr AIRDRIE ML6 99 F2
Moorcroft Rd NMRNS G77 161 F2
Moore Dr BSDN G61 34 C5
Moore Gdns HMLTN ML3 181 E1
Moore St DMNK/BRGTN G40 90 C3
MTHW ML1 137 F4
Moorfield Crs AIRDRIE ML6 99 F2
Moorfield Rd
BLTYR/CAMB G72 151 F4
Moorfoot Av GIF/THBK G46 126 D4
PSLYS PA2 104 A3
Moorfoot Dr WISHAW ML2 173 G2
Moorfoot Gdns EKILS G75 177 G5
Moorfoot St CAR/SHTL G32 91 H3
Moorfoot Wy BSDN G61 16 A5
Moorhill Crs NMRNS G77 161 F2
Moorhill Rd NMRNS G77 161 F1
Moorhouse Av KNTSWD G13 50 A5
PSLYS PA2 103 G2
Moorhouse St
BRHD/NEIL G78 124 B5
The Moorings PSLYS PA2 103 H1
Moorland Dr AIRDRIE ML6 99 F2
Moorlands Wk
UD/BTH/TAN G71 134 B2
Moorpark Av AIRDRIE ML6 99 F2
BAIL/MDB/MHD G69 58 B4
CARD/HILL/MSPK G52 86 A3
Moorpark Ct GOV/IBX G51 87 H2
Moorpark Dr
CARD/HILL/MSPK G52 86 B3
Moorpark Sq RNFRW PA4 63 E4
Moor Rd MLNGV G62 17 F3
Morag Av BLTYR/CAMB G72 151 F1
Moraine Av DRUM G15 50 B2
Moraine Circ DRUM G15 50 B2
Moraine Dr
CRMNK/CLK/EAG G76 145 F2
DRUM G15 50 B2
Moraine Pl DRUM G15 50 C2
Morar Av CLYDBK G81 32 A4
Morar Ct CUMB G67 25 F5
HMLTN ML3 169 F4
Morar Crs AIRDRIE ML6 75 H5
BSHPBGS G64 54 C1
BSHPTN PA7 46 B1
CLYDBK G81 32 A4
CTBR ML5 74 A5
Morar Dr BSDN G61 35 E5
CLYDBK G81 32 A4
CUMB G67 44 A1
PSLYN/LNWD PA3 101 H1
PSLYS PA2 103 E2
RUTH G73 130 A4
Morar Pl CLYDBK G81 32 A4
EKILN G74 166 C2
NMRNS G77 144 A3
RNFRW PA4 63 E2
Morar Rd
CARD/HILL/MSPK G52 87 F4
CLYDBK G81 32 A4
Morar St WISHAW ML2 173 H4
Morar Ter RUTH G73 130 C4
UD/BTH/TAN G71 115 G5
Moravia Av UD/BTH/TAN G71 134 B4
Moray Av AIRDRIE ML6 98 B4
Moray Ct RUTH G73 110 D4
Moray Dr BSHPBGS G64 19 F4
CRMNK/CLK/EAG G76 146 A3
Moray Gdns BALLOCH G68 10 B5
CRMNK/CLK/EAG G76 146 A2
UD/BTH/TAN G71 115 E4
Moray Ga UD/BTH/TAN G71 134 A3
Moray Pl BAIL/MDB/MHD G69 58 C3
BLTYR/CAMB G72 151 F4
BSHPBGS G64 55 F2
KKNTL G66 22 A4
PLKSD/SHW G41 108 D2
PSLYN/LNWD PA3 81 H5
Moray Qd BLSH ML4 135 H2
Mordaunt St
DMNK/BRGTN G40 110 D1
Moredun Crs CAR/SHTL G32 92 D2
Moredun Dr PSLYS PA2 103 G3
Moredun Rd PSLYS PA2 103 G3
Moredun St CAR/SHTL G32 92 D2
Morefield Rd GOV/IBX G51 87 E2
Morgan Ms GVH/MTFL G42 109 G2
Morgan St HMLTN ML3 170 A3
Morina Gdns PLK/PH/NH G53 125 H5
Morion Rd KNTSWD G13 51 E3
Moriston Ct WISHAW ML2 158 A4
Morland EKILN G74 150 A5
Morley St GVH/MTFL G42 109 F5
Morna La SCOT G14 65 F4
Morningside Rd
WISHAW ML2 175 F1
Morningside St
STPS/GTHM/RID G33 91 G1
Morrin St SPRGB/BLRNK G21 68 B3
Morris Crs BLTYR/CAMB G72 151 G3
MTHW ML1 156 B1
Morrishall Rd EKILN G74 167 F3
Morrison Dr KKNTL G66 4 C3
Morrison Qd CLYDBK G81 49 H2
Morrison St CLYDBK G81 31 G2
GBLS G5 89 F3
Morris St HMLTN ML3 170 A4
Morriston Crs RNFRW PA4 64 A5
Morriston Park Dr
BLTYR/CAMB G72 112 B5
Morriston St
BLTYR/CAMB G72 131 F1
Morton Gdns
PLKSD/SHW G41 108 B3
Morton St MTHW ML1 154 D2
Morven Av BLTYR/CAMB G72 151 F1
BSHPBGS G64 55 F2
PSLYS PA2 104 A4
Morven Dr
CRMNK/CLK/EAG G76 145 G2
PSLYN/LNWD PA3 101 H1
Morven Gait ERSK PA8 48 B3
Morven Gdns
UD/BTH/TAN G71 115 E4
Morven Rd BLTYR/CAMB G72 131 E4
BSDN G61 34 B2
Morven St
CARD/HILL/MSPK G52 87 F4
CTBR ML5 96 D1
Mosesfield St
SPRGB/BLRNK G21 68 C1
Mosque Av GBLS G5 89 H4
Mossacre Rd WISHAW ML2 174 B1
Moss Av PSLYN/LNWD PA3 82 A3
Mossbank BLTYR/CAMB G72 151 G4
EKILS G75 165 E5
Mossbank Av
STPS/GTHM/RID G33 70 A2
Mossbank Crs MTHW ML1 138 C3
Mossbank Dr
STPS/GTHM/RID G33 70 A2
Mossbank Rd WISHAW ML2 174 B1
Mossbell Rd BLSH ML4 135 G1
Mossburn Rd WISHAW ML2 174 C2
Mossburn St WISHAW ML2 174 C4
Mosscastle Rd
STPS/GTHM/RID G33 70 D4
Mossdale EKILN G74 165 H2
Mossdale Gdns HMLTN ML3 168 D3
Moss Dr BRHD/NEIL G78 123 H2
ERSK PA8 47 G4
Mossend La
STPS/GTHM/RID G33 93 E1
Mossend St
STPS/GTHM/RID G33 93 E2
Mossgiel EKILS G75 177 G1
Mossgiel Av RUTH G73 129 H2
Mossgiel Crs
CRMNK/CLK/EAG G76 146 A5
Mossgiel Dr CLYDBK G81 32 B5
Mossgiel Gdns KKNTL G66 21 H4
UD/BTH/TAN G71 114 D4
Mossgiel Pl RUTH G73 129 H2
Mossgiel Rd CUMB G67 26 D3
PLKSW/MSWD G43 127 G1
Mossgiel Ter
BLTYR/CAMB G72 133 F5
Mosshall Gv MTHW ML1 138 C3
Mosshall Rd MTHW ML1 119 E5
Mosshall St MTHW ML1 138 C4
Mosshead Rd BSDN G61 34 C1
Moss Heights Av
CARD/HILL/MSPK G52 87 E4
Mosshill Rd BLSH ML4 117 E5
Moss Knowe CUMB G67 26 D3
Mossland Dr WISHAW ML2 174 B1
Mossland Rd
CARD/HILL/MSPK G52 85 G1
Mosslands Rd
PSLYN/LNWD PA3 84 A2
Mosslingal EKILS G75 178 B3
Mossmulloch EKILS G75 178 A3
Mossneuk Av EKILS G75 176 D1
Mossneuk Crs WISHAW ML2 174 B1
Mossneuk Dr EKILS G75 177 E1
PSLYS PA2 103 H4
WISHAW ML2 174 B1
Mossneuk Pk WISHAW ML2 174 B1
Mossneuk Rd EKILS G75 165 F5
Mossneuk St CTBR ML5 116 C1
Mosspark Av
CARD/HILL/MSPK G52 107 G1
MLNGV G62 17 E2
Mosspark Bvd
CARD/HILL/MSPK G52 107 G1
Mosspark Dr
CARD/HILL/MSPK G52 106 D1
Mosspark Ov
CARD/HILL/MSPK G52 107 F1
Mosspark Rd CTBR ML5 96 A1
MLNGV G62 17 E2
Mosspark Sq
CARD/HILL/MSPK G52 107 F1
Moss Rd AIRDRIE ML6 98 B3
BAIL/MDB/MHD G69 58 B4
BRWEIR PA11 79 H4
CRG/CRSL/HOU PA6 82 A1
CUMB G67 27 G1
EKILS G75 177 H4
GOV/IBX G51 87 E1
KKNTL G66 41 E1
KKNTL G66 39 G2
PSLYN/LNWD PA3 82 B3
WISHAW ML2 174 D2
Moss Side Av AIRDRIE ML6 97 H1
Moss-Side Rd
PLKSD/SHW G41 108 D3
Moss St PSLY PA1 84 B4
Mossvale La PSLYN/LNWD PA3 84 A3
Mossvale Rd
STPS/GTHM/RID G33 70 D4
Mossvale Sq
STPS/GTHM/RID G33 70 C4
Mossvale St PSLYN/LNWD PA3 84 A2
Mossvale Ter
BAIL/MDB/MHD G69 42 B5
Mossview Crs AIRDRIE ML6 98 B3
Mossview La
CARD/HILL/MSPK G52 86 D4
Mossview Qd
CARD/HILL/MSPK G52 87 E4
Mossview Rd
STPS/GTHM/RID G33 71 F1
Mosswater Wynd
BALLOCH G68 24 D3
Mosswell Rd MLNGV G62 17 F2
Mossywood Ct BALLOCH G68 43 G1
Mossywood Pl BALLOCH G68 43 G1
Mossywood Rd BALLOCH G68 43 G1
Mote Hl HMLTN ML3 170 B1
Mote Hill Ct HMLTN ML3 153 F5
Mote Hill Gv HMLTN ML3 153 F5
Motehill Rd PSLYN/LNWD PA3 85 E2
Mote Hill Rd PSLYN/LNWD PA3 84 D3
Motherwell Rd BLSH ML4 135 H2
HMLTN ML3 170 C2
MTHW ML1 154 A1
MTHW ML1 138 D1
Motherwell St AIRDRIE ML6 76 D5
Moulin Circ
CARD/HILL/MSPK G52 86 C5
Moulin Pl
CARD/HILL/MSPK G52 86 B5
Moulin Rd
CARD/HILL/MSPK G52 86 B5
Moulin Ter
CARD/HILL/MSPK G52 106 B1
Mountainblue St
DEN/PKHD G31 90 D4
Mount Annan Dr
LNPK/KPK G44 109 G5
Mountblow Rd CLYDBK G81 31 E2
Mount Cameron Dr North
EKILN G74 166 D5
Mount Cameron Dr South
EKILN G74 179 E1
Mountgarrie Rd GOV/IBX G51 87 E2
Mount Harriet Av
STPS/GTHM/RID G33 57 F5
Mount Harriet Dr
STPS/GTHM/RID G33 57 F5
Mountherrick EKILS G75 178 B3
Mount Lockhart
UD/BTH/TAN G71 114 A2
Mount Lockhart Pl
UD/BTH/TAN G71 114 A2
Mount Pleasant Crs KKNTL G66 5 F4
Mount Pleasant Dr OLDK G60 30 C1
Mount St MRYH/FIRH G20 67 E3
Mount Stuart St
PLKSD/SHW G41 108 D4
Mount Vernon Av
BAIL/MDB/MHD G69 113 F1
CAR/SHTL G32 93 F5
CTBR ML5 96 B2
Mournian Wy HMLTN ML3 170 A4
Mowbray EKILN G74 167 F1
Mowbray Av
BAIL/MDB/MHD G69 73 E1
Moyne Rd PLK/PH/NH G53 106 B2
Muckcroft Rd
BAIL/MDB/MHD G69 41 E4
Mugdock Rd MLNGV G62 17 E3
Muirbank Av RUTH G73 110 C5
Muirbank Gdns RUTH G73 110 C5
Muirbrae Rd RUTH G73 130 A3
Muirbrae Wy RUTH G73 130 A3
Muircroft Dr MTHW ML1 139 E5
Muirdrum Av
CARD/HILL/MSPK G52 107 E1
Muirdyke Rd AIRDRIE ML6 74 D1
CTBR ML5 96 A1
Muirdykes Av
CARD/HILL/MSPK G52 86 B4
Muirdykes Crs
PSLYN/LNWD PA3 83 G3
Muirdykes Rd
CARD/HILL/MSPK G52 86 B4
PSLYN/LNWD PA3 83 G3
Muiredge Ct
UD/BTH/TAN G71 134 A1
Muiredge Ter
BAIL/MDB/MHD G69 94 A5
Muirend Av LNPK/KPK G44 128 A2
Muirend Rd LNPK/KPK G44 127 H3
Muirfield Ct LNPK/KPK G44 128 A3
Muirfield Crs SMSTN G23 52 D2
Muirfield Mdw
UD/BTH/TAN G71 133 H5
Muirfield Rd BALLOCH G68 10 C5
Muirhead Dr MTHW ML1 138 C3
PSLYN/LNWD PA3 101 H1
Muirhead Gdns
BAIL/MDB/MHD G69 94 B5
Muirhead Ga
UD/BTH/TAN G71 115 F4
Muirhead Gv
BAIL/MDB/MHD G69 94 B5
Muirhead Rd
BAIL/MDB/MHD G69 114 A1
Muirhead Ter MTHW ML1 171 H1
Muirhead Wy BSHPBGS G64 55 G2
Muirhill Av LNPK/KPK G44 127 H3
Muirhill Ct HMLTN ML3 170 A1
Muirhill Crs KNTSWD G13 50 B4
Muirhouse Av MTHW ML1 172 C2
WISHAW ML2 158 C4
Muirhouse Dr MTHW ML1 172 D3
Muirhouse La EKILS G75 176 C2
Muirhouse Pk BSDN G61 16 B5
Muirhouse Rd MTHW ML1 172 C3
Muirhouse St
PLKSD/SHW G41 109 F1
Muirkirk Dr HMLTN ML3 168 C3
KNTSWD G13 51 G4
Muirlees Crs MLNGV G62 16 C3
Muirmadkin Rd BLSH ML4 136 A2
Muirmaillen Av MTHW ML1 157 F1
Muirpark Av RNFRW PA4 63 F4
Muirpark Dr BSHPBGS G64 54 D3
Muirpark St PTCK G11 66 A4
Muirpark Ter BSHPBGS G64 54 D3
Muir Rd DMBTN G82 13 H1
Muirsheil Av PLK/PH/NH G53 125 H1
Muirshiel Ct PLK/PH/NH G53 125 H2
Muirshiel Crs PLK/PH/NH G53 125 H1
Muirside Av CAR/SHTL G32 113 F1
KKNTL G66 22 A5
Muirside Pl WISHAW ML2 158 A4
Muirside Rd
BAIL/MDB/MHD G69 94 A5
Muirside St
BAIL/MDB/MHD G69 94 A5
Muirskeith Crs
PLKSW/MSWD G43 128 A1
Muirskeith Pl
PLKSW/MSWD G43 128 A1
Muirskeith Rd
PLKSW/MSWD G43 128 A1
Muir St BLTYR/CAMB G72 151 G4
BSHPBGS G64 54 D2
CTBR ML5 96 B2
HMLTN ML3 170 B1
MTHW ML1 154 C2
RNFRW PA4 63 G2
Muir Ter PSLYN/LNWD PA3 84 D2
Muirton Dr BSHPBGS G64 37 G5
Muiryfauld Dr DEN/PKHD G31 91 H5
Muiryhall St CTBR ML5 97 E2
Muiryhall St East CTBR ML5 97 F2
Mulben Crs PLK/PH/NH G53 106 A5
Mulben Pl PLK/PH/NH G53 106 A5
Mulben Ter PLK/PH/NH G53 106 A5
Mulberry Crs AIRDRIE ML6 119 F1
Mulberry Dr EKILS G75 177 H3
Mulberry Rd
PLKSW/MSWD G43 127 G2
UD/BTH/TAN G71 115 H3
Mulberry Wy EKILS G75 177 H3

Mulberry Wynd
BLTYR/CAMB G72 132 C4
Mull EKILN G74 179 F1
Mullardoch St SMSTN G23 52 C2
Mull Av PSLYS PA2 104 B5
RNFRW PA4 63 F5
Mull Ct HMLTN ML3 169 E4
Mullen Ct
STPS/GTHM/RID G33 71 G1
Mull Qd WISHAW ML2 157 H5
Mull St SPRGB/BLRNK G21 69 E4
Mulvey Crs AIRDRIE ML6 97 H2
Mungo Pk EKILS G75 166 A5
Mungo Pl UD/BTH/TAN G71 115 F3
Munlochy Rd GOV/IBX G51 87 E2
Munro Ct CLYDBK G81 31 G2
Munro Dr KKNTL G66 5 F5
Munro La KNTSWD G13 65 F1
Munro La East KNTSWD G13 65 F1
Munro Pl EKILN G74 167 E2
KNTSWD G13 51 F4
Munro Rd KNTSWD G13 65 F1
Murano Pl MRYH/FIRH G20 67 E2
Murano St MRYH/FIRH G20 67 E2
Murchison KVD/HLHD G12 51 H5
Murchison Dr EKILS G75 165 G5
Murchison Rd
CRG/CRSL/HOU PA6 80 D2
Murdoch Dr MLNGV G62 17 H5
Murdoch Pl MTHW ML1 137 E4
Murdoch Rd EKILS G75 166 B5
Murdoch Sq BLSH ML4 117 F5
Murdostoun Gdns
WISHAW ML2 157 E5
Murdostoun Rd WISHAW ML2 158 D1
Murdostoun Ter MTHW ML1 157 H1
Murdostoun Vw
WISHAW ML2 158 A4
Muriel La BRHD/NEIL G78 124 B4
Muriel St BRHD/NEIL G78 124 B4
Murray Av KSYTH G65 8 B2
Murray Ct HMLTN ML3 169 F2
Murray Crs BLTYR/CAMB G72 151 H4
WISHAW ML2 158 B3
Murrayfield Dr BSDN G61 51 F2
Murrayfield St CAR/SHTL G32 91 H2
Murrayhill EKILS G75 165 H5
Murray Pl BLSH ML4 116 B5
BRHD/NEIL G78 124 C3
DMBTN G82 13 H4
Murray Rd UD/BTH/TAN G71 134 B4
The Murray Rd EKILS G75 178 A1
The Murray Sq EKILS G75 178 B1
Murray St PSLYN/LNWD PA3 83 H3
RNFRW PA4 63 F3
Murray Ter MTHW ML1 154 A3
Murray Wk BLTYR/CAMB G72 151 H4
Murrin Av BSHPBGS G64 55 G2
Murroch Av DMBTN G82 13 H1
Murroes Rd GOV/IBX G51 87 E2
Musgrove Pl EKILS G75 165 H5
Muslin St DMNK/BRGTN G40 90 C5
Muttonhole Rd HMLTN ML3 168 A5
Mybster Pl GOV/IBX G51 87 E2
Myers Ct BLSH ML4 135 E1
Myers Crs UD/BTH/TAN G71 134 B2
Myreside Pl CAR/SHTL G32 91 G3
Myreside St CAR/SHTL G32 91 H3
Myres Rd PLK/PH/NH G53 107 E4
Myrie Gdns BSHPBGS G64 55 E1
Myrtle Av KKNTL G66 39 H3
Myrtle Dr MTHW ML1 137 G2
WISHAW ML2 173 E1
Myrtle Hill La GVH/MTFL G42 109 H4
Myrtle Pk GVH/MTFL G42 109 G3
Myrtle Pl GVH/MTFL G42 109 H4
Myrtle Rd CLYDBK G81 31 E4
UD/BTH/TAN G71 115 G4
Myrtle Sq BSHPBGS G64 54 D3
Myrtle St BLTYR/CAMB G72 151 G1
Myrtle View Rd
GVH/MTFL G42 109 H4
Myrtle Wk BLTYR/CAMB G72 131 E1
Myvot Av CUMB G67 44 A2
Myvot Rd CUMB G67 43 F4

N

Naburn Ga GBLS G5 89 H5
Nagle Gdns MTHW ML1 156 C2
Nairn Av BLSH ML4 135 H1
BLTYR/CAMB G72 133 F5
Nairn Crs AIRDRIE ML6 98 B5
Nairn Pl CLYDBK G81 31 G5
EKILN G74 167 F2
Nairn Qd WISHAW ML2 157 E5
Nairnside Rd
SPRGB/BLRNK G21 55 F4
Nairn St BLTYR/CAMB G72 151 F4
CLYDBK G81 31 C5
KVGV G3 66 C5
Nairn Wy BALLOCH G68 10 C5
Naismith St CAR/SHTL G32 112 D4
Naismith Wk BLSH ML4 117 F5
Nansen St MRYH/FIRH G20 67 F3
Napier Ct BALLOCH G68 11 F2
OLDK G60 30 D3
Napier Crs DMBTN G82 12 C4
Napier Dr GOV/IBX G51 88 A1
Napier Gdns PSLYN/LNWD PA3 82 B3
Napier Hl EKILS G75 166 B5
Napier La EKILS G75 166 B5
Napier Pk BALLOCH G68 11 E4
Napier Pl BALLOCH G68 11 E2
GOV/IBX G51 88 A1
OLDK G60 30 D3
Napier Rd BALLOCH G68 11 F3
CARD/HILL/MSPK G52 64 A5
GOV/IBX G51 88 A1
Napiershall La MRYH/FIRH G20 67 E4
Napiershall Pl
MRYH/FIRH G20 67 E4
Napiershall St
MRYH/FIRH G20 67 E4
Napier Sq BLSH ML4 117 F5
Napier St CLYDBK G81 49 G4
GOV/IBX G51 88 A1
JNSTN PA5 101 F3
PSLYN/LNWD PA3 82 B3
Napier Ter GOV/IBX G51 88 A1
Napier Wy BALLOCH G68 11 E3
Naproch Pl NMRNS G77 145 F5
Naseby Av PTCK G11 65 G3
Naseby La PTCK G11 65 G3
Nasmyth Av EKILS G75 178 D1
Nasmyth Pl EKILS G75 178 C1
Nasmyth Rd
CARD/HILL/MSPK G52 86 B2
Nasmyth Rd North
CARD/HILL/MSPK G52 86 B2
Nasmyth Rd South
CARD/HILL/MSPK G52 86 B2
Nassau Pl EKILS G75 165 F4
National Bank La CGLE G1 2 E5
Navar Pl PSLYS PA2 104 D2
Naver St STPS/GTHM/RID G33 69 H5
Naylor La AIRDRIE ML6 98 C1
Naysmyth Bank EKILS G75 178 C1
Neidpath Av CTBR ML5 116 D1
Neidpath Pl CTBR ML5 116 D1
Neidpath Rd East
GIF/THBK G46 144 D4
Neidpath Rd West
GIF/THBK G46 144 D3
Neilsland Dr HMLTN ML3 180 C1
MTHW ML1 154 A4
Neilsland Ov PLK/PH/NH G53 107 E4
Neilsland Rd HMLTN ML3 169 G3
Neilsland Sq HMLTN ML3 169 H4
PLK/PH/NH G53 107 E3
Neilsland St HMLTN ML3 169 H4
Neilson Ct HMLTN ML3 170 B3
Neilson St BLSH ML4 135 H2
Neilston Av PLK/PH/NH G53 125 H3
Neilston Pl KSYTH G65 7 H1
Neilston Rd BRHD/NEIL G78 141 F3
PSLYS PA2 104 B2
Neilston Wk KSYTH G65 8 B1
Neil St RNFRW PA4 63 G1
Neilvaig Dr RUTH G73 130 B4
Neistpoint Dr
STPS/GTHM/RID G33 92 B1
Nelson Av CTBR ML5 96 B5
Nelson Crs MTHW ML1 172 C1
Nelson Mandela Pl CGLW G2 2 E4
Nelson Pl BAIL/MDB/MHD G69 94 A5
Nelson St BAIL/MDB/MHD G69 94 A5
GBLS G5 89 G4
Nelson Ter EKILN G74 166 D5
Neptune St GOV/IBX G51 88 A2
Neptune Wy BLSH ML4 136 D2
Nerston Rd EKILN G74 148 C4
Ness Av JNSTN PA5 120 D1
Ness Dr BLTYR/CAMB G72 151 H1
EKILN G74 167 E4
Ness Gdns BSHPBGS G64 55 E2
Ness Rd RNFRW PA4 63 E2
Ness St STPS/GTHM/RID G33 69 H5
WISHAW ML2 174 A5
Ness Ter HMLTN ML3 169 F4
Nethan Av WISHAW ML2 172 D3
Nethan Ga HMLTN ML3 169 H2
Nethan Pl HMLTN ML3 180 D2
Nethan St GOV/IBX G51 87 H1
MTHW ML1 136 B5
Nether Auldhouse Rd
PLKSW/MSWD G43 127 F1
Netherbank Rd WISHAW ML2 173 E3
Netherbog Rd DMBTN G82 13 G3
Netherburn Av
CRG/CRSL/HOU PA6 81 F4
LNPK/KPK G44 128 A5
Netherburn Gdns
CRG/CRSL/HOU PA6 81 F3
Netherby Dr PLKSD/SHW G41 88 C5
Nethercairn Pl NMRNS G77 145 F5
Nethercairn Rd
PLKSW/MSWD G43 127 F3
Nethercliffe Av
LNPK/KPK G44 128 A5
Nethercraigs Dr PSLYS PA2 103 H4
Nethercraigs Rd PSLYS PA2 103 G5
Nethercroy Rd KSYTH G65 8 C5
Netherdale Crs MTHW ML1 172 D3
Netherdale Dr PSLY PA1 106 A1
Netherdale Rd WISHAW ML2 173 F3
Netherfield St DEN/PKHD G31 91 F3
Nethergreen Crs RNFRW PA4 63 E3
Nethergreen Wynd
RNFRW PA4 63 E3
Netherhall Rd WISHAW ML2 173 F3
Netherhill Av LNPK/KPK G44 146 A1
Netherhill Crs
PSLYN/LNWD PA3 84 D3
Netherhill Rd
BAIL/MDB/MHD G69 59 E2
PSLYN/LNWD PA3 85 E2
Netherhouse Av CTBR ML5 116 C1
KKNTL G66 40 B4
Netherhouse Pl ESTRH G34 94 D1
Netherhouse Rd
BAIL/MDB/MHD G69 94 D2
Nether Kirkton Av
BRHD/NEIL G78 141 F2
Netherlee Pl LNPK/KPK G44 128 B3
Netherlee Rd LNPK/KPK G44 128 B3
Nethermains Rd MLNGV G62 17 E5
Netherpark Av
LNPK/KPK G44 146 A1
Netherplace Crs NMRNS G77 161 F1
PLK/PH/NH G53 106 C4
Netherplace Rd NMRNS G77 160 C1
PLK/PH/NH G53 106 C4
Netherton Av KNTSWD G13 51 F4
Netherton Ct NMRNS G77 144 D4
Netherton Dr
BRHD/NEIL G78 124 C5
Netherton Farm La
KNTSWD G13 51 G3
Netherton Rd EKILS G75 177 E4
KNTSWD G13 51 G4
NMRNS G77 144 C4
WISHAW ML2 172 D3
Netherton St WISHAW ML2 173 G3
Nethervale Av LNPK/KPK G44 146 A1
Netherview Rd
LNPK/KPK G44 146 B1
Netherway LNPK/KPK G44 146 A1
Netherwood Av BALLOCH G68 24 D5
Netherwood Ct BALLOCH G68 25 E5
Netherwood Gv BALLOCH G68 25 E5
Netherwood Rd BALLOCH G68 24 D5
MTHW ML1 172 C2
Netherwood Wy
BALLOCH G68 25 E5
Neuk Av BAIL/MDB/MHD G69 58 B4
CRG/CRSL/HOU PA6 80 D2
Neuk Crs CRG/CRSL/HOU PA6 80 D1
The Neuk WISHAW ML2 173 F2
Neville EKILN G74 149 H5
Nevis Av HMLTN ML3 169 F4
Nevis Ct BRHD/NEIL G78 142 B1
MTHW ML1 171 H1
Nevis Dr BSHPBGS G64 19 F4
MTHW ML1 172 D3
Nevis Rd BSDN G61 33 G1
PLKSW/MSWD G43 127 E2
RNFRW PA4 63 E5
Nevis Wy PSLYN/LNWD PA3 62 B5
Newark Dr PLKSD/SHW G41 108 D1
PSLYS PA2 103 H4
WISHAW ML2 157 F4
Newark Ga SHOTTS ML7 159 G2
Newark Pl WISHAW ML2 157 G4
Newarthill Rd MTHW ML1 137 H5
New Ashtree St WISHAW ML2 173 F2
New Av HWWD PA9 120 A4
Newbank Ct DEN/PKHD G31 91 H5
Newbank Gdns
DEN/PKHD G31 91 G5
Newbank Rd DEN/PKHD G31 91 G5
Newbattle Av AIRDRIE ML6 118 C2
Newbattle Ct CAR/SHTL G32 112 C2
Newbattle Gdns
CAR/SHTL G32 112 C2
Newbattle Pl CAR/SHTL G32 112 C2
Newbattle Rd CAR/SHTL G32 112 B3
Newbold Av
SPRGB/BLRNK G21 54 B4
Newburgh St
PLKSW/MSWD G43 108 C5
Newcastleton Dr SMSTN G23 52 D2
New City Rd COWCAD G4 2 D1
Newcraigs Drive
CRMNK/CLK/EAG G76 147 E3
Newcroft Dr LNPK/KPK G44 129 E2
Newdyke Rd KKNTL G66 21 H5
New Edinburgh Rd
UD/BTH/TAN G71 134 D1
Newfield Crs HMLTN ML3 169 G1
Newfield Pl GIF/THBK G46 126 C5
RUTH G73 110 B5
Newfield Sq PLK/PH/NH G53 125 F1
Newford Gv
CRMNK/CLK/EAG G76 145 H5
Newgrove Gdns
BLTYR/CAMB G72 131 F1
Newhall St
DMNK/BRGTN G40 110 B1
Newhaven Rd
STPS/GTHM/RID G33 92 C1
Newhaven St CAR/SHTL G32 92 B2
Newhills Rd
STPS/GTHM/RID G33 93 F2
Newhousemill Rd EKILN G74 179 F1
Newhut Rd MTHW ML1 154 C2
New Inchinnan Rd
PSLYN/LNWD PA3 84 B2
Newington St CAR/SHTL G32 92 A3
New Kirk Rd BSDN G61 34 B3
New Lairdsland Rd KKNTL G66 21 F5
Newlands Dr HMLTN ML3 170 A5
Newlandsfield Rd
PLKSW/MSWD G43 108 C5
Newlands Gdns JNSTN PA5 102 B3
Newlandsmuir Rd EKILS G75 177 E2
Newlands Pl EKILN G74 166 B4
Newlands Rd EKILS G75 176 D4
PLKSW/MSWD G43 127 H1
UD/BTH/TAN G71 115 E4
Newlands St CTBR ML5 96 D5
New La AIRDRIE ML6 118 C2
Newliston Dr GBLS G5 110 A1
New Luce Dr CAR/SHTL G32 113 E1
Newmains Av RNFRW PA4 61 F1
Newmains Rd RNFRW PA4 63 F5
Newmill Rd
SPRGB/BLRNK G21 69 F1
Newmilns Gdns HMLTN ML3 168 C3
Newmilns St PLK/PH/NH G53 125 E1
Newnham Rd PSLY PA1 85 H5
Newpark Crs
BLTYR/CAMB G72 112 B5
New Park St HMLTN ML3 152 D5
New Plymouth EKILS G75 177 F1
New Rd BLTYR/CAMB G72 132 B3
Newrose Av BLSH ML4 117 E5
Newshot Dr ERSK PA8 47 H2
RNFRW PA4 47 H4
New Sneddon St
PSLYN/LNWD PA3 84 B4
Newstead Gdns SMSTN G23 52 D2
New Stevenston Rd
MTHW ML1 137 G5
New St BLTYR/CAMB G72 151 F3
CLYDBK G81 31 H2
KLBCH PA10 100 B3
PSLY PA1 84 B5
Newton Av BLTYR/CAMB G72 132 A1
BRHD/NEIL G78 142 C2
JNSTN PA5 102 D1
Newton Brae
BLTYR/CAMB G72 132 C2
Newton Ct
BLTYR/CAMB G72 132 A1
NMRNS G77 161 G2
Newton Dr JNSTN PA5 102 D1
UD/BTH/TAN G71 115 F5
WISHAW ML2 158 B5
Newton Farm Rd
BLTYR/CAMB G72 132 C1
Newtongrange Av
CAR/SHTL G32 112 C2
Newtongrange Gdns
CAR/SHTL G32 112 C2
Newton Gv NMRNS G77 161 G2
Newtonlea Av NMRNS G77 162 A1
Newton Pl KVGV G3 2 A2
NMRNS G77 161 H2
Newton Rd BSHPTN PA7 28 C5
KKNTL G66 40 B4
Newton St CGLW G2 2 A3
Newton Station Rd
BLTYR/CAMB G72 132 B3
Newton St PSLY PA1 83 H5
Newton Ter PSLYS PA2 103 E1
Newton Terrace La KVGV G3 89 E1
Newtown St KSYTH G65 8 B2
Newtyle Dr PLK/PH/NH G53 106 A3
Newtyle Pl BSHPBGS G64 55 G2
PLK/PH/NH G53 106 A3
Newtyle Rd PSLY PA1 85 F5
New View Dr BLSH ML4 135 H4
New View Pl BLSH ML4 135 H4
New Wynd CGLE G1 3 G7
Niamh Ct RNFRW PA4 47 H4
Nicholas St CGLE G1 3 J5
Nicholson St GBLS G5 89 G4
Nicklaus Wy MTHW ML1 119 F5
Nicolson Ct
STPS/GTHM/RID G33 71 E1
Nicol St AIRDRIE ML6 76 D5
Niddrie Rd GVH/MTFL G42 109 E2
Niddrie Sq GVH/MTFL G42 109 E3
Niddry St PSLYN/LNWD PA3 84 C4
Nigel Gdns PLKSD/SHW G41 108 C3
Nigel St MTHW ML1 154 C4
Nigg Pl ESTRH G34 93 H1
Nightingale Pl JNSTN PA5 121 E2
Nimmo Dr GOV/IBX G51 87 F2
Nimmo Pl WISHAW ML2 174 B2
Ninian Av CRG/CRSL/HOU PA6 80 D3
Ninian Rd AIRDRIE ML6 98 D4
Ninian's Ri KKNTL G66 40 C1
Nisbet St DEN/PKHD G31 91 G4
Nisbett Pl AIRDRIE ML6 119 F1
Nisbett St AIRDRIE ML6 119 F2
Nissen Pl PLK/PH/NH G53 106 A3
Nith Av PSLYS PA2 103 E3
Nith Dr HMLTN ML3 169 F5
RNFRW PA4 63 H4
Nith Qd MTHW ML1 137 H4
Nithsdale EKILN G74 167 G2
Nithsdale Crs BSDN G61 33 H2
Nithsdale Dr PLKSD/SHW G41 109 E2
Nithsdale Rd
PLKSD/SHW G41 109 E2
PLKSD/SHW G41 88 B5
Nithsdale St PLKSD/SHW G41 109 E2
Nith St STPS/GTHM/RID G33 69 G5
Nitshill Rd GIF/THBK G46 126 B5
PLK/PH/NH G53 125 F2
Niven St MRYH/FIRH G20 52 B5
Noble Rd BLSH ML4 135 H2
Nobles Pl BLSH ML4 135 G3
Nobles Vw BLSH ML4 135 G3
Noldrum Av CAR/SHTL G32 112 D4
Noldrum Gdns CAR/SHTL G32 112 D4
Norbreck Dr GIF/THBK G46 127 F3
Norby Rd PTCK G11 65 G3
Nordic Crs BLTYR/CAMB G72 151 H3
Nordic Gdns
BLTYR/CAMB G72 151 H3
Nordic Gv BLTYR/CAMB G72 151 H4
Noremac Wy BLSH ML4 116 C5
Norfield Dr LNPK/KPK G44 109 G5
Norfolk Ct GBLS G5 89 G4
Norfolk Crs BSHPBGS G64 37 F5
Norfolk St GBLS G5 89 G4
Norham St PLKSD/SHW G41 108 D3
Norman St
DMNK/BRGTN G40 110 C1
Norse La North SCOT G14 64 D2
Norse La South SCOT G14 64 D2
Norse Pl SCOT G14 64 D2
Norse Rd SCOT G14 64 D2
Northall Qd MTHW ML1 155 F1
Northampton Dr
KVD/HLHD G12 52 A5
North Av BLTYR/CAMB G72 131 E1
CLYDBK G81 48 D1
Northbank Av
BLTYR/CAMB G72 132 A1
North Bank Pl CLYDBK G81 49 F3
Northbank Rd KKNTL G66 21 E5
Northbank St
BLTYR/CAMB G72 132 A1
North Bank St CLYDBK G81 49 F3
North Barr Av ERSK PA8 47 F1
North Berwick Av
BALLOCH G68 10 B5
North Berwick Crs EKILS G75 177 F2
North Biggar Rd AIRDRIE ML6 98 C1
North Birbiston Rd KKNTL G66 4 C2
Northbrae Pl KNTSWD G13 50 C5
North Bridge St AIRDRIE ML6 98 A1
North British Rd
UD/BTH/TAN G71 134 A1
Northburn Av AIRDRIE ML6 76 C5
Northburn Pl AIRDRIE ML6 76 C4
Northburn Rd CTBR ML5 75 F5
North Bute St CTBR ML5 97 E5
North Caldeen Rd CTBR ML5 97 F4
North Calder Dr AIRDRIE ML6 99 E3
North Calder Gv
UD/BTH/TAN G71 114 A2
North Calder Pl
UD/BTH/TAN G71 113 H2
North Calder Rd
UD/BTH/TAN G71 115 H3
North Campbell Av
MLNGV G62 16 D4
North Canal Bank COWCAD G4 67 H4
North Canal Bank St
COWCAD G4 67 H4
North Carbrain Rd CUMB G67 26 B5
North Claremont La
MLNGV G62 17 E3
North Claremont St KVGV G3 66 D5
North Corsebar Rd
PSLYS PA2 103 H2
North Ct CGLE G1 3 F5
North Court La CGLE G1 3 F5
Northcroft Rd
BAIL/MDB/MHD G69 58 D1
North Croft St
PSLYN/LNWD PA3 84 B4
North Dean Park Av
UD/BTH/TAN G71 134 B4
North Douglas St CLYDBK G81 49 F3
North Dr CGLW G2 2 E6
PSLYN/LNWD PA3 82 A3
North Dryburgh Rd
WISHAW ML2 156 D5
North Dumgoyne Av
MLNGV G62 16 D3
North Elgin Pl CLYDBK G81 49 F4
North Elgin St CLYDBK G81 49 G3
North Erskine Pk BSDN G61 34 A3
Northfield EKILS G75 177 E1
Northfield Rd KSYTH G65 7 H1
Northfield St MTHW ML1 154 D2
North Frederick St CGLE G1 3 G5
North Gardner St PTCK G11 66 A4
Northgate Qd
SPRGB/BLRNK G21 55 F5
Northgate Rd
SPRGB/BLRNK G21 55 F4
North Gower St GOV/IBX G51 88 B4
North Grange Rd BSDN G61 34 B2
North Hanover St CGLE G1 3 G4
Northinch St SCOT G14 65 E4
North Iverton Park Rd
JNSTN PA5 101 H3
North Kilmeny Crs
WISHAW ML2 157 F4
Northland Av SCOT G14 64 D1
Northland Dr SCOT G14 64 D2
Northland Gdns SCOT G14 64 D2
Northland La SCOT G14 64 D2
North La PSLYN/LNWD PA3 82 B3
North Lodge Av MTHW ML1 171 H2
North Lodge Rd RNFRW PA4 63 F2
Northmuir Dr WISHAW ML2 174 C1
Northmuir Rd DRUM G15 33 G4
North Orchard St MTHW ML1 154 C3
North Park Av
BRHD/NEIL G78 124 A4
GIF/THBK G46 126 C3
Northpark St MRYH/FIRH G20 67 E2
North Portland St COWCAD G4 3 H5
North Porton Rd BSHPTN PA7 29 F4
North Rd BALLOCH G68 43 H1
BLSH ML4 135 H2
JNSTN PA5 101 F4
North & South Rd
MTHW ML1 157 H2
North St KVGV G3 2 A4
MTHW ML1 155 E2
PSLYN/LNWD PA3 84 B3
Northumberland St
MRYH/FIRH G20 66 D2
North Vw BSDN G61 51 E1
North View Rd BRWEIR PA11 80 A4
North Wallace St COWCAD G4 3 H2
Northway BLTYR/CAMB G72 151 F1
Northwood Dr WISHAW ML2 158 B4
North Woodside Rd
MRYH/FIRH G20 67 F4
Norval St PTCK G11 65 H4
Norwich Dr KVD/HLHD G12 66 A1
Norwood Av KKNTL G66 20 D4
Norwood Dr GIF/THBK G46 144 D1
Norwood Pk BSDN G61 34 C5
Norwood Ter
UD/BTH/TAN G71 115 F5
Nottingham Av
KVD/HLHD G12 52 A5
Nottingham La
KVD/HLHD G12 52 A5
Novar Dr KVD/HLHD G12 65 H2
Novar Gdns BSHPBGS G64 54 B2
Novar St HMLTN ML3 170 A3
Nuneaton St
DMNK/BRGTN G40 110 D1
Nurseries Rd
BAIL/MDB/MHD G69 93 G3
Nursery Av BSHPTN PA7 29 H4
Nursery La PLKSD/SHW G41 109 E2
Nursery Pl BLTYR/CAMB G72 151 G4
Nursery St PLKSD/SHW G41 109 F1
Nutberry Ct GVH/MTFL G42 109 G3

O

Oak Av BSDN G61 34 C1
EKILS G75 177 G2
Oakbank Av WISHAW ML2 173 F4
Oakbank Dr BRHD/NEIL G78 142 D2
Oakbank St AIRDRIE ML6 99 E2
Oakburn Av MLNGV G62 16 D4
Oakburn Crs MLNGV G62 16 D4
Oak Crs BAIL/MDB/MHD G69 93 H5
Oakdene Av BLSH ML4 116 D5
UD/BTH/TAN G71 115 G5
Oakdene Crs MTHW ML1 137 H3
Oak Dr BLTYR/CAMB G72 131 H3
KKNTL G66 39 G3
Oak Fern Dr EKILN G74 166 A1
Oak Fern Gv EKILN G74 166 A2
Oakfield Av KVD/HLHD G12 66 D4
Oakfield Dr MTHW ML1 154 D4
Oakfield La KVD/HLHD G12 66 D4
Oakfield Rd MTHW ML1 154 D5
Oak Gv AIRDRIE ML6 119 F1
Oakhill Av
BAIL/MDB/MHD G69 113 G1
Oak Lea HMLTN ML3 170 C3
Oaklea Crs BLTYR/CAMB G72 151 F2
Oakley Dr LNPK/KPK G44 128 A4
Oakley Ter DEN/PKHD G31 90 C2
Oak Pk BSHPBGS G64 55 E2
MTHW ML1 171 G1
Oak Pl CTBR ML5 97 F4
EKILS G75 177 G2
UD/BTH/TAN G71 115 H5
Oakridge Crs
PSLYN/LNWD PA3 83 G5
Oakridge Rd
BAIL/MDB/MHD G69 95 G3
Oak Rd CLYDBK G81 31 G3
CUMB G67 27 G1
PSLYS PA2 104 D3
Oakshaw Brae PSLY PA1 84 A4

Oakshaw St East *PSLY* PA1 ......84 B4
Oakshaw St West *PSLY* PA1 ......84 A4
The Oaks *JNSTN* PA5...........101 E4
Oak St *CGLW* G2.....................3 G6
Oaktree Gdns *CSMK* G45 ......129 G3
  DMBTN G82........................13 H5
Oakwood Av *PSLYS* PA2.........103 E5
Oakwood Crs *ESTRH* G34 ....94 C1
Oakwood Dr *CTBR* ML5............96 A4
  NMRNS G77........................162 A1
Oak Wynd *BLTYR/CAMB* G72...132 C4
Oates Gdns *MTHW* ML1 ....172 C1
Oatfield St *SPRGB/BLRNK* G21...69 E2
Oban Dr *MRYH/FIRH* G20..........66 D2
Oban La *MRYH/FIRH* G20...........66 D2
Oban Pl *AIRDRIE* ML6................99 E3
Obiston Gdns *CAR/SHTL* G32....92 B4
Observatory Rd
  KVD/HLHD G12....................66 C3
Ocean Fld *CLYDBK* G81.............31 G3
Ochil Ct *EKILS* G75................177 G4
Ochil Dr *BRHD/NEIL* G78........142 A2
  PSLYS PA2.........................104 A4
Ochil Pl *CAR/SHTL* G32.............92 B5
Ochil Rd *BSDN* G61...................33 G1
  BSHPBGS G64.....................55 F2
  RNFRW PA4..........................63 F5
Ochil St *CAR/SHTL* G32.............92 B5
  WISHAW ML2......................173 G1
Ochiltree Av *KNTSWD* G13.........51 G4
Ochiltree Crs *CTBR* ML5.............96 B5
Ochiltree Dr *HMLTN* ML3.........168 D4
Ochil Vw *UD/BTH/TAN* G71......115 F4
Odense Ct *EKILS* G75..............178 B2
Ogilvie Pl *DEN/PKHD* G31.........91 G5
Ogilvie St *DEN/PKHD* G31.........91 G5
Oki Wy *BALLOCH* G68..................1 E4
Old Aisle Rd *KNTL* G66.............40 C1
Old Avon Rd *HMLTN* ML3.........170 C5
Old Balmore Rd *BSHPBGS* G64...37 F1
Old Bars Dr
  BAIL/MDB/MHD G69.............42 B5
Old Bore Rd *AIRDRIE* ML6..........99 E1
Old Bothwell Rd
  UD/BTH/TAN G71................152 C2
Old Bridge of Weir Rd
  CRG/CRSL/HOU PA6.............80 B1
Old Castle Gdns
  LNPK/KPK G44...................128 C1
Old Castle Rd *LNPK/KPK* G44...128 B1
Old Church Gdns
  BAIL/MDB/MHD G69.............95 F4
Old Coach Rd *EKILN* G74.........166 C2
Old Dalmarnock Rd
  DMNK/BRGTN G40..............110 D1
Old Dalnottar Rd *OLDK* G60......30 C3
Old Dullatur Rd *BALLOCH* G68.....9 H4
Old Dumbarton Rd *KVGV* G3......66 C5
Old Edinburgh Rd
  UD/BTH/TAN G71................114 D3
Old Farm Rd *BSDN* G61.............51 G3
Old Gartloch Rd
  BAIL/MDB/MHD G69.............73 E2
Old Glasgow Rd *CUMB* G67.......26 C1
  UD/BTH/TAN G71................133 H2
Old Greenock Rd *BSHPTN* PA7...27 E5
  RNFRW PA4...........................47 E3
Oldhall Rd *PSLY* PA1.................85 G4
Old Humbie Rd *NMRNS* G77....161 H5
Old Manse Gdns *CTBR* ML5........96 D2
Old Manse Rd *CAR/SHTL* G32....93 E5
  WISHAW ML2......................173 F5
Old Mill Ct *CLYDBK* G81............31 H3
Old Mill La *UD/BTH/TAN* G71...134 A1
Old Mill Rd *BLTYR/CAMB* G72...132 A2
  CLYDBK G81........................31 H3
  EKILN G74..........................166 C3
  PSLY PA1............................103 G1
  SHOTTS ML7........................159 H1
  UD/BTH/TAN G71................134 A1
Old Mill Vw *KSYTH* G65.............24 D2
Old Monkland Rd *KLBCH* ML5...116 A1
Old Playfield Rd
  CRMNK/CLK/EAG G76...........147 E2
Old Quarry Rd *BALLOCH* G68......43 E3
Old Renfrew Rd *GOV/IBX* G51....64 B4
Old Rd *JNSTN* PA5..................102 B1
Old Rutherglen Rd *GBLS* G5.......89 H4
Old School Sq *KLBCH* PA10......100 B3
Old Shettleston Rd
  CAR/SHTL G32.....................92 B4
Old Sneddon St *PSLY* PA1.........84 B4
Old Stable Rw *CTBR* ML5............97 E2
Old St *CLYDBK* G81...................31 G2
Old Union St *AIRDRIE* ML6..........98 C2
Old Wood Rd
  BAIL/MDB/MHD G69.............113 H1
Old Wynd *CGLE* G1.....................3 G7
Olifard Av *UD/BTH/TAN* G71....134 C4
Oliphant Crs
  CRMNK/CLK/EAG G76...........145 H5
  PSLYS PA2.........................102 D4
Olive Bank *UD/BTH/TAN* G71...115 H3
Olive St *STPS/GTHM/RID* G33....70 A1
Olympia *EKILN* G74................166 C5
Olympia Pl *EKILN* G74.............166 C5
Olympia St *DMNK/BRGTN* G40...90 C4
Omoa Rd *MTHW* ML1................137 G4
O'Neill Av *BSHPBGS* G64...........55 E3
Onslow *EKILS* G75...................177 H1
Onslow Dr *DEN/PKHD* G31.........90 D2
Onslow Rd *CLYDBK* G81.............49 F1
Onslow Sq *DEN/PKHD* G31........90 D2
Ontario Pk *EKILS* G75..............165 G4
Ontario Pl *EKILS* G75...............165 G4
Onyx St *BLSH* ML4...................135 H5
Oran Gdns *MRYH/FIRH* G20........66 D1
Oran Ga *MRYH/FIRH* G20...........66 D1
Oran Pl *MRYH/FIRH* G20............66 D2
Oran St *MRYH/FIRH* G20............66 D2
Orbiston Dr *BLSH* ML4..............136 A4
  CLYDBK G81.........................31 H1
Orbiston Pl *CLYDBK* G81.............32 C1
Orbiston Rd *BLSH* ML4.............135 G3
Orbiston Sq *BLSH* ML4.............135 G4
Orbiston St *MTHW* ML1.............155 E1
Orcades Dr *LNPK/KPK* G44......128 C3
Orchard Av *HMLTN* ML3...........170 A2
Orchard Brae *HMLTN* ML3........170 A2

Orchard Ct *CAR/SHTL* G32 ......112 C4
  GIF/THBK G46....................126 D4
Orchard Dr *BLTYR/CAMB* G72...151 G2
  GIF/THBK G46....................127 E4
  RUTH G73............................110 C4
Orchard Fld *KKNTL* G66..............40 A4
Orchard Gn *EKILN* G74.............167 E1
Orchard Gv *CTBR* ML5................97 E5
Orchard Pk *GIF/THBK* G46........127 E5
Orchard Park Av
  GIF/THBK G46....................126 D4
Orchard Pl *BLSH* ML4...............135 G4
  HMLTN ML3........................170 A2
  KKNTL G66..........................40 C1
Orchard St
  BAIL/MDB/MHD G69.............113 G1
  HMLTN ML3........................170 B2
  MTHW ML1.........................154 C3
  PSLY PA1.............................84 B5
  RNFRW PA4..........................63 G2
Orchardton Rd *BALLOCH* G68.....42 D1
Orchid Pl *KKNTL* G66...................4 A2
Orchy Av
  CRMNK/CLK/EAG G76...........146 A2
Orchy Ct *CLYDBK* G81................32 B5
Orchy Crs *AIRDRIE* ML6............98 B5
  BSDN G61.............................51 E2
  PSLYS PA2.........................103 E5
Orchy Dr
  CRMNK/CLK/EAG G76...........146 A1
Orchy Gdns
  CRMNK/CLK/EAG G76...........146 A1
Orchy St *LNPK/KPK* G44..........128 B3
Orefield Pl *EKILN* G74..............166 B2
Oregon Pl *GBLS* G5....................89 H5
Orion Pl *BLSH* ML4...................136 D2
Orion Wy *BLTYR/CAMB* G72......131 F1
Orkney Pl *GOV/IBX* G51.............88 A2
Orkney Qd *WISHAW* ML2...........174 C1
Orkney St *GOV/IBX* G51.............88 A2
Orlando *EKILN* G74..................149 H5
Orleans Av *SCOT* G14.................65 F3
Orleans La *SCOT* G14..................65 F3
Ormiston Av *SCOT* G14...............64 A3
Ormiston Dr *HMLTN* ML3..........169 H5
Ormiston La *SCOT* G14...............64 D2
Ormiston La North *SCOT* G14.....64 D2
Ormiston La South *SCOT* G14.....64 D2
Ormonde Av *LNPK/KPK* G44.....128 A4
Ormonde Ct *LNPK/KPK* G44......127 H4
Ormonde Crs *LNPK/KPK* G44....128 A4
Ormonde Dr *LNPK/KPK* G44......128 A4
Ornsay St *PPK/MIL* G22..............54 A4
Oronsay Crs *BSDN* G61..............35 E5
  OLDK G60............................30 D2
Oronsay Gdns *OLDK* G60...........30 D2
Oronsay Pl *OLDK* G60...............30 D2
  WISHAW ML2......................174 A4
Oronsay Sq *AIRDRIE* ML6..........99 E4
Orr Sq *PSLY* PA1.......................84 B4
Orr St *DMNK/BRGTN* G40..........90 C4
  PSLY PA1..............................84 A4
  PSLYS PA2.........................104 B1
Orr Ter *BRHD/NEIL* G78............140 D4
Orton Pl *GOV/IBX* G51................87 H3
Osborne Crs *EKILN* G74............164 A2
Osborne St *CGLW* G2....................3 F7
  CLYDBK G81........................31 H5
Osprey Av *PSLY* PA1.................173 H1
Osprey Dr *UD/BTH/TAN* G71.....115 F5
Osprey Rd *PSLYN/LNWD* PA3....84 A1
Osprey Vw *PSLYN/LNWD* PA3....84 A2
Ossian Av *PSLY* PA1...................86 A4
Ossian Rd *PLKSW/MSWD* G43...127 H1
Oss Qd *MTHW* ML1....................172 D2
Oswald St *CGLE* G1......................2 D7
Oswald Wk *MLNGV* G62.............17 G5
Otago La *KVD/HLHD* G12............66 D4
Otago Pk *EKILS* G75.................165 H4
Otago Pl *DMBTN* G82.................13 H5
Otago St *KVD/HLHD* G12............66 D4
Othello *EKILN* G74...................149 G5
Otterburn Dr *GIF/THBK* G46......127 F5
Otterswick Pl
  STPS/GTHM/RID G33.............70 D4
The Oval
  CRMNK/CLK/EAG G76...........146 A1
  CTBR ML5.............................59 H5
Overbrae Gdns *DRUM* G15.........33 E3
Overbrae Pl *DRUM* G15..............33 E3
Overburn Av *DMBTN* G82...........13 E3
Overburn Crs *DMBTN* G82..........13 E2
Overdale Av *GVH/MTFL* G42.....109 E4
Overdale Gdns
  GVH/MTFL G42...................109 E4
Overdale Pl *GVH/MTFL* G42.....109 E4
Overjohnstone Dr
  WISHAW ML2......................172 D1
Overlea Av *RUTH* G73...............130 C1
Overlee Rd
  CRMNK/CLK/EAG G76...........145 H3
Overnewton Pl *KVGV* G3............88 C1
Overnewton Sq *KVGV* G3...........88 C1
Overnewton St *KVGV* G3............88 B1
Overton Crs *JNSTN* PA5...........102 A2
Overton Rd
  BLTYR/CAMB G72................132 B3
  JNSTN PA5.........................101 H4
Overton St *BLTYR/CAMB* G72...132 B3
Overtoun Av *DMBTN* G82...........13 G5
Overtoun Dr *CLYDBK* G81...........31 G4
  RUTH G73............................110 D5
Overtoun Rd *CLYDBK* G81..........31 G4
Overtown Av
  PLK/PH/NH G53..................125 F1
Overtown Pl *DEN/PKHD* G31.......90 D4
Overtown St *DEN/PKHD* G31......90 D4
Overwood Dr *DMBTN* G82...........13 G3
  LNPK/KPK G44...................128 D1
Owen Av *EKILS* G75..................177 H1
Owendale Av *BLSH* ML4............117 E3
Owen Pk *EKILS* G75.................177 H1
Owen St *MTHW* ML1.................154 D2
O'Wood Av *MTHW* ML1.............137 G1
Oxford Dr *PSLYN/LNWD* PA3......82 A3
Oxford La *GBLS* G5.....................89 G4
Oxford Rd *RNFRW* PA4...............63 F3

Oxford St *CTBR* ML5...................96 C3
  GBLS G5..............................89 G4
Oxgang Pl *KKNTL* G66................40 B1
Oxhill Pl *DMBTN* G82.................12 C4
Oxhill Rd *DMBTN* G82................12 C4
Oxton Dr
  CARD/HILL/MSPK G52...........86 C4

P

Pacific Dr *GOV/IBX* G51..............88 B3
Paddock St *CTBR* ML5................97 H5
The Paddock
  HMLTN ML3........................170 C1
Paidmyre Crs *NMRNS* G77........161 G2
Paidmyre Gdns *NMRNS* G77.....161 G2
Paidmyre Rd *NMRNS* G77........161 G2
Paisley Rd *BRHD/NEIL* G78.......124 A3
  GBLS G5..............................89 F3
  PLKSD/SHW G41...................88 D3
  PSLYN/LNWD PA3..................84 D1
  RNFRW PA4..........................63 F3
Paisley Rd West
  CARD/HILL/MSPK G52...........86 B5
  GOV/IBX G51........................88 B4
Palacecraig St *CTBR* ML5..........116 D1
Palace Grounds Rd
  HMLTN ML3........................170 C1
Paladin Av *KNTSWD* G13...........50 C3
Palladium Pl *SCOT* G14..............65 E3
Palmer Av *KNTSWD* G13............51 E4
Palmerston *EKILS* G75..............177 F1
Palmerston Pl *JNSTN* PA5.........120 D2
  KVGV G3...............................88 C1
Palm Pl *UD/BTH/TAN* G71.........115 G3
Pandora Wy
  UD/BTH/TAN G71................115 F5
Pankhurst Pl *EKILN* G74...........166 C3
Panmure Pl *BALLOCH* G68..........24 C5
Panmure Pl *PPK/MIL* G22............67 F2
Panmure St *MRYH/FIRH* G20......67 F2
Park Av *BRHD/NEIL* G78...........142 A1
  BSHPBGS G64......................37 H5
  DMBTN G82...........................13 E2
  JNSTN PA5..........................102 B2
  KKNTL G66............................21 E5
  KSYTH G65...........................24 B1
  KVGV G3...............................67 E4
  MLNGV G62..........................17 E4
  MTHW ML1..........................137 F2
  PSLYS PA2.........................103 H3
Park Bank *ERSK* PA8..................47 G2
Park Brae *ERSK* PA8..................47 G2
Parkbrae Av *MRYH/FIRH* G20.....53 F5
Parkbrae Gdns
  MRYH/FIRH G20....................53 F5
Parkbrae La *MRYH/FIRH* G20.....53 F5
Parkburn Av *KKNTL* G66.............39 H2
Park Burn Ct *HMLTN* ML3.........152 B4
Parkburn Rd *KSYTH* G65............8 B1
Park Circ *KVGV* G3.....................66 D5
Park Circus La *KVGV* G3.............67 E5
Park Circus Pl *KVGV* G3.............67 E5
Park Ct *BSHPBGS* G64................38 A5
  GIF/THBK G46.....................126 E4
Park Crs *BLTYR/CAMB* G72.......151 F4
  BSDN G61.............................33 H5
  BSHPBGS G64......................38 A5
  DMBTN G82...........................13 E2
  RNFRW PA4..........................63 G3
Park Dr *BLSH* ML4....................135 H5
  EKILN G74...........................164 B2
  ERSK PA8.............................47 H2
  HMLTN ML3.........................171 F4
  KVGV G3...............................67 E4
  RUTH G73............................110 D5
  WISHAW ML2......................158 B5
Parker Pl *KSYTH* G65...................8 B2
Parkfield *EKILS* G75.................178 B3
Parkfoot St *KSYTH* G65...............8 B1
Park Gdns *KLBCH* PA10............100 C2
  KVGV G3...............................66 D5
Park Ga *KVGV* G3.......................66 D5
Park Gate Pl *BLSH* ML4............135 G2
Park Gld *ERSK* PA8....................47 H3
Park Gn *ERSK* PA8....................47 H3
Park Gv *ERSK* PA8....................47 H3
Parkgrove Av *GIF/THBK* G46.....127 G4
Parkgrove Ter *KVGV* G3.............66 D5
Parkgrove Terrace La
  KVGV G3...............................66 D5
Parkhall Rd *EKILN* G74...............31 G4
Parkhall St *EKILN* G74..............166 B3
Parkhall Ter *CLYDBK* G81...........31 G3
Parkhead St *AIRDRIE* ML6..........98 B1
  MTHW ML1.........................154 D4
Park Hl *ERSK* PA8......................47 G2
Parkhill Dr *RUTH* G73...............110 D5
Parkhill Rd
  PLKSW/MSWD G43..............108 B4
Parkholm Dr *PLK/PH/NH* G53...125 F3
Park Holme Ct *HMLTN* ML3.......153 E5
Parkholm Gdns
  PLK/PH/NH G53..................125 F3
Parkholm La *GBLS* G5................89 E3
Parkhouse Rd
  PLK/PH/NH G53..................125 F3
Parkinch *ERSK* PA8....................47 H4
Parklands Ov
  PLK/PH/NH G53..................106 A2
Parklands Rd *LNPK/KPK* G44...128 C4
Parklands Vw
  PLK/PH/NH G53..................106 A2
Park La *BLTYR/CAMB* G72........151 G2
  DMNK/BRGTN G40................90 C4
  KSYTH G65............................8 B2
Parklee Dr
  CRMNK/CLK/EAG G76...........147 F3
Parkmanor Av
  PLK/PH/NH G53..................125 E4
Parkmanor Gn
  PLK/PH/NH G53..................125 E4

Park Moor *ERSK* PA8..................47 G3
Parkneuk Rd
  PLKSW/MSWD G43...............127 F3
Parkneuk St *MTHW* ML1...........154 D2
Park Pl *BLSH* ML4....................135 F4
  EKILN G74...........................166 B3
Park Qd *KVGV* G3......................66 D5
  WISHAW ML2......................173 F4
Park Rd *AIRDRIE* ML6...............118 C2
  BAIL/MDB/MHD G69.............95 F4
  BAIL/MDB/MHD G69.............58 D5
  BLSH ML4...........................135 H3
  BRWEIR PA11........................79 G2
  BSHPBGS G64......................54 C5
  CAR/SHTL G32....................112 D4
  CLYDBK G81.........................31 G5
  COWCAD G4..........................2 C1
  GIF/THBK G46....................127 F5
  HMLTN ML3........................170 A2
  JNSTN PA5..........................101 G5
  MLNGV G62..........................17 E4
  PSLYS PA2.........................104 A4
  RNFRW PA4..........................63 G3
Parksail *ERSK* PA8....................47 H4
Parksail Dr *ERSK* PA8................47 H3
Parkside Gdns
  MRYH/FIRH G20....................53 F5
Parkside Pl *MRYH/FIRH* G20......53 F5
Park St *CTBR* ML5......................97 E2
  CLYDBK G81.........................31 G5
  KKNTL G66............................41 E1
  MTHW ML1.........................154 D3
Park St South *KVGV* G3.............66 D5
Park Ter *EKILN* G74..................166 B3
  KVGV G3...............................66 D5
Park Terrace East La *KVGV* G3...66 D5
Park Terrace La *KVGV* G3...........66 D5
Parkvale Av *ERSK* PA8...............48 A3
Parkvale Crs *ERSK* PA8.............48 A3
Parkvale Dr *ERSK* PA8...............48 A3
Parkvale Gdns *ERSK* PA8...........48 A3
Parkvale Pl *ERSK* PA8................48 A3
Parkvale Wy *ERSK* PA8..............48 A3
Park Vw *HMLTN* ML3.................170 A2
  PSLYS PA2.........................103 H3
Parkview Av *KKNTL* G66.............40 A1
Parkview Ct *KKNTL* G66.............40 A1
Parkview Crs *WISHAW* ML2.......175 F1
Parkview Dr *CTBR* ML5................96 C2
  STPS/GTHM/RID G33.............57 H4
Parkville Dr *BLTYR/CAMB* G72...151 H4
Parkville Rd *BLSH* ML4..............117 F5
Park Wy *CUMB* G67....................26 D1
Parkway *ERSK* PA8.....................47 G4
Parkway Ct
  BAIL/MDB/MHD G69.............94 A2
Parkway Pl *CTBR* ML5................96 B3
Parkway Rd *CTBR* ML5...............97 E2
Park Winding *ERSK* PA8.............47 H3
Park Wd *ERSK* PA8....................47 H3
Parliament Rd *KKNTL* G66..........40 A1
Parnell St *AIRDRIE* ML6..............98 A4
Parnie St *CGLE* G1......................3 G6
Parry Ter *EKILS* G75.................165 G4
Parsonage Row *COWCAD* G4.......3 J6
Parsonage Sq *CGLE* G1................3 J6
Partick Bridge St *PTCK* G11........66 B5
Partickhill Av *PTCK* G11.............66 A4
Partickhill Rd *PTCK* G11.............66 A4
Partick St *CTBR* ML5..................97 F4
Paterson Pl *BSDN* G61................16 A5
Paterson's Laun *BSHPBGS* G64...37 F1
Paterson St *GBLS* G5..................89 F3
  MTHW ML1.........................158 D3
Paterson Ter *EKILS* G75............178 A1
Pather St *WISHAW* ML2............174 A3
Pathhead Gdns
  STPS/GTHM/RID G33.............56 A5
Pathhead Rd
  CRMNK/CLK/EAG G76...........147 E3
Patna St *DMNK/BRGTN* G40.....111 E4
Patna Pl *BLSH* ML4...................135 E1
Patrickbank Crs *JNSTN* PA5......102 C1
Patrick St *PSLYS* PA2...............104 C1
Patterton Dr *BRHD/NEIL* G78....142 C1
Pattison St *CLYDBK* G81.............31 F5
Paton St *DEN/PKHD* G31............91 E2
Paxton Ct *EKILN* G74................166 C1
Payne St *COWCAD* G4..................3 F1
Peace Av *BRWEIR* PA11..............79 E1
Peach Ct *MTHW* ML1................138 A5
Peacock Av *PSLYS* PA2.............103 E2
Peacock Dr *HMLTN* ML3...........169 H1
  PSLYS PA2.........................103 E2
Pearce La *GOV/IBX* G51.............87 H1
Pearce St *GOV/IBX* G51.............87 H1
Pearl St *BLSH* ML4....................136 A4
Pearson Dr *RNFRW* PA4.............63 G4
Pearson Pl *PSLYN/LNWD* PA3.....82 A4
Peathill Av
  BAIL/MDB/MHD G69.............58 A3
Peathill St *SPRGB/BLRNK* G21...67 H3
Peat Rd *BRWEIR* PA11................79 H4
  PLK/PH/NH G53..................125 F3
Pedmyre La
  CRMNK/CLK/EAG G76...........146 D3
Peebles Dr *RUTH* G73...............111 H5
Peebles Pth *CTBR* ML5..............117 G1
Peel Ct *BLTYR/CAMB* G72.........131 H1
Peel Glen Gdns *DRUM* G15..........33 F3
Peel Glen Rd *BSDN* G61.............33 F4
Peel La *PTCK* G11......................66 A4
Peel Park Pl *EKILN* G74.............165 E4
Peel Rd *EKILN* G74...................164 D5
  UD/BTH/TAN G71................115 G3
Peel St *PTCK* G11......................66 A4
Pegasus Av *PSLY* PA1................101 G2
  SHOTTS ML7........................159 E2
Pembroke *EKILS* G75................178 B3
Pembroke St *KVGV* G3................89 E1
Pencaitland Dr
  CAR/SHTL G32....................112 B1
Pencaitland Ov
  CAR/SHTL G32....................112 B2
Pencaitland Pl *SMSTN* G23.........52 D2

Pendale Ri *CSMK* G45..............129 E4
Pendeen Crs
  STPS/GTHM/RID G33.............93 F4
Pendeen Pl
  STPS/GTHM/RID G33.............93 G3
Pendeen Rd
  STPS/GTHM/RID G33.............93 G4
Pendicle Crs *BSDN* G61..............34 A5
Pendicle Rd *BSDN* G61...............34 A5
Pendle Ct
  BAIL/MDB/MHD G69.............59 E5
Penfold Crs *EKILS* G75.............166 A5
Penilee Rd
  CARD/HILL/MSPK G52...........85 G1
Penilee Ter
  CARD/HILL/MSPK G52...........85 H3
Peninver Dr *GOV/IBX* G51..........87 F1
Penman Av *RUTH* G73...............110 C4
Pennan Pl *SCOT* G14..................64 B1
Penneld Rd
  CARD/HILL/MSPK G52...........86 A4
Penneircroft Av *DMBTN* G82.......13 H2
Pennine Gv *AIRDRIE* ML6..........119 G3
Pennyroyal Ct *EKILN* G74.........166 A2
Penrioch Dr *EKILS* G75.............177 H4
Penrith Av *GIF/THBK* G46........127 F3
Penrith Dr *KVD/HLHD* G12.........51 H5
Penrith Pl *EKILS* G75................177 E2
Penryn Gdns *CAR/SHTL* G32....113 E1
Penston Rd
  STPS/GTHM/RID G33.............93 E1
Pentland Av *PSLYN/LNWD* PA3...101 H1
Pentland Crs *PSLYS* PA2...........104 A4
Pentland Dr *BRHD/NEIL* G78....142 B1
  BSHPBGS G64......................55 G1
  RNFRW PA4..........................62 D5
Pentland Pl *BSDN* G61...............33 G1
Pentland Rd
  BAIL/MDB/MHD G69.............58 C3
  EKILS G75..........................177 F5
  PLKSW/MSWD G43..............127 F2
  WISHAW ML2......................173 F1
Pentland Wy *HMLTN* ML3.........180 A1
Penzance Wy
  BAIL/MDB/MHD G69.............59 E1
Peockland Gdns *JNSTN* PA5......101 H3
Peockland Pl *JNSTN* PA5..........101 H3
Peploe Dr *EKILN* G74................150 A5
Percy Dr *GIF/THBK* G46............145 F1
Percy Rd *PSLYN/LNWD* PA3.......81 H5
Percy St *GOV/IBX* G51................88 B2
Perran Gdns
  BAIL/MDB/MHD G69.............58 D1
Perray Av *DMBTN* G82...............12 A2
Perth Av *AIRDRIE* ML6..............118 B4
Perth Crs *CLYDBK* G81...............31 E5
Perth St *KVGV* G3.......................2 A5
Peter D. Stirling Rd
  KKNTL G66............................21 F4
Petersburn Rd *AIRDRIE* ML6......99 F4
Petersburn Rd *AIRDRIE* ML6......99 E3
Petershill Ct
  SPRGB/BLRNK G21................69 E3
Petershill Dr
  SPRGB/BLRNK G21................69 F3
Petershill Pl
  SPRGB/BLRNK G21................69 E3
Petershill Rd
  SPRGB/BLRNK G21................68 D3
Peterson Dr *KNTSWD* G13..........49 H5
Peterson Gdns *KNTSWD* G13......49 H5
Petition Pl *UD/BTH/TAN* G71....134 B2
Pettigrew St *CAR/SHTL* G32.......92 B4
Peveril Av *PLKSD/SHW* G41.....108 C3
  RUTH G73............................130 B2
Pharonhill St *DEN/PKHD* G31.....91 H4
Philip Ct *BLSH* ML4..................135 E1
Philip Murray Rd *BLSH* ML4......135 E1
Philipshill Ga *EKILN* G74...........164 D2
Philipshill Rd *EKILN* G74..........164 D2
Phoenix Crs *BLSH* ML4.............116 C4
Phoenix Pl *JNSTN* PA5.............102 C1
  MTHW ML1.........................137 F4
Phoenix Rd *BLSH* ML4..............116 D4
Piccadilly St *KVGV* G3.................2 A6
Pickerstonhill *MTHW* ML1.........138 B3
Picketlaw Dr
  CRMNK/CLK/EAG G76...........147 E3
Picketlaw Farm Rd
  CRMNK/CLK/EAG G76...........146 D3
Pienchorran *ERSK* PA8...............47 H4
Piershill St *CAR/SHTL* G32..........92 A2
Pikeman Rd *KNTSWD* G13..........50 D5
Pillans Ct *HMLTN* ML3..............152 B4
Pilmuir Av *LNPK/KPK* G44........128 A3
Pilrig St *CAR/SHTL* G32..............91 H2
Pilton Rd *DRUM* G15...................33 F5
Pine Cl *CUMB* G67......................27 G1
Pine Ct *CUMB* G67.....................27 G1
  EKILS G75...........................177 G3
Pine Crs *CUMB* G67...................27 G1
  EKILS G75...........................177 G3
  HMLTN ML3........................180 A1
  JNSTN PA5..........................101 H5
Pine Gv *AIRDRIE* ML6...............118 C2
  BAIL/MDB/MHD G69.............59 F2
  CUMB G67............................27 G1
  UD/BTH/TAN G71................115 G4
Pine Lawn *WISHAW* ML2...........158 B3
Pine Pk *HMLTN* ML3.................170 B4
Pine Pl *CUMB* G67.....................27 G1
  GBLS G5..............................89 H5
Pine Qd *AIRDRIE* ML6...............119 F1
Pine Rd *CLYDBK* G81.................31 E4
  CUMB G67............................27 G1
  DMBTN G82...........................13 E1
Pine St *AIRDRIE* ML6................119 G1
  KKNTL G66............................4 C2
  PSLYS PA2.........................104 D2
Pinewood Av *KKNTL* G66............39 G3
Pinewood Ct *DMBTN* G82...........13 H2
  KKNTL G66............................39 G3
Pinewood Pl *KKNTL* G66.............39 G3
Pinewood Sq *DRUM* G15.............33 F4
Pinkerton Av *RUTH* G73............110 C4
Pinkerton La *RNFRW* PA4............63 G5
Pinkston Dr
  SPRGB/BLRNK G21................68 A3

Pinkston Rd COWCAD G4........68 A4
Pinmore Pl PLK/PH/NH G53..125 E2
Pinmore St PLK/PH/NH G53...125 E2
Pinwherry Dr
  STPS/GTHM/RID G33........56 A5
Pinwherry Pl
  UD/BTH/TAN G71...........134 B4
Piper Av CRG/CRSL/HOU PA6...80 D3
Piper Rd AIRDRIE ML6.........98 D4
  CRG/CRSL/HOU PA6..........80 D3
Pirnie Pl KSYTH G65...........8 B2
Pirnmill Av EKILS G75........177 C4
  MTHW ML1.................137 H5
Pitcairn Crs EKILS G75.......165 E5
Pitcairn Gv EKILS G75........165 E5
Pitcairn Pl EKILS G75........165 E5
Pitcairn St DEN/PKHD G31.....91 H5
Pitcaple Dr
  PLKSW/MSWD G43...........127 E1
Pitlochry Dr
  CARD/HILL/MSPK G52........86 C5
Pitmedden Rd BSHPBGS G64.....55 C1
Pitmilly Rd DRUM G15.........33 H4
Pitreavie Ct HMLTN ML3......169 C5
Pitreavie Pl
  STPS/GTHM/RID G33........70 D4
Pit Rd BLSH ML4..............135 C1
  KKNTL G66.................41 E1
Pittenweem Pth
  BLTYR/CAMB G72...........168 C2
Pitt St CGLW G2...............3 F5
Pladda Rd RNFRW PA4..........63 C5
Pladda St MTHW ML1..........154 A2
Plaintrees Ct PSLYS PA2.....104 B3
Plane Pl UD/BTH/TAN G71.....115 C5
Planetree Pl JNSTN PA5......101 H5
Planetree Rd CLYDBK G81......31 H4
Plantation Av MTHW ML1......137 C1
Plantation Park Gdns
  GOV/IBX G51...............88 C4
Plantation Sq GOV/IBX G51....88 D3
Plant St DEN/PKHD G31........91 F3
Platthorn Dr EKILN G74......166 C4
Platthorn Rd EKILN G74......166 C4
Playfair St DMNK/BRGTN G40..110 D1
Plaza EKILN G74.............166 B5
Pleaknowe Crs
  BAIL/MDB/MHD G69..........58 D1
Pleamuir Pl BALLOCH G68......25 C4
Plean St SCOT G14............64 B1
Pleasance St
  PLKSW/MSWD G43...........108 B4
Pleasance Wy
  PLKSW/MSWD G43...........108 B5
Plover Dr EKILS G75.........177 F5
Plover Pl JNSTN PA5.........120 D2
Pochard Wy BLSH ML4.........116 C4
Poet's Vw KKNTL G66..........40 C5
Poindfauld Ter DMBTN G82.....13 F3
Pointhouse Rd KVGV G3........88 B1
Polden Av EKILS G75.........177 F5
Polden Ct EKILS G75.........177 F5
Pollock Av HMLTN ML3.........54 C5
Pollock Rd BSDN G61..........34 D5
  NMRNS G77................161 F1
Pollock St BLSH ML4.........136 B2
Pollok Dr BSHPBGS G64........54 B2
Pollok La EKILN G74.........167 E2
Pollok Pl EKILN G74.........167 E2
Pollokshaws Rd
  GVH/MTFL G42.............109 F1
  PLKSW/MSWD G43...........108 B5
Pollokshields Sq
  PLKSD/SHW G41............108 D2
Polmadie Av GBLS G5.........110 A2
Polmadie Rd GVH/MTFL G42....109 H5
Polmadie St GVH/MTFL G42....109 H1
Polnoon Av KNTSWD G13........50 B5
Polquhap Ct PLK/PH/NH G53..106 B4
Polquhap Pl
  PLK/PH/NH G53............106 B4
Polquhap Rd
  PLK/PH/NH G53............106 B4
Poison Dr JNSTN PA5.........101 H4
Poisons Crs PSLYS PA2.......104 A2
Polwarth La KVD/HLHD G12.....66 A3
Polwarth St KVD/HLHD G12.....66 A3
Pomona Pl HMLTN ML3.........169 E5
Poplar Av BSHPTN PA7.........46 A1
  JNSTN PA5................102 A1
  NMRNS G77................161 H2
  PTCK G11..................65 G2
Poplar Dr CLYDBK G81.........31 C5
  KKNTL G66.................39 F3
Poplar Gdns EKILS G75.......177 H5
Poplar Pl BLTYR/CAMB G72....151 F1
  MTHW ML1.................137 C5
  UD/BTH/TAN G71............13 B3
The Poplars BSDN G61.........16 B5
Poplar St AIRDRIE ML6........98 D2
Poplar Wy BLTYR/CAMB G72....132 C4
  MTHW ML1.................158 A5
Poplin St DMNK/BRGTN G40....110 D1
Porchester St
  STPS/GTHM/RID G33........71 E4
Portal Rd KNTSWD G13.........50 D3
Port Dundas Pl CGLW G2.......3 F3
Port Dundas Rd COWCAD G4.....2 E1
Porterfield Rd RNFRW PA4.....63 E4
Porter St COV/IBX G51........88 B4
Porters Well
  UD/BTH/TAN G71...........133 H2
Portessie ERSK PA8...........47 F1
Portland Pl MTHW ML1........154 D3
Portland Pk HMLTN ML3.......170 B3
Portland Rd HMLTN ML3.......170 B3
Portland Rd BALLOCH G68......10 D5
  PSLYS PA2................105 G1
Portland Sq HMLTN ML3.......170 B3
Portland St CTBR ML5.........97 E1
Portman St PLKSD/SHW G41....108 B1
Portmarnock Dr SMSTN G23.....52 C3
Portreath Rd
  BAIL/MDB/MHD G69..........42 A5

Portree Av CTBR ML5..........96 B5
Portree Pl DRUM G15..........32 D4
Portsoy Av KNTSWD G13........49 H3
Portsoy Pl KNTSWD G13........50 A3
Port St KVGV G3...............2 D6
Portugal St GBLS G5..........89 C4
Portwell HMLTN ML3..........170 B1
Possil Rd COWCAD G4..........67 C4
Postgate HMLTN ML3..........170 B1
Potassels Rd
  BAIL/MDB/MHD G69..........58 B4
Potrail Pl HMLTN ML3........169 F2
Potter Cl CAR/SHTL G32......111 H1
Potter Gv CAR/SHTL G32......111 H1
Potter Pl AI PSLYS PA2.......104 B4
Potterhill Rd PLK/PH/NH G53.106 B2
Potter St CAR/SHTL G32......111 H1
Potts Wy MTHW ML1...........154 B1
Powbrone EKILS G75..........178 B3
Powburn Crs
  UD/BTH/TAN G71...........114 C5
Powfoot St DEN/PKHD G31.....91 H4
Powrie St
  STPS/GTHM/RID G33........70 D3
Prentice La UD/BTH/TAN G71..114 F4
Prentice Rd MTHW ML1........154 A5
Prestonfield MLNGV G62.......16 C5
Preston Pl GVH/MTFL G42....109 G2
Preston St GVH/MTFL G42....109 G2
Prestwick Ct BALLOCH G68.....26 B1
Prestwick Pl NMRNS G77.....162 B1
Prestwick St
  PLK/PH/NH G53............125 F1
Pretoria St EKILS G75.......177 C4
Priestfield St
  BLTYR/CAMB G72...........151 F4
Priesthill Av PLK/PH/NH G53.125 H1
Priesthill Crs PLK/PH/NH G53.125 H1
Priesthill Gdns
  PLK/PH/NH G53............125 H1
Priesthill Rd PLK/PH/NH G53.125 G1
Prieston Rd BRWEIR PA11......79 C4
Primrose Av BLSH ML4........116 D5
Primrose Crs MTHW ML1......154 D5
Primrose Pl CUMB G67........27 F2
  UD/BTH/TAN G71...........115 H4
Primrose St SCOT G14.........64 D5
Prince Albert Rd
  KVD/HLHD G12..............66 A3
Prince Edward St
  GVH/MTFL G42.............109 F2
Prince of Wales Gdns
  MRYH/FIRH G20.............52 B3
Prince Pl WISHAW ML2........158 B4
Prince's Gdns KVD/HLHD G12...66 A3
Prince's Gardens La
  KVD/HLHD G12..............66 A3
Princes Ga RUTH G73.........110 D4
  UD/BTH/TAN G71...........133 F1
Princes Ml EKILN G74........166 C4
Princes Pk BSHPTN PA7........29 H4
Prince's Pl KVD/HLHD G12.....66 A3
Princess Crs PSLY PA1........85 C3
Princess Dr
  BAIL/MDB/MHD G69..........95 F4
Princes Sq BRHD/NEIL G78....124 C4
  EKILN G74................166 B4
Princess St MTHW ML1........154 C2
  RUTH G73.................110 D4
Prince's Ter KVD/HLHD G12....66 B3
Prince's Terrace La
  KVD/HLHD G12..............66 B3
Printers Lea KKNTL G66........4 A2
Priorwood Gdns
  KNTSWD G13................51 E5
Priorwood Ga NMRNS G77......160 D1
Priorwood Pl KNTSWD G13.....51 E5
Priorwood Rd NMRNS G77.....160 D1
Priory Av PSLYN/LNWD PA3.....84 D2
Priory Dr UD/BTH/TAN G71...114 C5
Priory Pl BALLOCH G68........24 C4
  KNTSWD G13................51 E4
Priory Rd KNTSWD G13.........51 E4
Priory St BLTYR/CAMB G72....151 F4
Priory Ter WISHAW ML2.......172 D3
Procession Rd PSLYS PA2.....123 E2
Prosper St CAR/SHTL G32.....111 H1
Prospect Av
  BLTYR/CAMB G72...........131 G1
  UD/BTH/TAN G71...........133 H1
Prospect Ct
  BLTYR/CAMB G72...........151 G5
Prospecthill Circ
  GVH/MTFL G42.............110 B3
Prospecthill Crs
  GVH/MTFL G42.............110 C3
Prospecthill Dr
  GVH/MTFL G42.............109 H4
Prospecthill Gv
  GVH/MTFL G42.............109 H4
Prospecthill Rd
  GVH/MTFL G42.............110 B3
Prospecthill Sq
  GVH/MTFL G42.............110 C3
Prospecthill Wy
  GVH/MTFL G42.............109 H4
Prospect Rd BALLOCH G68.......9 G4
  PLKSD/SHW G41............108 D3
Provand Hall Crs
  BAIL/MDB/MHD G69..........114 A1
Provanhill St
  SPRGB/BLRNK G21...........68 C5
Provanmill Rd
  STPS/GTHM/RID G33........69 H4
Provan Rd
  STPS/GTHM/RID G33........69 F5
Purdie EKILN G74............150 A5
Purdie St HMLTN ML3.........152 B5
Purdon St PTCK G11...........66 B4

Quadrant Rd
  PLKSW/MSWD G43...........127 H2
The Quadrant
  CRMNK/CLK/EAG G76........146 A2
Quantock Dr EKILS G75.......177 F5
Quarrelton Gd JNSTN PA5....101 C5
Quarrelton St JNSTN PA5....101 F4
Quarry Av BLTYR/CAMB G72...132 A4
Quarrybank KLBCH PA10......100 D4
Quarrybrae Av
  CRMNK/CLK/EAG G76........145 G3
Quarrybrae Gdns
  UD/BTH/TAN G71...........134 D1
Quarry Dr KNTL G66...........21 C5
Quarry Knowe DMBTN G82......12 C2
Quarryknowe RUTH G73........110 C1
Quarryknowe Gdns
  DEN/PKHD G31..............91 H4
Quarry Knowe Pl BLSH ML4...135 C4
Quarryknowe St CLYDBK G81....32 D1
Quarry La KKNTL G66...........4 B1
Quarry Pk EKILS G75.........166 B5
Quarry Pl BLTYR/CAMB G72....131 H5
  DMBTN G82.................12 C2
Quarry Rd AIRDRIE ML6........76 A5
  BRHD/NEIL G78............123 H5
  EKILS G75................178 A3
  PSLYS PA2................104 B3
Quarryside St AIRDRIE ML6....75 H2
Quarry St CTBR ML5...........97 C5
Quaywell Crs BLSH ML4.......135 C4
Raglan St COWCAD G4..........67 H4
Quay Pend DMBTN G82..........12 D4
Quay Rd RUTH G73............110 D4
Quay Rd North RUTH G73.....110 D3
Quay St DMBTN G82............13 E4
Quebec Dr EKILS G75.........165 H4
Quebec Wynd CAR/SHTL G32...112 D4
Queen Elizabeth Av
  CARD/HILL/MSPK G52........85 H2
Queen Elizabeth Ct
  CLYDBK G81.................31 H5
Queen Elizabeth Gdns
  CLYDBK G81.................31 H5
  GBLS G5...................89 H5
Queen Elizabeth Sq GBLS G5...89 H5
Queen Margaret Ct
  MRYH/FIRH G20.............66 D3
Queen Margaret Rd
  MRYH/FIRH G20.............66 D3
Queen Mary Av CLYDBK G81.....49 G1
  GVH/MTFL G42.............109 F3
Queen Mary Gdns
  CLYDBK G81.................31 H5
Queen Mary St
  DMNK/BRGTN G40............90 D5
Queen's Av BLTYR/CAMB G72..131 C1
Queensbank Av
  BAIL/MDB/MHD G69..........58 D4
Queensberry Av BSDN G61.....34 B1
  CARD/HILL/MSPK G52........86 A2
  CRMNK/CLK/EAG G76........145 H3
Queensborough Gdns
  KVD/HLHD G12..............65 H2
Queensby Av
  BAIL/MDB/MHD G69..........94 A4
Queensby Pl
  BAIL/MDB/MHD G69..........94 B3
Queensby Rd
  BAIL/MDB/MHD G69..........94 A3
Queen's Ct MLNGV G62.........17 E5
Queen's Crs AIRDRIE ML6.....119 E5
  BAIL/MDB/MHD G69..........95 E4
  BLSH ML4.................135 C5
  COWCAD G4.................67 F4
  MTHW ML1.................155 H3
  MTHW ML1.................137 H3
Queens Dr BALLOCH G68........10 A4
  BSHPTN PA7................29 F5
  GVH/MTFL G42.............109 F3
  HMLTN ML3................180 D2
Queen's Drive La
  GVH/MTFL G42.............109 C3
Queensferry St BLSH ML4....135 H1
Queen's Gdns KVD/HLHD G12....66 B3
Queen's Ga
  CRMNK/CLK/EAG G76........145 H2
Queens Gate La
  KVD/HLHD G12..............66 B3
Queens Gv KKNTL G66..........39 H4
Queenside Crs ERSK PA8......47 E2
Queensland Dr
  CARD/HILL/MSPK G52........86 D3
Queensland Gdns
  CARD/HILL/MSPK G52........86 D3
Queensland La East
  CARD/HILL/MSPK G52........86 D3
Queensland La West
  CARD/HILL/MSPK G52........86 D3
Queenslie St
  STPS/GTHM/RID G33........69 G4
Queen's Park Av
  GVH/MTFL G42.............109 G3
Queen's Pk KVD/HLHD G12.....66 B3
Queen's Sq PLKSD/SHW G41...109 E2
Queen's Rd JNSTN PA5........102 B2
Queen St CGLW G2.............3 H5
  HMLTN ML3................152 B5
  KKNTL G66.................21 E5
  MTHW ML1.................154 C3
  PSLY PA1..................83 H5
  RNFRW PA4.................63 G3
  RUTH G73.................110 D4
Queens Vw BSHPBGS G64........19 F5
Queensway EKILN G74.........166 C5
  EKILS G75................166 C5
Queen Victoria Dr SCOT G14...64 D2

Queen Victoria Ga
  KNTSWD G13................64 D1
Queen Victoria St
  AIRDRIE ML6................98 A2
Quendale Dr CAR/SHTL G52....112 A1
Quentin St PLKSD/SHW G41...108 D3
Quinton Gdns
  BAIL/MDB/MHD G69..........93 H4

Raasay Crs AIRDRIE ML6.......99 E3
Raasay Dr PSLYS PA2.........104 A5
Raasay Gdns NMRNS G77.......143 C5
Raasay St PPK/MIL G22........53 H5
Racecourse Vw HMLTN ML3....153 F5
Rachan St ESTRH G34..........72 C5
Radnor St CLYDBK G81.........31 H5
  KVGV G3...................66 C5
Raeberry St
  MRYH/FIRH G20.............67 E3
Raebog Crs AIRDRIE ML6.......76 A4
Raebog Rd AIRDRIE ML6........76 B1
Raeburn Av EKILN G74........167 E1
Raeburn Pl EKILN G74........167 E1
Raeburn Crs HMLTN ML3......168 C2
Raeside Av NMRNS G77........161 C2
Raeswood Dr
  PLK/PH/NH G53............106 A4
Raeswood Rd
  PLK/PH/NH G53............106 A4
Raewell Crs BLSH ML4........135 C4
Raglan St COWCAD G4..........67 H4
Railway Rd AIRDRIE ML6.......97 C2
Raith Av CSMK G45...........129 E3
Raithburn Av CSMK G45.......128 D3
Raithburn Rd CSMK G45.......128 D3
Raith Dr BALLOCH G68.........44 A3
  BLSH ML4.................136 A3
Ralston Av PSLY PA1.........106 A1
Ralston Ct
  CARD/HILL/MSPK G52........86 A5
Ralston Dr
  CARD/HILL/MSPK G52........86 A5
Ralston Rd BRHD/NEIL G78...124 B5
  BSDN G61..................34 B3
Ralston St AIRDRIE ML6.......97 H2
  PSLY PA1..................84 B5
Rampart Av KNTSWD G13........50 B3
Ramsay Av JNSTN PA5.........101 F5
Ramsay Ct NMRNS G77.........161 H3
Ramsay Crs KLBCH PA10......100 C4
Ramsay Hl EKILN G74.........167 F1
Ramsay Pl CTBR ML5..........116 A1
  JNSTN PA5................101 F5
Ramsay St CLYDBK G81.........31 C5
Ranald Gdns RUTH G73........130 C4
Randolph Av
  CRMNK/CLK/EAG G76........146 A1
Randolph Dr
  CRMNK/CLK/EAG G76........146 A1
Randolph Gdns PTCK G11.......65 C2
Randolph La PTCK G11.........65 C2
Randolph Rd PTCK G11.........65 C2
Ranfurly Dr BALLOCH G68......26 A1
Ranfurly Pl BRWEIR PA11......79 H5
Ranfurly Rd BRWEIR PA11......79 H5
  CARD/HILL/MSPK G52........86 A4
Range Av MTHW ML1...........172 D2
Range Pl HMLTN ML3..........170 B4
Rangerhouse Rd EKILS G75...178 C1
Range Rd MTHW ML1...........172 C1
Rankin Dr NMRNS G77.........143 H4
Rankin St KLBCH PA10........100 C4
Rankine Pl EKILS G75........178 A3
Rankine St JNSTN PA5........101 G5
Rankin Rd WISHAW ML2........174 D1
Rannoch Av BSHPBGS G64......54 A5
  CTBR ML5..................74 A5
  HMLTN ML3................169 F4
  NMRNS G77................144 A3
Rannoch Ct BALLOCH G68.......44 A2
  CUMB G67..................44 A2
  KKNTL G66.................22 B4
  RNFRW PA4.................63 C2
  WISHAW ML2...............173 H2
Rannoch Dr BSDN G61..........35 E5
  KKNTL G66.................21 F5
  RNFRW PA4.................63 C2
  WISHAW ML2...............173 H1
Rannoch Gn EKILN G74........166 C2
Rannoch Pl PSLYS PA2........104 D1
Rannoch Rd AIRDRIE ML6......76 A5
  JNSTN PA5................101 G5
  UD/BTH/TAN G71...........115 E4
Rannoch St LNPK/KPK G44.....128 B1
Raploch Av SCOT G14..........64 C2
Raploch La SCOT G14..........64 C2
Rashielee Av ERSK PA8........47 F1
Rashielee Rd ERSK PA8........47 F1
Rathlin St GOV/IBX G51.......87 H2
Rathlin Ter DMBTN G82........12 C2
Ratho Dr BALLOCH G68.........9 H5
  SPRGB/BLRNK G21...........68 C2
Ravel Rw DEN/PKHD G31........91 E4
Ravelston Rd BSDN G61........51 F1
Ravelston St CAR/SHTL G32...91 C4
Ravel Wynd
  UD/BTH/TAN G71...........115 C4
Ravenscliffe Dr
  GIF/THBK G46.............127 E4
Ravenscraig Av PSLYS PA2...103 H2
Ravenscraig Ct BLSH ML4....136 A3
Ravenscraig Dr
  PLK/PH/NH G53............125 C1
Ravenscraig Ter
  PLK/PH/NH G53............125 H2
Ravenshall MTHW ML1........157 H2

Ravenshall Rd
  PLKSD/SHW G41............108 B4
Ravenshill Dr MTHW ML1.....157 F1
Ravenstone Dr
  GIF/THBK G46.............127 E3
Ravenswood Av PSLYS PA2....102 D5
Ravenswood Dr
  PLKSD/SHW G41............108 C3
Ravenswood Rd
  BAIL/MDB/MHD G69..........94 B5
Raven Wynd WISHAW ML2......174 A2
Rawyards Av AIRDRIE ML6......76 C4
Raymond Pl EKILS G75........165 H4
Ream Av AIRDRIE ML6..........99 G3
Reay Av EKILN G74...........165 C5
Reay Gdns EKILN G74.........165 C5
Redan St DMNK/BRGTN G40.....90 D4
Redbrae Rd KKNTL G66.........21 F4
Redburn Av GIF/THBK G46....145 E2
Redburn Ct CUMB G67..........11 H4
Redburn Pl CUMB G67..........11 H5
Redburn Rd CUMB G67..........11 H4
Redcastle Sq
  STPS/GTHM/RID G33........71 E5
Redcliffe Dr EKILS G75......165 H4
Redcroft St HMLTN ML3......165 H3
Redford St
  STPS/GTHM/RID G33........91 C5
Redgate Pl SCOT G14.........64 C2
Redgrave EKILN G74..........149 H5
Redhill Rd BALLOCH G68.......25 H4
Redhills Vw KKNTL G66........4 C3
Redhurst Crs PSLYS PA2.....103 C5
Redhurst La PSLYS PA2.......103 C5
Redlands La KVD/HLHD G12.....66 C3
Redlands Rd KVD/HLHD G12....66 C3
Redlands Ter KVD/HLHD G12...66 C3
Redlands Terrace La
  KVD/HLHD G12..............66 B2
Redlawood Pl
  BLTYR/CAMB G72...........132 D1
Redlawood Rd
  BLTYR/CAMB G72...........132 D1
Redmoss Rd CLYDBK G81........31 C2
  KKNTL G66.................67 F5
Redmoss St PPK/MIL G22.......67 C1
Rednock St PPK/MIL G22.......67 C1
Redpath Dr BLTYR/CAMB G72..132 A1
  CARD/HILL/MSPK G52........86 C3
Red Road Ct
  SPRGB/BLRNK G21...........69 E3
Redshank Av RNFRW PA4........63 C2
Redwing Crs CTBR ML5........117 H2
Redwing Gdns WISHAW ML2....174 A4
Redwood Av EKILN G74........164 D4
Redwood Ct EKILN G74........164 D4
  SPRGB/BLRNK G21...........68 D3
Redwood Dr EKILN G74........164 D4
  SPRGB/BLRNK G21...........68 D3
Redwood Pl CTBR ML5.........117 E3
Redwood Pl EKILN G74........164 C4
Redwood Rd CUMB G67.........27 F5
  MTHW ML1.................137 C2
Reelick Av KNTSWD G13........49 H3
Reelick Qd KNTSWD G13........49 H3
Reema Rd BLSH ML4...........116 B5
Reen Pl UD/BTH/TAN G71.....134 C3
Regency Wy HMLTN ML3.......170 D5
  MTHW ML1.................137 E5
Regent Dr RUTH G73..........110 D4
Regent Moray St KVGV G3......66 C5
Regent Park Sq
  PLKSD/SHW G41............109 E2
Regent Sq UD/BTH/TAN G71...133 C5
Regent Sq KKNTL G66.........21 E5
Regent St CLYDBK G81.........31 F5
  KKNTL G66.................21 E5
  PSLY PA1..................85 E4
Reid Av BLSH ML4...........135 H4
Register Av BLSH ML4........135 H1
Register Rd KSYTH G65........8 B2
Reid Gv MTHW ML1............172 C1
Reidhouse St
  SPRGB/BLRNK G21...........68 C2
Reid Pl DMNK/BRGTN G40.......90 D5
Reid St AIRDRIE ML6..........98 C1
  CTBR ML5..................96 D1
  DMNK/BRGTN G40...........110 D1
  HMLTN ML3................152 A5
  RUTH G73.................111 E4
Reidvale St DEN/PKHD G31.....90 D5
Reith Dr EKILS G75..........178 A1
Remus Pl BLSH ML4...........136 D2
Renfield La CGLW G2...........2 E5
Renfield St CGLW G2...........2 E5
  RNFRW PA4.................63 G2
Renfrew Ct CGLW G2...........2 E4
Renfrew Rd PSLYN/LNWD PA3...84 B4
  RNFRW PA4.................63 G2
  STPS/GTHM/RID G33........69 G4
Rennie Pl EKILN G74.........165 H1
Rennie Rd KSYTH G65..........8 B2
Renshaw Dr
  CARD/HILL/MSPK G52........86 C3
Renshaw Rd BSHPTN PA7.......29 G5
Renshaw Rd JNSTN PA5........102 A3
Renton Rd DMBTN G82.........13 F3
Renton St COWCAD G4..........3 F1
Resipol Rd
  STPS/GTHM/RID G33........71 F1
Reston Dr
  CARD/HILL/MSPK G52........86 C5
Reuther Av RUTH G73.........111 E5
Revoch Dr KNTSWD G13........50 B4

Reynolds Av EKILS G75 ...178 D1
Reynolds Dr
  STPS/GTHM/RID G33 ...71 G1
Reynolds Pth WISHAW ML2 ...174 C4
Rhannan Rd LNPK/KPK G44 ...128 B2
Rhannan Ter LNPK/KPK G44 ...128 B2
Rhindhouse Pl
  BAIL/MDB/MHD G69 ...94 C4
Rhindmuir Av
  BAIL/MDB/MHD G69 ...94 C4
Rhindmuir Ct
  BAIL/MDB/MHD G69 ...94 B4
Rhindmuir Av
  BAIL/MDB/MHD G69 ...94 B4
Rhindmuir Crs
  BAIL/MDB/MHD G69 ...94 C3
Rhindmuir Dr
  BAIL/MDB/MHD G69 ...94 B3
Rhindmuir Gdns
  BAIL/MDB/MHD G69 ...94 B3
Rhindmuir Pth
  BAIL/MDB/MHD G69 ...94 C3
Rhindmuir Rd
  BAIL/MDB/MHD G69 ...94 C3
Rhindmuir Wynd
  BAIL/MDB/MHD G69 ...94 C3
Rhindsdale Crs
  BAIL/MDB/MHD G69 ...94 B4
Rhinds St CTBR ML5 ...95 G5
Rhymer St SPRCB/BLRNK G21...68 C5
Rhymie Rd CAR/SHTL G32 ...113 E1
Rhynie Dr GOV/IBX G51 ...88 A4
Riach Gdns MTHW ML1 ...154 B1
Ribblesdale EKILN G74 ...165 H2
Riccarton EKILS G75 ...177 G1
Riccarton St GVH/MTFL G42 ...109 H2
Riccartsbar Av PSLYS PA2 ...103 H1
Rice Wy MTHW ML1 ...172 C1
Richmond Av
  CRMNK/CLK/EAG G76...145 H3
Richmond Ct RUTH G73 ...111 F4
Richmond Dr
  BLTYR/CAMB G72 ...130 D2
  PSLYN/LNWD PA3 ...81 H4
  RUTH G73 ...111 G5
Richmond Gdns
  BAIL/MDB/MHD G69 ...58 A2
Richmond Gv RUTH G73 ...111 F5
Richmond Rd RUTH G73 ...111 F4
Richmond Rd RUTH G73 ...111 G5
Richmond St CGLE G1 ...3 H1
  CTBR ML5 ...49 F2
Riddell St CLYDBK G81 ...32 A3
  CTBR ML5 ...97 F2
Riddon Av KNTSWD G13 ...49 H3
Riddon Pl KNTSWD G13 ...49 H3
Riddrie Crs
  STPS/GTHM/RID G33 ...91 H1
Riddrie Knowes
  STPS/GTHM/RID G33 ...91 H1
Riddrievale Ct
  STPS/GTHM/RID G33 ...69 H5
Riddrievale St
  STPS/GTHM/RID G33 ...69 H5
Ridge St CLYDBK G81 ...91 G3
Rigghead Av CUMB G67 ...10 D5
Rigg Pl STPS/GTHM/RID G33 ...93 F2
Riggside Rd
  STPS/GTHM/RID G33 ...70 D4
The Riggs MLNGV G62 ...17 E2
Riglands Ga RNFRW PA4 ...63 F2
Riglaw Pl KNTSWD G13 ...50 B4
Rimsdale St
  DMNK/BRGTN G40 ...90 D4
Ringford St
  SPRCB/BLRNK G21 ...68 C3
Ripon Dr KVD/HLHD G12 ...51 H5
Risk St CLYDBK G81 ...31 G4
  DMBTN G82 ...12 D4
Ritchie Crs JNSTN PA5 ...102 B1
Ritchie Pk JNSTN PA5 ...102 A1
Ritchie St NMRNS G77 ...161 F1
Ritchie St GBLS G5 ...89 F5
  WISHAW ML2 ...173 E2
Riverbank Dr BLSH ML4 ...136 C4
Riverbank St
  PLKSW/MSWD G43 ...108 B5
River Ct
  CRMNK/CLK/EAG G76...146 A4
Riverdale Gdns HMLTN ML3 ...170 B4
River Dr RNFRW PA4 ...61 H1
Riverford Rd
  PLKSW/MSWD G43 ...108 B5
  RUTH G73 ...111 F3
River Rd CAR/SHTL G32 ...112 C4
Riversdale La SCOT G14 ...64 B1
Riverside Ct LNPK/KPK G44 ...128 A5
Riverside Gdns
  CRMNK/CLK/EAG G76...146 A5
Riverside La DMBTN G82 ...12 D4
Riverside Pl
  BLTYR/CAMB G72 ...132 B1
Riverside Rd
  CRMNK/CLK/EAG G76...163 F5
  PLKSW/MSWD G43 ...108 D5
Riverside Ter
  CRMNK/CLK/EAG G76...146 A5
Riverton Dr EKILS G75 ...165 G5
Riverview Dr GBLS G5 ...2 E7
Riverview Gdns GBLS G5 ...2 E7
Riverview Pl GBLS G5 ...2 E7
Roaden Av PSLYS PA2 ...103 E5
Roaden Rd PSLYS PA2 ...103 E5
Roadside CUMB G67 ...10 C1
Robert Burns Av CLYDBK G81...32 B5
  MTHW ML1 ...138 B3
Robert Burns Qd BLSH ML4 ...135 G2
Robert Dr GOV/IBX G51 ...88 A2
Robert Gilson Gdns CTBR ML5 ...97 E5
Roberton Av PLKSD/SHW G41...108 B2
Roberton St AIRDRIE ML6 ...119 F2
Robertson Av RNFRW PA4 ...63 E5
Robertson Crs
  BRHD/NEIL G78 ...141 E3

Robertson Dr BLSH ML4 ...135 H3
  EKILN G74 ...167 E3
  RNFRW PA4 ...63 E3
Robertson Gait PSLYS PA2 ...104 B1
Robertson La ST AIRDRIE ML6 ...97 H1
  BRHD/NEIL G78 ...124 A4
  CGLW G2 ...2 D7
Robertson St AIRDRIE ML6 ...152 A5
Roberts Qd BLSH ML4 ...136 A4
Roberts St WISHAW ML2 ...173 H2
Robert St GOV/IBX G51 ...87 H2
Robert Templeton Dr
  BLTYR/CAMB G72 ...131 G2
Robert Wynd WISHAW ML2 ...158 B3
Robin Pl WISHAW ML2 ...174 A2
Robroyston Av
  STPS/GTHM/RID G33 ...69 H3
Robroyston Rd
  STPS/GTHM/RID G33 ...69 G3
Roblees Crs GIF/THBK G46 ...126 D4
Roblee Dr GIF/THBK G46 ...127 E4
Roblee Rd GIF/THBK G46 ...126 D4
Robson Gv GVH/MTFL G42 ...109 G5
Rochsoles Crs AIRDRIE ML6 ...76 B4
Rochsoles Dr AIRDRIE ML6 ...76 B4
Rochsolloch Rd AIRDRIE ML6...97 G3
Rockall Dr LNPK/KPK G44 ...128 C3
Rockbank Pl
  DMNK/BRGTN G40 ...90 D4
Rockbank St
  DMNK/BRGTN G40 ...90 D4
Rockburn Crs BLSH ML4 ...116 D5
Rockburn Dr
  CRMNK/CLK/EAG G76...145 F2
Rockcliffe Pth AIRDRIE ML6...119 G3
Rockcliffe St
  DMNK/BRGTN G40 ...110 C1
Rock Dr KLBCH PA10 ...100 C4
Rockfield Pl
  SPRCB/BLRNK G21 ...69 F1
Rockfield Rd
  SPRCB/BLRNK G21 ...69 F1
Rockhampton Av EKILS G75...177 G1
Rockmount Av
  BRHD/NEIL G78 ...142 C1
  GIF/THBK G46 ...126 D4
Rockwell Av PSLYS PA2 ...103 H4
Roddinghead Rd
  GIF/THBK G46 ...144 D4
Rodger Av NMRNS G77 ...143 H5
Rodger Dr RUTH G73 ...129 H1
Rodger Pl RUTH G73 ...129 H1
Rodil Av LNPK/KPK G44 ...128 D3
Rodney St MRYH/FIRH G20 ...67 E3
Roebank Dr BRHD/NEIL G78 ...142 B1
Roebank St DEN/PKHD G31 ...91 E1
Roffey Park Rd PSLY PA1 ...85 G4
Rogart St DMNK/BRGTN G40 ...90 C4
Rogerfield Rd ESTRH G54 ...72 B4
Rokeby La KVD/HLHD G12 ...66 D3
Roland Crs NMRNS G77 ...162 A2
Roman Av BDSN G61 ...34 C3
  DRUM G15 ...50 B2
Roman Ct BDSN G61 ...34 C3
  CLYDBK G81 ...31 H2
Roman Crs OLDK G60 ...30 A1
Roman Dr BLSH ML4 ...136 A3
  BDSN G61 ...34 C3
Roman Gdns BDSN G61 ...34 C3
Roman Hill Rd CLYDBK G81 ...31 H1
Roman Pl BLSH ML4 ...135 F4
Roman Rd CLYDBK G81 ...31 H2
  CLYDBK G81 ...31 H2
  KKNTL G66 ...20 D5
  MTHW ML1 ...154 D3
Roman Wy UD/BTH/TAN G71 ...134 D1
Romney Av LNPK/KPK G44 ...128 D3
Romulus Ct MTHW ML1 ...154 B1
Ronaldsay Dr BSHPBGS G64 ...55 G1
Ronaldsay Pl CUMB G67 ...25 H5
Ronaldsay St PPK/MIL G22 ...53 H4
Ronald St CTBR ML5 ...117 E1
Rona St SPRCB/BLRNK G21 ...69 E4
Rona Ter BLTYR/CAMB G72 ...131 E4
Ronay St PPK/MIL G22 ...54 A4
  WISHAW ML2 ...157 H4
Rooksdell Av PSLYS PA2 ...103 H3
Ropework La CGLE G1 ...89 H3
Rosa Burn Av EKILS G75 ...177 G4
Rosebank Av
  BLTYR/CAMB G72 ...151 H1
  KKNTL G66 ...21 G5
Rosebank Dr
  BLTYR/CAMB G72 ...131 H3
  UD/BTH/TAN G71 ...114 A2
Rosebank Gdns
  UD/BTH/TAN G71 ...114 A2
Rosebank Pl BALLOCH G68 ...9 G4
  HMLTN ML3 ...169 F2
Rosebank Rd BLSH ML4 ...117 E4
Rosebank St AIRDRIE ML6 ...99 F1
Rosebank Ter
  BAIL/MDB/MHD G69 ...95 E5
Roseberry Av AIRDRIE ML6 ...119 F1
Roseberry Pl HMLTN ML3 ...169 F1
Roseberry Rd AIRDRIE ML6 ...99 E5
Roseberry St GBLS G5 ...110 B2
Roseburn Ct CUMB G67 ...11 H5
Rose Crs HMLTN ML3 ...169 E1
Rose Dl BSHPBGS G64 * ...55 E3
Rosedale EKILN G74 ...165 H2
Rosedale Av PSLYS PA2 ...102 C5
Rosedale Dr
  BAIL/MDB/MHD G69 ...93 H5
Rosedale Gdns
  MRYH/FIRH G20 ...52 B3
Rosedene Ter BLSH ML4 ...135 H1
Rosefield Gdns
  UD/BTH/TAN G71 ...114 D5
Rose Gdns CTBR ML5 ...116 D1
Rosegreen Crs BLSH ML4 ...116 D4
Rosehall Av CTBR ML5 ...97 E5
Rosehall Rd BLSH ML4 ...135 H1
Rosehall Ter WISHAW ML2 ...173 F4
Rosehill Dr CUMB G67 ...43 H2
Rosehill Rd BSHPBGS G64 ...19 G5
Rose Knowe Rd
  GVH/MTFL G42 ...110 B2
Roselea Dr MLNGV G62 ...17 F2
Roselea Gdns KNTSWD G13 ...51 G4

Roselea Pl BLTYR/CAMB G72...151 F1
Roselea Rd UD/BTH/TAN G71...114 D4
Rosemary Crs EKILN G74 ...166 A1
Rosemary Pl EKILN G74 ...166 A1
Rosemount BALLOCH G68 ...10 B5
Rosemount Av NMRNS G77 ...161 G5
Rosemount Ct NMRNS G77 ...161 G5
Rosemount La BRWEIR PA11 ...79 E5
Rosemount Mdw
  UD/BTH/TAN G71 ...133 H5
Rosemount St
  SPRGB/BLRNK G21 ...90 D1
Rosendale Wy
  BLTYR/CAMB G72 ...151 H3
Roseness Pl
  STPS/GTHM/RID G33 ...92 B1
Rosenheath Ga EKILN G74 ...165 H3
Rosepark Av
  UD/BTH/TAN G71 ...134 C1
Rose St CGLW G2 ...2 D3
  CUMB G67 ...44 A2
  KKNTL G66 ...21 F5
  MTHW ML1 ...155 F5
Rosevale Crs BLSH ML4 ...136 B3
  HMLTN ML3 ...169 G3
Rosevale Rd BDSN G61 ...34 B4
Rosevale St PTCK G11 ...65 H4
Rosewood Av BLSH ML4 ...117 E5
  PSLYS PA2 ...103 G3
Rosewood Pth BLSH ML4 ...135 F2
Rosewood Pl
  BAIL/MDB/MHD G69 ...95 F3
Rosewood St KNTSWD G13 ...51 F4
Roslea Dr DEN/PKHD G31 ...90 D2
Roslin Pl AIRDRIE ML6 ...119 F2
Roslyn Dr BAIL/MDB/MHD G69 ...95 A4
Rosneath St GOV/IBX G51 ...87 H1
Ross Av KKNTL G66 ...21 H5
  RNFRW PA4 ...62 D2
Ross Crs MTHW ML1 ...154 B5
Ross Dr AIRDRIE ML6 ...97 H5
  MTHW ML1 ...154 B5
  UD/BTH/TAN G71 ...115 H3
Rossendale Ct
  PLKSW/MSWD G43 ...108 B4
Rossendale Rd
  PLKSW/MSWD G43 ...108 B4
Ross Gdns MTHW ML1 ...154 B5
Rosshall Av PSLY PA1 ...85 F5
Rosshall Pl RNFRW PA4 ...63 G3
Rosshill Av
  CARD/HILL/MSPK G52 ...86 A4
Rosshill Rd
  CARD/HILL/MSPK G52 ...86 A4
Rossie Crs BSHPBGS G64 ...55 F3
Rossie Gv NMRNS G77 ...143 G5
Rosslea Dr GIF/THBK G46 ...127 F5
Rosslyn Av RUTH G73 ...111 F5
Rosslyn Rd BDSN G61 ...33 G2
Rosslyn Ter KVD/HLHD G12 ...66 B2
Ross Pl RUTH G73 ...130 C5
Ross St CTBR ML5 ...96 D2
  DMNK/BRGTN G40 ...90 A3
  PSLY PA1 ...104 D1
Ross Ter HMLTN ML3 ...171 F4
Rostan Rd
  PLKSW/MSWD G43 ...127 F2
Rosyth Rd GBLS G5 ...110 B2
Rosyth St GBLS G5 ...110 B2
Rotherwick Dr PSLY PA1 ...85 H5
Rotherwood Av KNTSWD G13 ...50 D2
Rotherwood La
  KNTSWD G13 ...50 D1
Rotherwood Pl KNTSWD G13 ...51 E1
Rothes Dr SMSTN G23 ...52 B4
Rothesay Crs CTBR ML5 ...117 E1
Rothesay Pl CTBR ML5 ...117 E1
Rothes Dr SMSTN G23 ...52 B3
Rottenrow CGLE G1 ...3 H4
Rottenrow East COWCAD G4 ...3 J5
Roughcraig St AIRDRIE ML6 ...99 H1
Roughrigg Rd AIRDRIE ML6 ...99 H3
Roukenburn St
  GIF/THBK G46 ...126 B3
Rouken Glen Rd
  GIF/THBK G46 ...144 D1
The Roundel WISHAW ML2 ...174 B2
Roundhill Dr JNSTN PA5 ...102 D1
Roundknowe Rd
  UD/BTH/TAN G71 ...114 B3
Round Riding Rd DMBTN G82 ...13 F3
Rowallan Gdns PTCK G11 ...65 G3
Rowallan La
  CRMNK/CLK/EAG G76...145 G3
Rowallan La East PTCK G11 ...65 G3
Rowallan Rd GIF/THBK G46 ...126 C5
Rowallan Ter
  STPS/GTHM/RID G33 ...70 C2
Rowan Av KKNTL G66 ...5 F5
  RNFRW PA4 ...63 F2
Rowanbank Pl AIRDRIE ML6 ...97 G2
Rowan Ct WISHAW ML2 ...174 D2
Rowan Crs AIRDRIE ML6 ...119 F1
  KKNTL G66 ...39 H3
Rowandale Av
  BAIL/MDB/MHD G69 ...93 H5
Rowand Av GIF/THBK G46 ...127 F5
Rowanden Av BLSH ML4 ...135 H1
Rowan Dr BSDN G61 ...34 A1
  CLYDBK G81 ...31 G4
Rowan Gdns PLKSD/SHW G41 ...88 A5
Rowan Gv HMLTN ML3 ...181 F5
Rowanlea Av PSLYS PA2 ...102 C5
Rowanlea Dr GIF/THBK G46 ...127 G3
Rowanpark Dr
  BRHD/NEIL G78 ...123 H2
Rowan Pl BLTYR/CAMB G72 ...131 H1
  CTBR ML5 ...96 B5
Rowan Ri HMLTN ML3 ...170 B3
Rowan Rd CUMB G67 ...27 F2

  PLKSD/SHW G41 ...88 A5
  PSLYN/LNWD PA3 ...81 G4
Rowans Gdns UD/BTH/TAN G71 ...134 C3
Rowans Ga PSLYS PA2 ...104 C2
The Rowans BSHPBGS G64 ...54 C2
Rowan St PSLYS PA2 ...104 C2
  WISHAW ML2 ...173 G3
Rowantree Av JNSTN PA5 ...119 E5
Rowantree Av RUTH G73 ...130 A3
  UD/BTH/TAN G71 ...115 H5
Rowantree Gdns RUTH G73 ...130 A3
Rowantree Pl JNSTN PA5 ...101 G5
Rowantree Rd JNSTN PA5 ...101 G5
Rowantree Ter KKNTL G66 ...4 C3
  MTHW ML1 ...138 A2
Rowanwood Crs CTBR ML5 ...96 A4
Rowena Av KNTSWD G13 ...51 E2
Roxburgh Dr BSDN G61 ...34 B1
  CTBR ML5 ...97 G5
Roxburgh Pk EKILN G74 ...166 C4
Roxburgh Rd PSLYS PA2 ...102 C5
Roxburgh St KVD/HLHD G12 ...66 C3
Royal Bank Pl CGLE G1 ...3 F5
Royal Crs KVGV G3 ...88 D1
Royal Dr HMLTN ML3 ...170 D3
Royal Exchange Ct CGLE G1 ...3 F5
Royal Exchange Sq CGLE G1 ...3 F5
Royal Gdns UD/BTH/TAN G71 ...133 H5
Royal Inch Crs RNFRW PA4 ...63 G1
Royal Ter KVGV G3 ...66 D5
Royal Terrace La KVGV G3 ...66 D5
Royellen Av HMLTN ML3 ...169 E3
Roystonhill SPRGB/BLRNK G21 ...68 C5
Roystonhill Pl
  SPRGB/BLRNK G21 ...68 C5
Royston Rd
  SPRGB/BLRNK G21 ...68 C5
  STPS/GTHM/RID G33 ...69 H3
Royston Sq
  SPRGB/BLRNK G21 ...68 C5
Roy St SPRGB/BLRNK G21 ...68 A3
Rozelle Av DRUM G15 ...33 G5
  NMRNS G77 ...161 E1
Rozelle Dr NMRNS G77 ...161 E1
Rozelle Pl NMRNS G77 ...161 E1
Rubislaw Dr BSDN G61 ...34 B5
Ruby St DMNK/BRGTN G40 ...90 D5
Ruby Ter BLSH ML4 ...135 H3
Ruchazie Pl
  STPS/GTHM/RID G33 ...92 A1
Ruchazie Rd CAR/SHTL G32 ...92 A3
Ruchill Pl MRYH/FIRH G20 ...67 E1
Ruchill St MRYH/FIRH G20 ...66 D1
Ruel St LNPK/KPK G44 ...109 F5
Rufflees Av BRHD/NEIL G78 ...124 C4
Rugby Av KNTSWD G13 ...50 C3
Rullion Pl
  STPS/GTHM/RID G33 ...92 A1
Rumford St DMNK/BRGTN G40 ...110 C1
Runciman Pl EKILN G74 ...167 E1
Rundell Dr KKNTL G66 ...5 E5
Rupert St COWCAD G4 ...67 E4
Rushyhill St
  SPRGB/BLRNK G21 ...68 D2
Ruskin La KVD/HLHD G12 ...66 D3
Ruskin Pl KSYTH G65 ...7 G2
Ruskin Ter KVD/HLHD G12 ...66 D3
Russell Colt St CTBR ML5 ...96 D1
Russell Dr BSDN G61 ...34 B1
Russell Gdns
  UD/BTH/TAN G71 ...115 F4
Russell La WISHAW ML2 ...173 H3
Russell Pl
  CRMNK/CLK/EAG G76...146 B5
  EKILS G75 ...177 H1
  PSLYN/LNWD PA3 ...81 G5
Russell Rd CLYDBK G81 ...31 F1
Russell St AIRDRIE ML6 ...119 F2
  BLSH ML4 ...135 G1
  HMLTN ML3 ...152 A5
  JNSTN PA5 ...101 H3
  PSLYN/LNWD PA3 ...84 A2
  WISHAW ML2 ...173 H3
Rutherford Av BSDN G61 ...16 C4
Rutherford Ct CLYDBK G81 ...49 F1
Rutherford Gra EKILS G75 ...178 C3
Rutherford La EKILS G75 ...166 D5
Rutherford Sq EKILS G75 ...166 B5
Rutherglen Rd GBLS G5 ...110 A1
Ruthven Av GIF/THBK G46 ...145 G1
Ruthven La KVD/HLHD G12 ...66 C3
Ruthven Pl BSHPBGS G64 ...55 F3
Ruthven St KVD/HLHD G12 ...66 C3
Rutland Crs GOV/IBX G51 ...88 D3
Rutland Ct GOV/IBX G51 ...88 D3
Rutland Pl GOV/IBX G51 ...88 D3
Ryan Rd BSHPBGS G64 ...55 E2
Ryan Wy RUTH G73 ...130 B4
Ryat Dr NMRNS G77 ...143 H4
Ryat Gn NMRNS G77 ...143 H5
Ryatt Linn ERSK PA8 ...47 F3
Rydal Gv EKILS G75 ...177 E2
Rydal Pl EKILS G75 ...177 E2
Ryden Mains Rd AIRDRIE ML6...75 H2
Ryde Rd WISHAW ML2 ...174 B2
Rye Crs SPRGB/BLRNK G21 ...54 D5
Ryecroft Dr
  BAIL/MDB/MHD G69 ...94 A4
Ryedale Pl DRUM G15 ...33 F4
Rye Dr SPRGB/BLRNK G21 ...54 D5
Ryefield Av JNSTN PA5 ...101 E5
Ryefield Pl JNSTN PA5 ...101 E5
Ryefield Rd SPRGB/BLRNK G21...69 E1
Ryehill Pl SPRGB/BLRNK G21 ...69 F1
Ryehill Rd SPRGB/BLRNK G21 ...69 F1
Ryemount Rd
  SPRGB/BLRNK G21 ...69 F1
Rye Rd SPRGB/BLRNK G21 ...54 D5
Ryeside Rd SPRGB/BLRNK G21...69 E1
Ryewraes Rd
  PSLYN/LNWD PA3 ...82 A4
Rylands Dr CAR/SHTL G32 ...93 E5
Rylands Gdns CAR/SHTL G32 ...93 F5
Rylees Crs
  CARD/HILL/MSPK G52 ...85 H2
Rylees Rd
  CARD/HILL/MSPK G52 ...85 H2

  PLKSD/SHW G41 ...88 A5
  PSLYN/LNWD PA3 ...81 G4
Rysland Av NMRNS G77 ...144 B5
Rysland Crs NMRNS G77 ...144 B5
Ryvra Rd KNTSWD G13 ...51 E5

S

Sachelcourt Av BSHPTN PA7 ...46 A2
Sackville Av KNTSWD G13 ...65 G1
Sackville La KNTSWD G13 ...65 G1
Saddell Rd DRUM G15 ...33 G4
Saffron Crs WISHAW ML2 ...173 G4
Saffronhall Crs HMLTN ML3 ...170 A1
Saffronhall La HMLTN ML3 ...170 A1
St Abb's Dr PSLYS PA2 ...103 E3
St Aidan's Pth WISHAW ML2 * ...157 F4
Saint Andrew's Av
  BSHPBGS G64 ...54 B1
St Andrews Av
  UD/BTH/TAN G71 ...152 B1
St Andrew's Brae DMBTN G82 ...13 G1
St Andrew's Ct EKILS G75 ...13 G2
St Andrews Dr DMBTN G82 ...88 D5
  PLKSD/SHW G41 ...61 H5
  PSLYN/LNWD PA3 ...10 D4
St Andrews Dr BALLOCH G68 ...79 E4
  BRWEIR PA11 ...34 A1
  BSDN G61 ...168 C1
  HMLTN ML3 ...108 B2
  PLKSD/SHW G41 ...84 A1
  PSLYN/LNWD PA3 ...62 B5
St Andrew's Dr West
  PSLYN/LNWD PA3 ...83 H1
St Andrews Gdns
  AIRDRIE ML6 ...98 C1
St Andrew's La CGLE G1 ...3 H1
St Andrew's Rd
  PLKSD/SHW G41 ...89 E5
  RNFRW PA4 ...63 F2
St Andrew's Sq CGLE G1 ...90 A3
St Andrew's St CGLE G1 ...3 H7
  MTHW ML1 ...137 F2
St Andrew's Wy
  WISHAW ML2 ...157 F4
St Annes Av ERSK PA8 ...48 A3
St Anne's Ct HMLTN ML3 ...170 A5
St Annes Wynd ERSK PA8 ...47 H3
St Ann's Dr GIF/THBK G46 ...127 F5
St Barchan's Rd KLBCH PA10 ...100 C4
St Blane's Dr RUTH G73 ...129 F1
St Boswell's Dr PSLYS PA2 ...103 F3
St Boswells Dr CTBR ML5 ...96 C5
St Bride's Av
  UD/BTH/TAN G71 ...115 H5
St Bride's Rd
  PLKSW/MSWD G43 ...127 G1
St Brides Wy
  UD/BTH/TAN G71 ...134 B5
St Bryde St EKILN G74 ...166 C3
St Catherine's Rd
  GIF/THBK G46 ...127 G5
St Clair Av GIF/THBK G46 ...127 E4
St Clair St MRYH/FIRH G20 ...67 E4
Saint Columba Dr KKNTL G66 ...40 B1
St Cuthbert Wy HMLTN ML3 ...152 A5
St Cyrus Gdns BSHPBGS G64 ...55 F2
St Cyrus Rd BSHPBGS G64 ...55 F2
St Davids Dr AIRDRIE ML6 ...98 D5
St Denis Wy CTBR ML5 ...96 C1
St Edmunds Gv MLNGV G62 ...17 E2
St Enoch Av
  UD/BTH/TAN G71 ...115 H4
St Enoch Sq CGLE G1 ...2 E7
St Fillans Dr
  CRG/CRSL/HOU PA6 ...80 B1
St Fillans Rd
  STPS/GTHM/RID G33 ...70 D1
St Flanan Rd KKNTL G66 ...22 D3
St Francis Rigg GBLS G5 ...90 A5
St George's Pl MRYH/FIRH G20...67 F4
St George's Rd COWCAD G4 ...67 F4
St Germains BSDN G61 ...34 B4
St Giles Pk HMLTN ML3 ...169 G5
St Giles Wy HMLTN ML3 ...169 G5
St Helena Crs CLYDBK G81 ...32 B2
St Helens Gdns
  PLKSD/SHW G41 ...108 D1
St Ives Rd
  BAIL/MDB/MHD G69 ...42 A5
St James Av PSLYN/LNWD PA3...83 G2
St James Ct CTBR ML5 ...116 B1
St James Rd COWCAD G4 ...3 J4
St James' St PSLYN/LNWD PA3...84 B4
St James Wy CTBR ML5 ...116 B1
St Johns Bvd
  UD/BTH/TAN G71 ...134 D1
St John's Ct PLKSD/SHW G41 ...88 D5
St John's Qd PLKSD/SHW G41 ...88 D5
St John's Rd PLKSD/SHW G41 ...88 D5
St John St CTBR ML5 ...96 D2
St Johns Wy KSYTH G65 ...8 B2
St Joseph's Ct
  SPRGB/BLRNK G21 ...68 C5
St Joseph's Vw
  SPRGB/BLRNK G21 ...68 C5
St Kenneth Dr GOV/IBX G51 ...87 E1
St Kilda Dr SCOT G14 ...65 F2
St Kilda Wy WISHAW ML2 ...157 H5
St Leonards Dr GIF/THBK G46 ...127 F4
St Leonards Rd EKILN G74 ...167 H3
St Leonards Wk CTBR ML5 ...117 F1
St Lukes Pl GBLS G5 ...89 H4
St Lukes Ter GBLS G5 ...89 H4
St Machan's Wy KKNTL G66 ...4 A1
St Machars Rd BRWEIR PA11 ...79 H4
St Margarets Av
  PSLYN/LNWD PA3 ...84 C2
St Margaret's Ct
  PSLYN/LNWD PA3 ...84 C2
St Margaret's Dr
  WISHAW ML2 ...173 H4
St Margaret's Pl CGLE G1 ...89 H3

St Mark Gdns *CAR/SHTL* G32.....92 A4
St Mark's Ct *WISHAW* ML2.....157 F4
St Mark St *CAR/SHTL* G32.....91 H4
Marnock St
  DMNK/BRGTN G40.....90 D4
St Martins Ga *CTBR* ML5.....96 D5
St Mary's La *BRHD/NEIL* G78.....124 B5
St Marys Gdns
  BRHD/NEIL G78.....124 B5
St Mary's La *CGLW* G2.....2 E5
St Mary's Rd *BLSH* ML4.....135 F2
St BSHPBGS G64.....55 G4
St Mary's Wy *DMBTN* G82.....13 E4
St Michael Rd *WISHAW* ML2.....172 D4
St Michael's La *DEN/PKHD* G31.....91 H1
St Mirren's Rd *KSYTH* G65.....8 C2
St Mirren St *PSLY* PA1.....84 B5
St Monance St
  SPRGB/BLRNK G21.....68 C1
St Mungo Av *COWCAD* G4.....3 G3
St Mungo Ct *BRWEIR* PA11.....79 H5
St Mungo Pl *COWCAD* G4.....3 J3
  HMLTN ML3.....168 C1
St Mungos Crs *MTHW* ML1.....137 G5
St Mungo's Rd *CUMB* G67.....26 B4
St Mungo St *BSHPBGS* G64.....54 C3
St Ninian's Av *PSLYS* PA2.....104 C2
St Ninian's Pl *HMLTN* ML3.....168 D2
St Ninian's Rd *HMLTN* ML3.....168 D2
  PSLYS PA2.....104 C2
St Ninian Ter *GBLS* G5.....89 H4
St Peter's La *CGLW* G2.....2 C5
St Peter's St *COWCAD* G4.....67 F4
St Roberts Gdns
  PLK/PH/NH G53.....125 H2
St Ronan's Dr *HMLTN* ML3.....169 H5
  PLKSD/SHW G41.....108 C3
  RUTH G73.....129 H2
St Stephens Av *RUTH* G73.....130 B4
St Stephens Ct *CLYDBK* G81.....31 G5
St Stephen's Crs *RUTH* G73.....130 C4
St Valentine Ter *GBLS* G5.....90 A5
St Vigeans Av *NMRNS* G77.....161 E2
St Vigeans Pl *NMRNS* G77.....161 F2
St Vincent Ct *KVGV* G3.....88 C1
St Vincent Crescent La
  KVGV G3.....2 A4
St Vincent La *CGLW* G2.....2 C4
St Vincent Pl *CGLE* G1.....3 F5
  EKILS G75.....165 F5
  MTHW ML1.....154 D5
St Vincent St *CGLW* G2.....89 E1
  KVGV G3.....2 A4
St Vincent Ter *KVGV* G3.....2 A4
St Winifred's Wy
  WISHAW ML2.....173 H1
Salamanca St *DEN/PKHD* G31.....91 G4
Salasaig Ct
  STPS/GTHM/RID G33.....92 B2
Salen St *SPRGB/BLRNK* G21.....87 G4
Saline St *AIRDRIE* ML6.....98 A4
Salisbury *EKILN* G74.....167 G1
Salisbury St *MTHW* ML1.....154 A1
Salisbury St *PLKSD/SHW* G41.....89 G5
Salkeld St *GBLS* G5.....89 G5
Salmona St *PPK/MIL* G22.....67 G2
Saltaire Av *UD/BTH/TAN* G71.....134 B2
Salterland Rd
  PLK/PH/NH G53.....124 D2
Saltmarket *CGLE* G1.....89 H1
Saltmarket Pl *CGLE* G1.....89 H3
Saltoun La *KVD/HLHD* G12.....66 C5
Saltoun St *KVD/HLHD* G12.....66 C5
Salvia St *BLTYR/CAMB* G72.....130 D3
Sandaig Rd
  STPS/GTHM/RID G33.....93 F4
Sandalwood Av *EKILN* G74.....166 A1
Sandalwood Ct *EKILN* G74.....166 A1
Sanda St *MRYH/FIRH* G20.....66 D2
Sandbank Crs *MRYH/FIRH* G20.....52 C5
Sandbank Dr *MRYH/FIRH* G20.....52 C4
Sandbank Ter *MRYH/FIRH* G20.....52 C4
Sandend Rd *PLK/PH/NH* G53.....106 B5
Sanderling Pl *JNSTN* PA5.....121 E3
Sanderling Rd
  PSLYN/LNWD PA3.....84 A1
Sanders Ct *BRHD/NEIL* G78.....124 B4
Sanderson Av
  UD/BTH/TAN G71.....135 E1
Sandfield Av *MLNGV* G62.....17 E2
Sandfield St *MRYH/FIRH* G20.....52 D5
Sandgate Av *CAR/SHTL* G32.....113 E1
Sandhaven Pl
  PLK/PH/NH G53.....106 B5
Sandhead Crs *AIRDRIE* ML6.....119 F3
Sandhead Ter
  BLTYR/CAMB G72.....168 C3
Sandholes Rd *JNSTN* PA5.....100 D1
Sandholes St *PSLY* PA1.....84 A5
Sandholm Pl *SCOT* G14.....64 A1
Sandholm Ter *SCOT* G14.....64 A1
Sandiefield Rd *GBLS* G5.....89 H5
Sandielands Av *ERSK* PA8.....48 A2
Sandilands St *MTHW* ML1.....154 A5
Sandilands St *CAR/SHTL* G32.....92 D4
Sandmill St *SPRGB/BLRNK* G21.....68 D5
Sandpiper Crs *CTBR* ML5.....117 G2
Sandpiper Dr *EKILS* G75.....177 F3
Sandpiper Pl *EKILS* G75.....177 F3
Sandpiper Wy *BLSH* ML4.....117 G5
Sandra Rd *BSHPBGS* G64.....55 F1
Sandringham Av *NMRNS* G77.....144 D4
Sandringham Dr *JNSTN* PA5.....102 A3
Sandringham La
  KVD/HLHD G12.....66 C3
Sandwood Rd
  CARD/HILL/MSPK G52.....86 B3
Sandyfaulds St *GBLS* G5.....90 A5
Sandyford Av *MTHW* ML1.....119 E4
Sandyford Pl *MTHW* ML1.....119 E4
Sandyford Place La *KVGV* G3.....88 D1
Sandyford Rd *MTHW* ML1.....119 F5
  PSLYN/LNWD PA3.....84 B1
Sandyford St *KVGV* G3.....88 B1
Sandyhills Crs *CAR/SHTL* G32.....112 C1
Sandyhills Dr *CAR/SHTL* G32.....112 C1
Sandyhills Gv *CAR/SHTL* G32.....112 D2
Sandyhills Pl *CAR/SHTL* G32.....112 C1
Sandyhills Rd *CAR/SHTL* G32.....112 D1
Sandyknowes Rd *CUMB* G67.....26 B5
Sandy Rd *PTCK* G11.....65 F5
  RNFRW PA4.....63 F5
Sanford Pl *KVGV* G3.....88 B1
Sannox Dr *MTHW* ML1.....154 A3
Sannox Gdns *DEN/PKHD* G31.....91 E1
Sannox Pl *EKILS* G75.....177 G4
Sanquhar Dr *PLK/PH/NH* G53.....106 B4
Sanquhar Gdns
  BLTYR/CAMB G72.....133 E5
  PLK/PH/NH G53.....106 B4
Sanquhar Pl *PLK/PH/NH* G53.....106 B4
Sanquhar Rd
  PLK/PH/NH G53.....106 B4
Sapphire Rd *BLSH* ML4.....135 H4
Saracen Head Rd *CGLE* G1.....3 K7
Saracen St *PPK/MIL* G22.....67 H2
Sarazen Ct *MTHW* ML1.....156 B2
Sardinia La *KVD/HLHD* G12.....66 C3
Saskatoon Pl *EKILS* G75.....165 G4
Saturn Av *PSLY* PA1.....83 G5
Saucel Crs *PSLY* PA1.....84 B5
Saucel Hill Ter *PSLYS* PA2.....104 B1
Saucel Pl *PSLY* PA1.....104 B1
Saucel St *PSLY* PA1.....84 C5
Sauchenhall Pth
  BAIL/MDB/MHD G69.....42 B5
Sauchiehall La *CGLW* G2.....2 B3
Sauchiehall St *CGLW* G2.....2 D4
  KVGV G3.....66 C5
Saughs Av
  STPS/GTHM/RID G33.....56 A5
Saughs Dr
  STPS/GTHM/RID G33.....56 A5
Saughs Ga
  STPS/GTHM/RID G33.....56 A5
Saughs Pl
  STPS/GTHM/RID G33.....56 A5
Saughs Rd
  STPS/GTHM/RID G33.....56 B5
Saughton St *CAR/SHTL* G32.....91 H2
Savoy St *DMNK/BRGTN* G40.....90 C1
Sawmillfield St *COWCAD* G4.....67 G4
Saxon Rd *KNTSWD* G13.....51 E4
Scadlock Rd *PSLYN/LNWD* PA3.....83 G5
Scalloway Rd
  BAIL/MDB/MHD G69.....72 B2
  BLTYR/CAMB G72.....130 D4
Scalpay Pl *PPK/MIL* G22.....54 A4
Scalpay Pl *PPK/MIL* G22.....53 H4
Scapa St *SMSTN* G23.....52 D5
Scapa Wy
  STPS/GTHM/RID G33.....57 F5
Scaraway Dr *PPK/MIL* G22.....54 A3
Scaraway Pl *PPK/MIL* G22.....54 A3
Scaraway St *PPK/MIL* G22.....53 H3
Scaraway Ter *PPK/MIL* G22.....54 A3
Scarba Dr *PLKSW/MSWD* G43.....127 E1
Scarba Od *WISHAW* ML2.....157 H4
Scarffe Av *PSLYN/LNWD* PA3.....101 G1
Scarhill Av *AIRDRIE* ML6.....98 A4
Scarhill La *AIRDRIE* ML6.....98 B4
Scarhill St *CTBR* ML5.....116 C1
  MTHW ML1.....139 E5
Scarrel Dr *CSMK* G45.....129 H5
Scarrel Gdns *CSMK* G45.....129 H5
Scarrel Rd *CSMK* G45.....129 H4
Scarrel Ter *CSMK* G45.....129 H5
Scavaig Crs *DRUM* G15.....32 D4
Schaw Dr *BSDN* G61.....34 B2
Schaw Rd *PSLYN/LNWD* PA3.....84 D3
  CLYDBK G81.....32 C2
Scholar's Ga *EKILS* G75.....178 A2
School Av *BLTYR/CAMB* G72.....131 G2
Schoolhouse La
  BLTYR/CAMB G72.....151 H3
School La *BLTYR/CAMB* G72.....132 B3
  DMBTN G82.....12 C3
  KNTL G66.....4 A5
School Od *AIRDRIE* ML6.....76 A4
School Rd *BSHPBGS* G64.....19 G4
  NMRNS G77.....161 G1
  PSLY PA1.....85 E3
  STPS/GTHM/RID G33.....57 F5
  WISHAW ML2.....175 G2
School St *AIRDRIE* ML6.....119 E2
  HMLTN ML3.....170 A4
School Wynd *PSLY* PA1.....84 B4
Scioncroft Av *RUTH* G75.....111 F5
Scone St *SPRGB/BLRNK* G21.....47 H4
Sconser St *SMSTN* G23.....52 D2
Scorton Gdns
  BAIL/MDB/MHD G69.....93 G5
Scotia Gdns *HMLTN* ML3.....180 C1
Scotia St *MTHW* ML1.....154 B3
Scotland St *GBLS* G5.....89 E4
Scotland St West
  GBLS G5.....88 C4
Scotsblair Av *KNTL* G66.....39 H1
Scotsburn Rd
  SPRGB/BLRNK G21.....69 F2
Scotstoun St *SCOT* G14.....64 D3
Scott Av *JNSTN* PA5.....121 F1
  KNTL G66.....21 G4
  OLDK G60.....15 G5
Scott Crs *CUMB* G67.....44 C1
Scott Dr *BSDN* G61.....33 G1
  CUMB G67.....44 C1
Scott Gv *HMLTN* ML3.....170 A3
Scott Hl *EKILN* G74.....166 D2
Scott Hill *BLSH* ML4.....117 E5
Scott Rd
  CARD/HILL/MSPK G52.....86 A1
Scott's Pl *AIRDRIE* ML6.....98 C1
Scott's Rd *PSLYS* PA2.....105 F1
Scott St *BAIL/MDB/MHD* G69.....41 F4
  CLYDBK G81.....31 G3
  HMLTN ML3.....170 A4
  KVGV G3.....2 C2
  MTHW ML1.....154 D3
Seafar Rd *CUMB* G67.....26 A4
Seafield Av *BSDN* G61.....34 C1
Seafield Crs *BALLOCH* G68.....24 C4
Seafield Dr *RUTH* G73.....130 C4
Seaforth Crs *BRHD/NEIL* G78.....124 A4
Seaforth Rd *BLSH* ML4.....116 D5
Seaforth Rd
  CARD/HILL/MSPK G52.....86 B2
  CLYDBK G81.....49 E2
Seaforth Rd North
  CARD/HILL/MSPK G52.....86 B2
Seaforth Rd South
  CARD/HILL/MSPK G52.....86 B2
Seagrove St *CAR/SHTL* G32.....91 F3
Seamill Gdns *EKILN* G74.....166 A5
Seamill St *PLK/PH/NH* G53.....125 E2
Seamore St *MRYH/FIRH* G20.....67 E4
Seath Av *AIRDRIE* ML6.....97 H1
Seath Rd *RUTH* G73.....110 D5
Seath St *GVH/MTFL* G42.....109 H2
Seaton Ter *HMLTN* ML3.....169 F1
Seaward La *PLKSD/SHW* G41.....88 D4
Seaward Pl *PLKSD/SHW* G41.....89 E4
Seaward St *PLKSD/SHW* G41.....88 D4
Second Av *BSDN* G61.....34 D5
  CLYDBK G81.....49 E1
  CLYDBK G81.....31 H5
  DMBTN G82.....13 H2
  KKNTL G66.....40 B1
  LNPK/KPK G44.....128 C1
  RNFRW PA4.....63 F5
  STPS/GTHM/RID G33.....70 C1
  UD/BTH/TAN G71.....115 E4
Second Gdns *PLKSD/SHW* G41.....87 H5
Second Rd *BLTYR/CAMB* G72.....151 H5
Second St *UD/BTH/TAN* G71.....115 E4
Seedhill *PSLY* PA1.....84 C5
Seedhill Rd *PSLY* PA1.....84 C5
Seggielea La *KNTSWD* G13.....51 E5
Seggielea Rd *KNTSWD* G13.....51 E5
Seil Dr *LNPK/KPK* G44.....128 C3
Selborne Pl *KNTSWD* G13.....65 F1
Selborne Place La
  KNTSWD G13.....65 F1
Selborne Rd *KNTSWD* G13.....65 F1
Selby Gdns *CAR/SHTL* G32.....93 E4
Selby Pl *CTBR* ML5.....74 A4
Selby St *CTBR* ML5.....74 A4
Selkirk Av
  CARD/HILL/MSPK G52.....86 D5
  PSLYS PA2.....105 F4
Selkirk Dr *RUTH* G73.....111 F5
Selkirk Pl *EKILN* G74.....167 G2
  HMLTN ML3.....170 B3
Selkirk St *BLTYR/CAMB* G72.....151 G3
  WISHAW ML2.....157 F5
Selkirk Wy *CTBR* ML5.....117 H1
Sella Rd *BSHPBGS* G64.....55 G1
Selvieland Rd
  CARD/HILL/MSPK G52.....85 H4
Semphill Gdns *EKILN* G74.....167 E3
Semple St *HMLTN* ML3.....169 E1
Sempill Av *ERSK* PA8.....47 E1
Semple Av *BSHPTN* PA7.....29 E5
Semple Pl *PSLYN/LNWD* PA3.....82 A3
Semple Vw *HWWD* PA9.....120 A4
Senate Pl *MTHW* ML1.....154 B1
Senga Crs *BLSH* ML4.....116 C4
Seres Rd
  CRMNK/CLK/EAG G76.....145 G2
Sergeantlaw Rd *PSLYS* PA2.....122 A2
Service St *KKNTL* G66.....4 A1
Seton Ter *DEN/PKHD* G31.....90 C2
Settle Gdns
  BAIL/MDB/MHD G69.....93 G5
Seven Sisters *KKNTL* G66.....40 B3
Seventh Av *UD/BTH/TAN* G71.....115 E4
Seventh Rd
  BLTYR/CAMB G72.....151 H5
Severn Rd *EKILS* G75.....176 D1
Seymour Gn *EKILS* G75.....165 G5
Seyton Av *GIF/THBK* G46.....145 F1
Seyton Ct *GIF/THBK* G46.....145 F1
Seyton La *EKILN* G74.....166 B2
Shaftesbury St *CLYDBK* G81.....48 C1
  KVGV G3.....2 A4
Shafton Pl *KNTSWD* G13.....51 F3
Shafton Rd *KNTSWD* G13.....51 F3
Shakespeare Av *CLYDBK* G81.....31 G4
Shakespeare St
  MRYH/FIRH G20.....66 D1
Shamrock St *COWCAD* G4.....2 D1
  KKNTL G66.....21 F5
Shandon Crs *BLSH* ML4.....116 D5
Shandon Ter *HMLTN* ML3.....169 E6
Shand St *WISHAW* ML2.....174 B3
Shandwick St *ESTRH* G34.....93 H1
Shanks Av *BRHD/NEIL* G78.....124 B5
Shanks Crs *JNSTN* PA5.....101 F4
Shanks St *AIRDRIE* ML6.....76 B5
  MRYH/FIRH G20.....66 D1
Shanks Wy *BRHD/NEIL* G78.....124 B2
Shannon St *MRYH/FIRH* G20.....67 E1
Shapinsay St *PPK/MIL* G22.....54 A3
Sharp Av *CTBR* ML5.....95 H5
Sharp St *MTHW* ML1.....154 A3
Sharp Av *BSHPTN* PA7.....29 F5
Shawbridge St
  PLKSW/MSWD G43.....108 B3
Shawburn St *HMLTN* ML3.....169 G1
Shaw Ct *ERSK* PA8.....47 F1
Shawfield Dr *GBLS* G5.....110 C2
Shawfield Rd *GBLS* G5.....110 D1
Shawfoot Rd *MTHW* ML1.....118 A4
Shawhead Av *CTBR* ML5.....97 E5
Shawhead Dr *CTBR* ML5.....97 E5
Shawhill Rd
  PLKSD/SHW G41.....108 B3
Shawhill Rd *PLKSD/SHW* G41.....108 C4
Shawholm Crs
  PLKSW/MSWD G43.....108 A3
Shawmoss Rd
  PLKSD/SHW G41.....108 A3
Shawpark St *MRYH/FIRH* G20.....52 D5
Shaw Pl *PSLYN/LNWD* PA3.....82 A4
Shawrigg Rd *HMLTN* ML3.....170 C3
Shaw St *GOV/IBX* G51.....88 A2
Shawwood Crs *NMRNS* G77.....161 H2
Shearer Dr *HMLTN* ML3.....180 C1
Sheddens Pl *CAR/SHTL* G32.....91 H4
Sheepburn Rd
  UD/BTH/TAN G71.....114 D5
Sheila St *STPS/GTHM/RID* G33.....69 H2
Sheiling Hl *HMLTN* ML3.....170 B1
Sheldaig Rd *PPK/MIL* G22.....53 H3
Sheldrake Pl *JNSTN* PA5.....121 E3
Shelley Dr *CLYDBK* G81.....31 H4
  UD/BTH/TAN G71.....115 G5
Shelley Rd *KVD/HLHD* G12.....65 G1
Shells Rd *KKNTL* G66.....21 H5
Shepford Pl *CTBR* ML5.....96 A2
Sherbrooke Av
  PLKSD/SHW G41.....108 B2
Sherbrooke Dr
  PLKSD/SHW G41.....108 B1
Sherbrooke Gdns
  PLKSD/SHW G41.....108 B1
Sherbrooke Pl *EKILS* G75.....165 H4
Sherburn Gdns
  BAIL/MDB/MHD G69.....93 G5
Sherdale Av *AIRDRIE* ML6.....99 G5
Sheriff Park Av *RUTH* G73.....110 D5
Sherry Av *MTHW* ML1.....137 F2
Sherry Dr *HMLTN* ML3.....169 F4
Sherwood Av *PSLY* PA1.....84 D5
  UD/BTH/TAN G71.....134 B2
Sherwood Dr *GIF/THBK* G46.....126 D4
Sherwood Pl *DRUM* G15.....33 G5
Shetland Dr *LNPK/KPK* G44.....128 C3
Shettleston Rd
  DEN/PKHD G31.....91 H4
  CAR/SHTL G32.....166 C2
Shielbridge Gdns *SMSTN* G23.....52 D2
Shiel Ct *BRHD/NEIL* G78.....124 A4
Shieldaig Dr *RUTH* G73.....130 A3
Shieldburn Rd *GOV/IBX* G51.....86 D2
Shieldhall Gdns *GOV/IBX* G51.....86 D2
Shieldhall Rd *GOV/IBX* G51.....86 C2
Shields Ct *MTHW* ML1.....172 D1
Shields Dr *MTHW* ML1.....172 C2
Shields Dr *MTHW* ML1.....172 C2
Shields Rd *MTHW* ML1.....172 C2
  PLKSD/SHW G41.....89 E5
Shiel Pl *CTBR* ML5.....74 A4
  EKILN G74.....166 C2
Shiel Rd *BSHPBGS* G64.....55 E2
Shiel Ter *WISHAW* ML2.....158 A4
Shilford Av *KNTSWD* G13.....50 B5
Shillay St *PPK/MIL* G22.....54 B2
Shillingworth Pl *BRWEIR* PA11.....79 G5
Shilton Dr *PLK/PH/NH* G53.....125 H2
Shilton La *BSHPTN* PA7.....29 E3
Shinwell Av *CLYDBK* G81.....49 G3
Shipbank La *CGLE* G1.....89 H1
Shira Ter *EKILN* G74.....167 E4
Shirley Od *MTHW* ML1.....171 G2
Shirrel Av *BLSH* ML4.....116 D5
Shirrel Rd *MTHW* ML1.....137 F5
Shirva Lea *KSYTH* G65.....23 F1
Shiskine Pl *MRYH/FIRH* G20.....52 B3
Shiskine Pl *MRYH/FIRH* G20.....52 B3
Shiskine St *MRYH/FIRH* G20.....52 B3
Sholto Crs *BLSH* ML4.....116 A5
Shore St *DMNK/BRGTN* G40.....110 C2
Shortridge St *MRYH/FIRH* G20.....67 E2
Shortroods Av
  PSLYN/LNWD PA3.....84 A2
Shortroods Crs
  PSLYN/LNWD PA3.....84 A2
Shotts St *STPS/GTHM/RID* G33.....93 E1
Shuna Crs *MRYH/FIRH* G20.....66 D1
Shuna Gdns *MRYH/FIRH* G20.....66 D1
Shuna Pl *MRYH/FIRH* G20.....66 D1
  NMRNS G77.....143 G4
Shuna St *MRYH/FIRH* G20.....52 D5
Shuttle St *CGLE* G1.....3 J6
  KLBCH PA10.....100 B3
  KSYTH G65.....8 A1
  PSLY PA1.....84 B5
Sidland Rd *SPRGB/BLRNK* G21.....69 F1
Sidlaw Av *BRHD/NEIL* G78.....142 B1
  HMLTN ML3.....169 E3
Sidlaw Dr *WISHAW* ML2.....157 G5
Sidlaw Rd *BSDN* G61.....33 G2
Sidlaw Wy *AIRDRIE* ML6.....119 G3
Sielga Pl *ESTRH* G34.....93 H1
Siemens Pl *SPRGB/BLRNK* G21.....68 D4
Siemens St *SPRGB/BLRNK* G21.....68 D4
Sievewright St *RUTH* G73.....111 F3
Sikeside Pl *CTBR* ML5.....97 G4
Sikeside St *CTBR* ML5.....97 G4
Silkin Av *CLYDBK* G81.....49 G2
Silk St *PSLY* PA1.....84 C4
Silvan Pl
  CRMNK/CLK/EAG G76.....146 B5
Silver Birch Dr *GOV/IBX* G51.....87 E2
Silver Birch Gdns
  GOV/IBX G51.....87 E2
Silverbirch Gv *HMLTN* ML3.....181 F5
Silverburn Crs *MTHW* ML1.....138 A4
Silverburn St
  STPS/GTHM/RID G33.....91 H1
Silverdale *EKILN* G74.....165 H2
Silverdale St *DEN/PKHD* G31.....91 F5
Silverdale Ter *AIRDRIE* ML6.....77 G5
Silver Firs *MTHW* ML1.....137 G4
Silverfir St *GBLS* G5.....110 A1
Silvergrove St
  DMNK/BRGTN G40.....90 B5
Silverton Av *DMBTN* G82.....13 F4
Silverton Av *HMLTN* ML3.....170 B5
Silvertonhill La *DMBTN* G82.....13 G4
Silvertonhill Pl *HMLTN* ML3.....180 D1
Silverwells *UD/BTH/TAN* G71.....152 B1
Silverwells Crs
  UD/BTH/TAN G71.....152 A1
Simons Crs *RNFRW* PA4.....63 G1
Simpson Ct *CLYDBK* G81.....48 D1
  UD/BTH/TAN G71.....134 A1
Simpson Dr *EKILS* G75.....178 A1
Simpson Gdns *BRHD/NEIL* G78.....142 A1
Simpson Pl *EKILS* G75.....178 A1
Simpson St *MRYH/FIRH* G20.....67 E3
Simpson Wy *BLSH* ML4.....117 F5
Simshill Rd *LNPK/KPK* G44.....128 C3
Sinclair Av *BSDN* G61.....34 B2
Sinclair Dr *CTBR* ML5.....96 A2
  GVH/MTFL G42.....109 E5
Sinclair Gdns *BSHPBGS* G64.....55 E3
Sinclair Gv *BLSH* ML4.....135 G5
Sinclair Pk *EKILS* G75.....166 C5
Sinclair Pl *EKILS* G75.....166 C5
Sinclair St *CLYDBK* G81.....49 G3
  MLNGV G62.....17 G3
Singer Rd *CLYDBK* G81.....31 G5
  EKILS G75.....178 C2
Singer St *CLYDBK* G81.....49 G1
Sir Michael Pl *PSLY* PA1.....84 A5
Siskin Wy *CTBR* ML5.....117 G5
Sixth Av *RNFRW* PA4.....63 F5
Sir Michael Pl *PSLY* PA1.....114 D5
Skaethorn Rd *MRYH/FIRH* G20.....52 A5
Skaterigg La *KNTSWD* G13.....65 F1
Skelbo Pl *ESTRH* G34.....72 C5
Skene Rd *GOV/IBX* G51.....87 H4
Skerne Gv *EKILS* G75.....177 E2
Skerray Qd *PPK/MIL* G22.....53 H3
Skerray St *PPK/MIL* G22.....53 H3
Skerryvore Pl
  STPS/GTHM/RID G33.....92 C1
Skerryvore Rd
  STPS/GTHM/RID G33.....92 C1
Skibo La *GIF/THBK* G46.....126 B4
Skibo Dr *GIF/THBK* G46.....126 B4
Skimmers Pl *GOV/IBX* G51.....87 E1
Skipness Dr *GOV/IBX* G51.....86 C2
Skirsa Ct *SMSTN* G23.....53 E4
Skirsa Pl *SMSTN* G23.....53 E4
Skirsa Sq *SMSTN* G23.....53 E3
Skirsa St *SMSTN* G23.....53 E3
Skirving St *PLKSD/SHW* G41.....108 D4
Skovlunde Wy *EKILS* G75.....178 B2
Skye *EKILN* G74.....167 G4
Skye Av *RNFRW* PA4.....63 F5
Skye Ct *CUMB* G67.....25 H5
Skye Crs *OLDK* G60.....30 D3
  PSLYS PA2.....104 A5
Skye Dr *CUMB* G67.....25 H5
  OLDK G60.....30 D3
Skye Gdns *BSDN* G61.....33 G2
Skye Pl *AIRDRIE* ML6.....99 E3
  CUMB G67.....25 H5
Skye Od *WISHAW* ML2.....157 H5
Skye Rd *CUMB* G67.....25 H5
  RUTH G73.....130 C4
Skye Wynd *HMLTN* ML3.....169 E4
Skylands Gv *HMLTN* ML3.....169 F5
Skylands Rl *HMLTN* ML3.....169 F5
Slakiewood Av
  BAIL/MDB/MHD G69.....58 D4
Slatefield *EKILN* G74.....167 G1
Slatefield St *DEN/PKHD* G31.....90 D3
Sleaford Av *MTHW* ML1.....171 G1
Slenavon Av *RUTH* G73.....130 C4
Slessor Dr *EKILS* G75.....178 B1
Sloy St *PPK/MIL* G22.....67 H2
  WISHAW ML2.....173 H4
Small Crs *BLTYR/CAMB* G72.....151 G3
Smeaton Av *BSHPBGS* G64.....19 E5
Smeaton Dr *BSHPBGS* G64.....37 H4
Smeaton Gv *MRYH/FIRH* G20.....53 E5
Smeaton St *MRYH/FIRH* G20.....53 E5
Smith Cl *BSHPBGS* G64.....55 G3
Smith Crs *CLYDBK* G81.....32 A3
Smith Gdns *BSHPBGS* G64.....55 G3
Smith Gv *BSHPBGS* G64.....55 G3
Smithhills St
  PSLYN/LNWD PA3.....84 B4
Smith Od *CTBR* ML5.....117 H1
Smithstone Crs *KSYTH* G65.....8 A2
Smithstone Rd *BALLOCH* G68.....24 D5
Smith St *SCOT* G14.....65 G3
Smith Wy *BSHPBGS* G64.....55 G3
Smithycroft *HMLTN* ML3.....170 B5
Smithycroft Rd
  STPS/GTHM/RID G33.....69 H5
Smithyends *CUMB* G67.....10 B5
Smollett Rd *DMBTN* G82.....13 G4
Snaefell Av *RUTH* G73.....130 B3
Snaefell Crs *RUTH* G73.....130 B2
Snead Vw *MTHW* ML1.....156 B1
Sneddon Av *WISHAW* ML2.....174 B4
Sneddon Dr *HMLTN* ML3.....152 B4
Sneddon Ter *HMLTN* ML3.....152 A4
Snowdon St *GBLS* G5.....90 A5
Snuff Mill Rd *LNPK/KPK* G44.....128 C2
Society St *DEN/PKHD* G31.....91 E4
Solias Pl *KNTSWD* G13.....49 H5
Solsgirth Gdns *KKNTL* G66.....22 D5
Solway Ct *HMLTN* ML3.....169 G5
Solway Pl
  BAIL/MDB/MHD G69.....58 C2
Solway Rd *BSHPBGS* G64.....55 G1
Solway St *DMNK/BRGTN* G40.....110 C2
Somerford Rd *BSDN* G61.....51 G2
Somerled Av
  PSLYN/LNWD PA3.....62 C3
Somerset Av *HMLTN* ML3.....169 G1
Somerset Pl *KVGV* G3.....67 E5
Somerset Place Ms *KVGV* G3.....67 E5
Somervell St
  BLTYR/CAMB G72.....131 E1
Somerville Dr *EKILS* G75.....178 C1
  GVH/MTFL G42.....109 G4
Somerville La *EKILS* G75.....178 C1
Sorby St *DEN/PKHD* G31.....91 F4
Sorn St *DMNK/BRGTN* G40.....111 E1
Souterhouse Pth *CTBR* ML5.....96 C4
Souterhouse Rd *CTBR* ML5.....96 C4
Southampton Dr
  KVD/HLHD G12.....52 A5
Southampton La
  KVD/HLHD G12.....52 A5
South Annandale St
  GVH/MTFL G42.....109 G2
South Av *BLTYR/CAMB* G72.....151 H5
  CLYDBK G81.....48 D1
  PSLYS PA2.....104 C2
  RNFRW PA4.....63 H5
Southbank Av *EKILS* G75.....21 E5
Southbank Rd *KKNTL* G66.....39 G1
Southbank St *HMLTN* ML3.....153 E1
Southbar Av *KNTSWD* G13.....50 B4
Southbar Rd *ERSK* PA8.....47 G2
Southbrae Dr *KNTSWD* G13.....65 E1
South Barrowood Rd *KSYTH* G65.....8 D3
South Biggar Rd *AIRDRIE* ML6.....98 C2
South Brae *KKNTL* G66.....5 E1
Southbrae Av *BRWEIR* PA11.....79 F4
Southbrae Dr *KNTSWD* G13.....65 E2
Southbrae Gdns *KNTSWD* G13.....65 E1

Southbrae La KNTSWD G13....65 F1
South Bridge St AIRDRIE ML6....98 B1
South Burn Rd AIRDRIE ML6....97 G2
South Caldeen Rd CTBR ML5....97 F4
South Campbell St PSLYS PA2....104 B1
South Carbrain Rd
  CUMB G67....26 C5
South Chester St
  CAR/SHTL G32....92 B4
South Circular Rd CTBR ML5....96 D3
South Claremont La
  MLNGV G62....17 E4
South Commonhead Av
  AIRDRIE ML6....76 A5
Southcroft Rd RUTH G73....110 B3
Southcroft St GOV/IBX G51....88 A2
South Crosshill Rd
  BSHPBGS G64....54 D2
South Dean Park Av
  UD/BTH/TAN G71....134 B5
Southdeen Av DRUM G15....33 G5
Southdeen Rd DRUM G15....33 F5
South Douglas St CLYDBK G81....49 F3
South Dr PSLYN/LNWD PA3....82 A3
South Dumbreck Rd
  KSYTH G65....7 H2
Southend Pl CLYDBK G81....49 F4
South Elgin Pl CLYDBK G81....49 F4
South Elgin St CLYDBK G81....49 F4
Southend Pl BLSH ML4....135 G5
Southern Av RUTH G73....130 A2
Southerness Dr BALLOCH G68....13 H1
South Erskine Pk BSDN G61....34 A5
Southesk Av BSHPBGS G64....37 G5
South Exchange Ct CGLE G1....3 F6
Southfield CTBR ML5....97 F4
Southfield Av PSLYS PA2....104 B4
Southfield Crs CTBR ML5....97 F4
  PLK/PH/NH G53....106 D4
Southfield Rd BALLOCH G68....25 G4
South Frederick St CGLE G1....3 G6
Southgate EKILN G74....166 B5
  MLNGV G62....17 E4
South Glassford St
  MLNGV G62....17 F4
Southhill Av RUTH G73....130 B2
Southinch Av SCOT G14....49 H5
Southinch La SCOT G14....49 H5
Southlea Av GIF/THBK G46....126 D4
South Line Vw WISHAW ML2....173 F5
Southloch Gdns
  SPRGB/BLRNK G21....68 C3
Southloch St
  SPRGB/BLRNK G21....68 C3
South Mains Rd MLNGV G62....16 D4
South Medrox St CTBR ML5....59 H4
South Mound
  CRG/CRSL/HOU PA6....80 B1
South Muirhead Rd CUMB G67....26 C3
Southmuir Pl MRYH/FIRH G20....66 A1
South Nimmo St AIRDRIE ML6....98 C2
South Park Av
  BRHD/NEIL G78....124 A4
Southpark Av KVD/HLHD G12....66 D4
South Park Dr PSLYS PA2....104 B2
Southpark La KVD/HLHD G12....66 D4
South Park Rd HMLTN ML3....170 A4
South Pk BLSH ML4....135 G3
South Portland St GBLS G5....89 G4
South Rd
  CRMNK/CLK/EAG G76....146 B5
South Robertson Pl
  AIRDRIE ML6....97 H2
South Scott St
  BAIL/MDB/MHD G69....94 A5
Southside Crs GBLS G5....89 G5
South St CRG/CRSL/HOU PA6....80 C1
  RNFRW PA4....61 G2
  SCOT G14....64 B2
South Vesalius St
  CAR/SHTL G32....92 B4
South Vw CLYDBK G81....31 G5
  BLSH ML4....135 F3
  BLTYR/CAMB G72....151 F1
Southview BSDN G61....33 H3
Southview Av
  CRMNK/CLK/EAG G76....145 H5
Southview Ct BSHPBGS G64....54 C5
Southview Crs BRWEIR PA11....79 G2
Southview Dr BSDN G61....33 H3
Southview Pl
  BAIL/MDB/MHD G69....58 D5
Southview Ter BSHPBGS G64....54 C5
South William St JNSTN PA5....101 G4
Southwold Rd PSLY PA1....85 H4
Southwood Dr
  LNPK/KPK G44....128 D2
South Woodside Rd
  COWCAD G4....66 D4
  MRYH/FIRH G20....67 E3
Soutra Pl STPS/GTHM/RID G33....92 C1
Spairdrum Rd AIRDRIE ML6....45 E4
Spalehall Dr MTHW ML1....138 C4
Spateston Rd JNSTN PA5....120 D3
Spean Av EKILN G74....166 C3
Spean St LNPK/KPK G44....109 F5
Speirsfields Gdns PSLYS PA2....104 B1
Speirshall St SCOT G14....64 A1
Speirshall Ter SCOT G14....49 H5
Speirs Pl PSLYN/LNWD PA3....82 A3
Speirs Rd BSDN G61....34 D5
Spencer Dr PSLYS PA2....102 C5
Spencer Field Gdns
  HMLTN ML3....170 C2
Spencer St CLYDBK G81....31 H5
  KNTSWD G13....51 G4
Spey Av PSLYS PA2....102 D3
Speyburn Pl AIRDRIE ML6....76 B4
  STPS/GTHM/RID G33....57 F5
Spey Ct AIRDRIE ML6....98 C4
Spey Dr CTBR ML5....96 B5
  RNFRW PA4....63 H4
Spey Gdns HMLTN ML3....169 G5
Spey Pl JNSTN PA5....120 D1
Spey Rd BSDN G61....33 G5
Spey St STPS/GTHM/RID G33....92 A1
Spey Ter EKILS G75....177 E4

Spiersbridge Av
  GIF/THBK G46....126 C4
Spiersbridge La
  GIF/THBK G46....126 B4
Spiersbridge Rd
  GIF/THBK G46....126 C5
Spiersbridge Ter
  GIF/THBK G46....126 C5
Spiersbridge Wy
  GIF/THBK G46....126 C4
Spiers Gv GIF/THBK G46....126 C4
Spiers Rd
  CRG/CRSL/HOU PA6....80 C1
  JNSTN PA5....102 A1
Spindlehowe Rd
  UD/BTH/TAN G71....134 B1
Spindleside Rd MTHW ML1....157 G5
Spinners Gdns PSLYS PA2....103 G1
Spinners La CLYDBK G81....32 A1
Spittal Rd RUTH G73....129 H2
Spoolers Rd PSLY PA1....103 G1
Spoutmouth CGLE G1....3 J7
Springbank Crs HMLTN ML3....180 A1
  MTHW ML1....155 F1
Springbank Rd
  PSLYN/LNWD PA3....84 A2
Springbank St
  MRYH/FIRH G20....67 F2
Springbank Ter AIRDRIE ML6....77 G3
  PSLYN/LNWD PA3....84 A2
Springbank Vw AIRDRIE ML6....77 G3
Springboig Av CAR/SHTL G32....92 D5
Springboig Rd CAR/SHTL G32....92 D2
Springburn Pl EKILN G74....165 F2
Springburn Rd
  SPRGB/BLRNK G21....68 B4
Springburn Wy
  SPRGB/BLRNK G21....68 C2
Springcroft Av
  BAIL/MDB/MHD G69....94 A3
Springcroft Crs
  BAIL/MDB/MHD G69....94 A3
Springcroft Dr
  BAIL/MDB/MHD G69....93 H3
Springcroft Gdns
  BAIL/MDB/MHD G69....94 A3
Springcroft Gv
  BAIL/MDB/MHD G69....94 A3
Springcroft Rd
  BAIL/MDB/MHD G69....94 A3
Springcroft Wynd
  BAIL/MDB/MHD G69....94 A3
Springfield Av BSHPBGS G64....54 D5
  PSLY PA1....85 E3
  UD/BTH/TAN G71....134 A2
Springfield Ct CGLE G1....3 F6
Springfield Crs
  BLTYR/CAMB G72....151 F4
  BSHPBGS G64....54 D5
  UD/BTH/TAN G71....134 A2
Springfield Dr
  BRHD/NEIL G78....142 D1
Springfield Gv
  BRHD/NEIL G78....142 C2
Springfield Pk JNSTN PA5....101 H4
Springfield Park Rd
  RUTH G73....130 B1
Springfield Quay GBLS G5....2 A7
Springfield Rd AIRDRIE ML6....99 F1
  BRHD/NEIL G78....141 G3
  BSHPBGS G64....54 D5
  CUMB G67....26 C1
  DEN/PKHD G31....91 F5
  DMNK/BRGTN G40....111 E1
Springfield Sq BSHPBGS G64....54 D5
Springfield Woods JNSTN PA5....101 H4
Springhead Rd SHOTTS ML7....159 H2
Springhill Av AIRDRIE ML6....98 C1
  CTBR ML5....95 H5
Springhill Dr North
  BAIL/MDB/MHD G69....93 H2
Springhill Dr South
  BAIL/MDB/MHD G69....93 H3
Springhill Farm Gv
  BAIL/MDB/MHD G69....93 H3
Springhill Farm Pl
  BAIL/MDB/MHD G69....93 H3
Springhill Farm Rd
  BAIL/MDB/MHD G69....93 H3
Springhill Farm Wy
  BAIL/MDB/MHD G69....93 H3
Springhill Gdns
  PLKSD/SHW G41....108 D3
Springhill Pkwy
  BAIL/MDB/MHD G69....94 D1
Springhill Pl CTBR ML5....95 H5
Springhill Rd
  BAIL/MDB/MHD G69....93 G3
  BRHD/NEIL G78....141 H5
  CRMNK/CLK/EAG G76....146 A3
Springholm Dr AIRDRIE ML6....76 A4
Springkell Av
  PLKSD/SHW G41....108 A1
Springkell Dr
  PLKSD/SHW G41....108 A2
Springkell Gdns
  PLKSD/SHW G41....108 B2
Springkell Ga
  PLKSD/SHW G41....108 C2
Springside Gdns DRUM G15....33 F3
Springside Pl DRUM G15....33 F4
Springvale Dr PSLYS PA2....103 E2
Springvale Ter
  SPRGB/BLRNK G21....68 B2
Springwells Crs
  BLTYR/CAMB G72....152 A3
Springwells Av AIRDRIE ML6....98 D1
Springwells Crs AIRDRIE ML6....98 D1
Spring Wynd GBLS G5....89 H5
Spruce Av BLTYR/CAMB G72....151 F2
  HMLTN ML3....170 A1
  JNSTN PA5....101 H5
Spruce Ct HMLTN ML3....170 B4
Spruce Dr BLTYR/CAMB G72....151 F2
  KKNTL G66....39 F3
Spruce Rd CUMB G67....27 F1
  UD/BTH/TAN G71....115 H3
Spruce St PPK/MIL G22....68 A1
Spruce Wy BLTYR/CAMB G72....132 C5
Squire St SCOT G14....65 E4

Stable Gv PSLY PA1....103 G1
  PSLY PA1....83 G5
Stable Pl MLNGV G62....16 D2
Stable Rd MLNGV G62....16 D2
Staffa EKILN G74....167 F5
Staffa Av RNFRW PA4....63 F5
Staffa Dr AIRDRIE ML6....99 G2
  KKNTL G66....22 B5
Staffa Pl PSLYS PA2....104 B5
Staffa Rd BLTYR/CAMB G72....131 E4
Staffa St DEN/PKHD G31....91 E1
Staffin Pl SMSTN G23....52 C2
Staffin St SMSTN G23....52 D2
Staffin St BLSH ML4....135 G3
  COWCAD G4....H2
Stag Ct UD/BTH/TAN G71....134 D1
Stag St GOV/IBX G51....88 A2
Staig Wynd MTHW ML1....172 B5
Staineybraes Pl AIRDRIE ML6....76 A4
Stalker St WISHAW ML2....172 D1
Stamford Ga DEN/PKHD G31....91 F4
Stamford Pl DEN/PKHD G31....91 E4
Stamford Rd DEN/PKHD G31....91 E4
Stamford St DEN/PKHD G31....91 E4
Stamperland Av
  CRMNK/CLK/EAG G76....146 A2
Stamperland Gdns
  CRMNK/CLK/EAG G76....146 A3
Stamperland Hl
  CRMNK/CLK/EAG G76....145 H2
Stanalane St GIF/THBK G46....126 C3
Standburn Rd
  SPRGB/BLRNK G21....55 G5
Staneacre Pk HMLTN ML3....170 C2
Stanecraigs Pl WISHAW ML2....158 A4
Stanefield Dr MTHW ML1....138 B3
Stanely Av PSLYS PA2....103 G3
Stanely Crs PSLYS PA2....103 H3
Stanely Dr PSLYS PA2....103 H3
Stanely Gra PSLYS PA2....103 G4
Stanely Rd PSLYS PA2....103 H3
Stanford St CLYDBK G81....49 F2
Stanhope Dr RUTH G73....130 C2
Stanhope Pl WISHAW ML2....173 H5
Stanley Bvd BLTYR/CAMB G72....168 C1
Stanley Dr BLSH ML4....135 H1
  BSHPBGS G64....55 E1
  JNSTN PA5....100 D1
Stanley La JNSTN PA5....100 D1
Stanley Pl BLTYR/CAMB G72....151 G1
Stanley St HMLTN ML3....169 E1
  PLKSD/SHW G41....88 D4
Stanley Street La
  PLKSD/SHW G41....88 D4
Stanmore Rd GVH/MTFL G42....109 G4
Stanrigg St AIRDRIE ML6....78 A1
Stark Av CLYDBK G81....31 F2
Starling Wy BLSH ML4....116 B4
Startpoint St
  STPS/GTHM/RID G33....92 B1
Station Brae BRHD/NEIL G78....140 D2
Station Rd RNFRW PA4....63 H2
Station Pk
  BAIL/MDB/MHD G69....94 B5
Station Rd AIRDRIE ML6....94 B5
  BAIL/MDB/MHD G69....94 B5
  BLTYR/CAMB G72....151 E4
  BRHD/NEIL G78....141 E3
  BSDN G61....34 A3
  BSHPTN PA7....46 A1
  CRMNK/CLK/EAG G76....146 B5
  DMBTN G82....12 D3
  GIF/THBK G46....126 D4
  KKNTL G66....40 A4
  KLBCH PA10....100 B4
  KSYTH G65....8 B1
  MLNGV G62....36 B1
  MTHW ML1....157 E1
  MTHW ML1....137 G4
  OLDK G60....30 C2
  PSLY PA1....84 D5
  RNFRW PA4....63 H2
  STPS/GTHM/RID G33....70 B1
  UD/BTH/TAN G71....133 H1
  WISHAW ML2....173 H3
Station Wynd KLBCH PA10....100 C4
Staybrae Dr PLK/PH/NH G53....106 A3
Staybrae Gv PLK/PH/NH G53....106 A3
The Steading WISHAW ML2....157 F5
Steel Pl WISHAW ML2....173 F5
Steel St CGLE G1....90 A3
  WISHAW ML2....174 A3
Steeple St KLBCH PA10....100 B3
Stenhouse Av
  BAIL/MDB/MHD G69....58 B4
Stenton Crs WISHAW ML2....173 E4
Stenton Pl WISHAW ML2....173 E4
Stenton St CAR/SHTL G32....91 H2
Stenzel Pl STPS/GTHM/RID G33....71 G1
Stepford Pl
  STPS/GTHM/RID G33....93 G2
Stepford Rd
  STPS/GTHM/RID G33....93 H2
Stephen Crs
  BAIL/MDB/MHD G69....93 G4
Stephenson Pl EKILS G75....166 A5
Stephenson St
  CARD/HILL/MSPK G52....85 H1
Stepps Rd KKNTL G66....57 F1
  STPS/GTHM/RID G33....70 D5
Stevenson Pl BLSH ML4....117 G5
Stevenson St CLYDBK G81....31 H3
  DMNK/BRGTN G40....90 B4
  PSLYS PA2....104 B1
Stevenston Ct MTHW ML1....137 F3
Stevenston St MTHW ML1....137 F3
Stewart Av BLTYR/CAMB G72....151 F2
  HMLTN ML3....180 A1
  NMRNS G77....144 B4
  RNFRW PA4....63 E5
Stewart Ct BRHD/NEIL G78....124 B3
Stewart Crs BRHD/NEIL G78....124 C3

WISHAW ML2....158 B4
Stewart Dr
  BAIL/MDB/MHD G69....95 G3
  CLYDBK G81....32 A2
  CRMNK/CLK/EAG G76....145 G2
Stewartfield Crs EKILN G74....165 H2
Stewartfield Dr EKILN G74....166 A1
Stewartfield Rd EKILN G74....165 H2
Stewartfield Wy EKILN G74....165 E1
Stewarton Dr
  BLTYR/CAMB G72....131 E4
Stewarton Rd NMRNS G77....143 H3
Stewarton St WISHAW ML2....174 B3
Stewart Pl BRHD/NEIL G78....124 C3
Stewart Qd MTHW ML1....137 G1
Stewart Rd PSLYS PA2....104 C4
Stewarts La WISHAW ML2....174 B2
Stewart St BLSH ML4....136 C2
  BRHD/NEIL G78....124 C3
  CGLE G1....31 F5
  COWCAD G4....2 C1
  CTBR ML5....96 D1
  HMLTN ML3....152 D1
  MLNGV G62....17 E3
Stewartville St PTCK G11....66 A4
Stirling Av BSDN G61....51 G3
  EKILN G74....166 D2
Stirling Dr BSDN G61....33 H2
  BSHPBGS G64....54 A1
  HMLTN ML3....168 D1
  JNSTN PA5....101 E4
  RUTH G73....130 A2
Stirlingfauld Pl GBLS G5....89 G5
Stirling Gdns BSHPBGS G64....37 F5
Stirling Rd AIRDRIE ML6....99 E5
  AIRDRIE ML6....45 F4
  COWCAD G4....3 G2
  DMBTN G82....13 G3
  KSYTH G65....H2
Stirling St AIRDRIE ML6....98 A2
  CTBR ML5....96 A5
  CUMB G67....26 D1
  MTHW ML1....172 C1
Stirrat St MRYH/FIRH G20....52 B5
  PSLYN/LNWD PA3....83 G2
Stobcross Rd KVGV G3....88 E1
Stobcross St CTBR ML5....96 B4
Stobcross Wynd KVGV G3....88 B1
Stobhill Rd SPRGB/BLRNK G21....54 C4
Stobo EKILN G74....167 F1
Stobo Ct EKILN G74....167 F1
Stobo St WISHAW ML2....157 F5
Stobs Dr BRHD/NEIL G78....124 A3
Stock Av PSLYS PA2....104 B1
Stockholm Crs PSLYS PA2....104 B1
Stockiemuir Av BSDN G61....34 B1
Stockiemuir Rd BSDN G61....16 A4
Stock St PSLYS PA2....104 B2
Stockwell Pl CGLE G1....3 F7
Stockwell St CGLE G1....89 H3
Stonebank Gv CSMK G45....129 E4
Stonebyres Ct HMLTN ML3....169 G3
Stonecraig Rd WISHAW ML2....174 B3
Stonedyke Gv DRUM G15....50 C1
Stonefield Av KVD/HLHD G12....52 A5
  PSLYS PA2....104 C3
Stonefield Crs
  BLTYR/CAMB G72....151 F4
  CRMNK/CLK/EAG G76....145 F2
  PSLYS PA2....104 C3
Stonefield Dr PSLYS PA2....104 C3
Stonefield Gdns PSLYS PA2....104 C3
Stonefield Pk PSLYS PA2....104 B3
Stonefield Park Gdns
  BLTYR/CAMB G72....151 H2
Stonefield Pl
  BLTYR/CAMB G72....151 F3
Stonefield Rd
  BLTYR/CAMB G72....151 F3
Stonefield St AIRDRIE ML6....76 B5
Stonehall Av HMLTN ML3....169 G3
Stonehaven Crs AIRDRIE ML6....97 H4
Stonelaw Dr RUTH G73....111 E5
Stonelaw Rd RUTH G73....111 E5
Stoneside Dr
  PLKSW/MSWD G43....127 E1
Stoneside Sq
  PLKSW/MSWD G43....126 D1
Stoney Brae PSLYN/LNWD PA3....84 B4
  PSLYS PA2....104 B4
Stoneyetts Rd
  BAIL/MDB/MHD G69....59 E1
Stoneymeadow Rd
  BLTYR/CAMB G72....150 C5
  EKILN G74....149 G5
Stonyflatt Av DMBTN G82....13 G2
Stonyflatt Rd DMBTN G82....13 G2
Stonyhurst St PPK/MIL G22....67 H2
Stonylee Rd CUMB G67....26 C4
Storie St PSLY PA1....84 B5
Stormyland Wy
  BRHD/NEIL G78....124 B5
Stornoway Crs WISHAW ML2....174 D1
Stornoway St PPK/MIL G22....53 H4
Stow Brae PSLY PA1....104 B1
Stow St PSLY PA1....84 B5
Strachan Pl BLTYR/CAMB G72....168 C2
Strachur Crs PPK/MIL G22....53 F4
Strachur Gdns PPK/MIL G22....53 F4
Strachur St PPK/MIL G22....53 F4
Strain Crs AIRDRIE ML6....98 C3
Straiton Dr HMLTN ML3....168 C3
Straiton Pl
  STPS/GTHM/RID G33....91 H2
Stranka Av PSLYS PA2....103 H1
Stranraer Dr DRUM G15....50 D1
Stratford EKILN G74....166 C2
Stratford St MRYH/FIRH G20....66 D1
Strathallan Av EKILS G75....165 F5
Strathallan Ga EKILS G75....165 F5
Strathallan Wynd EKILS G75....165 F4
Strathallon Pl RUTH G73....130 C4
Strathaven Rd EKILN G74....166 D5
  EKILS G75....179 E3
  HMLTN ML3....180 B5
Strathavon Crs AIRDRIE ML6....76 B4

Strathblane Crs AIRDRIE ML6....76 B3
Strathblane Dr EKILS G75....164 D5
Strathblane Gdns
  KNTSWD G13....51 G3
Strathblane Rd MLNGV G62....17 F3
Strathbran St DEN/PKHD G31....91 G5
Strathbrock Rd AIRDRIE ML6....76 B3
Strathcairn Crs PSLYS PA2....105 F3
Strathcarron Dr PSLYS PA2....105 F3
Strathcarron Crs
  MRYH/FIRH G20....66 C1
Strathcarron Gv PSLYS PA2....105 E4
Strathcarron Pl PSLYS PA2....105 E4
  MRYH/FIRH G20....66 C1
Strathcarron Rd PSLYS PA2....105 F3
Strathcarron Wy PSLYS PA2....105 F3
Strathclyde Gdns
  BLTYR/CAMB G72....132 B4
Strathclyde Rd DMBTN G82....154 A4
  MTHW ML1....154 A4
Strathclyde St
  DMNK/BRGTN G40....110 D2
Strathclyde Vw
  UD/BTH/TAN G71....152 C1
Strathclyde Wy BLSH ML4....117 F5
Strathcona Dr KNTSWD G13....51 G4
Strathcona Gdns KNTSWD G13....51 H4
Strathcona La EKILS G75....178 B3
Strathcona Pl EKILS G75....178 B3
  RUTH G73....130 C2
Strathcona St KNTSWD G13....51 G5
Strathcorn Gdns EKILS G75....164 D5
Strathdearn Gv EKILS G75....164 D5
Strathdee Av CLYDBK G81....32 A2
Strathdee Rd LNPK/KPK G44....127 H5
Strathdon Av LNPK/KPK G44....127 H5
  PSLYS PA2....103 H1
Strathdon Dr LNPK/KPK G44....128 A5
Strathdon Pl EKILS G75....164 D5
Strathearn Gv KKNTL G66....22 A1
Strathearn Rd
  CRMNK/CLK/EAG G76....145 H4
Strathendrick Dr
  PLKSW/MSWD G43....127 H3
Strathfillan Rd EKILN G74....166 A3
Strathgoil Crs AIRDRIE ML6....76 B3
Strathgryffe Crs BRWEIR PA11....79 F2
Strathhalladale Ct EKILS G75....164 D5
Strathisla Wy MTHW ML1....137 G5
Strathkelvin Av BSHPBGS G64....54 A4
Strathkelvin La EKILS G75....164 D5
Strathmiglo Ct EKILS G75....164 D5
Strathmore Av
  BLTYR/CAMB G72....151 F1
  PSLY PA1....105 F1
Strathmore Crs AIRDRIE ML6....76 B3
Strathmore Gdns RUTH G73....130 C3
Strathmore Gv EKILS G75....164 D5
Strathmore Pl CTBR ML5....97 G4
Strathmore Rd HMLTN ML3....170 B2
  PPK/MIL G22....53 G4
Strathmungo Crs
  AIRDRIE ML6....76 A4
Strathnairn Av EKILS G75....164 D5
Strathnairn Ct EKILS G75....164 D5
Strathnairn Dr EKILS G75....164 D5
Strathnairn Wy EKILS G75....164 D5
Strathnaver Crs AIRDRIE ML6....76 A3
Strathnaver Gdns EKILS G75....164 D5
Strathord Pl
  BAIL/MDB/MHD G69....42 B5
Strathord St CAR/SHTL G32....112 B1
Strathpeffer Crs AIRDRIE ML6....76 B3
Strathrannoch Wy EKILS G75....164 D5
Strathspey Av EKILS G75....164 D5
Strathspey Crs AIRDRIE ML6....76 B3
Strathtay Av EKILS G75....164 D5
  LNPK/KPK G44....127 H5
Strathtummel Crs
  AIRDRIE ML6....76 B3
Strathview Gv
  LNPK/KPK G44....127 H5
Strathview Pk
  LNPK/KPK G44....127 H5
Strathview Rd BLSH ML4....135 G4
Strathvithie Gv EKILS G75....164 D5
Strathyre Gdns AIRDRIE ML6....76 A1
  BSDN G61....35 E3
  EKILS G75....164 D5
Strathyre Rd
  BLTYR/CAMB G72....151 H4
Strathyre St PLKSD/SHW G41....108 D4
Stratton Dr GIF/THBK G46....127 E1
Strauss Av CLYDBK G81....49 H2
Stravaig Pth PSLYS PA2....103 E5
Stravaig Wk PSLYS PA2....103 F5
Stravanan Av CSMK G45....129 E5
Stravanan Gdns CSMK G45....129 E5
Stravanan Pl CSMK G45....129 E5
Stravanan Rd CSMK G45....128 D5
Stravanan St CSMK G45....129 E5
Strawberry Field Rd
  CRG/CRSL/HOU PA6....80 C2
Strawhill Rd
  CRMNK/CLK/EAG G76....145 H5
Streamfield Gdns
  STPS/GTHM/RID G33....55 H4
Streamfield Ga
  STPS/GTHM/RID G33....55 G4
Streamfield Lea
  STPS/GTHM/RID G33....55 H3
Streamfield Pl
  STPS/GTHM/RID G33....55 H4
Strenabey Av RUTH G73....130 C3
Striven Crs WISHAW ML2....173 H3
Striven Gdns MRYH/FIRH G20....67 E3
Striven Ter HMLTN ML3....169 F4
Stroma St SPRGB/BLRNK G21....69 F4
Stromness St GBLS G5....89 F5
Stronend St PPK/MIL G22....53 G4
Stronsay Pl KKNTL G66....22 A1
  SPRGB/BLRNK G21....69 G4
Stronvar Dr SCOT G14....64 C2
Stroud Rd EKILS G75....177 H3
Strowan Crs CAR/SHTL G32....92 C5

Strowan's Rd DMBTN G82.....13 H4
Strowan St CAR/SHTL G32.....92 C5
Strowan's Well Rd DMBTN G82.13 H4
Struan Av GIF/THBK G46.....127 H4
Struan Gdns LNPK/KPK G44.....128 B2
Struan Rd LNPK/KPK G44.....128 B2
Strule St ESTRH G34.....93 H1
Struma Dr
  CRMNK/CLK/EAG G76.....145 E1
Struthers Crs EKILN G74.....167 E1
Stuart Av OLDK G60.....30 C2
  RUTH G73.....130 A2
Stuart Dr BSHPBGS G64.....54 B3
Stuarton Pk EKILN G74.....166 B3
Stuart Rd WISHAW ML2.....173 H4
Stuart Rd BSHPTN PA7.....29 E4
  CRMNK/CLK/EAG G76.....147 E1
  DMBTN G82.....13 H3
Stuart St EKILN G74.....166 C3
  OLDK G60.....30 C3
Succoth St KNTSWD G13.....51 G4
Sudbury Crs EKILS G75.....165 G4
Sugworth Av
  CRMNK/CLK/EAG G76.....145 G4
Suilnish ERSK PA8.....47 H4
Sumburgh St
  STPS/GTHM/RID G33.....92 A2
Summerfield Rd CUMB G67.....45 H2
Summerfield St
  DMNK/BRGTN G40.....111 E2
Summerhill Dr DRUM G15.....33 G4
Summerhill Gdns DRUM G15.....33 G4
Summerhill & Garngibbock Rd
  CUMB G67.....44 C5
Summerhill PI DRUM G15.....33 G4
Summerhill Rd
  CRMNK/CLK/EAG G76.....146 A5
  DRUM G15.....33 G4
Summerlea Rd GIF/THBK G46.146 C6
Summerlee St WISHAW ML2.172 D1
Summerlee St CTBR ML5.....96 D2
  STPS/GTHM/RID G33.....90 C4
Summer St DMNK/BRGTN G40.90 C4
Summertown Rd GOV/IBX G51.88 A2
Sunart Av RNFRW PA4.....63 E2
Sunart Gdns BSHPBGS G64.....55 F2
Sunart Rd BSHPBGS G64.....55 F2
  CARD/HILL/MSPK G52.....87 E3
Sunart St WISHAW ML2.....173 H4
Sunbury Av
  CRMNK/CLK/EAG G76.....145 F3
Sundale Av
  CRMNK/CLK/EAG G76.....145 G4
Sunderland Av DMBTN G82.....12 B3
Sunflower Gdns MTHW ML1.154 C2
Sunningdale Av NMRNS G77.144 C5
Sunningdale Dr BRWEIR PA11.79 F3
Sunningdale Rd SMSTN G23.....52 C3
Sunningdale Wynd
  UD/BTH/TAN G71.....133 H4
Sunnybank Dr
  CRMNK/CLK/EAG G76.....145 G4
Sunnybank Gv
  CRMNK/CLK/EAG G76.....145 G4
Sunnyhill KSYTH G65.....23 F2
Sunnylaw Dr PLSYS PA2.....103 G2
Sunnylaw St PPK/MIL G22.....67 H2
Sunnyside Av MTHW ML1.....137 G3
  UD/BTH/TAN G71.....134 A3
Sunnyside Crs MTHW ML1.137 G3
Sunnyside Dr
  BAIL/MDB/MHD G69.....95 E4
  CRMNK/CLK/EAG G76.....145 G2
  DRUM G15.....50 B2
Sunnyside Ga MTHW ML1.....137 G3
Sunnyside Ov PLSYS PA2.....104 B3
  DRUM G15.....50 B2
  MTHW ML1.....137 F2
Sunnyside Rd CTBR ML5.....137 F2
  HMLTN ML3.....181 G4
  MTHW ML1.....157 F2
  PLSYS PA2.....104 A3
Surrey La GBLS G5.....89 G5
Surrey St GBLS G5.....89 G5
Sussex St PLKSD/SHW G41.....88 B4
Sutcliffe Ct KNTSWD G13.....51 F4
Sutcliffe Rd KNTSWD G13.....51 G4
Sutherland Av BSDN G61.....34 B1
  PLKSD/SHW G41.....108 B1
Sutherland Crs HMLTN ML3.169 F1
Sutherland Dr AIRDRIE ML6.....98 A4
  KVD/HLHD G12.....66 C4
Sutherland La
  KVD/HLHD G12.....66 C4
Sutherland St
  BLTYR/CAMB G72.....151 F5
  PSLY PA1.....84 A4
Sutherland Wy EKILN G74.167 F2
Sutherness Dr
  STPS/GTHM/RID G33.....92 B2
Swaledale EKILN G74.....165 H2
Swallow Dr JNSTN PA5.....120 D2
Swallow Gdns KNTSWD G13.....50 A4
Swallow Rd CLYDBK G81.....32 A1
  WISHAW ML2.....174 A2
Swan PI JNSTN PA5.....120 D2
Swanston St
  DMNK/BRGTN G40.....110 D2
Swan St CLYDBK G81.....31 G5
  COWCAD G4.....3 G1
Sween Av LNPK/KPK G44.....128 B4
Sween Dr HMLTN ML3.....169 F4
Sweethope Gdns
  UD/BTH/TAN G71.....134 C5
Sweethope PI
  UD/BTH/TAN G71.....134 B4
Swift Bank HMLTN ML3.....168 D4
Swift Crs KNTSWD G13.....50 A3
Swift PI EKILS G75.....176 D2
  JNSTN PA5.....120 D2
Swinstie Ct CLYDBK G81.....31 F5
Swinstie Rd MTHW ML1.....157 F1
Swinstie Vw MTHW ML1.....157 F1
Swinton Av
  BAIL/MDB/MHD G69.....94 C4

Swinton Crs
  BAIL/MDB/MHD G69.....94 B4
  CTBR ML5.....95 C5
Swinton Dr
  CARD/HILL/MSPK G52.....86 C4
Swinton Gdns
  BAIL/MDB/MHD G69.....94 C4
Swinton Pth
  BAIL/MDB/MHD G69.....94 C4
Swinton PI
  CARD/HILL/MSPK G52.....86 C4
Swinton Rd
  BAIL/MDB/MHD G69.....94 B4
Swinton Vw
  BAIL/MDB/MHD G69.....94 B4
Swisscot Av HMLTN ML3.....169 G5
Swisscot Wk HMLTN ML3.....169 G5
Switchback Rd BSDN G61.....51 G2
Swordale PI ESTRH G34.....93 H1
Sword St AIRDRIE ML6.....98 A2
  DEN/PKHD G31.....90 C3
Sycamore Av JNSTN PA5.....101 H5
  KKNTL G66.....40 A3
  UD/BTH/TAN G71.....115 H5
Sycamore Ct EKILS G75.....178 A2
Sycamore Crs AIRDRIE ML6.....99 E3
  EKILS G75.....178 A2
Sycamore Dr AIRDRIE ML6.....99 E3
  CLYDBK G81.....31 G4
  HMLTN ML3.....170 C3
Sycamore Gv
  BLTYR/CAMB G72.....151 F2
Sycamore PI EKILS G75.....178 A2
  MTHW ML1.....137 H4
Sycamore Wy
  BLTYR/CAMB G72.....132 C5
  CRMNK/CLK/EAG G76.....147 E5
Sydenham La KVD/HLHD G12.....66 B3
Sydney Dr EKILS G75.....177 H1
Sydney PI EKILS G75.....165 H5
Sydney St CLYDBK G81.....31 E4
  DEN/PKHD G31.....90 B3
Sykehead Av BLSH ML4.....136 A2
Sykeside Rd AIRDRIE ML6.....97 H5
Symington Dr CLYDBK G81.....48 D1
Syriam PI SPRGB/BLRNK G21.....68 C1
Syriam St SPRGB/BLRNK G21.....68 C1

T

Tabard PI KNTSWD G13.....50 D1
Tabard Rd KNTSWD G13.....50 D1
Tabernacle La
  BLTYR/CAMB G72.....131 F2
Tabernacle St
  BLTYR/CAMB G72.....131 F2
Taggart Rd KSYTH G65.....24 D2
Taig Rd KKNTL G66.....41 E1
Tain Ter BLTYR/CAMB G72.168 B2
Tait Av BRHD/NEIL G78.....124 C3
Talbot EKILN G74.....167 F1
Talbot Ct KNTSWD G13.....64 C1
Talbot Crs CTBR ML5.....116 B1
Talbot Dr KNTSWD G13.....64 C1
Talbot PI KNTSWD G13.....64 C1
Talbot Ter KNTSWD G13.....64 C1
  UD/BTH/TAN G71.....114 D4
Talisman Av DMBTN G82.....12 B5
Talisman Crs MTHW ML1.....136 C5
Talisman Rd KNTSWD G13.....64 C1
  PSLYS PA2.....102 D5
Tallant Rd DRUM G15.....33 G5
Tallant Ter DRUM G15.....33 H5
Talla Rd CARD/HILL/MSPK G52.86 C4
Tamarack Crs
  UD/BTH/TAN G71.....115 H3
Tamar Dr EKILS G75.....177 E2
Tambowie Av MLNGV G62.....16 D3
Tambowie Crs MLNGV G62.....16 D3
Tambowie St MRYH/FIRH G20.51 F4
Tanar Av RNFRW PA4.....64 A5
Tandlehill Rd KLBCH PA10.....100 B5
Tanera Av LNPK/KPK G44.....128 D3
Tanfield PI CAR/SHTL G32.....92 D2
Tanfield St CAR/SHTL G32.....92 D2
Tankerland Rd
  LNPK/KPK G44.....128 B1
Tannadice Av
  CARD/HILL/MSPK G52.....106 D1
Tanna Dr
  CARD/HILL/MSPK G52.....107 G1
Tannahill Crs JNSTN PA5.....121 F1
Tannahill Dr EKILN G74.....167 F2
Tannahill Rd
  PLKSW/MSWD G43.....108 B1
  PSLYN/LNWD PA3.....83 G3
Tannahill Ter
  PSLYN/LNWD PA3.....83 G3
Tannoch Dr CUMB G67.....45 E1
  MLNGV G62.....16 D3
Tannoch PI CUMB G67.....45 E1
Tannochside Dr
  UD/BTH/TAN G71.....115 G3
Tannock St PPK/MIL G22.....67 G2
Tantallon Dr CTBR ML5.....73 H5
  PSLYS PA2.....103 F3
Tantallon PK EKILN G74.....166 A3
Tantallon Rd
  BAIL/MDB/MHD G69.....113 H1
  PLKSD/SHW G41.....108 D5
Tanzieknowe Av
  BLTYR/CAMB G72.....131 G3
Tanzieknowe Dr
  BLTYR/CAMB G72.....131 G4
Tanzieknowe PI
  BLTYR/CAMB G72.....131 F4
Tanzieknowe Rd
  BLTYR/CAMB G72.....131 F4
Taransay St GOV/IBX G51.....87 H1
Tarbert Av BLTYR/CAMB G72.151 H3
  WISHAW ML2.....173 H4
Tarbert Ct HMLTN ML3.....169 F4
Tarbert Wy CTBR ML5.....96 B5
Tarbolton EKILN G74.....167 G2
Tarbolton Crs AIRDRIE ML6.119 E3

Tarbolton Dr CLYDBK G81.....32 B5
Tarbolton Rd CUMB G67.....26 D3
  PLKSW/MSWD G43.....127 G1
Tarbrax Wy HMLTN ML3.....169 F2
Tarfside Av
  CARD/HILL/MSPK G52.....87 E5
Tarfside Gdns
  CARD/HILL/MSPK G52.....87 E5
Tarfside Ov
  CARD/HILL/MSPK G52.....107 E1
Target Rd AIRDRIE ML6.....98 C5
Tarland St GOV/IBX G51.....87 G3
Tarn Gv STPS/GTHM/RID G33.....69 H5
Tarquin PI MTHW ML1.....154 B2
Tarras Dr RNFRW PA4.....63 H5
Tarsan Dr EKILS G75.....177 G1
Tasmania Qd WISHAW ML2.174 D2
Tassie PI EKILN G74.....166 D3
Tassie St PLKSD/SHW G41.....108 C4
Tattershall Rd
  STPS/GTHM/RID G33.....70 D4
Tavistock Dr
  PLKSW/MSWD G43.....127 G2
Tay Av RNFRW PA4.....63 H3
Tay Ct EKILS G75.....164 D5
Tay Crs BSHPBGS G64.....55 E2
  STPS/GTHM/RID G33.....69 H5
Tay Gv EKILS G75.....164 D5
Taylor Av KLBCH PA10.....100 A3
  MTHW ML1.....138 A5
Taylor PI COWCAD G4.....3 J4
Taylor St CLYDBK G81.....49 G3
  COWCAD G4.....3 J5
Taymouth St CAR/SHTL G32.112 C1
Taynish Dr LNPK/KPK G44.....128 D3
Tay PI EKILS G75.....176 D1
  JNSTN PA5.....120 D1
Tay Rd BSDN G61.....51 E1
  BSHPBGS G64.....55 E2
Tayside AIRDRIE ML6.....76 A5
Tay St CTBR ML5.....73 G4
Tay Ter EKILS G75.....164 D5
Teak PI UD/BTH/TAN G71.....116 A3
Teal Ct BLSH ML4.....116 B4
Teal Crs EKILS G75.....177 E3
Teal Dr KNTSWD G13.....50 B4
Tealing Av
  CARD/HILL/MSPK G52.....86 D5
Tealing Crs
  CARD/HILL/MSPK G52.....86 D5
Teasel Av PLK/PH/NH G53.125 C4
Teawell Rd NMRNS G77.....144 A5
Technology Av
  EKILN G74.....168 B1
Teesdale EKILN G74.....165 H2
Teign Cv EKILS G75.....177 E2
Teith Av RNFRW PA4.....64 A4
Teith Dr BSDN G61.....33 H5
Teith St STPS/GTHM/RID G33.....69 H5
Telephone La KVD/HLHD G12.66 B4
Telford PI CUMB G67.....45 F1
Telford Rd CUMB G67.....26 C5
  EKILS G75.....166 B5
Telford St BLSH ML4.....116 A5
Teme PI EKILS G75.....177 E1
Templar Vw KNTSWD G13.....51 G4
Temple Gdns KNTSWD G13.....51 G4
Templeland Rd
  PLK/PH/NH G53.....106 D2
Temple Locks Ct KNTSWD G13.51 G4
Temple Locks PI KNTSWD G13.51 G4
Temple Rd KNTSWD G13.....51 H4
Templeton Ct
  DMNK/BRGTN G40.....90 B4
Templeton St
  DMNK/BRGTN G40.....90 B4
Tennant Av EKILN G74.....165 F4
Tennant St RNFRW PA4.....63 G2
Tennant Wynd BLSH ML4.....116 D4
Tennent St CTBR ML5.....97 E4
Tennyson Dr DEN/PKHD G31.91 H5
Tennyson Gdns
  BLTYR/CAMB G72.....151 G3
Tenters Wy PLSYS PA2.....103 G1
Tern PI JNSTN PA5.....121 E2
Tern Wy CTBR ML5.....117 H1
Terregles Av PLKSD/SHW G41.108 B2
Terregles Crs PLKSD/SHW G41.108 B2
Terregles Dr PLKSD/SHW G41.108 B2
Teviot Av BSHPBGS G64.....37 H5
  PSLYS PA2.....102 C4
Teviot Crs BSDN G61.....51 G1
Teviot Dr BSHPTN PA7.....46 B1
Teviot St CTBR ML5.....74 A4
  KVGV G3.....88 C1
Teviot Ter JNSTN PA5.....120 D1
Tewkesbury Rd EKILN G74.150 C4
Thane Rd KNTSWD G13.....50 D5
Thanes Ga UD/BTH/TAN G71.133 H2
Thankerton Av MTHW ML1.137 E2
Tharsis St SPRGB/BLRNK G21.68 C5
Third Av DMBTN G82.....13 H5
  KNTL G66.....57 E2
  LNPK/KPK G44.....109 G5
  RNFRW PA4.....63 H4
  STPS/GTHM/RID G33.....70 C1
Third Gdns PLKSD/SHW G41.88 A5
Thirdpart Crs KNTSWD G13.49 H4
Third Rd BLTYR/CAMB G72.151 H5
Thirlmere EKILS G75.....177 E3
Thistle Bank KKNTL G66.....40 A1
Thistledown Gv CTBR ML5.116 B3
Thistle Gdns MTHW ML1.....137 H1
Thistle Neuk OLDK G60.....30 C3
Thistle PI EKILN G74.....166 A2
Thistle Qd AIRDRIE ML6.....76 C5
Thistle St AIRDRIE ML6.....98 A2
  GBLS G5.....89 G5
  KKNTL G66.....21 E5
  MTHW ML1.....137 H1
  PSLYS PA2.....103 H2
Thistle Ter GBLS G5.....89 G5
Thomas Muir Av BSHPBGS G64.54 D3
Thomas St PSLY PA1.....83 G5
Thompson Brae PSLYS PA2.104 B2
Thompson PI CLYDBK G81.....32 B2
Thompson St DEN/PKHD G31.90 D3

Thomson Av JNSTN PA5.....101 F3
  KKNTL G66.....21 G5
  WISHAW ML2.....173 F3
Thomson Dr AIRDRIE ML6.....98 A3
  BLSH ML4.....135 G2
  BSDN G61.....34 C2
Thomson Gv
  BLTYR/CAMB G72.....112 B5
Thomson St JNSTN PA5.....101 F4
  RNFRW PA4.....63 F4
Thorn Av KEILN G74.....164 B2
Thornbank St KVGV G3.....88 B1
Thorn Brae JNSTN PA5.....101 H5
Thornbridge Av
  BAIL/MDB/MHD G69.....94 A4
  KVD/HLHD G12.....66 B1
Thornbridge Gdns
  BAIL/MDB/MHD G69.....93 H4
Thornbridge Rd
  BAIL/MDB/MHD G69.....93 H4
Thorncliffe Gdns
  PLKSD/SHW G41.....108 D2
Thornden Dr LNPK/KPK G44.129 E3
Thorndean Av BLSH ML4.....136 A3
Thorndean Crs BLSH ML4.....136 A3
Thorndene AIRDRIE ML6.....102 A1
Thorndene Av MTHW ML1.....137 F1
Thornden La SCOT G14.....64 B2
Thorn Dr BSDN G61.....34 A3
  RUTH G73.....130 A3
Thorndyke EKILN G74.....149 H5
Thornhill JNSTN PA5.....101 H4
Thornhill Av
  BLTYR/CAMB G72.....151 G2
  JNSTN PA5.....102 A2
Thornhill Dr JNSTN PA5.....102 A2
Thornhill Gdns JNSTN PA5.101 H3
  NMRNS G77.....161 G3
Thornhill Rd HMLTN ML3.....168 D1
Thorniecroft Dr CUMB G67.....44 D5
Thorniecroft PI CUMB G67.....44 D5
Thorniecroft Rd CUMB G67.....44 B2
Thorniewood Gdns
  UD/BTH/TAN G71.....115 E4
Thorniewood Rd
  UD/BTH/TAN G71.....115 E4
Thornkip PI CTBR ML5.....97 G4
Thornlea Dr GIF/THBK G46.127 G3
Thornley Av KNTSWD G13.....50 C5
Thornliebank Rd
  PLKSW/MSWD G43.....127 G2
Thornlie Gill WISHAW ML2.174 A3
Thornly Park Av PSLYS PA2.104 B4
Thornly Park Dr PSLYS PA2.104 B4
Thornly Park Rd PSLYS PA2.104 A4
Thorn Rd BLSH ML4.....136 A2
  BSDN G61.....34 A2
Thornside Rd JNSTN PA5.....101 H3
Thornton La MRYH/FIRH G20.52 D4
Thornton PI HMLTN ML3.....180 D2
Thornton Rd EKILN G74.....164 B2
Thornton St CTBR ML5.....52 D4
  MRYH/FIRH G20.....52 D4
Thorntree Av HMLTN ML3.152 A5
Thorntree Dr CTBR ML5.....96 B5
Thorntree Wy
  UD/BTH/TAN G71.....134 C4
Thornwood Av KKNTL G66.....39 F3
  PTCK G11.....65 H4
Thornwood Crs PTCK G11.....65 G4
Thornwood Dr BRWEIR PA11.79 E4
  PLSYS PA2.....103 G3
  PTCK G11.....65 G4
Thornwood Gdns PTCK G11.65 H4
Thornwood PI PTCK G11.....65 H3
Thornwood Rd PTCK G11.....65 G4
Thornwood Ter PTCK G11.....65 G4
Thornyburn Dr
  BAIL/MDB/MHD G69.....94 C5
Thornyburn PI
  BAIL/MDB/MHD G69.....94 B5
Thrashbush Av WISHAW ML2.174 C1
Thrashbush Crs WISHAW ML2.174 C1
Thrashbush La AIRDRIE ML6.76 C4
Thrashbush Rd AIRDRIE ML6.76 B4
  WISHAW ML2.....174 C1
Threave PI
  NMRNS G77.....143 G5
Threestonehill Av
  CAR/SHTL G32.....92 C3
Threshold EKILN G74.....166 D3
Threshold Pk EKILN G74.....166 D3
Thriplee Rd BRWEIR PA11.....79 E3
Thrums EKILN G74.....150 A5
Thrums Av BSHPBGS G64.....55 F2
Thrushbush Qd AIRDRIE ML6.76 B4
Thrushcraig Crs PSLYS PA2.104 C2
Thrush PI JNSTN PA5.....121 E2
Thurso St PTCK G11.....66 B5
Thurston Rd
  CARD/HILL/MSPK G52.....86 B4
Thyme Sq MTHW ML1.....154 D2
Tibbermore Rd PTCK G11.....65 H3
Tiber Av MTHW ML1.....154 B1
Tillanburn Rd MTHW ML1.138 C4
Tillet Ov PSLYN/LNWD PA3.84 B3
Tillie St MRYH/FIRH G20.....67 E3
Till St WISHAW ML2.....157 F4
Tillycairn Av
  STPS/GTHM/RID G33.....71 E4
Tillycairn Dr
  STPS/GTHM/RID G33.....71 E4
Tillycairn PI
  STPS/GTHM/RID G33.....71 E4
Tillycairn St
  STPS/GTHM/RID G33.....71 E4
Tilt Rd WISHAW ML2.....158 A4
Tilt St STPS/GTHM/RID G33.....69 H4
Timmons Gv BLSH ML4.....136 C2
Timmons Ter AIRDRIE ML6.119 E3
Tinker's La MTHW ML1.....154 B4
Tintagel Gdns
  BAIL/MDB/MHD G69.....42 A5
Tintock Dr KKNTL G66.....21 H4
Tintock PI BALLOCH G68.....9 H4
Tinto Crs WISHAW ML2.....174 B3

Tinto Dr BALLOCH G68.....25 H3
  BRHD/NEIL G78.....142 B3
Tinto Rd AIRDRIE ML6.....98 C3
  BAIL/MDB/MHD G69.....35 G2
  BSDN G61.....33 G2
  PLKSW/MSWD G43.....127 F2
Tinto St WISHAW ML2.....174 B3
Tinto Vw HMLTN ML3.....170 B5
Tinto Wy EKILS G75.....177 G3
Tinwald Pth
  CARD/HILL/MSPK G52.....86 B3
Tiree EKILN G74.....179 F1
Tiree Av RNFRW PA4.....63 F1
Tiree Ct CUMB G67.....25 H5
Tiree Crs WISHAW ML2.....158 A3
Tiree Dr CUMB G67.....25 H5
Tiree Gdns AIRDRIE ML6.....76 A1
  BSDN G61.....33 G2
  OLDK G60.....30 D2
Tiree Gra HMLTN ML3.....169 E4
Tiree PI CTBR ML5 *.....96 B5
  NMRNS G77.....143 G5
  OLDK G60.....30 D2
Tiree Rd CUMB G67.....25 H5
Tiree St SPRGB/BLRNK G21.....69 F4
Tirry Av RNFRW PA4.....64 B4
Titwood Rd NMRNS G77.....161 H4
  PLKSD/SHW G41.....108 B2
Tiverton Av CAR/SHTL G32.113 E1
Tivoli Ct EKILS G75.....178 B2
Tobago PI DMNK/BRGTN G40.90 B4
  EKILS G75.....165 F4
Tobago St DMNK/BRGTN G40.90 B4
Tobermory Gdns AIRDRIE ML6.76 B3
Tobermory Rd RUTH G73.....130 C4
Todburn Dr PSLYS PA2.....104 C5
Todd St DEN/PKHD G31.....91 F2
Todhills North EKILS G75.166 C5
Todhills South EKILS G75.178 C1
Todholm Crs PSLYS PA2.....105 E2
Todholm Rd PSLYS PA2.....105 E2
Todholm Ter PSLYS PA2.....105 E2
Tofthill Av BSHPBGS G64.....54 C1
Tofthill Gdns BSHPBGS G64.54 B1
Tollbrae Av AIRDRIE ML6.....98 C2
Tollcross Park Gdns
  CAR/SHTL G32.....111 H1
Tollcross Park Gv *
  CAR/SHTL G32.....112 A1
Tollcross Park Vw
  CAR/SHTL G32.....111 H1
Tollcross Rd CAR/SHTL G32.112 C1
  DEN/PKHD G31.....91 G4
Tollhouse Gdns BLSH ML4.136 B4
Toll La GOV/IBX G51.....88 B3
Tollpark Crs WISHAW ML2.158 B5
Tollpark PI BALLOCH G68.....11 G2
Tollpark Rd BALLOCH G68.....11 G2
Toll St MTHW ML1.....155 E5
Toll Wynd HMLTN ML3.....180 C1
Tolsta St SMSTN G23.....52 D2
Tomtain Brae BALLOCH G68.....45 E3
Tomtain Ct BALLOCH G68.....45 E3
Tontine La CLGE C1.....3 H7
Tontine PI RUTH G73.....130 D3
Topaz Ter BLSH ML4.....135 H3
Toppersfield KLBCH PA10.....100 C4
Torbeg Gdns EKILS G75.....177 G4
Torbracken HWWD PA9.....120 B3
Torbreck St
  CARD/HILL/MSPK G52.....87 G4
Torbrex Rd CUMB G67.....26 C4
Torburn Av GIF/THBK G46.127 E3
Tordene Pth BALLOCH G68.....25 H2
Torgyle St SMSTN G23.....52 C2
Tormeadow Rd NMRNS G77.144 A5
Tormore St
  STPS/GTHM/RID G33.....57 F5
Tormusk Dr CSMK G45.....129 H3
Tormusk Gv CSMK G45.....129 H3
Tormusk Rd CSMK G45.....129 H3
Torness St PTCK G11.....66 B4
Torogay St PPK/MIL G22.....54 B3
Torogay Ter PPK/MIL G22.....53 H4
  PPK/MIL G22.....53 H4
Torphin Crs CAR/SHTL G32.....92 B2
Torrance Av AIRDRIE ML6.....99 E2
  EKILS G75.....179 E3
Torrance Gait EKILS G75.179 E4
Torrance La EKILS G75.....179 E4
Torrance Rd BSHPBGS G64.....38 B1
  EKILN G74.....166 B3
Torrance Wynd EKILS G75.179 E4
Torran Dr ERSK PA8.....48 B4
Torran Rd
  STPS/GTHM/RID G33.....93 G2
Torranyard Ter HMLTN ML3.168 D4
Torr Av BRWEIR PA11.....78 B1
Torr Gdns PPK/MIL G22.....68 A2
Torriden PI CTBR ML5.....96 A4
Torriden St CTBR ML5.....96 A4
Torridon Av MTHW ML1.....138 A4
  PLKSD/SHW G41.....108 A1
Torridon Gdns NMRNS G77.162 C1
Torrington Av GIF/THBK G46.144 D2
Torrington Crs CAR/SHTL G32.113 E1
Torrin Rd SMSTN G23.....52 C2
Torrisdale PI CTBR ML5.....96 B2
Torrisdale St CTBR ML5.....96 B2
  PLKSD/SHW G41.....109 E2
Torr La BRWEIR PA11.....78 B1
Torr PI PPK/MIL G22.....68 A2
Torr Rd BRWEIR PA11.....79 F3
  BSHPBGS G64.....55 G2
Torr St PPK/MIL G22.....68 A2
Torryburn Rd
  SPRGB/BLRNK G21.....69 F2
Torwood Brae HMLTN ML3.169 E3
Torwoodhill Rd RUTH G73.....110 B5
Toryglen Rd RUTH G73.....110 B4
Toryglen St GBLS G5.....110 A2
Tourmaline Ter BLSH ML4.....136 A4
Toward Ct BLTYR/CAMB G72.151 H1
Toward Rd
  STPS/GTHM/RID G33.....92 D2
Tower Av BRHD/NEIL G78.....124 C3
Tower Crs RNFRW PA4.....63 E4

Tower Dr RNFRW PA4....63 E4
Towerhill Rd KNTSWD G13...50 D1
Tower PI JNSTN PA5...101 G5
  MLNGV G62...17 F3
Tower Rd BSHPBGS G64...53 C4
  CUMB G67...45 F2
  JNSTN PA5...101 G5
Towerside Crs
  PLK/PH/NH G53...106 B2
Towerside Rd
  PLK/PH/NH G53...106 B2
Towers Rd AIRDRIE ML6...99 G2
Tower St PLKSD/SHW G41...88 D4
Tower Ter PSLY PA1...84 A5
Towie PI UD/BTH/TAN G71...134 A1
Townend Rd DMBTN G82...13 F2
Townhead Av MTHW ML1...117 H5
Townhead Dr MTHW ML1...138 C4
Townhead Dr
  UD/BTH/TAN G71...115 F4
Townhead Rd CTBR ML5...75 F5
  NMRNS G77...161 F1
Townhead St HMLTN ML3...170 C2
  KSYTH G65...8 B3
Townhead Ter PSLY PA1...84 A5
Townhill Rd HMLTN ML3...168 D2
Townhill Ter HMLTN ML3...168 D2
Townmill Rd DEN/PKHD G31...90 D1
Townsend St COWCAD C4...3 F1
Tradeston St GBLS C5...89 F4
Trafalgar Ct BALLOCH G68...9 H4
Trafalgar St CLYDBK G81...31 G5
  DMNK/BRGTN G40...110 C1
Trainard Av CAR/SHTL G32...92 A5
Tranent PI MTHW ML1...139 F5
  STPS/GTHM/RID G33...91 H1
Traquair Av WISHAW ML2...157 F5
Traquair Dr
  CARD/HILL/MSPK G52...86 C5
Treeburn Av GIF/THBK G46...127 E4
Treemain Rd GIF/THBK G46...144 D2
Treespark Av BRHD/NEIL G78...124 A3
Trefoil Av PLKSD/SHW G41...108 C1
Trent PI EKILS G75...176 D2
Trent St CTBR ML5...74 A4
Tresta Rd SMSTN G23...53 E5
Trinidad Gn EKILS G75...165 F4
Trinity Av
  CARD/HILL/MSPK G52...86 D5
Trinity Dr BLTYR/CAMB G72...131 H4
Trinley Rd KNTSWD G13...51 E2
Triton PI BLSH ML4...137 G3
Trondra Pth ESTRH G34...93 G1
Trondra PI ESTRH G34...93 G1
Trongate CGLE G1...3 H7
Troon Av EKILS G75...177 F2
Troon Ct EKILS G75...177 G2
Troon Dr BRWEIR PA11...79 F4
Troon Gdns BALLOCH G68...10 B4
Troon PI NMRNS G77...162 B1
Tulloch-ard PI RUTH G73...130 C4
Trossachs Av MTHW ML1...137 F2
Trossachs Rd RUTH G73...130 C5
Trossachs St MRYH/FIRH G20...67 F3
Troubridge Av KLBCH PA10...100 C5
Troubridge Crs KLBCH PA10...100 C4
Trovaig ERSK PA8...47 H4
Truce Rd KNTSWD G13...50 C3
Truro Av BAIL/MDB/MHD G69...42 A5
Tryst Rd CUMB G67...26 A4
Tudor La South SCOT G14...65 F3
Tudor Rd SCOT G14...65 F3
Tudor St BAIL/MDB/MHD G69...111 G1
Tulley Wynd MTHW ML1...136 C5
Tullallan PI EKILN G74...166 D1
Tullis Ct DMNK/BRGTN G40...90 B5
Tullis St DMNK/BRGTN G40...90 B5
Tulloch-ard PI RUTH G73...130 C4
Tulloch Gdns MTHW ML1...172 C1
Tulloch St LNPK/KPK G44...128 C2
Tullymet Rd HMLTN ML3...170 A5
Tummel Av EKILN G74...166 A4
Tummel St
  STPS/GTHM/RID G33...69 H5
Tummel Wy CUMB G67...26 A3
Tunnel St KVGV C3...88 D2
Tuphall Rd HMLTN ML3...170 A3
Turnberry Av PTCK G11...66 A3
Turnberry Crs AIRDRIE ML6...119 F3
  CTBR ML5...96 D4
Turnberry Dr BRWEIR PA11...79 F5
  HMLTN ML3...168 C4
  NMRNS G77...161 G2
  RUTH G73...129 G3
Turnberry Gdns BALLOCH G68...10 C5
Turnberry PI EKILS G75...177 G2
  RUTH G73...129 G2
Turnberry Rd PTCK G11...65 H3
Turnberry Wynd
  UD/BTH/TAN G71...133 H4
Turnbull St CGLE G1...90 A3
Turner Rd PSLYN/LNWD PA3...84 C1
Turners Av PSLY PA1...103 G5
Turner St CTBR ML5...96 C5
Turnhill Av ERSK PA8...47 F4
Turnhill Crs ERSK PA8...47 G4
Turnhill Dr ERSK PA8...47 G4
Turnhill Gdns ERSK PA8...47 F4
Turnlaw EKILS G75...178 A3
Turnlaw Rd BLTYR/CAMB G72...131 F5
Turnlaw St GBLS C5...90 A5
Turnyland Mdw ERSK PA8...47 G4
Turnyland Wy ERSK PA8...47 G4
Turquoise Ter BLSH ML4...135 H4
Turret Crs KNTSWD G13...50 D3
Turret Rd KNTSWD G13...50 D3
Turriff St GBLS C5...89 G5
Tweed Av PSLYS PA2...103 E2
Tweed Crs AIRDRIE ML6...98 D4
Tweed Crs RNFRW PA4...63 H4
  STPS/GTHM/RID G33...69 H4
  WISHAW ML2...157 F5
Tweed Dr BSDN G61...34 A5
Tweedmuir PI CTBR ML5...117 F1
Tweed PI JNSTN PA5...120 D1
Tweedsmuir BSHPBGS G64...55 E1
Tweedsmuir Crs BSDN G61...34 B1

Tweedsmuir Pk HMLTN ML3...169 H3
Tweedsmuir Rd
  CARD/HILL/MSPK G52...86 C5
Tweed St CTBR ML5...116 D1
  EKILS G75...176 D1
Tweedvale Av SCOT G14...49 H5
Tweedvale PI SCOT G14...49 H5
Twinlaw St ESTRH G34...72 C5
Tylney Rd PSLY PA1...85 G4
Tyndrum Rd BSDN G61...35 E5
Tyndrum St COWCAD C4...3 F1
Tynecastle Crs CAR/SHTL G32...92 C2
Tynecastle PI CAR/SHTL G32...92 C2
Tynecastle St CAR/SHTL G32...92 C2
Tyne PI EKILS G75...176 D2
Tynron Ct HMLTN ML3...168 B4
Tynwald Av RUTH G73...130 B3

U

Udston Rd HMLTN ML3...168 D1
Udston Ter HMLTN ML3...152 A5
Uig PI STPS/GTHM/RID G33...93 F3
Uist Crs STPS/GTHM/RID G33...71 F2
Uist Dr KKNTL G66...22 A5
Uist PI AIRDRIE ML6...99 F3
Uist St GOV/IBX G51...87 G2
Uist Wy WISHAW ML2...157 H5
Ullswater EKILS G75...177 E5
Ulundi Rd JNSTN PA5...101 F4
Ulva St CARD/HILL/MSPK G52...87 G4
Ulverston Ter HMLTN ML3...180 D2
Umachan ERSK PA8...47 H1
Underwood Ct
  PSLYN/LNWD PA3...84 A4
Underwood Dr WISHAW ML2...158 B3
Underwood La PSLY PA1...84 A4
Underwood Rd
  PSLYN/LNWD PA3...84 A4
  RUTH G73...130 B1
Underwood St
  PLKSD/SHW G41...108 D4
Union PI KVD/HLHD G12...66 C4
Union St CGLE G1...2 E5
  HMLTN ML3...170 A1
  KKNTL G66...21 E5
  MTHW ML1...137 F5
  PSLYS PA2...104 B2
Unitas Rd BLSH ML4...136 B2
Unity PI COWCAD C4...67 F4
University Av KVD/HLHD G12...66 C4
University Gdns
  KVD/HLHD G12...66 C4
University PI KVD/HLHD G12...66 C4
Unsted PI PSLY PA1...84 D5
Unst La BLTYR/CAMB G72...130 D5
Unthank Rd BLSH ML4...135 H3
Uphall PI STPS/GTHM/RID G33...91 H1
Upland La SCOT G14...64 D2
Upland Rd SCOT G14...64 D2
U.P. La KSYTH G65...8 B2
Upper Bourtree Ct RUTH G73...130 B3
Upper Bourtree Dr RUTH G73...130 A3
Upper Glenburn Rd BSDN G61...34 A3
Upper Mill St AIRDRIE ML6...98 B1
U.P. Rd KSYTH G65...8 B2
Urquhart Crs RNFRW PA4...63 F4
Urquhart Dr EKILN G74...166 D2
Urquhart PI
  BAIL/MDB/MHD G69...72 D2
Urrdale Rd PLKSD/SHW G41...88 A4
Usmore PI
  STPS/GTHM/RID G33...93 F4

V

Vaila La BLTYR/CAMB G72...131 H4
Vaila St SMSTN G23...53 E4
Valerio Ct BLTYR/CAMB G72...151 G2
Valetta PI CLYDBK G81...31 E5
Valeview Ter DMBTN G82...13 F1
  GVH/MTFL G42...109 F4
Vallantine Crs
  UD/BTH/TAN G71...115 F4
Vallay St PPK/MIL G22...54 A3
Valley Ct HMLTN ML3...169 H3
Valleyfield EKILS G75...166 A4
  KKNTL G66...5 E4
Valleyfield Dr BALLOCH G68...24 C4
Valleyfield St
  SPRGB/BLRNK G21...68 B3
Valley Vw MTHW ML1...154 D3
Vancouver Dr EKILS G75...165 G4
Vancouver La SCOT G14...64 D2
Vancouver PI CLYDBK G81...31 E5
Vancouver Rd SCOT G14...64 D3
Vanguard St CLYDBK G81...49 H1
Vardar Av
  CRMNK/CLK/EAG G76...145 F2
Vardon Lea MTHW ML1...156 B1
Varna La SCOT G14...65 F3
Varna Rd SCOT G14...65 F3
Varnsdorf Wy AIRDRIE ML6...99 E3
Vassart PI MRYH/FIRH G20...67 E2
Veir Ter DMBTN G82...12 D4
Veitches Ct CLYDBK G81...31 H1
Veitch PI KNTSWD G13...50 A5
Vennacher Rd RNFRW PA4...62 D1
Vennard Gdns
  PLKSD/SHW G41...109 E2
Vermont Av RUTH G73...110 D5
Vermont St PLKSD/SHW G41...88 D4
Vernon Bank EKILN G74...166 B3
Vernon Dr PSLYN/LNWD PA3...81 H5
Verona Av SCOT G14...64 D2
Verona Gdns SCOT G14...64 D2
Verona La SCOT G14...64 D2
Vesalius St CAR/SHTL G32...92 B4
Viaduct Rd
  BLTYR/CAMB G72...131 F2
Vicars Wk BLTYR/CAMB G72...131 G2

Vickers St MTHW ML1...154 A2
Victoria Av BRHD/NEIL G78...124 A3
Victoria Br GBLS C5...89 H3
Victoria Circ KVD/HLHD G12...66 B3
Victoria Crs AIRDRIE ML6...97 H3
  BRHD/NEIL G78...124 A3
  CRMNK/CLK/EAG G76...146 A3
  KSYTH G65...7 H2
  WISHAW ML2...173 E1
Victoria Crescent La
  KVD/HLHD G12...66 B3
Victoria Crescent PI
  KVD/HLHD G12...66 B3
Victoria Crescent Rd
  KVD/HLHD G12...66 B3
Victoria Dr BRHD/NEIL G78...124 A3
Victoria Dr East RNFRW PA4...63 F4
Victoria Dr West RNFRW PA4...63 E3
Victoria Gdns BRHD/NEIL G78...124 A3
  PSLYS PA2...103 H2
Victoria Gv BRHD/NEIL G78...124 A3
Victoria La NMRNS G77...161 G5
Victoria Pk KSYTH G65...7 H2
Victoria Park Cnr SCOT G14...65 E2
Victoria Park Dr North
  SCOT G14...65 F3
Victoria Park Dr South
  SCOT G14...65 F3
Victoria Park Gdns North
  PTCK G11...65 G3
Victoria Park Gdns South
  PTCK G11...65 G3
Victoria Park La South
  SCOT G14...65 F3
Victoria Park St SCOT G14...65 E3
Victoria PI AIRDRIE ML6...98 A3
  BLSH ML4...135 G4
  BRHD/NEIL G78...124 B3
  KSYTH G65...8 A2
  MLNGV G62...17 F2
Victoria Qd MTHW ML1...137 F2
Victoria Rd BALLOCH G68...9 H4
  BRHD/NEIL G78...124 A3
  CVH/MTFL G42...109 F3
  JNSTN PA5...101 E1
  KKNTL G66...39 H4
  PSLYS PA2...103 H2
  RUTH G73...130 A1
  STPS/GTHM/RID G33...71 H1
Victoria St BLTYR/CAMB G72...151 G4
  DMBTN G82...13 E3
  HMLTN ML3...152 C4
  KKNTL G66...21 E5
  RUTH G73...110 D4
  WISHAW ML2...175 F1
Victor St AIRDRIE ML6...77 H4
Victory Dr KLBCH PA10...100 B2
Viewbank GIF/THBK G46...126 D4
Viewbank Av AIRDRIE ML6...118 C2
Viewbank St CTBR ML5...74 C1
Viewfield AIRDRIE ML6...97 H3
Viewfield Av
  BAIL/MDB/MHD G69...93 G4
  BLTYR/CAMB G72...151 H1
  BSHPBGS G64...54 B3
  KKNTL G66...39 H5
Viewfield Dr
  BAIL/MDB/MHD G69...93 F4
Viewfield La KVD/HLHD G12...66 C4
Viewfield Rd BLSH ML4...135 G4
  BSHPBGS G64...54 B3
  CTBR ML5...95 H5
Viewglen Ct CSMK G45...147 E1
Viewmount Dr MRYH/FIRH G20...52 C4
Viewpark Av DEN/PKHD G31...91 E1
Viewpark Dr RUTH G73...130 A1
Viewpark Gdns RNFRW PA4...63 E3
Viking Crs CRG/CRSL/HOU PA6...81 E3
Viking Rd AIRDRIE ML6...98 C4
Viking Ter EKILS G75...178 B2
Viking Wy GIF/THBK G46...126 C2
Villafield Av BSHPBGS G64...37 H5
Villafield Dr BSHPBGS G64...37 H5
Village Gdns
  BLTYR/CAMB G72...151 H1
Village Rd BLTYR/CAMB G72...132 B2
Vinicombe La KVD/HLHD G12...66 C3
Vinicombe St KVD/HLHD G12...66 C3
Viola PI BSHPBGS G64...19 G5
Violet PI MTHW ML1...157 G1
Violet St PSLY PA1...85 E4
Virginia Ct CGLE G1...3 G6
Virginia Gdns MLNGV G62...17 G5
Virginia Gv HMLTN ML3...169 H5
Virginia PI CGLE G1...3 G6
Virginia St CGLE G1...3 G6
Virtue Well Vw AIRDRIE ML6...95 H5
Viscount Av RNFRW PA4...63 F4
Viscount Ga UD/BTH/TAN G71...133 H2
Vivian Av MLNGV G62...16 D4
Voil Dr LNPK/KPK G44...128 B3
Vorlich Ct BRHD/NEIL G78...142 B1
Vorlich Gdns BSDN G61...33 H1
Vryburg Crs EKILS G75...177 F4
Vulcan St MTHW ML1...154 D2
  SPRGB/BLRNK G21...68 B2

W

Waddell Av AIRDRIE ML6...75 G2
Waddell St AIRDRIE ML6...76 B5
  GBLS C5...89 H5
Waid Av NMRNS G77...143 H4
Waldemar Rd KNTSWD G13...50 D4
Waldo St MTHW ML1...137 G1
Walkerburn Dr WISHAW ML2...157 F4
Walkerburn Rd
  CARD/HILL/MSPK G52...86 C5
Walker Ct PTCK G11...66 A5
Walker Dr JNSTN PA5...102 A2
Walker Pth UD/BTH/TAN G71...115 H4
Walker St PSLY PA1...84 A5
  PTCK G11...66 A5

Walkinshaw Crs
  PSLYN/LNWD PA3...83 G3
Walkinshaw Rd RNFRW PA4...61 G3
Walkinshaw St
  DMNK/BRGTN G40...90 D5
  JNSTN PA5...101 H3
Wallace Av BSHPTN PA7...29 E5
Wallace Dr BSHPBGS G64...55 G3
Wallace Ga BSHPBGS G64...55 G3
Wallace PI BLTYR/CAMB G72...151 H1
  BSHPBGS G64...55 G3
Wallace Rd MTHW ML1...137 G5
  RNFRW PA4...62 D5
Wallace St AIRDRIE ML6...98 B1
  CLYDBK G81...49 E3
  DMBTN G82...13 E3
  GBLS C5...89 F4
  MTHW ML1...154 C3
  PSLYN/LNWD PA3...84 B3
  RUTH G73...110 D5
Wallacewell Crs
  SPRGB/BLRNK G21...69 E1
Wallacewell PI
  SPRGB/BLRNK G21...69 E1
Wallacewell Qd
  SPRGB/BLRNK G21...55 F5
Wallacewell Rd
  SPRGB/BLRNK G21...55 F5
Wallace Wynd
  BLTYR/CAMB G72...131 F4
Wallbrae Rd CUMB G67...26 C5
Wallneuk PSLY PA1...84 C4
Wallneuk Rd PSLYN/LNWD PA3...84 C4
Walls St CGLE G1...3 H6
Walmer Crs GOV/IBX G51...88 B4
Walnut CI EKILS G75...177 H2
Walnut Crs JNSTN PA5...102 A2
  PPK/MIL G22...68 A1
Walnut Dr KKNTL G66...39 G2
Walnut Ga BLTYR/CAMB G72...132 C3
Walnut Gv EKILS G75...177 H2
Walnut PI UD/BTH/TAN G71...115 H4
Walnut Rd PPK/MIL G22...67 H1
Walpole PI JNSTN PA5...120 D2
Walter St DEN/PKHD G31...91 E2
  PPK/MIL G22...68 A1
Walton Av NMRNS G77...143 H4
Walton St BRHD/NEIL G78...124 B4
  PLKSD/SHW G41...108 D4
Wamba Av KNTSWD G13...51 E3
Wamphray PI EKILS G75...176 D1
Wandilla Av CLYDBK G81...49 G1
Wanlock St GOV/IBX G51...65 H5
Wardend Rd BSHPBGS G64...37 H5
Warden Rd KNTSWD G13...51 E4
Wardhill Rd SPRGB/BLRNK G21...55 E5
Wardhouse Rd PSLYS PA2...103 H5
Wardie PI STPS/GTHM/RID G33...93 G2
Wardie Rd ESTRH G34...93 H2
Wardlaw Av RUTH G73...111 E5
Wardlaw Crs EKILS G75...178 C3
Wardlaw Dr RUTH G73...111 E4
Wardlaw Rd BSDN G61...51 G2
Wardpark Ct CUMB G67...11 F4
Wardpark PI CUMB G67...11 F4
Wardpark Rd CUMB G67...11 E4
Wardrop PI EKILN G74...166 C2
Wardrop St GOV/IBX G51...87 H1
  PSLY PA1...84 B5
Wards Crs CTBR ML5...96 B4
Ware Rd ESTRH G34...93 G2
Warilda Av CLYDBK G81...49 F1
Warlock Dr BRWEIR PA11...79 G2
Warlock Rd BRWEIR PA11...79 G2
Warnock Crs BLSH ML4...136 A3
Warnock Rd NMRNS G77...143 H3
Warnock St DEN/PKHD G31...90 B1
Warren St GVH/MTFL G42...109 G3
Warren Wk KKNTL G66...4 C1
Warriston Crs
  STPS/GTHM/RID G33...91 G1
Warriston PI CAR/SHTL G32...92 C2
Warriston St
  STPS/GTHM/RID G33...91 G1
Warroch St KVGV C3...2 A6
Warwick EKILN G74...167 F1
Warwick Gv HMLTN ML3...168 D3
  HMLTN ML3...151 H5
Washington Rd KKNTL G66...20 D5
  PSLYN/LNWD PA3...84 C1
Washington St KVGV C3...2 C6
Watchmeal Crs CLYDBK G81...32 B1
Waterbank Rd
  CRMNK/CLK/EAG G76...147 E4
Waterfoot Av
  PLK/PH/NH G53...106 D4
Waterfoot Rd NMRNS G77...162 A4
Waterfoot Rw
  CRMNK/CLK/EAG G76...163 F2
Waterfoot Ter
  PLK/PH/NH G53...106 D4
Waterford Rd GIF/THBK G46...127 E4
Waterhaughs Gdns
  STPS/GTHM/RID G33...55 G4
Waterhaughs Gv
  STPS/GTHM/RID G33...55 G4
Waterloo Cl KKNTL G66...21 F4
Waterloo La CGLW G2...2 D5
Waterloo St CGLW G2...2 C5
Watermill Av KKNTL G66...40 A1
Water Rd BRHD/NEIL G78...124 B4
Water Rw GOV/IBX G51...87 H1
Watersaugh Dr MTHW ML1...139 G3
Waterside Av NMRNS G77...161 H2
Waterside Dr NMRNS G77...161 H1
Waterside Gdns
  BLTYR/CAMB G72...132 B4
  CRMNK/CLK/EAG G76...147 E3
  HMLTN ML3...170 B4
Waterside Rd
  CRMNK/CLK/EAG G76...147 E5
  KKNTL G66...40 B1
Waterside St GBLS C5...90 A5
Watling PI EKILS G75...165 H4
Watling St MTHW ML1...154 B1
  UD/BTH/TAN G71...114 D3

Watson Av PSLYN/LNWD PA3...82 A4
  RUTH G73...110 C5
Watson Crs KSYTH G65...8 C2
Watson PI BLTYR/CAMB G72...151 E5
Watson St BLTYR/CAMB G72...151 F3
  CGLE G1...3 H7
  MTHW ML1...154 D3
  UD/BTH/TAN G71...134 A2
Watsonville Pk MTHW ML1...154 D4
Watt Av STPS/GTHM/RID G33...71 G1
Watt La BRWEIR PA11...117 E5
Watt PI BLSH ML4...117 E5
Watt PI MLNGV G62...16 D2
Watt Rd BRWEIR PA11...79 G4
  CARD/HILL/MSPK G52...86 B2
Watt St AIRDRIE ML6...76 D5
  GBLS C5...89 E4
Waukglen Av
  PLK/PH/NH G53...125 G5
Waukglen Crs
  PLK/PH/NH G53...125 H4
Waukglen Dr
  PLK/PH/NH G53...125 G4
Waukglen Gdns
  PLK/PH/NH G53...125 G5
Waukglen Pth
  PLK/PH/NH G53...125 G4
Waukglen Rd PLK/PH/NH G53...125 G4
Waulking Mill Rd BLTYR/CAMB G72...32 A1
Waukmill Av BRHD/NEIL G78...124 C3
Waukmill La CLYDBK G81...32 A2
Waukmill St GIF/THBK G46...126 B3
Waukmill Wy BRHD/NEIL G78...124 C3
Waverley EKILN G74...167 G1
Waverley Crs CUMB G67...44 C1
  HMLTN ML3...169 E1
  KKNTL G66...21 G5
Waverley Dr AIRDRIE ML6...77 H4
  RUTH G73...111 F5
  WISHAW ML2...174 B3
Waverley Gdns JNSTN PA5...102 C2
  PLKSD/SHW G41...108 D3
Waverley Pk KKNTL G66...21 G5
Waverley Rd PSLYS PA2...103 E4
Waverley St CTBR ML5...75 E5
  HMLTN ML3...169 E1
  PLKSD/SHW G41...108 D3
Waverley Ter
  BLTYR/CAMB G72...151 F5
  DMBTN G82...12 A3
Weardale La
  STPS/GTHM/RID G33...92 D1
Weardale St
  STPS/GTHM/RID G33...92 D1
Weaver Av NMRNS G77...144 A4
Weaver Crs AIRDRIE ML6...98 B4
Weaver PI EKILS G75...176 D1
Weavers Av PSLYS PA2...103 G1
Weavers Ct KLBCH PA10...100 B3
Weavers Ga PSLYS PA2...103 G1
Weavers St COWCAD C4...3 G5
Weaver Ter PSLYS PA2...104 D1
Webster Groves WISHAW ML2...157 G5
Webster St CLYDBK G81...49 H3
  DMNK/BRGTN G40...110 D1
Wedderlea Dr
  CARD/HILL/MSPK G52...86 C3
Weensmoor Rd
  PLK/PH/NH G53...125 F5
Weeple Dr PSLYN/LNWD PA3...81 H5
Weighhouse Cl PSLY PA1...84 B5
Weir Av BRHD/NEIL G78...124 B5
Weir St CTBR ML5...96 D2
  GBLS C5...89 H4
Weirwood Av
  BAIL/MDB/MHD G69...93 G5
Weirwood Gdns
  BAIL/MDB/MHD G69...93 G5
Welbeck Rd PLK/PH/NH G53...125 G3
Weldon PI KSYTH G65...24 D2
Welfare Av BLTYR/CAMB G72...132 C3
Welland PI EKILS G75...176 D1
Wellbank PI UD/BTH/TAN G71...134 A2
Wellbrae Rd HMLTN ML3...169 G4
Wellcroft PI GBLS C5...89 G5
Wellcroft Ter HMLTN ML3...168 D3
Wellesley Crs BALLOCH G68...24 B4
  EKILS G75...177 E1
Wellesley Dr BALLOCH G68...24 B4
  EKILS G75...165 E5
Wellfield Av GIF/THBK G46...127 E4
Wellfield St SPRGB/BLRNK G21...68 C2
Well Gn PLKSW/MSWD G43...108 B4
Wellhall Ct HMLTN ML3...169 G1
Wellhall Rd HMLTN ML3...169 E3
Wellhouse Crs
  STPS/GTHM/RID G33...93 F2
Wellhouse Gdns
  STPS/GTHM/RID G33...93 G2
Wellhouse Gv
  STPS/GTHM/RID G33...93 G2
Wellhouse Rd
  STPS/GTHM/RID G33...93 G1
Wellington EKILS G75...177 G1
Wellington La CGLW G2...2 C4
Wellington PI CLYDBK G81...31 E5
  CTBR ML5...95 H4
  WISHAW ML2...174 C5
Wellington Rd BSHPBGS G64...38 B4
Wellington St AIRDRIE ML6...76 B5
  CGLW G2...2 D4
  PSLYN/LNWD PA3...84 A4
  WISHAW ML2...155 H5
Wellknowe Av EKILN G74...164 B3
Wellknowe PI EKILN G74...164 A2
Wellknowe Rd EKILN G74...164 B2
Well La KKNTL G66...4 C1
Wellmeadow CI NMRNS G77...144 A5
Wellmeadow La NMRNS G77...144 A5
Wellmeadow Rd
  PLKSW/MSWD G43...126 D1
Wellmeadows La HMLTN ML3...169 F3
Wellmeadow St PSLY PA1...84 A5
Wellmeadow Wy NMRNS G77...144 A5
Wellpark Rd MTHW ML1...154 B4
Wellpark St COWCAD C4...90 B2

Wellpark Ter BRHD/NEIL G78....141 E4
Well Rd KLBCH PA10........100 B5
Wellshot Dr BLTYR/CAMB G72..131 G2
Wellshot Rd CAR/SHTL G32....92 A5
Wellside Av AIRDRIE ML6......76 B5
Wellside La AIRDRIE ML6......31 G5
Wellside Qd AIRDRIE ML6......76 B4
Wellsquarry Rd EKILN G74....165 H1
Wells St CLYDBK G81..........83 H4
Wells St PSLY PA1
Wellview Dr MTHW ML1........154 C5
Wellwynd AIRDRIE ML6.........98 A1
Welsh Dr BLTYR/CAMB G72....151 G4
  HMLTN ML3..............180 C1
Welsh Rw AIRDRIE ML6........118 D1
Wemyss Av NMRNS G77........143 H3
Wemyss Dr BALLOCH G68.......24 C4
Wemyss Gdns
  BAIL/MDB/MHD G69.........113 H1
Wenlock Rd PSLYS PA2........104 C2
Wensleydale EKILN G74.......165 H2
Wentworth Dr SMSTN G23......52 D2
Wesley St AIRDRIE ML6........98 A2
West Academy St
  WISHAW ML2..............173 F2
Westacres Rd NMRNS G77.....161 E4
West Av AIRDRIE ML6..........77 H3
  BLTYR/CAMB G72..........151 H5
  PSLYN/LNWD PA3...........63 H3
  RNFRW PA4...............63 F5
  STPS/GTHM/RID G33........71 E1
  UD/BTH/TAN G71..........134 C1
Westbank Gv
  BSHPBGS G64.............19 F4
Westbank La KVD/HLHD G12....66 D4
Westbank Qd KVD/HLHD G12....66 D4
Westbourne Crs BSDN G61......33 H3
Westbourne Dr BSDN G61.......33 H3
Westbourne Gardens La
  KVD/HLHD G12............66 A2
Westbourne Gdns South
  KVD/HLHD G12............66 B2
Westbourne Gdns West
  KVD/HLHD G12............66 B2
Westbourne Rd
  KVD/HLHD G12............66 A2
Westbourne Terrace La North
  KVD/HLHD G12............66 B2
Westbourne Terrace La South
  KVD/HLHD G12............66 B2
West Brae PSLY PA1...........84 A5
Westbrae Dr KNTSWD G13......65 F2
Westbrae Rd NMRNS G77......144 C4
West Bridgend DMBTN G82......12 D1
Westburn Av
  BLTYR/CAMB G72..........132 A1
  PSLYN/LNWD PA3...........83 F4
Westburn Crs CLYDBK G81......32 A1
  RUTH G73................110 C5
Westburn Farm Rd
  BLTYR/CAMB G72..........131 G1
Westburn Rd
  BLTYR/CAMB G72..........132 B2
West Burnside St KSYTH G65....8 B2
West Campbell St CGLW G2
  PSLY PA1................83 G5
West Canal St CTBR ML5.......96 C3
Westcastle Ct CSMK G45......129 E4
Westcastle Crs CSMK G45.....129 E4
Westcastle Gdns CSMK G45....129 E4
Westcastle Gv CSMK G45......129 E4
West Chapelton Av BSDN G61...34 C4
West Chapelton Crs BSDN G61..34 C4
West Chapelton Dr BSDN G61...34 C4
West Chapelton La BSDN G61...34 C4
Westcliff DMBTN G82..........12 A3
Westclyffe St PLKSD/SHW G41.108 D3
West Coats Rd
  BLTYR/CAMB G72..........131 E3
Westdale Dr
  BAIL/MDB/MHD G69.........42 B5
West Dr AIRDRIE ML6..........99 F4
West End Dr BLSH ML4.......135 G3
Westend Park St KVGV G3......4 A1
West End Pl BLSH ML4.......135 G3
Westerburn St CAR/SHTL G32...92 A3
Wester Carriagehill
  PSLYS PA2...............104 B2
Wester Cleddens Rd
  BSHPBGS G64.............54 D1
Wester Common Dr
  PPK/MIL G22.............67 F2
Wester Common Rd
  PPK/MIL G22.............67 G2
Westercraigs DEN/PKHD G31....90 C2
Westercraigs Ct
  DEN/PKHD G31............90 C2
Westerdale EKILN G74........165 H2
Westerfield Rd EKILN G74....164 C1
Westergill Av AIRDRIE ML6....99 F3
Westergreens Av KKNTL G66....39 H4
Westerhill Rd BSHPBGS G64....38 A4
Westerhouse Rd ESTRH G34....71 H5
Westerkirk Dr SMSTN G23......52 C2
Westerlands KVD/HLHD G12....51 G5
Westerlands Dr NMRNS G77....161 E1
Westerlands Gv NMRNS G77...161 E1
Westerlands Pl NMRNS G77....143 G5
Westermains Av KKNTL G66....39 G4
Wester Mavisbank Av
  AIRDRIE ML6.............97 H1
Wester Moffat Av AIRDRIE ML6.99 F1
Wester Moffat Crs
  AIRDRIE ML6.............99 H1
Wester Myvot Rd CUMB G67....43 H4
Wester Rd CAR/SHTL G32.......93 E5
Western Av RUTH G73.........110 C4
Western Isles Rd OLDK G60....30 D3
Western Rd BLTYR/CAMB G72..131 G4
Westerpark Av
  BLTYR/CAMB G72..........168 D2
West Rd CAR/SHTL G32.......113 G1
Westerton KKNTL G66..........66 D5
  CRMNK/CLK/EAG G76......146 B5
Westerton La
  CRMNK/CLK/EAG G76......146 B5
Westfarm Crs
  BLTYR/CAMB G72..........132 A1

Westfarm Gv
  BLTYR/CAMB G72..........132 A1
Westfarm Wynd
  BLTYR/CAMB G72..........113 E5
Westfield DMBTN G82.........12 B3
Westfield Av RUTH G73.......110 C5
Westfield Crs BSDN G61......51 F1
Westfield Dr BALLOCH G68....43 G1
  BSDN G61................51 F1
  CARD/HILL/MSPK G52......86 B4
Westfield Rd BALLOCH G68....43 E2
  BALLOCH G68.............24 D5
  GIF/THBK G46............126 D5
  KSYTH G65...............8 A1
  MTHW ML1................118 D5
Westfields BSHPBGS G64......37 F5
Westgarth Pl EKILN G74.....165 F2
West Ga WISHAW ML2.........174 C2
West George La CGLW G2......2 C4
West George St CGLE G1.......3 F5
  CGLW G2.................2 B4
  CTBR ML5................96 D1
West Glebe Ter HMLTN ML3...169 H5
West Graham St COWCAD G4....2 C2
West Greenhill Pl KVGV G3....88 D1
West High St KKNTL G66......21 E4
Westhorn Dr CAR/SHTL G32...112 B5
Westhouse Av RUTH G73.......110 B5
Westhouse Gdns RUTH G73....110 B5
West Kirk St AIRDRIE ML6.....98 A2
Westland Dr SCOT G14........65 E4
Westland Dr Gdns PSLYS PA2..104 A2
West La PSLY PA1............83 G5
Westlea Pl AIRDRIE ML6.......98 B3
West Lodge Rd RNFRW PA4.....63 E2
West Mains Rd EKILN G74....165 G3
Westmoreland St
  GVH/MTFL G42...........109 F2
Westmuir Pl RUTH G73........110 B5
Westmuir St DEN/PKHD G31....91 G4
West Nile St CGLE G1.........2 D4
Westpark Dr PSLYN/LNWD PA3..83 F4
West Pl WISHAW ML2.........158 B5
Westport EKILN G75..........165 G4
Westport St KSYTH G65.........8 B2
West Princes St COWCAD G4....66 D4
Westray Av NMRNS G77.......143 H5
Westray Circ PPK/MIL G22.....53 H5
Westray Ct CUMB G67.........67 H3
Westray Pl PPK/MIL G22.......54 A4
Westray Rd CUMB G67.........67 H3
Westray Sq PPK/MIL G22.......53 H4
Westray St PPK/MIL G22.......53 H4
West Regent St CGLW G2.......2 D4
West Rd KLBCH PA10..........100 B2
West Scott Ter HMLTN ML3...170 A4
West Stewart St HMLTN ML3..169 H1
West St CLYDBK G81..........49 H5
  GBLS G5.................89 G6
  PSLY PA1................83 H5
West Thomson St CLYDBK G81...31 H5
West Thornlie St
  WISHAW ML2..............173 H3
West Wellbrae Crs
  HMLTN ML3...............169 H5
West Whitby St
  DEN/PKHD G31............91 F5
Westwood Av GIF/THBK G46...127 F4
Westwood Crs HMLTN ML3....169 H5
Westwood Dr MTHW ML1.......157 H1
Westwood Gdns
  PSLYN/LNWD PA3...........83 G4
Westwood Hl EKILS G75......177 G1
Westwood Qd CLYDBK G81......49 G2
Westwood Rd EKILS G75......165 H5
  PLKSW/MSWD G43.........127 G1
  WISHAW ML2..............158 B4
Weymouth Dr KVD/HLHD G12...51 H5
Weymouth La KVD/HLHD G12...66 A1
Whamflet Av
  BAIL/MDB/MHD G69.........94 B2
Wheatfield Rd BSDN G61......51 E1
Wheatholm St AIRDRIE ML6....76 C5
Wheatland Av
  BLTYR/CAMB G72..........151 F2
Wheatlandhead Ct
  BLTYR/CAMB G72..........151 F2
Wheatlands Dr KLBCH PA10...100 B2
Wheatlands Farm Rd
  KLBCH PA10..............100 B2
Wheatley Ct CAR/SHTL G32....92 B4
Wheatley Crs KSYTH G65.......8 B3
Wheatley Dr CAR/SHTL G32....92 B4
Wheatley Loan BSHPBGS G64...55 F3
Wheatley Pl CAR/SHTL G32....92 B4
Whifflet St CTBR ML5.........96 B1
Whimbrel Wy RNFRW PA4......63 H2
Whin Av BRHD/NEIL G78......123 H5
Whinfell Dr EKILS G75.......177 E2
Whinfell Rd EKILS G75.......177 E2
Whinfield Rd PLK/PH/NH G53..125 F5
Whinhall Av AIRDRIE ML6......75 H5
Whinhall Rd AIRDRIE ML6.....75 H5
Whin Hl EKILN G74...........167 E1
Whinhill Rd PLK/PH/NH G53...106 C4
  PSLYS PA2...............105 E2
Whin Loan KSYTH G65..........6 D1
Whinney Gv WISHAW ML2.....174 D1
Whinny Burn Ct MTHW ML1...172 C2
Whinpark Av BLSH ML4.......135 H4
Whin Pl EKILN G74...........149 G5
Whins Rd PLKSD/SHW G41.....108 B3
Whin St CLYDBK G81..........31 H4
Whirlie Dr CRC/CRSL/HOU PA6..80 C3
Whirlie Rd CRC/CRSL/HOU PA6..80 D3
Whirlow Gdns
  BAIL/MDB/MHD G69.........93 H4
Whirlow Rd
  BAIL/MDB/MHD G69.........93 H4
Whistleberry Crs HMLTN ML3..152 B1
Whistleberry Dr HMLTN ML3..152 C4
Whistleberry La HMLTN ML3..152 C4
Whistleberry Pk HMLTN ML3..152 B5
Whistleberry Rd HMLTN ML3..152 B5
Whistlefield Ct BSDN G61.....34 B5
Whitacres Rd
  PLK/PH/NH G53..........125 E3
Whitburn St CAR/SHTL G32....92 A2

Whiteadder Pl EKILS G75....176 C1
White Av DMBTN G82.........13 G4
White Cart Ct
  PLKSW/MSWD G43.........108 C5
White Cart Rd
  PSLYN/LNWD PA3...........84 B1
Whitecraigs Ct GIF/THBK G46.144 D2
Whitecraigs Pl SMSTN G23....52 D2
Whitecrook St CLYDBK G81....49 F3
Whitefield Av
  BLTYR/CAMB G72..........131 F3
Whitefield Rd GOV/IBX G51....88 B3
Whitefield Ter KKNTL G66......4 A1
Whiteford Av DMBTN G82......13 G1
Whiteford Crs DMBTN G82.....13 H2
Whiteford Ct HMLTN ML3.....180 C2
Whiteford Pl DMBTN G82.....13 H2
Whiteford Rd PSLYS PA2.....104 D2
Whiteford Rd
  STPS/GTHM/RID G33........71 G1
Whitehall St KVGV G3.........2 A6
Whitehaugh Av PSLY PA1......85 E4
Whitehaugh Crs
  PLK/PH/NH G53..........125 F3
Whitehaugh Dr PSLY PA1......85 E4
Whitehaugh Rd
  PLK/PH/NH G53..........125 F3
Whitehill Av AIRDRIE ML6.....76 B4
  BALLOCH G68.............25 H3
  KKNTL G66...............21 G4
  STPS/GTHM/RID G33........57 E5
  KKNTL G66...............21 H4
Whitehill Farm Rd
  STPS/GTHM/RID G33........70 D1
Whitehill Gdns DEN/PKHD G31..90 D2
Whitehill Gv NMRNS G77.....162 A3
Whitehill La BSDN G61........34 A4
Whitehill Pl DEN/PKHD G31....90 D2
Whitehill Rd BSDN G61........34 A4
  HMLTN ML3...............152 C5
Whitehills Dr EKILS G75.....178 B1
Whitehills Pl EKILS G75.....178 B1
Whitehills Ter EKILS G75....178 B2
Whitehill St DEN/PKHD G31...90 D2
Whitehill Street La
  DEN/PKHD G31............90 D2
Whitehurst BSDN G61.........33 H2
Whitehurst Pk BSDN G61......33 H2
Whitekirk Pl DRUM G15.......50 B1
Whitelaw Av CTBR ML5........73 F2
Whitelaw Crs BLSH ML4......136 C3
Whitelaw Gdns BSHPBGS G64...37 H5
Whitelaw St MRYH/FIRH G20...52 B4
Whitelaw Ter KSYTH G65.......23 F1
Whitelee EKILS G75..........178 A3
Whitelee Crs NMRNS G77....143 G4
Whitelee Ga NMRNS G77.....143 G4
Whitelee Rd CUMB G67........11 H4
Whiteloans UD/BTH/TAN G71..134 C4
Whitemoss Av EKILN G74.....166 C4
  LNPK/KPK G44...........128 A3
Whitemoss Gv EKILN G74.....166 D3
Whitemoss Rd EKILN G74.....166 C4
Whitepond Av BLSH ML4......135 G4
Whites Bridge Av PSLY PA1....85 E5
Whites Bridge Cl
  PSLYN/LNWD PA3...........83 F5
White St CLYDBK G81.........49 G3
  PTCK G11................66 A4
Whitevale St DEN/PKHD G31...90 D2
Whithope Rd
  PLK/PH/NH G53..........125 E2
Whithope Ter
  BAIL/MDB/MHD G69.........42 B5
Whitlawburn Av
  BLTYR/CAMB G72..........130 D3
Whitlawburn Rd
  BLTYR/CAMB G72..........130 D3
Whitlawburn Ter
  BLTYR/CAMB G72..........130 D3
Whitriggs Rd
  PLK/PH/NH G53..........125 E2
Whitslade St ESTRH G34......71 H5
Whitslade St ESTRH G34......71 H5
Whitsun Dl EKILN G74.......165 H2
Whittagreen Av MTHW ML1...138 A4
Whittagreen Crs MTHW ML1..138 A5
Whittinghame Dr
  KVD/HLHD G12............65 G1
Whittinghame La
  KNTSWD G13..............65 G1
Whittinghame Pk
  KVD/HLHD G12............65 G1
Whittington St CTBR ML5......96 D3
Whittlemuir Av
  LNPK/KPK G44...........128 A3
Whitton Dr GIF/THBK G46....127 G3
Whitton St MRYH/FIRH G20....52 B3
Whitworth Dr CLYDBK G81.....48 D1
  MRYH/FIRH G20...........67 F3
Whitworth Gdns
  MRYH/FIRH G20...........53 F5
Whitworth Ga
  MRYH/FIRH G20...........67 G1
Whyte Av BLTYR/CAMB G72...130 D2
Whyte Cnr DMBTN G82........14 C4
Wick Av AIRDRIE ML6.........97 H5
The Wickets PSLY PA1.......104 D1
Wickham Av NMRNS G77.....144 A4
Wigton Av NMRNS G77.......143 H2
Wigtoun Pl CUMB G67.........26 D1
Wilfred Av KNTSWD G13.......51 E4
Wilkie Rd UD/BTH/TAN G71..134 B2
William Dr HMLTN ML3......180 C5
William Mann Dr NMRNS G77.161 F1
Williamsburgh Ter PSLY PA1...84 D4
Williamson Av DMBTN G82.....13 F3
Williamson Pl JNSTN PA5....102 A2
Williamson St CLYDBK G81....32 A4
  DMNK/BRGTN G40..........91 E5
William St CLYDBK G81.......31 H1
  CTBR ML5................97 E5
  HMLTN ML3...............152 D5
  JNSTN PA5...............101 G5
  KSYTH G65...............8 C2
  KVGV G3.................2 A4
  PSLY PA1................83 H5
William Ure Pl BSHPBGS G64..38 A3
William Wilson Ct KSYTH G65..8 B1

Williamwood Dr
  LNPK/KPK G44...........127 H5
Williamwood Pk
  LNPK/KPK G44...........128 A5
Williamwood Pk West
  LNPK/KPK G44...........128 A5
Willie Ross La RUTH G73.....111 E3
Willock Pl MRYH/FIRH G20.....52 D2
Willoughby Dr KNTSWD G13....51 G5
Willoughby La KNTSWD G13....51 G5
Willow Av BSHPBGS G64.......54 D3
  JNSTN PA5...............102 B2
  KKNTL G66...............39 H1
  MTHW ML1................137 F5
Willowbank Crs KVGV G3......67 E4
Willowbank Gdns KKNTL G66...21 H4
Willowbank St KVGV G3.......67 E5
Willow Crs CTBR ML5.........96 D5
Willowdale Crs
  BAIL/MDB/MHD G69.........93 H5
Willowdale Gdns
  BAIL/MDB/MHD G69.........93 H5
Willow Dr AIRDRIE ML6........98 C3
  BLTYR/CAMB G72..........151 F2
  JNSTN PA5...............102 B1
  KKNTL G66...............5 C5
Willowford Rd
  PLK/PH/NH G53..........125 E3
Willow Gv MTHW ML1.........137 G2
Willow La CAR/SHTL G52.....112 C2
Willow Pl JNSTN PA5.........101 H4
  UD/BTH/TAN G71..........116 A4
The Willows
  CRMNK/CLK/EAG G76......147 F2
Willow St KNTSWD G13........51 H4
Willow Wy HMLTN ML3........170 B4
Willwood Dr WISHAW ML2....157 F5
Wilmot Rd KNTSWD G13.......51 H5
Wilsgait St MTHW ML1.......139 F5
Wilson Av PSLYN/LNWD PA3....81 H5
Wilson Ct BLSH ML4.........135 G2
Wilson Pl EKILN G74.........166 D1
  NMRNS G77...............161 F1
Wilson St AIRDRIE ML6........98 A1
  CGLE G1.................3 G6
  CTBR ML5................97 F2
  HMLTN ML3...............169 G1
  MTHW ML1................155 E5
  RNFRW PA4...............63 G2
Wiltonburn Rd
  PLK/PH/NH G53..........125 F3
Wilton Crescent La
  MRYH/FIRH G20...........67 E3
Wilton Dr MRYH/FIRH G20.....67 E3
Wilton St CTBR ML5..........74 A4
  MRYH/FIRH G20...........66 D3
Wilverton Rd KNTSWD G13....51 F5
Winburne Crs HMLTN ML3....169 G5
Winchester Dr KVD/HLHD G12..52 A3
Windemere Gdns HMLTN ML3..180 C3
Windemere EKILS G75........177 E3
Windhill Crs
  PLKSW/MSWD G43.........127 E2
Windhill Rd
  PLKSW/MSWD G43.........127 E2
Windlaw Gdns LNPK/KPK G44.128 A4
Windlaw Park Gdns
  LNPK/KPK G44...........128 A3
Windmill Ct CSMK G45.......147 E1
Windmillcroft Qd
  GBLS G5.................89 G5
Windmillhill St MTHW ML1...170 H1
  MTHW ML1................155 H5
Windmill Rd HMLTN ML3......155 H5
Windrow Ter WISHAW ML2....157 F3
Windsor Av NMRNS G77......144 C5
Windsor Crs CLYDBK G81......31 H5
  JNSTN PA5...............102 A3
  PSLY PA1
Windsor Crescent La
  CLYDBK G81..............31 H5
Windsor Dr AIRDRIE ML6.......78 C2
Windsor Gdns HMLTN ML3....152 B5
Windsor Rd MTHW ML1.......137 F2
  RNFRW PA4...............63 F5
Windsor St CTBR ML5........116 B1
  MRYH/FIRH G20...........67 F4
Windsor St CLYDBK G81.......31 H5
Windward Rd EKILS G75......165 H3
Windyedge Crs KNTSWD G13...64 D1
Windyedge Pl KNTSWD G13....64 D1
Windyedge Rd MTHW ML1.....139 H4
Windyhill Pk
  CRMNK/CLK/EAG G76......163 F4
Windyridge Pl
  BLTYR/CAMB G72..........151 F3
Windy Yetts KSYTH G65.......23 F2
Wingate Crs EKILN G74......167 F1
Wingate Dr EKILN G74.......167 F1
Wingate Pk EKILN G74.......167 F1
Wingate St WISHAW ML2......173 G3
Wingfield Gdns
  UD/BTH/TAN G71..........152 C1
Winifred St
  STPS/GTHM/RID G33........69 G2
Winning Ct BLTYR/CAMB G72..151 H1
Winning Rw DEN/PKHD G31....91 H4
Winnipeg Dr EKILS G75......165 G5
Winston Crs KKNTL G66........4 A1
Wintergreen Dr EKILN G74...166 A1
Wintergreen Ct EKILN G74...166 A1
Winter St COWCAD G4.........67 H6
Winton Dr GIF/THBK G46.....127 F5
Winton Crs BLTYR/CAMB G72..151 H4
Winton Dr KVD/HLHD G12......66 B1
Winton Gdns
  UD/BTH/TAN G71..........115 E5
Winton La GIF/THBK G46.....127 F5
Winton Pk EKILS G75........165 H3
Wishart Av CLYDBK G81.......32 B1
Wishart St DEN/PKHD G31.....90 C2
Wishaw High Rd MTHW ML1...157 F2
Wishawhill St WISHAW ML2...157 E3
Wishaw Low Rd MTHW ML1....157 H2
Wishaw Rd WISHAW ML2......174 C4

Wisner Ct GIF/THBK G46......126 C5
Wiston St BLTYR/CAMB G72...132 A2
Witcutt Wy WISHAW ML2......173 F4
Woddrop St
  DMNK/BRGTN G40..........111 E2
Wolcott Dr BLTYR/CAMB G72..151 G2
Wolfe Av NMRNS G77.........143 H5
Wolseley St GBLS G5.........110 A1
Wood Aven Dr EKILN G74.....166 A1
Woodbank Crs
  CRMNK/CLK/EAG G76......145 H4
  JNSTN PA5...............101 G4
Woodburn Av AIRDRIE ML6.....98 A3
  BLTYR/CAMB G72..........151 F4
  CRMNK/CLK/EAG G76......146 A5
Woodburn Ct RUTH G73.......130 A1
Woodburn Gv HMLTN ML3....170 A2
Woodburn Pl
  CRG/CRSL/HOU PA6
  PLKSW/MSWD G43.........127 G2
Woodburn Rd MTHW ML1......119 E5
  MTHW ML1................154 D2
Woodburn Wy BALLOCH G68....25 G5
Wood Crs MTHW ML1.........154 D2
Woodcroft Av PTCK G11.......65 G2
Woodend UD/BTH/TAN G71....113 F2
Woodend Dr AIRDRIE ML6.....98 A3
  KNTSWD G13.............65 F1
  PSLY PA1...............85 G5
Woodend Gdns
  CAR/SHTL G32...........113 G2
Woodend La KNTSWD G13.....65 F1
Woodend Pl JNSTN PA5.......102 A2
Woodend Rd CAR/SHTL G32...113 F2
  RUTH G73...............130 A3
Wood Farm Rd GIF/THBK G46..144 D1
Woodfield UD/BTH/TAN G71...134 C5
Woodfield Av BSHPBGS G64...55 E3
Woodford Pl PSLYN/LNWD PA3..81 H5
Woodford St
  PLKSW/MSWD G43.........108 C5
Woodgreen Av
  LNPK/KPK G44...........128 C1
Woodhall Av AIRDRIE ML6....118 C4
  CTBR ML5...............116 D1
  HMLTN ML3..............169 G1
  MTHW ML1...............155 E5
Woodhall Cottage Rd
  AIRDRIE ML6............118 D3
Woodhall Mill Rd
  AIRDRIE ML6............116 D1
Woodhall Pl CTBR ML5.......116 C1
Woodhall Rd AIRDRIE ML6....118 C4
  WISHAW ML2.............175 E2
Woodhall St AIRDRIE ML6....118 E3
  DMNK/BRGTN G40.........110 D2
Woodhead Av BALLOCH G68...43 G1
  KKNTL G66..............40 A1
  UD/BTH/TAN G71.........152 C2
Woodhead Ct BALLOCH G68...43 G1
Woodhead Crs AIRDRIE ML6..118 C4
  HMLTN ML3..............169 F5
  UD/BTH/TAN G71.........115 F5
Woodhead Gdns
  UD/BTH/TAN G71.........152 C2
Woodhead Gv BALLOCH G68...43 G1
Woodhead Pl BALLOCH G68...43 G1
Woodhead Rd
  BAIL/MDB/MHD G69.......58 A5
  BALLOCH G68............43 G1
  PLK/PH/NH G53..........125 H2
Woodhead Ter
  BAIL/MDB/MHD G69.......58 A4
  UD/BTH/WALL BALLOCH G68.43 G1
Woodhill Rd
  SPRGB/BLRNK G21........55 E5
Woodholm Av LNPK/KPK G44..128 D1
Woodhouse St KNTSWD G13...51 H4
Woodilee Rd KKNTL G66......40 B2
Woodland Av AIRDRIE ML6...118 B5
  KKNTL G66..............20 D5
  PSLYS PA2..............104 B4
Woodland Crs
  BLTYR/CAMB G72.........131 G3
Woodland Gdns
  CRMNK/CLK/EAG G76......147 E2
  HMLTN ML3..............170 B3
Woodlands Av
  BAIL/MDB/MHD G69.......58 D4
  UD/BTH/TAN G71.........134 A3
Woodlands Crs
  GIF/THBK G46...........126 C5
  JNSTN PA5..............101 E5
  UD/BTH/TAN G71.........134 B4
Woodlands Dr CTBR ML5.....96 A2
  KVGV G3................67 E4
  MTHW ML1...............154 D1
Woodlands Gdns
  UD/BTH/TAN G71.........134 A4
Woodlands Ga GIF/THBK G46..126 C5
  KVGV G3................67 E5
Woodlands Gv MLNGV G62....17 E2
Woodlands Pk GIF/THBK G46..145 H1
  KVGV G3................67 E5
  MTHW ML1...............119 E5
Woodlands Rd GIF/THBK G46.145 H2
  KVGV G3................67 E5
  MTHW ML1...............155 G1
Woodlands Ter KVGV G3......66 D5
The Woodlands BLSH ML4....136 C4
Woodland Wy CUMB G67......26 D2
Woodlea Av AIRDRIE ML6.....98 D5
Woodlea Dr GIF/THBK G46...127 F4
  HMLTN ML3..............170 A5
Woodlea Pl AIRDRIE ML6.....98 D5
Woodlinn Av LNPK/KPK G44.128 C2
Woodmill Dr BSHPBGS G64...38 C4
Woodmill Gdns CUMB G67....67 G4
Woodneuk Rd
  BAIL/MDB/MHD G69.......73 E1
  PLK/PH/NH G53..........125 G2
Woodneuk St AIRDRIE ML6...119 E1

Woodneuk Ter BAIL/MDB/MHD G69 ....73 E1
Wood Qd PLKSD G81 ....49 H3
Woodrow MTHW ML1 ....118 C4
Woodrow Av MTHW ML1 ....137 G5
Woodrow Circ PLKSD/SHW G41 ....88 C5
Woodrow Pl PLKSD/SHW G41 ....88 B5
Woodrow Rd PLKSD/SHW G41 ....88 C5
Woodside CRS/CRSL/HOU PA6 ....81 E2
Woodside Av MTHW ML1 ....117 H4
Woodside Av BRWEIR PA11 ....79 G3
  GIF/THBK G46 ....126 D4
  HMLTN ML3 ....170 B3
  KKNTL G66 ....40 A5
  KSYTH G65 ....8 D2
  RUTH G73 ....111 F5
Woodside Crs BRHD/NEIL G78 ....124 C5
  CRMNK/CLK/EAG G76 ....163 E3
  KVGV G3 ....
  PSLY PA1 ....83 H5
  WISHAW ML2 ....158 C4
Woodside Dr AIRDRIE ML6 ....118 B4
Woodside Gdns CRMNK/CLK/EAG G76 ....147 E3
  CRMNK/CLK/EAG G76 ....145 G3
  CTBR ML5 ....96 A5
Woodside La JNSTN PA5 ....80 D5
Woodside Pl KVGV G3 ....67 E5
  UD/BTH/TAN G71 ....115 H4
Woodside Place La KVGV G3 ....67 E5
Woodside Rd CRMNK/CLK/EAG G76 ....147 E3

Woodside St AIRDRIE ML6 ....119 E2
  CTBR ML5 ....116 A1
  MTHW ML1 ....172 C1
  MTHW ML1 ....137 F4
Woodside Ter KVGV G3 ....67 E5
Woodside Terrace La KVGV G3 ....67 E5
Woodside Wk HMLTN ML3 ....170 B3
Woodside Gv RUTH G73 ....111 F5
Woodstock Av KKNTL G66 ....21 H5
  PLKSD/SHW G41 ....108 C4
  PSLYS PA2 ....102 D4
Woodstock Dr WISHAW ML2 ....174 B1
Wood St AIRDRIE ML6 ....76 D5
  CTBR ML5 ....96 B2
  DEN/PKHD G31 ....91 E1
  MTHW ML1 ....155 E2
  PSLYS PA2 ....105 E1
Woodvale Av AIRDRIE ML6 ....99 E5
  BSDN G61 ....52 A1
  GIF/THBK G46 ....145 E2
Woodvale Dr PSLYN/LNWD PA3 ....83 F4
Woodview Av UD/BTH/TAN G71 ....116 A4
Woodview Dr AIRDRIE ML6 ....98 B4
  BLSH ML4 ....117 F5
Woodville Pl KVGV G3 ....67 E5
Woodville St GOV/IBX G51 ....88 A3
Woodyard Rd DMBTN G82 ....12 D4
Woodyett Pk CRMNK/CLK/EAG G76 ....146 A5

Woodyett Rd CRMNK/CLK/EAG G76 ....146 A5
Wordsworth Wy UD/BTH/TAN G71 ....134 C4
Worrall Gdns HMLTN ML3 ....171 E5
Worsley Crs NMRNS G77 ....143 H4
Wraes Av BRHD/NEIL G78 ....124 C3
Wraes Vw BRHD/NEIL G78 ....124 D3
Wraisland Crs BSHPTN PA7 ....28 C4
Wrangholm Crs MTHW ML1 ....137 G4
Wrangholm Dr MTHW ML1 ....137 F4
Wren Ct BLSH ML4 ....116 B4
Wren Pl JNSTN PA5 ....121 E2
Wright Av BRHD/NEIL G78 ....123 H5
Wrightlands Crs ERSK PA8 ....48 B3
Wright St RNFRW PA4 ....62 C5
Wye Crs CTBR ML5 ....74 A5
Wykeham Pl KNTSWD G13 ....50 D5
Wykeham Rd KNTSWD G13 ....50 D5
Wylie EKILN G74 ....150 A5
Wylie Av NMRNS G77 ....144 A3
Wylie St HMLTN ML3 ....170 A3
Wyndford Dr MRYH/FIRH G20 ....66 C1
Wyndford Pl MRYH/FIRH G20 ....66 C1
Wyndford Rd MRYH/FIRH G20 ....66 B1
Wyndford Ter UD/BTH/TAN G71 ....115 G5
Wyndham Ct KVD/HLHD G12 ....66 C2
Wyndham St KVD/HLHD G12 ....66 C2
The Wynd CUMB G67 ....10 D5
Wynyard Gn EKILS G75 ....177 G1
Wyper Pl DEN/PKHD G31 ....90 D3
Wyvil Av KNTSWD G13 ....51 F2

Wyvis Av BSDN G61 ....33 H1
  KNTSWD G13 ....49 H3
Wyvis Ct NMRNS G77 ....161 F3
Wyvis Pl KNTSWD G13 ....50 A3
  NMRNS G77 ....161 G3
Wyvis Qd KNTSWD G13 ....50 A3
Wyvis Wy MTHW ML1 ....173 E2

Y

Yair Dr CARD/HILL/MSPK G52 ....86 B3
Yarrow Crs BSHPTN PA7 ....46 B1
Yarrow Gdns MRYH/FIRH G20 ....67 E3
Yarrow Gardens La MRYH/FIRH G20 ....67 E3
Yarrow Pk EKILN G74 ....166 D4
Yarrow Rd BSHPBGS G64 ....37 H4
Yate Gv DEN/PKHD G31 ....91 E4
Yate Rd DEN/PKHD G31 ....91 E4
Yate St DEN/PKHD G31 ....91 E4
Yetholm Gdns CARD/HILL/MSPK G52 ....166 C1
Yetholm St SCOT G14 ....64 A1
Yetholm Ter HMLTN ML3 ....168 D2
Yett Rd MTHW ML1 ....138 A4
Yetts Crs KKNTL G66 ....21 H5
Yetts Hole Rd AIRDRIE ML6 ....75 E5
Yew Dr SPRGB/BLRNK G21 ....68 B3
Yew Pl JNSTN PA5 ....101 G5
Yokerburn Pl KNTSWD G13 ....49 H4

Yokerburn Ter CLYDBK G81 ....49 G4
Yoker Ferry Rd SCOT G14 ....49 H5
Yoker Mill Gdns KNTSWD G13 ....49 H4
Yoker Mill Rd KNTSWD G13 ....49 H4
York Dr RUTH G73 ....130 C2
Yorkhill Pde KVGV G3 ....66 B5
Yorkhill St KVGV G3 ....88 C1
York Rd AIRDRIE ML6 ....119 E4
York St CGLW G2 ....2 C6
  CLYDBK G81 ....49 G1
  WISHAW ML2 ....174 A3
Young Pl EKILS G75 ....178 D3
  UD/BTH/TAN G71 ....115 F4
  WISHAW ML2 ....158 C5
Young St CLYDBK G81 ....32 A4
  WISHAW ML2 ....174 A3
Young Ter SPRGB/BLRNK G21 ....68 D2
Young Wynd BLSH ML4 ....116 D4
Yukon Ter EKILS G75 ....165 G5
Yule Wy CUMB G67 ....26 C3

Z

Zambesi Dr BLTYR/CAMB G72 ....151 F1
Zena Crs STPS/GTHM/RID G33 ....69 F2
Zena Pl SPRGB/BLRNK G21 ....69 G2
Zena St STPS/GTHM/RID G33 ....69 G2
Zetland Rd CARD/HILL/MSPK G52 ....86 A1

Index - featured places

Abbey Cemetery JNSTN PA5 ....102 A2
Abbey Mill Business Centre PSLY PA1 ....84 C5
ABC Cinema LNPK/KPK G44 ....128 A3
Abercorn Industrial Estate PSLYN/LNWD PA3 ....84 B2
Abercorn School COWCAD G4 ....67 G4
Abode Hotel 2 D4
Abronhill Health Centre CUMB G67 ....27 G1
Abronhill High School CUMB G67 ....27 G1
Abronhill Primary School CUMB G67 ....27 F2
Agricultural Museum CRMNK/CLK/EAG G76 ....147 G5
Airdrie Academy AIRDRIE ML6 ....76 A5
Airdrie Golf Club AIRDRIE ML6 ....76 A4
Airdrie Health Centre AIRDRIE ML6 ....97 H2
Airdrie United FC (Excelsior Stadium) AIRDRIE ML6 ....98 D3
Air Link Industrial Estate PSLYN/LNWD PA3 ....84 B1
Aitkenhead Primary School DMBTN G82 ....13 H2
Aitkenhead Primary School UD/BTH/TAN G71 ....115 E3
Albert Primary School AIRDRIE ML6 ....98 C1
  SPRGB/BLRNK G21 ....68 C1
Albion Rovers FC (Cliftonhill) CTBR ML5 ....97 F3
Alexander Hospital CTBR ML5 ....96 B1
Alexandra Golf Club DEN/PKHD G31 ....91 E1
Alexandra Parade Primary School DEN/PKHD G31 ....90 D2
Alexandra Primary School AIRDRIE ML6 ....98 B2
Alison Lea Medical Centre EKILN G74 ....167 E2
Allandar Sports Centre BSDN G61 ....35 E1
Allanshaw Industrial Estate HMLTN ML3 ....169 H2
All Saints Secondary School SPRGB/BLRNK G21 ....69 F1
AMF Bowling KVGV G3 ....89 E2
The Anderson Doe Podiatry Clinic PTCK G11 ....65 G2
Anderson Primary School KVGV G3 ....89 E1
Anderston Medical Centre KVGV G3 ....88 D1
Annette Street Primary School GVH/MTFL G42 ....109 F2
Annfield Medical Centre DEN/PKHD G31 ....90 D2
Anniesland College KVD/HLHD G12 ....65 H1
  MRYH/FIRH G20 ....52 D5
  PPK/MIL G22 ....54 B4
  PTCK G11 ....65 G4
Anniesland Industrial Estate KNTSWD G13 ....51 F3
The Antonine Sports Centre CLYDBK G81 ....31 H2
Antonine Wall: Bearsden Bath-House BSDN G61 ....34 C4
Aquatec Leisure Centre MTHW ML1 ....154 D3
Arcadia Business Centre CLYDBK G81 ....48 B3

Arches Theatre CGLE G1 ....2 D7
Arden Primary School GIF/THBK G46 ....126 A3
Ardoch Medical Centre BLTYR/CAMB G72 ....131 E1
Argo Sports Centre DRUM G15 ....32 D5
Argyle Indoor Market CGLE G1 ....3 F6
Arkleston Primary School RNFRW PA4 ....63 G5
Ashcraig School STPS/GTHM/RID G33 ....70 C3
Ashfield Medical Practice MLNGV G62 ....17 E4
Atholl Preparatory School MLNGV G62 ....17 E2
Auchenback Primary School BRHD/NEIL G78 ....142 C1
Auchenlodment Primary School JNSTN PA5 ....101 H5
Auchinairn Primary School BSHPBGS G64 ....55 E3
Auchinloch Primary School KKNTL G66 ....57 E1
Auchinraith Primary School BLTYR/CAMB G72 ....151 G3
Auldhouse Retail Park PLKSW/MSWD G43 ....127 F1
Auld Kirk Museum KKNTL G66 ....21 E4
The Avenue Shopping Centre NMRNS G77 ....161 F1
Baillieston FC BAIL/MDB/MHD G69 ....94 B5
Baillieston Health Centre BAIL/MDB/MHD G69 ....94 A5
Baird Memorial Primary School CUMB G67 ....44 B1
Balaffray Primary School BSDN G61 ....16 A5
Ballaffray Shopping Centre BSDN G61 ....16 A5
Balmalloch Primary School KSYTH G65 ....8 A1
Balmore Golf Club BSHPBGS G64 ....18 B5
Balmuildy Primary School BSHPBGS G64 ....37 G5
Balornock Primary School SPRGB/BLRNK G21 ....68 D2
Bankhead Primary School KNTSWD G13 ....50 B5
  RUTH G73 ....110 C5
Bannerman High School BAIL/MDB/MHD G69 ....93 H5
Bargarran Primary School ERSK PA8 ....30 A5
Bargeddie Primary School BAIL/MDB/MHD G69 ....95 F3
Barlanark Primary School STPS/GTHM/RID G33 ....93 F3
Barmulloch Primary School SPRGB/BLRNK G21 ....69 F2
Barncluith Business Centre HMLTN ML3 ....170 C2
Barras Market DMNK/BRGTN G40 ....90 B3
Barratt Trading Estate COWCAD G4 ....67 G4
Barrhead Bowling Club BRHD/NEIL G78 ....124 B4
Barrhead High School BRHD/NEIL G78 ....124 C4
Barrhead Sports Centre BRHD/NEIL G78 ....124 B4
Barsail Primary School ERSK PA8 ....47 H3
Battlefield Primary School GVH/MTFL G42 ....109 E5
BBC Scotland GOV/IBX G51 ....88 C2
Beardmore Hotel CLYDBK G81 ....31 E5

Bearsden Academy BSDN G61 ....34 B2
Bearsden Golf Club BSDN G61 ....33 H3
Bearsden Primary School BSDN G61 ....34 B3
The Beatson West of Scotland Cancer Centre KVD/HLHD G12 ....65 H2
Beckford Primary School HMLTN ML3 ....152 D5
Beckford Street Business Centre HMLTN ML3 ....152 D5
Bellahouston Academy PLKSD/SHW G41 ....88 B4
Bellahouston Leisure Centre CARD/HILL/MSPK G52 ....87 G5
Bellahouston Primary School GOV/IBX G51 ....88 A3
Bell College HMLTN ML3 ....170 A1
The Bell Leisure Centre DMBTN G82 ....12 D4
Bellshill Academy BLSH ML4 ....136 A2
Bellshill Golf Club BLSH ML4 ....136 A4
Bellshill Industrial Estate BLSH ML4 ....135 G1
Belmont House School NMRNS G77 ....144 C4
Belvidere Primary School BLSH ML4 ....135 H3
Benburb Football Club GOV/IBX G51 ....87 F3
Bent Cemetery HMLTN ML3 ....169 H2
Berryhill Primary School WISHAW ML2 ....173 F2
Best Western Garfield House Hotel STPS/GTHM/RID G33 ....57 G4
Bewleys Hotel CGLW G2 ....2 E4
Birkenshaw Industrial Estate UD/BTH/TAN G71 ....114 D3
Bishopbriggs Golf Club BSHPBGS G64 ....54 C1
Bishopbriggs High School BSHPBGS G64 ....54 D2
Bishopbriggs Sports Centre BSHPBGS G64 ....37 H4
Bishoploch Primary School ESTRH G34 ....72 B5
Bishopton Health Centre BSHPTN PA7 ....46 A1
Bishopton Primary School BSHPTN PA7 ....28 D5
Blackfriars Primary School GBLS G5 ....89 H5
Blacklaw Primary School EKILN G74 ....167 E4
Blackwoods Medical Centre BAIL/MDB/MHD G69 ....94 B5
Blairbeth Golf Club CSMK G45 ....129 H4
Blairdardie Primary School DRUM G15 ....50 C2
Blairtummock Primary School ESTRH G34 ....94 A1
Blantyre Cemetery BLTYR/CAMB G72 ....151 F4
Blantyre High School BLTYR/CAMB G72 ....151 G3
Blantyre Victoria FC BLTYR/CAMB G72 ....152 A3
Blawarthill Hospital KNTSWD G13 ....50 B5
Blythswood Estate RNFRW PA4 ....63 E2
Bobbys Leisure Centre CUMB G67 ....26 B3
Boclair Academy BSDN G61 ....35 F4
Bothwell Bridge Hotel UD/BTH/TAN G71 ....134 B5

Bothwell Castle UD/BTH/TAN G71 ....133 G4
Bothwell Castle Golf Club UD/BTH/TAN G71 ....134 A1
Bothwell Cemetery BLSH ML4 ....135 E2
Bothwell Medical Centre UD/BTH/TAN G71 ....134 B5
Bothwell Park High School MTHW ML1 ....172 B1
Bothwell Park Industrial Estate UD/BTH/TAN G71 ....134 B3
Bothwell Primary School UD/BTH/TAN G71 ....134 B5
Braehead Arena RNFRW PA4 ....64 A2
Braehead Business Park RNFRW PA4 ....64 A3
Braehead Primary School DMBTN G82 ....13 F3
Braehead Retail Park GOV/IBX G51 ....64 C4
Braehead Shopping Centre GOV/IBX G51 ....64 C4
Braidbar Primary School GIF/THBK G46 ....127 G4
Braidcraft Medical Centre PLK/PH/NH G53 ....106 C3
Braidfield High School CLYDBK G81 ....49 F1
Braidhurst Business Centre MTHW ML1 ....136 B5
Braidhurst High School MTHW ML1 ....154 C1
Braidhurst Industrial Estate MTHW ML1 ....154 C2
Brannock High School MTHW ML1 ....137 H4
Braidland Primary School PSLYS PA2 ....103 F3
Bridge of Weir Primary School BRWEIR PA11 ....79 G2
Bridgeton Business Centre DMNK/BRGTN G40 ....90 B4
Bridgeton Health Centre DMNK/BRGTN G40 ....90 C4
The Bridgewater Shopping Centre ERSK PA8 ....47 G1
Broomhill Industrial Estate KKNTL G66 ....21 G3
Broomhill Primary School PTCK G11 ....65 G2
Broomlee School PTCK G11 ....65 G4
Brownsburn Industrial Estate AIRDRIE ML6 ....98 C4
Bruce Medical Centre BLSH ML4 ....136 A2
Buchanan Business Park STPS/GTHM/RID G33 ....57 G5
Buchanan Galleries & Shopping Centre CGLE G1 ....3 G4
Burgh Primary School RUTH G73 ....110 D4
Burnbank Medical Centre HMLTN ML3 ....152 B5
Burnbrae Primary School PLK/PH/NH G55 ....126 A2
Burnhead Primary School UD/BTH/TAN G71 ....116 A4
Burnhill Sports Centre RUTH G73 ....110 C4
Burnside Primary School RUTH G73 ....130 A2
Burrell Collection PLKSW/MSWD G43 ....108 A3
Busby Primary School CRMNK/CLK/EAG G76 ....146 A4
Bushes Primary School PSLYS PA2 ....104 A4
Butterbiggins Medical Centre GVH/MTFL G42 ....109 G1
Byres Road Market PTCK G11 ....66 B2

Cadder Primary School SMSTN G23 ....53 E4
Cadzow Business Centre HMLTN ML3 ....170 A1
Cadzow Health Centre HMLTN ML3 ....170 A1
Cadzow Industrial Estate HMLTN ML3 ....170 A1
Cairnhill Industrial Estate ESTRH G34 ....94 A3
Cairnhill Trading Estate AIRDRIE ML6 ....98 B3
Cairns Primary School BLTYR/CAMB G72 ....131 H3
Calderbank Primary School AIRDRIE ML6 ....118 D1
Calderbraes Golf Club UD/BTH/TAN G71 ....114 B3
Caldercuilt Primary School SMSTN G23 ....52 D2
Calderglen Country Park EKILS G75 ....179 F2
Calder Primary School MTHW ML1 ....155 E3
Caldervale High School AIRDRIE ML6 ....99 G2
Calderwood Lodge Jewish Primary School PLKSW/MSWD G43 ....127 H2
Calderwood Primary School EKILN G74 ....130 B1
Caledonian University CGLW G2 ....2 E3
Caledonia Primary School BAIL/MDB/MHD G69 ....114 A1
Callander Street Clinic MRYH/FIRH G20 ....67 E3
Cambuslang Avory Club BLTYR/CAMB G72 ....131 F3
Cambuslang College BLTYR/CAMB G72 ....131 G2
  EKILN G74 ....166 C3
Cambuslang Golf Club BLTYR/CAMB G72 ....112 C5
Cambuslang Rangers FC BLTYR/CAMB G72 ....131 E1
Cambuslang Recreation Centre BLTYR/CAMB G72 ....132 A2
Cambuslang RFC RUTH G73 ....130 C2
Cambusnethan Primary School WISHAW ML2 ....174 C1
Campanile Hotel KVGV G3 ....88 D2
Campsie Recreation Centre KKNTL G66 ....4 B2
Campsie View School KKNTL G66 ....39 F3
Canberra Primary School EKILS G75 ....165 G5
Canniesburn Hospital BSDN G61 ....51 F1
Carbrain Primary School CUMB G67 ....26 D3
Cardinal Newman High School BLSH ML4 ....135 F2
Cardonald Clinic CARD/HILL/MSPK G52 ....86 D4
Cardonald College CARD/HILL/MSPK G52 ....107 E1
Cardonald Primary School CARD/HILL/MSPK G52 ....86 C5
Carfin Industrial Estate MTHW ML1 ....137 F4
Carfin Primary School CLYDBK G81 ....31 F2
Carlibar Primary School BRHD/NEIL G78 ....124 B4
Carmichael Hall GIF/THBK G46 ....127 E5
Carmunnock Cemetery CSMK G45 ....146 C1
Carmunnock Primary School CRMNK/CLK/EAG G76 ....147 E5

Carmyle Medical Centre
CAR/SHTL G32 .... 112 C4
Carmyle Primary School
CAR/SHTL G32 .... 112 D3
Carnbooth Residential Care
CRMNK/CLK/EAG G76 ...... 146 C3
Cambroe Primary School
CTBR ML5 .... 97 G5
Carntyne Primary School
STPS/GTHM/RID G33 .... 91 G1
Carntradric Primary School
GIF/THBK G46 .... 126 C3
Caroisdale Medical Centre
CRMNK/CLK/EAG G76 ...... 145 H3
Caroisdale Primary School
CRMNK/CLK/EAG G76 ...... 145 H4
Carsemeadow School
BRWEIR PA11 .... 78 A1
Cart Vale Secondary School
GOV/IBX G51 .... 88 A2
Castlebank Industrial Estate
PTCK G11 .... 65 H5
Castlecary House Hotel
BALLOCH G68 .... 11 H1
Castlefield Primary School
EKILS G75 .... 177 G3
Castlehead High School
PSLYS PA2 .... 104 A1
Castlehill Primary School
BSDN G61 .... 33 G2
WISHAW ML2 .... 173 H5
Castlemilk Health Centre
CSMK G45 .... 129 F4
Castlemilk High School
CSMK G45 .... 129 F5
Castlemilk Pool
CSMK G45 .... 129 F4
Castlemilk Sports Centre
CSMK G45 .... 129 F4
Castleton Primary School
CSMK G45 .... 128 D4
Cathcart Castle Golf Club
CRMNK/CLK/EAG G76 ...... 145 F3
Cathedral Primary School
MTHW ML1 .... 154 D3
Cathkin Braes Country Park
CSMK G45 .... 147 G1
Cathkin Braes Golf Club
RUTH G73 .... 148 A1
Cathkin High School
BLTYR/CAMB G72 .... 130 D3
Cathkin Primary School
RUTH G73 .... 130 C4
Cawder Golf Club
BSHPBGS G64 .... 37 G2
Celtic FC (Celtic Park)
DEN/PKHD G31 .... 91 E4
Central College of Commerce
CGLE G1 .... 3 G4
Central Health Centre
CUMB G67 .... 26 B4
Chapelgreen Primary School
KSYTH G65 .... 7 E3
Chapelhall Industrial Estate
AIRDRIE ML6 .... 99 F5
AIRDRIE ML6 .... 119 E1
Chapelhall Primary School
AIRDRIE ML6 .... 119 E2
Chapelside Primary School
AIRDRIE ML6 .... 76 B5
Chapel Street
Industrial Estate
MRYH/FIRH G20 .... 52 D5
Charing Cross Clinic
KVGV G3 .... 2 A2
Chatelherault Country Park
HMLTN ML3 .... 181 H1
Chatelherault Primary School
HMLTN ML3 .... 170 B4
Chatelherault Visitor Centre
HMLTN ML3 .... 170 D5
Child Health Clinic
PLKSW/MSWD G43 .... 108 B4
Chimnsyde Primary School
PPK/MIL G22 .... 54 A5
Christ the King Primary School
MTHW ML1 .... 137 G1
Chryston High School
BAIL/MDB/MHD G69 .... 58 B3
Chryston Primary School
BAIL/MDB/MHD G69 .... 58 B3
Chryston Valley
Business Centre
BAIL/MDB/MHD G69 .... 58 B3
Cineworld
CGLW G2 .... 2 E3
DEN/PKHD G31 .... 91 F4
City Chambers
CGLE G1 .... 3 G5
Claremont High School
EKILN G74 .... 167 F5
Clarkston Primary School
AIRDRIE ML6 .... 99 E1
Cleland Athletics Track
MTHW ML1 .... 156 B2
Cleland Hospital
MTHW ML1 .... 157 F1
Cleland Primary School
MTHW ML1 .... 157 E1
Cleveden Secondary School
KVD/HLHD G12 .... 66 A1
MRYH/FIRH G20 .... 66 D2
Clippens Special School
PSLYN/LNWD PA3 .... 82 B3
Clober Golf Club
MLNGV G62 .... 16 D2
Clober Primary School
MLNGV G62 .... 16 C3
Clyde Auditorium
KVGV G3 .... 88 C2
Clydebank Business Centre
CLYDBK G81 .... 49 F3
Clydebank College
CLYDBK G81 .... 32 A5
DMBTN G82 .... 12 C3
Clydebank Crematorium
CLYDBK G81 .... 31 E2
Clydebank & District Golf
Course
CLYDBK G81 .... 32 B2

Clydebank Health Centre
CLYDBK G81 .... 32 A4
Clydebank High School
CLYDBK G81 .... 31 H4
Clydebank Town Hall
CLYDBK G81 .... 48 C1
Clydebuilt
GOV/IBX G51 .... 64 B3
Clyde FC
(Broadwood Stadium)
BALLOCH G68 .... 24 D4
Clyde Industrial Estate
RUTH G73 .... 111 G4
Clydemuir Primary School
CLYDBK G81 .... 31 E4
Clydesdale Cricket Club
PLKSD/SHW G41 .... 108 C2
Clyde Tunnel
SCOT G14 .... 65 F5
Clydeview Primary School
GOV/IBX G51 .... 154 A2
Clydeview Shopping Centre
BLTYR/CAMB G72 .... 151 G3
Clydeway Business Centre
KVGV G3 .... 88 D2
Coatbridge Business Centre
CTBR ML5 .... 97 F3
Coatbridge College
CTBR ML5 .... 97 E2
Coatbridge Health Centre
CTBR ML5 .... 96 D3
Coatbridge High School
CTBR ML5 .... 96 D2
Coatbridge Outdoor Sports
Complex Track
CTBR ML5 .... 96 C4
Coathill Hospital
CTBR ML5 .... 96 D5
Coats Observatory
PSLY PA1 .... 84 A4
Cochrane Castle Golf Club
JNSTN PA5 .... 121 F1
Cochrane Castle Primary
School
JNSTN PA5 .... 121 E1
College of Building & Printing
CGLE G1 .... 3 G4
Coighunun Park Primary
School
BSDN G61 .... 33 H5
Coltness High School
WISHAW ML2 .... 174 C1
Coltness Primary School
WISHAW ML2 .... 157 F4
Columba High School
CTBR ML5 .... 97 E4
Colville Park Golf Club
MTHW ML1 .... 155 E1
Commonhead
Primary School
CTBR ML5 .... 94 C1
Condorrat Health Centre
CUMB G67 .... 43 H2
Condorrat Primary School
CUMB G67 .... 44 A1
Copeland Primary School
GOV/IBX G51 .... 88 A2
Corpus Christi
Primary School
AIRDRIE ML6 .... 118 C1
KNTSWD G13 .... 50 D5
Corseford School
KLBCH PA10 .... 120 C2
Cotton Street Business Park
DMNK/BRGTN G40 .... 110 D2
Cowglen Golf Club
PLKSW/MSWD G43 .... 107 G5
Cowglen Hospital
PLK/PH/NH G53 .... 107 E5
Craigdhu Primary School
MLNGV G62 .... 16 D3
Craighead Primary School
KKNTL G66 .... 5 G4
Craighead School
HMLTN ML3 .... 152 C3
Craigholme School
PLKSD/SHW G41 .... 108 B1
Craigielea Primary School
PSLYN/LNWD PA3 .... 83 F3
Craigton Crematorium
CARD/HILL/MSPK G52 ...... 87 E4
Craigton Primary School
CARD/HILL/MSPK G52 ...... 87 F4
Croftcroighn Special School
STPS/GTHM/RID G33 .... 71 F5
Crofthead Industrial Estate
BRHD/NEIL G78 .... 140 D3
Crookfur Primary School
NMRNS G77 .... 144 A3
Crookston Castle (NTS)
PLK/PH/NH G53 .... 106 C2
Cross Arthurlie
Primary School
BRHD/NEIL G78 .... 123 H3
Crosshouse Primary School
EKILS G75 .... 177 F3
Crowne Plaza Hotel
KVGV G3 .... 88 C2
Crowngate Business Centre
DMNK/BRGTN G40 .... 90 C4
Crownpoint Sports Complex
DMNK/BRGTN G40 .... 90 C3
Crow Wood Golf Club
BAIL/MDB/MHD G69 .... 57 H5
Cumbernauld Airport
BALLOCH G68 .... 11 E2
Cumbernauld College
CUMB G67 .... 26 B4
Cumbernauld High School
CUMB G67 .... 27 E4
Cumbernauld Primary School
BALLOCH G68 .... 10 D4
Cumbernauld Shopping Centre
CUMB G67 .... 26 B4
Cumbernauld Theatre
CUMB G67 .... 26 D1
Cunard Primary School
CLYDBK G81 .... 49 F2
Cuthbertson Primary School
PLKSD/SHW G41 .... 109 F1

Daily Record & Sunday Mail
Offices
KVGV G3 .... 89 E2
Dairsie House School
PLKSW/MSWD G43 .... 127 H1
Daldowie Crematorium
UD/BTH/TAN G71 .... 114 A4
Dalmarnock Industrial Estate
RUTH G73 .... 111 E2
Dalmarnock Primary
School Annexe
DMNK/BRGTN G40 .... 90 D5
Dalmarnock Primary School
DMNK/BRGTN G40 .... 90 D5
Dalmarnock Trading Estate
RUTH G73 .... 110 D3
Dalmuir Municipal Golf Club
CLYDBK G81 .... 31 F4
Dalreoch Primary School
DMBTN G82 .... 12 B2
Dalshoim Industrial Estate
MRYH/FIRH G20 .... 52 A4
Dalzell House
MTHW ML1 .... 172 B3
Dalziel Business Centre
MTHW ML1 .... 154 D4
Dalziel High School
MTHW ML1 .... 154 C4
Darnley Outdoor
Recreation Centre
BSHPBGS G64 .... 54 C3
Darnley Primary School
PLK/PH/NH G53 .... 125 H3
Darrows Estate
BLSH ML4 .... 135 E1
David Dale College
DMNK/BRGTN G40 .... 90 C4
David Livingstone Centre
(NTS)
UD/BTH/TAN G71 .... 133 H1
David Livingstone Primary
School
BLTYR/CAMB G72 .... 151 G1
David Lloyd Sports Centre
PSLYN/LNWD PA3 .... 84 D1
Dental Hospital & School
CGLW G2 .... 2 C3
The Dollan Aqua Centre
EKILN G74 .... 166 B4
Donald Dewar
Leisure Centre
DRUM G15 .... 50 B1
Douglas Academy
MLNGV G62 .... 16 B2
Douglas Inch Centre
KVGV G3 .... 2 A2
Douglas Park Golf Club
BSDN G61 .... 34 D3
Downanhill Primary School
PTCK G11 .... 66 B4
Dr D'Silva & Partners
UD/BTH/TAN G71 .... 115 H5
Drumchapel Health Centre
DRUM G15 .... 33 E5
Drumchapel High School
DRUM G15 .... 33 E5
Drumchapel Hospital
DRUM G15 .... 50 B1
Drumchapel Pool
DRUM G15 .... 50 A1
Drummore School
DRUM G15 .... 33 H4
Drumoyne Industrial Estate
GOV/IBX G51 .... 87 F3
Drumoyne Primary School
GOV/IBX G51 .... 87 F2
Drumpark School
BAIL/MDB/MHD G69 .... 95 G3
Drumpellier Country Park
CTBR ML5 .... 95 H1
Drumpellier Cricket Club
CTBR ML5 .... 96 A3
Drumpellier Golf Club
CTBR ML5 .... 95 H3
Drumry Primary
School Annexe
DRUM G15 .... 33 E4
Drumry Primary School
DRUM G15 .... 49 H1
Duchess Industrial Estate
RUTH G73 .... 111 F3
Dullatur Golf Club
BALLOCH G68 .... 9 H4
Dumbarton Academy
DMBTN G82 .... 13 F3
Dumbarton Castle
DMBTN G82 .... 13 F5
Dumbarton FC (Strathclyde
Homes Stadium)
DMBTN G82 .... 13 E5
Dumbarton Golf Club
DMBTN G82 .... 13 E2
Dumbarton Health Centre
DMBTN G82 .... 13 E3
Dumbarton Joint Hospital
DMBTN G82 .... 12 B3
Dumbarton Peoples Theatre
DMBTN G82 .... 13 G4
Dunard Primary School
MRYH/FIRH G20 .... 67 E2
Duncanrig Secondary School
EKILS G75 .... 165 G4
Duncanrig Sports Centre
EKILS G75 .... 165 G5
Dundas Business Centre
COWCAD G4 .... 3 G2
Dundyvan Industrial Estate
CTBR ML5 .... 96 C5
Dunrobin Primary School
AIRDRIE ML6 .... 99 F2
Dykebar Hospital
PSLYS PA2 .... 105 E5
Earnock High School
HMLTN ML3 .... 169 F3
Eastbank Academy
CAR/SHTL G32 .... 92 C5
Eastbank Primary School
CAR/SHTL G32 .... 92 D4
Easterhouse Day Care
ESTRH G34 .... 94 A1

Easterhouse Pool
ESTRH G34 .... 93 H1
Easterhouse Sports Centre
ESTRH G34 .... 71 G5
Eastfield Primary School
BALLOCH G68 .... 25 F4
East Fulton Primary School
PSLYN/LNWD PA3 .... 81 G5
Easthall Primary School
ESTRH G34 .... 94 B3
East Kilbride Arts Centre
Cinema
EKILN G74 .... 166 C2
East Kilbride Golf Club
EKILN G74 .... 149 G4
East Kilbride Ice Rink
EKILN G74 .... 166 C2
East Kilbride
Shopping Centre
EKILN G74 .... 166 B4
East Kilbride Sports Club
EKILS G75 .... 179 F3
East Kilbride Stadium
EKILN G74 .... 166 D3
East Milton Primary School
EKILS G75 .... 165 H4
Eastmuir Special School
CAR/SHTL G32 .... 93 E3
East Park Home School
MRYH/FIRH G20 .... 66 D1
East Renfrewshire Golf Club
NMRNS G77 .... 160 C5
Eastside Industrial Estate
KKNTL G66 .... 21 F4
Eastwood High School
NMRNS G77 .... 144 B3
Eastwood Recreation Centre
GIF/THBK G46 .... 127 E5
Eastwood Theatre
GIF/THBK G46 .... 127 E5
Elderpark Clinic
GOV/IBX G51 .... 87 G2
Elder Park Primary School
GOV/IBX G51 .... 87 F1
Elderslie Cottage Hospital
JNSTN PA5 .... 102 A2
Elderslie Golf Club
JNSTN PA5 .... 102 D1
Elmvale Primary School
SPRGB/BLRNK G21 .... 68 B3
Elmwood Medical Centre
NMRNS G77 .... 144 C4
Empire Cinema
CLYDBK G81 .... 49 E1
Erskine Golf Club
BSHPTN PA7 .... 29 E3
Erskine Health Centre
ERSK PA8 .... 30 B5
Erskine Hospital
BSHPTN PA7 .... 29 H3
Erskine Swimming Pool
ERSK PA8 .... 47 G1
Erskine View Clinic
OLDK G60 .... 30 B2
Esporta, Dougalston Golf Club
MLNGV G62 .... 17 G2
Eurocentral International
Freight Terminal
MTHW ML1 .... 118 A5
Failside Secondary School
UD/BTH/TAN G71 .... 135 E1
Faraday Retail Park
CTBR ML5 .... 96 D3
Farm Castle Industrial Estate
RUTH G73 .... 111 F4
Farmeloan Industrial Estate
RUTH G73 .... 111 E4
Fereneze Golf Club
BRHD/NEIL G78 .... 123 H4
Ferguslie Cricket Club
PSLYS PA2 .... 103 H1
Ferguslie Primary School
PSLYN/LNWD PA3 .... 83 G3
Fernhill School
RUTH G73 .... 130 B4
Festival Business Centre
GOV/IBX G51 .... 88 B3
Firhill Business Centre
MRYH/FIRH G20 .... 67 F2
Firpark School
MTHW ML1 .... 172 A1
Flemington Industrial Estate
BLTYR/CAMB G72 .... 132 B3
Florence Street Clinic
GBLS G5 .... 89 H4
Flowerhill Industrial Estate
AIRDRIE ML6 .... 98 C1
Fordbank Primary School
JNSTN PA5 .... 120 D1
Forge Shopping Centre
DEN/PKHD G31 .... 91 F3
The Fort Theatre
BSHPBGS G64 .... 54 C2
Fountain Business Centre
CTBR ML5 .... 96 D2
French Street Industrial Estate
RNFRW PA4 .... 63 E4
Fullwood Health Centre
MTHW ML1 .... 137 F5
Fullwood Industrial Estate
HMLTN ML3 .... 152 C5
HMLTN ML3 .... 169 C1
Gadburn Special School
SPRGB/BLRNK G21 .... 69 F1
The Gait
CGLE G1 .... 3 H6
Gallery of Modern Art
CGLE G1 .... 3 H5
Gallowgate Market
CGLE G1 .... 90 A3
Gallowhill Primary School
PSLYN/LNWD PA3 .... 85 E2
Garnetbank Primary School
KVGV G3 .... 2 B2
Garrell Business Centre
KSYTH G65 .... 8 A2
Garrion Business Park
WISHAW ML2 .... 173 H5
Garrowhill Primary School
BAIL/MDB/MHD G69 .... 93 H4

Garscadden Primary School
KNTSWD G13 .... 50 A4
Gartconner Primary School
KKNTL G66 .... 22 C5
Gartcosh Primary School
BAIL/MDB/MHD G69 .... 73 E1
Gartcosh Works Sports Club
BAIL/MDB/MHD G69 .... 73 F1
Garthamlock Primary School
STPS/GTHM/RID G33 .... 70 D5
Garthamlock Secondary
School
STPS/GTHM/RID G33 .... 71 E4
Gartnavel General Hospital
KVD/HLHD G12 .... 65 H2
Gartnavel Royal Hospital
KVD/HLHD G12 .... 65 H2
Gartsherrie Industrial Estate
CTBR ML5 .... 74 C5
Gartsherrie Primary School
CTBR ML5 .... 96 B1
Gask House School
BSHPBGS G64 .... 54 C4
Gavinburn Primary School
OLDK G60 .... 30 A1
Georgian Hotel
CTBR ML5 .... 96 B2
GHK RFC
KNTSWD G13 .... 51 G5
Giffnock Primary School
GIF/THBK G46 .... 127 F4
The Glasgow Academy
KVD/HLHD G12 .... 66 D3
Glasgow Airport
RNFRW PA4 .... 62 A4
Glasgow Airport Terminals
PSLYN/LNWD PA3 .... 62 A5
Glasgow Botanic Gardens
KVD/HLHD G12 .... 66 C2
Glasgow Caledonian
University
COWCAD C4 .... 3 F2
KVD/HLHD G12 .... 51 H5
KVGV G3 .... 66 D5
Glasgow Cathedral
COWCAD C4 .... 3 K4
Glasgow College of Nautical
Studies
GBLS G5 .... 89 H4
Glasgow Cross
CGLE G1 .... 3 H7
The Glasgow Gaelic School
KVGV G3 .... 88 D1
Glasgow Golf Club
BSDN G61 .... 52 B1
Glasgow Marriott Hotel
KVGV G3 .... 88 B3
Glasgow Metropolitan College
CGLE G1 .... 3 G4
Glasgow Museums Resource
Centre (The Open Museum)
PLK/PH/NH G53 .... 125 E2
Glasgow Nuffield Hospital
KVD/HLHD G12 .... 66 A1
Glasgow Royal Infirmary
DEN/PKHD G31 .... 3 K3
Glasgow School of Art
COWCAD C4 .... 2 C3
COWCAD C4 .... 2 D2
Glasgow Science Centre &
IMAX Theatre
GOV/IBX G51 .... 88 C2
Glasgow Ski
& Snowboard Centre
PLKSD/SHW G41 .... 87 H5
Glasgow Tower
GOV/IBX G51 .... 88 B2
Glenboig Primary School
CTBR ML5 .... 74 C1
Glenburn Clinic
PSLYS PA2 .... 104 A4
Glencairn Primary School
MTHW ML1 .... 155 E5
Glencryan School
CUMB G67 .... 44 D1
Glendale Primary School
PLKSD/SHW G41 .... 89 E5
Glenduffhill Cemetery
CAR/SHTL G32 .... 93 E3
Glen Family Centre
GIF/THBK G46 .... 126 D5
Gleniffer Braes Country Park
CUMB G67 .... 11 G5
Gleniffer High School
PSLYS PA2 .... 103 F4
Glenlee Primary School
HMLTN ML3 .... 152 B5
Glenmanor Primary School
BAIL/MDB/MHD G69 .... 58 D1
Glenpark Industrial Estate
DEN/PKHD G31 .... 91 E3
Glenvale FC
PSLYS PA2 .... 83 H5
Glenwood Business Centre
CSMK G45 .... 129 F4
Glenwood Business Park
CSMK G45 .... 129 F4
Golfhill Hotel
RNFRW PA4 .... 63 E5
Goethe Institute
KVGV G3 .... 66 D5
Goldenhill Primary School
CLYDBK G81 .... 32 A2
Golfhill Primary School
AIRDRIE ML6 .... 75 H4
DEN/PKHD G31 .... 90 C1
Gorbals Health Centre
GBLS G5 .... 89 H5
Gorbals Leisure Centre
GBLS G5 .... 90 A4
Govan Health Centre
GOV/IBX G51 .... 87 F1
Govan High School
GOV/IBX G51 .... 87 F2
Govanhill Health Centre
GVH/MTFL G42 .... 109 G2
Gowanbank Primary School
PLK/PH/NH G53 .... 125 F4

Greenbank Garden (NTS)
CRMNK/CLK/EAG G76 ....145 E4
Greenburn Primary School
EKILN G74 ....167 G3
Greenfaulds High School
CUMB G67 ....44 C1
Greenfield Primary School
GOV/IBX G51 ....87 G2
Greenhill Industrial Estate
CTBR ML5 ....74 D5
Greenhill Primary School
CTBR ML5 ....96 D1
Greenhills Health Centre
EKILS G75 ....177 F2
Greenhills Primary School
EKILS G75 ....177 H3
Grenview School
PPK/MIL G22 ....54 A5
Grovewood Business Centre
BLSH ML4 ....116 B4
Gryffe High School
CRG/CRSL/HOU PA6 ....80 B1
Haggs Castle Golf Club
CARD/HILL/MSPK G52 ....107 H1
Haghill Park Primary School
DEN/PKHD G31 ....91 E2
Hairmyres & Stonehouse
Hospitals
EKILS G75 ....165 E4
Halfmerke Primary School
EKILN G74 ....166 D2
Hallside Primary School
BLTYR/CAMB G72 ....132 B3
Hamilton Academical FC
(New Douglas Park)
HMLTN ML3 ....152 D5
Hamilton Business Park
HMLTN ML3 ....153 E5
Hamilton College
HMLTN ML3 ....153 E5
Hamilton Golf Club
HMLTN ML3 ....171 F5
Hamilton Grammar School
HMLTN ML3 ....170 A2
Hamilton Industrial Estate
PPK/MIL G22 ....67 G2
Hamilton Park Racecourse
HMLTN ML3 ....153 E3
Hamilton Public Baths
HMLTN ML3 ....170 A1
Hamilton School for the Deaf
HMLTN ML3 ....169 F3
Hamilton Water Palace
HMLTN ML3 ....153 E5
Hampden (Scotland's
National Stadium)
GVH/MTFL G42 ....109 H4
Hampden Special School
GVH/MTFL G42 ....110 A4
Harestanes Primary School
KKNTL G66 ....22 A4
Hartfield Clinic
DMBTN G82 ....13 F3
The Harvest Clinic
COWCAD G4 ....2 B1
Hawkhead Cemetery
PSLYS PA2 ....105 F1
Hawkhead Hospital
PSLYS PA2 ....105 F2
Hayston Golf Club
KKNTL G66 ....20 D3
Healthcare International (HCI)
CLYDBK G81 ....48 C1
Heathery Knowe Primary
School
EKILS G75 ....178 A1
Heriot Primary School
PSLYS PA2 ....103 E4
High Blantyre Primary School
BLTYR/CAMB G72 ....151 E3
High School of Glasgow
BSDN G61 ....34 A4
The High School of Glasgow
KNTSWD G13 ....51 F5
High Street Industrial Estate
KKNTL G66 ....21 E4
Hillhead High School
KVD/HLHD G12 ....66 D4
Hillhead Primary School
KVD/HLHD G12 ....21 G5
KVD/HLHD G12 ....66 D5
Hillhead RFC
KVD/HLHD G12 ....66 A2
Hillington Industrial Estate
CARD/HILL/MSPK G52 ....86 A2
Hillington Park Retail &
Amenities Centre
CARD/HILL/MSPK G52 ....86 B1
Hillington Primary School
CARD/HILL/MSPK G52 ....86 B3
Hillpark Secondary School
PLKSW/MSWD G43 ....127 F2
Hill's Trust Primary School
GOV/IBX G51 ....87 G1
HM Prison
BSHPBGS G64 ....55 H4
STPS/GTHM/RID G33 ....70 A5
Hollybrook Special School
GVH/MTFL G42 ....109 G2
Hollywood Bowl
BAIL/MDB/MHD G69 ....115 H1
Holm Industrial Estate
PSLYS PA2 ....104 C2
Holmwood House (NTS)
LNPK/KPK G44 ....128 C3
Holy Cross High School
HMLTN ML3 ....170 B1
Holy Cross Primary School
GVH/MTFL G42 ....109 G2
KSYTH G65 ....24 D1
Holy Family Primary School
HMLTN ML3 ....136 B2
KKNTL G66 ....40 A4
Holyrood Secondary School
& Sports Centre
GVH/MTFL G42 ....109 H3
Holytown Primary School
MTHW ML1 ....137 G1
Hotel 377
CGLW G2 ....2 C6

Hotel du Vin
KVD/HLHD G12 ....66 A2
Hotel Ibis
CGLW G2 ....2 C3
House for an Art Lover
PLKSD/SHW G41 ....87 H4
Househillmuir
Primary School
PLK/PH/NH G53 ....125 G2
Houston Primary School
CRG/CRSL/HOU PA6 ....80 C2
Howford Special School
PLK/PH/NH G53 ....106 B2
Howwood Primary School
HWWD PA9 ....120 A4
The Hunter Health Centre
EKILN G74 ....166 C4
Hunter High School
EKILN G74 ....167 F3
Hunterhill Tutorial Centre
PSLYS PA2 ....104 D1
Hunterian Museum
KVD/HLHD G12 ....66 C4
Hunter Primary School
EKILN G74 ....167 E3
Hutchesons Grammar Junior
School
KVD/HLHD G12 ....66 C4
Hutchesons Grammar
Preparatory School
GVH/MTFL G42 ....109 F2
Hutchesons Grammar School
PLKSD/SHW G41 ....108 D1
Hutchesons' Hall
CGLE G1 ....3 G6
Hutchesons St Aloysians RFC
GIF/THBK G46 ....126 D2
Hyndland Primary School
PTCK G11 ....66 A4
Hyndland Secondary School
KVD/HLHD G12 ....65 H3
Ibrox Industrial Estate
GOV/IBX G51 ....88 A3
Ibrox Primary School
GOV/IBX G51 ....87 H4
IKEA Store Glasgow
GOV/IBX G51 ....64 B4
Inchinnan Business Park
RNFRW PA4 ....61 H2
Inchinnan Primary School
RNFRW PA4 ....48 A4
International Christian College
COWCAD G4 ....3 J4
Isobel Mair School
CRMNK/CLK/EAG G76 ....145 G1
Italian Centre
CGLE G1 ....3 G6
Jackton Business Centre
EKILS G75 ....176 B1
James Aiton Primary School
BLTYR/CAMB G72 ....131 F1
James Hamilton Heritage
Park
EKILN G74 ....148 C5
John Hillhouse Industrial
Estate
BLTYR/CAMB G72 ....111 G5
John Ogilvie High School
HMLTN ML3 ....168 D1
John Paul Academy
SMSTN G23 ....52 B2
John Paul II Primary School
CSMK G45 ....129 G5
UD/BTH/TAN G71 ....115 H5
John Smith Memorial
Swimming Pool
AIRDRIE ML6 ....98 B2
Johnstone Health Centre
JNSTN PA5 ....101 H4
Johnstone High School
JNSTN PA5 ....121 E1
Johnstone Hospital
JNSTN PA5 ....101 H2
Johnstone Swimming Pool
JNSTN PA5 ....101 G3
John Wheatley College
CAR/SHTL G32 ....92 C4
STPS/GTHM/RID G33 ....92 D2
The John Wright Sports Centre
EKILN G74 ....166 D3
Jordanhill School
KNTSWD G13 ....65 F1
Keil School
DMBTN G82 ....12 C4
Keir Hardie Memorial Primary
School
MTHW ML1 ....138 A4
Keir Hardie Sports Centre
MTHW ML1 ....137 F1
Kelbourne School
MRYH/FIRH G20 ....66 D1
Kelburne Cricket Club
PSLY PA1 ....84 D4
Kelvindale Primary School
KVD/HLHD G12 ....65 H1
Kelvingrove Art Gallery &
Museum
PTCK G11 ....66 C5
Kelvin Hall International
Sports Arena
KVGV G3 ....66 B5
Kelvin School
KVGV G3 ....66 B5
Kelvinside Academy
KVD/HLHD G12 ....66 C2
Kenilworth Medical Centre
CUMB G67 ....26 A5
Kennyhill School
DEN/PKHD G31 ....91 F1
Kersland School
PSLYS PA2 ....104 C3
Kibble Education
& Care Centre
PSLYN/LNWD PA3 ....83 H1
Kilbarchan Cemetery
JNSTN PA5 ....100 C1
Kilbarchan Primary School
KLBCH PA10 ....100 B2

Kilbowie Cemetery
CLYDBK G81 ....49 F1
Kilbowie Primary School
CLYDBK G81 ....32 A5
Kilbowie Retail Park
CLYDBK G81 ....49 F1
Kildrum Primary School
CUMB G67 ....26 D3
Killermont Primary School
BSDN G61 ....34 D4
Kilpatrick School
CLYDBK G81 ....31 F2
Kilsyth Academy
KSYTH G65 ....8 A1
Kilsyth Health Centre
KSYTH G65 ....8 C2
Kilsyth Primary School
KSYTH G65 ....8 B2
Kilsyth Swimming Pool
KSYTH G65 ....8 A1
Kingsgate Retail Park
EKILN G74 ....149 E4
Kings Park Secondary School
LNPK/KPK G44 ....128 D2
Kings Theatre
CGLW G2 ....2 B3
Kinning Park Medical Centre
PLKSD/SHW G41 ....88 D3
Kirkhill Golf Club
BLTYR/CAMB G72 ....131 F4
Kirkhill Primary School
NMRNS G77 ....145 E5
Kirkintilloch Foot Clinic
KKNTL G66 ....21 G5
Kirkintilloch Golf Club
KKNTL G66 ....20 C4
Kirkintilloch High School
KKNTL G66 ....21 H5
Kirkintilloch Industrial Estate
KKNTL G66 ....21 F3
Kirkintilloch Leisure Centre
KKNTL G66 ....40 A1
Kirkland Hospital
UD/BTH/TAN G71 ....134 C3
Kirklandneuk Primary School
RNFRW PA4 ....63 E3
Kirk Lane Cemetery
PLKSW/MSWD G43 ....108 B5
Kirkriggs School
CSMK G45 ....129 H2
Kirkshaws Primary School
CTBR ML5 ....96 B5
Kirktonholme
Primary School
EKILN G74 ....165 H3
Kirkwood Health Clinic
CTBR ML5 ....95 H5
Kittoch School
EKILS G75 ....178 A1
Knightswood Golf Club
KNTSWD G13 ....50 C4
Knightswood Primary School
KNTSWD G13 ....51 F4
Knightswood Secondary
School
KNTSWD G13 ....51 E5
Knockburn Primary School
SPRCB/BLRNK G21 ....55 F4
Knowetop Primary School
MTHW ML1 ....172 A4
Knoxland Primary School
DMBTN G82 ....13 F4
Ladywell Primary School
MTHW ML1 ....154 C3
Ladywell School
SCOT G14 ....65 H2
Lagoon Leisure Centre
PSLY PA1 ....84 C5
Laigh Bent Sports Club
HMLTN ML3 ....170 C1
Laird Business Park
DMNK/BRGTN G40 ....110 D2
Lairdsland Primary School
KKNTL G66 ....21 E5
Lambhill Cemetery
SMSTN G23 ....53 E2
Lamlash Primary School
STPS/GTHM/RID G33 ....92 C1
Lammermoor Primary School
WISHAW ML2 ....174 A1
Lanarkshire Ice Rink
HMLTN ML3 ....170 B1
Langcraigs Primary School
PSLYS PA2 ....103 H5
Langfaulds Primary School
DRUM G15 ....33 E4
Langlands School
GOV/IBX G51 ....87 F2
Langloan Primary School
CTBR ML5 ....96 B3
Langs Hotel
CGLW G2 ....3 F3
Langside College
CSMK G45 ....129 G4
GVH/MTFL G42 ....109 F4
RUTH G73 ....111 F5
Langside Primary School
PLKSD/SHW G41 ....108 C4
Lansdowne Clinic
KVD/HLHD G12 ....65 H1
Lawmuir Primary School
BLSH ML4 ....135 H4
Lennoxtown Primary School
KKNTL G66 ....4 B2
Lenzie Academy
KKNTL G66 ....39 H2
Lenzie Golf Club
KKNTL G66 ....40 A3
Lenzie Hospital
KKNTL G66 ....40 B3
Lenzie Moss Primary School
KKNTL G66 ....39 G3
Lenzie Primary School
KKNTL G66 ....39 H3
Lethamhill Golf Club
STPS/GTHM/RID G33 ....70 A3
Leverndale Hospital
PLK/PH/NH G53 ....106 A2
Lightburn Hospital
CAR/SHTL G32 ....92 C2

The Lighthouse
CGLE G1 ....2 E6
Linburn Special School
CARD/HILL/MSPK G52 ....86 A3
The Linn Cemetery
CSMK G45 ....146 C1
The Linn Crematorium
CSMK G45 ....128 B5
Linn Park Gardens
LNPK/KPK G44 ....128 B4
Linn Park Golf Club
LNPK/KPK G44 ....128 C3
Linnpark Industrial Estate
CSMK G45 ....128 C5
Linnvale Primary School
CLYDBK G81 ....49 G2
Linwood Health Centre
PSLYN/LNWD PA3 ....82 B4
Linwood High School
PSLYN/LNWD PA3 ....81 G5
Linwood Moss Sports Centre
PSLYN/LNWD PA3 ....81 H4
Littlehill Golf Club
BSHPBGS G64 ....54 C4
Lochend Community High
School
ESTRH G34 ....94 B1
Lochend Secondary School
ESTRH G34 ....94 B1
Lochfield Primary School
PSLYS PA2 ....104 C3
Lochinch Playing Fields
& Sports Club
PLKSD/SHW G41 ....107 G3
Loch Primary School
RUTH G73 ....130 C3
Logans Primary School
MTHW ML1 ....154 A2
Long Calderwood Primary
School
EKILN G74 ....149 H5
Lorne Street Primary School
GOV/IBX G51 ....88 C3
Lourdes Primary School
CARD/HILL/MSPK G52 ....86 D5
Lourdes Secondary School
CARD/HILL/MSPK G52 ....87 E5
Low Parks Museum
HMLTN ML3 ....153 F5
Low Waters Medical Centre
HMLTN ML3 ....169 H5
Macdonald Crutherland
House Hotel
EKILS G75 ....179 F3
Macmillan School of Music
& Drama
PSLY PA1 ....83 H5
Madhok Medical Centre
GVH/MTFL G42 ....109 F5
Maiden Castle
KKNTL G66 ....5 E1
Malmaison Hotel
CGLW G2 ....2 C4
Manse Road Medical Centre
WISHAW ML2 ....158 B5
Martyr's Public School
COWCAD G4 ....3 J3
Maryhill Crematorium
SMSTN G23 ....52 D3
Maryhill FC
MRYH/FIRH G20 ....52 D5
Maryhill Health Centre
MRYH/FIRH G20 ....52 D5
Maryhill Primary School
MRYH/FIRH G20 ....52 C4
The Mary Russell School
PSLYS PA2 ....105 F2
Mavisbank Special School
AIRDRIE ML6 ....98 A1
Maxwellton Primary School
EKILN G74 ....167 E3
McGill Primary Annexe
Bonnyholm Campus
CARD/HILL/MSPK G52 ....106 B1
McGill Primary Annexe
Leithland Campus
PLK/PH/NH G53 ....106 C4
McGill Primary School
PLK/PH/NH G53 ....106 D2
McLellan Galleries
KVGV G3 ....2 C3
Meadowburn Primary School
BSHPBGS G64 ....37 H5
Meadowside Industrial Estate
RNFRW PA4 ....49 G5
Mearns Castle High School
NMRNS G77 ....162 B2
Mearns Cemetery
NMRNS G77 ....162 A3
Mearns Primary School
NMRNS G77 ....161 F2
Megabowl
CLYDBK G81 ....49 F2
Merchiston Hospital
CRG/CRSL/HOU PA6 ....101 F1
Merkland School
KKNTL G66 ....21 H4
Merrylee Annex
LNPK/KPK G44 ....128 C3
Merrylee Primary School
PLKSW/MSWD G43 ....128 A2
Middlefield Residential School
PTCK G11 ....66 A4
Middlemuir School
CLYDBK G81 ....31 G5
Midlock Medical Centre
GOV/IBX G51 ....88 A4
Millarston Industrial Estate
PSLY PA1 ....103 F1
Millennium Hotel
CGLE G1 ....3 F5
Millersneuk Primary School
KKNTL G66 ....40 B4
Milncroft Primary School
STPS/GTHM/RID G33 ....92 D1
Milngavie & Bearsden Sports
Club
MLNGV G62 ....35 G1
Milngavie Business Centre
MLNGV G62 ....17 E3

Milngavie Primary School
MLNGV G62 ....17 E3
Miltonbank Primary School
PPK/MIL G22 ....53 H3
Milton Clinic
PPK/MIL G22 ....53 H4
Milton School
PPK/MIL G22 ....54 B4
Mitchell Theatre & Library
KVGV G3 ....2 A3
Modryvale Medical Centre
MTHW ML1 ....155 E5
Monklands District General
Hospital
AIRDRIE ML6 ....97 G2
Monklands Industrial Estate
CTBR ML5 ....116 C2
Moorpark Primary School
RNFRW PA4 ....63 E4
Morningside Primary School
WISHAW ML2 ....175 G1
Mossedge Industrial Estate
PSLYN/LNWD PA3 ....82 B2
Mossend Primary School
BLSH ML4 ....136 B3
Mosshead Primary School
BSDN G61 ....34 B1
Mossneuk Primary School
EKILS G75 ....177 E1
Mosspark Primary School
CARD/HILL/MSPK G52 ....107 F1
Mossvale School
PSLYN/LNWD PA3 ....84 A2
Motherwell Business Centre
MTHW ML1 ....155 E3
Motherwell College
MTHW ML1 ....172 A2
Motherwell Cricket Club
MTHW ML1 ....172 B2
Motherwell FC (Fir Park)
MTHW ML1 ....172 A1
Motherwell Heritage Centre
MTHW ML1 ....154 C3
Mount Cameron Primary
School
EKILS G75 ....179 E1
Mount Ellen Golf Club
BAIL/MDB/MHD G69 ....59 G5
Mount Florida Medical
Centre
GVH/MTFL G42 ....109 F4
Mount Florida Primary
School
GVH/MTFL G42 ....109 G5
Mount Manor Business Park
KVGV G3 ....88 C1
Mount Vernon
Primary School
CAR/SHTL G32 ....113 E1
M8 Trading Estate
PLKSD/SHW G41 ....88 C1
Muiredge Primary School
UD/BTH/TAN G71 ....134 A1
Muirhouse Primary School
MTHW ML1 ....172 D3
Muir Street Primary School
MTHW ML1 ....154 C2
Munro Business Centre
KNTSWD G13 ....51 F4
Murano Business Centre
MRYH/FIRH G20 ....67 E2
Murray Primary School
EKILS G75 ....166 B5
Museum of Scottish
Country Life
CRMNK/CLK/EAG G76 ....165 G1
Museum of Scottish Football
GVH/MTFL G42 ....109 G3
Museum of Transport
PTCK G11 ....66 B5
National Piping Centre
COWCAD G4 ....3 F2
National Swimming Centre at
Tollcross Leisure Centre
CAR/SHTL G32 ....92 A5
Neilsland Primary School
HMLTN ML3 ....169 F4
Neilston Cemetery
BRHD/NEIL G78 ....141 H1
Neilston Primary School
BRHD/NEIL G78 ....141 F3
Neilston Swimming Pool
BRHD/NEIL G78 ....141 F3
Nerston Residential School
EKILN G74 ....149 F3
Nethercommon Industrial
Estate
PSLYN/LNWD PA3 ....84 B2
Nethercraigs Sports Centre
PLK/PH/NH G53 ....107 G2
Netherlee Primary School
LNPK/KPK G44 ....128 A5
Netherton Primary School
WISHAW ML2 ....173 F4
Netherton School
CSMK G45 ....128 D5
New Albion Industrial Estate
KNTSWD G13 ....49 H4
Newarthill Primary School
MTHW ML1 ....138 B4
Newhills School
STPS/GTHM/RID G33 ....93 F2
Newhouse Industrial Estate
MTHW ML1 ....118 D5
MTHW ML1 ....154 C3
Newmains Primary School
RNFRW PA4 ....63 F5
WISHAW ML2 ....175 E1
New Monkland Primary
School
AIRDRIE ML6 ....75 H2
New Stevenston Primary
School
MTHW ML1 ....137 E3
The Nicholas Geraghty Clinic
MTHW ML1 ....155 E3
Nitshill Primary School
PLK/PH/NH G53 ....125 F3
Noble Primary School
BLSH ML4 ....116 D5

North Glasgow College
  SPRGB/BLRNK G21 ....68 C2
North Woodside Swimming
  Pool
  COWCAD G4 ....67 F4
Notre Dame High School
  KVD/HLHD G12 ....66 B3
Notre Dame Primary School
  KVD/HLHD G12 ....66 B3
Novotel
  CGLW G2 ....2 C5
Nuneaton Industrial Estate
  DMNK/BRGTN G40 ....110 D1
Oakbank Industrial Estate
  MRYH/FIRH G20 ....67 F3
Oakgrove Primary School
  COWCAD G4 ....67 F4
Odeon Cinema
  CGLW G2 ....2 E3
  EKILN G74 ....166 C5
  GOV/IBX G51 ....89 E3
Ogilvie Primary School
  STPS/GTHM/RID G33 ....93 G2
Old Aisle Cemetery
  KKNTL G66 ....40 C2
Old Course Ranfurly Golf Club
  BRWEIR PA11 ....79 F4
Old Kilpatrick Cemetery
  OLDK G60 ....53 G2
Old Monkland Cemetery
  CTBR ML5 ....116 A1
Old Monkland Primary School
  CTBR ML5 ....95 H5
Optimax Laser Eye Clinic
  KVGV G3 ....2 A2
Orbiston Business Centre
  BLSH ML4 ....135 H4
Our Holy Redeemers Primary
  School
  CLYDBK G81 ....49 G4
Our Lady of Loretto Primary
  School
  CLYDBK G81 ....31 E5
Our Lady of Lourdes Primary
  School
  EKILS G75 ....165 H5
Our Lady of Peace Primary
  School
  PSLYN/LNWD PA3 ....101 H1
Our Lady of the Annunciation
  Primary School
  PLKSW/MSWD G43 ....127 H2
Our Lady of the Assumption
  Primary School
  MRYH/FIRH G20 ....67 F1
Our Lady of the Missions
  Primary School
  GIF/THBK G46 ....126 D5
Our Lady of the Rosary
  Primary School
  CARD/HILL/MSPK G52 ....87 E5
Our Lady & St Francis Primary
  School
  MTHW ML1 ....137 H5
Our Lady & St Patricks High
  School
  DMBTN G82 ....12 B2
Our Ladys High School
  CUMB G67 ....25 H4
  MTHW ML1 ....172 B2
Oxgang Primary School
  KKNTL G66 ....21 H5
Paisley Abbey
  PSLY PA1 ....84 C4
Paisley Crematorium
  PSLY PA1 ....83 H4
Paisley Golf Club
  PSLY PA2 ....122 C2
Paisley Grammar School
  PSLY PA1 ....84 C4
Paisley Maternity Hospital
  PSLYS PA2 ....103 H2
Paisley Museum & Art Galleries
  PSLY PA1 ....84 A5
Palacerigg Country Park
  CUMB G67 ....27 H5
Palacerigg Golf Club
  CUMB G67 ....45 C1
Parkburn Industrial Estate
  BLTYR/CAMB G72 ....152 A4
Parkhead Hospital
  DEN/PKHD G31 ....91 G4
Park Mains High School
  ERSK PA8 ....47 G2
Parkview Business Centre
  KVGV G3 ....2 A2
Parkview Primary School
  SMSTN G23 ....52 C3
Partick Market
  PTCK G11 ....66 B4
Partick Thistle FC
  (Firhill Stadium)
  MRYH/FIRH G20 ....67 F2
The Pavilion Theatre
  CGLW G2 ....2 E3
Peacock Cross Industrial
  Estate
  HMLTN ML3 ....152 D5
Penilee Secondary School
  CARD/HILL/MSPK G52 ....86 A3
Pentagon Business Centre
  KVGV G3 ....2 B6
Pentland School
  CTBR ML5 ....73 H5
People's Palace
  DMNK/BRGTN G40 ....90 B4
Petersburn Primary School
  AIRDRIE ML6 ....98 D4
Petershill FC
  SPRGB/BLRNK G21 ....68 C3
Petershill Recreation Centre
  SPRGB/BLRNK G21 ....69 E5
Phoenix Business Park
  PSLYN/LNWD PA3 ....82 C5
Phoenix Industrial Estate
  PSLYN/LNWD PA3 ....84 B2
Phoenix Retail & Business Park
  PSLY PA1 ....82 D4
Pinewood Primary School
  DRUM G15 ....33 H5

Plains Primary School
  AIRDRIE ML6 ....77 H4
The Play Drome
  CLYDBK G81 ....49 E2
Pollok Leisure Centre
  PLK/PH/NH G53 ....106 D5
Pollok Shopping Centre
  PLK/PH/NH G53 ....106 D5
Pollok Country Park
  PLKSD/SHW G41 ....107 H3
Pollok Golf Club
  PLKSW/MSWD G43 ....107 H5
Pollok House
  PLKSW/MSWD G43 ....107 G4
Pollokshields Primary School
  PLKSD/SHW G41 ....109 E1
Portland High School
  CTBR ML5 ....97 E2
Portland Park Medical Centre
  HMLTN ML3 ....170 B3
Possilpark Health Centre
  PPK/MIL G22 ....67 H2
Premier Travel Inn
  BSDN G61 ....34 D1
  CAR/SHTL G32 ....112 B3
  CGLE G1 ....3 H5
  CUMB G67 ....26 C3
  EKILS G75 ....165 G4
  EKILS G75 ....166 C5
  HMLTN ML3 ....153 F4
  KVGV G3 ....2 B3
  MLNGV G62 ....17 E5
  MTHW ML1 ....119 H5
  PSLY PA1 ....82 C4
  PSLYN/LNWD PA3 ....84 B1
  STPS/GTHM/RID G33 ....57 C5
  UD/BTH/TAN G71 ....114 A3
Priestfield Industrial Estate
  BLTYR/CAMB G72 ....151 C5
Prince's Square Shopping
  Centre
  CGLE G1 ....2 E6
Princess Royal
  Maternity Hospital
  DEN/PKHD G31 ....90 B1
Pro Bowl
  KKNTL G66 ....21 E3
Pro Lane Bowl
  EKILS G75 ....178 D2
Provand's Lordship
  COWCAD G4 ....3 K4
Provan Hall (NTS)
  ESTRH G34 ....71 G1
Provanmail Primary School
  ESTRH G34 ....71 H5
Quadrant Shopping Centre
  CTBR ML5 ....96 D2
Quality Hotel
  CGLE G1 ....2 D5
Quarry Brae Primary School
  DEN/PKHD G31 ....91 H4
Quarter Primary School
  HMLTN ML3 ....181 F5
Queen Margaret Hall of
  Residence
  KVD/HLHD G12 ....66 B1
Queenslie Industrial Estate
  STPS/GTHM/RID G33 ....93 F1
Queen's Park FC
  (Hampden Park)
  GVH/MTFL G42 ....109 H4
Radisson SAS Glasgow
  CGLE G1 ....2 D6
Ralston Golf Club
  PSLY PA1 ....85 G5
Ralston Primary School
  PSLY PA1 ....85 H4
Ramada Hotel
  CGLE G1 ....3 F6
  PSLYN/LNWD PA3 ....84 A1
Ramoy Business Centre
  PSLY PA1 ....83 H5
Ramshorn Theatre
  CGLE G1 ....3 H5
Ranfurly Castle Golf Club
  BRWEIR PA11 ....79 E4
Range Road
  Industrial Estate
  MTHW ML1 ....172 D1
Rangers FC
  GOV/IBX G51 ....87 H3
Rashielea Primary School
  ERSK PA8 ....30 C5
Ravenswood Primary School
  CUMB G67 ....26 A5
Redburn School
  CUMB G67 ....27 E3
Red Deer Day Hospital
  EKILS G75 ....165 H5
Regency Medical Clinic
  KVGV G3 ....66 D5
Reid Kerr College
  PSLYN/LNWD PA3 ....84 C3
Reid Kerr Learning Centre
  PSLYN/LNWD PA3 ....83 F3
Renfrew District Welfare
  Clinic
  PSLYS PA2 ....103 E3
Renfrew Golf Club
  RNFRW PA4 ....63 E1
Renfrew Health Centre
  RNFRW PA4 ....63 F4
Renfrew High School
  RNFRW PA4 ....63 G4
Richmond Park School
  GBLS G5 ....110 A1
Riddrie Park Cemetery
  STPS/GTHM/RID G33 ....69 G5
Righead Industrial Estate
  BLSH ML4 ....135 F1
Robertsons Sports Centre
  PSLYS PA2 ....104 C5
Rob Roy Football Club
  KKNTL G66 ....20 C5
Robslee Primary School
  GIF/THBK G46 ....127 E5
Rochsolloch Primary School
  AIRDRIE ML6 ....97 H3
Rogerfield Primary School
  ESTRH G34 ....94 B1

Rosehall High School
  CTBR ML5 ....116 C1
Rosehall Industrial Estate
  CTBR ML5 ....116 C1
Rosevale School
  PPK/MIL G22 ....54 A4
Rosshall Academy
  CARD/HILL/MSPK G52 ....86 B5
Ross Hall Hospital
  CARD/HILL/MSPK G52 ....106 B1
Rouken Glen Park
  GIF/THBK G46 ....144 C1
Royal Alexandra Hospital
  PSLYS PA2 ....104 A2
Royal College of Nursing
  KVGV G3 ....67 E5
Royal Concert Hall
  CGLE G1 ....3 G3
Royal Highland Fusiliers
  Museum
  KVGV G3 ....67 E5
Royal Hospital for Sick Children
  & Maternity Hospital
  KVGV G3 ....66 B5
Royal Scottish Academy of
  Music
  CGLW G2 ....2 E2
Royston Primary School
  SPRGB/BLRNK G21 ....68 C5
RSPB Nature Reserve
  MTHW ML1 ....171 H3
Ruchazie Primary School
  STPS/GTHM/RID G33 ....70 B5
Ruchill Primary School
  MRYH/FIRH G20 ....53 E5
Rutherglen Cemetery
  RUTH G73 ....129 H1
Rutherglen Health Centre
  RUTH G73 ....111 E5
Rutherglen High School
  RUTH G73 ....111 E4
Rutherglen Swimming Pool
  RUTH G73 ....110 D5
Sacred Heart Primary School
  BLSH ML4 ....135 H4
  DMNK/BRGTN G40 ....90 C5
SAE Institute
  PLKSD/SHW G41 ....88 D4
St Agathas Primary School
  KKNTL G66 ....22 B5
St Agnes Primary School
  SMSTN G23 ....52 D3
St Aidans High School
  WISHAW ML2 ....174 A1
St Aidans Primary School
  WISHAW ML2 ....157 F4
St Aidans School
  CAR/SHTL G32 ....91 G3
St Alberts Primary School
  PLKSD/SHW G41 ....88 C5
St Aloysius College
  KVGV G3 ....2 C2
St Aloysius Preparatory School
  KVGV G3 ....2 C2
St Ambrose High School
  CTBR ML5 ....96 B1
St Andrews Academy
  PSLYS PA2 ....105 F3
St Andrews Cathedral
  CGLE G1 ....2 E7
St Andrews Clinics for Children
  KVD/HLHD G12 ....66 C3
St Andrews High School
  CLYDBK G81 ....49 F3
  EKILS G75 ....178 A2
St Andrews Primary RC School
  BALLOCH G68 ....10 D4
St Andrews Primary School
  AIRDRIE ML6 ....75 H5
  BSDN G61 ....33 H2
St Andrews RC Secondary
  School
  CAR/SHTL G32 ....92 B2
St Angelas Primary School
  PLK/PH/NH G53 ....125 H4
St Annes Primary School
  DEN/PKHD G31 ....90 D3
  ERSK PA8 ....47 H5
  HMLTN ML3 ....170 A4
St Anthonys FC
  GOV/IBX G51 ....87 H3
St Anthonys Primary School
  GOV/IBX G51 ....87 G1
  HWWD PA9 ....120 D2
  RUTH G73 ....130 B3
St Augustine's Primary School
  CTBR ML5 ....96 C3
St Augustines Primary School
  PPK/MIL G22 ....53 H4
St Barbaras Primary School
  BAIL/MDB/MHD G69 ....58 C4
St Bartholomews Primary
  School
  CTBR ML5 ....73 H5
St Benedicts Primary School
  ESTRH G34 ....94 C1
St Bernadette's Primary
  School
  MTHW ML1 ....154 A2
St Bernards Primary School
  CTBR ML5 ....117 E1
  PLK/PH/NH G53 ....125 E2
St Blanes Primary School
  BLTYR/CAMB G72 ....151 F2
  CLYDBK G81 ....32 C1
St Brendans High School
  PSLYN/LNWD PA3 ....82 B3
St Brendan's Primary School
  KNTSWD G13 ....49 H4
St Brides High School
  EKILN G74 ....166 D4
St Bride's Primary School
  BLTYR/CAMB G72 ....131 F2
St Brides RC Primary School
  GVH/MTFL G42 ....109 F2
  UD/BTH/TAN G71 ....134 B3

St Bridgets Primary School
  BAIL/MDB/MHD G69 ....94 A4
St Brigids Primary School
  GVH/MTFL G42 ....110 A4
  WISHAW ML2 ....158 B5
St Cadoc's Primary School
  BLTYR/CAMB G72 ....131 H5
St Cadocs Primary School
  NMRNS G77 ....143 H5
St Catherine's Primary School
  PSLYN/LNWD PA3 ....84 C3
St Catherines Primary School
  SPRGB/BLRNK G21 ....69 F1
St Charles Primary School
  BLTYR/CAMB G72 ....132 C1
  MRYH/FIRH G20 ....67 E2
St Charles' Primary School
  PSLYS PA2 ....104 C3
St Clares Primary School
  DRUM G15 ....33 F4
St Columbas High School
  CLYDBK G81 ....32 B1
St Columbkilles Primary
  School
  RUTH G73 ....110 D5
St Convals Primary School
  CARD/HILL/MSPK G52 ....108 C4
St Cuthberts High School
  KLBCH PA10 ....120 D2
St Cuthberts Primary School
  HMLTN ML3 ....152 B5
  PPK/MIL G22 ....67 G2
St David's Primary School
  AIRDRIE ML6 ....77 G4
  JNSTN PA5 ....101 E5
St Denis Primary School
  DEN/PKHD G31 ....91 E2
St Dominic's RC
  Primary School
  AIRDRIE ML6 ....98 D3
St Edmunds Primary School
  PLK/PH/NH G53 ....107 E3
St Edwards Primary School
  AIRDRIE ML6 ....98 D2
St Elizabeth Seton Primary
  School
  STPS/GTHM/RID G33 ....92 C1
St Elizabeths Primary School
  HMLTN ML3 ....180 D1
St Enoch Business Centre
  CGLE G1 ....2 E7
St Enoch Shopping Centre
  CGLE G1 ....3 F7
St Eunans Primary School
  CLYDBK G81 ....49 F1
St Fergus Primary School
  PSLYN/LNWD PA3 ....83 G4
St Fillan's Primary School
  CRG/CRSL/HOU PA6 ....80 C2
St Fillans Primary School
  LNPK/KPK G44 ....128 C1
St Flannans Primary School
  KKNTL G66 ....21 H4
St Francis of Assisi Primary
  School
  BAIL/MDB/MHD G69 ....113 G1
  BALLOCH G68 ....43 H1
St Francis Primary School
  GBLS G5 ....90 A5
St Gabriel's Primary School
  UD/BTH/TAN G71 ....116 A4
St Georges Medical Centre
  KVGV G3 ....2 A1
St Georges Primary School
  CARD/HILL/MSPK G52 ....86 A4
St George's School
  CARD/HILL/MSPK G52 ....86 B4
St Gerards Primary School
  BLSH ML4 ....116 D5
St Gilberts Primary School
  SPRGB/BLRNK G21 ....69 F3
St Gregorys Primary School
  MRYH/FIRH G20 ....68 A2
St Helens Primary School
  BLTYR/CAMB G72 ....151 G2
  CLYDBK G81 ....32 C1
  CRMNK/CLK/EAG G76 ....145 H4
  MLNGV G62 ....16 D4
  MRYH/FIRH G20 ....53 G4
  STPS/GTHM/RID G33 ....71 F1
St Judes Primary School
  STPS/GTHM/RID G33 ....93 F3
St Julies Primary School
  LNPK/KPK G44 ....129 E5
St Kenneths Primary School
  EKILN G74 ....166 A2
St Kevins Primary School

St Kevins Special School
  SPRGB/BLRNK G21 ....68 B4
St Leonards Primary School
  EKILN G74 ....167 G2
St Louise Primary School
  GIF/THBK G46 ....126 A3
St Louises Primary School
  EKILS G75 ....178 A1
St Lucys Primary School
  CUMB G67 ....27 G1
St Lukes High School
  BRHD/NEIL G78 ....142 B2
St Machans RC Primary School
  KKNTL G66 ....4 B1
St Margaret Marys Secondary
  School
  CSMK G45 ....129 E5
St Margaret of Scotland
  Primary School
  CUMB G67 ....26 C4
St Margarets High School
  AIRDRIE ML6 ....98 C5
St Margarets Primary School
  JNSTN PA5 ....101 F4
St Marks Primary School
  BRHD/NEIL G78 ....142 B1
  HMLTN ML3 ....169 G4
  RUTH G73 ....130 A2
St Mark's Primary School
  DEN/PKHD G31 ....91 H4
St Marthas RC Primary School
  PLK/PH/NH G53 ....106 D3
St Martins RC Primary School
  SPRGB/BLRNK G21 ....69 E1
St Marys Cathedral
  MRYH/FIRH G20 ....67 G4
St Mary's Kenmure Primary
  School
  BSHPBGS G64 ....54 B2
St Marys (Maryhill) Primary
  School
  MRYH/FIRH G20 ....52 B4
St Marys Primary School
  CLYDBK G81 ....31 G2
  CTBR ML5 ....96 D4
  CUMB G67 ....26 D4
  HMLTN ML3 ....170 A1
  KKNTL G66 ....20 C5
  MTHW ML1 ....157 E1
  PSLY PA1 ....83 H5
St Matthews Primary School
  BSHPBGS G64 ....55 E1
St Matthew's Primary School
  WISHAW ML2 ....173 F1
St Maurices High School
  BALLOCH G68 ....25 E5
St Michaels Primary School
  BAIL/MDB/MHD G69 ....59 F1
  DMBTN G82 ....12 B3
St Michael's Primary School
  DEN/PKHD G31 ....91 F4
St Mirins High School
  PSLY PA1 ....83 G5
St Mirins Primary School
  LNPK/KPK G44 ....128 D2
St Mirren FC (St Mirren Park)
  PSLYN/LNWD PA3 ....84 B3
St Modans Primary School
  STPS/GTHM/RID G33 ....92 B1
St Monicas Primary School
  CTBR ML5 ....95 H5
  PLK/PH/NH G53 ....106 D3
St Mungo Museum of
  Religious Life & Art
  COWCAD G4 ....3 K4
St Mungo's Academy
  DEN/PKHD G31 ....90 D3
St Ninians High School
  GIF/THBK G46 ....126 C5
  GIF/THBK G46 ....127 E5
  KKNTL G66 ....20 D5
St Ninians Primary School
  HMLTN ML3 ....168 D1
St Ninian's Primary School
  KNTSWD G13 ....50 D2
St Oswald's School
  LNPK/KPK G44 ....128 D2
St Patrick's Cemetery
  MTHW ML1 ....137 E4
St Patricks High School
  CTBR ML5 ....97 E2
St Patricks Primary School
  CTBR ML5 ....97 E2
  DMBTN G82 ....13 F3
  KSYTH G65 ....8 B1
  KVGV G3 ....2 A4
St Patrick's Primary School
  MTHW ML1 ....137 E4
St Paul's High School
  PLK/PH/NH G53 ....107 E4
St Pauls Primary School
  CAR/SHTL G32 ....112 B1
  HMLTN ML3 ....152 A3
  PSLYS PA2 ....103 E3
  SCOT G14 ....64 D5
St Peters Primary School
  DMBTN G82 ....13 G1
  HMLTN ML3 ....169 G4
St Peter's Primary School
  PSLYS PA2 ....103 H4
  PTCK G11 ....66 B4
St Philip's Primary School
  STPS/GTHM/RID G33 ....70 B5
St Phillips School
  AIRDRIE ML6 ....77 G5
St Philomena's
  Primary School
  STPS/GTHM/RID G33 ....69 G3
St Pius Primary School
  DRUM G15 ....33 F4
St Raymond's Special School
  CSMK G45 ....128 C5
St Robert's Primary School
  PLK/PH/NH G53 ....125 H1
St Rochs Primary School
  SPRGB/BLRNK G21 ....68 C4
St Rochs Secondary School
  SPRGB/BLRNK G21 ....68 B5
St Rose of Lima Primary
  School
  STPS/GTHM/RID G33 ....70 C4

St Saviours Primary School
GOV/IBX G51 ....88 A2
St Serfs Primary School
AIRDRIE ML6 ....76 C4
St Stephens Primary School
CLYDBK G81 ....31 G5
St Stephen's Primary School
SPRGB/BLRNK G21 ....68 B4
St Teresas Primary School
MTHW ML1 ....138 A4
St Teresa's Primary School
SPRGB/BLRNK G21 ....67 H3
St Thomas Aquinas RC
Secondary School
SCOT G14 ....65 F2
St Thomas Primary School
BRHD/NEIL G78 ....141 E3
STPS/GTHM/RID G33 ....69 H5
St Thomas' Primary School
WISHAW ML2 ....173 G3
St Timothys Primary School
CAR/SHTL G32 ....92 B2
CTBR ML5 ....96 C5
St Vincents Primary School
EKILS G75 ....177 G3
St Vincent's Primary School
GIF/THBK G46 ....126 B3
St Vincents School Tollcross
CAR/SHTL G32 ....112 B2
Sandaig Primary School
STPS/GTHM/RID G33 ....93 F3
Sanderson High School
EKILN G74 ....167 F5
Sandwood Primary School
CARD/HILL/MSPK G52 ....86 B4
Saracen Health Centre
PPK/MIL G22 ....67 G2
Saracen Primary School
PPK/MIL G22 ....67 G2
School of Art
KVGV G3 ....2 C2
Scotland Street School
Museum
GBLS G5 ....89 E4
Scotland's Theme Park
MTHW ML1 ....153 F1
Scotstoun Leisure Centre
SCOT G14 ....65 E2
Scotstoun Primary School
SCOT G14 ....64 D2
Scotstoun Stadium
SCOT G14 ....64 D2
The Scottish Centre for Children
with Motor Impairments
BALLOCH G68 ....25 G2
Scottish Exhibition
& Conference Centre
KVGV G3 ....88 C2
The Scottish Hotel School
COWCAD G4 ....3 J4
Scottish Maritime Museum
DMBTN G82 ....13 F4
Scottish School of Herbal
Medicine
GOV/IBX G51 ....65 F5
Scottish TV
CCLW G2 ....2 E3
Scottish Youth Theatre
CGLE G1 ....2 E5
Scotus College
BSDN G61 ....33 H4
Shawbridge Industrial Estate
PLKSW/MSWD G43 ....108 B5
Shawhead Industrial Estate
CTBR ML5 ....117 E2
Shawhead Primary School
CTBR ML5 ....117 E1
Shawlands Academy
PLKSD/SHW G41 ....108 C3
Shawlands Primary School
PLKSD/SHW G41 ....108 C3
Shettleston Day Hospital
CAR/SHTL G32 ....92 A5
Shettleston Health Centre
CAR/SHTL G32 ....92 B4
Showcase Cinema
BAIL/MDB/MHD G69 ....95 G5
Showcase Cinemas
PSLY PA1 ....82 D4
Sighthill Cemetery
SPRGB/BLRNK G21 ....68 B3
Sighthill Primary School
SPRGB/BLRNK G21 ....68 A3

Sikeside Primary School
CTBR ML5 ....97 G4
Sir John Maxwell Primary
School
PLKSW/MSWD G43 ....108 B5
Sir Matt Busby Sports
Complex
BLSH ML4 ....135 G2
Smithycroft Secondary School
STPS/GTHM/RID G33 ....69 H5
Somerset Eye Clinic
KVGV G3 ....88 D1
Southern General Hospital
GOV/IBX G51 ....87 E1
South Lanarkshire College
BLTYR/CAMB G72 ....131 G2
EKILN G74 ....166 C5
South Lanarkshire Lifestyle
Leisure Centre
RUTH G73 ....130 D1
South Park Primary School
EKILS G75 ....177 H2
South Primary School
PSLYS PA2 ....104 B2
Spark of Genius
PSLY PA1 ....84 D5
Spectrum Business Centre
RUTH G73 ....110 D4
Splersbridge Business Park
GIF/THBK G46 ....126 B4
Spittal Primary School
RUTH G73 ....129 G2
Springboig St Johns School
STPS/GTHM/RID G33 ....93 E2
Springburn Academy
SPRGB/BLRNK G21 ....68 C1
Springburn Health Centre
SPRGB/BLRNK G21 ....68 C2
Springburn Sports Centre
SPRGB/BLRNK G21 ....68 C2
Springhill Primary School
BRHD/NEIL G78 ....142 A1
Stepps Primary School
STPS/GTHM/RID G33 ....57 F5
Stirling Road Industrial Estate
AIRDRIE ML6 ....76 C3
Stirling's Library
CGLE G1 ....3 G6
Stobcross Street Industrial
Estate
CTBR ML5 ....96 D3
Stobhill General Hospital
SPRGB/BLRNK G21 ....54 D5
Stonedyke Primary School
DRUM G15 ....50 C1
Stonelaw High School
RUTH G73 ....130 B1
Stow College
COWCAD G4 ....2 C1
Strathclyde Art Centre
KVGV G3 ....2 B6
Strathclyde Business Centre
GOV/IBX G51 ....88 C3
MTHW ML1 ....137 E3
PLKSD/SHW G41 ....88 D4
Strathclyde Country Park
MTHW ML1 ....153 G2
Strathclyde Country Park
Camping & Caravan Site
MTHW ML1 ....153 H4
Strathclyde Hospital
MTHW ML1 ....154 C2
Strathclyde Park Golf Club
HMLTN ML3 ....153 F5
Strathkelvin Retail Park
BSHPBGS G64 ....38 A4
Summerhill Primary School
DRUM G15 ....33 G4
Summeree Heritage Trust
CTBR ML5 ....96 C2
Sunnyside Primary School
STPS/GTHM/RID G33 ....70 C3
Swinton Primary School
BAIL/MDB/MHD G69 ....94 C3
The Tall Ship at Glasgow
Harbour
KVGV G3 ....88 B1
Tannochside Primary School
UD/BTH/TAN G71 ....115 F4
Taylor High School
MTHW ML1 ....137 F4
Temple Primary School
KNTSWD G13 ....51 G4

Templeton Business Centre
DMNK/BRGTN G40 ....90 B4
Tenement House
KVGV G3 ....2 B2
Tennant Caledonian Brewery
DEN/PKHD G31 ....90 B2
Thames Open College
CGLW G2 ....2 D5
Thistle Hotel
CGLW G2 ....2 D3
Thomas Muir High School
BSHPBGS G64 ....55 G2
Thorniewood Football Club
UD/BTH/TAN G71 ....115 G5
Thorniebank Health Centre
GIF/THBK G46 ....126 C3
Thorniebank
Industrial Estate
GIF/THBK G46 ....126 A5
Thornliebank Primary School
GIF/THBK G46 ....126 D3
Thornlie Primary School
WISHAW ML2 ....173 H3
Thorn Primary School
JNSTN PA5 ....101 H4
Thorntree Primary School
CAR/SHTL G32 ....92 B3
Thornwood Primary School
PTCK G11 ....65 G4
Tinto Primary School
PLKSW/MSWD G43 ....127 F1
Todholm Primary School
PSLYS PA2 ....105 E2
Tolbooth Steeple
CGLE G1 ....3 H7
Tollbrae Primary School
AIRDRIE ML6 ....98 D2
Tollcross Industrial Estate
CAR/SHTL G32 ....112 B1
The Toonspeak Young
Peoples Theatre
SPRGB/BLRNK G21 ....68 C4
Tormusk Primary School
CSMK G45 ....129 H4
Torrance House Golf Club
EKILS G75 ....179 F2
Torrance Primary School
BSHPBGS G64 ....19 F1
Toryglen Primary School
GVH/MTFL G42 ....110 B4
Toss Theatre
BLSH ML4 ....136 B2
Town Hall Business Centre
MTHW ML1 ....154 C4
Townhead Clinic
CTBR ML5 ....96 B1
KKNTL G66 ....40 A1
Townhead Health Centre
DEN/PKHD G31 ....90 B1
Townhead Primary School
CTBR ML5 ....74 A4
Townhill Primary School
HMLTN ML3 ....168 D3
Trades Hall
CGLE G1 ....3 G6
Travelodge
DMBTN G82 ....14 C4
GBLS G5 ....89 E3
KVGV G3 ....2 D2
PSLYN/LNWD PA3 ....84 A1
The Triangle
Shopping Centre
BSHPBGS G64 ....54 D2
Trinity High School
RNFRW PA4 ....63 G2
RUTH G73 ....111 H5
Tron Steeple
CGLE G1 ....3 G7
Tron Theatre
CGLE G1 ....3 H7
Tryst Sports Centre
CUMB G67 ....26 C4
Tulip Inn
GBLS G5 ....89 H4
Turnbull High School
BSHPBGS G64 ....54 B1
Turret Theatre
KKNTL G66 ....21 E4
Twechar Primary School
KSYTH G65 ....23 F2
Uddingston Cricket & Sports
Club
UD/BTH/TAN G71 ....133 H2

Uddingston
Grammar School
UD/BTH/TAN G71 ....133 H1
Udston Hospital
HMLTN ML3 ....169 E1
Udston Primary School
HMLTN ML3 ....168 D1
University of Glasgow
BSDN G61 ....51 H3
CGLW G2 ....2 C3
KNTSWD G13 ....51 F4
KVD/HLHD G12 ....66 B3
KVGV G3 ....66 D4
PTCK G11 ....66 B4
University of Glasgow
Visitor Centre
PTCK G11 ....66 C4
University of Paisley
PSLY PA1 ....84 A5
PSLYS PA2 ....104 A1
University of Strathclyde
CGLE G1 ....2 E7
CGLW G2 ....2 B2
COWCAD G4 ....3 H4
KNTSWD G13 ....51 G4
University of Strathclyde RFC
STPS/GTHM/RID G33 ....70 C2
Victoria Buildings Business
Centre
PSLY PA1 ....84 D5
Victoria Infirmary
PLKSD/SHW G41 ....109 E4
Victoria Memorial Cottage
Hospital
KSYTH G65 ....7 G1
Victoria Primary School
AIRDRIE ML6 ....97 G2
GVH/MTFL G42 ....109 G2
Victory Baths
RNFRW PA4 ....63 G2
Village Theatre
EKILN G74 ....166 C3
Walker Clinic
KVGV G3 ....89 E1
Wallace Primary School
JNSTN PA5 ....102 C2
Wallacewell Primary
School Annexe
STPS/GTHM/RID G33 ....69 G4
Waverley Park
Day Hospital
KKNTL G66 ....21 F4
Weaver's Cottage (NTS)
KLBCH PA10 ....100 B3
Wellgreen Health Centre
PLKSW/MSWD G43 ....108 B4
Wellhall Medical Centre
HMLTN ML3 ....169 F2
Wellhouse Primary School
STPS/GTHM/RID G33 ....93 F2
Wellshot Primary School
CAR/SHTL G32 ....92 A5
Westburn Cemetery
BLTYR/CAMB G72 ....131 H1
West Cemetery
HMLTN ML3 ....169 F2
West Coats Primary School
BLTYR/CAMB G72 ....131 E2
Wester Cleddens Primary
School
BSHPBGS G64 ....54 D1
Westercommon Primary
School
MRYH/FIRH G20 ....67 F2
Western Infirmary & Accident
& Emergency
KVD/HLHD G12 ....66 B4
Westerton Primary School
BSDN G61 ....51 E1
The Westerwood Hotel
BALLOCH G68 ....10 D4
Westfield Health Clinic
CARD/HILL/MSPK G52 ....86 B4
Westfield Industrial Estate
BALLOCH G68 ....42 D2
Westfield Primary School
BALLOCH G68 ....43 C1
West Mains School
EKILN G74 ....166 D2
Westmuir Medical Centre
DEN/PKHD G31 ....91 G4
West of Scotland CC
PTCK G11 ....66 A4

West of Scotland
Science Park
MRYH/FIRH G20 ....51 H2
West of Scotland
Snowsports Centre
BSDN G61 ....34 A2
West Primary School
PSLY PA1 ....83 H5
Westwood Business Centre
ESTRH G34 ....94 A1
Whistleberry Industrial Park
HMLTN ML3 ....152 B4
The Whitecraigs Golf Club
NMRNS G77 ....144 D3
Whitecraigs RFC
NMRNS G77 ....143 F5
Whitecrook Business Centre
CLYDBK G81 ....49 F2
Whitehill Pool
DEN/PKHD G31 ....91 E2
Whitehill Secondary School
DEN/PKHD G31 ....91 E2
Whiteinch Business Park
SCOT G14 ....65 E4
Whiteinch Indoor Bowling
Stadium
SCOT G14 ....65 E4
Whiteinch Primary School
SCOT G14 ....65 F3
Whitelees Primary School
CUMB G67 ....11 H5
Whitlawburn Shopping Centre
BLTYR/CAMB G72 ....130 D4
Williamsburgh Primary
School
PSLY PA1 ....84 D4
William Street Clinic
KVGV G3 ....2 A4
Williamwood Golf Club
LNPK/KPK G44 ....145 H1
Williamwood High School
CRMNK/CLK/EAG G76 ....145 G2
Williamwood Medical Centre
CRMNK/CLK/EAG G76 ....145 G2
Willowbank Primary School
COWCAD G4 ....67 E4
Willowbank Special School
CTBR ML5 ....96 A3
Windlaw Primary School
CSMK G45 ....147 F1
Wishaw Academy Primary
School
WISHAW ML2 ....174 A3
Wishaw General Hospital
WISHAW ML2 ....173 F2
Wishaw Health Centre
WISHAW ML2 ....174 A2
Wishaw Sports Centre
WISHAW ML2 ....173 G3
Woodfarm High School
GIF/THBK G46 ....126 D4
Woodhead Primary School
HMLTN ML3 ....169 F5
Woodhill Primary School
BSHPBGS G64 ....55 F1
Woodilee Industrial Estate
KKNTL G66 ....40 B2
Woodlands Primary School
CUMB G67 ....44 D1
PSLYN/LNWD PA3 ....101 H1
Woodside Place Business
Centre
KVGV G3 ....2 A2
Woodside Primary School
HMLTN ML3 ....170 B3
Woodville Park Industrial
Estate
GOV/IBX G51 ....87 H3
Wyndford Primary School
MRYH/FIRH G20 ....52 C5
Wyndford Recreation Centre
KVD/HLHD G12 ....66 C1
Xscape
RNFRW PA4 ....64 A2
XS Superbowl
PSLYN/LNWD PA3 ....84 C3
Yoker Primary School
SCOT G14 ....50 A5
Yoker Sports Centre
SCOT G14 ....50 A5

Glasgow Underground Map

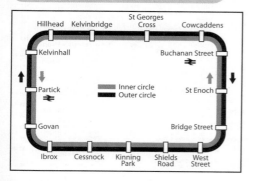

Schools address data provided by Education Direct

Petrol station information supplied by Johnsons

Garden centre information provided by:

Garden Centre Association   Britains best garden centres

    Wyevale Garden Centres

The statement on the front cover of this atlas is sourced, selected and quoted
from a reader comment and feedback form received in 2004

How do I find the perfect place?

AA Lifestyle Guides
Britain's largest travel publisher
order online at www.theAA.com/travel